ALL ABOUT
OSCAR®

ALL ABOUT
OSCAR®

THE HISTORY
AND POLITICS
OF THE
ACADEMY AWARDS®

EMANUEL LEVY

continuum
NEW YORK • LONDON

2003

The Continuum International Publishing Group Inc
370 Lexington Avenue, New York, NY 10017

The Continuum International Publishing Group Ltd
The Tower Building, 11 York Road, London SE1 7NX

Printed in the United States of America

Library of Congress Cataloging-in-Publication Data
Levy, Emanuel
All about Oscar : the history and politics of the Academy Awards /
Emanuel Levy.
p.   cm.
ISBN 0-8264-1452-4
1. Academy Awards (Motion pictures)   I. Title.
PN1993.92 .L47 2002
791.4307979494 – dc21
2002012016

To my sister Vivi
A Woman for All Seasons

CONTENTS

Film stills will be found between pages 256 and 257.

PREFACE

My interest in studying the Oscar Awards in a systematic way began twenty-five years ago, in 1977, when I was asked to teach a course on popular culture at Hunter College. But my curiosity about the Oscars as a uniquely American spectacle goes back much further, to my childhood in Israel. Television was introduced to the Israeli public rather late, in 1967, and in a limited way. There was one channel that broadcast only several hours per evening. Hence, movies were — and in many ways still are — the primary medium of entertainment.

My parents were both avid moviegoers. My father, a great womanizer, loved beautiful women, on-screen and off. His favorites in the 1950s were Ava Gardner and Susan Hayward. But he also loved John Wayne and Gary Cooper Westerns, Hitchcock thrillers, screwball comedies, and gangster pictures. So, my early movie education was well rounded. After my parents' divorce in 1955, at least once a week I was taken to the movies by my mother and aunt.

As a symbol that captures the essence of the American Dream, I couldn't have found a more appropriate topic for my professional life than the Academy Awards. I have forever been amazed by the immense popularity of the Oscars, which was established by the Academy of Motion Picture Arts and Sciences in 1927, and the show, which first took place in 1929. I thought that exploring this subject from socio-cultural and historical points of view would be of great interest — and tremendous fun, too.

It certainly has been.

Several of my books, *John Wayne: Prophet of the American Way of Life, Small-Town America in Film, Cinema of Outsiders: The Rise of American Independent Film, Citizen Harris, American Film Critic,* all deal with uniquely American phenomena. *All about Oscar: The History and Politics of the Academy Awards* adds another panel to what has emerged as a coherent research agenda, representing nearly thirty years of teaching and writing about film. Singly and jointly, these books also indicate various phases of my assimilation into American society and culture, first as an outsider and then as an insider, particularly after becoming a film scholar and critic.

I began to collect data on the Oscars in 1981, which resulted in the first edition of this book, *And the Winner Is: The History and Politics of the Academy Awards,* a very different chronicle in both style and format from the second edition, which was called *Oscar Fever,* as well as from the present book — a new, considerably revised, and expanded chronicle.

My goal to be thorough and comprehensive forced me to go back to the very beginnings, the establishment of the Academy of Motion Picture Arts and Sciences in 1927, the very year in which the first talkie was released. I soon realized that due to constraints of space, the book would have to focus on the important award categories: Best Picture, Best Director, the four acting awards (Best Actor, Best Actress, Best Supporting Actor, Best Supporting Actress), and the two writing awards (Best Original and Best Adapted Screenplay).

For the present *All about Oscar,* I not only updated the information but also substantially expanded the scope of the book, which includes six all-new chapters, among them: New investigations of the Best Foreign-Language Oscar; "Is the Oscar a White Man's Award?," on the under-representation of women and ethnic minorities in the awards' process; "The Importance of Being Eccentric," a detailed examination of kinds of roles and performances that tend to be nominated for, and win, Oscars (these include the use of foreign accents, heavy makeup, and the depiction of physical and mental disabilities and illnesses); and an account of the Oscars' "Middlebrow Sensibility," that is, the preference among the Academy for films that are "soft," uplifting, noble, heroic, and soothing rather than provocative.

This book is not a chronological, year-by-year, history of the Oscars. Rather, it provides a sociological view of the historic, cultural, and political contexts within which specific films and filmmakers have been nominated for, and have won, the Oscar Award over the past seventy-four years.

The Oscar Award assumes a very special emotional place and offers a great many pleasures to *one billion viewers annually,* all over the world, who know the text, context, and subtext of the Oscar Awards and the annual Oscar show. I would therefore briefly like to provide several clarifications about the ways I use data.

First, when I discuss nominated or winning films, I reference the year in which they were released. But when I refer to the Oscar show, I use the date in which the show took place. For example, when analyzing Julia Roberts's role in *Erin Brockovich,* I call it a 2000 film. But when describing Roberts's acceptance speech, I refer to it as the presentation that took place at the 2001 Oscar ceremonies.

Second, it is often impossible to determine accurately the age of the nominees. I have tried to use different sources and not to rely on information provided by studios' publicity departments. It is indicative of the culture and society in which we live that often an actress's age is revealed after death. (A prime example is Marlene Dietrich, whose date of birth is often listed as 1904 although it was really 1901.) I therefore acknowledge and apologize should readers find inconsistent information regarding age and related attributes.

Third, I take full responsibility for the specific genre designation of the Oscar-nominated and/or Oscar-winning film. A number of filmgoers and readers have claimed that *Terms of Endearment,* for example, is a melodrama, whereas I describe it as a serio-comedy. Ditto for *Driving Miss Daisy.* Furthermore, I analyze *Tom Jones* and *Shakespeare in Love* as historic (and epic) comedies rather than costume or period pieces, as they are often described.

A word about the title of this book. Avid moviegoers and avid viewers of the Oscar show need no explanation. But I would like to acknowledge two of my all-time favorite films, which have given me immeasurable gratification and have also inspired the title of the present book: Joseph L. Mankiewicz's 1950 Oscar-winning *All About Eve* and Pedro Almodóvar's 2000 Oscar-winning *All About My Mother,* a film that makes explicit references to the 1950 film as well as to another cherished movie, *A Streetcar Named Desire.* I have enjoyed meeting the late Mankiewicz and the very-much-alive Almodóvar, both professionally and socially, and though these gentlemen could not be more different, they do share one thing — a passion for film.

Friends and colleagues have read and commented on earlier drafts of this book as well as on papers presented at various conferences. I would like to thank Judith Blau, Herman Enzer, Gary Alan Fine, Wendy Griswold, Edward Johnson, Rob Remley, Pamela J. Riley, Yaffa Schlesinger, Bill Shepard, and Andrea Walsh for providing helpful comments. I have benefited immensely from conversations about film and popular culture with two of my professors and friends at Columbia University, the late Sigmund Diamond and Allan Silver.

This book owes an intellectual debt to my teacher Harriet A. Zuckerman, whose excellent study of the Nobel Prize contributed to the way I formulated significant research problems about the Oscars as a unique and peculiar reward system. The application of the cumulative-advantage theory to the film world is based on the influential ideas on the sociology of science and the profession of my teacher Robert K. Merton.

During the past almost-thirty years, I have shown numerous Oscar-winning and Oscar-nominated films to my students at The City University of New York, Columbia University, Wellesley College, UCLA, and ASU West. These students have contributed immeasurably to my evolution as a scholar and commentator by incessantly challenging my ideas about the intricate links between film, popular culture, politics, and society. Their candid, often spontaneous, remarks have continued to make the teaching of film studies a stimulating and rewarding enterprise.

The collection of data for this book took place in several libraries and collections. I would like to thank the personnel of the Margaret Herrick Library of the Academy of Motion Picture Arts and Sciences, particularly Linda Maer and Sondra Archer; the Lincoln Center Library for the Performing Arts; and the libraries of the AFI, the Museum of Modern Art (MOMA), UCLA, and USC. My special thanks go to Bruce Davis, the Executive Administrator of the Academy, for the useful information that he provided, and to Mary Corliss and Terry Geesken of MOMA's Film Stills Archive for their always-patient guidance in selecting stills for this book. (I note with considerable regret the decision to close their department and move the invaluable collection of photographs outside New York City.)

I am grateful to Dr. Thomas Keil, former Dean of Arts and Sciences at ASU West, for providing financial support for my film research. I would like to single out the work of three research assistants: Tamara Blaich, Lauren Caputo, and especially the resourceful and indefatigable Beth A. Mooney, who helped gather information, conducted meticulous library work, and prepared various appendixes and statistical tables.

It gives me great pleasure to thank Evander Lomke of Continuum International for the interest he has shown in my work and for improving the manuscript in its various incarnations. This is our fourth book! I also thank Russell Wolinsky for lending his considerable knowledge of popular culture and invaluable proofreading services.

All about Oscar could not have been written without the continuous support of two close friends, Nathan Waterman, who passed away in 1989, and particularly Rob Remley. No writer could ever hope for more inspirational encouragement and blissful support than are provided by Rob. His painstaking criticism and high standards of thinking, writing, and editing have contributed immeasurably to the depth, clarity, and quality of my writing over the past two decades.

Although I am trained as an academician, for *All about Oscar* I have resorted to a more-popular style that reduces scholarly jargon to a bare minimum. This book aims to reach educated readers all over the world who go to the movies and are interested in knowing more about Hollywood and the Academy Awards. It is my hope that *All about Oscar* will increase the general understanding of the many aspects of the Oscars, and will also serve as a valuable text for filmmakers, teachers, students, and viewers who want to know more about the history and politics of Hollywood.

I have left the best news for last. Just as *All about Oscar* is ready to go to press, I have begun work on a new book to be called *The Oscar Encyclopedia: Everything You Always Wanted to Know about the Academy Awards (and Were Courageous Enough to Ask!)*, with a target publication of early 2005. The projected *Oscar Encyclopedia* will include information that, due to the limitations of space, could not be contained or fully accommodated within *All about Oscar.* This includes discussions of each and every film nominated for the Best Picture, and important new inside-biographical entries on actors, directors, writers, editors, and cinematographers.

EMANUEL LEVY
Los Angeles
November 2002

ALL ABOUT
OSCAR®

· 1 ·

THE GREATEST SHOW ON EARTH

The Academy Award is the Nobel Prize of motion pictures.
— Leroy Johnston

Nothing denotes success so visibly and tangibly as the Oscars.
— British journalist

The Oscar is the most particular of American phenomenon.
— Vincent Canby, film critic

Aside from the campaign for President, the Oscar derby is America's most contentious horse race.   — Richard Corliss, film critic

When people see the label Academy Award Winner, they go to see that movie.   — Martin Scorsese, Oscar nominee

The Oscar show is Hollywood's orgy of self-congratulation.
— Anonymous executive

In the mythology of the cinema, the Oscar is the supreme prize.
— Federico Fellini

The Oscars are classic American Kitsch.
— Lily Tomlin, Oscar nominee

The Oscar is as valid as any award around.
— Jack Nicholson, three-time Oscar winner

$\mathbb{A}$s the quotes suggest, the Oscar Award and the Oscar telecast fulfill various functions, and convey different meanings in American pop culture.

Why Do We Watch the Oscars?

When I was a young boy, the two seminal television events in my family were the World Series and the Academy Awards.
— Harvey Weinstein, Miramax's co-president

The journalist Joyce Millman tried to explain in *Variety* the significance of awards in general, and the Oscar in particular: "We sneer at awards shows, we second-guess them. We hold viewing parties and yell catty comments at the tube. We complain about how long and dull they are. Yet, every year, when the awards telecast cycle begins anew, we're there."

For Millman, the Oscars, the Emmys, the Grammys, and the Golden Globes "invite us into the inner circle of the gods and goddesses, allowing us to witness them at their vulnerable moments when the envelopes are opened and the tribe has spoken." Perhaps more importantly, "awards are the canvas upon which we project our desire for fame, beauty, and, above all, popularity. Who hasn't experienced that fantasy moment in front of the bathroom mirror, where you clutch a shampoo bottle in lieu of a bronzed statuette and deliver the witty yet gracious acceptance speech you've been working on since you were a kid?"

Is it too much to suggest that standing on the Oscar podium and thanking your family and friends — and every person you have ever met in your life — has become the ultimate American fantasy? The strong need to be recognized, the urge to be acknowledged in public, the desire to grab the spotlight. Not for fifteen minutes of fame, as Andy Warhol predicted in the 1960s — that's too long. A forty-five-second speech, which is the Academy's prescribed norm, will do, or swelling music will interrupt your speech mid-sentence. Unless, of course, you're Julia Roberts or Warren Beatty, whose speeches have been some of the longest in Oscar's history.

The hype and hoopla around the Oscars have only increased. Every year, during the crucial Oscar season, roughly from mid-December, when the first critics' groups announce their selections, to late March, when the Oscar ceremonies are broadcast, the whole film industry — and the rest of the world — seem to be talking about one issue: The Oscars, their fairness, their meaning, their effect and, of course, their scandals and controversies.

The countdown to Oscar night, known in the industry as Super Sunday, kicks into high gear as soon as the nominations are made, in the second week of February. For six interminable weeks, the Oscar candidates, from front-runners to the underdogs, flood the airwaves with ads, tearing to shreds the campaign tactics of their opponents.

The 2002 Oscar campaigns were no exception, with a particularly nasty mudslinging over *A Beautiful Mind*'s alleged distortions of the real-life the film celebrated, that of schizo-mathematician John Forbes Nash Jr. Unfazed, the film's co-producers (Universal and DreamWorks) reacted with an effective counter-campaign that ultimately brought them the Best Picture.

Racial issues, both on-screen and off, featured prominently in the 2001 and the 2002 Oscars. As *Entertainment Weekly* (*EW*) noted: "In the dizzying and downright nasty weeks of campaigning leading up to this year's Oscars, race had become both a cause for celebration and rebuke." Race is the proper word, describing both the contest and the issue at its center: White versus black contenders in the acting categories. The color breakthrough that took place inside Oscar's new home on Hollywood Boulevard may be one of the most significant moments in Oscar's history.

The 2002 show, to quote *EW* again, pitted Old versus New Hollywood: "Old, sturdy, clubby, dependable Hollywood was acknowledged with a win for an old-fashioned Hollywood biopic — *A Beautiful Mind,* directed by the industry's favorite son, Ron Howard. But a fresh prince and princess (Halle Berry and Denzel Washington, recipients of the top acting awards) of a modern era in progressive Hollywood also reign."

There are scandals and there are scandals — though you can always count on their regular occurrence and blitz coverage by the national and international media, not just our gossipy tabloids. In 2001, the deadline to turn in the ballots to the Academy was extended by two days. Then when new ballots were mailed out to replace wayward ones that had been lost in the mail, thousands of ballots were mistakenly diverted to another location.

There was another disgrace that year: Fifty-five Oscar statuettes were stolen. A few days later, fifty-two of them were rescued by Willie Fulger, a man who rebuilds car parts. Three were still missing. Fulger, who found the missing Oscars in a trash bin, was promised a $50,000 reward. Significantly, Fulger called the media before notifying the police and, sure enough, he became an instant hero. Later, the police arrested two suspects in connection with the theft. Both men worked for Roadway Express, which had shipped the Oscars. The Oscars host that year, Billy Crystal, was thus handed a ready-made issue that screamed for jokes — and he used the opportunity well.

Another potentially embarrassing disgrace almost occurred when the Academy confirmed that actor Robin Williams would croon "Blame Canada," the Oscar-nominated Best Song from the rowdy and profane comedy, *South Park: Bigger, Longer & Uncut.* The tune's raunchy lyrics caused some consternation and gave the show's producers a workout. However, without giving specifics, producers Richard and Lili Fini Zanuck gave assurance that even conservative audiences would be fine with the presentation.

Earlier that evening, Trey Parker, who co-wrote the song with composer Marc Shaiman, arrived at the Oscar ceremonies dressed in a copy of Jennifer Lopez's green tropical-print, low-cut outfit that she had worn for the Grammys. Befuddled, the security guards gave him a hard time and a thorough inspection. Lopez's scandalous attire had occupied the national headlines, salons' talk, and bedroom gossip for weeks, as if there were no other pressing issues on the national agenda.

The Oscar Show

The Oscar show is the Super Bowl of awards.

> —Louis J. Horvitz, director of the Oscarcast

The Oscar show is Hollywood's Holiest Night. —Studio executive

The Oscar telecast is a peculiar event: Part variety show, part news event, part horse race, part fashion display — and all promotion. As *Premiere* magazine wrote: "Like everything else in Hollywood, the Oscar show is a big production surrounded by gushes of hype and hoopla, climaxing with a showbiz extravaganza, and ending with more bucks spent at the box office."

The Oscar shows are a mirror of their times. "They reflect America," said Gilbert Cates, long-time producer of the show. "When you look at the Oscar show from 1960, you learn something about American society in 1960." Each Oscar show reflects the fashion, the mores, the humor, the politics — in short the zeitgeist.

Every year, the Academy produces the most complex live-awards show on television. Amazingly, despite persistent fears, the producers have never really failed or come up short. Drawing on a solid budget of $17 million (for the 2002 show), the telecast employs the top talents in the industry, from the best set designers to the "hottest" presenters to the trendiest performers.

The challenge to produce a show that combines the best of film and the best of television entertainment is not an easy one. The producers feel that the Oscar spectacle should be much more than a tribute to film, that it should also be a thrilling television show in its own right since the ceremonies are watched by people who are not movie fans. The Oscar telecast is itself ultimately a far more important global media event than the Academy Awards and the honored film artists. John O'Connor observed in the *New York Times,* "The viewer gets not only the event, but also the overall television context." One can add to this observation that the viewer gets not only the television context but also the overall cultural context, both onstage and offstage, beginning with red-carpet arrivals (coverage of which is getting longer and longer), through the comments of the hosts and the winners' speeches.

Length is always an issue. Emcee Johnny Carson described the 1979 Oscar show as "two hours of sparkling entertainment spread over four hours." This was an understatement, compared to the dullness of other shows. The *New York Times*'s Vincent Canby compared the 1983 show to "taking an extremely slow Seventh Avenue Local to heaven in a long and over-crowded ride, and the arrival — by which time one is exhausted — is always a bit of an anticlimax." For Canby, the show's atmosphere combines "the solemnity of the annual Nobel ceremonies in Stockholm with the cheerful bad taste of the grand opening of a shopping center in Los Angeles." Little did Canby realize back in 1983 that in two decades the Oscar show *would* take place in a shopping mall!

The Oscar as Symbolic Ritual

The Oscar show has become an integral part of American culture, an annual symbolic ritual with a seventy-five-year tradition. Rain or shine, the Oscar show must — and will — go on.

On occasion, the Oscar ceremonies have been postponed, but never canceled. The first disturbance occurred in 1938, when heavy floods delayed the show by one week. In 1967, a national network-television strike threatened the April 10 telecast, which, among other things, would have meant a substantial loss of money. However, the Academy's board of directors decided to keep the ceremonies on schedule, with or without television. Fortunately, the strike was settled just three hours before the show was to begin. The second delay, by two days, occurred in 1968, when Dr. Martin Luther King Jr. was assassinated. The Academy's president, Gregory Peck, felt that "postponement was the only appropriate gesture of respect," a feeling that was embraced by the entire industry. In 1981, the ceremonies were suspended after an assassination attempt on President Ronald Reagan on March 30, the day of the telecast. Ironically, the Oscar show was going to begin with a pre-taped greeting from the President. Emcee Johnny Carson commented: "Because of the incredible events of yesterday, that old adage, the show must go on, seemed relatively unimportant." But ultimately the show did go on — a day later — signaling the eminence of the Oscar as a sacred ritual in American culture.

Surprise, Surprise

When you have eliminated the impossible, whatever remains, however improbable, must be truth. — Sherlock Holmes

The unpredictability of the Oscars is another critical attribute of the show. The telecast is live — "that's what makes it a white-knuckler," said Stefan Kanter, one of the show's writers. "You can't make people stick to the script. You can't plan a thing like Jack Palance's one-armed push-ups, but you can take advantage of it in a series of running gags so perfect you might have thought the whole thing was rigged." The writers sit backstage with the host, and they continue to write and modify jokes, even while the event is still in progress, monitoring and exploiting every gesture.

The final choice of winners is uncertain, abounding with last-moment upsets. Could anyone have predicted a month, or even two weeks, before the 2002 show that the Best Actor and Best Actress awards would go to African American players, Halle Berry and Denzel Washington? Could anyone have been sure that in 2001 director Steven Soderbergh would *not* cancel himself out and grab a Best Director Oscar for *Traffic,* one of his two nominated pictures; the other being *Erin Brockovich?*

As critic Kenneth Turan wrote in the *Los Angeles Times:* "The Oscars are so important in the international film cosmos as well as Hollywood and so ultimately unpredictable, that once you get the urge to handicap them, you're hooked for life." When it comes to the Oscars, the only sure bet is that there are no sure bets. Surprises are what keeps the Oscar show quirky and exciting.

A dark horse emerges every year — often just weeks before the voting — in one of the major categories. In the 1976 race, the buzz focused on two Best Picture contenders, *Network* and *All the President's Men,* but the Oscar winner was *Rocky.*

In 1977, Richard Dreyfuss's Best Actor award (for *The Goodbye Girl*) was an upset victory. Industryites in the know predicted Richard Burton, at his seventh nomination, would finally win an Oscar (for *Equus*). Besides, it was a strong year for male performers. The other nominees were Woody Allen for *Annie Hall,* which would win Best Picture; Marcello Mastroianni as a gay man in *A Special Day;* and John Travolta for his breakthrough performance in the blockbuster musical, *Saturday Night Fever.*

In 1981, the talk was high on *Reds* and *On Golden Pond* as potential winners for Best Picture, but the Oscar went to the British import *Chariots of Fire.* In 1989, *My Left Foot,* another low-budget British import, about paraplegic artist-writer Christy Brown, became the dark horse after winning Best Picture from the New York Film Critics Circle.

The Silence of the Lambs, the 1991 Best Picture, was unlikely material — a horror flick (a genre that seldom wins), and one released in February rather than the crucial months of November and December, as most Oscar nominees are. However, Jonathan Demme won the Directors Guild Award (DGA) for the film, which, coming just before the Oscars, was a strong indicator for the Best Director and Best Picture.

"You have to keep it interesting," said Miramax's Harvey Weinstein while campaigning for the Best Picture contender, *The Piano,* in 1993. "No one wants to be told by the media that the whole thing is wrapped up." Despite predictions that *Schindler's List* would sweep the Oscars that year (as it did), Weinstein's point was a reminder that "we're still here and the race isn't over." In the same year, the Spanish entry for the Best Foreign-Language Oscar, Fernando Trueba's comedy *La Belle Epoque,* unexpectedly won over the favorite, Chen Kaige's *Farewell, My Concubine,* which won most of the critics' prizes and shared the Palme d'Or (with *The Piano*) at the Cannes Film Festival.

Unlike years in which there were clear front-runners, such as *Schindler's List* in 1993, or *Forrest Gump* in 1994, the 1995 Best Picture race was wide-open. The feeling was that *Braveheart* won by a narrow margin over *Apollo 13.*

The proliferation of guild awards (PGA, DGA, WGA, and SAG), have made the Oscar process less predictable than it used to be. Consider 2002: "Just when you thought it was safe to go back into the water of Oscar predicting," wrote Jonathan Taylor in *Variety,* "the Producers Guild of America (PGA) Awards once again threw the Best Picture Oscar race into turmoil." The usually reliable Oscar predictor — the PGA winner has matched the Academy's choice 75 percent of the time — gave the award to Baz Luhrmann's avant-garde musical, *Moulin Rouge,* which was not handicapped as an Oscar frontrunner.

Earlier, in January 2002, the American Film Institute (AFI) named *The Lord of the Rings: The Fellowship of the Ring* as its top choice. The Golden Globes, which split their prizes by genre, honored *A Beautiful Mind* in the drama department and *Moulin Rouge* in the musical/comedy division. Then on March 10, two weeks before the Oscar ceremonies, the Screen Actors Guild (SAG) award went to Halle Berry (*Monster's Ball*) rather than Sissy Spacek (*In the Bedroom*), who had swept all the critics' kudos, an AFI honor, and a Golden Globe. Russell Crowe (*A Beautiful Mind*) won the acting award; Robert Altman's *Gosford Park* was cited for its ensemble acting, which is the closest Award the SAG has for Best Picture.

Despite the fact that 2002 was an especially weak year for mainstream Hollywood fare — and the kinds of films the Academy voters favor — it was still possible to narrow the field of Best Picture contenders. As could be expected, the two front runners: *The Lord of the Rings,* which swept 13 nominations, and *A Beautiful Mind,* with *The Lord of the Rings*'s co-front-runner status, was enhanced by a Best Picture at the British Academy of Film and Television Awards (BAFTA), which awards its prizes a month before the Oscars. But there was really no way of knowing until Oscar night which of the two pictures would triumph.

Long Night's Journey into Day

This is the shortest Oscar show of this century.
— Billy Crystal commenting on the 2000 show

Critics have long had a field day with the Oscar program. Year after year, the show is criticized. "The Oscars are one renewable source of negative energy," observed Joyce Millman. The usual rap on the Oscars is that it's too long and too boring. The 2002 show might have achieved a record running time — four hours and twenty minutes — but from the very first years, there were complaints about the show's length.

Consider the 1931 show, a banquet at the Ambassador Room in the Biltmore Hotel. Since seating arrangements were not sent in advance, it took an hour for the guests to be seated. The dinner started at 9:00 P.M., instead of 8:00 P.M., and the presentation of the awards began at midnight. Fortunately, there were only a few categories then. However, the Academy's guest of honor, Vice President Charles Curtis, who lectured about the movie industry's "glorious opportunity to render a great and steadying influence to your fellow Americans," is considered to be one of Oscar's all-time low-points. According to *Variety,* the show was "long winded, verbose, political and dull."

Every year some winners are reproached for "wasting valuable time" in acknowledging their families, or for reading boring, prepared notes, as Supporting Actress Jennifer Connelly did in at the 2002 show. Yet every March, even Hollywood's biggest cynics fall for the annual glitter parade. As one industryite noted: "We all tune in despite the grotesqueness of watching an entire industry congratulate itself on the pretenses that it's still an art form."

Some viewers watch the show with condescension, even borderline contempt, but they keep watching. No one has ever accused the Academy of displaying exquisite taste or radical sympathies — after all, Chaplin, Garbo, and Cary Grant, to name a few, had never won a competitive Oscar. The critic Andrew Sarris once noted: "The Oscars have fascinated me purely as a betting proposition. I enjoy matching my wits and presumed expertise against those of my colleagues, friends, students, and readers."

Despite recurrent complaints, overall, the public approves of the telecast. According to one study, 66 percent of the viewers enjoyed the show, 20 percent did not, and 12 percent had no opinion. That same poll found that the two prime motives for watching the show were "to see the celebrities," and "to find out the winners."

The Oscars as a Fashion Show

There are a few more important things in the world than fashion, but that's what's so crazy about the Oscars. It [fashion] ends up being the thing that's on your mind the whole time.
— Frances McDormand, Best Actress, *Fargo*

You know you've entered into a new territory when you realize your outfit costs more than your film.
— Jessica Yu, Oscar-winner, Documentary Short, *Breathing Lessons*

The Academy announcer, Randy Tomans, intoned in 1997: "Second only in interest to the Oscars themselves is what the ladies are wearing." This feeling was echoed by Oscar nominee Mare Winningham (for *Georgia*), who told reporters: "I watch the show every year with my popcorn and my kids, but mostly I look at what people are wearing."

But men are not exempt from scrutiny either. White tuxedos are anathema on Oscar night. Ben Kingsley made the same mistake twice, showing up for the show decked out in a white tux in 1982, when he won for *Gandhi,* and again years later as a presenter. "I just felt that I had enough darkness this year and I would try to go a little lighter," said Kevin Spacey in response to criticism of wearing a white tuxedo. The press was not pleased, and Spacey would not dare violate the code again.

The times when a top contender like Joanne Woodward could make her own simple evening gown are long gone. Woodward felt good about her achievement, claiming, "I spent $100 on the material, designed the dress and worked on it for two weeks. I'm almost as proud of that dress as I am of my Oscar." However, Woodward was criticized by Joan Crawford, for giving the Oscars a bad name and "setting the cause of Hollywood glamour back at least twenty years."

Edith Head, Hollywood's best-known costume designer, herself a winner of numerous Oscars and Oscar nominations, served as the Academy's fashion consultant for decades. The fashion aspect of the show has increased over the past decades. Audiences now expect to see the latest trends in haute couture worn by the presenters and the nominees. For director Joel Schumacher, Oscar night draws millions of fans, because "it means glamour, glamour, glamour, just as the Super Bowl means fun, fun, fun."

Indeed, before the 1979 show, costume consultant Rob Talsky instructed the female nominees: "No comfort, not what's in style but glamour with a capital G." Talsky's advice was in sharp divergence to what Jerry Wald, the producer of the 1959 ceremonies, told the women that year: "Please avoid deep cleavage at any cost." Yet both pieces of advice highlight the importance attached to the Oscars' fashion angle.

Who can forget Cher's notorious appearance as a presenter in the 1986 show? Snubbed by the Acting Branch, which ignored her performance in *Mask* (for which she won an acting prize in Cannes), Cher wore black pants, knee-high boots, loin cloth, a black wool jersey with metal brass plate and a big Mohawk head-piece. Flaunting her belly button, she said, "As you can see, I received my Academy booklet on how to dress like a serious actress."

In the 1996 show, the producers decided that models should parade the Costume Design nominees. The new James Bond, Pierce Brosnan, surrounded by Naomi Campbell and Claudia Schiffer, hosted the segment. There was a faux runway and faux photographers. The announcer intoned the models' names as if they were the real thing, Hollywood movie stars. But for Stephen Hunter of the *Baltimore Sun,* the show suggested a concession — "it's as if Hollywood was acknowledging that it had lost its grip on glamour and beauty, and that those values have been entirely appropriated by the fashion industry."

Also in 1996, presenter Winona Ryder, wearing a beaded black tulle Chanel, prompted the *Washington Post*'s Tom Shale's nasty quip: "Her dress looked as if an angry mob tried tearing it from her pale little body on her way to the show." The even stranger Sean Young was criticized for carrying a parasol that matched her blue Bob Mackie gown and made her look like a displaced Southern Belle.

In contrast, Brenda Blethyn, who was nominated for playing a frumpy mother in *Secrets & Lies,* shocked the public with her elegant outfit. Barely recognizable, Blethyn wore a lime green Armani with matching stole, and a 122-carat diamond necklace with a 13-carat pendant courtesy of designer Harry Winston, and valued at $1.5 million.

During and after the 1998 show, people were talking about presenter Ashley Judd's Richard Tyler dress with its extremely high slit, though they couldn't decide if Judd's outfit were "shockingly revealing" or "revealingly shocking." In the same year, Kate Winslet, the Oscar-nominee for *Titanic,* received the most positive reports for her standout look. There were more body-guards from Harry Winston than from any other designer due to the fact that Winslet's *Titanic* colleague, nominee Gloria Stuart, wore a $20-million diamond sapphire necklace.

Viewers talked for years about Angelina Jolie's appearance in the 2000 show. In a black Versace gown, and long dyed-black hair and skull ring, she looked like Morticia of the Addams Family. No wonder *EW* labeled Jolie, "Oscar's latest glimpse of Gothic."

In 2001, viewers saw the shadow of Ava Gardner looming large over the female nominees. Both Marcia Gay Harden and Catherine Zeta-Jones wore long, elegant red dresses that evoked Hollywood's glorious past (Harden had earlier played Gardner in a TV-Movie-of the Week). "I think the Oscars may only come once in a lifetime," Harden, the talented but not typical Hollywood celeb, told Joan Rivers, "and I just wanted to feel and look like a movie star."

That year, Best Actress nominee Laura Linney also wore a red dress — courtesy of Valentino. The dress cost considerably more than Linney's paycheck for *You Can Count on Me,* the indie responsible for her nomination, though Linney claimed, "I would have made that movie for free."

Joan Rivers, who was covering the red carpet for *E!,* wore a Vera Wang dress and a pair of Harry Winston earrings estimated at $6 million. This kind of excess prompted the *Los Angeles Times* fashion reporter Valli Hermann-Cohen to comment: "Amid all of the commotion, it's easy to forget that this almost-gross display of wealth (most of it borrowed or granted gratis) takes place near USC, in a working-class neighborhood."

Singer Bjork, who performed the Oscar-nominated song from *Dancer in the Dark,* wore an outfit that became the year's fashion faux pas: A giant swan dress, a full-body stocking that was covered with a giant swan whose neck wrapped around her with its head and beak resting on her breasts. For the same show, Jennifer Lopez decided to go modest for a change, and wore pale-green Chanel, a departure from the notorious Versace outfit she had worn for the Grammys.

The Obsession with Celebs

I get a kick out of watching movie stars. — Jack Nicholson

Celebrity considerations affect every aspect of the Oscar show, beginning with the choice of presenters. There are about forty slots available for presenters who get no pay but receive unparalleled publicity. When it comes to appearing at the Oscars, no adage is more appropriate than "you can't buy this kind of publicity."

The show's producers have often relied on literary figures, like Tennessee Williams, who presented the writing awards in the 1972 show, or Lillian Hellman, to lend added cachet. But celebs are important even if they come from other fields, like boxing champion Muhammad Ali, who made a surprise appearance at the 1977 show. Ali burst on stage exclaiming, " 'I'm the real Apollo Creed," before accusing Sylvester Stallone, the Supporting Actor presenter, of "stealing my script," referring, of course to *Rocky.*

The choice of presenters is imbued with political correctness. The producers try to satisfy age, race, and sex quotas. And presenters must meet at least one "celebrity" requirement. They must be stars who can generate good ratings. They must be newsworthy types, like artists who have won Oscars and might win that night. Among the women, the presenters must make a fashion statement, preferably like Cher's in 1986.

Oscar also loves stars who have been out of the public eye for a while. Media celebrities elevate the show's visibility — and ratings. In 1961, fans mobbed the entrance of the Santa Monica auditorium to catch a glimpse of the convalescing Liz Taylor, who was nominated for *Butterfield 8.* After accepting the Best Actress Oscar from Yul Brynner, Taylor walked to a backstage bathroom and fainted. The same show witnessed another emotional moment: Gary Cooper, dying of cancer in a hospital, received an Honorary Oscar from his friend Jimmy Stewart. "We're all very proud of you," Stewart said with tears in his eyes. Cooper died on May 13, 1961, a month after the ceremony.

In 2000, Jane Fonda fit the bill of a celeb returning to the show after a long absence. Recently estranged from media mogul Ted Turner, Fonda made a grand Hollywood comeback after a decade of retirement, as presenter of the Honorary Oscar to Polish filmmaker Andrzej Wajda. It was Fonda's fourth time as participant since she was first nominated for *They Shoot Horses, Don't They?* thirty-one years earlier.

Woody Allen made his first appearance at the Oscars in 2002, not to collect an award, but to deliver a homage to New York, a city celebrated in so many of his movies. In the wake of the September 11 terrorist attacks, Allen's graceful appearance became a highlight of the show. How on earth did this show's first-time producer, Laura Ziskin, persuade the notorious Oscar-avoider Allen to attend? Allen had not even been present at the show in which it was predicted *Annie Hall* would win the Best Picture and Best Director. "That was just a miracle," Ziskin told the *Los Angeles Times*. "Every Oscar show producer has wanted Woody Allen."

Early on, Ziskin wanted to integrate a film about New York City into the show. She asked her friend, director Nora Ephron, to put a montage together, and she wanted Allen to introduce it. With the help of DreamWorks's Jeffrey Katzenberg, who has been distributing Allen's films, Ziskin's dream came true. But Allen wouldn't let Ziskin tell anybody — not even the ABC network brass. Allen arrived half an hour before the show, slipped in through the rear entrance, and stayed in Ziskin's office until it was time to go onstage. There was no script, no TelePrompTer. He left immediately afterward. For a live TV show, it was thrilling.

Backstage, Allen said he "felt honored to do it." He explained, "I'm not a big awards person, so when I had an opportunity to do this for the city, it was a different thing. I was able to just talk about New York City and show it in a light that I sincerely feel about it." Allen said he would not avoid shooting the New York skyline without the World Trade Center towers for his next project. "I feel it's ridiculous to pussyfoot around and reframe the shots and not show it," Allen said. "It's a terrible tragedy, but it's reality. New York still has a spectacular skyline, and I'm sure what they build in its place will enhance it."

Oscar and the Power Elite

From the beginning, it has been important to bestow prestige on the event by including dignitaries from the cultural and political milieux. Guests of honor in the first event were stage actor Sir Gilbert Parker and novelist Fannie Hurst, whose books were adapted to the screen, including numerous versions of *Back Street*. In that show, the link between Hollywood and Washington's power elite began when MGM's Louis B. Mayer singled out President Herbert Hoover for a life dedicated to service. "Life without service isn't worth living," said Mayer by way of explaining the goal of the Academy Awards — "give flowers to the living, don't wait until they're dead." The Hollywood-Washington connection proved to be mutually beneficial, and the Oscars have received the formal endorsement of several presidents.

For the 1931 banquet, Louis B. Mayer invited Governor of California Will Hays, an admiral, and leaders of the American Newspaper Publishers Association, which was holding its convention in Los Angeles at the same time. Mayer's guest of honor was Herbert Hoover's Vice President, Charles Curtis, who arrived with his sister, society lady Dolly Gann. The Oscar show thus became a political event. The admiral paid tribute to democracy, and the Governor saluted the movie industry and Louis B. Mayer as a man "beloved in the halls of Congress." Curtis was later criticized for his "dull Republican" speech, but his presence helped put the Academy Awards into the national spotlight. In the same evening, Conrad Nagel, one of the Academy's founders, paid tribute to Thomas Edison, the recipient of the previous year's Lifetime Membership, who had just died.

In 1941, Franklin D. Roosevelt became the first president to address the motion picture industry via radio. Three years earlier, his son, Hollywood producer James Roosevelt, presented the Best Picture Award to Frank Capra for *You Can't Take It With You*. President Harry S. Truman followed in Roosevelt's footsteps, when he sent a congratulatory message to the Academy in 1949.

In 1981, President Ronald Reagan, a former Hollywood B-actor and SAG president, participated in the proceedings via a pre-taped one-minute greeting. "I've been trapped in some film forever myself," Reagan said, "It's surely no state secret that Nancy and I share your interest in the results of this year."

The Oscars as a Global Event

Apart from wheat and auto parts, America's biggest export is now the Oscar. — Billy Crystal, Oscar host

The Oscar show is the most closely scrutinized and most widely watched entertainment event on global television. — Andrew Sarris, film critic

The Oscar show is a global event generating extensive coverage in the media all over the world. This became clear in 1986, when China, India, and France received the Oscar telecast for the first time, and emcee Robin Williams translated salutations into various languages. The fact that once a year people around the world talk about the same movies at the same time is an amazing phenomenon. Few media events can boast the Oscars' global dimensions.

How did the Oscars become such a global event? When the Academy was founded, its purpose was to "establish the industry in the public mind as a respectable and legitimate institution, and its people as reputable individuals." The Oscars were designed as a local gesture by Hollywood insiders to recognize and honor film achievements. They were an afterthought on the Academy's agenda, barely mentioned in the 1927 statement of goals: "The Academy will encourage the improvement and advancement of the arts and sciences of the profession by the interchange of constructive ideas and by awards of merit for distinctive achievements." For Louis B. Mayer, the Academy's chief architect, the Academy Awards had a dual purpose: "To recognize fine achievements today and to inspire others to give finer achievements tomorrow."

The initial idea was to bestow the awards in an open meeting or a dinner. The board decided in favor of the dinner, a format that prevailed for many years. The guests of the first Oscar ceremonies, on May 16, 1929, at the Blossom Room of the Hollywood Roosevelt Hotel, dined on jumbo squab périgeaux, Lobster Eugènie, Los Angeles salad, terrapin, and fruit supreme. About three hundred people occupied 36 tables, each bearing a replica of the statuette in waxed candy. The banquet was more of a private party than a big public event, and the awards were handed out in less than ten minutes. Veteran members were shocked by the attention accorded to the Oscars. "It was just a small group getting together for a pat on the back," Janet Gaynor, the first Best Actress, recalled. "It wasn't open to anyone but Academy members, and as you danced, you saw the most important people in Hollywood." In the first years, the banquet was an intimate "family affair," with little media coverage.

No one knew if the banquet would become a lasting tradition. Then-Academy president, Douglas Fairbanks, handed out all of the awards under the organization of chair William C. DeMille (the brother of director Cecil B. DeMille). As if foreseeing that the show would get out of control, Fairbanks asked for brevity in acceptance speeches.

Achievements in 1928–29 were celebrated on April 30, 1930, at the Coconut Grove of the Ambassador Hotel. The next banquet was held on November 5, 1930, only seven months later, in order to make up for lost time and get the annual event on a regular schedule. The brief presentation of the awards by Academy president William C. DeMille began after dinner, and one of the Academy founders, Conrad Nagel, acted as emcee.

Will Hays, then head of the industry's self-censorship board, gave a lecture on morality and business: "Good taste is good business, and to offend good taste is to fortify sales resistance." Hays's bombastic lecture lasted more than half an hour, during which he said "nothing unclean can maintain growth and vitality. When a tree begins to collect blights, it begins to wither. So does reputation. So does business."

Reputation and respectability were indeed key words which featured prominently from the very first year. When Louis B. Mayer presented the Best Picture to *All Quiet on the Western Front,* he noted, rather pretentiously: "There's talk that the motion picture we honor tonight may win a Nobel Prize."

The Academy Award got its nickname, Oscar, during the 1934 show (honoring 1933 films), which took place on March 16 at a banquet held at the Fiesta Room of the Ambassador Hotel. The Academy decided to delay the ceremony until 1934 in order to include all the 1933 films, a practice which has continued to the present. It was hosted by Will Rogers who, like his predecessors, presented all the awards. Emcee Rogers (then one of the country's most popular stars) said: "This looks like the last roundup of the ermine ... I got the courage to come here and talk to the highbrows and brains of the industry after I read that Sam Goldwyn had lectured at Harvard." Rogers showed nostalgia for "the old days of Republican rugged individualism, when Louis B. Mayer was photographed on the steps of the White House and when actors signing a contract at MGM had an Academy Award thrown in for good measure."

The Hollywood press ignored the Academy's labor disputes and emphasized the excitement and festivity of the ceremonies, with Duke Ellington's band playing music. Despite wars and resignations that shook the Academy during the past year, several celebs attended the show (see chapter 2).

The 1935 show, on February 27, at a banquet at the Biltmore Bowl of the Biltmore Hotel, was hosted by Irvin S. Cobb who again presented all the awards.

On December 17, 1941, with the United States entering World War II, the Academy's board announced that there would be no banquet. But then, on January 30, 1942, the group reversed itself, and reinstated the banquet in order to boost civil morale. It would be called a dinner, instead of a banquet, there would be music but no dancing, and women would be asked to wear modest attire. This prompted gossip columnist Hedda Hopper to quip: "Would it break down our soldiers' morale to see our women beautifully dressed?"

In 1944, due to the war situation, the dinner banquet seemed too conspicuously luxurious and the practice was discontinued for good; the Academy has always been sensitive to its public image. There was also a pragmatic reason: The group had expanded so much that it was impossible to accommodate all members and their guests for dinner. The new ceremonies were open to the public and took place at the Graumann's Chinese Theater. Displaying its version of patriotism, the Academy advertised the fact that many passes were given to the armed forces.

The dramatic increase in the Oscars' public profile baffled the Academy, which motivated the board of directors to issue the following statement: "Somewhat to the embarrassment of the traditional dignity of the Academy, the words 'Oscar' and 'Academy Awards' have slipped into the popular language like 'Sterling' and 'Nobel,' as recognized symbols of quality." The board was unaware that in a few years the Oscar would stand for something both more and less than "recognized symbols of quality."

The Oscar Statuette—The Latest Hot Commodity

If you think the Oscar is mostly about prestige and symbolic value, think again. The statuettes themselves have become a hot commercial commodity, sought in public auctions and private transactions. It wasn't always this way. It began with the publicity around Vivien Leigh's 1939 Oscar for *Gone With the Wind*, which was sold at Sotheby's for a then record-breaking $510,000.

In 1950, the Academy began to demand that recipients offer their Oscars back to the Academy before selling them. All Oscar nominees are now required to sign a written agreement to this effect before the ceremonies.

Producer Sid Luft was barred by a 1993 Academy-solicited court order from selling his ex-wife Judy Garland's Oscar. In 1958, Garland received a replacement statuette for the 1940 Special Oscar she had received as a juvenile and lost. Luft wanted to sell her statuette.

In July 2001, Steven Spielberg turned out to be the "anonymous" bidder who paid $578,000 for Bette Davis's Best Actress Oscar for *Jezebel* at a Christie's auction. Spielberg won the statuette in a telephone bidding war that started at $250,000. The Oscar was among various items auctioned from the actress's collection by her assistant, Kathryn Sermak. Spielberg later presented the Oscar to the Academy, as he had done in 1996, when he acquired Clark Gable's Oscar for *It Happened One Night* (for $607,000). Former Universal mogul Lew Wasserman also bought an Oscar at auction — Harold Russell's Supporting Award for *The Best Years of Our Lives.*

The "mystery" man who paid more than $150,000 for an Oscar in September 2001 turned out to be two-time Oscar-winner Kevin Spacey. The statuette, which honored composer George Stoll and his score for the 1945 musical *Anchors Aweigh,* was purchased anonymously by Spacey at an estate sale at Butterfield's auction house. "I strongly feel that Academy Awards should belong to those who have earned them," Spacey told the *Los Angeles Times,* "not those who simply have the financial means to acquire them." Bidding anonymously by phone, Spacey paid $156,875 for Stoll's Oscar, which was offered as part of the family's estate.

Year after year, Oscar sagas continue: Whoopi Goldberg's Supporting Oscar was found on February 5, 2002, at an Ontario airport in a trash bin. Goldberg had shipped her Oscar, which she had won for *Ghost,* for cleaning via UPS to R. S. Owens Co., the Chicago company that makes the statuettes. When the box arrived back, it was empty. Someone had opened the package, removed the Oscar, and resealed the box. UPS returned the Oscar to the Academy, which then sent it back to Goldberg. The actress no longer plans to have it cleaned, vowing that "polished or unpolished, the Oscar will never leave my house again!"

UPS spokesperson Robin Roberts confirmed the recovery, and said that the Goldberg case was under investigation. As a result, the Academy, which routinely sends Oscar statuettes by UPS for maintenance work, is now reexamining its shipping procedures. The statuettes are numbered, and Goldberg's was inscribed with her name, making it difficult for a thief to sell. "I don't know how in the world they would ever fence the darn thing," said Jon Pavlik, the Academy's spokesperson.

Oscar and the Mass Media

Sidney Kent, then Twentieth Century-Fox President, was the one to propose the use of radio "to sell our pictures," an idea that was immediately and wholeheartedly embraced by the studios. Consequently, the third Academy banquet, on April 3, 1931, was broadcast on radio station KNX. However, in 1931 and for the next fifteen years, only a portion of the show was broadcast. The entire ceremony was broadcast for the first time on March 15, 1945, over the ABC

Network and the Armed Forces Radio Service. This signaled the true beginning of what members would describe as the Oscars getting out of control.

Funding for the ceremonies initially came from the studios, which had vested interests in supporting the awards. The banquets in the 1930s were modest affairs that kept the annual deficits low. For example, the combined cost for Duke Ellington's band and the statuettes amounted to slightly over $1,000. By 1949, however, several of the major studios refused to underwrite the costs, even though the amount of money needed was minuscule. Their decision to discontinue support was conveyed to the Academy in December 1948, before the announcement of that year's nominations, which interestingly favored British movies such as *Hamlet* and *The Red Shoes* over American ones.

Jean Hersholt, the Academy's president, explained that the moguls didn't want "Academy standards foisted upon them," and that they favored the making of "commercial pictures unhampered by consideration of artistic excellence." And while Hersholt saw in the studios' decision "the highest praise for our organization," he was upset that MGM, Paramount, Fox, and Warner each gave $12,500, whereas Universal, Columbia, and Republic didn't support the event at all. In their statement, the defecting studios claimed that their decision was not commercially motivated, stressing that "the companies as companies were never members of the Academy," which was created as an organization to include only the most accomplished individual artists. Though few believed this, the studios declared they were "heartily in accord with the principle of individuals democratically selecting the best in artistic achievement." It was "in the interest of this principle," that they decided "to remove any suspicion of company influence."

However, *Hamlet*'s 1948 Best Picture win and the multiple awards showered on *The Red Shoes,* made the situation worse. Bosley Crowther wrote in the *New York Times:* "Prides had been wounded by the bombshell bestowal of the Academy upon *Hamlet,* making the timing of the studios' exposé sound like very sour grapes." The moguls were upset that the Academy favored British art films over what they considered superb American movies. In 1948, John Huston's *The Treasure of the Sierra Madre* was nominated in four categories, Jean Negulesco's *Johnny Belinda* in twelve, and Anatole Litvak's *The Snake Pit* in six. *The Snake Pit* was predicted to win the Best Picture, but received only one minor award (sound recording).

The studios denied any link between their actions and the prominence of British films. The British winners were bewildered to say the least. "I can't believe American companies would do such a thing," said director Emeric Pressburger (who collaborated on films with Michael Powell), and producer Alexander Korda noted, "I'm sure Americans are too generous for any ill-feeling to arise." But the studios' withdrawal of support, and the separation of the Oscar from the major companies, was seen by many as a positive move that would make the members freer to vote. In the past, the studios put pressure on their employees to vote for their own pictures and personnel.

Emmet Lavery expressed that feeling in the *Saturday Review:*

So we come now, in the twenty-first year of the Academy's existence, to the parting of the ways between the major Hollywood studios and the Academy as co-sponsors of the annual awards program. And a happy parting it is. The only cause for wonderment is that it did not happen sooner, preferably at the very beginning of the Academy's existence. This does not mean the end of the Academy. On the contrary, it means an expansion and development on a completely independent level. There can now be little question that the annual awards are the free choice of the 1800 members. This is the moment, and a very good moment, when Oscar comes into his own. At the ripe old age of 21, Oscar has shown that he is free to vote as he chooses.

For the next three years, 1949 to 1951, the Academy faced some challenges in producing the ceremony. Radio commercials, increased annual dues, and a fund drive barely managed to finance the Oscar ceremonies. In 1952, a turning point occurred. Television, Hollywood's long-time enemy, came to the rescue in a totally unexpected move. In the past, the studios either prohibited or restricted the appearances of their stars on television, so intense was the animosity between the media. But the new cooperation was mutually beneficial: Television needed stars, as it had not yet developed its own celebs, and the Academy was desperate for funds to cover the show's escalating costs.

The Oscar Telecast

RCA Victor sponsored the 1953 ceremony, and NBC televised it. The date, March 19, 1953, was appropriate: Oscar was celebrating its twenty-fifth anniversary. A new era had begun.

Simultaneous ceremonies took place in New York and Los Angeles from 1953 to 1956: Viewers were switched back and forth, depending on the winners' location, a practice that was discontinued in 1957. The ceremonies were televised in black and white, but in 1967 the show switched to color, which contributed to its popularity. American households that could not afford to buy a TV set were not forgotten. The Oscars were simultaneously broadcast on radio as late as 1969, when the Academy realized that few people listened to the ceremonies on radio anymore. By then, television had established itself as the dominant medium of entertainment in America.

The show's public grew rapidly. In 1948, an unprecedented fifty million listened to the proceedings, when ABC beamed the event to all its national affiliates and the Armed Forces Radio Service broadcast to American soldiers overseas. A decade later, in 1959, the audience had doubled: Eighty million Americans watched the show on television or listened to it on the radio, and another hundred million people were reached via overseas radio.

The dramatic increase in audiences had a direct impact on the amount of money paid to the Academy by the networks. In 1952, the rights were purchased for $100,000, and in 1964, they jumped to a million. No one could have predicted that in a few decades, the Oscar telecast would become the jewel in the Academy's crown.

At present, the Academy's financial well-being rests entirely on the Oscar. Under a new contract that runs through 2008, ABC is paying the Academy over $40 million for broadcast rights to the Sunday-night event. In 2001, after clearing all expenses, the Academy generated an Oscar-night profit of over $20 million.

For decades, the Oscar ceremonies took place on a Monday night, with a dress rehearsal on the preceding Sunday. In 1999, in an effort to broaden their reach, they were moved to Sunday. The Academy produces its own telecast as a way of ensuring quality. "This way we can control our fortunes," President Robert Rehme said. "We control everything, down to the number of commercials on the show. We look at every commercial and pass on the content. We want to protect the Oscar and the Academy as our brand."

ABC takes advantage of this extraordinary exposure. The ads usually sell out the summer before the show. In 1998, ABC charged $1 million for each of the fifty-eight commercial spots slated for the four-hour show. Two years later, the Academy broke the seven-figure barrier for a thirty-second ad. Madison Avenue calls the Academy Awards the "Super Bowl for Women," which is no doubt why companies are willing to pay an average of $1.25 million for a spot. Without television, the Oscar ceremonies as we know them would be impossible.

Using TV, the movies' old competitor, the Academy tries to put on an entertaining show. Exciting ceremonies depend on the intensity of the competition, caliber of potential winners, and the shows intrinsic entertainment value. It took several years to find a winning format, and the show continues to evolve. In 1955, a reporter noted that for the first time, "every word, every motion was designed for the camera. No more was the glittering festival a self-conscious performance with television's cameras guiltily watching what they could. Oscar has broken the twenty-five-year shroud of dignity, dullness, and routines for its sprightly marriage partner, television."

Popular figures such as movie star Will Rogers, humorist Irving S. Cobb, and comedian Jack Benny were among the show's hosts. But the emcee still most closely identified with the Oscars is comedian Bob Hope, serving as host twenty-two times, nine of which were solo. Hope was the perfect choice. He was a popular movie star, especially in his Road Movies with Bing Crosby. But Hope was more than a star, he was an American institution, having entertained soldiers in World War II, Korea, and Vietnam. Critic Walter Kerr described Hope as "Oscar's Constant Uncle," but a better term would be "America's comic consciousness," as Hope was described in his prime.

"I should have grabbed an Oscar, but they don't recognize comedies," Bob Hope once said, "and they don't have a comedy category. I have two Oscars and a plaque and a gold medal from the Academy, but I never won for acting."

Johnny Carson, of NBC's "The Tonight Show," hosted for a few years. Unlike Hope, Carson was uniquely a television creation, a genuine star of the small screen. Carson didn't last long as host: In 1984, the Oscar show changed to a multi-host format. For the fifty-eighth ceremonies, there were three hosts, Jane Fonda, Alan Alda, and Robin Williams, all familiar faces on both the large and small screens. The idea, of course, was to appeal to audiences of both film and television.

Robin Williams, the 1986 emcee, proved to be a fortuitous choice as he provided the show's funniest moments with his quirky humor. Appearing with two Price and Waterhouse representatives, carrying the winners' names in briefcases, Williams suggested they "open up the suckers right now." Rejected, the comedian told the public, "I'm afraid we have to do this show." Williams's one-liners were so fast that there was no time to be offended by them, as Jack Valenti could well have been, when he was introduced as "the man you never heard of but you have to listen to anyway."

Two hosts who have defined the Oscars' last decade are Billy Crystal and Whoopi Goldberg. In the 1991 show, Billy Crystal made a colorful entrance on a horse, a plug for his upcoming summer movie, *City Slickers,* in which he played a New York yuppie who goes to a dude ranch. Crystal rode bareback on a twenty-foot Oscar statuette that veteran actor Jack Palance dragged in by his teeth to open the 1992 show. Palance, who won Supporting Oscar for *City Slickers* the year before, had dropped to the stage for one-armed push-ups during his acceptance speech, a gesture that became the most-remarked about Oscar bit for years.

Making her debut as host in 1994, Whoopi Goldberg replaced Billy Crystal, thus becoming the first female — and first black — solo host. Goldberg spiced up the show with irreverent remarks and made good on her promise not to shy away from politics. People were nervous to see if Whoopi's ad libs would be "proper" for early evening network television. Buz Kohan, one of the show's writers, commented: "When you buy a Whoopi Goldberg, you buy the whole package and part of the package is that she is a free spirit who just might say anything that comes to mind at the moment."

Whoopi was back in 1997, after David Letterman's fiasco as host the year before. Her friend Quincy Jones, who had co-produced Goldberg's feature debut, *The Color Purple,* was the show's producer. Nervous due to the mixed reviews for her first hosting, Goldberg made her displeasure known during the telecast with satirical skits comparing herself to Crystal.

Though the 1997 Academy Awards were hosted and produced by African Americans, only one black artist was nominated for an Oscar, and there was not a single black performer among the twenty acting nominees. As a result, there were both formal and informal pressures on host Goldberg to take a stance. Reverend Jesse Jackson publicly urged African Americans attending the Oscars to wear a rainbow ribbon as a symbol of their opposition to Hollywood's "race exclusion and cultural violence." Jackson even threatened to stage a grass-roots protest against the Academy, but his idea backfired with the mainstream media.

The all-time, top-rated Oscarcast was in 1956, when *Marty* won Best Picture, garnering a 46.7/82 (rating/share). In contrast, the 1986 Oscarcast saw the lowest results ever, with 27.3/43. That year, *Out of Africa* won Best Picture, and the acting awards went to non-celebs, William Hurt (*Kiss of the Spider Woman*) and Geraldine Page (*The Trip to Bountiful*), both associated with the New York stage and independent movies.

One of the most popular Oscar shows was in 1970, with an impressive 43.4 rating, attributable to the anticipation of veteran star John Wayne winning the Best Actor for *True Grit*, which he did. In the 1970s, the ratings of the Oscar show ranged from 38.7 in 1972 to 34.6 in 1979. From 1992 to 1998, the Oscarcast averaged a 31.0/51, which reflected a significant boost since the Oscars' worst slump, from 1985 to 1991, which averaged a 28.3/47.

The 1999 Oscar telecast, while down from the previous year's *Titanic*-boosted numbers, ranked second-best among the 18–49 demographic over the past four years. Overall, though, the ratings were down 18 percent from 1998, despite expectations of an increase after switching the telecast to Sunday. The logic for the move was that the average Sunday viewership level would be higher because of less work-related distractions in time zones where the show begins before prime time. The 28.6 rating of 1999 was comparable to that of 1997, when *The English Patient* led the mostly independent nominees.

The solid results with the 18–49 group suggested that the Academy and ABC have made progress in their quest to lasso in a younger viewership. Reacting to the numbers positively, Michael Davies, one of ABC's executive vice presidents, said, "This is exactly where our ratings estimates were. We looked at last year's show as a huge spike. *Titanic* brought into the show people who hadn't been to the movies in twenty years, resulting in an impressive 34.9/55 rating/share." These were the highest numbers in fifteen years — eighty-seven million Americans tuned in to see at least part of the program.

Overall, the Academy Awards ranked as the third-highest-rated prime-time telecast of the 1999 season, behind the Super Bowl (40.2/61) and the *20/20* Barbara Walters show with Clinton intern Monica Lewinsky (33.4/48). ABC estimates that about seventy-eight million viewers watched at least part of the Oscars' coverage, down 10 percent from *Titanic*'s eighty-seven million. ABC was encouraged that the Academy Awards' national rating dropped just 11 percent from the telecast's average in Nielsen-metered markets. In past years, the drop had generally been about 15 percent, suggesting the 2000 coverage had stronger-than-usual appeal in the American heartland. In urban markets, the Oscars did best in Los Angeles (44.0/64), San Diego (41.4/60), and New York City (37.4/55).

Themes and Motifs of Oscar Shows

Nostalgia has served as a key theme of several Oscar shows. The 1985 show, for example, paid tribute to film achievements of 1934 and audiences were treated to clips of Shirley Temple who later appeared in person, and spectacular dancing by Fred Astaire and Ginger Rogers. There were also images from the 1934 Best Picture, *It Happened One Night*, directed by Frank Capra, who later served as the presenter of the top award. The homage to Hollywood's glorious past came in response to criticism that the show had become too much of a television spectacle. In the 1980s, many of the presenters were young performers who had little to do with movies; their popularity among TV viewers was the reason for their standing on the Oscar platform.

A tribute to MGM musicals, featuring its surviving female stars, Jane Powell, Cyd Charisse, June Allyson, Leslie Caron, Kathryn Grayson, Marge Champion, Anne Miller, and Esther Williams made up the show's nostalgic highlight. Gene Kelly, Debbie Reynolds, and Donald O'Connor, who presented the music award, reprised their classic number from *Singin' in the Rain*. There was another touching gesture when all the nominees were asked to stand up and were applauded as a group. Celebrating Old Hollywood was also the theme of "hymn to the losers," sung by Irene Cara and accompanied by impressive clips from the Best Picture losers, including *The Wizard of Oz, Citizen Kane, Sunset Boulevard,* and *Tootsie.* Stanley Donen, who produced the Oscar show, copped it by asking Billy Wilder, John Huston, and Akira Kurosawa to present the Best Picture.

In 1987, the Academy nominations were announced live on national television for the first time. Oscar winners Anjelica Huston and Don Ameche joined Academy president Robert Wise as hosts of the predawn show, scheduled at 5:30 A.M. to accommodate the New York-based network morning shows.

In 1989, the phrase "And the Oscar goes to," replaced "And the winner is," in an attempt to spare the feeling of the losers, or as the Academy calls them, "the non-winners."

The sixty-third show in 1991 celebrated the centennial of motion pictures with an impressive kickoff. Actor Michael Caine, stationed in Paris at the Hotel Scribe, where the first films were exhibited, gave the order for the projector to start for an 1891 audience, which spilled out of the room (in a technological whizbang) onto the stage of the Shrine Auditorium. Madonna's off-key, shake-your-bootie rendition of "Sooner or Later I Always Get My Man" and Stephen Sondheim's Oscar-winning song from Warren Beatty's *Dick Tracy,* also drew attention in the 1991 show. "It's the NC-17 portion of our show," Billy Crystal quipped. Another of the show's highlights was Michael Blake's acceptance speech for the script of *Dances With Wolves.* Blake was accompanied by Doris Leader Charge, who translated his words into a Native American language.

For the 1994 show, film supervisor Douglas M. Stewart gathered clips from nominated pictures and assembled a series of special presentations. One montage was dedicated to famous screen dogs (from Toto in *The Wizard of Oz* to Asta in The Thin Man series), and another to actors winking. In the same year, Tom Hanks delivered a lauded acceptance speech after winning Best Actor for Hollywood's first AIDS drama, *Philadelphia,* thanking his gay high-school drama teacher, Rawley Farnsworth. Hank's remarks, which outed the teacher, would inspire Paul Rudnick to write the comedy *In & Out* with Kevin Kline.

Certainly, the Oscar show has become a big family event. For the 1995 ceremonies, the lead contenders, Tom Hanks (*Forrest Gump*) and Jessica Lange (*Blue Sky*), had their kids rooting for them up in the balcony. And Spielberg—

announcing the Best Director, addressed a child in the audience, "Alex, your father just won the Academy Award." Spielberg was talking to Robert Zemeckis's son, who was sitting on his mother's lap.

The show has continued to display politically correct family values, as when Clint Eastwood brought his elderly mother to the ceremony. And when Mira Sorvino won a supporting Oscar for Woody Allen's 1995 *Mighty Aphrodite,* TV viewers witnessed her father, actor Paul Sorvino, sobbing in the audience. Kirk Douglas's sons were also seen crying in the audience when their father was accorded an Honorary Oscar, a compensation for never having won a competitive Oscar and a celebration for surviving a helicopter accident as well as a severe stroke.

As always, the most memorable Oscar moments are the small, personal ones. In 1996, actor Christopher Reeve, paralyzed after a horse-riding accident, received a standing ovation when, in a special wheelchair, he hosted a segment on the movies' power to deal with social issues. In 1997, when Cuba Gooding Jr. won the Supporting Actor for *Jerry Maguire,* he unleashed a long aria of joy. The show's director Louis J. Horvitz recalled: "We were standing up in the booth at that point, dreaming of a 40 share of the ratings."

Nineteen-ninety-seven show was dubbed "the year of the indies," because of the prominence of small-budget films made outside mainstream Hollywood, such as *Fargo, Secrets & Lies,* and *Shine.* In response to such a large number of indies being nominated, director Joel Schumacher told the *Los Angeles Times:* "People get more excited when the contest seems to be between people they know and have invested in for years. They don't know who these people are. I hope they find out." Unfortunately, Schumacher proved right, and the ratings for the show were poor.

The 1998 show saw the revenge of the majors against the indies, with big pictures like *Titanic* representing a return to Hollywood's tradition of grand cinema with strong production values. The potential threat of a predictable *Titanic* sweep was not ideal for the show's producers, always hoping for the live, spontaneous moments — the surprises that come with upsets and speeches. As Horvitz noted: "You hope they're meaty with meaningful words about filmmaking and its contribution to life, and have something more than a long list of thank yous."

In 1999, Roberto Benigni stole the show in one of Oscar's indelible moments, akin to Jack Palance's one-armed push-ups, or Sally Field's 1985 nakedly vulnerable, "You like me. You really like me!" A bouncing ball of unself-conscious energy, Benigni made his way to the stage to accept Best Foreign-Language Picture for *Life Is Beautiful* by climbing over the backs of chairs and audience members, bunny-hopping up the stairs to the stage. This was followed by his emotional "Ocean of Love" speech.

In the following year, the *Wall Street Journal* created a furor when it announced its intent to poll 6 percent of the Academy voters and reveal the results prior to the show. President Robert Rehme reacted with anger: "I canceled my subscription. They should go back to Wall Street and leave Hollywood alone."

The first show of the millennium saw studios and indies, veterans and new-comers, blockbusters and upstarts, all competing for Oscars. As always, the most treasured moments were the spontaneous ones, like the winner of Best Documentary Short, "Defending Our Lives," who blurted out: "Domestic violence is the leading cause of violence to women in the U.S. Please, we need all your help to stop this."

The 2000 event was not the condensed kudofest that producers Richard and Lili Fini Zanuck had promised. In fact, at four hours and nine minutes, it was one of the longest, exceeding the previous year's show, which ran four hours and two minutes. But it was also one of the best. Billy Crystal was digitally introduced into a variety of classic scenes from *Taxi Driver, Spartacus, The Graduate, The Godfather,* and *Deliverance* with hilarious results. Another highlight was a medley of movie music, orchestrated by Burt Bacharach.

In his introduction, Robert Rehme said that the nominees represented "the least predictable year in Academy history," an apt remark since many Oscar races were wide open. There was head-to-head competition between *American Beauty* and *The Cider House Rules.* DreamWorks refused to call *American Beauty* a shoo-in, lest history repeat itself. (In 1998, the studio's *Saving Private Ryan* was considered to be the easy front-runner, but it lost to Miramax's *Shakespeare in Love.*)

Steve Martin, the new host of the 2001 show, was described by some critics as "the perfect mix of class and class clown." Smart and fresh, Martin flaunted urbanc sophistication, refusing to appeal to the lowest common denominator of his mass audience. The show, one of the shortest in a long time (three hours and a few minutes), didn't suffer either, pulling in forty-six million viewers.

Martin was helped by the fact that the telecast was full of surprises, including a Bob Dylan win. No single movie dominated the awards. Instead, it was a three-way-tie among *Gladiator, Traffic,* and *Crouching Tiger, Hidden Dragon.* As Kenneth Turan observed in the *Los Angeles Times,* "Finally, eerily, it was a cliffhanger not unlike the one that decided the other election, back in November, with the winner in doubt until the final envelope was opened."

Coming Home—Back to Hollywood Boulevard

In 2002, the Oscars moved into a new, permanent home, the Kodak Theater, at Hollywood Boulevard and Highland Avenue. The plan is for the Kodak to host the Oscar ceremony annually, which has long been shuttled between various Los Angeles venues. It was an exciting occasion and a significant event in the rebirth of Hollywood. "Kodak is pictures and the Academy Awards honor the best pictures," said Joerg Agin, president of Kodak's Entertaining Imaging. "We expect it to be one of the most photographic locations in Hollywood." A decaying area that has resisted previous clean-up efforts was finally restored to what's close to its Golden Age glory.

The new home offers many advantages, though wheelchair accessibility was an issue. The return to Hollywood fulfills the Academy's wish for the show to originate from the mythical showbiz capital. The Academy gets its own home and will no longer be a vagabond, moving from one venue to another. The Dorothy Chandler Pavilion was elegant, but too small. The Shrine Auditorium was large, but timeworn. In comparison, the Kodak Theater is brand new and just the right size — three thousand seats. The theater has intimacy — its "pushed forward" steepness ought to help the host establish a rapport with the audience.

There's also efficiency in the venue's consolidation of elements — the telecast, the governor's ball, and the press are all in one place. The Academy hopes that having a designated arrival area will add to the theatricality of the pre-show experience. The red carpet leading to the Kodak Theater, which was actually burgundy, was cordoned off by an army of security guards. The extended area with fans in bleachers on the right and the press on the left added excitement to the arrivals. To avoid criticism that the Oscars are being held in a shopping mall, the Academy spent a fortune paying businesses to close down their stores and cover their signs. Considerable efforts were made to obscure the tackiness of Hollywood and Highland's mercantile side.

Observers were pondering the nature of the 2002 award ceremonies, considering the somber mood that loomed over the Emmys show — which had been postponed twice — after the tragedy of the September 11 terrorist attacks and the political events that followed. Whoopi Goldberg, the show's host, told the *Hollywood Reporter:* "We're all coming in a little shell-shocked from the last six months, and everybody's carrying that. My job is to get us across the rapids with some fun, humor, grace, and dignity, and make it a great night."

Goldberg did acknowledge the fact that she was "throwing a housewarming because that's what the Oscars are, a housewarming." Her task, to strike a balance between jokes for the industry and the need to relate to a vast TV audience, was met with relative success. Goldberg held that the national obsession with pop culture and celebs makes her hosting job easier, because, "there's very little inside information left. Most of the things that you talk about are things that everybody has heard or seen on 'Entertainment Tonight' or somewhere else."

Year one at the Kodak seems to have been fairly successful. In 2002, the Oscarcast's 41.8 million viewers was the fourth highest-rated telecast of the season, following the Super Bowl with 86.8 million, the Opening Ceremonies of the Winter Olympics with 45.6, and the Women's Figure-Skating competition with 43.3.

"Do the Oscars still function as *the* cultural event of the year, or are they just an ode to the culture of celebrity?" asked Paul Brownfield in the *Los Angeles Times.* As a shared experience, few occasions outside spectator sports merit the collective attention of the Academy Awards. For Brownfield, the show's laborious nature is dictated by the Academy's philosophy that television exists for the Oscar Awards — not the other way around. Grousing about the length of the broadcast is common, with attention span strained to the breaking point by the time the Thalberg Memorial Award is presented. Yet, we shouldn't forget that no matter how entertaining the show is, complaining about the Oscars, has become a global habit and a major part of the fun.

2

THE HISTORY OF THE OSCAR AWARD

The Academy Award is universally nicknamed the Oscar, which was first used at the 1934 banquet. There's still uncertainty as to who exactly had come up with that nickname.

Various people have claimed credit for the title, though the issue has never been resolved. Actress Bette Davis said that she was the one to label the award "Oscar" because it looked like the backside of her then-husband, Harmon Oscar Nelson.

Librarian Margaret Herrick, later the Academy's Executive Secretary, reported to her first day of work in 1931. After having been formally introduced to the gold statuette, she looked it over carefully and said it reminded her of her Uncle Oscar (Oscar Pierce was actually her second cousin, not uncle). Columnist Sidney Skolsky was reported on the scene and he immediately seized on the name and used it in his byline: "Employees have affectionately dubbed their famous statuette 'Oscar.'"

But according to Skolsky, he was the first to use the name Oscar for the following reason: "I got tired of using statuette in my story. I wanted to give the guy a name, not only to make it easier to write about, but to give the thing an identity and a personality. I thought Oscar wouldn't be too dignified a name for a banquet that had so much dignity."

The statuette was designed by MGM's art director Cedric Gibbons, and created by sculptor George Stanley. The Oscars were first printed on scroll, then cast in gold. Gibbons sketched a knight standing on a reel of film holding a two-edged sword. The five holes on the base represented the Academy's five original branches: Producers, writers, directors, actors, and technicians. A minor streamlining of the base is the only addition to the Oscar since it was created. Stanley sculpted Gibbons's design in clay, and Alex Smith cast the statue in tin and copper and then gold-plated it over a composition of 92.5 percent tin and 7.5 percent copper. The Oscar statuette is thirteen and a half inches tall and weighs about eight and a half pounds.

Screenwriter Frances Marion, who won Oscars for Writing Achievement (as it was then called) for *The Big House* and Original Story for *The Champ,* observed in her memoir that the statuette was perceived as a bit amateurish, but she saw it as a perfect symbol of the film business: "a powerful athletic body clutching a gleaming sword with half of his head, that part which held his brains, completely sliced off." Marion also recalled that, "Those who had never won the gold-plated honor referred to it disparagingly as the 'Oscar.' " It was only when Walt Disney mentioned the Oscar in his speech, that the name took on a different meaning since it was spoken with "sincere appreciation."

The Academy bestows different kinds of Oscars:

- The Annual Merit Awards honor various film categories, the number of which has changed over the years. At present, achievements are honored in twenty-four fields, including the new Oscar for Best Animated Feature, given for the first time at the 2002 ceremonies.
- The Scientific or Technical Achievement Awards.
- The Irving G. Thalberg Award "to a creative producer whose body of work reflects consistently high quality of motion picture productions."
- The Jean Hersholt Humanitarian Award "to an individual in the motion picture industry whose humanitarian efforts have brought credit to the industry."
- The Gordon E. Sawyer Award "to an individual in the motion picture industry whose technological contributions have brought credit to the industry."
- The Honorary Awards "for outstanding achievements not strictly within the other categories, for exceptionally distinguished service in the making of the motion pictures or for outstanding service to the Academy."

The winners of Annual Merit Awards, Class I Scientific or Technical Awards, Special Achievement Awards, the Jean Hersholt Humanitarian Award, and Honorary Awards receive the Oscar statuette. The Irving G. Thalberg Award is a bronze head of the distinguished producer.

During World War II, plaster statuettes were awarded as every piece of metal was needed for the war effort. After the War, though, the Academy went back to the original gold statuettes. The Oscars are awarded to winners without any fee, though the Academy charges for duplicates in cases of loss, theft, or disposal.

Every year the Academy orders fifty statuettes from Southern California Trophy, which began producing them in 1930, to make sure there will be no shortage. While only twenty-four categories are honored, there have often been collaborations of two or three artists, particularly in the writing and technical areas, and there are also Honorary Oscars. Shortly after the nominees are announced, a count is made of the maximum number of awards that could conceivably be handed out in a given year. The statuettes were not numbered until 1949, when the Academy's Board decided on the number 501 as a convenient starting point, even though it's estimated that more than five hundred statuettes were awarded in the first two decades.

The Idea for an Academy

The idea for a film academy emerged under the leadership of Louis B. Mayer, the powerful head of Metro-Goldwyn-Mayer. A prime motive for the Academy's foundation was the unionization of the industry in November 1926, when nine major studios and five unions signed the Studio Basic Agreement. But this agreement applied only to technical workers; the creative groups, directors, writers and actors still lacked standardized contracts.

Before the talent groups established their guilds, Mayer decided to take action, and, in December 1926, met with three industry leaders: Actor Conrad Nagel, director Fred Niblo (*Ben-Hur*), and Fred Beetson, head of the Association of Motion Picture Producers. The quartet conceived of an organization that would mediate labor disputes and also improve the public image of Hollywood by helping the Hays office to control controversial screen content.

Mayer thought of an elite association confined to the top members of the industry's branches: Actors, directors, writers, producers, and technicians. With the support of his colleagues, he appointed himself to be in charge of member selection. On January 11, 1927, Mayer invited thirty-six industry leaders to a formal meeting at the Ambassador Hotel. He proposed an International Academy composed of members "who had contributed in a distinguished way to the arts and sciences of motion picture production." However, Mayer's lawyers, who drafted the by-laws, suggested to drop "International" from the association's name, which was then called the Academy of Motion Picture Arts and Sciences. The thirty-six founders set out to achieve the following goals:

> The Academy will take aggressive action in meeting outside attacks that are unjust.
>
> It will promote harmony and solidarity among the membership and among the different branches.
>
> It will reconcile internal differences that may exist or arise.
>
> It will adopt such ways and means as are proper to further the welfare and protect the honor and good repute of the profession.
>
> It will encourage the improvement and advancement of the arts and sciences of the profession by the interchange of constructive ideas and by awards of merit for distinctive achievements.
>
> It will take steps to develop greater power and influence of the screen.
>
> The Academy proposes to do for the motion picture profession in all its branches what other great national and international bodies have done for other arts and sciences and industries.

It's interesting to note that in 1927 the bestowal of merit awards was only of, and not the most, important goal of the Academy.

The Academy became a legal corporation on May 4, 1927, when it was granted nonprofit status by the state of California. The group then elected its first officers, actor Douglas Fairbanks Sr. as president and director Frank Woods as secretary. Mayer invited three hundred people to a banquet at the Biltmore which was paid for by his own studio. That night, Fairbanks sold 231 Academy memberships at $100 apiece. At that first banquet, Fairbanks told the gathering that "the screen and all its people were under a great and alarming cloud of public censure and contempt." Some constructive action seemed imperative to stop the assaults, and establish the industry in the public mind as a "respectable legitimate institution and its people as reputable individuals."

As for the Merit Awards, Fairbanks stressed that they should be "the highest distinction attainable in the motion picture profession," and that this goal would be attained "only by the impartial justice and wisdom displayed by the membership in making their nominations." In July 1928, a Merit Awards Committee proposed the following voting system: Each member would cast a nominating vote in his branch, a Board of Judges from each branch would then count the nominations, and, finally, a Central Board of Judges with one representative from each branch would choose the winners.

From the first year, there were arguments as to which kinds of films should be honored. One of the Academy's first "scandalous" decisions was to rule *The Jazz Singer,* the first talkie which caused a national sensation, as ineligible for the top awards. There were two top awards at the time: One for the Best Production, defined as "the most outstanding motion picture considering all elements that contribute to a picture's greatness," and the other for Artistic Quality of Production which honored the film's producing company or an individual producer.

On February 15, 1929, the Central Board of Judges met all night. The board decided to honor *The Crowd* with the Artistic Quality of Production, and they even called on its director, King Vidor. But Mayer argued against *The Crowd* due to its downbeat tone. Instead, he championed *Sunrise,* by German director F. W. Murnau, who was a respected filmmaker. Additionally, *Sunrise* starred all-American Janet Gaynor, had a happy ending, and was made by Paramount. Mayer feared charges of favoritism since *The Crowd* was an MGM picture. Mayer prevailed and the voting results were published in the "Academy Bulletin," on February 16, with the winners announced right away.

The Academy's Functions

In its first years, the Academy regarded itself as a labor organization that represented the interests of all talent groups. As such, it was neither limited to the production studios nor to any particular creative group. However, since the studios were instrumental in creating the Academy, film artists feared that the Academy would become the studios' stronghold and thus control and restrict the other talent groups.

Most people relate to the Oscar Awards and to the Oscar show interchangeably. For them, the Academy's raison d'être is to bestow the Oscars, an organization that "comes to life" once a year for the "Oscar season." Few are aware of the Academy's other functions, which ambitiously include conducting cooperative research, providing common meeting grounds for the various film arts and crafts, serving as an impartial clearing house of records and statistics, and cooperating in educational activities between the public and the film industry.

The Academy has always emphasized its public and cultural roles. One important goal was to create a forum in which artists of various expertise could exchange ideas. During the 1929 ceremonies, a Stanford University professor invited Academy members to visit his school. Then, long before film studies became a discipline, the Dean of USC enthused about the school's new course, "Introduction to Photoplay." The Academy would not let the public forget its aims aside from "recognizing outstanding achievements." The board reminded the public that the Academy was conceived as "an honorary association," whose "prime object is to advance the arts and sciences of motion pictures and to foster cooperation among the creative leadership of the industry for cultural, educational, and technological progress." Affiliated with the Academy of Motion Picture Arts and Sciences is the Academy Foundation, which sponsors educational and cultural activities including scholarship programs, student film awards, and film preservation.

The Academy publishes "The Players Directory," a major casting tool with lists of actors and actresses. "The Players Directory," the casting bible of the industry since its inception in 1937, moved its offices in January 2002 from the Academy's headquarters in Beverly Hills to Vine Street in Hollywood. There's also an online version of "The Players Directory." Taking full advantage of the Internet's immediacy, enlisted actors now have the ability to update virtually all of their contacts, credits, representation and union affiliation information on a daily basis. As a result of the increased tendency of casting people to use the Internet-based version, the printed version of the directory is now published only twice (instead of three times) each year. Other Academy publications include "The Screen Achievement Records Bulletin," which serves as a guide for individuals and organizations, and "Who Wrote the Movie," which enlists screenwriters and screenplays, and is prepared in collaboration with the Screen Writers Guild.

That the functions of the Academy were not entirely clear to its founders is apparent from the power struggle between the Academy and the Actors Equity Association (founded in 1911) over the issue of representation. The matter was unclear, because many players came from the New York stage and thus were Equity members. The Academy won the battle in 1929, when it announced a contract for freelance actors, the first standardized contract to arbitrate disagreements.

The Academy managed, as historians Larry Ceplair and Steven Englund have observed, "to forestall serious labor organizing among the Hollywood artists for five years," up to the creation of the various screen guilds. The Academy was a strange association: On the one hand, it lacked enforcement procedures for its labor code, but on the other, of all talent groups, it best represented the interests of the production companies. Even so, as a labor organization, the Academy was innovative in structure and ambition, aiming to give equal representation to both employers (studio executives) and employees (artists and craftsmen).

The Academy faced a major crisis in 1933 when President Roosevelt signed the National Industry Recovery Act, which suspended anti-trust laws and allowed industries to regulate themselves through "fair competition." The talent groups were concerned that the code would increase the studio's control over them, which it did. The studios used the Recovery Act as an excuse to reduce salaries. The Academy attempted to mediate, but the resulting compromise, which stipulated that the reductions would be temporary, pleased no one. The studios withdrew their support from the Academy, and, as a counter-measure, the talent groups — writers, actors, directors — formed their own guilds.

In October 1933, several Hollywood stars — James Cagney, Jeanette MacDonald, Gary Cooper, Paul Muni among them — met at the house of Frank Morgan and founded the Screen Actors Guild. (SAG). Like the writers before them, the actors resigned from the Academy. Fredric March, winner of Best Actor, and two former acting nominees Adolphe Menjou and Ann Harding, were elected as the Guild's vice presidents.

The SAG President Eddie Cantor spent Thanksgiving with President Franklin Roosevelt and persuaded him to remove some of the anti-labor provisions from the producers' code via executive order. Cantor calmed down the creative community, but members continued to regard the producer-dominated Academy with suspicion. Large numbers of the talent groups left the Academy in protest. The main dispute was over who should have the authority to represent talent groups in their labor negotiations with the studios. The SAG accused the Academy of trying to jeopardize the possibility of an organization representing the interests of actors. As a result, Academy membership was reduced dramatically, its very existence threatened. Those remaining were described by Frank Capra, then-Academy president, as "very staunch Academy-oriented visionaries, dedicated to the cultural recognition and preservation that has become the Academy's strong card."

President Franklin D. Roosevelt's bank holiday, on March 5, 1933, was a severe blow to Hollywood, as most of the studios were operating on credit alone. The Academy's labor-negotiating wing formed an Emergency Committee which recommended a 50 percent pay cut for all studio employees for two months. The Academy quickly revised its recommendations so that a sliding percentage of cuts would spare the lower-income employees, but the deal didn't satisfy the writers. In retaliation, the scribes formed the Screen Writers Guild of America on April 6, 1933. The writer-members resigned from the Academy, but other groups accepted the pay cut. When Sam Goldwyn and Jack Warner refused to restore full salaries at the end of the two months period, the Academy audited their books and showed solvency, which led to more resignations.

Conrad Nagel resigned as Academy president, to be replaced by J. Theodore Reed, an assistant director at Paramount. Under Reed's leadership, the Academy adopted a new policy: "The Academy as a whole will be free from politics, and any taint of self-preservation in office." In October 1933, the Motion Picture Committee, of which the Academy president was a member, announced its new regulatory code, approved by the National Recovery Administration (NRA).

The code put a ceiling on the salaries of writers, actors, directors, though not on studio executives. It stated, among other things, that artists could not accept bids from other studios when their contracts were up for renewal until the original studio had definitely decided not to renew them.

Neither the Actors nor the Writers guilds had forgiven the Academy for siding with the producers over the NRA controversy the year before. SAG's bulletin, *Screen Player,* denounced the Academy as "policing the industry by an oligarchy. Membership in SAG, which required resignation from the Academy, had increased. As a result, the Acting Branch was reduced substantially. It's estimated that in 1934, less than a hundred actors participated in the nominations.

On May 27, 1935, the Supreme Court declared Roosevelt's National Recovery Act unconstitutional. The SAG asked its members to boycott the eighth Academy banquet, on March 5, 1936, and indeed, only a few members attended the awards ceremonies. But despite conflicts and resignations that have shaken the Academy during past year, celebrities attended the show. Several of the guilds' members were nominated despite the resignations: Writer Frances Marion for Original Story for *The Prizefighter and the Lady,* and actor Paul Muni for *I Am a Fugitive from a Chain Gang.*

Labor strikes continued, but under Capra's leadership, the Academy survived. In 1939, the guilds won the battle, and the Academy membership began to grow under a newly structured constitution which was "non-economic and non-political in theory and in fact." From this point on, the focus of the Academy became cultural and educational, though not always by choice.

The debate over the Academy's historical significance continues. Some critics think that the Academy was a major force in industrial relations because it helped artists to obtain standard contracts. They emphasize that, while AMPAS was not exactly a labor union (as some wished it to be), it introduced the principle of collective bargaining, which was later adopted by the guilds.

Needless to say, the Academy didn't fulfill all of its original objectives. And it's doubtful whether the Academy Awards have contributed "to raising the standard of production," as intended. But the Academy succeeded in elevating the status of film as a medium among the more respected arts, which was a major goal.

The Academy Membership

Originally, the Academy consisted of five branches, each representing a distinct talent group: Producers, writers, directors, actors, and technicians. However, the increasing specialization of the industry has resulted in a more complex structure, composed at present of fourteen branches of craftsmanship. They include four of the original groups (producers, writers, directors, actors), additional administrative units (executives, public relations), and subdivisions within the technical units (art directors, cinematography, editing, sound, art direction).

Membership has always been by invitation only. From the start, the idea was to create an association of Hollywood's creative elite. Artists are invited to join "when their services to the motion picture industry have been prominent enough to make the Academy members feel they would like to have them as brother members." Section I of the Academy constitution formalized the qualifications: "Any person who has accomplished distinguished work or acquired distinguished standing in, or made valuable contributions to the production branches of the motion picture industry, directly or indirectly, and who is of good moral and personal standing may become an active member of the Academy by vote of the Board of Directors or recommendation of the Committee on Membership."

In 1931, the Academy distinguished between two classes of members: Academy members, who "have all the privileges, are entitled to vote on all Academy matters, and may serve on the Board of Directors," and associate members, who "have voting privileges limited to branch policies and action." The new policy required for all invitees to be first admitted as associate members. And once a year, the Board of Directors, upon recommendation of the Branch Committee, would select from the associate members those entitled to "special distinction" of Academy membership. The rules allowed the membership to grow steadily, from the 270 artists who attended the second Academy banquet in 1929, to 1,200 members in 1932.

During World War II, the political climate overrode industry concerns, and the strife between the Academy and the guilds subsided. After the war, the Academy membership increased dramatically: In 1939, there were 600 members; in 1947, 1,433; and in 1956, 1,770 members. In the 1960s, the Academy saw a further increase of its ranks from 2,084 members in 1959 to 3,030 in 1968.

The annual net gain growth is estimated at about 150 members. In 2002, there were 5,739 voting members, divided as follows:

Actors	1,315
Art directors	364
Cinematographers	170
Directors	364
Documentarians	110
Executives	430
Film editors	216
Music	247
Producers	459
Public Relations	368
Shorts	299
Sound	409
Visual effects	217
Writers	409
Members at large	362

The Actors Branch has always been the largest, amounting to one-fourth of the membership. In 1928, there were 362 Academy members, of which 91 were actors, 78 directors, 70 writers, 69 technicians, and 54 producers. In 2002, the Actors Branch amounted to 23 percent of the entire membership.

Compared with the guilds, the Academy is small. The membership of the Actors Branch amounts to only 2 percent of the Screen Actors Guild. The Academy's Writers and Directors Branches are even smaller and more elitist in relation to their respective guilds. In 2002, the Academy's Directors Branch was composed of 364 members, compared with the 12,400 members of the Directors Guild of America (DGA), which includes in addition to filmmakers, TV directors, associate directors, stage managers, and unit production managers.

The Academy's small size and elitist nature account for its prestige, thus making membership a desirable goal for every artist. Defenders of its small size claim that democratizing its structure, by opening it to a larger number of industry workers, would defeat one of the Academy's original purposes — to be an elite organization of the most accomplished film artists. The Academy was never meant to be an egalitarian organization representing all filmmakers.

Membership requirements differ from one branch to another. The easiest and fastest way to become a member is by getting a nomination — all Oscar nominees are invited to become members. The Academy has seldom used its right to withhold an invitation to a nominee. Beyond that, each branch has its own criteria. In most branches, it is necessary to have several film credits, a few years of experience, and sponsorship by two established members.

The Actors Branch requires "a minimum of three feature film credits, in all of which the roles played were scripted roles, one of which was released in the past five years, and all of which are of a caliber that reflect the high standards of the Academy." But actors are also invited to join if, "in the judgment of the Actors Branch Executive Committee, (they) otherwise achieved unique distinction, earned special merit or made an outstanding contribution as a motion picture actor."

Yet there are exceptions. There was a good deal of criticism and resentment when Barbra Streisand was invited to become a voting member before she had even made her first film, *Funny Girl.* Gregory Peck, the Academy president, tried to rationalize the invitation by saying, "when an actress has played a great role on the stage and is coming into films for what will obviously be an important career, it is ridiculous to make her wait three years for membership."

The Streisand issue was raised again when a Best Actress tie was declared between she and Katharine Hepburn (*The Lion in Winter*). If, as the accounting firm claimed, it was "a precise tie," and assuming that Streisand had voted for herself, it meant that had Streisand not been a voting member, she would have lost by one vote and the winner would have been Hepburn.

Academy membership is for life, though occasionally members are transferred from active to associate members, which means they cannot vote for the Oscars. Needless to say, few voters have relinquished their membership voluntarily. The Academy's prestige and the power to determine which films will win Oscars are crucial rewards for maintaining membership. Composer David Raksin is the notable exception. Raksin resigned from the Music Branch "in disgust" after the "Theme from *Shaft*" won Best Song in 1971.

The member composition is a controversial issue about which the Academy is very sensitive. Critics feel that artists who have retired or have not been active in the industry should not be eligible to vote. Others propose a distinction between members who have retired from their careers to pursue other lines of work and those who have retired as a result of old age. It's one thing to criticize the membership of actors like Susan Kohner or Pat Boone, who are no longer involved in film, but quite another to criticize veteran members who are old but have spent most of their lives making films.

Life membership and old age of the average Academy voters pose a number of problems. The age difference between older members and those actively involved in filmmaking (writers, directors, players) suggests a generation gap with both sociological and artistic implications. The members' older age makes them less expert in evaluating current film work, thus impairing judgment of quality, which is, after all, the Oscars' official goal. Secondly, the increasingly younger age of frequent moviegoers in the United States contributes to an even wider gap between audiences and Academy members. There is at least one generation difference between Academy members and active filmmakers (those nominated for awards), and two generations between Academy members and average filmgoers. Age differences and generation gaps inevitably make the Academy vote more conservative, lagging behind the industry's aesthetic and technical innovations. This built-in conservative bias in the Academy vote, which is reflected in the kinds of movies that win Best Picture, is almost inescapable. Indeed, most of the Best Picture winners are soft, noble, middlebrow movies that reflect the dominant culture, steering clear of provocative issues or innovative experimental styles (see my preface and chapter 21).

The age of the typical Academy member has decreased over the last decade, and younger artists have been admitted. However, as Vincent Canby observes, younger members may be more sophisticated than their veteran counterparts, but they are still more conservative in their tastes and values than avid moviegoers. The teenage movie, a dominant genre in American cinema of the 1980s, is conspicuously missing from the Oscar race. None of the commercially popular or more artistically acclaimed (John Hughes's *Sixteen Candles,* 1984; *The Breakfast Club,* 1985) teen movies has received nomination. And no member of the young performers, labeled by the media as "The Brat Pack" (Emilio Estevez, Ally Sheedy, Molly Ringwald), was nominated for an acting award during their prime.

A more severe criticism of the Academy concerns its gender structure. With the exception of the Actors Branch, which consists of equal proportions of men and women, the other branches are still male-dominated. In the Directors Branch, only a small group of the 364 members are women, including Martha Coolidge, Randa Haines, Elaine May, Joan Micklin Silver, and Claudia Weill. And there are even fewer women among the 170 Academy cinematographers.

Due to the balloting's secret nature, it's impossible to assess the differences between the male and female choices. But one can assume that because the Actors Branch consists of both male and female members, the nominated performances are more balanced.

The large size of the Actors Branch vis-à-vis the other branches means that the Best Picture nominees are often movies that flaunt strong acting. A movie like *The Dresser* would probably not have been nominated for Best Picture if one-fourth of the members, all of whom nominate in this category, had not been players. It's not that *The Dresser* was not a high-quality film (it was), but that its subject matter (backstage life through the relationship between an aging, selfish actor and his dresser in World War II England) and extraordinary performances by Albert Finney and Tom Courtenay made it a likely Best Picture candidate in the opinion of the Acting Branch.

This is the reason why so many films about showbiz or entertainment have been nominated for Best Picture: *The Great Ziegfeld, Stage Door, A Star Is Born, All About Eve, Sunset Boulevard, The Country Girl, Funny Girl, Hello, Dolly!, Cabaret, Lenny, Nashville, The Turning Point, All That Jazz, Coal Miner's Daughter, Tootsie, Amadeus, Shine, Shakespeare in Love,* and most recently, *Moulin Rouge.*

By contrast, because of the small size of other branches, it takes fewer votes to nominate achievements. Thus, 20 or 30 members of the Directors Branch, which consists of only 364 filmmakers, can nominate a director. The Directors Branch is not only small but cliquish as well. This explains why respected filmmakers such as David Lynch, Martin Scorsese, and Ridley Scott can earn directing nominations for *Blue Velvet* and *Mulholland Drive* (both by Lynch), *The Last Temptation of Christ,* and *Black Hawk Down,* without their movies being nominated. Amounting to only 6 percent of the entire membership, the directors have less clout than the actors in determining which films are nominated for Best Picture.

Procedures for Nomination

In the first year, the Academy asked the entire membership to nominate achievements by the August 15, 1928, deadline. Five boards of judges, one from each branch, were appointed to consider the nominations. The ten nominees who received the highest number of votes were turned over to the board of judges, who narrowed them down to three in each category. A central board of judges, one from each branch, then examined the finalists and determined the winner and the two honorable mentions. The winners were announced immediately, though the ceremonies took place at the Academy's annual banquet.

However, Mary Pickford's Best Actress win for her performance in *Coquette,* a movie that few people liked or saw, was an upset that created an uproar. Pickford's win had more to do with her status as a silent movie star and Academy charter members than with the quality of work per se. The other contending performers, Ruth Chatterton in *Madame X* and Jeanne Eagles in

The Letter, were both deemed worthier of the Oscar. (A legendary stage actress, Eagles never fulfilled her potential as a movie star — she died of a heroin overdose in 1929.)

As a result, a reform took place, and in the next six years, the selection process was broadened. The nominations were now made in primary elections by the branches, and the final voting by the entire membership. The regulations stated: "Each Branch will vote separately for nominations, like a primary election. The five highest persons, or achievements, for each award will be certified and placed on a ballot for submission to all members of the Academy. Academy members will then select from the submitted nominees, one for each award and those votes will govern the final selections."

The new procedures came under severe attack in 1935, when Bette Davis's breakthrough performance in *Of Human Bondage* failed to get a nomination. Under contract to Warner, Davis engaged in fights over her demand to get more challenging roles, pleading with Jack Warner to loan her out to RKO, where John Cromwell was making a big-screen adaptation of W. Somerset Maugham's *Of Human Bondage* with Leslie Howard as the crippled artist. Davis wished to play Mildred, the female lead, a slatternly Cockney waitress who torments the disabled intellectual.

The critics thought Davis was a major new talent; *Life* magazine declared that "Davis gave the best performance ever recorded on the screen by an American actress." Novelist Maugham himself praised Davis publicly. But the film's downbeat tone resulted in a box-office flop, and not many viewers — or Academy members — saw it. The *Hollywood Reporter* was so incensed that it demanded so see the votes — the Hollywood community simply refused to let the Davis scandal go without a battle. The Academy was besieged by telegrams from various Hollywood celebs demanding a write-in ballot to give Davis a fair chance. Out of noblesse oblige, even Oscar-nominated Norma Shearer (*The Barrets of Wimpole Street*) supported Davis's cause.

Just days after the nominations were announced, then-Academy president, the writer Howard Estabrook, issued a statement: "Despite the fact that the criticism fails to take into consideration that the nominations have been made by the unrestricted votes of each branch, the awards committee has decided upon a change in the rules to permit unrestricted selection of any voter, who may write on the ballot his personal choice for the winner." In February 1935, the voting was thrown wide-open and write-in were permitted; members were allowed to name anyone they chose. The write-in votes were then counted exactly as the votes for the official nominations.

When Bette Davis announced she would attend the awards banquet, the three Best Actress nominees declined the invitation. The anxiety-ridden Davis recorded in her memoir: "The air was thick with rumors. It seemed inevitable that I would receive the coveted award. The press, the public and the members of the Academy who did the voting were sure I would win! Surer than I!" At least Davis lost to a good performance, Claudette Colbert's in *It Happened One Night.*

One artist, Hal Mohr, who won an Oscar for cinematography in *A Midsummer Night's Dream* (1935) became the first and last write-in winner. In the same year, it was revealed that through the write-in campaign for Paul Muni in *Black Fury*, he came second to Victor McLaglen (the Best Actor for *The Informer*). But the confusion and technical problems involved in the write-in procedures eventually brought about their demise.

In 1936, the nominations were made again by a committee of fifty members which represented the branches, but the final vote was retained by the entire membership. The labor problems and internal conflict, which resulted in the resignation of many members, led to other procedural changes. Frank Capra, then the Academy president, decided on a novel strategy — to open the Academy up and extend voting privileges to the actors, writers, and directors guilds. Getting the guilds' members to vote was not easy, however, as they accused the Academy of being anti-union. But Capra succeeded.

For the acting nominations, only members of the Senior Screen Actors Guild (Class A) took part, but final ballots were also sent to the Junior Screen Actors Guild and the Writers and Directors Guilds. In 1936, the industry's participation in the Oscars was active: Out of fifteen thousand ballots mailed, 80 percent came back. The Academy wanted to prove that it kept abreast of the times by making the awards representative of the entire industry. Again in 1938, the nominations for the acting awards were made by Class A SAG members, and twelve thousand guild professionals took part in the final balloting. Never shy of positive publicity, the Academy emphasized that the Oscars "are awarded on the basis of ballots which receive industry-wide distribution, representing the majority evaluation of those who work in the medium.

This practice continued well into the 1940s. In 1946, however, nomination ballots were sent to all 11,669 creative workers in the industry, but final ballots were mailed only to the 1,600 Academy members. This procedure was repeated in 1956, when nomination ballots were sent to the 16,721 industry employees and final ballots to the 1,770 Academy members.

Voting was again restricted to active Academy members in 1957, excluding guild and union participation. Director George Seaton, the Academy president, was instrumental in bringing about this change, urging members "to exercise the privilege now reserved solely for Academy members." In a personal letter Seaton wrote: "Since the number of eligible voters has been reduced, you can see how important it is that we get as nearly 100 percent return as possible, so that the nominations and final selections may truly reflect the majority choices of the Academy membership."

The 1957 rules for nomination and final balloting are still in effect. One of the few original practices that has proved effective is the reminder list. From the first year, a list of productions in the eligible year has been sent to all members to refresh their memories. The reminder list was first arranged according to studios; then according to movies, alphabetically. The list is not guaranteed to be complete. The Academy suggests, "If any film you wish to nominate is not included here, or if you need any further information, please telephone the Academy office."

Each studio is asked to furnish its own inventory of movies. Rule Six of the nominations states: "The Academy shall prepare reminder lists of all eligible pictures, but before distribution to voters, studios must check and assume full responsibility for errors and omissions." The list refers "only to the motion picture in which the achievement was made, and not to any individual responsible, except in the case of acting nominations which name both the individual and the one picture wherein the achievement occurred." The Academy assists members in coming to "intelligent decisions" in their voting by sending lists of screening dates of the nominated pictures, which they see without admission charge.

Achievements are eligible for nomination if they have met the general rule of "The Awards Year":

Academy Awards of Merit shall be bestowed for achievements in connection with feature-length motion pictures (defined as motion-pictures over 30 minutes in running time) first publicly exhibited by means of 35mm or 70mm film for paid admission (previews excluded) in a commercial motion picture theater in the Los Angeles Area, defined as Los Angeles, West Los Angeles or Beverly Hills, between January 1 and midnight of December 31 (of a given year), such exhibition being for a consecutive run of no less than a week after an opening prior to midnight of December 31.

Several categories allow exceptions. Documentaries and short films are entered by their producers, and music awards require the creator to file official submission forms. Foreign-language films are submitted by each country's equivalent of the Academy, and there is a limit of one picture per country. There are also exceptions to the location rule. Documentary features need not play in the Los Angeles area, and Foreign-language films need not have opened in the United States, but must have English subtitles.

The first Oscars were presented on May 16, 1929, for films released in 1927 and 1928. The period of eligibility was a specific twelve-month period, from August 1, 1927, to July 31, 1928. This eligibility period remained in effect for the next four years. In 1934, however, the time frame was changed to cover the calendar year, from January 1 to December 31, which required the addition of five months to the previous awards year. The 1932–33 awards covered the period from August 1, 1932, to December 31, 1933. The 1934 Oscar ceremony was held only seven months after the previous one to make up for lost time and to get the annual event on a regular schedule.

The voting timetable for the seventy-fifth-anniversary 2003 awards is:

December 1, 2002	Deadline for receipt of official screen credit forms to qualify feature films for award consideration
December 31, 2002	Awards year ends at midnight
January 13, 2003	Nomination ballots mailed

January 30	Nominations polls close at 5:00 P.M.
February 11	Nominations announced at 5:30 A.M. at the Samuel Goldwyn Theater
March 1	Final ballots mailed
March 4	Scientific and Technical Awards presentations at the Beverly Wilshire
March 18	Final Ballots close 5:00 P.M.
March 23	Seventy-fifth Annual Academy Awards presentation at the Kodak televised live by ABC at 5:30 P.M. Pacific Time

In 1931, the Academy made an important decision to withhold announcement of the Oscar winners until the banquet. British actor Lawrence Grant, who was in *Bulldog Drummond,* revealed that Ronald Colman had lost the Best Actor to George Arliss, cited for *Disraeli.* Arliss and Norma Shearer (*The Divorcee*) knew well in advance of their win since the Academy had asked them to pose with their statuettes before the banquet. To avoid the embarrassment of a last-moment Best Actor tie (which was held in suspicion since a single vote separated Fredric March and Wallace Beery in 1931–32), the Academy announced the exact ranking of votes in each category. Helen Hayes (*The Sin of Madelon Claudet*) had received more votes than Marie Dressler and Lynn Fontanne put together.

In the 1934 show (honoring films of 1932–33), emcee Will Rogers disclosed the Best Picture votes: Fox's *Cavalcade* received 50 percent more votes than first runner-up, Paramount's *A Farewell to Arms,* and RKO's *Little Women,* which came in third. Frank Lloyd won Best Director for *Cavalcade.* Frank Capra (*Lady for a Day*) was in second place, followed by George Cukor for *Little Women,* who received only two votes less than Capra.

The 1932–33 acting races were much tighter. For Best Actress, May Robson ran a close second to Katharine Hepburn, who won for *Morning Glory,* though she also featured prominently in the popular Oscar-nominated *Little Women.* And Paul Muni was a close second to Charles Laughton, who won for *The Private Life of Henry VIII.* In 1934, the voting results were also disclosed: Clark Gable (*It Happened One Night*) narrowly defeated Frank Morgan (*Affairs of Cellini*), but Claudette Colbert won by far, with Norma Shearer a second, and Grace Moore a distant third.

Price, Waterhouse and Company, a firm of certified public accountants, began counting the Oscar ballots in 1936. During the first twelve years, the results of the final balloting were released to the press prior to the presentation to accommodate newspaper deadlines. However, in 1940, when a newspaper printed the winners' names before the ceremonies, advance notice was discontinued. In 1941 the Academy declined to give out any advance release, and the practice of sealed envelopes began. Since then, the winners' identity is unknown until they are actually called to the podium to be handed the award.

The winners receive a blank Oscar; after the show their names are engraved on its base. This secrecy undoubtedly contributes to the tension and excitement of the ceremonies.

The only exceptions to the rule of secrecy are the Honorary, Scientific-Technical, the Jean Hersholt Humanitarian, and the Irving Thalberg Memorial Awards, which are announced in advance.

The Oscars differ from other prestigious awards. The Nobel Prize Nomination Committees are silent about the names proposed for the awards, always abiding by the rule of secrecy. However, the winners' names are made public weeks before the actual ceremonies to accommodate their arrival in Stockholm from all over the world. By contrast, the Academy nominees are publicly disclosed six weeks before the ceremonies, but the winners' identity is kept in utmost secrecy up to the last moment. When the presenters say, "May I have the envelope please," the nominees, the voters, and the viewers are in genuine suspense.

Award Categories

The number of award categories has changed over the years reflecting developments within the film industry, such as the advent of sound and color. In 1927–28, all the nominees for the first Best Picture were silent films (the winner was *Wings*) and only one award was given to a "talkie."

In the first year, there were eleven categories: Actor, Actress, Director of Drama, Director of Comedy, Outstanding Picture (Producer), Outstanding Quality (Production Company), Original Screenplay, Adaptation of Story, Cinematography, Art Direction, and Engineering Effects. The writers branch established three categories: Best Original Story, Best Adaptation, and Title Writing.

The production awards distinguished between the Best Producer, "who produced the most outstanding motion picture, considering all elements that contribute to a picture's greatness," and Best Production Company, "which produced the most artistic, unique, and/or original motion picture without reference to cost or magnitude." As for acting, members were asked to choose the best performance, "with special reference to character portrayal and effectiveness of dramatic or comedy rendition."

In the second year (1928–29), awards were given in only seven categories. The distinction between the direction of a comedy and a drama was dropped as well as that between original and adapted screenplay. And there was no longer differentiation between Best Producer and Best Production Company — the top award was named Best Picture. In the third year, Sound Recording and Scientific-Technical Achievement were added. In the fourth year (1930–31), the writing award was divided again into Original Story and Adaptation. By 1934, the number of categories had increased to thirteen, with new areas for Editing, Short Subjects, and Music. In the following year, due to the popularity of musical films, a new category was created to honor Dance Direction. For a few years, there was a distinction between Original Musical/Comedy Score and Original Dramatic Score. But in 1999 it was abolished.

For close to a decade, there were only two acting categories: Best Actor and Best Actress. In 1936, the Academy decided to create two more divisions, Supporting Actor and Supporting Actress, which required new rules to distinguish between lead and supporting performances (see chapter 4).

In keeping abreast of the advent of color, the Cinematography and Art Direction Awards were subdivided in 1939 into black-and-white and color. The first winners in these areas were Gregg Toland for his distinguished black-and-white cinematography in *Wuthering Heights,* and Ernest Haller and Ray Rennahan for their color work in *Gone With the Wind.*

The largest number of awards bestowed by the Academy was in 1956, with twenty-seven categories, including a special award for Best Foreign-Language Film, which would become a permanent category. In 1957, the Academy eliminated Best Scoring of a Musical, due to the genre's decline, along with several other categories. The tendency was toward compressing categories, keeping the number of awards to a minimum.

A major change occurred in 1967, when the duplicate awards in Art Direction, Set Decoration, and Cinematography, previously given for black-and-white and color, was discontinued. The feeling was that these awards would be more prestigious and meaningful if each named only one winner, though it made the competition in these categories much more intense.

Achievements in Makeup were given for the first time in 1982, after a lengthy battle by the makeup artists. In previous years, honorary awards were given to makeup artists, such as William Tuttle for *Seven Faces of Dr. Lao* in 1964, and John Chambers for *Planet of the Apes* in 1968, but there was no regular award. A competitive category was established following the Academy's failure to honor the makeup achievement in David Lynch's *The Elephant Man.*

The newest award category is animation. Before 2001, the only animated feature to be nominated for Best Picture was Disney's *Beauty and the Beast* in 1991. In 2001, nine animated pictures were eligible for the first new Oscar category in twenty years: Feature-length animation. The contenders were *Final Fantasy: The Spirits Within; Jimmy Neutron, Boy Genius; Marco Polo: Return to Xanadu; Monsters, Inc.; Osmosis Jones; The Prince of Light; Shrek; The Trumpet of the Swan;* and *Waking Life.* An Academy committee then pared the list down to three nominations: *Jimmy Neutron; Monsters, Inc.;* and *Shrek —* which won.

For decades, the term "animated film" referred to traditional cel animation, but with new innovations in the medium the definition now is much broader. The nine features offered a wide range of styles; only two are completely cel-animated; *Marco Polo* and *Trumpet of the Swan. Jimmy Neutron; Monsters, Inc.;* and *Shrek* are computer animated. *Final Fantasy* is a hotorealistoc computer-animated toon, and *Osmosis Jones* blends live-action sequences with cel animation.

The animated films were viewed by a hundred-member screening committee chaired by Academy governor Tom Hanks. The committee members — half animators, half members of the Academy's other branches — chose the nominees. Academy president Frank Pierson suggested to the committee that they consider all elements of the film, not just animation work, but also script, performances, score, etc. Films submitted in the animated feature category also qualify for Academy awards in other areas, including Best Picture, provided they meet the criteria governing those categories.

At present, merit awards are conferred in twenty-four categories: Picture, Director, four acting awards (Actor, Actress, Supporting Actor, Supporting Actress), Animated Feature, Foreign-Language Picture, two writing (Original Screenplay and Adaptation), two documentary (Feature and Short Subject), two music (Original Score and Original Song), two short-film awards (Animated and Live Action), Art Direction, Cinematography, Costume Design, Editing, Sound, Sound Effects, Visual Effects, and Makeup.

Three men were nominated for Best Actor in the first year: Richard Barthelmes for two films, *The Noose* and *The Patent Leather Kid,* Emil Jannings, also for two films, *The Last Command* and *The Way of All Flesh.* Charlie Chaplin, then the most respected artist in Hollywood — The Little Tramp — was nominated for *The Circus,* his first film since *The Gold Rush,* three years earlier. Jannings won, but as a consolation prize, the Academy gave Chaplin a Special Award for "versatility and genius in writing, acting, directing and producing *The Circus.*"

In the same year, three actresses were nominated for five performances: Janet Gaynor, the winner, for three films, *Seventh Heaven, Street Angel,* and *Sunrise;* Louise Dressler for *A Ship Comes In,* and Gloria Swanson for *Sadie Thompson.* Swanson was so offended when she received an Honorary Mention that she decided not to attend the banquet.

Five nominees were singled out in each category in the second year. In the third year, four actors were nominated for six roles (George Arliss and Maurice Chevalier were each nominated for two performances), and five actresses were nominated for seven roles (Greta Garbo was nominated for two, *Anna Christie* and *Romance;* and Norma Shearer also for two, *The Divorcee* and *Their Own Desire*).

For three years (1932–34), the two acting categories had three performers, each nominated for one role. But in 1935, there were four nominees in the Best Actor and six nominees in the Best Actress category. It wasn't until 1936 that the number of nominees was standardized to five in each group.

In the first year, there were two directing awards, one for comedy and one for drama, and three directors competed for each. The first directing winners were Frank Borzage for the drama *Seventh Heaven* and Lewis Milestone for the comedy *Two Arabian Nights.* This distinction was dropped in the following year. For two years, five nominees competed for Best Director, but in 1932, the number of contestants was reduced again to three. From 1936 on, the number of nominated directors was standardized to five.

Unlike the Actors Branch, which stipulates that actors may receive only one nomination per category, the Directors Branch allows for the same filmmaker to be nominated more than once in the same year. This has happened only twice. In 1938, Michael Curtiz was nominated for two directing achievements, *Angels With Dirty Faces* and *Four Daughters.* Curtiz lost both; the winner that year was Frank Capra for *You Can't Take It With You,* which also grabbed the Best Picture Award.

In 2000, Steven Soderbergh became the second director ever to nab two nominations, for *Erin Brockovich* and *Traffic.* In a major upset (pre-Oscar polls predicted that Ang Lee would be the winner for *Crouching Tiger, Hidden Dragon*), Soderbergh didn't cancel himself out and won Best Director for *Traffic,* though the Best Picture went to *Gladiator.*

There have also been fluctuations in the number of films nominated for Best Picture. In the first four years, five movies were nominated; in 1931–32, the number was increased to eight. Ten films were nominated in 1932–33, and in 1934 and 1935, twelve. Over the next seven years (1936–43), ten movies competed for Best Picture. The competition in these years was extremely fierce, as was evident in 1939, a watershed year in Hollywood's history, with so many excellent movies nominated: *Dark Victory, Gone With the Wind* (the winner), *Goodbye, Mr. Chips, Love Affair, Mr. Smith Goes to Washington, Ninotchka, Of Mice and Men, Stagecoach, The Wizard of Oz,* and *Wuthering Heights.* But nominating ten movies for Best Picture made the competition intense, and split the votes into too many subgroups. In 1944, the Academy standardized the Best Picture category to contain the same number of contestants — five — as in the other categories.

3

THE OSCAR—
KING OF THE SHOWBIZ AWARDS?

The Oscar is the most popular and the most prestigious award in the film industry. But the Oscar goes beyond the film world — it enjoys an extraordinary preeminence in the entertainment world and American culture at large. The Oscar's prestige and visibility surpass those of other showbiz awards, such as the Tony, the top award in the Broadway theater, the Emmy, which honors television achievements, and the Grammy, the most prestigious award in the recording industry.

While the Oscar is "the King of Awards" in the international film world, it is not the only award. Various awards are bestowed by film academies and institutes, international film festivals, and film critics groups. How did the Oscar Award and the Oscar telecast acquire such remarkable dimensions?

Film Institutes

The BAFTA (The British Film and Television Awards) are nothing more than a free trip to London. — Anonymous Hollywood Executive

Most countries with established film industries have national academies or institutes, which, among other activities, bestow merit awards. The Academy of Motion Picture Arts and Sciences is the oldest academy in the world. That most people refer to it as *The Academy,* not the *American Academy,* attests to its status as the world's most famous film organization.

The British Film Academy (BFA) was established in 1946 for the "advancement of film." In 1975, after a series of mergers and reorganizations, it became the British Academy of Film and Television Arts (BAFTA). BAFTA's annual awards honor achievements in film and television. In the United States the separation between the Academy of Motion Picture Arts and Sciences, and the Academy of Television Arts and Sciences, underscores both functional and symbolic differences. The Academy and its Oscar have always been more prestigious than television and its Emmy. In the United States, film and television are very different media, performing different functions in popular culture.

The awards season used to begin with the National Board of Review announcements in early December, and climaxed with the Oscars in late March. It has always been an all-American affair. But in 2000, the British attempted to crash the Oscar party when BAFTA shifted its awards from its old April slot to late February, in a bold bid to redraw the Oscar campaign map. Positioned between the Golden Globes (late January) and the Oscars (late March), the BAFTA situated itself as a stepping stone toward the ultimate prize. The prizes are officially labeled the Orange British Academy Film Awards, but in deference to their sponsor, everyone calls them the BAFTAs. There were speculations as to whether Hollywood would embrace the interloper or give it the cold shoulder. Some of the big American players are already pouring significant cash and effort into wooing BAFTA members — three thousand industry insiders in England and approximately eight hundred expatriates who live in Los Angeles and New York.

"We've had a fantastic response from the studios and big independents," Steve Woolley, the chairman of BAFTA's film section, told *Variety*. "We have a larger budget and more leverage to get the talent over," confirmed Richard Napper, managing director of Columbia TriStar U.K. "Everyone is looking at it as a stepping stone," said Andrew Cripps, president of United International Pictures. Woolly admitted that the BAFTAs can't compete with the Golden Globes for public impact. The one-two Globes-to-Oscars punch is a proven prescription for Hollywood marketers, and that's not likely to change easily, especially given the perception that the BAFTAs represent, as one top studio executive put it, "nothing more than a free trip to London."

The question is whether the British awards could eventually establish themselves as a more accurate Oscar predictor than the Golden Globes. Universal's London-based president of international marketing plays down the Oscar link. A couple of years ago, *The Truman Show* won consolation prizes at the BAFTAs after its Oscar shutout. In 1999, Spaniard Pedro Almodóvar beat Sam Mendes, the British-born Oscar winner, for the director award (*All About My Mother*). BAFTA's nightmare would be to find films ineligible for the Oscars' scooping up awards. In 2000, there were two top-quality contenders that stole BAFTA's thunder: Paul Thomas Anderson's *Magnolia,* which was eligible for the 1999 Oscars, and Christopher Nolan's *Memento,* which opened in the U.S. a year later, in 2001.

In France, the Oscar equivalent is the César, created in 1976 by publicist Georges Cravenne. The award is voted on by the entire membership of the French Motion Picture Academy, consisting of about three thousand members of the industry. The French Academy and the César are modeled after the Academy and its Oscar, honoring various film categories. The awards ceremony is sponsored and produced by Canal+, the French pay-TV giant.

At the latest Césars, on March 2, 2002, Jean-Pierre Jeunet's *Amélie* took four awards, including best director and film. Jeunet's box-office smash had been up for thirteen awards, making it a strong contender to beat record-holding Jean-Paul Rappeneau's *Cyrano* and François Truffaut's *The Last Metro,* each of which won ten Césars. In front of a celebrity crowd at Theatre de Chatelet in Paris, *Amélie* had to share the spotlight with Jacques Audiard's *Read My Lips,* winner of three Césars, including a surprise actress honor for Emanuelle Devos, who beat out *Amélie*'s Audrey Tautou. Best Actor nod also went to an unlikely, though not unpopular, choice, first-time nominee Michel Bouquet, seventy-six, for Anne Fontaine's *The Way I Killed My Father.*

David Lynch's Studio Canal-produced *Mulholland Drive* snagged best foreign film, beating Nanni Moretti's *The Son's Room,* Baz Luhrmann's *Moulin Rouge,* Steven Soderbergh's *Traffic,* and Joel Coen's *The Man Who Wasn't There.* Best first film went to the Bosnian Danis Tanovic's *No Man's Land.* Out of four nominations, Christopher Gans's *Brotherwood of the Wolf* nabbed the César for designer Dominique Borg's costumes. Honorary Césars went to Anouk Aimée, Claude Rich, and Britain's Jeremy Irons, one of the few non-French stars to be honored.

With general and presidential elections only a couple of months away, the French Prime Minister and presidential candidate Lionel Jospin, made the first appearance by a French head of government in the César's twenty-seven-year-history. Interestingly, former Vivendi Universal chief Jean-Marie Messier — out of favor with the French film community after his remark that France's cultural exception is dead — did not attend.

The top film award in Italy is the David Di Donatello Award, which is now administered by the Italian film industry. The bylaws of this award have changed, and its emphasis now is on European films. The Italian Academy, like many other national academies but unlike the Oscar, distinguishes between achievements by local and foreign artists, which increases the number of awards and decreases the intensity of competition.

Awards are also bestowed by the American Film Institute (AFI), which was established in 1967. Its Life Achievement Award, conferred since 1973, is highly respected, but it differs from most awards by honoring "the total career contributions of a filmmaker, regardless of place of birth, whose talent has fundamentally advanced the art of film or television, whose accomplishments have been acknowledged by scholars, critics, professional peers, and the general public, and whose work has withstood the test of time." The award is based on the judgment of the AFI's board, but the entire membership can suggest candidates. The annual ceremonies take place in February and are televised, but not live. Most of the winners have been directors (John Ford, Orson Welles, William Wyler, Alfred Hitchcock, Frank Capra, John Huston, Billy Wilder) or actors (James Cagney, Henry Fonda, James Stewart, Fred Astaire, Jack Nicholson, Dustin Hoffman). So far, only four women have been cited: Bette Davis, Lillian Gish, Barbara Stanwyck, and Barbra Streisand.

The inaugural AFI Awards for movies and television, broadcast live from the Beverly Hills Hotel on January 5, 2001, was as unappealing to viewers, with a paltry TV audience of 5.5 million, as it was to nominees, few of whom bothered to show up. Only four winners out of the fifteen individual achievements attended the subdued ceremony, including Sissy Spacek (*In the Bedroom*). Elijah Wood and Sean Astin were on hand to pick up the Best Film statuette for *The Lord of the Rings.* Absent winners included Denzel Washington, Gene Hackman, and Jennifer Connelly.

Why all the missing stars? "It's hard to fly someone to L.A. when you have to fly them back two weeks later for the Golden Globes," one publicist told *Variety*. CBS would have liked to have seen bigger numbers and more stars, but it was Year One, and then the event would build." But CBS declined to speculate on the show's future, though the network has had a successful partnership with AFI on recent highly rated 100 Years Specials. Comparisons might be made with the Screen Actors' Guild Awards, which ran for three years on NBC before being relegated to the TNT cable network in 1998. The SAG awards simply didn't make it. Even so, despite a lackluster debut, the AFI kicked off the year's round of awards.

The Oscar is more internationally visible than these awards. Unlike the AFI Life Achievement Award or the Kennedy Center Awards, which honor career achievements, the Oscar honors single achievement in a single film. And since the Oscar winners are younger, the award exerts a stronger impact on their careers.

International Film Festivals

Most international film festivals bestow awards based on a competition of films from all over the world. Venice, the oldest international film festival, was first held in 1932 under the auspices of the Venice Biennial. At its inception, the festival served as a vehicle for Fascist propaganda, receiving the sponsorship of Mussolini, who was highly aware of film's potential as a tool of political propaganda. In its first years, no merit awards were conferred, but prizes based on public referendum were given to "the most touching," "the most amusing," and "the most original" film. That first year, awards for "the favorite actor and actress" went to Fredric March (*Dr. Jekyll and Mr. Hyde*) and Helen Hayes (*The Sin of Madelon Claudet*), both of whom won an Oscar for their performances.

The Venice festival is held late August to early September and awards the Golden Lion as its top prize. Its reputation was seriously damaged in the 1930s and 1940s, when political favoritism proved to be a crucial factor in the selection of winners. However, in the next three decades, the festival restored its credibility, getting more Hollywood pictures for international premieres and honoring more respected films, such as Krzystof Zanussi's *A Year of the Quiet Sun* in 1984, Agnes Varda's *Vagabond* in 1985, Zhang Yimou's *Not One Less* in 1999, and Mira Nair's *Monsoon Wedding* in 2001. But in 2002, politics again intervened with the festival's operation, when director Alberto Barbera was ousted before his contract expired, and the government decided to take a more active role in the festival's operations.

The best-known of all international festivals, Cannes, emerged in opposition to Venice. It was originally scheduled to open in 1939, but because of World War II, the first festival was held in September 1946. Cannes has always enjoyed tremendous publicity and not just because of its cinematic functions. Over the years Cannes has become a highly commercial event, attended by celebs from all over the world. Cannes is also the biggest festival, screening hundreds of films, in and outside the official program. Until 1950, it took place in the fall. After that, it moved to May — mostly in order to precede Venice.

The highest prize in Cannes is the Palme d'Or (Golden Palm), which honors the best film from twenty-two entries in the official competition. The festival also honors juried achievements in acting, directing, and cinematography (or artistic contribution). For decades, Cannes has been an important force in presenting the latest developments in international cinema from the best auteurs. As in Venice, politics, in and outside the film world, have afflicted Cannes. In 1968, political demonstrations forced the festival to close while in progress, but it was a minor setback. And despite an increasing number of international festivals, Cannes has not lost its uniqueness or premier status.

Founded in 1951, the Berlin Film Festival has enjoyed immense publicity and official support due to the city's special political status. As a festival, it is less commercial than both Venice and Cannes, and more committed to the exhibition of documentaries and independent films. Until 1957, it was held in the summer, but currently, it takes place in February so that it will come well in advance of Cannes. In its first years, the bestowal of awards was democratic, a jury and the public participated in the process, but this practice was discontinued in 1957 due to growing criticism. The top prizes are the Golden Bear for best film and the Silver Bear for directing and acting achievements.

Established in 1963, under the auspices of the Lincoln Center Film Society (which also publishes the magazine *Film Comment*), the New York Film Festival is a prestigious forum. In its first twenty-five years, it was guided under the leadership of Richard Roud, a British cineaste and film critic. The New York event was the most important in the United States until the Sundance Film Festival was taken under the wing of Robert Redford in 1985, and emerged as the premiere festival in the country, second only to Cannes as far as the discovery of new talent is concerned.

During the New York festival's two-week duration (in late September to early October), about twenty-six features and some shorts are screened. The purpose of the festival is "to bring the most interesting films with the greatest artistic merit from all over the world to the attention of the New York film community." The films, selected by a five-member committee, tend to be either innovative, or solid, well-made features.

New York is the only major festival that does not bestow awards, attempting to steer clear of the political favoritism and negative aspects of competitiveness. Appalled by "the shenanigans that go on at other festivals when there are prizes and pressures to win," Roud claimed that, "prizes are for the one who wins," and that for New York, "all of the great filmmakers have won a prize by being in the festival." Indeed, competition to be included in the New York Festival is fierce. The twenty-six selections are drawn from a pool of over four hundred films, though about half of them come from Cannes. In the 1990s, the New York Festival has featured few world premieres, which is what usually gives festivals the cachet, opting instead to screen the best films from other festivals.

Most international festivals serve as arenas in which lively aesthetic and political conflicts take place. Selections are often criticized as inadequate due to the operation of special-interest politics and other biases. On many occasions, prizes are given to those filmmakers and national cinemas the jury felt deserved recognition for political reasons. However, the politics of film festivals also have positive effects, since they call attention to the variety of yardsticks — aesthetic, moral, and ideological — that come into play when evaluating film as an art form. Another charge often raised against Cannes, New York, and other festivals is that they consistently showcase the same favorite filmmakers — Truffaut, Godard, Fassbinder, Andrzej Wajda, — while disregarding the work of younger, more innovative and experimental filmmakers.

Unlike the Academy, festivals depend on the good will of studios, producers, and directors to submit their films for competition. By contrast, every film released in the United States within a calendar year is eligible to compete for Oscars regardless of the studio's or filmmaker's wishes. For festivals, availability of films is also a determining factor. Martin Scorsese's *After Hours,* for instance, was not included in the 1985 New York Film Festival because its producers demanded that it be shown on either opening or closing night. Moreover, some producers fear that displaying their films in festivals will label them as "arthouse" or "esoteric" films, thus limiting their potential commercial prospects.

Film Critics Associations

The New York Film Critics Award is more important to me than anything except my children. — Sally Field

I got so excited when I heard that I won the Lost Angeles Film Critics Award that I could not sleep for three days. — John Travolta

The New York Film Critics Circle was founded in 1935 with a twofold goal: To recognize the finest film achievements and to maintain high standards of film criticism. For three decades the circle recognized accomplishments in four categories: Picture, actor, actress, and director. In 1969, it created additional categories for supporting actor and actress, screenplay and cinematography. The Circle announces its winners at its annual meeting in December and certificates of honor are conferred in a dinner gathering, for many years held at Sardi's.

The National Society of Film Critics was founded in 1968 as a "highbrow" association to counter the other "middlebrow" film circles, whose tastes were considered to be too similar to the Academy's. In its first years, the Society was accused of being "too harsh and snobbish" toward commercial Hollywood pictures, and too "avant-garde" in its preference of European art films. One of the National Society's major goals was "to annually recognize the best films without distinction of nationality." Unlike other circles, in the first years each critic's votes and the complete tabulations were published in an annual volume. In the 1980s, the National Society broadened its base to include new members (it is composed of only fifty-two critics), a democratic procedure that led to the departure of some of its more elitist founders.

The National Society of Film Critics enjoys greater prestige than either the New York or the Los Angeles groups because it is small, elitist, and represents reviewers from all over the nation. In some circles, the choices of the New York Film Critics are considered to be less biased by commercial considerations than those by their California counterparts. (However, when *Brazil* was chosen as Best Picture by the Los Angeles Film Critics, it had tremendous influence on the conflict between director Terry Gilliam and his studio, Universal, over the film's running time and ending. There's also no denying that the selection of *Brazil* by the Los Angeles Film Critics resulted in an earlier release, in December, so that it could be eligible for Oscar nominations — initially, the film wasn't scheduled for release until the following year.)

The Los Angeles Film Critics Association (LAFCA), which consists of both print and television reviewers in the Los Angeles area, is one of the most recent circles, presenting its first awards in 1975. Its proximity to the film industry makes its influence on the Academy more direct and pervasive than that of the other associations.

The Broadcast Film Critics Association (BFCA) is the most recent and largest association of critics, amounting to close to 200 professionals, who cover the entertainment industry on radio, television, and the Internet.

Film critics' awards perform several crucial roles in the film world. Critics confer prestige on the winning films and artists. Critics are considered to be "experts" who use in their evaluations more dispassionate and matter-of-fact yardsticks than the Academy voters or large public. Critics also serve as tastemakers and guides for the public. As moviegoers can't possibly see all movies released in a given year, they often rely on the judgment of critics. But critics also exert influence on the Oscar Award. Most critics' circles announce their choices in mid-December, about two months prior to the mid-February nominations. Like moviegoers, Academy members cannot possibly see all the eligible films, and the critics' annual awards assist in focusing their attention on a smaller number of films.

As far as the Oscar goes, the critics' function is to shape the race, to narrow down the number of contenders to those films that are the worthiest of Academy attention. "Ten Best Lists" by influential critics who write for publications such as the *New York Times,* the *Los Angeles Times,* and *Entertainment Weekly* get special consideration from the Academy. It's been really rare for the Academy voters to ignore that critics' choices, unless they are small, arthouse films on the order of *Topsy-Turvy,* which won the 1999 Best Picture from the New York Film Critics Circle, but was only nominated for technical awards by the Academy.

However, with all their prestige, critical awards, unlike the Oscars, have little impact on films' standing at the box office. Furthermore, the critics' status remains ambiguous and suspicious. As Andrew Sarris once put it, "At best, movie reviewers are considered a necessary evil; at worst, a positive plague of locusts." If reviews are favorable, they are used in advertising; if they are negative, they are ignored and their writers are chastised for their "damaging impact on the industry."

Actors, too, attribute different meaning to the prizes given by the various critics groups. James Cagney was appreciative of the New York Film Critics when he learned that it took nine ballots before a consensus was reached over his performance in *Angels With Dirty Faces*. And after being honored for her performance in *I Want to Live!*, Susan Hayward said: "The big treat was winning the New York Film Critics Award. That's a tough one to win, not because they know so much, but because they're such rats and they don't like to give anyone a prize, especially anybody from Hollywood."

Other Awards

The National Board of Review is the country's oldest film association. Established in New York in 1909 by a voluntary group of film-oriented citizens, it was first called the National Board of Censorship of Motion Pictures, serving as a voluntary censorship agency and enjoying the industry's full support. In 1922, however, its powers were diminished when the industry established its own regulatory board under the leadership of Will H. Hays. Changing its name to the National Board of Review, it devoted its activities to the evaluation of films. In its first years, it honored the best film (American and foreign), but since 1930, it selects "Ten Best" films, best players, and other achievements.

Founded in 1940, the Hollywood Foreign Press Association consists of about ninety journalists who represent over a hundred million readers in more than fifty different countries. Its awards, the Golden Globes, were first presented in 1943. All members vote for the nominees in December, and for the winners in January. Due to its international nature, the occasion has enjoyed extensive media coverage. The Golden Globes were modeled on the Oscars, with several exceptions. They distinguish between achievements in drama and in comedy/musical, thus including genres that are usually overlooked by the Academy. The association also honors achievements in television, not just in film, and it presents career achievement awards, like Harrison Ford, the 2002 honoree.

The Golden Globes telecast combines movie and TV awards, which makes it a convenient one-stop gawking trip for celeb watchers. Journalist Joyce Millman admires the way the Hollywood Foreign Press seems unfazed by the Byzantine politics of other award-bestowing groups. George Clooney and Tom Cruise may be too pretty for Oscar voters, Jim Carrey too weird, and Madonna, too, well, Madonna, but all of those superstars have gone home with Golden Globes.

Millman noted last year: "In light of the Emmys' somber post-September 11 telecast, I hope the 2002 Golden Globes don't go all austere on us and institute a ban on champagne, cleavage, and Jack Nicholson. If ever we needed the Golden Globes' carefree vibe, it is now. Not that the fear of a well-behaved Golden Globes would keep us away. After all, it is an awards show. And the sordid truth is whenever we're watching the likes of Julia Roberts or Kevin

Spacey collecting their prizes and feeling the love, we're secretly picturing ourselves up there, basking in the glow of affirmation. Awards are the canvas upon which we project our desire for fame, beauty, and, above all, popularity." Many people have experienced that fantasy moment in front of the bathroom mirror, clutching a shampoo bottle in lieu of the Oscar statuette and delivering their witty yet gracious acceptance speeches.

The power of the HFPA was demonstrated in 1991, when *Beauty and the Beast* earned more Golden Globes than any other film. As David Fox observed in the *Los Angeles Times:* "The Globes have begun to take on a role in the Oscar race akin to New Hampshire's role in presidential politics. Like New Hampshire, the Globe voters may not be a big group, but they have influence." It's doubtful that an animated feature like *Beauty and the Beast* would have won a Best Picture nomination without the Globes's assistance.

The Golden Globes and the SAG Awards are two bellwethers with a better prophecy rate than the more esoteric critics awards. Film critics are often envious of the HFPA because of its power. As far as visibility and box-office impact are concerned, the Globes are much more influential than all the critics' awards. In 2001, an upset occurred at the Globes when, contrary to expectations, *Amélie,* the popular French picture, lost to the Bosnian entry *No Man's Land,* which went on to win the Best Foreign-Language Picture Oscar as well.

Popularity awards are also given by several associations and magazines. The oldest, most comprehensive, survey of America's "Top Box-Office Stars" is the Quigley Publications Poll, first conducted in 1932, and known in the industry as "The Poll." All movie exhibitors in the United States are asked to name the year's Top Ten Box-Office Attractions, namely, the ten players whose names on the marquees have drawn the largest audiences to the theaters.

The disparity between the country's commercial stars and its acclaimed actors, reflected in Oscar nominations and awards, has widened considerably since the 1980s. In 1985, the ten box-office stars in America were: Sylvester Stallone, Eddie Murphy, Clint Eastwood, Michael J. Fox, Chevy Chase, Arnold Schwarzenegger, Chuck Norris, Harrison Ford, Michael Douglas, and Meryl Streep. Note that only one of the ten stars was a woman, and that most male stars specialized in action-adventure or comedy. Furthermore, only a few of the aforementioned stars have been nominated for an Oscar. By contrast, in 1932, seven of the nation's top stars were or would become Oscar winners: Marie Dressler, Janet Gaynor, Joan Crawford, Norma Shearer, Wallace Beery, Clark Gable; Greta Garbo would not win a competitive award despite multiple nominations.

In recent years, there has been a proliferation of film awards. The People's Choice Awards, the MTV Awards, and the American Movie Awards honor the public's favorite performers in film, television, and music. Based on a national sample of moviegoers, and reaching large audiences, these awards cash in on the suspenseful excitement that precede the Oscar ceremonies.

The Guilds Awards

The Screen Actors Guild (SAG) began to celebrate acting achievements in 1994, immediately exerting influence on the Oscar race. The reason is simple: Actors represent about 24 percent of the Oscar ballot-casting members. Nominations for the SAG awards are based on poll results from 4,200 randomly selected SAG members, and the winners are determined via ballots sent to the entire 97,000 membership.

The SAG Awards are good indicators of what might happen on Oscar night. About 80 percent of the SAG winners in the lead categories (Best Actor and Best Actress) have also won the Oscar. The few exceptions have been Jodie Foster, who won the SAG award in 1994 for *Nell,* but lost the Oscar to Jessica Lange for *Blue Sky.* The SAG's supporting categories are less reliable. In 1998, the SAG Supporting Awards went to Robert Duvall for *A Civil Action* and Kathy Bates for *Primary Colors,* but the supporting Oscars went to James Coburn for *Affliction* and Dame Judi Dench for *Shakespeare in Love.*

Highlights of the 2000 SAG Awards show, which is telecast live, included Roberto Benigni's (the previous year's Best Actor) appearance as a presenter of Best Actress to Hilary Swank, and Sidney Poitier receiving a Lifetime Achievement Award from Denzel Washington. In 2002, the SAG Awards proved better predictors for the Oscars than the Golden Globes, when they chose Halle Berry as Best Actress for *Monster's Ball.*

The Preeminence of the Oscars

For awards to bear motivational significance, they have to fulfill at least three functions: They have to be visible and known to every artist; they have to carry a high degree of prestige; and they have to be within reach. The Oscar Awards meet all of these conditions. Almost every year, a performer comes out of nowhere to claim the Oscar, as Halle Berry did in 2002.

The importance of the Oscars goes beyond the American film world. The Oscars are now universally embraced as symbols of achievement in global entertainment. There are a number of reasons for this. First and foremost is the longevity of the award. The Oscar is the oldest film prize in history. A tradition of seventy-four years has made the Oscar a respectable symbol with historical heritage. Other major entertainment awards are children and grandchildren of the Oscar. The Antoinette Perry Awards (Tonys), given by the League of New York Theaters and Producers and the American Theater Wing, were first presented in April 1947. The Emmys, awarded by the National Academy of Television Arts and Sciences, were presented for the first time in January 1949. The Grammys, the youngest showbiz awards, were first bestowed by the National Academy of Recording Arts and Sciences in May 1959.

Aside from longevity, there are differences in scope. The Tony, for example, is essentially a local award, given for achievements in Broadway theater. Most people can't relate to the Tonys because they are confined to shows produced in New York. A growing criticism of the Tonys is that they exclude the off Broadway and off off Broadway theater, where the more innovative work is done. Film, by contrast, is a global medium. Even people who don't live in the United States and don't speak English can relate to the Oscar show and the Oscar-winning movies.

The Oscar's prestige also stems from the Academy's status within the industry. The Academy has always been elitist, yet despite its elitism, the Academy's selection procedures are more democratic than most other associations. The Academy, with its various branches, gives equal representation to all artists, regardless of specialty (writers, directors, players). Nomination and selection are based on peer evaluation. The Actors Branch selects nominees for acting awards, the Directors Branch for directing awards, etc. However, each Academy member proposes nominees for the Best Picture, and the entire membership votes for the winners in all the categories.

In contrast, the selection of nominees for the Tony Awards is done by a committee. Final ballots are sent out to about seven hundred eligible Tony voters, members of the governing boards of the Actors Equity Association, the Dramatists Guild, the Society of Stage Directors and Choreographers, the Board of Directors of the American Theater Wing, members of the League of the New York Theaters and Producers, and those on the first and second night press lists. Unlike the Oscar, which was always based on nominations, until 1956 there were no nominations for the Tonys.

The Oscar is awarded by peers, not by the public. Film artists, like other professionals, attribute utmost importance to recognition from their peers because they consider them the only experts with the necessary knowledge to make a competent evaluation of their work. For most filmmakers, the significant reference group, which sets standards to be emulated and also serves as a frame for judging one's performance, consists of fellow-workers. Film artists compare the rewards of their work (money, power, prestige) with those gained by their peers.

The scarcity of awards also contributes to the prestige of the Oscars. In the entire Academy history, only 608 players have been nominated for, and only 188 won, an acting Oscar. Every year, just twenty players are nominated in four categories, and only four win. These twenty performances are selected out of thousands of eligible performances.

Similarly, the five films competing for Best Picture are chosen from a large pool of over two hundred eligible films annually. Production in Hollywood over the years, however, has declined. In the 1940s, over four hundred eligible films were released in an average year, and in the 1960s over three hundred. Compare that to the Tonys. In some years, the Broadway theater is in such a dismal state that the Tony Committee has problems filling the categories with competent candidates, particularly in the musical fields. But even in better times, no more than forty new plays and ten musicals open in a given season.

Superlative performances by foreign players may be unfairly ignored, but the Academy refuses to create an additional category for excellence in a foreign-language film. The suggestion to divide the categories by genre, say, best achievement in drama and comedy, has also been turned down. The Tonys have separate sets of categories for dramatic plays and musicals. Those in favor of one prize, regardless of genre or artists' nationality, claim that increasing the number of awards decrease their prestige; too many categories belittle the award. The Grammys, for example, are awarded in over seventy categories, and singers can be nominated in three or four categories for the same song.

The Oscar is open to film artists of all nationalities: One fourth of the nominees have been foreign artists. This international dimension extends the visibility of the Oscar and contributes to its prestige. And the Oscar's prestige and scarcity of awards in turn makes for intense international competition. Whereas other national industries distinguish between local and foreign achievements, the only Oscar category specifically designed to honor foreign achievements is the Best Foreign-Language Picture.

The immense effects, both symbolic and pragmatic, on the winning films and winning artists, is another unique feature of the Oscars. Unlike the prestigious Nobel Prize, there is no financial honorarium, though the Oscar's economic worth is extraordinary — the winners' salaries skyrocket overnight! Winning an Oscar means hard cash at the box office: The Best Picture Award can add up to twenty to thirty million dollars in tickets sales. Winning the lead acting award can add four to six million dollars to a film's profitability. Hilary Swank's Best Actress nomination and then award for *Boys Don't Cry* almost doubled the film's gross, and Halle Berry's Oscar did the same for *Monster's Ball*.

The Oscars are visible and influential in both the domestic and global markets. Nowadays, foreign box-office receipts can amount to more than half of movies' overall grosses. Along with prestige and money, the Oscar winners also gain negotiating power for better roles with better directors, and they also enjoy increased popularity outside the film industry and outside the United States.

No other entertainment award has comparable effects. The Emmys are less influential for the very reason that reruns of Emmy-winning programs, unlike rereleases of Oscar-winning films, add little more money. As for the Tonys, many of the winning productions are no longer on the boards by the time of the ceremonies. However, winning a Tony for Best Play or Best Musical is more important for commercial appeal than winning the Pulitzer Prize for drama or the New York Drama Critics Award. In 1978, *The Wiz,* the all-black musical which opened to lukewarm reception, became a long-running show only after winning the Best Musical Tony. Plays that received favorable reviews, such as *The Elephant Man* and *Children of a Lesser God,* became more successful at the box office after winning Best Play in their respective years.

The Grammys do have an impact on record sales. Quincy Jones's 1982 album "The Dude" hit the top ten after winning five Grammys. The 1981 Grammy-winning album of singer-songwriter Christopher Cross leaped back up the charts and eventually sold more than four million copies, compared to the two million sale prior to winning. Still, these figures do not begin to compare to the financial bonanza of performers and films after winning the Oscar.

The four showbiz awards divide the calendar year, with one big event every season: The Oscar show takes place in the spring, the Tonys in the early summer, the Emmys in the fall, and the Grammys in the winter. However, the Oscar telecast is the most popular event of the four. The Oscars' preeminence in the entertainment world is enhanced through extensive coverage in all the media: Print and radio in the first two decades, and television in the last fifty years. This media blitz is not confined to the United States: The Oscar show is a popular TV program, watched live or on tape by over one billion people, as noted, in over 170 countries.

Every profession is stratified, though some more sharply than others. In the acting profession, the inequality in rewards (money, prestige, popularity, power) between the elite and the rank-and-file is particularly sharp. There are three relevant audiences and three corresponding evaluations in the film world: Evaluation by peers, evaluation by critics, and evaluation by the public. The first is internal to the film world, the other two are outside the industry. However, all three evaluations are important since they operate at the same time, and each exerts some impact on the film world.

Most film artists, particularly actors, aim at achieving two distinct goals in their careers: Professional attainment, as defined by peers and critics, and a broader commercial popularity, as determined by the general public. Actors are aware of the potential conflicts in fulfilling these goals. They know that to be respected by peers and critics is one thing; to be popular, quite another. In film, more than in other arts, outsiders, namely moviegoers, exercise power over artists' careers. By choosing to see a particular film or a particular actor, the public determines not only their present status, but also their chances to work in the future.

What makes the Oscar such an influential award is its combination of all three evaluations. Through the Oscar, the Academy voters function as peers, as critics, and as tastemakers. No other award so well combines the usually disparate critical and popular judgment. The Oscar is the only award to exert a direct, pervasive influence on every element of the film world: The movies, their filmmakers, and their audiences.

4

HUNKS, LEADING LADIES,
AND SECOND BANANAS—THE NOMINATION

The Oscar race is loaded with storylines featuring fresh faces, old pros, frontrunners, long shots, and years in the wilderness.

—John Clark, *Los Angeles Times*

Is the Oscar Race Democratic?

How democratic is the Oscar race? Do we really see young and fresh talent at the annual Oscar nominations? Or are the Oscar awards and nominations concentrated within a familiar elite?

In the first years, with few exceptions, the "usual suspects," specifically MGM players, were nominated year after year. MGM dominated most categories, not just in acting, which was a result of both the almighty Louis B. Mayer, the Academy architect, and the kinds of movies that studio was making. The situation began to change with the decline of the studio system in the late 1950s and early 1960s, when the Oscar race became wider and more open. There are always new faces, and in some years, fresh talent dominates.

Every once in a while, there's an anomaly, an exceptional year such as 1995, in which there were ten new faces in the supporting acting categories, all first-time nominees. In 1997, too, all five nominated directors were fresh faces: British Peter Cattaneo for *The Full Monty*, indie icon Gus Van Sant for *Good Will Hunting*, Curtis Hanson for *L.A. Confidential*, Canadian arthouse filmmaker Atom Egoyan for *The Sweet Hereafter*, and another Canadian, albeit one working within the big Hollywood tradition, James ("King of the World") Cameron for *Titanic*. (Of the five, Cattaneo was previously nominated for his 1990 Live Short, "Dear Rosie.")

In 1999, Hollywood opened its gates again, and seven out of the ten actresses (in both lead and supporting roles) were new faces. In 2000, of the thirty-one individuals who won competitive Oscars, more than half (nineteen) were first-time nominees. However, of the five female supporting nominees in 2002, only one, Jennifer Connelly (*A Beautiful Mind*), was a first-timer in her category. The other four were Oscar veterans: Maggie Smith with six nominations, Kate Winslet with three, and Helen Mirren and Marisa Tomei with two each.

The First Nomination

Just being nominated is a kind of vindication. — Ann-Margret

I'm not sure that winning is that important, but the nomination lets people know you are there. — Peter Finch

Earning an Oscar nomination means getting recognition, and getting recognition early on can make or break a career. The first Oscar nomination often serves as a predictor of future success since it places the nominee on a different level of prestige and visibility within the industry.

Actresses receive their first nomination at a much younger age than actors: About half of the women earn their first nomination prior to the age of thirty, compared with only one-tenth of the men. Supporting players gain their first nomination either at a very young or at a very old age. For example, about 10 percent of the supporting players, but only 3 percent of the leads, were older than sixty when first nominated.

The youngest nominees in the Academy's history are in the supporting leagues. Justin Henry was only eight when first nominated for *Kramer vs. Kramer,* a remarkable achievement since he had never acted before. The youngest nominees among the supporting actresses are Tatum O'Neal, who won for *Paper Moon* in 1973, at the age of ten, and Quinn Cummings for *The Goodbye Girl,* who, at eleven, earned a nomination for her first picture, though she had appeared on television before. New Zealander Anna Paquin, who at eleven won the Supporting Oscar, is one of the youngest performers in Oscars' history to have received the award. Paquin attained early attention for her riveting performance as Holly Hunter's emotionally complex daughter in 1993's *The Piano.* Like Tatum O'Neal, Paquin was an engaging, knowing-beyond-her-years girl. However, unlike O'Neal, whose career was short, Paquin has proved herself to be a capable actress in both studio and indie movies (*Hurly Burly, A Walk on the Moon, X-Men*).

Earning a nomination at an early age is more prevalent in the supporting categories since these players tend to be cast in younger screen roles. The Academy voters are also less discriminating in appraising performances by children and teenagers — sentimentality has always played a considerable role.

Children have been nominated for Oscars ever since the Supporting Oscars were created in 1936. Bonita Granville was the first child to earn a nomination in 1936, for *These Three,* based on Lillian Hellman's play *The Children's Hour.* In 1962, two young girls competed for the Supporting award: Patty Duke (*The Miracle Worker*) and Mary Badham (*To Kill a Mockingbird*); Duke won. The same situation prevailed in 1973, when Tatum O'Neal (*Paper Moon*) and Linda Blair (*The Exorcist*) were Supporting nominees; O'Neal won. At fourteen, playing a teen prostitute in *Taxi Driver,* Jodie Foster became one of the Academy's youngest nominees. In 1977, Quinn Cummings was nominated for *The Goodbye Girl,* but the winner was Vanessa Redgrave for *Julia.* No child actress was nominated from 1977 until Paquin received the supporting award for *The Piano*. In later years, Juliette Lewis was a young lady of sixteen when nominated for *Cape Fear* (1991).

By comparison, fewer child actors have been nominated: Brandon De Wilde (*Shane*) in 1953, Jack Wilde (*Oliver!*) in 1968, and Justin Henry in 1979. In 1999, at age eleven, child-actor Haley Joel Osment co-starred with Bruce Willis in *The Sixth Sense*. More than any other members of the cast, which also included Oscar-nominated Toni Collette, who played his mom, Osment deserves credit for contributing to what became the most popular horror thriller in the genre's history.

No child actress has ever been nominated for Best Actress. The youngest nominees in this category are Marlee Matlin (who won at twenty-one for *Children of a Lesser God*); Janet Gaynor and Kate Winslet, who each was twenty-two when nominated — Gaynor for three roles, Winslet for *Titanic*.

Jackie Cooper, nominated at the age of ten for *Skippy*, is the only boy to compete for the Best Actor. But Cooper was a known quantity, a nephew of film director Norman Taurog (who helmed *Skippy*), and a veteran who began performing in Bobby Clark and Lloyd Hamilton comedies, and was later in the popular Our Gang series, in which he made audiences laugh and cry with his antics and mishaps.

The Academy has acknowledged the importance of star-children as box-office champions with Special (Junior) Awards. In 1939, Deanna Durbin and Mickey Rooney were awarded miniature Oscar trophies. Durbin was honored for her performance in her first feature, *Three Smart Girls*, which made her a star and also saved Universal from bankruptcy. Rooney received the award in recognition of the Andy Hardy movies, "for significant contribution in bringing to the screen the spirit and personification of youth and as a juvenile player setting a high standard of ability and achievement."

In 1940, Judy Garland won a Special Oscar as "the year's best juvenile performer," for her appearance in the musical *The Wizard of Oz*, one of MGM's all-time smash hits. Other children were honored with a Special Oscar in the 1940s, but later, performances by young players qualified for nominations in the legitimate categories.

One of the youngest Best Actress nominees is Isabelle Adjani, who was nominated at the age of twenty-one for the title role of François Truffaut's *The Story of Adele H*. Adjani began her career in amateur productions at twelve, and made her film debut two years later. She rejected a tempting twenty-year contract with the noted Comédie-Française theater in order to appear in *The Story of Adele H*. It paid off: The movie, assisted by her nomination, put her at the forefront of international stars. In 1989, the Academy conferred on Adjani a second Best Actress nomination for another French film, *Camille Claudel*. That she played mentally disturbed women in both pictures was certainly a bonus, given the kinds of female roles for which the Academy goes.

Consistent differences prevail between the careers of female and male nominees. Women receive their first nomination at a younger age than men: The average age at first nomination is thirty-one for the women but forty for the men. Of the four groups, the Best Actresses are the youngest. The average age at receiving the first nomination is twenty-nine for the Best Actresses, thirty-three for the Supporting Actresses, thirty-eight for the Best Actors, and forty-three for the Supporting Actors. Within each category, women have an advantage over men when it comes to getting recognition at an early age. Supporting players tend to be younger or older than the lead nominees, based on the kinds of roles they play. Character roles are typically much younger or older than leading parts.

Not many Best Actresses are older than forty at their first nomination. Joan Crawford (*Mildred Pierce*) was the only actress in this age category in the 1940s, and in the 1950s there were only two, Shirley Booth (*Come Back, Little Sheba*) and Anna Magnani (*The Rose Tattoo*). Jessica Tandy, who at eighty-one became the oldest actress to be nominated for (and win) the Best Actress (for *Driving Miss Daisy*), is the exception. Actresses rightly complain that once they reach the age of forty they either have to switch to supporting roles or retire because of the dearth of scripts with middle-aged heroines as the central roles. Leading ladies in American films are typically young and attractive. Sadly, chances for an Oscar are rather slim if actresses don't receive a nomination by the age of thirty.

The position of middle-aged actresses in the film industry began to change in the 1970s. Slowly reflecting these changes, over the past two decades the Academy has cited more middle-aged actresses than ever before. Gena Rowlands (*A Woman Under the Influence, Gloria*), Ellen Burstyn (*Same Time Next Year, Resurrection*), Mary Tyler Moore (*Ordinary People*), and Sissy Spacek (*In the Bedroom*) were all mature actresses playing mature women.

Another encouraging development is the nomination of elderly actresses for lead roles, such as Katharine Hepburn (*On Golden Pond*), Geraldine Page (*The Trip to Bountiful*), Jessica Tandy (*Driving Miss Daisy*), and Ellen Burstyn (*Requiem for a Dream*). In the past, elderly actresses were mostly nominated in the supporting categories.

Nominating older players has also characterized the male categories over the last two decades. In the 1950s, only two supporting actors (Eric Von Stroheim in *Sunset Boulevard* and Sessue Hayakawa in *The Bridge on the River Kwai*) were in their sixties. But since the 1970s, a substantial cohort belongs to this age group, including John Mills (*Ryan's Daughter*), Lee Strasberg (*The Godfather, Part II*), Burgess Meredith (*Rocky*), Robert Preston (*Victor/Victoria*), Denholm Elliott (*A Room With a View*), and Armin Mueller-Stahl (*Shine*).

Hollywood has finally caught up with the growing awareness of ageism in American society. Though not nearly enough, more screenplays and more movies about elderly protagonists are being produced. The Academy has expressed its concern for elderly players with a larger number of nominations.

As Richard Farnsworth's career shows, it *is* possible to get a Best Actor nomination at an old age. More than half a century ago, Farnsworth swore off speaking roles after his first crack in a Roy Rogers Western. The director wanted the then-stuntman to say a few lines, but every time Farnsworth tried, he broke out in giggles. Eventually, the director gave up, and Farnsworth promised himself, never again. Decades later, Farnsworth was persuaded to give acting another shot by Alan J. Pakula in the Western, *Comes a Horseman,* for which he was rewarded with a 1978 Best Supporting nod.

Playing a Mongol horseman, in the twilight of a career that began in 1938 with *The Adventures of Marco Polo,* Farnsworth found himself nominated for a powerful performance in David Lynch's *The Straight Story,* as the real-life, stubborn Alvin Straight, who insisted on driving a lawnmower hundreds of miles to visit his ailing brother. "I'm pretty limited in a lot of ways," Farnsworth told *Entertainment Weekly.* "But if I feel the character, it's damn easy to do." In truth, it hurt to connect with Straight. Bum hips were killing the actor during the driving scenes, and then there was the agony of recounting Straight's World War II memories — a vet himself, Farnsworth won't talk about his war experience.

The oldest nominees in the four categories are:

> Best Actor: Richard Farnsworth (*The Straight Story*) 78, George Arliss (*Disraeli*) 63, and Art Carney (*Harry and Tonto*) 57
>
> Supporting Actor: Ralph Richardson (*Greystoke: The Legend of Tarzan, Lord of the Apes*) 82, George Burns (*The Sunshine Boys*) 80, and Don Ameche (*Cocoon*) 77;
>
> Best Actress: Dame May Robson (*Lady for a Night*) 76, and Ida Kaminska (*The Shop on Main Street*) 68
>
> Supporting Actress: Gloria Stuart (*Titanic*) 87, Jessica Tandy (*Fried Green Tomatoes*) 82, Eva Le Galienne (*Resurrection*) 80, Dame Edith Evans (*Tom Jones*) 76, Lauren Bacall (*The Mirror Has Two Faces*) 72.

In the supporting categories, it is possible to receive a nomination at any age. The supporting nominees' age has ranged from eight (Justin Henry) to eighty-two (Ralph Richardson) among the men, and from ten (Quinn Cummings) to eighty-seven (Gloria Stuart) among the women.

In each lead category, however, one age group is dominant. The lead leagues are more rigid concerning age: Most Best Actresses were in their late twenties, and most Best Actors in their late thirties, at their first nomination. A difference of a full decade, which is significant in performers' careers, reflects a double standard in American society regarding age.

Early Recognition: Nomination for First Film

How long does it take to get a nomination once a film career has been launched? At what phase of their careers will film artists receive their first nomination? Surprisingly, a considerable proportion of players (over 10 percent) have received a nomination for their very first film, particularly among the supporting players. The time span between film debut and first nomination is shorter for the women than for the men. Half of the actresses, but only one-third of the actors, were nominated within five years after their first movie. This means that the women's talent is certified by the Academy much faster than men's, and that the career "fate" of leading ladies is determined early on. Actresses failing to impress the Academy in their first five movies stand slim chances to get a nomination in the future.

Supporting players tend to receive their first nomination either very early or very late in their careers. About 20 percent of supporting, but only 5 percent of lead performers, had to wait two decades after their debuts to be nominated. About one-tenth of the Best Actors have earned a nomination for their first film or first major film. These actors include Paul Muni (*The Valiant*), Montgomery Clift (*The Search*), Anthony Franciosa (*A Hatful of Rain*), Alan Arkin (*The Russians Are Coming, the Russians Are Coming*), Ryan O'Neal (*Love Story*), and Dexter Gordon (*'Round Midnight*).

A similar percentage of Best Actresses were nominated for their first film, some for re-creating successful stage roles on-screen. Among these women are Julie Harris (*The Member of the Wedding*), Maggie McNamara (*The Moon Is Blue*), Jane Alexander (*The Great White Hope*), and Julie Walters (*Educating Rita*). Other lucky actresses singled out for their film debuts include Carrie Snodgress (*Diary of a Mad Housewife*), Diana Ross (*Lady Sings the Blues*), Bette Midler (*The Rose*), Whoopi Goldberg (*The Color Purple*), Emily Watson (*Breaking the Waves*), and Janet McTeer (*Tumbleweeds*).

Dustin Hoffman was particularly fortunate to earn a nomination for his first major film, *The Graduate,* in 1967; his first film, *The Tiger Makes Out,* was made the same year. After graduating from the Pasadena Playhouse in Los Angeles, Hoffman moved to New York, where he was forced to make his living as a typist and moving man. For a while he could not get any acting job and, at one point, even considered quitting. Then, after working as an assistant director off Broadway, Hoffman was cast in *Journey of the Fifth Horse,* which enjoyed a short life but won him an Obie Award. Director Mike Nichols was impressed with his performance and, looking for an unknown actor to play the lead in *The Graduate,* summoned Hoffman to Hollywood for a screen test. Hoffman became an instant star after this film.

Luck — being in the right place at the right time — plays a significant role in earning early recognition. Accidents and coincidences have accounted for a considerable number of actors being cast in what later became their Oscar-nominated roles.

The Academy is more generous in conferring nominations for film debuts on the supporting players. Among the actors who have immediately grabbed the Academy's attention are John Garfield (*Four Daughters*), Robert Morley (*Marie Antoinette*), Sidney Greenstreet (*The Maltese Falcon*), Richard Widmark (*Kiss of Death*), Don Murray (*Bus Stop*), Terence Stamp (*Billy Budd*), Brad Dourif (*One Flew Over the Cuckoo's Nest*), Howard Rollins Jr. (*Ragtime*), John Malkovich (*Places in the Heart*), Leonardo DiCaprio (*What's Eating Gilbert Grape*), and Ralph Fiennes (*Schindler's List*).

A talented actor like Edward Norton, "the chameleon of his generation," would have made it without Oscar's help, but early recognition catapulted him more quickly to a level of stardom. The circumstances surrounding Norton's first nomination are notable. In one year, 1996, he turned in three vastly different performances: As a pyschopathic choirboy in *Primal Fear* (for which he was nominated as supporting actor), a lawyer in *The People vs. Larry Flynt,* and as Woody Allen's twitchy, alter ego in *Everyone Says I Love You.* In 1998, Norton received a second, this time lead, nomination for his role as Derek, a racist skin-head in *American History X.* That same year he played an ex-con poker hustler in *The Rounders.* Wrote *Entertainment Weekly:* "The range he continues to exhibit is phenomenal, as is the insight he manages to bring to diverse characters. As Derek, he mesmerizes even as he repels, and the actor fully exposes the human being behind the tough poses."

Among the supporting actresses nominated for their very first or first major film are: Maria Ouspenskaya (*Dodsworth*), Teresa Wright and Patricia Collinge (both for *The Little Foxes*), Angela Lansbury (*Gaslight*), Lee Grant (*Detective Story*), Diane Varsi (*Peyton Place*), Shirley Knight (*The Dark at the Top of the Stairs*), Carol Channing (*Thoroughly Modern Millie*), Cathy Burns (*Last Summer*), Glenn Close (*The World According to Garp*), Oprah Winfrey (*The Color Purple*), and Julia Roberts (*Steel Magnolias*),

Hope Lange secured a supporting nomination for *Peyton Place* in the first year of her career, during which she also appeared in *Bus Stop.* She competed in 1957 with another young and talented actress, Diane Varsi, who also made a splashy debut in *Peyton Place* as Lana Turner's rebellious, illegitimate daughter. Varsi too received a supporting nomination. Most recently, Marianne Jean-Baptiste made a strong impression with her first film, Mike Leigh's *Secrets & Lies,* as the illegitimate daughter given to adoption, for which she secured a supporting nomination.

As James Dean's tough mother, who flees from her husband and then runs a bordello, Jo Van Fleet was nominated for *East of Eden,* her very first film though she was only eleven years older than Dean. An acclaimed Broadway actress — a graduate of the Actors Studio — Van Fleet made just a few films after her Supporting Oscar turn, among them *Wild River* and *Cool Hand Luke.* In contrast, Maureen Stapleton had a long and thriving career after her 1958 Oscar nomination for her first film, *Lonely Hearts.*

Interestingly, some of the nominated performances were not delivered by professional actors. Harold Russell won two Oscars, a competitive and a Special Award (*The Best Years of Our Lives*), for re-creating on-screen his real-life experience as a paratroop sergeant who lost both hands in World War II. It was Russell's first and for many years only picture.

Born in Cambodia and trained as a doctor, Haing S. Ngor was captured and tortured by the Khmer Rouge after their takeover of the country. Ngor escaped to Thailand and finally settled in the United States, where he worked at various jobs before making his debut in *The Killing Fields* (1984), for which he won a Supporting Oscar. Ngor made a number of other movies before he was tragically murdered in 1996.

Several singers and dancers have received nominations for their debuts — if their pictures were box-office hits. Miliza Korjus, a Polish opera singer, was nominated for her first and only movie, *The Great Waltz*. Mikhail Baryshnikov and Leslie Browne, both dancers of the American Ballet Theater, earned supporting nods for playing dancers in *The Turning Point*.

Some noted writers were also singled out for their acting debuts. Jason Miller, a successful Broadway playwright (*That Championship Season*), was nominated for portraying a priest in *The Exorcist*. Michael V. Gazzo, who wrote *A Hatful of Rain,* earned a nomination for his first movie, *The Godfather, Part II.* Both Miller and Gazzo earned nominations not so much for distinguished acting, but for performances within high-profile blockbusters. Deservedly or not, commercial hits tend to earn nominations in a disproportionately large number of categories.

Receiving a nomination for a first film, thus reaching a professional height with only one credit, is unique to acting careers. In most professions, a lengthy period of formal training and working experience are required before praise and promotion are granted. But in the performing arts, neither formal education nor training are prerequisites for entry into the profession or for climbing to the top. One film, especially if it is a commercial hit, can make or break a career. Besides, many factors, not just acting talent, are responsible for making a particular performance (or a particular film) Oscar-worthy.

Late Bloomers or Late Oscar Recognition

In contrast to those recognized early for their work, some artists have had to wait for a long time (over two decades) to earn a nomination. This is particularly true for foreign actors. Though foreign actors might begin at a young age, it often takes a long time to be cast in American movies or to make foreign films that are visible in the American market.

Anna Magnani received her first nomination (and Oscar) for *The Rose Tattoo,* as noted — twenty-one years after her Italian film debut. Had it not been for Tennessee Williams's demand that she play the title role, Magnani might never have been nominated for the Oscar, despite being one of the world's greatest screen actresses.

The crucial factor in the foreign players' career is the age at which they are brought to Hollywood. Many actors have shown promise in their own countries, but for a variety of reasons have not gotten international recognition. Maximilian Schell did not establish a reputation as a movie star in Europe, despite good work early on in his career. He arrived in Hollywood mostly known as Maria Schell's younger brother, but it took only one American film, *The Young Lions* (cast at the suggestion of Marlon Brando), to make him an actor of international caliber. Three years later, Stanley Kramer assigned Schell the role of the German counselor in 1961's *Judgment at Nuremberg,* for which he received the Best Actor Award.

Several British players became movie stars only after their relocation to Hollywood. Rex Harrison began his film career in England when he was twenty-two, but his first American movie (*Anna and the King of Siam*) occurred sixteen years later; he received his first nomination (for *Cleopatra*) thirty-three years after his film debut, at the age of fifty-five. Peter Finch, another excellent actor, began his career in Australia in his late teens, and established himself as a prominent actor in the British industry in the 1950s. However, he too received his first nomination (*Sunday, Bloody Sunday*) thirty-six years after his first movie. Directed by John Schlesinger, the UK *Sunday* received considerable attention in the United States.

Richard Burton's first five pictures in England failed to launch him as a major international star, despite acclaim for his acting. In America, however, it took one Broadway play, Christopher Frye's *The Lady's Not for Burning,* and one movie, *My Cousin Rachel,* which earned him a supporting nomination, to make Burton a star.

Whereas movies are seemingly dominated by young up-and-comers, Hollywood discovered Dame Judi Dench when she was in her sixties. In 1997, Dench became a star with her very first Oscar-nominated performance as Queen Victoria in *Mrs. Brown,* for which she won the Golden Globe. The next year, she played another royal figure, Queen Elizabeth, in *Shakespeare in Love,* for which she won the Supporting Oscar. Dench followed with a Tony Award for *Amy's View,* her first Broadway play in forty years, though she's a staple of the London stage.

Dench only has eight minutes of screen time in *Shakespeare in Love,* and yet she is unforgettable. "I just played her like I imagined she would be," Dench told *Premiere.* "She was a fierce woman. People didn't like messing with her. I was in all those clothes and I couldn't do much but stay very still and pray I didn't have to go to the loo in the middle." Interestingly, Cate Blanchett was nominated in 1998 (*Elizabeth*) for playing Dench's character as a younger woman.

In contrast to the British, American players who received delayed recognition were box-office stars who developed as actors later in their careers. John Wayne made his film debut in his early twenties, but received his first nomination (*Sands of Iwo Jima*) twenty-one years later, at the age of forty-two. Wayne became a movie star after his breakthrough role as the Ringo Kid in John Ford's *Stagecoach,* and he matured as a screen actor a decade later when Howard Hawks cast him in an epic character part in *Red River.* This performance and the Oscar nomination a year later certified Wayne a major talent.

Late recognition also characterizes popular performers who appeared in commercially successful films but failed to gain peer esteem. Later on, for a reasonably good performance, preferably in a successful film, they were honored with a nomination, which served as both acknowledgment of their skills and tribute to their endurance. Doris Day made her film debut in 1948, after which she appeared in musicals and romantic comedies. As a tribute to her popularity, the Academy conferred on her a nomination for the romantic comedy *Pillow Talk.*

Harrison Ford, too, was a box-office champion before earning recognition as a "serious" actor. Ford has appeared in more box-office hits than any other contemporary star; his pictures have grossed collectively more than $2 billion at the box office. Among others, Ford's screen credits include Han Solo in George Lucas's Star Wars trilogy and the archeological soldier of fortune Indiana Jones in Steven Spielberg's *Raiders of the Lost Ark* and its sequels. Some of these films were nominated in several categories, including Best Picture, but their special effects overshadowed Ford the actor. In 1985, when Ford played a more substantial dramatic character in *Witness,* the Academy rewarded him with a Best Actor nomination at the age of forty-three.

Actresses who managed smooth transition from being child performers to ingenues and leading ladies have also been rewarded. This group includes Carole Lombard, Mary Astor, Loretta Young, Natalie Wood, and Tuesday Weld. A striking beauty, Elizabeth Taylor made her first film at the age of ten in *There's One Born Every Minute*. In 1942, she was signed by MGM to a long-term contract. In the decade that followed, Taylor matured into one of Hollywood's most beautiful and popular screen personalities. She somehow skipped adolescence, moving almost directly from child roles to romantic leads. Taylor received her first nomination for playing a troubled Southern belle in *Raintree County,* fifteen years after her debut.

A small group of Academy players began their careers in the silent era, long before the Oscars existed, then made the transition to talkies. These actresses, usually nominated for featured roles, include Alice Brady, Jane Darwell, Ethel Barrymore, Marjorie Rambeau, and Billie Burke. The most distinguished among them is Lillian Gish, a pioneer of the American cinema, joining D. W. Griffith's troupe when she was sixteen. In the 1930s, Gish retired from the screen, but a decade later she returned, this time as a character actress. In 1946, Gish received a supporting nomination for playing a wife driven to drink by her brutal cattle baron husband in King Vidor's lushly shot Western, *Duel in the Sun,* a sweeping box-office success. This nomination was as much a symbolic tribute to Gish's comeback and lengthy career as a legitimate honor for a particular role.

The Oscar Comeback Kids

I've decided to keep making one movie every thirty-six years. You get to be new again. — George Burns, Supporting Winner, *The Sunshine Boys*

"I don't think it perceives me. Maybe as an old lady. What I find strange is a kind of respect. Where did I earn that respect?" Julie Chritsie told *Premiere* magazine, upon receiving a third nomination for *Afterglow,* twenty-six years after her nomination for *McCabe and Mrs. Miller* and thirty-two years after her Oscar for *Darling.*

Hollywood loves triumph-over-adversity stories. The Academy, just like Hollywood, has shown tremendous respect for comeback performances by distinguished players who, after years of absence from the screen, or after years of mediocre work, can still surprise with effective acting.

A major silent star who began performing in her early teens, Gloria Swanson was nominated for the silent movie *Sadie Thompson,* and for her first talkie, *The Trespasser.* However, her subsequent movies were unsuccessful, and in 1934 she retired. Swanson made an abortive comeback in the comedy *Father Takes a Wife,* and then, after a decade, rendered a memorable comeback performance in *Sunset Boulevard,* in which she played neurotic, fading movie queen Norma Desmond. Hollywood couldn't deny Swanson a nomination for her comeback as well as for her indelible portrayal.

The Academy's history is replete with comeback stories, some successful, others less so. Rosalind Russell was a popular star in the 1940s with three Best Actress nominations to her credit, but in the 1950s her career declined. Instead of despairing, or waiting for the right role, Russell went back to the stage and bounced back with a triumphant performance in *Auntie Mame,* which she first played on Broadway, then repeated on-screen. The Academy honored her with a fourth nomination, eleven years after her third (*Mourning Becomes Electra*).

In nominating comeback performances, Hollywood shows loyalty to its champions, based on the belief that they should get a second chance. Several of these comeback nominations have proven instrumental in providing second chapters to previously faltering careers. Since *Easy Rider,* for which he received a writing nomination, Peter Fonda has made peace with both mainstream Hollywood and his late father, Henry, whom he credits for inspiring his characterization in *Ulee's Gold,* a strong comeback role for which he received his first and only Best Actor nomination.

The first Oscar nomination of Lynn Redgrave came in 1966 for her role in *Georgy Girl.* In the 1970s, Redgrave's film career stagnated, but she worked steadily in television, until her 1996 career-reviving role in *Shine.* Two years later, and thirty-two years after her first nomination, Lynn received a second, this time supporting, nod for *Gods and Monsters* in which she played James Whale's devoted housekeeper, speaking with a thick accent.

Nominated at the age of eighty-seven for a supporting role in *Titanic,* Gloria Stuart, a founding member of SAG back in 1933, also qualifies as an Oscar "comeback kid." By *Titanic,* it had been ten years since Stuart had made a film and decades since she starred in one. She's still best remembered for her role in the 1933 horror picture *The Invisible Man,* and as the Queen in the 1939 version of *The Three Musketeers.*

First and Second Bananas: Lead Versus Supporting Oscars

> I guess the Academy is trying to tell me something.
>
> —Gene Hackman

For eight years, there were two acting awards: Best Actor and Best Actress. In 1936, the Academy created two additional categories: Best Supporting Actor and Best Supporting Actress. New rules were required to clarify the distinction between lead and supporting roles. At first, the Academy asked the studios to designate lead and supporting roles in their annual reminder lists, which gave them power. For instance, Luise Rainer's role in *The Great Ziegfeld,* as the showman's first wife, was so small that by today's standards she would have been nominated for another, lesser category. Nonetheless, with the backing of MGM's publicity machine, Rainer was nominated for (and won) Best Actress. Internal studio politics accounted for the fact that John Garfield ended up in the supporting league for his stunning debut in *Four Daughters,* in 1938. Warners was pushing hard for James Cagney to receive a Best Actor nomination in *Angels With Dirty Faces* (which he did), particularly after Cagney won a citation from the New York film Critics Circle. To avoid competition between two of their contract players, Warner's top brass decided to demote Garfield to the secondary category, even though he played a leading role.

The criteria designating lead and supporting roles were often controversial. In 1942, Agnes Moorehead was nominated for a supporting role in Orson Welles's *The Magnificent Ambersons* because the studio (RKO) believed she had no chance to win the Best Actress. Competition that year was particularly fierce, and Greer Garson (*Mrs. Miniver*) was considered to be the industry favorite. But Moorehead's role as the neurotic spinster aunt was of considerable size, which persuaded many that she deserved a Best Actress nomination. Moorehead was also cited as Best Actress by the New York Film Critics Circle. The Academy instructed its members: "Actors marked in the Reminder List by a star are considered leads and can be nominated only for the Best Acting Awards." However, members were given the option "to nominate any supporting player for both the Supporting Award and the Best Performance Award." Hence, in 1944, Barry Fitzgerald became the first (and only) player to be nominated for the same role (*Going My Way*) in both the lead and supporting categories. A compromise was reached in the final vote, when Bing Crosby, also nominated for that film, won Best Actor and Fitzgerald Supporting Actor. Many were disappointed, because they believed Fitzgerald's role was clearly a major one; once again, the New York Film Critics Circle cited Fitzgerald's work as Best Actor.

To avoid any ambiguity, in the following year the Academy changed its rules. It determined that "performance by an actor or actress in any leading role shall be eligible for nomination only for the General Awards for acting achievements." But performance by an actor or actress in a supporting role may be nominated for either the lead or the supporting category. The rules still allowed players to be nominated in both the lead and supporting categories, but for different screen roles.

Not surprisingly, a nomination in both categories in the same year has occurred only a few times in the Academy's history. In 1938, Fay Bainter was nominated for Best Actress in *White Banners* and for Supporting Actress in *Jezebel.* In 1942, Teresa Wright became the second actress to be nominated twice in the same year, for a lead in *The Pride of the Yankees* and a featured role in *Mrs. Miniver.* In 1982, Jessica Lange won two nominations, both for portraying an actress: Lead for the fiery and doomed Frances Farmer in *Frances,* and supporting for the soft and submissive TV actress in *Tootsie.* In 1988, Sigourney Weaver was nominated for a lead in *Gorillas in the Mist* and for a supporting role in the comedy *Working Girl.* Only once, in 1993, were two actresses nominated in both categories: Holly Hunter for a lead in *The Piano* and supporting in *The Firm,* and Emma Thompson for a lead in *The Remains of the Day* and supporting turn in the Irish political drama *In the Name of the Father.*

Three of these actresses, Fay Bainter, Teresa Wright, and Jessica Lange, won the Supporting Oscar. The Best Actress winners in those years were Bette Davis for *Jezebel,* Greer Garson for *Mrs. Miniver,* and Meryl Streep for *Sophie's Choice.* Holly Hunter won Best Actress for *The Piano,* but Thompson (who had won an Oscar the year before for *Howards End*) and Weaver failed to win an Oscar in either category.

In 1950, a further clarification was introduced: "If a performance by an actor or actress should receive sufficient votes to be nominated for both the Best Actress and Supporting Award, only the achievement which, in the preferential tabulation process, first received the quota shall be placed on the ballot. The votes for the second achievement shall thereupon be redistributed."

Classifications of nominations continued to be made by the studios, regardless of role size and billing considerations. In 1950, Anne Baxter persuaded Fox to campaign for her for a lead nomination in *All About Eve,* thereby running against Bette Davis, who was the film's chief star. Had Baxter been nominated for a featured role, as many believed she should have, Davis would have won Best Actress. Baxter had already earned the Supporting Oscar in 1946 for *The Razor's Edge,* which was her reason for competing in the Best Actress league. The industry's feeling was that Davis and Baxter canceled each other out, leaving the award to the least expected nominee that year, Judy Holliday in *Born Yesterday.*

By contrast, Betsy Blair's 1955 performance in *Marty,* as the shy and lonely schoolteacher, was nominated for a supporting Oscar despite the fact that it was considered to be a lead role. Earlier, Blair was honored with the chief acting prize at the Cannes Film Festival. However, the competition for Best Actress that year, headed by Anna Magnani (*The Rose Tattoo*), was intense, and Blair had no chance of winning.

A serious dispute erupted the following year, when Dorothy Malone volunteered, at her studio's "suggestion," to lower her standing in *Written on the Wind* in order to qualify for a supporting nomination. Malone received co-star billing, but Universal designated her performance as supporting because her chances to win were better in this league, which turned out to be true. However, Malone's switch was seen as "grossly unjust" to performers who deserved recognition as supporting players. This resulted in a new rule in 1957: "The Academy, not the studios, would make final determination as to the appropriate classification of screen roles. The Academy would consider the information provided by the studios, but should any screen credit be questioned, the matter would be submitted to a special committee for arbitration."

Unexpected nominations continued to be made. In 1961, Piper Laurie was nominated for Best Actress as Paul Newman's alcoholic girlfriend in *The Hustler,* in which she received co-star billing with George C. Scott and Jackie Gleason. It was a pleasant surprise as Scott and Gleason were nominated for featured roles.

Another major change in the rules occurred in 1964, when the Academy decided that "the determination as to whether a role was a lead or supporting is made individually by members of the Actors Branch at the time of the balloting." Branch members could nominate any player in either lead or supporting league, regardless of studio billings and publicity. The Academy felt that members should have the right to exercise judgment without interference from other sources.

Nonetheless, politicking through ad campaigns have prevailed and chances to win often still determine the specific designation. This became clear in 1966, when Walter Matthau was nominated for a supporting role in Billy Wilder's *The Fortune Cookie,* despite the fact that his role was major, and the whole film was based on team acting by him and co-star Jack Lemmon (who was not nominated). But Matthau's prospects were better in the supporting classification because there were two strong lead performances that year — Paul Scofield in *A Man for All Seasons,* and Richard Burton in *Who's Afraid of Virginia Woolf?* When the results were announced, the validity of these political concerns were reaffirmed: Scofield won Best Actor and Matthau Supporting Actor.

In 1980, Columbia campaigned for Meryl Streep for a supporting nomination in *Kramer vs. Kramer.* Streep's role, as the confused wife-mother, was small but constituted the center of the movie. The studio's decision, however, had nothing to do with the role's size but with the realization that she had no chance of beating Sally Field in *Norma Rae,* particularly after Field had been honored with all the critics awards (New York, Los Angeles, and the National Society).

It goes without saying that players attribute greater importance to star billing and lead roles. The winning of lead nominations and awards is more prestigious and has far more influence on their careers. Shelley Winters has not forgotten to this day that her two Oscars were for supporting roles. Peter Finch was upset at his publicists' suggestion that they try for the supporting award in *Network,* which the actor felt represented his best work. Finch was determined "to go for the top award or be out of the competition altogether." Samuel L. Jackson was upset in 1994 by Miramax's decision to campaign for him in the supporting league for *Pulp Fiction,* despite the fact that he played a co-starring role with John Travolta who was pushed by the studio for the lead Oscar.

The new rules sometimes lead to surprising results. Marlon Brando's role in *The Godfather* was considered to be suitable for a supporting nomination, but he was nominated for (and won) Best Actor. Valerie Perrine would have had better chances to win, as Lenny Bruce's sluttish wife in *Lenny,* had she been nominated for a featured role. Perrine was cited as Supporting Actress by both the New York Film Critics and the National Board of Review, but the Actors Branch nominated her for a lead because it was a weak year for actresses.

In 1981, the biggest surprise of the acting branch was placing *Susan Sarandon* for Best Actress in *Atlantic City*. Paramount had been pushing for a supporting nomination, and Sarandon herself admitted that she had voted for herself in the supporting category.

The criteria that distinguish lead from supporting roles are also unclear and confusing in other voting groups as well. In 1985, Peggy Ashcroft's role as Mrs. Moore, the bright elderly lady in David Lean's *A Passage to India*, received rave reviews and won a number of critical citations. But even the critics were divided as to the appropriate category to place her. The New York Film Critics cited Ashcroft as lead actress, but the Los Angeles Film Critics singled her out as supporting actress. The Academy followed the Los Angeles group and honored her with the Supporting Actress Award. Judy Davis, her co-star, playing the mysterious young woman, was nominated for Best Actress. The feeling was that had Ashcroft been nominated for the lead, she and Davis would canceled each other out. A few years later, Miramax's Harvey Weinstein held that Michael Caine had a better chance to receive a supporting nod for *Little Voice*, but the actor disagreed based on his winning of a Golden Globe in the lead category (for Musical/Comedy).

Single and Multiple Nominations

Tracy needs another Oscar like Zsa Zsa Gabor needs Ann Landers's lovelorn advice." — Emcee Bob Hope

The fact that I have lost five times intrigues me even more.
         — Peter O'Toole, at his sixth (but not last) nomination

Is earning a nomination a once-in-a-lifetime achievement? Apparently not, judging by the high percentage (one-third) of actors and directors who have received multiple nominations.

There are differences between the lead and supporting players. The vast majority (80 percent) of supporting players have received a single nomination, but a considerable proportion (about 50 percent) of the lead nominees have been cited more than once. Since the pool of leading players is smaller, the competition for major roles is tougher, though it increases the chances of those who get them to earn a second nomination.

The average number of nominations is 3.6 for the women and 2.8 for the men. However, women tend to receive multiple nominations after their first Oscar, whereas men tend to get them prior to winning. This difference stems from the fact that women tend to win the Oscar at their first nomination, whereas men win at their second or third nomination (see chapter 6).

The vast majority (84 percent) of the Best Actresses have received two or more nominations. In the Oscars' entire history, only ten of the sixty-two female winners have received a single nomination: Mary Pickford, Ginger Rogers,

Judy Holliday, Shirley Booth, Louise Fletcher, Marlee Matlin, and the four past winners, Helen Hunt, Gwyneth Paltrow, Hilary Swank, and Halle Berry. It is obviously premature to assess their future Oscar prospects since all four are young and just beginning their careers. But winning an Oscar almost ensures another nomination. The female-acting elite is even smaller than that of the males. In each era, the best screen roles circulate among a small group of women who are popular with the public, sought by the studios, and in control of their careers.

By contrast, one-fourth (seventeen) of the Best Actors have received only one nomination: Warner Baxter, Lionel Barrymore, Paul Lukas, Ray Milland, Broderick Crawford, Ernest Borgnine, Yul Brynner, David Niven, Charlton Heston, Lee Marvin, Cliff Robertson, Art Carney, F. Murray Abraham, Michael Douglas, Jeremy Irons, Nicolas Cage, and Roberto Benigni. Emil Jannings and George Arliss were each nominated for two different roles in the same year: The former in *The Last Command* and *The Way of All Flesh* (winning the 1927–28 Best Actor for both), and the latter for *Disraeli* and *The Green Goddess* (winning the 1929–30 Oscar for *Disraeli*). Two Best Actors have received a second (Paul Scofield for *Quiz Show*) and third (Ben Kingsley for *Bugsy* and *Sexy Beast*) Supporting nomination.

Multiple nominations take in either one or two different categories (lead and/or supporting). Most of the multiple nominations have been within the same category. For better or worse, once players are labeled by agents, producers, and directors as lead or character actors, these labels are hard to change — a phenomenon well known as the curse of typecasting. In the last two decades, however, it has become easier to cross from one category to another. In the past, the direction was usually one-sided, from leading to supporting roles. One of the recent positive developments within the film industry is that the rigid concepts of leading versus character players are not as formidable or clearly defined as they used to be.

About one-tenth of all players have been nominated in both lead and supporting categories. Most of the men began in character roles, then earned nominations in the lead categories. For years, this was considered to be the natural evolution of acting careers. For example, John Garfield's first nomination (*Four Daughters*) was for a featured role, and his second (*Body and Soul*) was for a lead. Rod Steiger's three nominations include one in the supporting (*On the Waterfront*) and two in the lead (*The Pawnbroker* and *In the Heat of the Night*) categories.

The other direction, from lead to character roles, marks the careers of more-senior actors. James Mason's first nomination (*A Star Is Born*) was for a lead, but his two subsequent nominations (*Georgy Girl* and *The Verdict*) were for supporting roles.

By contrast, few of the actresses who began in supporting roles were able to make the transition to leading ladies. Women are much more limited by cultural restrictions concerning their range of roles. Several actresses who began as leading ladies found themselves relegated to playing character roles. Thus, British actress Wendy Hiller, who won her first nomination for playing Eliza Doolittle in *Pygmalion,* always commanded leading roles on stage, but in Hollywood she was classified as a supporting actress, earning second (*Separate Tables*) and third (*A Man for All Seasons*) nominations for featured roles.

Shelley Winters also played leads early on in her career, earning a Best Actress nomination for her portrayal of the pregnant factory girl in *A Place in the Sun.* However, shortly after this nomination, producers and casting directors relegated her to supporting roles, and she remained in this league for the rest of her career, winning three supporting nominations (*The Diary of Anne Frank, A Patch of Blue,* and *The Poseidon Adventure*).

Recently though, women in Hollywood have been more flexible in their choice of roles, often beginning in one category and moving to another, or switching back and forth between lead and supporting roles. Ellen Burstyn, Meryl Streep, Glenn Close, and Frances McDormand all began their careers by playing supporting roles but later succeeded in becoming leading ladies. At the same time, for a good role in an interesting film, these women are still willing to play secondary roles. The "stigma" of being a supporting and thus "second-class" player, is less evident and less detrimental to acting careers than it had been in the past.

Academy nominations have been concentrated within a small group of players: One-fifth of the Best Actors and Best Actresses have earned more than four nominations. Among those nominated four times were: Barbara Stanwyck, Rosalind Russell, Jane Wyman, Charles Boyer, Mickey Rooney, Anthony Quinn, and Anthony Hopkins. A smaller group of actors, including Irene Dunne, Audrey Hepburn, Glenn Close, Fredric March, Paul Muni, Arthur Kennedy, and, most recently, Denzel Washington, earned five nominations.

The top of the pyramid is composed of only twenty-five players with six or more nominations.

6 nominations:	Norma Shearer,* Vanessa Redgrave, Thelma Ritter, Deborah Kerr, Robert Duvall, Ellen Burstyn, Jessica Lange, Sissy Spacek
7 nominations:	Greer Garson, Ingrid Bergman, Richard Burton, Peter O'Toole, Jane Fonda, Dustin Hoffman
8 nominations:	Marlon Brando, Jack Lemmon, Geraldine Page, Paul Newman, Al Pacino
9 nominations:	Spencer Tracy
10 nominations:	Bette Davis, Laurence Olivier
11 nominations:	Jack Nicholson
12 nominations:	Katharine Hepburn, Meryl Streep

*Norma Shearer was nominated for two performances in the same year, 1929–30.

Multiple Nominations in Other Categories

If you think the acting nominations are concentrated within a very small group of actors, you would be wrong. In other branches, such as Writing, Music, Cinematography, Costume Design, and Art Direction, the inequality is much sharper, with winners who have been nominated a dozen times for the Oscar.

Art Direction:	MGM's Cedric Gibbons received thirty-nine nominations and ten Oscars.
	Richard Day won seven Oscars out of twenty nominations, the last of which for *On the Waterfront*.
Costume Design:	Edith Head was nominated thirty-five times and won a record-setting eight Oscars.
Music:	Alfred Newman holds the all-time record of forty-five nominations and eleven Oscars.
Cinematography:	Leon Shamroy was nominated eighteen times and won four Oscars.
Sound:	MGM's Douglas Shearer, better known as Norma's brother, received nineteen nominations and seven Oscars.

The time span between first and last nominations may serve as an indicator of the viability of acting careers. Along with peer recognition, the Oscar nominations reflect the standing (and popularity) of the nominees in the movie colony.

Surprisingly, the viability of players' careers as measured by the number of years between first and last nomination is rather short. For half of the players, this time span is about a decade. For another one-third, two decades elapsed between first and last nominations, and only one-sixth received their multiple nominations in a period longer than two decades.

The span between first and last nominations is much shorter for actresses. For two-thirds of the women, it is less than a decade. With few exceptions, actresses' careers are shorter (fifteen to twenty years), because they cannot find rewarding or suitable roles upon reaching middle-age. In contrast, men's careers last three or four decades, and aging has less impact on their range of roles. It's therefore possible to describe most actresses' careers in terms of the one decade (or at most two) in which they were popular and in demand. Greta Garbo and Irene Dunne were stars of the 1930s; Olivia de Havilland, Rosalind Russell, and Greer Garson of the 1940s. Audrey Hepburn, Susan Hayward, and Deborah Kerr did their best work in the 1950s; and Anne Bancroft, Patricia Neal, and Shirley MacLaine in the 1960s. The 1970s were dominated by Ellen Burstyn, Faye Dunaway, and Diane Keaton. The 1980s saw the rise of a new group of actresses, headed by Sally Field, Sissy Spacek, Meryl Streep, Jessica Lange, and Glenn Close. The 1990s have been good for Susan Sarandon (a late bloomer), Holly Hunter, Jodie Foster, Emma Thompson, Michelle Pfeiffer, and Winona Ryder.

In contrast, male careers are viable for a much longer period of time, spanning three, four, or even five decades. Men who do consistently good work are rewarded with multiple nominations. Laurence Olivier's film career began in 1930 and continued for half a century. His ten nominations spanned thirty-nine years, from *Wuthering Heights* in 1939 to *The Boys from Brazil* in 1978. Olivier's brilliant career was rewarded with one nomination in the 1930s, three in the 1940s, one in the 1950s, two in the 1960s, and three in the 1970s. Spencer Tracy, another Hollywood giant, began his career in 1930, and continued to make movies up to his death in 1967. His thirty-seven-year-career brought him, as noted, nine nominations: Three in the 1930s, three in the 1950s, and three in the 1960s. His first nomination was in 1936 for *San Francisco* and the last, for *Guess Who's Coming to Dinner,* was awarded posthumously. Jack Lemmon earned seven nominations, from *Mister Roberts* in 1955 to *Missing* in 1982.

Of the current generation of actors, Jack Nicholson and Al Pacino continue to enjoy spectacular screen careers. Nicholson is the only actor to receive eleven nominations, including three Oscars: Two Best Actor (*One Flew Over the Cuckoo's Nest,* 1975; *As Good As It Gets,* 1997) and one Supporting (*Terms of Endearment,* 1983).

For the supporting players, the span between first and last nomination is shorter since most were older when first gaining Academy recognition. Among this distinguished group are Walter Brennan, Charles Coburn, Charles Bickford, and Gladys Cooper, all of whom won multiple nominations, usually within a short period.

Claude Rains, who made his stage debut as a choirboy in London at the age of eleven, went on to hold every possible position in the theater world, from call boy and prompter to stage manager and leading actor. However, Rains's impressive debut, *The Invisible Man,* in which he appeared faceless, occurred when he was forty-four. He won his first nomination in 1939, at the age of fifty, for playing the corrupt senator in *Mr. Smith Goes to Washington.* Rains soon established himself as one of Hollywood's finest character actors, winning four supporting nominations within seven years; his second nomination was for *Casablanca,* his third for *Mr. Skeffington.* Most memorable of all was Rains's role in Hitchcock's *Notorious* as the mother-ridden Nazi betrayed by the woman (Ingrid Bergman) he loves, for which he received his fourth and last nomination. Rains, who distinguished himself in numerous films, worked up to his death in 1967 yet never won an Oscar.

As Rains's career attests, the Academy does not hesitate to nominate the same players year after year. Over one-third of all the nominees have won consecutive nominations at one time or another in their careers. As expected, their numbers are much higher among the lead players. The peak of Bette Davis's career occurred between 1938 and 1942, during which she received five successive nominations. In the 1940s, Greer Garson and Gary Cooper were perennial nominees; Garson was nominated five consecutive years, from 1941 to 1945, and Cooper three times between 1941 and 1943. Marlon Brando won his first Oscar (*On the Waterfront*) in 1954, which was followed by three consecutive nominations. Of Elizabeth Taylor's five nominations, four were in successive years, from 1957 to 1960. Jessica Lange was a perennial Academy nominee in the 1980s, earning nominations in 1982, 1984, and 1985; and Susan Sarandon in the 1990s, with Best Actress nominations in 1991, 1992, 1994, and 1995. Not all of these citations were justified; critics raised eyebrows when Sarandon received a nomination for *The Client*.

As noted, Meryl Streep is the ultimate Academy nominee with twelve nominations. She is tied with Oscar favorite Katharine Hepburn. Streep was nominated in 1978, 1979, 1981, 1982, 1983, 1985, 1987, 1988, 1990, 1995, 1998, and 1999. Since Streep has just turned fifty-three, chances are she will surpass Hepburn and become the Academy's most celebrated actress.

The Longest Gap between First and Last Nomination

Katharine Hepburn: 48 years (from *Morning Glory* in 1932–33 to *On Golden Pond* in 1981)

Henry Fonda: 41 years (from *The Grapes of Wrath* in 1940 to *On Golden Pond* in 1981)

Mickey Rooney: 40 years (from *Babes in Arms* in 1939 to *The Black Stallion* in 1979)

Helen Hayes: 38 years (from *The Sin of Madelon Claudet* in 1931–32 to *Airport* in 1970)

Jack Palance: 38 years (from *Shane* in 1953 to *City Slickers* in 1991)

Albert Finney: 37 years (from *Tom Jones* in 1963 to *Erin Brockovich* in 2000

Note: Fonda was one of the producers of *Twelve Angry Men*, which received a 1957 Best Picture nomination.

The Effects of the Nominations

I have a legitimate career now.
> — Robert Foster on his nomination in *Jackie Brown*

I've been taking more showers and worry much more about clothes and matching shoes than ever before in my life.
> — Frances McDormand, Best Actress, *Fargo*

The very nomination for an Oscar can have a pervasive impact on artists' careers, expanding their visibility and exposure. Once artists are nominated, their careers are watched more carefully by producers, directors, and colleagues. The nomination elevates artists' status and popularity. Many artists were unknown prior to their nomination, but leaped into stardom afterward, particularly if their performances were in commercial pictures. Gregory Peck's first nomination in *The Keys of the Kingdom,* which was only his second movie, made him a star. Kirk Douglas did not make much of an impression in Hollywood until he earned a nomination for *Champion.* Joan Fontaine played small undistinguished parts in several movies like *The Women,* until she won a nomination for *Rebecca.*

Clifton Webb returned to the screen in 1944, after twenty years' absence, as the fastidious and elegant villain in *Laura,* for which he won a supporting nomination. He was cast in the film by director Otto Preminger over the objections of his almighty producer Darryl Zanuck. Born in 1891 as Webb Parmmallee Hollenbeck, Webb was trained as a dancer and actor from early childhood, becoming a seasoned performer by the age of ten. At thirteen, he quit school to study painting and music, and at seventeen sang with the Boston Opera Company. Turning to dance in earnest at nineteen, Webb soon became a ballroom dancer in New York, often partnering with Bonnie Glass. In the 1920s he played in musical comedies and dramatic parts in London, on Broadway, and in some silent movies.

After his Academy nod for *Laura,* Webb was nominated again for *The Razor's Edge,* becoming typecast as a waspish, acidulous, pedantic bachelor. But he found his greatest popularity as the pompous babysitter, Mr. Belvedere, in the hilarious comedy *Sitting Pretty* (1948), for which he received his third nomination in four years — and first Best Actor. Clifton Webb worked steadily until his death four years later, at the age of 75. (*Satan Never Sleeps* was his last picture, in 1962.)

In 1969, *Midnight Cowboy* brought Jon Voight the kind of instant stardom that *The Graduate* had brought Dustin Hoffman in 1967. Voight and Hoffman would have become international stars without getting nominations for their major debuts, but the nomination expedited the process.

Ann-Margret's career not only benefited from her first nomination, but got a tremendous boost when she appeared at the 1962 Oscar show. After singing "Bachelor in Paradise," one of the nominated songs, the former nightclub singer became "The Hottest Name in Town." That appearance got Ann-Margret work, but not recognition as a serious actress. It took an imaginative director like Mike Nichols, and a good supporting part as Bobbie Templeton, Jack Nicholson's love-starved actress-girlfriend in *Carnal Knowledge* (1971), to change her teenage sex-kitten (*Bye Bye Birdie, Viva Las Vegas*) screen image. The nomination brought critical acclaim and bolstered Ann-Margret's self-confidence, forcing her to mature as an actress.

Foreign players became international stars only after their Oscar nominations. British Laurence Harvey established himself as a screen actor after *Room at the Top,* which earned him a nomination, was released in the United States. The nomination of countryman Albert Finney in *Tom Jones,* and the film's commercial success, made him a household name in America. Richard Harris's first starring role, *This Sporting Life,* established him as an actor of the first rank with the help of a nomination; it was the kind of movie that would have received limited release had it not been for the Academy's recognition. *Alfie* performed

the same function for Michael Caine, and *Georgy Girl* for Lynn Redgrave —
both Caine and Redgrave became international stars after their nominations.

Equally important is the effect of the first nomination on filmmakers' status
and power in Hollywood. Most artists are eager to receive a nomination at
a young age because they know that it will bring them not only work but
more nominations. In some cases, only the first nod was actually deserved and
subsequent nominations were conferred because of increased visibility.

Of Marsha Mason's four nominations, only the first (*Cinderella Liberty*) and
possibly the fourth (*Only When I Laugh*) were justified. Mason received her
second (*The Goodbye Girl*) and third (*Chapter Two*) nominations for lukewarm
performances because, by that time, she had established herself as an Oscar-
caliber performer. Her new status meant that greater attention was paid to each
of her subsequent movies — at least in the short run.

Glenn Close's meteoric rise to stardom also owes a debt to her first nomination. Close earned a supporting nomination for her screen debut, *The World
According to Garp,* in which she played the plum role of Robin Williams's eccentric and liberated mother. In the following year, Close was the only actress
from *The Big Chill*'s gifted ensemble to be singled out by the Academy. In truth,
the success of *The Big Chill* was based on ensemble acting by Kevin Kline,
William Hurt, JoBeth Williams, and others. Yet only Close's performance was
nominated, indicating that it wasn't just the high-quality of her acting, but also
her newly gained status as an Oscar-caliber actress.

In 1984, Close earned her third consecutive nomination for *The Natural,* as
Robert Redford's naive girlfriend. Neither the role nor her acting were extraordinary, and had the same role been played by another actress it would probably
not have been recognized. Yet while watching *The Natural,* her fellow-actors
focused their attention on her acting because of her Academy status. Close became a perennial nominee in the 1980s, making an effective transition from
secondary to lead roles.

Ironically, it took a villainess role, that of the "Other Woman," in the suspenseful blockbuster *Fatal Attraction,* to put Close at the forefront of leading
ladies, for which she was rewarded with a fourth (and first Best Actress) nomination. "I wanted to break out of the kinds of roles I used to do, because I was
boring myself," Close said about her typecasting as an earth mother. Close's
new, more sexual look convinced producers of her versatile talent and wider
range. In 1988, she was cast by Stephen Frears in the sumptuous costume picture *Dangerous Liaisons,* playing another unsympathetic role, a manipulative
French aristocrat, for which she received her fifth nomination. The cumulative
effect of all this is that Close became a bankable star and one of Hollywood's
most respected actresses.

If Glenn Close was the greatest beneficiary of the nominations' effects in the
1980s, James Cromwell is the beneficiary of the immediate and positive effects
of a supporting nomination in the 1990s. The son of Hollywood veteran director
John Cromwell (who specialized in glossy melodramas like *The Razor's Edge*),
Cromwell was not young when he was nominated for playing the farmer in

Babe, a fantasy tale about a talking piglet who endeared the hearts of moviegoers and critics. As Kenneth Turan wrote in the *Los Angeles Times:* "In this age of hype, over-hype and still more hype, what is sweeter than a genuine sleeper, a captivating film that dares to arrive without advance notice? *Babe* is such an unanticipated treat." Even though he didn't nab an Oscar (the winner that year was Kevin Spacey for *The Usual Suspects*), Cromwell defied the Hollywood adage to beware of children and animals. In the next five years, Cromwell went on to become one of the busiest character actors around, appearing in a number of high-profile studio pictures.

· 5 ·

THE LUCK OF THE BRITISH

Apart from wheat and auto parts, America's biggest export is now the Oscar. — Billy Crystal, Oscarcast Host

The Oscar has always been regarded as much more than an American prize. Film artists from all over the world can compete for any of the Oscars. The only exception is the Best Picture category, which differentiates between films in English (Best Picture) and film in other languages (Best Foreign-Language).

As seen in chapter 3, most countries with established film industries bestow film awards, usually through their film academies. However, none of these awards is nearly as visible or prestigious as the Oscar, and none disregards nationality as fully as the Oscar. From the very beginning, the rules stated that "No national or Academy membership distinctions are to be considered." The awards were to be conferred with no regard to geographical or political boundaries. The Academy was proud that the first Best Actor, the German Emil Jannings, "was not even a citizen of our country," and that the first Best Actress, Janet Gaynor, "was not even a member of the Academy." As merit awards, the Oscars were based on the philosophy that true art knows no boundaries. Philosophy, however, is one thing, practice another. And to what extent the Oscars are truly global awards that easily cross national borders is still a very relevant question.

The Oscar's International Dimension

By and large, Americans have dominated the Oscar race. The majority (over 70 percent) of the Oscar nominees have been American, about 20 percent British, and about 10 percent of other nationalities. The proportion of foreign players in the lead categories is bigger than that in the supporting league. This is mostly because lead players are more visible and hence attract greater attention to the films in which they appear. Women who have won lead awards represent a larger number of countries than the men, who have mostly been British.

Do foreign players have better chances to get the nomination than the actual award? A clear case of favoritism, of preferential treatment based on nationality, would prevail if there were significant differences between the nominees and the winners. In actuality, there are no such differences. The same proportion of foreign winners and nominees exists in all four acting categories. Despite accusations of favoring American over foreign artists, nationality has had little impact on the chances of winning. About 30 percent of all winners and nominees have come from other countries, attesting to Oscar's internationalism, which extends its visibility beyond the borders of the United States. For instance, in only one-third of Oscar's seventy-four years have all four acting winners been American. In other years, at least one of the four was of foreign origin.

Despite annual fluctuations, roughly two out of every three foreign players have been British, indicating a clear British dominance of the Oscar contest. Is it the high quality of British films and British acting that accounts for their preeminence in the Oscar race? Or is it simply the fact that the films are English-speaking?

The British Are Coming, the British Are Coming

You really are incredibly generous to aliens.
— Robert Bolt, Oscar winner, *A Man for All Seasons*

The British representation in the Oscar race has ranged from 11 percent in the 1950s to an all-time high of 31 percent in the 1960s. The 1960s were the most hospitable decade to all foreign artists, not just the British: 40 percent of the acting nominees in that decade were from outside the U.S. British players also made a strong showing in the 1940s, commanding one-fifth of the acting nominations. In other decades, the British contingent is about 15 percent of all acting nominees. The poorest British presence was in the 1950s, the most conservative and "patriotic" decade in the Oscars' history.

The share of non-British foreign artists in the Oscar contest has been more or less stable, ranging from 6 to 10 percent of all acting nominees. There's one notable exception: In the early 1980s, only 2 percent of the acting nominees were drawn from foreign countries. Under the Reagan administration, the 1980s resembled the 1950s in several ways.

In the 1930s, the American movie market was accused by the British of being insular, of denying support to British fare. Alexander Korda's *The Private Life of Henry VIII* (1933) was the first British commercial hit in the United States since the advent of sound. The film's lead, Charles Laughton, who won Best Actor, became one of Hollywood's most celebrated — and busiest — actors after winning the award. Not many other British other films were nominated for major awards in that decade. Anthony Asquith's *Pygmalion* (1938) is the exception, bringing acting nominations to its stars, Leslie Howard and Wendy Hiller, and two writing awards for Best Writing Adaptation and Best Screenplay to playwright Bernard Shaw. It was one of the high "literary" moments in Oscar's history, though the famously acerbic writer greeted the award with a bemused irony: "It's an insult for them to offer me any honor, as if they had never heard of me before — and it's very likely they never have."

In 1939, the two lead acting awards went to British players for the first time, though Vivien Leigh (*Gone With the Wind*) was honored for an American movie, and Robert Donat (*Goodbye, Mr. Chips*) for a film that was financed by MGM but drew mostly on British cast and crew. Ironically, Vivien Leigh won two Best Actress Oscars (the second was for *A Streetcar Named Desire*) for portraying two of the most famous Southern belles in American literature. The casting of *Gone With the Wind* received such extensive coverage in the press that apparently some Southern women threatened to boycott the movie if Leigh did not measure up to their expectations of how Scarlett O'Hara should be portrayed.

This generosity to English performers was used by the Academy for public relations, promoting the notion of a matter-of-fact, nonsentimental voting that disregards political or national considerations. At the same time, it prompted speculation as to "whether England would have done the same for us," to which ultra-patriotic gossip columnist Louella Parsons answered unequivocally, "I doubt it."

In the early 1940s, two British movies were nominated for Best Picture, both dealing with the war. Michael Powell's *The Invaders* (1942), about the survival attempts of a group of Nazis, also earned Emeric Pressburger an Oscar for best original story. The second, *In Which We Serve* (also 1942), co-directed by David Lean and Noel Coward, won the latter a Special Award for his outstanding production. Coward also wrote the music and starred in the film. Prior to that, British movies had won only a few technical awards. In 1940, *The Thief of Bagdad,* also directed by Michael Powell, won Oscars for Cinematography, Color Art Direction, and Special Effects. Alexander Korda's *That Hamilton Woman,* a huge success in America, starring Laurence Olivier and Vivien Leigh, won the Oscar for Sound Recordings.

It wasn't until the late 1940s that British films began to make a real impact on the Academy and the American movie market. The Best Picture and Best Actor nominations for Laurence Olivier's screen version of *Henry V* (1946) annoyed the major Hollywood studios, which regarded the nominations as close to acts of treason. But *Henry V* was such a box-office hit — it ran in New York for forty-six consecutive weeks — that the Academy couldn't ignore it. Though losing in each of its four categories (the other two were Color Interior Decoration and Scoring), *Henry V* was cited with a Special Award to Olivier for "outstanding achievement as actor, producer, and director."

As if that were not enough, three other British pictures were nominated for important awards in 1946. David Lean's exquisitely tender tale of an uncon-summated adulterous affair, *Brief Encounter,* was nominated for Best Actress (Celia Johnson), Director, and Screenplay. Compton Bennett's *The Seventh Veil,* the film that made James Mason an international star, won Original Screenplay for Muriel and Sydney Box. Gabriel Pascal's *Caesar and Cleopatra,* the most expensive British movie to that time, based on Bernard Shaw's droll play about the social and moral "education" of the young Cleoptara (Vivien Leigh), was nominated for its lavish color interior design, but didn't win.

The resentment against the Academy's seemingly preferential treatment of British movies increased in the following year, when David Lean's version of Charles Dickens's *Great Expectations* was nominated for Best Picture, Director, and Screenplay, and most deservedly earned the Black-and-White Cinematography (by Guy Green) and Black-and-White Art Direction-Set Decoration (John Bryan and Wilfred Shingleton) Awards. Journalists who took the matter seriously wrote that the "United States helped the British win the war, but shouldn't help them win 'our Oscars.' "

The British, however, were disappointed as they believed that *Great Expectations* should have won the 1947 Best Picture; the winner was *Gentleman's Agreement.* "A certain amount of bias influences Hollywood's Oscar Awards," said J. Arthur Rank, the powerful British producer. But he also expressed hopes that the number of bookings for British films in the United States would double from six to twelve thousand a year, which was the number that American films received in Britain. Curiously, Rank reported that exhibitors complained about difficulties some American audiences experienced in understanding the speech of British players and that "efforts are being made to correct this."

A turning point in the Anglo-American relationship occurred in 1948 when, against all expectations, *Hamlet* was named Best Picture and Laurence Olivier won Best Actor. *Hamlet* also won Black and White Art Direction-Set Decoration and Black-and-White Costume Design. It was the first time that a British movie won the top award, an act which reinforced the moguls' earlier decision to withdraw their financial support from the ceremonies. In the same year, another British film, Michael Powell's *The Red Shoes,* a romantic drama set in the ballet world, was also nominated for Best Picture, and won Color Art Direction-Set Decoration and Scoring. With the assistance of the nominations and awards, and good notices, *The Red Shoes* became the top money-maker of the year, grossing $5 million.

The *Hamlet* "incident" was recalled in 1956, when Mike Todd's *Around the World in 80 Days* won Best Picture. Its British director, Michael Anderson, received a nomination but not the award; the winner was George Stevens for *Giant.* It was one of the few occasions in which the Academy split its votes for Best Picture and Best Director.

In the 1950s, few British movies were nominated for or won important awards. Carol Reed's masterpiece, *The Third Man* (1950), based on Graham Greene's mystery novel, was singled out for Robert Frasker's evocative black-and-white cinematography of postwar Vienna, and was also nominated for its direction and editing. Charles Crichton's *The Lavender Hill Mob* (1952), which made Oscar-nominated Alec Guinness a star in the United States, won Best Story and Screenplay for T. E. B. Clarke.

Most of the nominations for British films in this decade were in the writing categories, reaffirming the belief that British pictures are better scripted than their American counterparts. In 1953, two British screenplays competed in the same category, *The Cruel Sea,* based on Nicholas Monsarrat's best-seller, and the comedy *The Ladykillers,* featuring Alec Guinness as a sinister lodger plotting to kill his old landlady. Neither won.

David Lean became the first British filmmaker to ever win Best Director in 1957, for the epic World War II prison drama *The Bridge on the River*

Kwai, which was named Best Picture and also won Best Actor (Alec Guinness), Screenplay (Based on Material from Another Medium), Editing, Cinematography, and Score. Though financed and distributed by Columbia, *The Bridge on the River Kwai* used a mostly British cast and crew.

The British representation in the Oscar contest improved dramatically in the 1960s, undoubtedly the best decade for British movies. A considerable number of movies were nominated for Best Picture: Jack Clayton's *Room at the Top* (1959), John Schlesinger's *Darling* (1965), Lewis Gilbert's sex farce *Alfie* (1966), and Anthony Harvey's historical melodrama *The Lion in Winter* (1968), which co-starred the very American Katharine Hepburn and the very British Peter O'Toole.

Four British-made films won the top award in the 1960s: *Lawrence of Arabia* (1962), *Tom Jones* (1963), *A Man for All Seasons* (1966), and *Oliver!* (1968). The directors of these movies (David Lean, Tony Richardson, Fred Zinnemann, and Carol Reed, respectively) were also singled out by the Academy for their achievements.

A fifth British filmmaker, John Schlesinger, won the directing Oscar for *Midnight Cowboy* (1969), made with American stars Dustin Hoffman and Jon Voight. The victory of *Midnight Cowboy* was symptomatic of Hollywood's tendency to co-opt young British talent at the time. Schlesinger, who two years later would be nominated for *Sunday, Bloody Sunday,* was brought to America, following in the footsteps of other gifted Brits. His "co-optation" helped cause a brain drain from which the always frail British film industry would continue to suffer, at least for another decade, until 1981 and 1982, with the back-to-back Best Picture wins of *Chariots of Fire* and *Gandhi.*

In the 1970s, few British films were nominated for important awards, perhaps reflecting the depression of the British industry. Two movies, *A Clockwork Orange* (1971) and *Barry Lyndon* (1975), both financed with American money but made in England by expatriate director Stanley Kubrick, were nominated for Best Picture. Neither won the top award. *Barry Lyndon* was cited for Cinematography, Art Direction, Scoring-Original Song Score and/or Adaptation, and Costume Design; *Clockwork Orange* lost each of its four nominations. British-filmmaker Alan Parker's *Midnight Express* (1978), a thriller about Billy Hayes, an American student arrested in Turkey for carrying hashish, was also nominated for the Best Picture. The weak British presence in the Oscars was reflected in other film forums. In 1980, for the first time in thirty-three years, not even one British movie competed in the Cannes Film Festival.

But in the early 1980s, several movies about distinctly British subjects made their mark, both artistically and commercially. Based on the hit stage play, *The Elephant Man* (1980) was not really a British film. Though financed by Paramount, produced by Mel Brooks, and directed by David Lynch, the film had a distinctly British flavor. The tale of John Merrick — a grossly deformed man victimized and exploited by Victorian society — was cast with mostly British actors, headed by John Hurt in the title role (who won a nomination) and Anthony Hopkins, as his caring doctor. The Academy showed its appreciation with eight nominations, including Best Picture, though the film lost in every category. In the same year, Roman Polanski's romantic historical epic, *Tess,* beautifully mounted in England, was also nominated for six awards.

After *Oliver!* it took thirteen years for another British-made film, *Chariots of Fire* (1981), to win Best Picture. Directed by Hugh Hudson and based on the true story of two British runners in the 1924 Olympics, it was the upset winner, competing against such big-scale movies as Steven Spielberg's *Raiders of the Lost Ark* and Warren Beatty's *Reds.* Its success was attributed to its emotionally compelling narrative about the courage and passion of two characters (played by unknown actors), who triumphed against great odds.

Made in England on the modest budget of $6 million, *Chariots of Fire* was turned down by every major Hollywood studio. Despite the fact that the movie was considered "too British" and "too specialized," it became a commercial hit, after winning four Oscars. Many filmmakers resented the fact that American money (Fox partially financed it) was used to help a British product in a year in which *Reds,* an ambitious historical epic, failed at the box office, despite critical acclaim. The British had an even better reason to celebrate the following year, when Richard Attenborough's *Gandhi,* financed by Columbia, was nominated for eleven awards and swept most of them, including Best Picture, Director, and Actor. British movies continued to fare well throughout the decade. In 1983, Peter Yates's screen adaptation of *The Dresser* was nominated for five awards, including Best Picture.

In 1984, two British films were recognized with multiple nominations. Roland Joffe's *The Killing Fields,* which was based on Sydney Schanberg's 1980 *New York Times* magazine article, "The Death and Life of Dith Pran," recounted the political situation in Cambodia during its civil war. The film was nominated for seven awards and won three, including a citation for Chris Menges's exhilarating cinematography. David Lean's epic, *A Passage to India,* an adaptation of E. M. Forster's celebrated novel, was nominated for eleven awards, though won only two. The big winner that year was *Amadeus,* with eight awards.

Trevor Nunn's 1982 Tony Award acceptance speech (for his adaptation of Charles Dickens's *Nicholas Nickleby*), in which he exclaimed with bravado, "The British Are Coming, the British Are Coming," turned out to be true in 1986, when two Best Picture nominees were British. The production team of *The Killing Fields* returned to the Oscar arena with the high-minded but dull epic, *The Mission,* which received seven nominations and one award (for Menges's cinematography).

The other nominee, *A Room With a View,* producer Ismail Merchant and director James Ivory's adaptation of E. M. Forster's novel, won in three out of its eight nominated categories: Adapted Screenplay, Art Direction-Set Decoration, and Costume Design. John Boorman's charming autobiographical war saga, *Hope and Glory* (1987), which reconstructed his adolescence in war-torn London, was acclaimed by the critics and received five nominations, but no awards.

The Glory of British Acting

I am vastly intimidated by English actors. We American actors think we're just a bunch of slobs compared to them, and that they can quote all of Shakespeare by heart.

— Meryl Streep, twelve-time Oscar nominee

There's a feeling that being big in Britain is not quite enough, that you haven't really made it until you've made it in Hollywood.

— Peter Whittle, *Los Angeles Times*

The one category in which the British have always excelled, faring even better than their movies, is acting. British acting enjoys great prestige in the United States — it is a revered institution. Admired for their versatility and technical skills, British actors are deemed better trained than their American counterparts, as Meryl Streep's cited opinion demonstrates.

The prestige of English players is reflected in the number of nominations and awards they have won. Eighteen of the sixty-eight Best Actors (26 percent), sixteen of the sixty-two Best Actresses (also 26 percent), nine of the fifty-nine Supporting Actors (15 percent), and five of the sixty-four Supporting Actresses (8 percent) have been British. (Note: The number of winners in each category is different due to the fact that there have been multiple winners).

The first British player to win Best Actor was George Arliss, though he won for an American film, *Disraeli*. Charles Laughton was actually the first English player to win for a British film, *The Private Life of Henry VIII*. Other British or Irish-born winners include: Victor McLaglen, Robert Donat, Ray Milland, Ronald Colman, Laurence Olivier, Alec Guinness, David Niven, Rex Harrison, Paul Scofield, Peter Finch, and Ben Kingsley.

The British dominated the Best Actor category for three consecutive years: Daniel Day Lewis (*My Left Foot*) in 1989, Jeremy Irons (*Reversal of Fortune*) in 1990, and Anthony Hopkins (*The Silence of the Lambs*) in 1991, elevating the visibility of British players to an unparalleled level.

It's much easier for the British to win the Oscar if they appear in an American movie. Only Olivier (*Hamlet*), Day-Lewis, and a few others have won acting awards for British pictures. Most of the British-born Best Actresses, including Vivien Leigh, Greer Garson, Julie Andrews, Maggie Smith, Glenda Jackson, and Emma Thompson have won for American movies. The two exceptions are Julie Christie (*Darling,* the UK's Embassy Pictures production) and Glenda Jackson in her first Oscar-winning role (*Women in Love*). Her second Oscar was for an American picture (*A Touch of Class*).

Players from the United Kingdom who won supporting awards also appeared primarily in Hollywood pictures, such as Scottish-born Donald Crisp (*How Green Was My Valley*), Wales-raised Edmund Gwenn (*Miracle on 34th Street*), North Wales-born Hugh Griffith (*Ben-Hur*), Peter Ustinov (*Spartacus* and *Topkapi*), Londoner John Gielgud (*Arthur*), Michael Caine (*Hannah and Her Sisters* and *The Cider House Rules*), the very Scottish Sean Connery

(*The Untouchables*). The only supporting winners in British-made films, though some were financed with Hollywood money, were John Mills in David Lean's *Ryan's Daughter,* and most recently, Jim Broadbent in *Iris.*

Among the Supporting Actresses, too, Dame Peggy Ashcroft and Dublin-born Brenda Fricker were the only women to win for a British or Irish-made movie, *A Passage to India* and *My Left Foot,* respectively. The other English actresses won for American films: Wendy Hiller (*Separate Tables*), Margaret Rutherford (*The V.I.P.s*), Vanessa Redgrave (*Julia*), Maggie Smith (*California Suite*), and Dame Judi Dench (*Shakespeare in Love*).

The illustrious list of Oscar-nominated British players reads like the "Who's Who" register of honorary titles of Sirs and Dames. Sir Michael Redgrave, Sir Ralph Richardson, Sir John Gielgud, Sir Ian McKellen, Sir Anthony Hopkins, Sir Michael Caine, and, most recently, Sir Sean Connery, have all been nominated and several have won. Then there are Dame Edith Evans, Dame May Whitty, Dame Judith Anderson, Dame Gladys Cooper, Dame Flora Robson, Dame Peggy Ashcroft, and Dame Judi Dench. Both the Academy and the British actors benefit from playing the Oscar game. The Oscar has made these players into international movie stars, and the British players in turn have contributed to the prestige of the Academy as a reputable institution that recognizes talent.

The largest number of British players were nominated in the 1960s, a watershed decade for British films. They included Peter O'Toole, Michael Caine, Albert Finney, Ron Moody, Tom Courtenay, Alan Bates, Rachel Roberts, Deborah Kerr, Jean Simmons, and Janet Suzman.

The esteem of these players goes beyond the film world because of the different structure of the performing arts in Britain, where there's constant mutual fertilization among the theater, film, and television industries. (For the London press junket of *Harry Potter* and *Iris,* Judi Dench arrived for an hour of interviews, in between matinee and evening performances of her West End play *The Royal Family of Broadway.*) American players tend to specialize in one medium, often to the exclusion of the other two, but British players continue to commute successfully between theater and film, or film and television, to the appreciation of all three arts and their audiences.

Along with high-quality acting, there were other reasons for the favorable reception of British movies in the 1960s, which was not a particularly good decade for Hollywood. American films, still suffering from fierce competition with television, had not yet adjusted to their new status as the second cultural medium, having been for half a century the dominant form of entertainment.

The decline in American films was quantitative as well as qualitative. In 1963, the industry reached an all-time production low, with only 141 American movies released. Compare this poor figure with over 400 movies released in a typical year in the 1940s, and over 300 films in the 1950s. For years, American films ruled the market, but in the 1960s, their dominance was shattered. In 1960, of the 320 movies distributed in the United States, 208 were American and 112 were foreign, but in 1968, of the 380 new pictures, only 176 were American.

By contrast, in the 1960s, the British cinema witnessed a vibrant renaissance. Shortly after 1956, which saw the premiere of John Osborne's *Look Back in Anger,* a turning point in the history of British theater, a new generation of filmmakers that included Tony Richardson and Lindsay Anderson began to leave their mark on British culture. The flowering of British cinema in the 1960s, led by Anderson, Richardson, Schlesinger, Karel Reisz, and others, was a cross-fertilization of documentaries and works by playwrights and novelists such as Osborne and Shelah Delaney. As members of an innovative cultural movement known as The Free Cinema, they were the British equivalent of the French New Wave. Among their best works are Jack Clayton's *Room at the Top* (1959), Karel Reisz's *Saturday Night and Sunday Morning* (1960), Jack Cardiff's *Sons and Lovers* (1960), Tony Richardson's *The Loneliness of the Long Distance Runner* (1962), and Lindsay Anderson's *This Sporting Life* (1963). Each of these movies received major nominations for their directors and talented casts.

The prevailing mood of the new movies was bitter — they dealt with what critic David Denby called "declining-empire anguish." Chillingly bleak, they had a tartour and acerbic flavor, a humiliating familiarity with poverty and rage. The film critic Pauline Kael once noted that "Heaven seems to have sent English moviemakers the upper class so that they would have something to justify their malice." True, the 1960s saw the Harold Pinter-Joseph Losey exposes of decadence within the wealthy and educated classes in *The Servant* (1963) and *Accident* (1967), and screenwriter Frederic Raphael's acidulous lampoon of social climbing in *Nothing But the Best* (1964) and *Darling* (1965).

The popularity of British films and actors in the 1960s also indicated that the traditional provincialism and parochialism of American culture had subsided. This decade saw ideological changes that affected American culture and movies, specifically the repudiation of the 1950s' conservative and isolationist trends, represented by Senator Joseph McCarthy and the hearings of the House Un-American Activities Committee (HUAC).

Furthermore, the melting-pot ideology which had prevailed in American society for decades, ignoring racial and class differences, began to disintegrate. In the 1960s, the youth and ethnic segments of society became much more vocal in their demands for cultural representation. For the first time, youth not only required films specifically dealing with their issues and problems, but could also determine which movies would become box-office hits. Both younger and more sophisticated, these viewers greeted with enthusiasm the new European films, not just British, but also Italian, French, Swedish, and Japanese.

The number of foreign-made films, particularly British, among the top money-makers was the highest in the 1960s. In the 1940s and 1950s, only five of the hundred most commercial movies were foreign-made, but in the 1960s, their proportion increased dramatically to sixteen movies. The most successful British films, both Oscar nominated and top ranking money-grossers of their respective years were David Lean's *Lawrence of Arabia* (1962), Tony Richardson's *Tom Jones* (1963), Richard Lester's Beatles movie *A Hard Day's Night*

(1964), Lewis Gilbert's *Alfie* (1966), Silvio Narizzano's *Georgy Girl* (1966), Carol Reed's *Oliver!* (1968), and, of course, the James Bond movies starring Sean Connery.

The Oscar race reflected the popularity of British films. In 1963, four of the five supporting actresses were British: Diane Cilento, Dame Edith Evans, Joyce Redman (all for *Tom Jones*), and Dame Margaret Rutherford (*The V.I.P.'s*), who won. In 1964, all five Best Actor nominees were born outside the United States, four of whom were British: Richard Burton, Peter O'Toole (both for *Becket*), Peter Sellers (*Dr. Strangelove; or, How I Learned to Stop Worrying and Love the Bomb*), and Rex Harrison (*My Fair Lady*), who won. The fifth nominee was Mexican-born, American-educated Anthony Quinn, who gave the performance of a lifetime in *Zorba the Greek*.

Indeed, 1964 was probably the most "international" year in the Academy's history. In addition to Harrison, the other winners in the acting categories were all foreign-born: Britons Julie Andrews (*Mary Poppins*) and Peter Ustinov (*Topkapi*), and French-Russian Lila Kedrova (*Zorba the Greek*). "This will be an unusual night," emcee Bob Hope predicted at the beginning of the ceremonies, "Tonight Hollywood is handing out foreign aid." Indeed, Julie Andrews, overwhelmed by her win, said in her acceptance speech: "You Americans are famous for your hospitality, but this is ridiculous."

The *Hollywood Reporter* noted that the 1964 show was "a reminder that Hollywood has never been chauvinistic and that its great days are those when artists from throughout the world flocked here or were imported. The winners are reminders that the movies are the true international medium." This feeling was reaffirmed in 1965, when, once again, only one of the Best Actress nominees was American, Elizabeth Hartman, as the blind girl in *A Patch of Blue*. That year, three of the nominees were British: Julie Christie, who won for *Darling*, Julie Andrews for *The Sound of Music*, and Samantha Eggar for *The Collector;* the fifth was French actress Simone Signoret, for the American production *Ship of Fools*.

In 1983, when British actors again dominated the race, critics found it strange that four of the five Best Actors were English: Michael Caine (*Educating Rita*), Albert Finney and Tom Courtenay (both for *The Dresser*), and Tom Conti (*Reuben, Reuben,* an American film). The fifth nominee, American Robert Duvall (*Tender Mercies*), turned out to be the winner. *New York Times*'s Vincent Canby, who understood the root dynamics of the situation, observed that the Academy's customary respect for English players was no greater in 1983 than in previous years, and that "Hollywood today is no more or less Anglophile than it's ever been."

However, Canby explained, "If you are a good American actor and you want to make it big in contemporary American movies, you've got to be able to upstage special effects and futuristic hardware, with very little or no help from the screenwriters." Hence Roy Scheider was essentially upstaged by a marvelous space-age helicopter in *Blue Thunder*. And despite being a box-office star, Harrison Ford failed to get nominations for playing either Han Solo in *Star*

Wars or Indiana Jones in *Raiders of the Lost Ark.* In addition to competing with technology, American actors were stereotyped as hoodlums and/or psychopaths (Al Pacino in *Scarface,* Robert De Niro in *The King of Comedy*), roles that usually don't get Academy recognition. It was no accident that the British dominated the Best Actors, but not the Best Actress categories. As Canby noted, for the first time in years, the American cinema offered richer parts for women than for men.

The new British pictures of the 1980s explored feminism, racism, and multiculturalism in London. Stephen Frears's *My Beautiful Laundrette* (1985), which received a writing nomination, is a perfect example. Filmmakers such as Ken Loach (*Riff-Raff*), Mike Leigh (*High Hopes*) and others professed an anti-Thatcher message, spelling out their political position explicably and didactically. They enacted the British working class's revenge against years of Thatcherite callousness. For critic David Denby, the one emotion that always comes through and links the different styles of serious English cinema of the last generation is disgust — disgust at an empire maintained by force and then precipitously lost, disgust at mean industrial cities, disgust at the exploitation and destruction of the working class, disgust at social hypocrisy, even disgust at squalid sex.

But bleak British films, such as *Dance With a Stranger, Wetherby, Mona Lisa, Wish You Were Here, The Good Father,* or *Letter to Brezhnev,* don't win the Academy's attention; they're too small, too intimate — and too depressing. What wins is safer, broader fare, like the comedy *Four Weddings and a Funeral,* a movie celebrating the complacency of a circle of British Oxford yuppies, which was nominated for the 1994 Best Picture. Or *The Full Monty,* which was nominated for the top award in 1997. As critic John Powers noted, it is easier for Americans to digest the stereotypes of *Four Weddings* — stuttering vicars, idiot Yanks who think Oscar Wilde is still alive, clumsy aristocrats who step into every available cow pie — than face the harsh realities of the working class.

In some years, an entire category was dominated by British players. In 1992, three of the Supporting Actresses were British: Joan Plowright (*Enchanted April*), Miranda Richardson (*Damage*), and Vanessa Redgrave (*Howards End*); one was Australian, Judy Davis (*Husbands and Wives*); and one, the winner, was American, Marisa Tomei (*My Cousin Vinny*). Jack Palance, who presented the Supporting Actress Oscar, quipped: "This is the first time in the history of the Academy Awards that five foreign actresses are up for the same award: Four from England and one from Brooklyn."

Variety labeled 1992 as "the Year of the Visa," because, in addition to the nods to British and Irish artists, the Academy acknowledged French, Japanese and other foreign achievements. Foreign nominees won in ten different categories, the most international cross-section in decades. *Howards End,* which won three Oscars, embodied the international flavor of contemporary filmmaking. Based on a classic of English literature, it was technically a British production, except it was made by Indian producer Ismail Merchant, American director James Ivory, and German-born (to Polish-Jewish parents) writer Ruth Prawer Jhabvala, who received Best Adapted Screenplay.

The following year, 1993, again showed that the British film industry might be dead, but the United Kingdom certainly made its impact felt when acting nominations were concerned. Half of the male acting nominations went to the British. Daniel Day-Lewis was nominated for his portrayal of the wrongly accused Gerry Conlon in *In the Name of the Father,* and Pete Postlethwaite earned a supporting nod for playing his father. Welshman Anthony Hopkins played a repressed butler in the Oscar-nominated *The Remains of the Day,* which also earned a nomination for Emma Thompson. In the same year, Northern Ireland native Liam Neeson was nominated for the title role in *Schindler's List,* and Ralph Fiennes became a star after winning a supporting nomination for playing a Nazi commandant in the same film.

In a *Los Angeles Times* interview, producer Ismail Merchant attributed the British rule to strong theatrical training and solid technique. Merchant elaborated: "British actors have an extraordinary training and are very disciplined. They have a profound knowledge of the characters they are playing and exceptional acting ability." But for Oscar-winner Judi Dench, there's no difference between American and British acting. "Good acting is good acting," she told *Premiere,* "Sometimes people say it's the Method. The other day I heard Rod Steiger talking about the Method, and it didn't make any sense to me. He said that no longer do you come in, say, in mourning for *your* daughter. It's mourning for *your* daughter, not the character's. It's self-indulgent, and you can see self-indulgent acting all over the world. Good acting is not the things you say, it's the things you don't say. It's like in watercolor — it's what you leave out that's most important."

Who's right? Merchant or Dench? No matter. The trend continues. On the occasion of Mike Leigh's powerful family drama, *Secrets & Lies,* which was nominated for the 1996 Best Picture, the *Los Angeles Times* critic Kenneth Turan observed that "Britain's supposedly moribund film industry is turning into cinema's most celebrated invalid." Though economic difficulties have seriously curtailed its output, the British films that do get made are invariably models of strength and compassion. The ensemble riches of British acting help explain why a country with no financially viable film industry keeps turning out such good movies — and performances.

Four of the 1997 Best Actress nominees were British: Helena Bonham Carter for *The Wings of the Dove,* Julie Christie for *Afterglow,* Judi Dench for *Mrs. Brown,* and Kate Winslet for *Titanic.* The winner was the all-American nominee, Helen Hunt, for the comedy *As Good As It Gets.* Most critics attribute a lack of good women roles in American cinema to a brand of filmmaking typified by Hollywood studios that calls for big stars and high concepts heavy on special effects and fast-paced action. "A lot of our studio movies are boys' flicks and testosterone events," casting director Mali Finn told *USA Today,* "and the women get shoved into the background."

"The British are coming!" exclaimed British writer Colin Welland in 1981 after winning the Original Screenplay for *Chariots of Fire*, a statement that typified how the British measure the success of their own industry — in terms of how well they are doing "over there" in the United States. "Nothing denotes success so visibly and tangibly as the Oscars," wrote journalist Peter Whittle in the *Los Angeles Times*. "There's a feeling that being big in Britain is not quite enough, that you haven't really made it until you've made it in Hollywood."

But ambiguity prevails: "On the one hand, there is a superior disdain for the whole circus, and on the other a keenly patriotic desire to see Brits beating Americans at their own game." This ambiguity is not new. At their prime, Kenneth Branagh and Emma Thompson were chronic irritants to the British media, because they have achieved success at an early age — and in America — and because they showed every sign of relishing it. In 1989, when Branagh received two nominations, as Actor and Director for *Henry V,* his audacious directorial debut at the young age of twenty-nine, comparisons were made to the young Olivier, whose own version of *Henry V,* in 1946, also earned Best Picture and Best Actor nominations.

In 1999 Sam Mendes, the much-praised London theater director, won a directing Oscar for *American Beauty* and four countrymen were nominated for acting: Samantha Morton for *Sweet and Lowdown,* Janet McTeer for *Tumbleweeds,* Jude Law for *The Talented Mr. Ripley,* and Michael Caine, "that quintessence of a certain kind of Britishness," for *The Cider House Rules.* There was extensive coverage in the London media which hailed an outstanding lineup of British talent, on course for Oscar glory. When there is a big Oscar triumph featuring prominent British talent or British themes, as with *The English Patient, Shakespeare in Love,* or *American Beauty,* it may well seem that the British media often "forget" to mention that it was American money and American executives that got these movies made.

· 6 ·

WINNING THE OSCAR

I can only say I have been daydreaming about this since I was nine years old. — Joanne Woodward, Best Actress, *The Three Faces of Eve*

Winning the Award was like pretending to be an astronaut and finally making it to the moon.
　　　　— Kim Basinger, Best Supporting Actress, *L.A. Confidential*

Winning the Oscar Award is considered to be the ultimate achievement in the film world, the epitome of professional success. Filmmakers strive to win the Oscar at an early phase of their work since they clearly know that the award will have a vast impact on their future careers.

The Winners' Age

In theory, it is possible to win the Oscar at any age, and, indeed, there have been winners in every age group, young and old. In practice, however, the best chances to win the Oscar are between the ages of thirty and forty-nine; two-thirds of all winners are in those age bracket.

As with first nomination, actresses are much younger than actors when they receive their first Oscar. About 40 percent of the women, compared with 5 percent of the men, won an Oscar before the age of thirty. And two-thirds of the women, but only one-third of the men, win the Oscar by the time they reach forty. The gap in winning age is significant in the lead categories, over half of the Best Actresses, but only a small fraction of the Best Actors are younger than thirty-five at their first win.

Within each category, there's a concentration of winners in one or two age groups. Among the Best Actresses, the largest group of winners is in their late twenties and early thirties. By contrast, the dominant group among the Best Actors is winners in their early forties. There's no dominant norm in the two supporting categories, in which the age range of winners is wide, from early teens to late seventies.

The likelihood of winning at a particular age is determined by the kinds of screen roles available to men and women and to leading versus supporting players. Cultural norms have prescribed these roles, and these prescriptions are more rigid and confining for women and lead players. Compared with the lead roles, there are no specific requirements that character roles be played by young or attractive players, hence the greater age variability of supporting winners.

The impact of gender on the winning age is paramount: The average age at first win (lead and supporting combined) is thirty-four for the actresses and forty-four for actors. More specifically, the average winning age is thirty-one for the Best Actresses, thirty-eight for the Supporting Actresses, forty-one for the Best Actors, and forty-six for the Supporting Actors.

Is the Oscar a young artists' game? The answer is no, but it is a qualified no. Only one-fifth of all winners have received the award before thirty. Young women have an Oscar edge over young men. Fifteen percent of the Best Actresses, but no Best Actors, are in their early or mid-twenties. Middle-age seems to be the norm for the male winners: Most Best Actors are between thirty-five and fifty when they first win the Oscar.

Among directors, the youngest winners are: William Friedkin at thirty-two for *The French Connection;* Norman Taurog, also thirty-two, for *Skippy;* and Lewis Milestone, thirty-three, for *Two Arabian Nights.* Like the actors, most directors are in their late thirties and early forties when they first win the Oscar Award.

Some actors were particularly lucky to win the Oscar at a young age. The youngest winners in each category are:

Tatum O'Neal	10	Supp. Actress	*Paper Moon*
Timothy Hutton	19	Supp. Actor	*Ordinary People*
Marlee Matlin	21	Best Actress	*Children of a Lesser God*
Richard Dreyfuss	29	Best Actor	*The Goodbye Girl*

Several players had to wait until old age before winning. The oldest winners in each category are:

Jessica Tandy	81	Best Actress	*Driving Miss Daisy*
Henry Fonda	77	Best Actor	*On Golden Pond*
Peggy Ashcroft	77	Supp. Actress	*A Passage to India*
George Burns	79	Supp. Actor	*The Sunshine Boys*

Jessica Tandy and Marie Dressler (who was sixty-two when she won) are the exceptions. Few women in the Oscars' history have received their award after the age of sixty. However, older actresses have been more prominent over the last generation: Ellen Burstyn (*Alice Doesn't Live Here Anymore*) was forty-three, Shirley MacLaine (*Terms of Endearment*) fifty, and Geraldine Page (*The Trip to Bountiful*) sixty-one.

By contrast, elderly supporting winners have prevailed in each decade: Helen Hayes (*Airport*), John Houseman (*The Paper Chase*), Don Ameche (*Cocoon*), Jack Palance (*City Slickers*), and James Coburn (*Affliction*) were all over seventy when they won the Oscar.

Ruth Gordon's winning age, seventy-two, suggests the broader career opportunities available to supporting players when they reach older age. Though a late bloomer in film, Gordon was an accomplished stage actress. After a few appearances in silent movies and one substantial role, as Mary Todd Lincoln in *Abe Lincoln in Illinois* (1940), Gordon dedicated herself almost exclusively to the theater. In 1965, however, Gordon made an impressive comeback, as Natalie Wood's demented mother in *Inside Daisy Clover,* for which she earned her first supporting nomination. Three years later, Gordon won the supporting Oscar for her delicious portrait of a modern Manhattan witch in *Rosemary's Baby.* "Well, I can't tell you how encouraging a thing like that is!" enthused Gordon. "The first money I ever earned was as an extra in 1915, and here it is 1969."

Gordon's husband-writer Garson Kanin, with whom she collaborated on many Oscar-nominated screenplays (*Adam's Rib, Pat and Mike*), responded similarly: "Suddenly, Hollywood discovered Ruth. It's only taken them fifty years." Among the many congratulatory cables Gordon received was one from Mary Pickford, her old colleague and friend, which simply said: "Dear Ruth, why did you take so long?"

Gordon saw in her Oscar not only a tribute to past attainments, but also a prelude to a new career. And it was. For the next fifteen years, up to her death at the age of eighty-eight, Gordon worked nonstop, delivering some of her most vivid performances, including a memorable turn in the cult film *Harold and Maude,* and in Clint Eastwood's *Any Which Way You Can.*

The Oscar as an Instant Reward

How long does it take to win the Oscar Award once actors make their debut? Women tend to receive faster recognition for their talent than men. About 20 percent of the actresses, but only 5 percent of the actors, have won the Oscar during the first year of their careers. And over half of the actresses, compared with one-third of the actors, receive the Oscar within a decade after their first film.

As with the nomination, the Oscar functions as an instant reward for the women but not for the men. Actresses experience a shorter period of time between their debut and their win. The average number of years between the first film and the first Oscar is seven for the women and fourteen for the men. Quite consistently, of the four groups, the Best Actresses receive the quickest Academy recognition. The average number of years between the first film and the first win is six for the Best Actresses, eight for the Supporting Actresses, twelve for the Best Actors, and fifteen for the Supporting Actors.

Six women have received the Best Actress Oscar for their debuts or during the first year of their film careers: Katharine Hepburn (*Morning Glory*), Shirley Booth (*Come Back, Little Sheba*), Julie Andrews (*Mary Poppins*), Barbra Streisand (*Funny Girl*), Louise Fletcher (*One Flew Over the Cuckoo's Nest*), and Marlee Matlin (*Children of a Lesser God*). By contrast, only two Best Actors, Ben Kingsley (*Gandhi*) and Geoffrey Rush (*Shine*), have received the Oscar for their first major film.

Supporting players display one of two extremes, winning either very early or very late. On the one hand, twice as many supporting as lead players win the

Oscar during the first year of their careers, and, on the other, more supporting players had to wait a long time before winning.

The Academy is also more likely to bestow the Oscar for a debut or during the first year of a career on female supporting players. Of the winners in this group, more than half are women, including Gale Sondergaard (*Anthony Adverse*), Mercedes McCambridge (*All the King's Men*), Eva Marie Saint (*On the Waterfront*), Jo Van Fleet (*East of Eden*), Goldie Hawn (*Cactus Flower*), Meryl Streep (*Kramer vs. Kramer*), and Anna Paquin (*The Piano*).

Instant Oscar recognition is often achieved by players who repeated on-screen successful stage roles. When Lillian Hellman's 1941 stage hit, *Watch on the Rhine,* an antifascist play, was made into a movie two years later, two of its cast members, Paul Lukas, as the freedom fighter, and Lucille Watson, as the benevolent matriarch, were recast by director Herman Shumlin. Lukas won Best Actor for his stage to screen role, and Watson received a supporting nomination.

Three of the four principals in Tennessee Williams's prize-winning play, *A Streetcar Named Desire,* Marlon Brando, Karl Malden, and Kim Hunter, were cast in the 1951 film version. This was determined by filmmaker Elia Kazan, who had staged the Broadway production with great mastery before directing the film. Jessica Tandy, who had originated the role of Blanche DuBois, was not cast in the movie because the studio wanted a major star. Instead, they chose Vivien Leigh, the *Gone With the Wind* Oscar winner who had played the part in London under the direction of her husband-actor Laurence Olivier. At Oscar time, Vivien Leigh, Karl Malden, and Kim Hunter all won Oscars, and Brando earned his first nomination (the Best Actor that year was Humphrey Bogart for *The African Queen*).

Other stage players who have received nominations or awards for the screen versions of their work include: Nancy Kelly and Patty McCormack in *The Bad Seed,* Paul Newman and Burl Ives in *Cat on a Hot Tin Roof,* Rosalind Russell and Peggy Cass in *Auntie Mame,* Anne Bancroft and Patty Duke in *The Miracle Worker,* James Earl Jones and Jane Alexander in *The Great White Hope,* and Richard Burton and Peter Firth in *Equus.*

Four Best Actresses have won the Oscar for an acclaimed stage role with which they were intimately connected: Judy Holliday (*Born Yesterday*), Shirley Booth (*Come Back, Little Sheba*), Anne Bancroft (*The Miracle Worker*), and Barbra Streisand (*Funny Girl*). Streisand established herself as a major Broadway star in *Funny Girl,* winning a Tony Award nomination, and went on to become a movie star after the play was made into a movie. Director Herbert Ross (who later directed her in the sequel, *Funny Lady*) held that Streisand was extremely lucky to make her film debut in *Funny Girl:* "Having had the advantages of playing Fanny Brice for two years on Broadway, Streisand knew her role inside out. It was the perfect part for Streisand, ideally suited to her range as an actress and singer."

The proportion of women nominated for re-creating their stage roles on-screen is considerable, amounting to 10 percent of all Best Actresses. Despite the fact that they appeared in other pictures, some of these women are still identified with these memorable roles. This group of women includes Lynn Fontanne in *The Guardsman,* Katharine Hepburn in *The Philadelphia Story,* Julie Harris in *The Member of the Wedding,* Maggie McNamara in *The Moon Is Blue,* and Geraldine Page in *Sweet Bird of Youth.* Stockard Channing, still best known for her New York theater career and recently a regular on the TV series "The West Wing," was nominated for an Oscar for *Six Degrees of Separation,* the same role that had earned her a Tony nomination.

Of the Best Actors, no fewer than seven have received the Oscar for re-creating a famous stage role, beginning with George Arliss, who played the British statesman in *Disraeli* on stage, then in both the silent and sound film versions. Yul Brynner made the part of the King of Siam in Rodgers and Hammerstein's musical *The King and I* so much his own, that it was unthinkable for anyone else to play it when the film was made. For his royal turn Brynner won a supporting Tony Award, an Oscar Award, and a lifetime lease on this role, which he revived on Broadway and on the road for years. Brynner also starred as the Siamese monarch in the short-lived CBS series *Anna and the King* in 1972. This role offered Brynner his very last stage appearance in New York, just weeks before his death in 1985.

Rex Harrison scored such a huge triumph in Lerner and Lowe's *My Fair Lady,* on both sides of the Atlantic, that when the Bernard Shaw-based musical was made into a movie, he was the natural choice. Like Brynner, Harrison became intimately identified with the role of Henry Higgins, arguably his very best in a long and distinguished career that was marked by many Shaw plays.

The Academy could not deny the Oscar to other actors who excelled in transferring a stage role to the big screen, such as Jose Ferrer in *Cyrano de Bergerac* and Paul Scofield in *A Man for All Seasons.* A large number of Best Actor nominees received recognition for playing the same popular role on stage and on-screen: Walter Huston in *Dodsworth,* Raymond Massey in *Abe Lincoln in Illinois,* Anthony Franciosa in *A Hatful of Rain,* Ron Moody in *Oliver!,* Topol in the musical *Fiddler on the Roof,* James Whitmore in his one-man show, *Give 'Em Hell, Harry,* Tom Courtenay in *The Dresser,* Kenneth Branagh in *Henry V,* Nigel Hawthorne in *The Madness of King George.*

Getting instant recognition is often a result of luck or circumstances over which actors have little control. The "hand of fate" is an often-used term in showbiz, because it describes quite accurately how screen careers are created and sustained — from getting the first break, to being cast in an attention-grabbing feature, to being nominated and even winning the Oscar. Fluke, or as actors say, "being the right person at the right time in the right place," often is a more crucial factor in determining the shape of screen careers than acting talent or skill. During the heyday of the studio system, for example, many players gave their Oscar-winning performances not at their home studios but when they were loaned out, often as punishment. Producer Samuel Goldwyn let Warner borrow Gary Cooper for the title role of *Sergeant York* (Cooper's first Oscar) in exchange for Warner's difficult and rebellious contract player,

Bette Davis. At William Wyler's suggestion, Goldwyn cast Davis in *The Little Foxes,* which became one of her best-known roles, and earned her accolades and a Best Actress nomination.

Clark Gable and Claudette Colbert scored a great victory in Columbia's *It Happened One Night* despite the fact that both were at first reluctant to appear in the Frank Capra-directed comedy. Colbert, in fact, was about to sail for Europe, and Gable was loaned out to Columbia by Louis B. Mayer as a "disciplinary" act, having rejected several scripts that the studio had created for him. MGM considered *It Happened One Night* a minor project at a minor studio, which Columbia was at the time. Film history, however, proved otherwise; *It Happened One Night* won Best Picture, Director, and acting awards as well as elevating Columbia's status in Hollywood. The movie's unanticipated critical and commercial success showed again how serendipitous the industry is. The history of the Oscars is replete with cases of unpredictability; artists often are the worst judges of their own work and audiences' response can never be accurately predicted.

Warner Baxter was assigned, by default, the role of the Cisco Kid in the Western *In Old Arizona,* which garnered him an Oscar. The intended actor for the part was Raoul Walsh (better known as a director), who had an automobile accident in which he lost an eye.

Mercedes McCambridge believed that she might have never "stumbled onto an Oscar," for *All the King's Men,* "if it hadn't been for a pushy friend of mine who took me to a 'cattle call' in New York." Her part, as a corrupt politician's assistant and mistress, launched a vital screen career after McCambridge won a Supporting Oscar for it.

Numerous players have won their Oscars for parts in which they had not been the first or even second choice. Katharine Hepburn, who had the final say over her leading men at MGM, offered Cary Grant the choice between the two male leads in *The Philadelphia Story.* As Tracy Lord's ex-husband, or the canny journalist. Grant chose the former and Jimmy Stewart, cast as the reporter, went home with the Oscar. (Originally, with Hepburn's blessing, *The Philadelphia Story* was going to star Spencer Tracy and Clark Gable.) In hindsight, Grant committed another error, when he turned down the part of Judy Garland's down-and-out husband-actor in *A Star Is Born.* Director George Cukor begged Grant to do it, but rumors have it that Grant felt the role was too similar to his offscreen life at the time. The part was later played with great distinction by James Mason, who received a Best Actor nomination for it.

One can't guarantee, of course, that if the original actors played the roles intended for them, they would have been singled out by the Academy, but chances are they would at least have been nominated. In the absence of her husband, MGM's head of production Irving Thalberg (who died in 1936), Norma Shearer made major errors of judgment. Among others, Shearer turned down the title role in *Mrs. Miniver,* which then went to Greer Garson, bringing her an Oscar and her best-remembered role. Though she was in her early forties, Shearer was apprehensive about playing a woman who is old enough to have a teenage daughter. And it is true that Joan Crawford is best known for her eponymous heroine in *Mildred Pierce,* but few people know that role was first offered to Bette Davis, who turned it down. Davis herself delivered what is undoubtedly the finest performance of her career, Margo Channing in *All About Eve,* by accident. Claudette Colbert was initially cast in the role of the aging actress, but a back injury prevented her from doing it. Producer Darryl Zanuck then opted to replace Colbert with Ingrid Bergman, who was then in Italy, working and living with Roberto Rossellini. Davis was Zanuck's last-minute choice. In retrospect, it's hard to imagine any other actress in the role.

Director Anatole Litvak chose Ingrid Bergman to play the mentally disturbed woman in the intense drama *The Snake Pit,* but she declined, based on her feeling that "it all takes place in an insane asylum and I couldn't bear that." Instead, the role went to Olivia de Havilland, who scored a great victory, winning an Oscar nomination and a citation from the New York Film Critics. After the film's success, Litvak confronted Bergman, "look what you turned down!" "It was a very good part," Bergman replied, "but if I had played it, I wouldn't have got an Oscar for it." Bergman also turned down the part of the Swedish maid in *The Farmer's Daughter* because as she noted, "for me to play my own part as a Swedish girl was not what I wanted." Instead, Loretta Young was cast in this political comedy and received an Oscar for her very first nomination, after in twenty-two years in the business. Known for her strong instincts, the stubborn Bergman later said she had never regretted refusing either of those roles.

Marlon Brando's stunning performance in *On the Waterfront,* as the none-too-bright ex-prizefighter Terry Malloy, was first offered to Frank Sinatra, on the strength of his 1953 Supporting Oscar for *From Here To Eternity.* However, when director Kazan learned that Brando was available, he broke his promise to Sinatra and cast Brando. In 1962, Brando himself turned down the title role in David Lean's epic, *Lawrence of Arabia,* which went to a then-unknown British actor, Peter O'Toole. Though physically wrong for the role (and forced to undergo plastic surgery before shooting began), O'Toole became an international star overnight, receiving for this part the first of his seven Best Actor nominations.

Rod Steiger scored critical acclaim in Paddy Chayefsky's soggy television drama *Marty,* but when the play was transferred to the big screen, he refused to do it again. Instead, a relatively obscure thespian, Ernest Borgnine, until then cast in villainous roles (*From Here to Eternity*), was chosen. *Marty,* which won Best Picture, Best Actor, and other awards, broadened Borgnine's range and placed him on a higher-prestige list of actors.

Sophia Loren's part in *Two Women* was first intended for Anna Magnani under George Cukor's direction. The idea was to cast Magnani in the mother's role and Loren as her daughter. Magnani, however, rejected this proposition because Loren was "much taller than me," claiming that she could not perform with a daughter "I have to look up to." Loren was excited about the prospects of performing with Magnani, who at the time was the doyenne of Italian actresses. She tried to persuade Magnani, but to no avail. As it turned out, this part, which Loren ultimately played, was singlehandedly responsible for changing her image from a sex symbol to a dramatic actress of the first rank.

The hand of fate also accounted for Peter Finch's most accomplished screen roles. Ian Bannen was originally cast as the homosexual Jewish doctor in *Sunday, Bloody Sunday,* but after a month of shooting, he became sick and had to be replaced. Finch's first reaction when the role was offered to him was, "But I'm not queer." On a second thought, however, Finch was persuaded that "it was a fabulous script and a fabulous part." Director John Schlesinger later said that he "can't think of anyone who could have done it better," and that Finch's performance was "definitive." For his role as a gay-Jewish doctor, competing with Glenda Jackson for the love of a bisexual man, Finch won international recognition, his first Best Actor nomination.

Nor was Finch the top choice to play the demented television commentator in Sidney Lumet's satire *Network.* The role had been previously offered to — and rejected by — George C. Scott, Glenn Ford, and Henry Fonda. It was apparently screenwriter Paddy Chayefsky's idea to approach Finch for the juicy part. According to Finch's biographer, the arrival of *Network's* script in Jamaica, where Finch was vacationing, "absolutely galvanized him, his major concern being that someone else would take it before he could stake his claim." As soon as Finch finished reading the screenplay, he was frantic to let the producers know he was more than interested.

Finch knew that *Network* was a plum role — "Oscar material."

However, it is not always easy for actors to assess the quality of screen roles before or even after shooting begins. *Coming Home,* one of Hollywood's first anti-Vietnam War movies, was in various phases of pre-production for at least six years, until Jane Fonda's company, IPC, brought it to the screen. The film, which earned Fonda and Jon Voight acting laurels, is now considered to be a perfect piece of casting. But Voight's role, as the paraplegic war veteran, was first offered to Jack Nicholson (on the heels of his triumph in *One Flew Over the Cuckoo's Nest*) then to Sylvester Stallone (fresh from *Rocky*). United Artists wanted a more bankable star, but producer Jerome Hellman and director Hal Ashby managed to persuade the studio that Voight was the right actor for the part.

In 1997, industryites wondered why Holly Hunter turned down the lead role in the comedy *As Good As It Gets,* which, after all, was directed by the man who "discovered" her, James Brooks. Brooks's *Broadcast News* offered Hunter her first meaty screen role — and her first Best Actress nomination. As a result of Hunter's rejection, Helen Hunt, until then best known for her television series "Mad About You" and a few indie movies, became the eternally grateful beneficiary. Hunt won the Best Actress in her very first nomination, which catapulted her to the front rank of Hollywood leading ladies.

Nomination and Winning

Claiming that the number of nominations doesn't affect the candidates' chances to win the Oscar, the Academy points to the fact that two-thirds of all players have earned the Oscar in their first nomination. But those charging that previous nominations do count, use their evidence, namely, that 22 percent of the winners have been nominated twice, and 12 percent three or more times prior to winning. It's a matter of interpretation, depending on how statistics are read or misread.

It is easier for supporting players to win the Oscar at the first nomination: 80 percent compared with 50 percent of the lead winners. The competition for supporting awards is usually less intense. Besides, the Academy is more discriminating in evaluating lead performances; after all, the lead Oscars are more prestigious and influential.

But once again, of the four groups, the Best Actors are the least likely to get the Oscar the first time around. Twice as many Best Actresses as Best Actors have won the Oscar at their first nomination. The men's disadvantageous position derives from the fact that, until the late 1970s, American films provided better roles for men, thus making the competition within their category much fiercer.

In the Oscar's first decade, all the Best Actresses won at their first nomination. Joan Fontaine was the first actress to win the Oscar at her second nomination, for *Rebecca* in 1941. Until the 1970s, at least half of the Best Actresses won the Oscar for their first nominated roles. In the last two decades, however, Faye Dunaway (*Network*) won at her third nomination, Shirley MacLaine (*Terms of Endearment*) at her fifth, and Geraldine Page (*The Trip to Bountiful*) broke records by winning the Oscar at her eighth nomination.

By contrast, except for the first and last decades, it's been almost a rarity for men to win at their first, or even second, nomination. In the 1970s, only two winners, Art Carney (*Harry and Tonto*) and Richard Dreyfuss (*The Goodbye Girl*), received the award for their first nomination. The other actors were nominated three or four times before winning. However, since the 1980s, the trend has reversed itself, with many actors winning at their first nomination: Ben Kingsley (*Gandhi*), F. Murray Abraham (*Amadeus*), William Hurt (*Kiss of the Spider Woman*), Michael Douglas (*Wall Street*), Jeremy Irons (*Reversal of Fortune*), Nicolas Cage (*Leaving Las Vegas*), Geoffrey Rush (*Shine*), and Roberto Benigni (*Life Is Beautiful*). Kevin Spacey won the 1999 Best Actor (*American Beauty*) at his first nomination in this category, but by then he had already won a Supporting Actor for *The Usual Suspects* in 1995.

Players who had to wait a while before winning the Oscar:

Fourth nomination:	Lawrence Olivier, Marlon Brando, Elizabeth Taylor, Dustin Hoffman, Maureen Stapleton, Robert Duvall, Michael Caine, Robin Williams
Fifth nomination:	Susan Hayward, Gregory Peck, Jack Nicholson, Shirley MacLaine

Seventh nomination: Paul Newman

Eighth Nomination: Geraldine Page, Al Pacino

If chances to win increase with the number of nominations, the following actors are likely candidates for the award in the near future: Peter O'Toole (seven nominations), Albert Finney and Glenn Close (five each), Jane Alexander, Marsha Mason, Warren Beatty, and Jeff Bridges (four each), Morgan Freeman, Sigourney Weaver, Michelle Pfeiffer, and Tom Cruise (three each). The late Richard Burton was nominated seven times, six in the lead and once in the supporting category, but never won.

The careers of Oscar Directors resemble those of the women: About half won the Oscar at their first nomination, and one-fourth at their second. Only a handful of helmers had to wait for at least three nominations before winning.

Third nomination: Michael Curtiz, Fred Zinnemann, Carol Reed, Sydney Pollack

Fourth nomination: David Lean, Steven Spielberg

Fifth nomination: William Wyler, George Cukor

The greatest losers among the directors are Clarence Brown (six nominations, including two in the same year, 1929–30, for *Anna Christie* and *Romance*), King Vidor, Hitchcock, and Robert Altman (each with five nominations), Sidney Lumet, Federico Fellini and Stanley Kubrick (each with four), and Ernst Lubitsch, William A. Wellman, Sam Wood, Richard Brooks, Stanley Kramer, Ingmar Bergman, Martin Scorsese, Peter Weir, James Ivory, David Lynch, and Ridley Scott (each with three). Of these, judging by the status of their current work and careers, Altman, Scorsese, Weir, Ivory, Lynch, and Scott are likely to win an Oscar in the near future.

Ties and Multiple Oscars

Oscar ties have been a rare occurrence. Neither the Academy nor the filmmakers like the idea of sharing the coveted award. There has never been a tie in the Best Picture category, and only two in the acting awards. The first tie was declared in 1932, when Wallace Beery (*The Champ*) and Fredric March (*Dr. Jekyll and Mr. Hyde*) split the Best Actor award. Beery came within one vote of March, and in those years, such a narrow margin qualified for a tie.

Beery achieved acclaim in MGM's box-office hit *The Champ,* as a broken-down boxer rejuvenated by his adoring young son. Beery's co-star was box-office champion Jackie Cooper, 11, who had endeared himself with audiences the year before in *Skippy*. After winning the Oscar, Beery too became one of MGM's top-drawing stars.

Director Rouben Mamoulian chose Fredric March for the lead in *Dr. Jekyll and Mr. Hyde* based on his reputation; March had already been nominated for his parody of John Barrymore in *The Royal Family of Broadway*. The critics praised March's dual role, even though he was more convincing as Dr. Jekyll; his Hyde was not very scary by standards of Boris Karloff's Frankenstein or Bela Lugosi's Dracula. In fact, some critics believed that March won the Oscar because of his makeup, which took Wally Westmore three hours a day to apply. Acknowledging the importance of makeup in his acceptance speech, March said: "I must thank Wally, who made my task an easy one and is responsible for the greater measure of my success."

During the ceremony, one of the vote-checkers discovered that Beery was only one vote shy of March as Best Actor. Under Academy rules at the time, this qualified as a tie. Fortunately, both March and Beery were present at the ceremonies. Paramount's head, B. P. Schulberg, sent a messenger to find another statuette before calling Academy president Nagel. Nagel then called Beery to the stage and announced what became the first and only Best Actor tie. A cynical *Los Angeles Times* reporter observed the next day: "This time lapse made the second award seem more like a consolation prize." Since the two thespians were separated by a single vote, the Beery-March tie was held in suspicion for years.

The second tie occurred in the 1968 Best Actress award, which was shared by Katharine Hepburn (*The Lion in Winter*) and Barbra Streisand (*Funny Girl*). This time, however, the Academy insisted that the two actresses received exactly the same number of votes.

In other groups, too, ties have been rare. In its sixty-seven years of existence, the New York Film Critics Circle has declared a tie only a few times. In 1960, two films were cited as Best Picture, *The Apartment* and *Sons and Lovers;* both films were nominated for Oscars, but the winner was *The Apartment.* In 1966, Elizabeth Taylor (*Who's Afraid of Virginia Woolf?*) and Lynn Redgrave (*Georgy Girl*) were singled out as Best Actresses; the Oscar winner was Taylor.

The Los Angeles Film Critics Association has generally refrained from splitting its awards, though in 1976, Sidney Lumet's *Network* and John Avildsen's *Rocky* were both named Best Picture; the Oscar winner was *Rocky.* In 1984, the Los Angeles group honored two male performances: Albert Finney in *Under the Volcano* and F. Murray Abraham in *Amadeus;* the Oscar winner was Abraham. The latest acting tie occurred in 1998, when Ally Sheedy (*High Art*) and veteran Brazilian actress Fernanda Montenegro (*Central Station*) were both cited. Against all odds, Montenegro received a Best Actress nomination, but Sheedy wasn't nominated; the Oscar that year went to Gwyneth Paltrow (*Shakespeare in Love*).

Winning a Second Oscar

For most actors, winning the Oscar is a once-in-a-lifetime achievement. Yet considering the intensity of competition, the percentage of players who have received multiple awards is quite impressive: About 20 percent of all winners. As expected, the leads have better chances than the supporting players to win a second Oscar. Quite consistently, the Best Actresses enjoy the best prospects: 30 percent, compared with 13 percent of the Best Actors.

The following players won two Oscars within the same category:

Best Actor: Fredric March, Spencer Tracy, Gary Cooper, Marlon Brando, Jack Nicholson, Tom Hanks

Best Actress: Bette Davis, Luise Rainer, Vivien Leigh, Ingrid Bergman, Olivia de Havilland, Elizabeth Taylor, Glenda Jackson, Jane Fonda, Sally Field, Jodie Foster

Supporting Actor: Anthony Quinn, Peter Ustinov, Melvyn Douglas, Jason Robards, Michael Caine

Supporting Actress: Shelley Winters, Diane Wiest

Two players stand out in their Oscar achievements. Katharine Hepburn, Hollywood's most respected screen actress, ties the record of the most nominations with Meryl Streep (each twelve), and holds the record for winning the largest number of Oscars (four). Hepburn's Oscars have been won over a period of half a century, from *Morning Glory* in 1932, to *Guess Who's Coming to Dinner* in 1967, to *The Lion in Winter* in 1968, to *On Golden Pond* in 1981.

One of the American screen's most versatile and prolific character actors, Walter Brennan holds another kind of a record, having won three Supporting Oscars within the shortest period of time (five years): *Come and Get It* in 1936, *Kentucky* in 1938, and *The Westerner* in 1940. Brennan, who played older men even when he was younger, won another nomination in 1941, for *Sergeant York,* and continued to turn in reliable work in many other films, including the cult Western *Rio Bravo.*

Ten players have won Oscars in both the leading and supporting categories: Five actors (Jack Lemmon, Robert De Niro, Jack Nicholson, Gene Hackman, and Kevin Spacey) and five actresses (Helen Hayes, Ingrid Bergman, Maggie Smith, Meryl Streep, and Jessica Lange).

With the exception of Nicholson and Hackman, the men first won a supporting, then a lead Oscar. The first two-time male winner was Jack Lemmon, who was cited for a featured role in *Mister Roberts* in 1955, then twenty-eight years later won Best Actor for the lead in *Save the Tiger.*

Three of the women first won Best Actress, then Supporting Actress. Helen Hayes was the first multiple winner, receiving Best Actress for *The Sin of Madelon Claudet* in 1932, and a second, Supporting Oscar for *Airport* in 1970. Never mind that she didn't deserve the award. Pauline Kael dismissed her work as "Helen Hayes does her lovable-old-trouper pixie," and even kinder critics, such as the *New York Times'* Vincent Canby, wrote that Hayes's performance was "a teensy-weensy bit terrible."

This different career pattern stems in part from the more rigid specifications for the women's roles, demanding that leading ladies be young and attractive. Nonetheless, the careers of Meryl Streep and Jessica Lange, two actresses who first won a supporting (*Kramer vs. Kramer* and *Tootsie,* respectively) then a lead

Oscar (*Sophie's Choice* and *Blue Sky*), is seen as an encouraging development for women's opportunities in Hollywood.

Multiple wins have been more prevalent among filmmakers, reflecting the different ratio of supply and demand of directing talent. The concentration of awards and nominations within a small group of talented filmmakers has been a consistent trend in Hollywood. Of the fifty-five Oscar-winning directors, sixteen (29 percent) have won multiple awards.

The all-time record is still held by John Ford, who won four Oscars, followed by Frank Capra and William Wyler, each with three. Ten directors have been nominated five or more times, including Frank Capra, Billy Wilder, Elia Kazan, John Huston, and Fred Zinnemann. Only seventeen (31 percent) of the winning directors have received a single nomination.

Consecutive Wins

Only five players have won two Oscars in a row: Luise Rainer in 1936 and 1937, Spencer Tracy in 1937 and 1938, Katharine Hepburn in 1967 and 1968, Jason Robards in 1976 and 1977, and Tom Hanks in 1993 and 1994.

Of the Oscar directors, only two have won consecutive Oscars: John Ford for *The Grapes of Wrath* in 1940 and *How Green Was My Valley* in 1941, and Joseph L. Mankiewicz for *A Letter to Three Wives* in 1949 and *All About Eve* in 1950.

Posthumous Nominations and Wins

The Academy is reluctant to bestow the Oscar posthumously. Some suggest that the Academy's reluctance stems from its belief that the awards should affect the careers of practicing artists. In some categories, such as the Irving G. Thalberg Memorial Award for distinguished producers, and the Honorary Oscars, the Academy rules state explicitly that awards "shall not be voted posthumously."

In 1939, Sidney Howard won a posthumous Screenplay Oscar for *Gone With the Wind,* to which several other writers contributed but remained uncredited. Unfortunately, Howard was killed in a tractor accident on his Massachusetts farm a few months before the picture's world premiere in Atlanta. Peter Finch is still the only player to have won the Oscar, for *Network,* after his death. In 1972, Raymond Rasch, Larry Russell, and Charlie Chaplin earned the Original Score for *Limelight,* a film that was made twenty years earlier. However, released in Los Angeles in 1972 for the first time, *Limelight* was eligible for the nominations. Both Rasch and Russell were dead, but Chaplin accepted the award for a film that had been shown in Europe, but banned in the United States for many years.

Posthumous nominations have been only slightly more frequent than the actual awards. James Dean is one of few exceptions, earning two Best Actor nominations posthumously, for *East of Eden* and *Giant.* Dean was killed in a car crash while driving his Porsche to Salinas to compete in a race. *East of Eden* was released a few weeks before his death on September 30, 1955, and *Giant,* which he did not entirely complete, about a year later. When the 1956 awards were presented, on March 27, 1957, Dean had been dead for eighteen months. Consensus held that Dean's second nomination was influenced by the sentimentality factor, though his achievements in both pictures were outstanding. Dean's Oscar nominations not only contributed to the box-office success of *East of Eden* and *Giant,* but helped to elevate his extremely brief career to a legendary status.

Spencer Tracy was also nominated posthumously for *Guess Who's Coming to Dinner,* a film that provided a grand acting reunion with Katharine Hepburn — their ninth film together. Were it not for Hepburn's support and care, Tracy would not have committed to do the film. Frightened that he might not get through with the picture, the sickly but ultimate pro Tracy told director Stanley Kramer four days before shooting ended: "You know, I read the script again last night, and if I were to die on the way home tonight, you can still release the picture with what you've got." Had Tracy lived, he would probably have won the Oscar, both for his acting and for sentimental reasons. Hepburn's third Best Actress award was probably influenced by sentimentality as well: She selflessly nursed Tracy throughout the demanding shoot. Acknowledging Tracy's contribution to her own performance, Hepburn said upon winning: "I'm sure mine is for the two of us."

Ralph Richardson received a posthumous supporting nomination for his bravura performance in *Greystoke: The Legend of Tarzan, Lord of the Apes* (1984), in which he played the eccentric Lord Greystoke. Undeterred by his death, the New York Film Critics Circle cited Richardson for his work. The Academy's Actors Branch followed suit with a nomination; the winner, however, was Haing S. Ngor for *The Killing Fields.*

In 1994, Italian actor Massimo Troisi (*Il Postino*) received the first posthumous Best Actor nod since Peter Finch in 1976. Troisi died just twelve hours after completing the shoot, a factor no doubt contributing to the film's immense popularity.

In other fields, too, posthumous awards and nominations are rare. Cult composer Bernard Hermann, best-known for his Hitchcock scores, received two posthumous nominations in the same year, 1976, for Scorsese's *Taxi Driver* and Brian DePalma's *Obsession* (the latter film was a tribute to Hitchcock's masterpiece, *Vertigo*). It was a fitting swan song for Hermann's distinguished career, though the Academy decided to honor Jerry Goldsmith for *The Omen* (which happened to be another Hitchcock-inspired thriller).

Individual Versus Ensemble Acting

Through the Oscars, the Academy, like American culture at large, emphasizes and celebrates *individual achievements,* even though film is essentially a collaborative art.

Year after year, the casts of large-ensemble pictures are entirely ignored because the Academy doesn't know what to do with ensembles. The only organization that formally acknowledges the importance of collective acting to a film's overall impact is the Screen Actors Guild (SAG), which has a separate category for Best Ensemble. In 1970, Altman's irreverent comedy *MASH,* about the antics of an American medical unit in Korea, set critics abuzz. But when the Oscar nominations were announced, only one performer out of the huge and talented cast, Sally Kellerman as Hot Lips, was recognized in the supporting league (the sentimental favorite was Helen Hayes in another all-star picture, albeit a lousy one, *Airport*).

Appearing in an ensemble film, as one Hollywood executive noted, "can be the kiss of death, as far as actors are concerned." "It's simple mathematics," observed producer Adam Fields (*Brokedown Palace*): "Your screen time in an ensemble film is reduced. A beautiful girl in a room full of models won't stand out as much as a beautiful girl alone. If your only goal is to get an Academy Award, star in a one-man show." Leonard Maltin agreed: "When there's a true ensemble with a lot of good performances, it's hard to single out one without insulting the others." When Kevin Spacey won a Supporting Oscar for the noir thriller *The Usual Suspects,* a film whose success depended on ensemble acting, he told reporters: "It's a little embarrassing to be picked out of an ensemble, because it was never considered as anything other than that." One can only guess how Spacey's peers, Stephen Baldwin, Gabriel Byrne, Chazz Palminteri, Kevin Pollak, and Pete Postlethwaite, felt.

The "ensemble dilemma" assumed special urgency in the 2001 Oscar season, due to the unusually large number of strong ensemble movies. Among the heavy contenders were: Peter Jackson's *The Lord of the Rings: The Fellowship of the Ring,* whose cast included Ian McKellen, Ian Holm, Elijah Wood, and Viggo Mortensen; Wes Anderson's *The Royal Tenenbaums,* with Gene Hackman, Anjelica Huston, Gwyneth Paltrow, Ben Stiller, Owen Wilson; and Altman's *Gosford Park,* which featured Britain's best-regarded acting talent, Kristin Scott Thomas, Alan Bates, Michael Gambon, Maggie Smith, Helen Mirren, Emily Watson, and Jeremy Northam among them. However, of *Gosford Park*'s forty-eight speaking parts, only two actresses, Helen Mirren and Maggie Smith, were singled out by the Academy. Talking to the London Film Critics Circle, supporting winner Helen Mirren said she felt embarrassed to accept an award for an ensemble film like *Gosford Park.* "Just look in the corners," she urged the critics, "In every corner of the screen there is an extraordinary performance going on."

History tends to repeat itself. Over the years, Altman, the quintessential ensemble director, has seen all or most of his actors overlooked in such acclaimed films as *The Player* or *Short Cuts.* Altman's first reaction to the nominations of Mirren and Smith in *Gosford Park* was "déjà vu all over again," having experienced the same problem when *Nashville* garnered Oscar nominations for only two of its large troupe: Lily Tomlin and Ronee Blakley.

Every once in a while, there are exceptions. Both *Pulp Fiction* and *Boogie Nights* brought nominations to their multiple cast members. The Academy singled out *Pulp Fiction*'s stars, John Travolta (lead), Samuel L. Jackson and Uma Thurman (supporting). Of the dozen members in Paul Thomas Anderson's *Boogie Nights,* only two were nominated: Julianne Moore and Burt Reynolds (for the first time in his career). Then again, rather unfairly, Tom Cruise was the only thespian to receive a supporting nomination for Anderson's next film, *Magnolia.*

Indeed, how do you handle a war film like *Black Hawk Down,* in which Josh Hartnett is nominally the star, but actually only the first among many talented men, all playing soldiers, including Ewan McGregor, Tom Sizemore, and Sam Shepard?

Here are Best Picture nominees with large ensembles that received one (or no) acting nomination:

Grand Hotel (1932)	None
Dinner at Eight (1933)	None
Forty-Second Street (1933)	None
David Copperfield (1935)	None
Stage Door (1937)	One: Andrea Leeds (supp)
Stagecoach (1939)	One: Thomas Mitchell (supp)
Great Expectations (1947)	None
Battleground (1939)	One: James Whitemore (supp)
Letter to Three Wives (1939)	None
An American in Paris (1951)	None
Twelve Angry Men (1957)	None
Gigi (1958)	None
Deliverance (1972)	None
American Graffiti (1973)	One: Candy Clark (supp)
The Big Chill (1983)	One: Glenn Close (supp)
JFK (1991)	One: Tommy Lee Jones (supp)
Apollo 13 (1995)	One: Ed Harris (supp)
Saving Private Ryan (1998)	One: Tom Hanks (lead)
The Thin Red Line (1998)	None
Traffic (2000)	One: Benicio Del Toro (supp)
The Lord of the Rings (2001)	One: Ian McKellen (supp)

The Nominees as a Social Community

The Oscar winners and nominees are members of a closely knit artistic community. To begin with, they form a small group comprised of the most distinguished artists. The Oscar-nominated artists amount to a small percentage of their respective guilds' memberships. The Oscar directors, for example, are a particularly select group: 55 winners and 133 nominees, amounting to a very small percentage of the Directors Guild membership.

Intensely stratified, the film professions are marked by sharp inequality between the elite and the rank-and-file. According to the Screen Actors Guild, on any randomly chosen day, over 85 percent of its members are unemployed, and only a minority makes more than $20,000 a year from acting. By contrast, Oscar-winning players make millions of dollars per picture and tend to work nonstop, moving from one project to another. The Oscar contest reflects this acute inequality. Nominations are concentrated within a small group. The average number of nominations is 3.6 for the Best Actresses, 3.2 for the Best Directors, and 2.8 for the Best Actors.

The winners and nominees form a social community in other significant ways. Many players were under contract to the same studio for the duration of their careers, thus appearing opposite the same performers and working with the same directors in film after film. Bette Davis, Humphrey Bogart, and James Cagney were Warner stars. Clark Gable, Spencer Tracy, Joan Crawford, and Norma Shearer defined MGM as much as the studio shaped their careers. During the studio system, lengthy affiliations meant that performers appeared in similar films and specialized in particular screen roles, a pattern that helped audiences distinguish a "Bette Davis" from a "Joan Crawford," film, a "Clark Gable" from a "James Cagney" movie.

To increase audience's personal interest in their stars, the studios' publicity machines went out of their way to create on-screen romantic couples. Janet Gaynor appeared so often with Charles Farrell that they became known as "America's lovebirds." Olivia de Havilland and Errol Flynn became a noted romantic team after making *Captain Blood* and *The Adventures of Robin Hood.* Katharine Hepburn and Spencer Tracy made nine pictures together, beginning with the sports comedy, *Woman of the Year,* continuing with the George Cukor comedies (*Adam's Rib, Pat and Mike*), and ending with *Guess Who's Coming to Dinner?* Margaret Sullavan ended up in James Stewart's arms in a number of pictures, the best of which was *The Shop Around the Corner.* Greer Garson and Walter Pidgeon were matched by Louis B. Mayer in *Mrs. Miniver* and other schmaltzy pictures.

Humphrey Bogart met and fell in love with Lauren Bacall on the set of *To Have and Have Not.* After their marriage, Bogie and Bacall made a number of memorable films, such as *The Big Sleep* and *Key Largo.*

Rock Hudson managed to conceal effectively his true sexual identity until 1985, when it was revealed that he had AIDS. In the 1950s, Hudson paired in several romantic melodramas and comedies that brought Oscar nominations to his leading ladies (Jane Wyman in *Magnificent Obsession,* Dorothy Malone in *Written on the Wind,* Doris Day in *Pillow Talk*). (Hudson also co-starred with the aforementioned women in other, non-nominated pictures.)

With the demise of the studio system, this distinctive aspect of the American cinema is gone forever. At present, we're more accustomed to the pairing of a director with a particular actor. For example, the collaboration between Martin Scorsese and Robert De Niro has been extremely fruitful for both, with De Niro receiving three Best Actor nominations for a Scorsese picture: *Taxi Driver,* *Raging Bull,* and *Cape Fear.*

Direct occupational inheritance, that is, children stepping into their parents' shoes, is also prominent in the film world, resulting in an even smaller, more intimate, and more coherent community. About 10 percent of the Oscar players had one parent in the acting profession, and 5 percent had both. If related professions (writing, producing, directing) are included, the proportion of players is even higher (15 percent), particularly among the women (20 percent).

In some cases, occupational inheritance has crossed three or more generations. Consider the acting dynasties of the Barrymores, the Powers, the Fondas, the Robards, and the Bridges in the United States, and the Redgraves in England.

Paul Muni (née Muni Weisenfreund) was literally reared in a theater trunk; his parents were strolling players who toured all over Europe and America with him and his brothers. Shunning the financial hazards of acting, Muni's parents hoped that he would pursue a career as a violinist. But he was stagestruck, and at thirteen became a regular member of his parents troupe. Muni never had to study acting, there was no need for it.

Another Academy nominee, Mickey Rooney, spent his infancy and childhood touring with his parents, who were both entertainers. Rooney made his stage debut at fifteen months, appearing as a midget in a vaudeville act in which he wore a tuxedo and smoked a big rubber cigar. The parents of Oscar-winner Jennifer Jones were the owners-stars of the Isley Stock Company, a tent show which toured the Midwest. After working as a ticket and soda seller, Jones made her stage debut at the age of ten, and her film debut (as Phyllis Isley) at twenty.

Marrying a spouse within the same profession is another distinctive characteristic of acting. These "in" marriages contribute to the integration of its members into a social and professional group that has its own lifestyle and subculture. At least two-thirds of the nominated players have married within the film colony; many more than once. The only difference between the genders is that actors usually marry actresses, whereas actresses also marry producers and directors.

The Academy's nominees could almost be accused of "incest," based on the high percentage (north of twenty) of all nominated actors and directors who have been married to other pros at one time or another in their careers. Many in fact have met their prospective spouses at work, while appearing in a play or shooting a movie. Some have fallen in love and subsequently married their leading men or leading ladies.

The Oscar ceremonies themselves have functioned as dating grounds. For the 1939 show, Oscar-nominated Bette Davis (*Jezebel*) was escorted by her then-lover, director William Wyler. Wyler's former wife, Margaret Sullavan, competed with Davis that year for her performance in *Three Comrades,* in which she played Robert Taylor's tubercular wife. Three of Sullavan's four husbands were Oscar-nominated: Henry Fonda, Wyler, and producer-agent Leland

Hayward. In 1994, Oscar-winning actress Holly Hunter (*The Piano*) and Oscar-winning cinematographer Janusz Kaminski (*Schindler's List*) met backstage during the ceremonies. Several months later they were married.

Merle Oberon (nominated for *The Dark Angel*) drew three of her four husbands from the showbiz milieu. Oberon's first husband was British film producer Alexander Korda, and her second, cinematographer Lucien Ballard. Oberon's third, and longest marriage, to an Italian industrialist was the exception. However, in 1973, Oberon wed her co-star, Robert Wolders, who was many years her junior. Ironically, it was a story in which Wolders was cast as a young man falling in love with an aging woman. Oberon is by no means unique. Oscar-nominee *James Earl Jones* (*The Great White Hope*) met his prospective wife, Julienne Marie, when she played Desdemona to his Othello in the New York Public production of this Shakespearean play in Central Park.

Along with occupational inheritance, marital and familial bonds are reflected in the Oscar contest by intergenerational nominations of parents and children, marital nominations of husbands and wives, and nominations of siblings.

Take the Huston family, for example. In 1948, John Huston won two Oscars for writing and directing *The Treasure of the Sierra Madre,* a film which provided his father, Walter Huston, with one of his richest roles. Huston père played the shrewd old gold prospector, for which he won the Supporting Oscar. This double win was the emotional highlight of the evening, after which Walter Huston jokingly remarked: "I always told my boy that if he ever became a director to find a part for his old man."

Thirty seven years later, John Huston's daughter, Anjelica Huston, accepted the Supporting Oscar for her stunning performance as the don's wild and wronged granddaughter in *Prizzi's Honor,* directed by none other than her father. The pre-Oscar polls predicted that John Huston would win a second directorial Oscar for *Prizzi's Honor,* and people in the industry were excited at the prospects of seeing father and daughter sharing the spotlight. The winner, however, was Sydney Pollack for *Out of Africa.* In her acceptance speech, Anjelica, who had made her debut in one of her father's earlier pictures, acknowledged her family debt: "This means a lot to me, especially since it comes for a role in which I was directed by my father, and I know it means a lot to him." John Huston became the only director to have directed both his father and his daughter to Oscar victories.

The 1975 awards ceremonies were described by some as "The Francis Ford Coppola Family Hour." *The Godfather, Part II,* won six Oscars, including Best Director (Coppola) and Original Dramatic Score for the director's father, Carmine Coppola, who composed the music with Nino Rotta. "I want to thank my son for my being up here," said Carmine, "Without him, I wouldn't be here. However, if I wasn't here, he wouldn't be here either, right?" Talia Shire, also related to Coppola, was nominated for a supporting award as Connie Corleone, Al Pacino's sluttish sister, but did not win.

A family reunion imbued with symbolic meaning on- and offscreen, took place at the 1982 Oscar show, when Henry Fonda won Best Actor for *On Golden Pond*. Jane Fonda purchased the screen rights to Ernest Thompson's stage play as a vehicle for her father. Though Jane had made her acting debut opposite her father Henry at the Omaha Community House Theater, *On Golden Pond* was the first and only movie they made together. Jane was cast as Chelsea, a middle-aged daughter and single mom at odds with her father over painful childhood misunderstandings. The film's reconciliation scene, under the sturdy guidance of Katharine Hepburn who plays Fonda's wife, in which Chelsea finally comes to terms with her past, was semiautobiographical to say the least. Jane's unhappy childhood and later radical politics had created tension with her distanced and more conservative dad. Rumors have it that it was Henry who told Jane not to use the Oscar podium for political declarations should she win Best Actress for *Klute,* which she did.

Jane agreed to play a thankless role in *On Golden Pond* for familial reasons. The Academy respectfully honored Henry Fonda and Katharine Hepburn with Oscars, and Jane with her sixth (and first supporting) nomination. In an emotional speech, Jane accepted the Oscar for her father, who was unable to attend the ceremonies due to poor health. After the show, the cameras followed the dutiful daughter as she drove to her father's house to present him with the statuette. Unfortunately, Fonda died four months later.

Jane Fonda also proved herself a dutiful sister, when she accompanied her brother Peter Fonda, to several awards ceremonies upon his first acting nomination for *Ulee's Gold.* Since *Easy Rider,* for which he was nominated for a writing Oscar (along with Dennis Hopper and Terry Southern), Peter has made peace with Hollywood and with his father Henry, whom he credited for inspiring his quiet but impressive performance in *Ulee's Gold.* Fonda played a taciturn beekeeper, forced to emerge out of his solitary life and face familial responsibilities as the father of an imprisoned son and grandfather of two girls ruthlessly abandoned by their drug-addict mother. That Peter resembled his father physically made the link between père and fils all the more apparent.

Angelina Jolie and Jon Voight joined Henry Fonda and Jane Fonda as another second father-daughter team to win acting Oscars; he as Best Actor for *Coming Home,* in 1978, she, as Supporting Actress for *Girl, Interrupted,* in 1999. An "awards darling," with three Golden Globes to her credit, Jolie's bad-girl reputation, eccentric personality, and the film's lukewarm box office obviously didn't hurt her chances.

Famous Hollywood families have become an integral part of Oscar's long history. In 1958, Vincente Minnelli was named Best Director for the musical *Gigi.* His ex-wife, Judy Garland, was not nominated for any of their previous collaborations (*Meet Me in St. Louis, The Clock*), but she was nominated twice for other films: As Best Actress for the musical drama *A Star Is Born,* and as Supporting Actress for the court drama *Judgment at Nuremberg.* Then at the age of two, Vincente and Judy's daughter, Liza Minnelli, made her film debut in a walk-on part in her mother's musical *In the Good Old Summertime.* Liza was later nominated twice: For *The Sterile Cuckoo,* which Judy urged her do though the film was released after her death, and *Cabaret,* which garnered Liza the Best Actress Oscar. "I don't want to think that I won the Oscar because of my mother," Liza told the press, "That's why I said in my speech, 'Thank you for giving me this award.'"

The Redgraves represent one of England's most renowned acting dynasties, so far consisting of five generations of players. Sir Michael Redgrave's grandfather and both of his parents were actors, and Redgrave was married to Rachel Kempson, mostly known for her stage and television work. All of Michael and Rachel's children — Vanessa, Lynn, and Corin — pursued acting careers. On the evening of Vanessa's birth, Michael was playing opposite Olivier in *Hamlet* at the Old Vic. Olivier was so excited by the event that in his curtain speech he announced: "Tonight a lovely new actress has been born. Laertes (played by Redgrave) has a daughter." Olivier's prophecy turned out to be self-fulfilling, when Vanessa made her first screen appearance in *Behind the Mask,* in which she played the daughter of her real-life father.

Talent has been in abundance in the Redgrave clan, some of which was certified by the Academy. Three family members have been nominated, beginning with Sir Michael, as Best Actor for the 1947 film version of Eugene O'Neill's *Mourning Becomes Electra.* Vanessa and Lynn received their first Best Actress nomination in the same year, 1966, the former for *Morgan!,* the latter for *Georgy Girl.* For the lead of *Georgy Girl,* a young woman who just missed being beautiful, the producers tried to get every girl in London, including Vanessa, who turned it down because of other commitments. The nomination of Vanessa and Lynn in the same year was taken in stride by the sisters, who both made sure to dispel any feelings of rivalry or animosity. Lynn told reporters: "We like each other's work and each other as people. Vanessa takes the spotlight one week, I get it the next." In the next decade, however, it was Vanessa who distinguished herself as a performer. Regarded as one of the best actresses in the English-speaking world, Vanessa has been nominated five times, winning a Supporting Oscar for *Julia.* As for Lynn, after a long dry period, a fine performance in *Gods and Monsters* (1998), as director James Whale's (played by Ian McKellen) heavily accented housekeeper earned her a second supporting nomination.

The Redgrave acting torch is passing down from generation to generation: All three of Vanessa's children have appeared on the stage or in film. Daughter Joely Richardson played Vanessa's character as an adolescent in David Hare's *Wetherby.* Vanessa's other daughter, Natasha Richardson, played Nina to her mother's Irina in a British production of Chekhov's *The Sea Gull,* which had been one of her mother's earlier screen roles in Sidney Lumet's 1968 film.

The Redgrave sisters' amicable sportsmanship didn't prevail in 1941, when another pair of ambitious sisters were nominated in the same year: Joan Fontaine for *Suspicion* and Olivia de Havilland for *Hold Back the Dawn.* Rumors of the "feuding sisters," who were close in age, circulated in the movie colony.

De Havilland's early career had been more auspicious than her sister's, having made a number of popular films opposite Errol Flynn. Fontaine's life as de Havilland's Cinderella sister was well covered by the press. Until 1939, Olivia seemed to get all the good breaks, and Joan all the bad ones. Fontaine's s stage debut was in an English comedy, *Call It a Day,* but when Warner bought the picture rights, her role was given to Olivia. Fontaine was determined to make her own way independent of her more famous sister. She tested for Scarlett O'Hara in *Gone With the Wind,* but lost to Vivien Leigh; Olivia was cast as Melanie in the picture. The childhood taunt, "Livva can, Joan can't" continued to haunt Fontaine for years.

The Oscar rivalry between the two sisters was more than a routine Hollywood publicity story. In 1941, the New York Film Critics had to cast five ballots before deciding between de Havilland and Fontaine for the Best Actress honor. It was one of the few times that the Academy and the New York Film Critics Circle selected the same actress for the award. When Fontaine won Best Actress for *Suspicion,* de Havilland clapped the loudest of all, exclaiming, "We've won." Fontaine recalled in her memoir, "Olivia took the situation very graciously. I am sure it was not a pleasant moment for her, as she'd lost the previous year for Melanie in *Gone With the Wind* in the supporting actress category." Privately, however, de Havilland was devastated, telling her friends that if the release of *Suspicion* had been delayed — originally it was intended to open in 1942 — she would have won the 1941 Oscar. Fontaine was well aware of this, telling the press: "If *Suspicion* had been delayed just a little it wouldn't have got under the wire for this year's award. I've been runner-up so often it isn't funny anymore. If it happens again, I'm likely to break something." Recalled Fontaine: "In later years, Olivia made it up with two Oscars, for *To Each His Own* and *The Heiress,* so the evening of *Suspicion* was only a temporary setback." Magazines, however, reported in great detail how de Havilland backed off and gave Fontaine the cold shoulder when she tried to shake her hand upon winning the Oscar for *Suspicion.*

Oscar anxieties and frustrations have also dominated the Barrymore family. Two of the Barrymore siblings have won Oscars. Lionel Barrymore earned the 1930–31 Best Actor (*A Free Soul*) as Norma Shearer's alcoholic lawyer-father. His sister, Ethel Barrymore, was nominated four times for supporting actress within five years, finally winning for *None But the Lonely Heart* as Cary Grant's poor mother. Nonetheless, John Barrymore, the most famous sibling, was never nominated. The Barrymores, like the Redgraves, have been an acting clan extending over five generations. Drew Barrymore is the most recent family member to have graced the screen, beginning with *E.T. The Extra-Terrestrial* in 1982. A prominent actress-producer (*Charlie's Angels*), Drew is likely to be nominated in the future.

The first, and so far only, team of brothers to be nominated for acting Oscars is in the Phoenix family: River Phoenix was nominated for a supporting actor in 1988, at the young age of eighteen, in Sidney Lumet's political melodrama, *Running on Empty.* Twelve years later, his younger brother, Joaquin, received *his* first supporting actor nomination as the weakling son in *Gladiator.* Unfortunately, River, was not there to share the joy. In 1993, he collapsed and died under mysterious, drug-related circumstances outside the Viper Room, a hip Los Angeles club owned by his friend, actor Johnny Depp.

The Oscar race has included several marital nominations. Three husband-and-wife teams have been nominated for the same film. Alfred Lunt and Lynn Fontanne were nominated for re-creating on-screen their famous Broadway roles, as the jealous husband-actor and his flirtatious wife-actress, in Hungarian-playwright Ferenc Molnar's comedy, *The Guardsman.* Charles Laughton and Elsa Lanchester (who made a number of films together) were similarly both nominated for Billy Wilder's *Witness for the Prosecution.* Laughton played Sir Wilfred Robards, the eccentric queen's Defense Counsel, and Lanchester his maidenly owlish nurse. In one memorable scene, Lanchester tells Laughton, "It's time for our nap," to which he replies, "You go ahead, start it without me." Neither Laughton nor Lanchester won for that film. In 1957, a year of intense competition, Alec Guinness won Best Actor for *The Bridge on the River Kwai,* and Miyoshi Umeki the Supporting Actress for *Sayonara.* Elizabeth Taylor and Richard Burton, one of Hollywood's most glamorous couples, were the third team to be nominated for the same film, also playing husband and wife. Taylor, as the earthy Martha, and Burton, as her husband-professor George, probably gave the finest performances of their careers in Mike Nichols's adaptation of Edward Albee's prize-winning *Who's Afraid of Virginia Woolf?* Taylor won a second Oscar, but Burton lost to Paul Scofield. (British couple Rex Harrison and Rachel Roberts were also nominated in the same year, 1963, but for different films — he for *Cleopatra,* she for *This Sporting Life.*)

Paul Newman and Joanne Woodward met while performing on Broadway in *Picnic.* They went on to appear in many films together — *From the Terrace, Paris Blues, A New Kind of Love,* among them. But none of their acting collaborations was as critically acclaimed as their director-actress teaming in *Rachel, Rachel* (1968). Woodward earned her second Best Actress nomination and, though Newman was not nominated as director, the film was nominated for Best Picture. In 1990 Woodward was again nominated, for her comeback performance in *Mr. and Mrs. Bridge,* but her co-star Paul Newman was not.

Amy Madigan was nominated for a supporting Oscar in *Twice in a Lifetime,* and her husband Ed Harris has been nominated three times: Twice for supporting roles (*Apollo 13* and *The Truman Show*) and once for a lead (*Pollock*).

A late bloomer as far as Academy recognition is concerned (as noted), Susan Sarandon stumbled into acting while married to Chris Sarandon, later nominated for the Supporting Oscar in *Dog Day Afternoon.* And Sarandon's companion of twelve years, Tim Robbins, directed her to her first Best Actress Oscar in *Dead Man Walking,* in which she played the real-life nun, Sister Helen Prejean.

In 1991, Diane Ladd and Laura Dern became the first real-life mother-daughter team to be nominated for the same film, *Rambling Rose,* though they didn't play mother-daughter in the story.

Father-and-son teams have included Raymond Massey, as Best Actor nominee for playing the president in *Abe Lincoln in Illinois,* and son Daniel Massey, as Supporting Actor for impersonating Noel Coward in the musical *Star!*

When Kevin Spacey and Mare Winningham were both nominated for supporting roles in 1995 — he for *The Usual Suspects,* and she for *Georgia* — no one suspected any link between them, but there was. Spacey fondly recalled a happy time in the twelfth grade at Chatsworth High, when he and Winningham co-starred in *The Sound of Music,* as Baron and Maria Von Trapp. This is yet another example of how small the film world is.

· 7 ·

IS THE OSCAR A WHITE MAN'S AWARD?

> Who will win this year's Best White Actor and Best White Actress?
> —Protesters, Oscar Show

In the Oscar's seventy-four-year history, the only African American to have received a directing nomination is John Singleton, for the 1991 urban crime drama, *Boyz 'N the Hood.* Spike Lee, the dean of contemporary African American filmmakers, has never been nominated for Best Director, despite impressive achievements in such timely films as *Do the Right Thing* and the epic biopicture *Malcolm X.* Both aroused controversy due to their inflammatory subject matter. In 1997, Lee's documentary-feature *4 Little Girls* was nominated, but the prize went to a Holocaust documentary, *The Long Way Home.*

Black-Themed Movies

Before Spike Lee, most black-themed and all-black cast pictures were directed by white filmmakers, including King Vidor's 1929 *Hallellujah* (for which he received Best Director nomination), Vincente Minnelli's 1943 feature debut, *Cabin in the Sky,* and others. The all-black *Carmen Jones* (1954), inspired by Bizet's famous opera, was also brought to the screen by a white filmmaker, Otto Preminger. In this reworking, a sexy black factory worker and whore (Dorothy Dandridge) elopes with a soldier named Joe (Harry Belafonte) and together they evade the law. Carmen is strangled by Joe after deserting him for a prizefighter.

Black-themed movies, whether helmed by white or black artists, have seldom won recognition for their filmmakers, though the films themselves have been nominated. Spielberg's *The Color Purple,* adapted to the screen from Alice Walker's best-selling novel, is one of the greatest losers in the Oscar annals. *The Color Purple* received a record of eleven nominations, yet when it came to the actual awards, the film lost out in each and every category. Spielberg, who earlier had won the Directors Guild Award, even failed to receive a Best Director citation. The big winner that year was *Out of Africa.*

The Color Purple was certainly not one of Spielberg's great pictures. What was missing from the movie was the unique voice of its protagonist Celie (Whoopi Goldberg), which gave the book such distinction. Spielberg turned an intimate and complex tale with strong lesbian overtones into what film scholar Donald Bogle describes as "a Disneyesque Victorian melodrama full of 'big' moments and simplified characters." For Bogle, it became "a family film that soft-pedaled its lesbian theme."

Even white directors of decent black-themed pictures have been snubbed by the Academy. Stanley Kramer's 1967 Oscar nominee, *Guess Who's Coming to Dinner,* opened to mixed reviews. For the harsher critics, it was "pure 1949 claptrap done up in 1940s high-gloss MGM style. By concentrating on nice decent people entangled in personal heartaches, director Kramer diverted the audience from any real issue."

Guess Who's Coming's major competitor was another black-themed film, *In the Heat of the Night.* The film won the 1967 Best Picture, but the directing Oscar that year went to Mike Nichols for *The Graduate* rather than Norman Jewison. In 1984, *A Soldier's Story* was nominated for Best Picture, but helmer Jewison again failed to receive a directing nod. The Academy finally compensated Jewison, who never won a legit Oscar despite three nominations (the other two were for *Fiddler on the Roof* and *Moonstruck*) with the Irving G. Thalberg Memorial Award, in 1999.

African American Actors

Black actors have fared slightly better than black writers and directors. The first black actor to be honored by the Academy was James Baskett, who received a Special Oscar in 1947. Baskett played Uncle Remus in Disney's *Song of the South,* co-directed by Wilfred Jackson and Harve Foster, a movie that required him to sing to cartoon animals. He was cited in recognition of his "able and heartwarming characterization of Uncle Remus, friend and storyteller to the children of the world." The film is out of circulation except in Japan.

Gossip columnist Hedda Hopper claimed that it was her idea to honor Baskett as a humanitarian gesture. Some Academy board members opposed the award because Baskett played a slave, feeling that Negroes should play only professionals, doctors, lawyers, scientists. Similar objections were raised in 1939, when Hattie McDaniel won the Supporting Actress for playing a servant in *Gone With the Wind.* According to Hopper, Jean Hersholt threatened after a heated argument that, if Baskett didn't receive an Oscar, "I shall stand up tomorrow night and tell the world the whole disgraceful story." The board gave in and asked Hollywood's then-most-popular star, Ingrid Bergman, to present Baskett the award.

In the Academy's history, only eight black performances have won the Oscar, three in the lead and five in the supporting category. Denzel Washington is the only black actor to have won two competitive Oscars. These performers are:

Hattie McDaniel, *Gone With the Wind* (1939)

Sidney Poitier, *Lilies of the Field* (1963)

Louis Gossett Jr., *An Officer and a Gentleman* (1982)

Denzel Washington, *Glory* (1989)

Whoopi Goldberg, *Ghost* (1990)

Cuba Gooding Jr., *Jerry Maguire* (1996)

Denzel Washington, *Training Day (2001)*

Halle Berry, *Monster's Ball* (2001)

Sidney Poitier was the first and only black actor to win the Best Actor Oscar until 2001, when Denzel Washington joined the Best Actor ranks. A veteran of fifty years of cinema, Poitier has carried the burden of the turbulent and contradictory history of blacks in American film. After winning the 1963 Best Actor for *Lilies of the Field,* Poitier's career soared to undreamed of heights with three pictures: *To Sir, With Love, Guess Who's Coming to Dinner,* and *In the Heat of the Night.*

When director Norman Jewison approached Poitier to star in the racially charged drama *In the Heat of the Night,* the actor said he would do it on one condition — that he would not have to travel south of the Mason-Dixie Line. Indeed, Jewison agreed to shoot the film in Indiana rather than Mississippi where it is set.

"Sidney represented such an important image in *In the Heat of the Night,*" Jewison told the *Hollywood Reporter,* "and he gave the character such a sense of dignity and strength and pride. I was worried about audience reaction to this very intense black-white relationship, but of course it was well-received." With the Civil Rights movement in full swing and the country's big cities burning with racial hatred, Poitier gracefully led the charge in smashing the color barriers of mainstream culture.

At seventy-five, Poitier received the Honorary Oscar "for his extraordinary performances and unique presence on the screen and for representing the motion picture industry with dignity, style and intelligence throughout the world." President Frank Pierson held that "when the Academy honors Sidney Poitier, it honors itself even more."

Oscar host Whoopi Goldberg introduced Poitier as a presenter in the 1996 show, as the man who "made a lot of other actors possible, including myself." She did not exaggerate. Poitier has survived, as Bogle observes, "through all the vicissitudes, the uphill battles, the change in public tastes and outlooks, the demands of audiences, black and white." For his survival and accomplishments against all odds, the Academy bestowed on Poitier an Honorary Oscar at the 2002 ceremonies. It was most appropriate that Poitier was presented with his second Oscar by Denzel Washington, who, a few minutes later, would make history by winning the Best Actor for *Training Day.*

Poitier and Washington comprise 3.3 percent (2 out of the 66) of the Best Actors. The percentage of African American Best Actor nominees is slightly higher: 5.5 percent, or 7 out of one 118 nominees. They are:

James Earl Jones, *The Great White Hope* (1970)

Paul Winfield, *Sounder* (1972)

Dexter Gordon, *'Round Midnight* (1986)

Morgan Freeman, *Driving Miss Daisy* (1989) and *The Shawshank Redemption* (1994)

Denzel Washington, *Malcolm X* (1992), *The Hurricane* (1999), and *Training Day (2001)*

Lawrence Fishburne, *What's Love Got to Do With It (1993)*

Will Smith, *Ali (2001)*

It took thirty-three years after the creation of the Supporting Actor/Actress categories for the first black performer to be nominated in that league, Rupert Crosse for *The Reivers* in 1969. Three black actors have won Supporting Oscars, all in the past twenty years:

Louis Gossett Jr., *An Officer and a Gentleman* (1982)

Denzel Washington, *Glory* (1989)

Cuba Gooding Jr., *Jerry Maguire* (1996)

The seven black supporting actors amount to a small percentage of all supporting nominees. They are:

Rupert Crosse, *The Reivers* (1969)

Howard E. Rollins, *Ragtime* (1981)

Adolph Caesar, *A Soldier's Story* (1984)

Morgan Freeman, *Street Smart* (1989)

Jaye Davidson, *The Crying Game* (1992)

Samuel Jackson, *Pulp Fiction* (1994)

Michael Clarke Duncan, *The Green Mile* (1999)

Jaye Davidson, born in California but reared in England, was working as a fashion assistant when director Neil Jordan spotted him for the pivotal role in his psycho-political mystery, *The Crying Game*. The focus of the film's shocking revelations, Davidson plays the transsexual lover of a British soldier-hostage (Forrest Whitaker) and then the lover of the Irish terrorist (Stephen Rae).

No black woman had won the Best Actress Oscar until the 2002 Academy Awards, when Halle Berry was selected for her breakthrough performance in *Monster's Ball*. Prior to Berry, only six black women were nominated in the lead category:

Dorothy Dandridge, *Carmen Jones* (1954)

Diana Ross, *Lady Sings the Blues* (1972)

Cicely Tyson, *Sounder* (1972)

Diahann Carroll, *Claudine* (1974)

Whoopi Goldberg, *The Color Purple* (1985)

Angela Bassett, *What's Love Got to Do With It (1993)*

Note that three of these women (Dandridge, Ross, and Bassett) played show-biz personalities, and that at least a decade elapsed between one nomination and the next. The three black female winners — McDaniel, Goldberg, and Berry — are a vast underrepresentation considering the proportion (about 12 percent) of blacks in American society.

In 1990, when Goldberg won the Supporting Actress for *Ghost,* she became the first black actress to win an Oscar since Hattie McDaniel in *Gone With the Wind,* back in 1939. So much for progress. Goldberg told the press rather revealingly: "I never say I'm black when I'm looking for work. I just don't admit it, because as soon as you say it, they tell you there's no work for you. You wouldn't say to a doctor that he couldn't operate on your kneecap because he is black. In the same way, art should have no color and no sex."

Goldberg, no doubt, benefited form the bonanza success of *Ghost,* and from the fact that the supernatural romantic melodrama was nominated for major Oscars, including Best Picture. Only a few critics at the time pointed out that Goldberg's role in *Ghost* was problematic and stereotypical. As Oda Mae Brown, a medium dressed in a gold-lamé dress and sporting long hair, Goldberg operates in the realm of otherworldly spirits, what Bogle has described as "an old stereotype revamped for a new generation."

The part certainly did not promote a more realistic view of black women, as Goldberg's character is an asexual oddball, with no personal life of her own, channeling all her energy toward uniting two lovers (played by Demi Moore and Patrick Swayze), and getting an epiphany while pulling off a bank scam at the end.

Along with McDaniel and Goldberg, six other black actresses were nominated for the Supporting Oscar:

Ethel Waters, *Pinky* (1949)

Juanita Moore, *Imitation of Life* (1959)

Bea Richards, *Guess Who's Coming to Dinner* (1967)

Alfre Woodard, *Cross Creek* (1983)

Margaret Avery and Oprah Winfrey, *The Color Purple* (1985)

Marianne Jean-Baptiste, *Secrets & Lies* (1996)

With the notable exception of *The Color Purple* and *Secrets & Lies,* which was a British film, the other films offered mostly stereotypical roles, such as Hattie McDaniel's Mammy in *Gone With the Wind* or Ethel Waters's Granny in *Pinky.* Juanita Moore played an all-suffering mother to an ungrateful daughter and housekeeper to a rich white family in *Imitation of Life.* And though Bea Richards played a liberal, middle-class mother in *Guess Who's Coming to Dinner,* she was given nothing of significance to do or say. The big "message" speeches were left for the men, particularly the white patriarch, played by Spencer Tracy.

It may be significant that most Oscar-nominated black characters are dead by the end of the film. *A Soldier's Story,* set in a Louisiana military base, is a court drama that begins with the murder of Sergeant Waters (Adolph Caesar), a foul-mouthed, conflicted military man, embittered by his own self-loathing and self-hatred. *Cry Freedom, Malcolm X, Training Day,* all featuring Denzel Washington, also conclude with their protagonist's death, albeit in different circumstances.

Furthermore, black-themed movies (by both white and black directors) are often safely set in the distant past, thus relieving both filmmakers and audiences from the challenge and responsibility of dealing in a direct and explicit manner with the painful realities of contemporary race relations. For example, *A Soldier's Story* is set in 1944, *The Color Purple* covers some forty years, *Driving Miss Daisy* spans from 1948 to 1973, and the biopicture *Ali* centers on one crucial decade, from 1964 to 1974, in the fighter's life. As with other controversial issues tackled by Hollywood, it's always safer to set a film in the past.

Black Artists in Other Categories

In other categories, too, black artists have been vastly underrepresented. No black writer has ever won the Best Screenplay and few have been nominated. The Academy neglected to nominate William Gunn, who did a wonderful adaptation of Hal Ashby's *The Landlord* (1970), a sharp, timely satire about gentrification, based on the novel written by black writer Kristin Hunter. *The Landlord* brought a supporting nomination to Lee Grant, who played the mother of Beau Bridges, the rich but naive white guy who buys a run-down house in the ghetto.

In 1984, Charles Fuller, the Pulitzer Prize-winner for the play *A Soldier's Tale,* was nominated for his adapted screenplay for the film version, retitled *A Solider's Story;* the winner that year was Peter Shafer for *Amadeus,* which swept most of the Oscars. Spike Lee was nominated for *Do the Right Thing*'s original screenplay but the winner was Tom Schulman for *Dead Poets Society.*

In 1970, Isaac Hayes became the first black musician to win the Best Song Oscar for his work in *Shaft.* In his emotional acceptance speech, Hayes thanked his grandmother.

Russell Williams has won two Oscars for achievements in sound, for *Glory* and *Dances With Wolves,* but he is the notable exception.

In 1995, Dianne Houston, the producer-director of "Tuesday Morning Ride," the live-action short contender, was the only African American among the 166 Oscar-nominated artists, an all-time low. This single nomination sparked cover stories in news magazines and the ire of political activist Jesse Jackson, who asked black performers to boycott the Oscar ceremonies. Reverend Jackson threatened to organize vigorous protests, "even civil disobedience," which didn't materialize. (The Shorts Oscar that year went to Christine Lahti, for her "Lieberman in Love." Ironically, Lahti, who had previously been nominated for a 1984 supporting turn in *Swing Shift,* decided to direct because of the limited acting opportunities for women. Explaining why she became a director, Lahti said: "There aren't a lot of great parts for women over thirty-five. They're all earnest moms waiting at home while the guys are having these great adventures. I didn't want to play these two-dimensional roles.")

Two weeks before the show, *People* magazine ran a cover story entitled "Hollywood Blackout" in which it wrote: "The film industry says all the right things, but its continued exclusion of African Americans is a national disgrace. A shocking level of minority exclusion remains." The condemning article revealed some alarming statistics:

Only 3.9 percent of the Academy members were black;

Only 2.3 percent of the DGA members were black;

Only 2.6 percent of the WGA members were black.

The magazine also pointed out that in the previous year's Oscar show, even the "seat fillers" — people who occupy empty chairs during the show for the benefit of TV cameras — were overwhelmingly white.

In a sidebar, the Oscar-show producer, musician Quincy Jones was described as "Hollywood Rarity: A Brother with Clout." For his part, Quincy acknowledged that racism existed in Hollywood, but he put the issue in a broader perspective. What about Asian Americans and Latinos? Are these minorities adequately represented in the Oscar race? Taiwanese-born helmer Ang Lee was overlooked in 1995 by the Directors Branch, though his film *Sense and Sensibility* received major nominations, including Best Picture. Lee received a directing nomination five years later for *Crouching Tiger, Hidden Dragon.*

Peter Bart, *Variety*'s editor-in-chief, wrote: "If 1995 proved not to be a good year for black Oscar nominees, it wasn't a good year for black movies, or for any movies. . . . But certainly the positioning of Quincy Jones and Whoopi Goldberg, not to mention Sidney Poitier as a presenter, should give some clue that the Academy is hardly a bastion of racist sentiment."

Most people would like to believe that 2001 was a turning point, with its three lead black nominations (Halle Berry, Will Smith, and Denzel Washington), the first time in thirty years (since 1972, when Diana Ross and Cicely Tyson) that multiple black nominations have occurred.

No doubt, progress has been slow. Yet the careers of two talented actors, Morgan Freeman and Denzel Washington, who belong to different generations, shed light on the changing status of black actors in Hollywood. Freeman received his first (supporting) nomination for *Street Smart,* in which he played a pimp, Fast Black, in conflict with his culture and aware of its deceptions and injustices. For a long time, Freeman's career looked, as Bogle has written, like "a series of dazzling starts, followed by troubling dead ends." Indeed, five years later, Freeman was nominated for Best Actor in *Driving Miss Daisy,* in which he played a loyal chauffeur who turns companion. Freeman, then fifty-two, had been meticulously honing his craft for years, acting in a style that was sternly natural and realistic.

In 1994, before it was cast with Freeman, the character of Red, a convicted murderer behind bars in *The Shawshank Redemption,* was originally written as an Irishman. Freeman showed his masterful acting in narrating the tale with the plain-spoken poetry of a seasoned storyteller. Playing this part, for which he received a second Best Actor nomination, proved a liberating experience for Freeman, catapulting him to a major star status. Good or bad, mainstream commercial films, such as *Kiss the Girls, Along Came a Spider, High Crimes,* and *The Sum of Fears,* are now built around his presence as either solo or co-starring vehicles.

Denzel Washington's five Oscar nominations also tell an interesting political story. His first nomination, the same year that Freeman was nominated, was for *Cry Freedom,* in which he played Steve Biko, the South African anti-apartheid activist. Except for Washington's performance, the reviews were mixed, claiming this was yet another black-themed picture told from a strictly white point of view. A year later, Washington was nominated and won the Supporting Oscar for *Glory.* He played Trip, the rebellious runaway slave who, having endured hardships, sees racism clearly and is eager to speak out. In a stirring sequence, Trip, having gone AWOL, returns to the military camp where he is whipped.

Glory was a career milestone for Washington. Two Best Actor nominations followed, for *Malcolm X* and *The Hurricane,* in both of which he played heroic figures. But in his Oscar-winning role, *Training Day,* Washington refreshingly deviated from his established screen image and played a corrupt and decadent cop, hence impressively expanding his range.

Latino Artists

Frustrations have been mounting for Latino actors in Hollywood, many of whom feel disenfranchised by the industry and their own unions, the Screen Actors Guild and the American Federation of Television and Radio Artists (AFTRA).

Although there are twenty-three million Latinos in the United States, roughly 10 percent of the nation's population, during the 1990s, Latinos accounted for only one percent of all characters in prime-time television programs. The percentage has actually declined from that of the 1980s, according to the Washington based Center for Media and Public Affairs. For movies, SAG reports that in 1992 Latino performers in feature films amounted only to 4 percent. Latino performers felt that the unions weren't doing enough to improve the situation. Among their top complaints were:

> Minority casting on theatrical productions is too low, and SAG is not releasing data about, or enforcing, the nondiscrimination clause in its contracts.

> English language commercials pay more than Spanish language commercials.

> Latino actors are being turned away when they try to audition for English language commercials.

Theatrical hiring for Latino actors remains lethargic, according to Victor Contreras, an AFTRA board member. "The vast majority of the roles that Hispanics are cast in are either as victims — poor and downtrodden and helpless — or they're the perpetrators, the criminals. Of those that are not, if it's a good Hispanic role, it has a fairly good chance of being cast white." A prime example was *The House of the Spirits* in 1993. With the exception of Antonio Banderas, most of the leads were white, among them, Meryl Streep, Jeremy Irons, and Glenn Close.

Javier Garcia Berumen's book, *The Chicano/Hispanic Image in American Film,* documents the narrow ways Hispanics are typically depicted in American movies as simpletons, ne'er-do-wells, drug dealers, bandits, and murderers. Latinos are invariably portrayed as lazy, unintelligent, over-sexed, or criminal. To remedy the situation, a number of Latino Film Festivals have sprung up in recent years to celebrate the Latino experience in all its variety, showing works that tell Latino stories never before published or seen on the big screen.

What could be more condemning of stereotyping and underrepresentation than the evidence that in the Academy's annals, only two Latino performers have won the Oscar, both in the supporting categories: Rita Moreno for *West Side Story* in 1961, and Benicio Del Toro for *Traffic* in 2000?

Moreno, the first Latina to win the Oscar, became completely identified with her feisty Puerto Rican heroine in *West Side Story.* Post-Oscar, all the offers she received were in tune with her stereotypical image as a "Latin spitfire." Moreno decided not to "get stuck" with this kind of role for the rest of her career and returned to the New York theater. After a decade of stage work, Moreno was ready to begin a second chapter in Hollywood with a more "neutral" screen image.

Del Toro, in a mostly Spanish-language role in *Traffic,* became the second Latino to win an acting Oscar and the fourth actor to win for a mostly foreign language performance.

The first and only Latino to be nominated for the Best Actor is Edward James Olmos, in 1988, for the biopicture, *Stand and Deliver,* in which he portrayed Jaime Escalante, the tough, inspirational high-school math teacher in the Los Angeles barrio. (Javier Bardem, a Spanish actor of Madrid, was nominated in 2000 for *Before Night Falls*). Among the few Latinos supporting nominees are Andy Garcia, for *The Godfather, Part III,* in 1990, and Rosie Perez, as an air-crash survivor in *Fearless* in 1993.

Asian Americans

In 1984, rather coincidentally, two Asians were nominated for the Supporting Actor Oscar: Haing S. Ngor (who won) for *The Killing Fields,* and Noriuki "Pat" Morita, as Ralph Macchio's instructor, Mr. Miyagi, in *The Karate Kid.* It took a long time for Asian American actors to be recognized by the Academy. Reflecting Hollywood's biases against Asian Americans, several white performers won the Oscar for playing Asian roles, a practice that would not be acceptable today. Luise Rainer won a second undeserved Best Actress for *The*

Good Earth, based on Pearl S. Buck's book, in which she played O-lan, the gentle wife of poor Chinese peasant Wang (Paul Muni).

In *Dragon Seed* (1944), also based on a Buck work, Katharine Hepburn was miscast as a bright, intelligent woman growing up in a Chinese village. Though not as prestigious as *The Good Earth,* the film was nominated for two Oscars: Supporting Actress to Aline MacMahon, as Hepburn's tradition-oriented mother, and cinematography to Sidney Wagner. Ironically, the few Asian actors who appeared in *Dragon Seed* played the villainous Japanese invaders. Ludicrously miscast from the leads to the secondary roles, the film also features Walter Huston, Agnes Moorehead, and J. Carrol Naish as Chinese villagers.

Naish deserves a note in this discussion. Though Irish by descent, he always played ethnic roles due to his dark skin and great capacity with accents. Naish received a supporting nomination for *A Medal for Benny* (1945), in which he played the father of a young man scorned by his villagers who becomes a war hero after his death in combat.

Naish was in "good" company. Flora Robson, one of Britain's finest actresses, received a supporting nomination for *Saratoga Trunk* (1946), a Gary Cooper vehicle, in which she was preposterously miscast as a mulatto servant.

Native Americans

Reflecting the discrimination against Native Americans in the U.S., Hollywood cast Native American roles with white actors for decades.

In one of its weakest moments, the Actors Branch nominated Jeff Chandler for playing Cochise in *Broken Arrow* (1950). Chandler was a Brooklyn Jew (née Ira Grossel), who achieved notoriety in actioners and melodramas due to his good looks and masculine appearance. As if to reward him for excellence, Chandler was cast again as Cochise in *The Battle at Apache Pass* (1952).

In this film, a typical product of the 1950s, James Stewart attempts to bring peace between the white settlers and the Apaches, led by Cochise. A blend of action and earnestness, *Broken Arrow* was one of the first popular movies to present the Indians' side of the conflict. The cast did feature some Native Americans, including Jay Silverheels, best known for playing Tonto on TV's "The Lone Ranger." But the Apache leads were played by Caucasians — Stewart's love interest, an Indian woman, was played by white actress Debra Paget. *Broken Arrow* became a cause célèbre for another, equally important reason. Its screenplay, credited to Michael Blankfort, was nominated for an Oscar, except that Blankfort served as a front to blacklisted writer Albert Maltz, one of the Hollywood Ten.

The image of the Native American in film changed with the 1970 revisionist Western, *Little Big Man.* Chief Dan George was nominated for a Supporting Oscar in this adaptation of Thomas Berger's comic-picaresque novel about the events that led up to Custer's Last Stand. It was brought to the screen during the era of protest against the Vietnam War by Arthur Penn, who put white brutality and racism at the center of the narrative. Dustin Hoffman plays Jack Crabb, an American Candide whose adventures take him back and forth between the red man's and the white man's culture. For a while, the comic tone is pleasantly askew with a gallery of amusing characters that includes Faye Dunaway as a preacher's wife, Jeff Corey as Wild Bill Hickok, and Martin Balsam as a swindler getting dismantled. Pauline Kael described Chief Dan George's Indian chief as "part patriarch, part Jewish mother." After the first hour, however, the massacres start coming, and the speeches, too. Author Berger suggested that the Indians looked like Orientals, but Crabb's Indian bride looked Vietnamese.

Two decades later, Graham Greene was one of several Native American actors to be hired by Kevin Costner for *Dances With Wolves,* in sharp departure from old Hollywood practices of using the likes of Jeff Chandler or Sal Mineo to play Native Americans. Experienced but unknown, Greene was soon in demand for television and screen roles, but he refused to be typecast. The Supporting Oscar went to Joe Pesci for *GoodFellas,* but, as a result of his nomination — and the picture's success — Greene has enjoyed a viable career, including an appearance in *Thunderheart* as a contemporary Sioux lawman.

Oscar's Distaff—Women

For decades, women's Oscar achievements outside acting were not much better than those of African American artists — or other ethnic minorities. Furthermore, in the women's case, contrary to popular notion, there was actually a backlash compared to their more visible status in Hollywood in the 1930s and 1940s, at the height of the studio system.

To begin with, in its entire history, the Academy has had only two female presidents: Bette Davis and Fay Kanin. It may have been a Freudian slip, but it's indicative that when the Oscar announcer, Hank Sims, introduced Fay to the TV viewers, he mistakenly referred to her as Mr. Fay Kanin.

In seventy-four years, only two women have received Best Director nominations. In 1993, Jane Campion became the first woman director to be nominated, for *The Piano,* since Lina Wertmuller had received the nod for *Seven Beauties,* in 1976. Several women-directed films were nominated for Best Picture, but their helmers were not. *Children of a Lesser God* was nominated in 1986, but not its director, Randa Haines. *Awakenings* was a 1990 Best Picture nominee, but helmer Penny Marshall was totally ignored. Women's track record in other branches is also far from being fair or impressive. Lyricist Dorothy Fields became the first woman to win the Best Song Oscar in 1936, for "The Way You Look Tonight" from *Swing Time,* though the song was a collaboration with Jerome Kern.

Barbra Streisand, the driving force behind *The Prince of Tides,* which grossed over $70 million, was also denied a 1991 Best Director nomination. The omission of Streisand was interpreted as a slight against women directors in general. Producer Lynda Obst (*The Fisher King*), explained: "When you're celebrating a woman behind the camera, that's a woman in power, and people are still uncomfortable with that." "Streisand's snub by the Academy may be less sexism than Barbarism," wrote *Newsweek:* "Many in Hollywood consider her self-absorbed, difficult and controlling."

Streisand did receive a nomination from the Directors Guild, which usually portends an Oscar nomination. But in 1991, John Singleton, the then-twenty-three-year-old black director of *Boyz N the Hood* fame, took Streisand's slot. To some, this act suggested the industry's political correctness at the moment, as though saying blacks, yes, women, no. Streisand, however, refused to let the Academy rain on her parade. She told the *Los Angeles Times:* "I can't honestly say that I was wronged in any way, since there are a lot of good movies in contention." At the same time, she allowed that sexism is still a problem: "It's as if a man were allowed to have passion and commitment to his work, but a woman is allowed that feeling for a man, but not her work."

A more prevalent trend is for women to produce their Oscar-nominated roles. It began with the entrepreneurial Mary Pickford, who produced *Coquette* as a vehicle for which she undeservedly won the Best Actress. Other Actresses, all in the past two decades, who produced their Oscar-nominated films, include: Jane Fonda, *The China Syndrome* (1979), Goldie Hawn, *Private Benjamin* (1980), Jessica Lange, *Country* (1985), Bette Midler, *For the Boys* (1991), and Jodie Foster, *Nell* (1994).

The late editor Margaret Booth, who had celebrated her 104th birthday in 2001, occupies a special place of honor in the Academy's annals. Booth began as a film cutter for D. W. Griffith at the age of sixteen, and went on to work on such prestigious productions as the silent *Ben-Hur,* the 1935 Oscar-winner *Mutiny on the Bounty,* and Garbo's best vehicle, *Camille.* After decades at MGM, Booth worked with producer Ray Stark on two Streisand pictures, *Funny Girl,* and *The Way We Were,* and many Neil Simon pictures. Booth received an Honorary Oscar in 1977, and retired from the business at the age of 88.

It took over half a century for a woman, Gloria S. Borders, to win the Sound Effects Oscar, for *Terminator 2: Judgment Day* in 1991 (though she did have a male collaborator, Gary Rydstrom).

In 1995, Anna Behlmer won the Sound Oscar for *Braveheart,* though, again, Behlmer was part of a male-dominated team. In the same year, Dutch director Marlen Gorris became the first and only female helmer to win the Best Foreign-Language Picture, for her feminist, multigenerational fable *Antonia's Line.*

In Editing, too, few women have won. Anne Bauchens, one of the industry's top editors who worked closely with Cecil B. DeMille, was nominated for *Cleopatra* in 1934, and won the Oscar in 1940 for *North West Mounted Police.* Other women who have won the Best Editing Oscar include Thelma Schoonmaker for *Raging Bull* in 1980 and Claire Simpson for *Platoon* in 1986.

Frances Marion, received the Writing Achievement Oscar for *The Big House* in 1929–30, and the Original Story Oscar for *The Champ* in 1931–32. More women were nominated for writing achievements in the 1930s and 1940s than in later decades. Indeed, between 1980 and 1999, of the two hundred films nominated for writing awards (both original and adapted), only 2.5 percent of the winners have been women. For solo winners, not husband-and-wife teams, it took forty years between Clemence Dane, who had won in 1947 for *Vacation from Marriage* (its British title is *Perfect Strangers*), and Ruth P. Jhabvala, who won in 1986 for *A Room With a View.* Jhabvala won a second writing Oscar for *Howards End* in 1992. Three other women have won the Writing Oscar in the past decade: Callie Khouri, *Thelma & Louise* (1991), Jane Campion, *The Piano* (1993), and Emma Thompson, *Sense and Sensibility* (1995). Thompson is the only individual, male or female, to have won competitive Oscars for acting (*Howards End*) and writing (Best Adapted Screenplay).

In 1991, Linda Woolverton became the first woman to write an animated feature for Disney, *Beauty and the Beast,* which received a Best Picture nomination and displayed a more overt "feminist" sensibility than the studio's other animated features. Ten years later, the Oscar-winning animated feature, *Shrek,* was co-directed by Vicky Jenson and Andrew Adamson. In music, Rachel Portman became the first woman to win the Oscar for composing a score (in the category of Best Original Musical or Comedy Score), for *Emma* in 1996.

Women have also been underrepresented in winning the Honorary Oscar or the Jean Hersholt Humanitarian Award. And only few Oscar-winning films were produced, or co-produced, by women such as Julia Phillips, *The Sting* in 1973, and Lili Fini Zanuck (with husband Richard Zanuck), *Driving Miss Daisy* in 1989.

8

THE OSCAR-WINNERS—
BIOPICTURES AND PROBLEM DRAMAS

Every year, hundreds of movies are eligible for Oscar nominations, but only five are chosen to compete for the top award, the Best Picture. In 2001, for example, 248 pictures were in the running to nab Oscar gold in the Best Picture category. To be eligible, films must have a running time longer than forty minutes and be displayed on 35mm film, 70mm film or a qualifying digital format in a commercial theater in Los Angeles between January 1 and December 31. In addition, the films must have played for at least seven consecutive days.

The rules sound quite simple, yet readers may still wonder what exactly made the Academy select the 2001 Best Picture nominees: *A Beautiful Mind, Gosford Park, In the Bedroom, The Lord of the Rings: The Fellowship of the Ring,* and *Moulin Rouge.* In other words, are there any discernible criteria of selection? Are there any patterns in the 432 films nominated for Best Picture between 1927 and 2001? Has the Academy displayed consistent biases in favor of — or against — particular kinds of films in its seventy-four years of operation? How important are the films' particular genre and subject matter in elevating their potential Oscar visibility?

From Real to Reel— Biopictures

The Academy has displayed a clear bias in favor of biopictures, that is, films inspired by actual events and real-life personalities. Twenty-four (32 percent) of the seventy-four Oscar-winning films are based on, or inspired by, real-life events and actual individuals. Diverse in both theme and locale, these movies have depicted showbiz personalities (*The Great Ziegfeld*), scientists (*The Story of Louis Pasteur*), writers (*The Life of Emile Zola*), historical figures (*Lawrence of Arabia, A Man for All Seasons*), Nobel-prize mathematicians (*A Beautiful Mind*), and even a heroic German industrialist (*Schindler's List*).

In 2000, four of the Best Actor nominees played a biographical role, most of some famous artist. The fourth Best Actor, Russell Crowe (who won) played the role of Maximus in the historical epic *Gladiator.*

In *Before Night Falls,* the Spanish actor Javier Bardem embodied the exiled Cuban poet and novelist Reinaldo Arenas, who smuggled his prose and himself out of Cuba to avoid imprisonment by Castro. He published several novels in New York before dying of AIDS in 1990.

Ed Harris received his first lead nomination for *Pollock* (which he also directed), in which he delves into the world of New York painter Jackson Pollock, who died in 1956 at the age of 44. In this first feature about the abstract expressionist, Harris revealed the creative process behind Pollock's masterpieces as well as the life plagued by alcoholism, insecurity, and turbulent marriage.

In *Quills,* Geoffrey Rush portrays the impious eighteenth century French novelist Marquis de Sade, his prurient madness and maverick writings, including the many years he spent in and out of prisons and asylums for sexual offense and for publishing banned novels, which melded philosophy and pornography.

We live in a time when biopictures carry a great burden in preserving a popular grasp of history, observed critic David Thomson. Audiences these days expect more realistic and more personal accounts of their heroes. In the past, the public was willing to accept on faith Charles A. Lindbergh's courage as he crossed the Atlantic (chronicled in the *The Spirit of St. Louis*), composer Glenn Miller's patriotism and good family values (*The Glenn Miller Story*), Louis Pasteur's selfless sacrifice to science. These movies were all respectable attempts at difficult subjects. But once you get past the inspirational — but uninspired — treatments, you begin to see the artifice, the blatancy of the messages, the way each scene is hermetically sealed.

The accuracy of biopictures in terms of their factual source materials is also variable, as demonstrated by the heated debate over *A Beautiful Mind,* an intensely dramatic tale of genius mathematician John Forbes Nash Jr., whose brilliance was undermined by a lifelong battle with schizophrenia. Inspired by events in the life of Nash, as described in Sylvia Nasar's book, the script details the tragedy of a scientist who makes an astonishing discovery early in life which almost — but not quite — catapults him to international acclaim. Unfortunately, Nash's white-hot climb into the intellectual stratosphere takes a drastic turn when his intuitive acumen is hampered by severe paranoia and schizophrenia.

Screenwriter Akiva Goldsman, who won the Adapted Writing Oscar, decided not to render a literal telling of Nash's life, but to delineate the "architecture of his existence." Hence, *A Beautiful Mind* was billed as a semifictional story, with Goldsman receiving a "written by" rather than "screenplay by" credit from the Writers Guild. But some of the tale's omissions are glaring and peculiar, specifically Nash's homosexual experiences, his extramarital sexual activities, his racial attitudes and anti-Semitic remarks, which real-life Nash later claimed he must have made while delirious.

A year earlier, there were fervent discussions about the distortions of *The Hurricane,* based on the black boxer Rubin "Hurricane" Carter, who was wrongly accused of murder. Some people believe that the nasty campaign against the film cost its star, Denzel Washington, the Best Actor Oscar (after winning a Golden Globe). In the same year, the indie *Boys Don't Cry,* which re-creates the life of Brandon Teena (née Teena Brandon), a girl who passed as a boy, also generated controversy, though not as fervent as that for *A Beautiful Mind* or *The Hurricane.*

Biopictures have featured more prominently in the last two decades: Five of the ten winners in the 1980s were inspired by real-life figures. In 1981, *Chariots of Fire,* the inspirational tale of two British runners, Harold Abrahams and Eric Liddell, in the 1924 Paris Olympics, won Best Picture. *Gandhi,* an earnest, noble biopicture about the venerable Indian politician, was the 1982 Oscar winner. In 1984, *Amadeus* offered an intriguing view of the musical genius Wolfgang Amadeus Mozart in eighteenth-century Vienna. Based on the life of Karen Blixen, the Danish writer who published under the name of Isak Dinesen, *Out of Africa* won Best Picture in 1985. Bertolucci's *The Last Emperor,* an expansive epic about Pu Yi, China's last Manchu emperor, was the big 1987 winner.

In the 1990s, too, *Schindler's List,* an epic film about Oskar Schindler (Liam Neeson), the Catholic war profiteer who initially flourished by collaborating with the Nazis but eventually saved more than a thousand Polish Jews, won the 1993 Best Picture. Mel Gibson's *Braveheart,* an epic tale of the thirteenth century Scottish rebel warrior William Wallace (played by Gibson), won the 1995 prize. James Cameron's bombastic and anachronistic *Titanic,* a fictionalized account of the 1912 ship disaster, swept the 1997 awards.

Biopictures have used the narrative conventions of various genres: Musicals (*Yankee Doodle Dandy*), war films (*Patton, Saving Private Ryan*), Westerns (*Butch Cassidy and the Sundance Kid*), historical epics (*Mutiny on the Bounty, Ben-Hur, Schindler's List, Braveheart*), psycho-political exposes (*Born on the Fourth of July, JFK*), action-adventures (*The French Connection, The Right Stuff*), and even horror-disaster movies (*Titanic*).

In the 1930s, the studio most associated with the production of biopictures was Warner. A biopicture cycle began with *Disraeli* (1929), starring George Arliss as the wily British statesman, and became more prominent the next decade with the release of two notable Warner movies, both starring Paul Muni. In 1936, *The Story of Louis Pasteur* recounted the life of the French chemist who discovered the anthrax vaccine which saved French cattle from the black plague. The Oscar winner of 1937 was *The Life of Emile Zola,* which dealt with the exposure of anti-Semitism in the French government. These films, as historian Lewis Jacobs suggested, were social in outlook, realistic in interpretation, and imbued with strong messages about democratic values. As such, they drew parallels between the past and the present, particularly in their condemnation of the rampant Fascism and Nazism in Europe.

The percentage of biopictures in the 1940s (23 percent of all nominees) was much higher than that in the 1950s (7 percent). The American involvement in World War II had a strong impact on Hollywood, which produced many war films inspired by actual military figures. Of these, perhaps the best-known was *Sergeant York* (1941), which celebrated the courage of the World War I hero. By contrast, the few 1950s films drawing on actual events or figures dealt with biblical (*The Ten Commandments*) and Christian heroes (*Quo Vadis?, The*

Robe). Unlike the 1940s biopictures, the next decade's historical epics didn't even attempt to be realistic or truthful to their source material.

The biopictures nominated in the 1960s either concerned showbiz personae (*Funny Girl*), or royalty intrigues and affairs (*Cleopatra, Becket, The Lion in Winter, Anne of the Thousand Days, Nicholas and Alexandra*). However, from the mid-1970s on, the range of nominated biopictures became wider. They included the perennial topic of entertainment, such as *Lenny* and *All That Jazz,* both directed by Bob Fosse, the latter drawing on his own life. But there were also movies about working-class protagonists, which in the past were neglected by mainstream American cinema. Sidney Lumet's *Dog Day Afternoon,* based on a Brooklyn bank robbery, depicted the lives of marginal people, centering on Sonny (Al Pacino), the doomed bisexual who turned to robbery to provide money for his lover's sex-change operation. *Norma Rae*'s protagonist would have been an unlikely heroine for a Hollywood film of yesteryear, but Martin Ritt made an uplifting movie, inspired by the life of a Southern hillbilly (Sally Field) who undergoes a major transformation after gaining political consciousness.

Biopictures reached an apogee in the 1980 Oscar contest, in which three of the Best Picture nominees were based to varying degrees of authenticity on real-life figures. *Coal Miner's Daughter* re-created the life of country and western singer Loretta Lynn (Sissy Spacek), from her backwoods childhood to national success. Martin Scorsese's *Raging Bull* offered an uncompromisingly tough look at the disintegrating life of the brutish and abusive middleweight champion Jake La Motta (Robert De Niro). *The Elephant Man* probed the life of John Merrick (John Hurt), the grossly deformed victim of neurofibromatosis, in the context of nineteenth century Victorian society. Nineteen-eighty was also the first year in which both lead acting awards, to De Niro and Spacek, celebrated contemporary personalities, with Jake La Motta and Loretta Lynn present as guests of honor at the ceremonies.

In 1989, *My Left Foot,* a low-budget British import about the paraplegic artist-writer Christy Brown, became a dark horse after winning the New York Film Critics Award for Best Picture and Best Actor for Daniel Day-Lewis. In 1990, Jeremy Irons won a well-deserved Best Actor for playing millionaire Claus von Bulow, accused of trying to kill his wife, in *Reversal of Fortune.* "I'd love to meet him and tell him what he's all about," Irons told the press. "But the man's had enough invasion of his privacy without my calling him."

The glamorous gangster Benjamin (Bugsy) Siegel (played by glamorous star Warren Beatty) in *Bugsy,* and the mythic politician, John F. Kennedy in Oliver Stone's *JFK,* dominated the 1991 Best Picture and acting nominations, though neither picture won the top prize; the winner was *The Silence of the Lambs.*

Year after year, biopictures have been nominated for the top award. In 1994, *Quiz Show,* Robert Redford's gracefully intelligent and engrossing story of the late-1950s' TV quiz-show scandal, was a top Oscar contender. Using the show as a metaphor for a nation newly hypnotized by television artifice, the story focuses on a hotheaded loser (John Turturro) and his successor on the game show "Twenty-One," instant hero Charles Van Doren (Ralph Fiennes), a scion of a socially prominent and intellectual family. *Quiz Show* brought the 1950s to life as no other movie has since *Diner,* directed by Barry Levinson, who had a cameo in Redford's picture.

In 1995, Ron Howard's *Apollo 13* provided an exhilarating chronicle of the ill-fated Apollo 13 mission to the moon, and how the heroic work of astronaut Jim Lovell and his crew, combined with the dogged persistence of the NASA team in Houston, averted tragedy. The 1996 Australian arthouse hit, *Shine,* recounts how the piano prodigy, David Helfgott (Oscar-winning Geoffrey Rush) was pushed to the breaking point by his domineering father (Oscar-nominated Armin Mueller-Stahl).

Of the five pictures nominated in 1998, two featured the British monarchy (*Elizabeth* and *Shakespeare in Love*), and three dealt with different aspects of World War II. *Saving Private Ryan* and *The Thin Red Line* re-created actual combats, and *Life Is Beautiful* was an Italian fable set in a concentration camp.

One of the 2000 Best Picture nominees was *Erin Brockovich,* directed by Steven Soderbergh. Though based on a true story, the film feels familiar from previous corporate-malfeasance thrillers, such as *Norma Rae* and *A Civil Action.* A lone-justice crowd-pleaser, like *Norma Rae* and *Silkwood, Erin Brockovich* pays tribute to a working-class woman who dares to fight the system because she's too stubborn or naive to know otherwise. Assigned to do some routine paperwork, Erin stumbles upon a hidden epidemic: Dozens of residents near Hinkley, California, had fallen victim to tumors, degenerative organs and other afflictions. The illnesses are caused by pollution from the Pacific Gas and Electric plant on the edge of town. They have used a deadly form of chromium as an antitrust agent, thereby contaminating the water supply.

Aside from favoring biopictures over fiction narratives, the Academy has endorsed specific genres while overlooking others. The two most dominant genres among Oscar-winning movies are the social-problem drama (about 40 percent) and the historical epic (about 20 percent). Other genres, such as comedies, musicals, war films, action-adventures, suspense-thrillers, and Westerns have been largely overlooked in the Oscar contest.

The Serious-Problem Picture

The most respected and honored genre in the Best Picture competition is the serious-problem film. About half of all nominated pictures have dealt with "important" social or political issues. This genre's strongest impact in the Oscar contest was in the 1930s and 1940s, and the weakest in the 1960s.

What distinguishes the serious-problem film is its reliance on other literary sources, such as best-selling novels and Broadway stage hits. This was particularly evident in the 1950s, when the primary source for the Hollywood problem drama was the Broadway theater. For example, three of Tennessee Williams's stage hits were nominated for Best Picture: *A Streetcar Named Desire* in 1951, *The Rose Tattoo* in 1955, and *Cat on a Hot Tin Roof* in 1958.

The impact of Broadway on Hollywood was apparent in every film genre at that time. Most film musicals in the 1950s, such as *The King and I* in 1956 originated on the New York stage. Along with stage plays, some television dramas were transferred to the big screen and received major Academy attention: *Marty* in 1955, *Twelve Angry Men* in 1957, *Judgment at Nuremberg* in 1961.

Serious-problem films are intimately linked with their broader socio-political contexts. Reflecting relevant issues, they tend to appear in cycles whose duration is three to five years. In the late 1940s, Hollywood produced a cycle of films dealing with racial prejudice and discrimination. Two of these films were nominated for Best Picture: *Crossfire* and *Gentleman's Agreement,* both in 1947. In the late 1960s and early 1970s, there was a cycle of films about the position of blacks in American society (*In the Heat of the Night* in 1967, *Sounder* in 1972). In 1979, *Kramer vs. Kramer* launched a cycle of high-profile family dramas, which included *Ordinary People, On Golden Pond,* and *Terms of Endearment.*

Social-problem films have centered on the public domain, dealing with careers and the work place, or on the political arena or focusing on racial hatred, discrimination, and violence. But many of these films are hybrids, dealing with both public and private lives, conflicts between work and family, career and marriage, and the impact of war and politics on individual behavior.

Few movies have dealt exclusively with political issues. This is characteristic of the American cinema in general, not just of the nominated pictures. Even politically committed filmmakers such as Costa-Gavras or Oliver Stone understand that in order to attract the mass public to serious "message" films, they must deal with issues in a more intimate and emotional way. Hence the two Costa-Gavras Oscar-nominated pictures, *Z* in 1969 and particularly *Missing* in 1982, are political films that convey their ideological messages through emotionally engaging personal stories. Similarly, Oliver Stone's *Platoon, Born on the Fourth of July, JFK,* and *Nixon* have approached their broad political issues through personal melodramas that often use the psychological-Freudian paradigms of intergenerational conflicts between parents and their biological or surrogate children.

The Woman's Picture

Problem pictures featuring male roles differ from those focusing on women. Most female-nominated roles are contained in what is known as "the woman's film," also labeled "the weepie." Boasting strong female protagonists, these films revolve around romantic issues that are specifically designed for mostly female audiences. The woman's film doesn't exist anymore as a pure form, but it was quite popular in the 1930s, 1940s, and 1950s, when it was appropriated by television, later in the disreputable format of TV Movie-of-the-Week.

Bette Davis distinguished herself in such melodramatic vehicles. In William Wyler's *Jezebel* (1938), a romantic melodrama of the Old South, advertised by Warner as "Half-angel, half-siren, all-woman," Davis won an Oscar for playing a Southern belle. Edmund Goulding's *Dark Victory,* from a screenplay by Casey Robinson, about a society girl who discovers she is dying of a brain tumor, was one of 1939's most popular films, earning Best Picture and Actress nominations.

Adapted from Rachel Field's book about the love of a nineteenth-century married French nobleman (Charles Boyer) for his governess (Davis), *All This and Heaven Too* (1940) was nominated for Best Picture but did not win any awards. In the same year, William Wyler's *The Letter* was a remake of the 1929 film based on Somerset Maugham's tale of an adulterous wife (Davis) who shoots her lover in a jealous rage. Marked by a distinctive visual style, courtesy of cinematographer Gaetano Gaudio, the film was nominated for Best Picture and five other awards. The role of Leslie Crosbie was played on stage by Katharine Cornell and by Jeanne Eagels in the first film version; both Eagels and Davis were nominated, though neither won. Director Wyler cast Davis again as the conniving and greedy Regina Giddens in Lillian Hellman's *The Little Foxes* (1941), which was nominated for nine awards, winning none.

None of the so-called woman's pictures has ever won the Best Picture Oscar, and after the 1940s few were even nominated. The only two Oscar-winners that approximate this genre, featuring strong women and dealing specifically with women's problems, were *Grand Hotel* and *All About Eve.*

Based on Vicki Baum's novel, adapted to the screen by William A. Drake, *Grand Hotel* was an MGM prestige production which won the 1931–32 Best Picture. *Grand Hotel* features an all-star cast, showing that MGM did indeed live up to its claim, "more stars than in heaven." There are five star performances, each exhibiting his/her particular screen persona, though the best are Greta Garbo, as the fading dancer, and John Barrymore, as the declining nobleman. Their scenes together are the strongest, and Garbo's line, "I want to be alone," became forever associated with her screen image. Also notable are Joan Crawford, as a determined secretary; Wallace Beery, as her brutish tycoon-employer; and Lionel Barrymore, as a pathetic dying man.

However, the movie is a patchwork of star performances and "big scenes." But obviously audiences didn't mind, as they turned *Grand Hotel* into the year's top-grossing movie. Seen from today's perspective, however, *Grand Hotel* serves as an example of a type of film that "Hollywood does not make anymore."

Seven other movies competed against *Grand Hotel* for Best Picture: John Ford's *Arrowsmith,* King Vidor's *The Champ, One Hour With You,* (co-directed by George Cukor and Ernst Lubitsch), Josef Von Sternberg's *Shanghai Express,* Melvyn LeRoy's newspaper drama, *Five Star Final,* and Lubitsch's charmer *The Smiling Lieutenant,* with Maurice Chevalier and Miriam Hopkins. Strangely enough, none of *Grand Hotel*'s stars or director Edmund Goulding was nominated. It is one of three Oscar-winning films to have received only one Oscar; the other two films are *The Broadway Melody* and *Mutiny on the Bounty.* Currently, the tendency is for a few films to get multiple nominations and awards, but in the 1930s and 1940s, Academy votes were spread among a larger number of pictures.

In contrast to *Grand Hotel,* the 1950 Oscar-winning *All About Eve* was the first movie to be nominated in fourteen categories (the largest number of nominations until *Titanic* equaled this in 1997). Of its six Oscars, Joseph L. Mankiewicz won two, as writer and director, and George Sanders won the Supporting Actor as an acerbic drama critic. Edith Head and Charles LeMaire won Black-and-White Costume Design, and W. D. Flick and Roger Herman won for sound. Its two leading ladies, Bette Davis and Anne Baxter, were nominated in the same category but must have canceled each other out.

All About Eve's major competitor that year was Billy Wilder's *Sunset Boulevard,* a darkly humorous probe of the movie industry. The noirish film, seen now more as a comic horror picture, contrasts old and new Hollywood through the relationship of a fading, demented silent-movie queen, played by Gloria Swanson, and a young gigolo-writer, played by William Holden. Neither film was very successful at the box office when initially released; each grossed less than $3 million. However, both have acquired cult status over the years and for the same reasons: The star performances of Davis in *All About Eve* and Swanson in *Sunset Boulevard.* Their wittily campy dialogue entered movie lore, with such lines as Davis exclaiming, "Fasten your seat belts, it's going to be a bumpy night," or Swanson's, "They don't make faces like that anymore," or "I'm still big, it's the pictures that got small."

The nominated features with strong female protagonists have usually dealt with showbiz, like *Stage Door* and *A Star Is Born,* both released in 1937. Gregory La Cava's *Stage Door,* nominated for four Oscars, focuses on a clique of would-be actresses living in a theatrical boarding house, all anxious to get their "big break." Katharine Hepburn, playing one of her many rich girls, and Ginger Rogers, have the best parts in an all-female cast that includes Eve Arden, Lucille Ball, and Ann Miller. The only actress to be nominated was Andrea Leeds for playing an ingenue who, after waiting a whole year for "the one role," commits suicide. Like *All About Eve* and *Sunset Boulevard, Stage Door* has become a cult item, with such memorable lines as Hepburn declaring: "If I can act I want the world to know it, but if I can't act, I want to know it."

Along with Bette Davis and Katharine Hepburn, Greer Garson was a third female star to appear in prestige Oscar-nominated films. Indeed, until 1950, only one Oscar-winning film featured a single female heroine, Greer Garson in *Mrs. Miniver.* Garson was MGM's most respected star and Louis B. Mayer's favorite actress for whom he chose the best vehicles. No other MGM actress has ever enjoyed as complete a support of MGM's top brass as Garson.

From 1939 to 1943, five of Garson's dramas were nominated for Best Picture. Garson was introduced to the American public in Sam Woods's *Goodbye, Mr. Chips,* as the actress who humanizes a public school teacher (Oscar-winning Robert Donat), rescuing him from feelings of failure. In Mervyn LeRoy's *Blossoms in the Dust,* based on Anita Loos's script, Garson plays child welfare crusader Edna Gladney, who proudly exclaims: "There are no illegitimate children; there are only illegitimate parents!" And in 1943, Garson re-created the life of the noted French scientist in *Madame Curie,* one of the era's more distorted and schmaltzy biopictures.

Except for the three aforementioned women, few leading female stars made films that were nominated for Best Picture. Rosalind Russell and Barbara Stanwyck received their nominations for films that for one reason or another weren't considered "Oscar stuff." Stanwyck was first nominated for her moving portrait of the self-sacrificing mother in King Vidor's *Stella Dallas* (1937), a prototype of the woman's film. Her second nomination was for playing a striptease queen in Howard Hawks's 1941 comedy, *Ball of Fire.* Neither film was Oscar-nominated.

As for Russell, she first received Academy recognition for the comedy *My Sister Eileen* (1942), then for the biopicture *Sister Kenny* (1946) as the woman who devoted her life to getting the medical profession's approval of her unorthodox method of treating infantile paralysis.

What could be more revealing — and condemning — about the status of the woman's film and the screen roles allotted to women than the weak correlation between the Best Picture and the Best Actress awards? Twenty-six (36 percent) of the seventy-five female-winning roles were contained in films that were not nominated for Best Picture, compared with thirteen (18 percent) of the male-winning roles. (Note: The number of winning roles is seventy-five and not seventy-four, due to ties in the 1931–32 Best Actor and the 1968 Best Actress.)

Movies that flaunted dynamic female roles weren't considered vigorous or "important" enough to compete for Best Picture. And conversely, films nominated for Best Picture featured few female leading roles. Feminist-themed films weren't taken as seriously by the Academy; up to the late 1970s, there was a strong correlation between the Best Picture and Best Actor but not between the Best Picture and Best Actress awards. This was particularly true during the heyday of the studio system. Mary Pickford (*Coquette*), Marie Dressler (*Min and Bill*), Helen Hayes (*The Sin of Madelon Claudet*), Katharine Hepburn (*Morning Glory*), Bette Davis (*Dangerous*), Olivia de Havilland (*To Each His Own*), Loretta Young (*The Farmer's Daughter*), all won Oscars for roles that were not contained in Oscar-nominated films. In the last decade, too, the winning roles of Kathy Bates (*Misery*), Jessica Lange (*Blue Sky*), and Hilary Swank (*Boys Don't Cry*) were in films that failed to earn the Best Picture nomination.

Message Movies: Race, Politics, and Crime

More male than female-winning roles were contained in the serious-problem film, attesting to the prestigious status of both film genre and male performances. The overwhelming majority of the Best Actors' roles were featured in message films that dealt with "important" social or political issues.

Warner's *The Life of Emile Zola* was nominated for the largest number of awards (ten) in 1937. It won three: Best Picture, Screenplay, and Supporting Actor to Joseph Schildkraut as the wrongly accused Captain Alfred Dreyfus. Had Paul Muni not won the previous year for another biopicture, *The Story of Louis Pasteur,* he would have taken home the Best Actor Oscar for portraying the French writer who exposed anti-Semitism in the French government. Reviewing *Emile Zola,* the critic Otis Fergusson suggested that "Along with *Louis Pasteur,* it ought to start a new category — the Warner crusading films, costume division."

Nine other movies competed with *The Life of Emile Zola* in 1937, including Leo McCarey's marital comedy *The Awful Truth,* with six nominations, and Gregory La Cava's *Stage Door,* with four. The other nominees were: *Captains Courageous;* William Wyler's social drama set in a New York City slum, *Dead End;* Sidney Franklin's *The Good Earth;* Frank Capra's utopian comedy *Lost Horizon;* Henry King's romantic adventure *In Old Chicago,* Henry Koster's *One Hundred Men and a Girl* starring Deanna Durbin and featuring conductor Leopold Stokowski playing himself; and *A Star Is Born. A Star Is Born* was nominated for seven Oscars but only won one: Writing (as the category was called then) for William A. Wellman (who directed) and Robert Carson.

The political crusading drama reappeared in the late 1940s, when Hollywood began to explore racial discrimination, first against Jews, then against blacks and Native Americans. The 1947 Oscar-winner was Elia Kazan's *Gentleman's Agreement,* based on Laura Z. Hobson's novel, adapted to the screen by Moss Hart. Gregory Peck plays a crusading journalist who decides to pose as a Jew so that he can experience first-hand racial prejudice. Like most serious films, *Gentleman's Agreement* also contains a romance, here between Peck and his publisher's daughter (Dorothy McGuire), who turns out to be bigoted herself. The film is preachy, particularly in the lengthy dialogue scenes between Peck and a Jewish military captain (John Garfield) who has just returned from occupied Germany. Even so, the movie was praised by most reviewers, with critic Howard Barnes finding it to be "more savagely arresting and properly resolved as a picture than it was as a book," and describing its script as "electric with honest reportage." *Gentleman's Agreement* also won Oscars for Director Kazan, and Supporting Actress Celeste Holm.

The major competitor for Kazan's agit-prop was Edward Dmytryk's similarly themed *Crossfire,* which lost in each of its five nominations. Its screenplay, by John Paxton, was based on Richard Brooks's novel *The Brick Foxhole,* though in a typically cowardly Hollywood manner, the book's homosexual protagonist was changed to a Jew. *Crossfire* is a better film than *Gentleman's Agreement* in every respect: Characterization, acting, and visual style. It was directed by Dmytryk as a tense noir thriller about an obsessive, psychopathic sergeant (Robert Ryan, who specialized in this kind of role) who beats a Jewish ex-sergeant to death. Detective Finlay (Robert Young), helped by sergeant

Keely (Robert Mitchum), sets out to trap the killer. Like *Gentleman's Agreement, Crossfire* is a message film replete with speeches against prejudice, but it boasts great supporting turns from Ryan and Gloria Grahame, as a floozy dance hall girl, both of whom were nominated.

That *Gentleman's Agreement* was voted Best Picture for ideological rather than artistic considerations is clear not only from its win over *Crossfire,* but also in its win over David Lean's masterpiece, *Great Expectations.* However, the Academy couldn't entirely ignore *Great Expectations'* exquisite technical innovations, honoring its Black-and-White Cinematography, Art Direction and Set Decoration. Yet the Academy proved once again that, ultimately, as far as winning the Oscar is concerned, a film's theme and content are far more important than its cinematic style.

None of the late 1940s films dealing with racial prejudice against African Americans or Native Americans was nominated for Best Picture. Stanley Kramer's *Home of the Brave* (1949) began this cycle, which was followed by two other films released in the same year, *Intruder in the Dust* and *Pinky.* One of the first films about racial identity among blacks, *Pinky* was singled out for its acting. All three of its female performers were nominated: Jeanne Crain, as a light-skinned black trying to pass as white, Ethel Waters, as her benign grandmother, and Ethel Barrymore, as an old Southern matriarch.

Considered at the time "courageous," because of its subject matter, *Pinky* was not the first nominated film about interracial relations. That honor went to the first version of *Imitation of Life* (1934), starring Claudette Colbert and Louise Beaver, a lone voice at the time. In 1959, *Imitation of Life* was remade by Douglas Sirk as a glossy melodrama, starring Lana Turner and Juanita Moore. Moore and Susan Kohner, who played the black mother and her dissident daughter, earned supporting nominations.

Sidney Lumet's first feature, *Twelve Angry Men,* was nominated for the 1957 Best Picture, but did not win any award. A courtroom drama, it is confined to one room where twelve jurors debate the fate of a black boy accused of murdering his father. In the course of the tumultuous trial, Henry Fonda as Mr. Davis, the liberal Juror No. 8, succeeds in reversing the majority's opinion.

In the following year, Stanley Kramer's Oscar-nominated *The Defiant Ones* was more successful, both critically and commercially. It's an intriguing tale of two escaped convicts, one black (Sidney Poitier) the other white (Tony Curtis), forced to spend their short-lived freedom together because they are chained by the wrist. *The Defiant Ones* was cited as Best Picture by the New York Film Critics Circle and won two Oscars, for Story and Screenplay (Nathan E. Douglas and Harold Jacob Smith) and for Sam Leavitt's Black-and-White Cinematography.

Otto Preminger's *Anatomy of a Murder* and Robert Mulligan's *To Kill a Mockingbird* were Best Picture nominees in 1959 and 1962 respectively. Among other things, *Anatomy* contains one of the longest — over an hour — trial scenes in film history, in which James Stewart's small-town lawyer defends a white

Army lieutenant (Ben Gazzara) accused of killing a black tavern owner for allegedly raping his wife (Lee Remick).

Universal's *To Kill a Mockingbird* featured more prominently in the Oscar race than *Anatomy,* which did not win any award. Based on Harper Lee's Pulitzer Prize-winning novel, the film featured Gregory Peck in his Oscar-winning role as a widowed liberal lawyer defending a black man against a rape accusation in a Southern town rampant with prejudice. Peck, in a perfectly suitable role, concentrated all his acting energies on the courtroom scene, the film's most powerful, in which he delivers a nine-minute close-up speech to the jury (i.e., the audience). *To Kill a Mockingbird* also won Adapted Screenplay for Horton Foote, as well as Black-and-White Art Direction and Set Decoration.

For unaccountable reasons other than a "noble" subject matter, Ralph Nelson's *Lilies of the Field* was nominated for five awards in 1963. Its only award, Best Actor, went to Sidney Poitier who played Homer Smith, a lighthearted ex-G.I. handyman who helps a group of nuns from behind the Iron Curtain to build a chapel in the Arizona desert. Poitier thus became the first black actor to win an Oscar for a lead role and the second black, following Hattie McDaniel as Supporting Actress in *Gone With the Wind,* to ever win an Oscar. It would take another twenty years for the next black performer, Louis Gossett Jr. in *An Officer and a Gentleman* (1982), to win an Oscar, albeit a supporting one.

Black players and black-themed films about racial prejudice left their most impressive mark in 1967 with the release of three films, all starring Sidney Poitier: *To Sir, With Love; Guess Who's Coming to Dinner;* and *In the Heat of the Night.* All of a sudden, black was not only beautiful but also good business at the box office. The Academy showered both *Guess Who's Coming to Dinner* and *In the Heat of the Night* with multiple nominations and awards.

A verbose and rather banal comedy, *Guess Who's Coming* centers on a liberal couple (Spencer Tracy and Katharine Hepburn), he a publisher, she an art-gallery owner, whose value system is challenged when their only daughter (Katharine Houghton) announces her intent to marry a world-renowned black surgeon (Poitier). Inexplicably nominated for ten Oscars, *Guess Who's Coming to Dinner* won two: Best Actress to Hepburn, and Screenplay and Story to William Rose. As historian Donald Bogle noted, the film was a "pure 1949 claptrap done up in 1940s high-gloss MGM style. By concentrating on nice decent people entangled in personal heartaches, the film diverted the audience from any real issue."

Norman Jewison's *In the Heat of the Night* is the only problem film about racial discrimination against blacks to have won Best Picture, though later pictures with similar issues, such as Martin Ritt's *Sounder* in 1972, and *A Soldier's Story* in 1984 (also directed by Jewison), were nominated. But in 1967, the timing seemed right to honor a topical film, and *In the Heat of the Night,* about the evolving camaraderie between an initially bigoted police chief (Rod Steiger) and an honest black homicide detective (Poitier), won five Oscars, including the Best Actor nod to Steiger.

Of the nominated films in 1967, the most exciting was Arthur Penn's *Bonnie and Clyde,* an innovative film in every sense of the word. However, its romantic attitude toward its gangster characters and the fact that Hollywood newcomer Warren Beatty served as producer and star must have worked against it. To think that the Academy honored *In the Heat of the Night* for best editing and sound over the amazing achievements in these areas in *Bonnie and Clyde* is still shocking, though it supports the theory of the Oscar sweep.

Social-Problems Movies

"Serious" winning films have dealt with such wide ranging themes as adjustment to a changing postwar society, political corruption, urban alienation, and rampant crime. Each of these Oscar-winners was representative, though not always the best, of a larger cycle of films.

The Best Years of Our Lives, 1946's most honored film, received the largest number of awards to date, seven legitimate and two Special Oscars. This social drama captured the mood of postwar America so effectively that even the harsher critics failed to see its flaws at the time. Independent producer Samuel Goldwyn, who released the film through RKO, was inspired by an August 7, 1944, article in *Time* magazine, which recounted the homecoming story of war veterans. Goldwyn commissioned MacKinlay Kantor to write a script, which was first published as a book, *Glory for Me,* then adapted to the screen by Robert Sherwood. Released in 1946, the movie was relevant and timely, as many Americans were still struggling with painful readjustment to civilian life after the war.

In his rave review, James Agee thought that *The Best Years* was "profoundly pleasing, moving and encouraging," singling out its script, which was "well differentiated, efficient, free of tricks of snap and punch and over-design," and its visual style, which was of "great force, simplicity and beauty." Agee found Wyler's direction to be "of great purity, directness and warmth, about as cleanly devoid of mannerisms, haste, superfluous motion, aesthetic or emotional overreaching." The movie was photographed by Gregg Toland in black and white, stressing long shots, deep-focus, and crisp imagery. The acting was also superb, particularly by Fredric March, who won a second Best Actor award for playing an anguished banking executive and ex-sergeant, who realizes that in his absence his family — as well as the larger society — have tremendously and irrevocably changed.

All the King's Men, a political drama about the corruptive nature of power and the danger of a populist dictatorship in America, won the 1949 Best Picture Oscar. Broderick Crawford won Best Actor as Willie Stark, a self-styled demagogue who starts as a rural self-made Louisiana lawyer and ends up building a fraudulent political empire, which leads to his assassination. Mercedes McCambridge won Supporting Actress as his tough and unscrupulous secretary-mistress. The film drew on Robert Penn Warren's 1946 Pulitzer Prize-winning and thinly disguised novel about the life of assassinated-Louisiana Senator Huey

Long. *All the King's Men* competed against four other films, each critical of some aspect of American life — two realistic analyses of men at war, *Battleground* and *Twelve O'Clock High;* a tale of a greedy courtship, *The Heiress;* and a satiric examination of bourgeois suburban life and marriage, *A Letter to Three Wives.*

James Jones's *From Here to Eternity,* about life in an Army base, was a best-seller before Fred Zinnemann decided to adapt it for the big screen. Set in Hawaii prior to the Pearl Harbor attack, it captures the essence of military life in all its complexity and detail. The main story centers on the conflict between individualism, embodied by Montgomery Clift's Private Prewitt, and rigid institutional authority, represented by the Army. Having once blinded a man in the ring, Prewitt refuses to fight for the unit's team, despite promises of rewards, and pressures from his superior. A stubborn yet decent soldier, Prewitt admires the Army but he's unwilling to compromise his notion that "if a man don't go his own way, he's nothin'," which sums up the film's message as well as a recurrent theme in all of Zinnemann's films.

Daniel Taradash's fine screenplay contains half a dozen sharply etched characterizations, including Burt Lancaster's Sergeant Warden, an efficient but human officer; Clift's Prewitt, an inner-directed soldier guided by his code of ethics; Frank Sinatra's Maggio, the cocky but honest Italian-American soldier; Deborah Kerr's Karen Holmes, the frustrated, adulterous wife married to a weakling (Philip Ober); and Donna Reed's Alma, a dance-hall hostess. Zinnemann's direction is tight and restrained, bringing to the surface the film's issues which, as Pauline Kael observed, represented new, more mature attitudes and touched a deep social nerve. *From Here to Eternity* is candid in its treatment of military life and personal frustrations, and most important of all, in its frank view of sexuality. The erotic beach scene between Lancaster and Kerr, which was daring and innovative at the time, has unfortunately been imitated and ridiculed to death.

From Here to Eternity was nominated in 1953 along with two historical features, *Julius Caesar* and *The Robe,* George Stevens's classic Western, *Shane,* and William Wyler's elegant comedy, *Roman Holiday.* Nominated in thirteen categories, *From Here to Eternity* won eight, the largest number of awards a movie has won since *Gone With the Wind.* "The industry which voted the honors now merits an appreciative nod," wrote the *New York Times*'s Bosley Crowther, having convinced his peers to honor the film, director Zinnemann and actor Lancaster with the New York Film Critic Awards.

The casting and acting by each member was perfect, due in part to the fact that Zinnemann rehearsed the entire film with props, an uncommon practice in Hollywood, which gave the actors a unique opportunity to develop their roles. All five players were nominated. Burt Lancaster and Montgomery Clift cancelled each other out as Best Actors (the winner was William Holden in *Stalag 17*); Kerr was nominated for Best Actress, but lost to Audrey Hepburn. It was the film's secondary players, Frank Sinatra and Donna Reed, who went home with Oscars.

Political corruption, this time in the context of labor unions, was the topic of Elia Kazan's *On the Waterfront,* the 1954 Oscar winner. The film works both as an exposé of union racketeering and as a thriller about the murder of an innocent longshoreman. Filmed on location, *On the Waterfront* was photographed in black-and-white, almost documentary style (Boris Kaufman won an Oscar), which suited its realistic subject matter and commonplace characters. Marlon Brando won the Best Actor for one of his most touching and memorable performances as Terry Malloy, an ex-prizefighter who transforms himself, with the assistance of his girl (Eva Marie Saint) and the neighborhood priest (Karl Malden), from a passive dock worker into a crusader against trade-union tyranny.

On the Waterfront brought Oscars to Director Kazan, Supporting Actress Saint, Story and Screenplay to Budd Schulberg, Art Direction, and Editing. The only categories in which the movie lost were Score (Leonard Bernstein) and Supporting Actor, probably because three actors from the film were nominated in the same category. Rod Steiger was nominated for playing Brando's brother, an opportunistic lawyer working for the arrogant racketeer-boss, played by Lee J. Cobb, who was also nominated. Karl Malden, who had previously won the Supporting Oscar for *A Streetcar Named Desire,* received a nomination for playing the militant yet sympathetic Father Barry.

Much has been written about Kazan as a friendly witness testifying before the HUAC, in which he repudiated his leftist past and named names. The movie itself has been interpreted as a "McCarthy film," one that favors informing, though the analogy between informing on Communists and informing on corrupt crooks is problematic. But *On the Waterfront* is a powerful and enjoyable film even without this ideological reading. And the picture would have won Oscars regardless of its politics considering the weak Best Picture competition of 1954. The other contenders were a courtroom drama based on Herman Wouk's novel, *The Caine Mutiny,* which starred Humphrey Bogart; Clifford Odets's stiff backstage melodrama *The Country Girl,* with Bing Crosby, Grace Kelly, and William Holden; MGM's musical *Seven Brides for Seven Brothers,* starring Jane Powell and Howard Keel; and the romantic comedy *Three Coins in the Fountain,* which did more for the encouragement of American tourism to Rome than for the advancement of film art.

The urban crime drama, which had been popular during the Depression, re-emerged in the late 1960s, as a result of changes in the urban landscape. *Midnight Cowboy,* John Schlesinger's 1969 Oscar-winner, is a touching yet disturbing tale of the strange friendship that evolves between the handsome Joe Buck (Jon Voight); an uneducated and naive Texan who under the influence of radio and television commercials fancies himself a stud, and Ratso Rizzo (Dustin Hoffman), a sickly and crippled drifter. The film captured the ambience of night life in Times Square and its alienated, lonely creatures, but it also perpetuated the myth of New York as a sleazy, dehumanized, impersonal city. Voight and Hoffman are superb — both were nominated for Best Actor. And

Waldo Salt's Oscar-winning screenplay, based on James Leo Herlihy's novel, is witty and sharp. *Midnight Cowboy* surprised audiences with its daring dialogue and blunt view of sex. It is the only X-rated film to ever win Best Picture, though by today's standards, the film is rather tame.

The phenomenal success of *Bonnie and Clyde* (1967) revived interest in the crime-gangster film. More crime films were nominated in the 1970s than in any other decade, and three won Best Picture: The action-thriller *The French Connection* in 1971, and the Francis Ford Coppola crime sagas, *The Godfather* in 1972 and *The Godfather, Part II,* in 1974. Of the two, *The Godfather, Part II,* was more critically acclaimed and more honored by the Academy, but the first was more popular, grossing over $80 million.

Less honored by the Academy than its sequel, *The Godfather* won two Oscars: A second Best Actor for Marlon Brando as Mafia boss Don Vito Corleone, and Adapted Screenplay for Coppola and Mario Puzo, upon whose best-seller the film was based. Its major competitor in 1972 was Bob Fosse's musical *Cabaret,* which swept eight awards, including Best Director. *The Godfather, Part II,* which won six awards in 1974, is the only sequel to have received the Best Picture Oscar. Breaking new grounds thematically and artistically, the two *Godfather* sagas are still the only crime-gangster movies to have won Best Picture.

Despite eager anticipation and public pressures, it took sixteen years for Coppola to make *The Godfather, Part III* (1990), which garnered seven nominations including Best Picture. Again teamed with Puzo, Coppola extended his history-making Mafia saga into an absorbing tale of an older and disillusioned Michael (Al Pacino) attempting to remove himself from the world of crime, and how fate and circumstances draw him back in, with his trigger-happy nephew (Andy Garcia) and the rest of the family in tow. Long (191 minutes) but masterfully told, the film had one nearly fatal flaw, the casting of Coppola's daughter, Sofia, in the pivotal role of Michael's daughter and Garcia's love interest.

In the same year, Martin Scorsese made one of his best films, *GoodFellas,* which swept all the critics awards, but lost the Oscar to *Dances With Wolves.* Joe Pesci won the Supporting Oscar for playing the year's "worst human being in the movies," Tommy DeVito, a Mafia killer who gleefully enjoys his pasta while a dying victim is locked in his car trunk. As written by Scorsese and Nicholas Pileggi, based on the latter's book *Wiseguy, GoodFellas* provides a fascinating look at the allure — and dark reality — of "routine" life in a Brooklyn Mafia family. The story is based on the experiences of Henry Hill (Ray Liotta) who wound up in the Federal Witness Protection Program. The film's violence was almost unnecessarily harsh — and inevitably divisive — but *GoodFellas* was brilliantly realized by Scorsese and cinematographer Michael Ballhaus. Pesci and Oscar-nominated Lorraine Bracco stood out in an exceptional cast that also included Robert De Niro.

As accomplished as they were, *The Godfather, Part III* and *GoodFellas* didn't break new ground thematically or artistically. And neither did *Casino,* a

1995 crime picture that reunited director Scorsese with De Niro, his quintessential actor, and co-screenwriter Nicholas Pileggi. An honest if cold and remote look at crime as a sordid business, *Casino* is a tale of greed and betrayal that explores the glittering, decadent world of Las Vegas in the 1970s. Scorsese felt that if a suave, Waspish actor like Warren Beatty (in *Bugsy*) can play a Jewish gangster, why can't De Niro, here cast as Sam "Ace" Rothstein, a gambler overcome by his personal ambitions and caught in a power struggle that transforms the legendary gaming capital? His romance with Ginger (Sharon Stone), an alluring young woman, soon begins to threaten his friendship with partner Nicky Santoro. The outstanding production, which outstrips the dramatic and human interest of the material, benefited from the work of Oscar-winning cinematographer Robert Richardson (*JFK*), Oscar-winning editor Thelma Schoonmaker (*Raging Bull*), and Oscar-nominated production designer Dante Ferretti (*The Age of Innocence*).

It would take another decade for an innovative urban crime film to take American cinema by storm, and it would be done by indie prodigy Steven Soderbergh. In *The New Yorker,* David Denby declared *Traffic* "the most exciting and complexly imagined American movie of the year," one "full of mysteries, double meanings, and sly, mocking falsehoods," with a mood that's "rushed, dazed, fraught with suspicion." Inspired by "Traffik," the British TV series, the American *Traffic* offers a vivid and wide-spanning view of the drug war — high and low, dealer and user, Mexican and American, whose encounters are imbued with ambiguity.

Director Soderbergh treats his epic-scope movie with a dazzling style and panoramic excitement. The brilliant cast includes Michael Douglas as the new U.S. drug czar and Benicio Del Toro as a Tijuana cop. The thematic link between Coppola's crime movies and *Traffic* is provided by the character played by Catherine Zeta-Jones. For critic Owen Gleiberman, Zeta-Jones created in this film "what may be the most lived-in portrayal of ruthless familial loyalty since Al Pacino in *The Godfather.*" Watching *Traffic,* American viewers were confronted with the "dirty capitalistic secret of the drug war: That when drugs are wired into a society's central nervous system, that society will behave, collectively, in as clawing and amoral a fashion as any addict."

Message Movies: Individual and the Family

Oscar-winning issue-oriented movies have also dealt with social-psychological problems such as alcoholism, physical deformity, mental anguish, deviance and insanity.

Billy Wilder's *The Lost Weekend,* which won the 1945 Oscar, was the first major Hollywood film to deal with alcoholism; before this film, screen alcoholics were either comic or secondary characters, never heroes or central figures. *The Lost Weekend* depicts the degradation and torment of Don Birnbaum (Ray Milland) who, unable to realize his writing ambitions, quickly turns to the bottle. Wilder painted a stark portrayal of alcoholism in all its misery and horror, but the changes made in adapting Charles Jackson's novel to the screen shed light on Hollywood's "morality" standards and screen hero conventions of the time. In the book, Birnbaum's frustrations derive from an indecisive sexuality (he's a confused and troubled bisexual, whereas in the film his frustrations derive from a creative block). The movie also changed the book's ending by providing a more hopeful resolution to Birnbaum's drinking problem, using the ploy of a patiently loving girl (played by Jane Wyman) who helps to rehabilitate him.

The Lost Weekend won the New York Film Critics Award, then under the leadership of Bosley Crowther, who found its most commendable distinction to be "a straight objective report, unvarnished with editorial comment or temperance morality" commendable. *The Lost Weekend* won the Best Picture over Hitchcock's *Spellbound* and Leo McCarey's *The Bells of St. Mary's,* both starring Ingrid Bergman. Surprisingly, Wilder's exposé also appealed to large numbers of moviegoers, ranking as the year's ninth most popular film.

Suffering and victimization have been almost exclusively women's domain in the American cinema, as evident in the Oscar-winning performances of Jane Wyman's deaf-mute girl in *Johnny Belinda,* Joanne Woodward's schizophrenic Eve in *The Three Faces of Eve,* and Patty Duke's blind-deaf Helen Keller in *The Miracle Worker.* It was the success of *The Lost Weekend* that opened the door to pictures about mental illness. Anatole Litvak's *The Snake Pit,* nominated for the 1948 Oscar, was based on Mary Jane Ward's partly autobiographic novel (screenplay by Millen Brand) about the harrowing experiences of a mentally ill woman (Olivia de Havilland) sent to an asylum. Considered at the time to be a breakthrough picture in its more realistic treatment of insanity, the film was honored with six nominations.

Hollywood has usually been careful in its treatment of mental problems on-screen for fear of alienating its movie patrons. However, *One Flew Over the Cuckoo's Nest,* the 1975 Oscar winner, was so popular that it even shocked its producers, Saul Zaentz and Michael Douglas. Ken Kesey's 1962 novel, which was first adapted to the stage, was well-received, but it was Jack Nicholson's flamboyant performance as Randle Patrick McMurphy, a free-spirited, anti-establishment hero, which made the difference. The film's conflict between individualistic, nonconformist behavior (Nicholson's) and the repressive established society, represented by Nurse Ratched (Louise Fletcher), the head of the mental ward, was embraced by younger audiences as timely, relevant, and entertaining in the immediate post-Vietnam era.

The *New York Times* critic Vincent Canby singled out the film's comic scenes, which he thought were the best, and the fact that director Milos Forman didn't patronize the patients as freaks but presented them as variations of "ourselves," as ordinary human beings. *One Flew Over the Cuckoo's Nest* won all five major Oscars and with box-office grosses of over $50 million became the most widely seen problem film, ranking second only to Spielberg's action thriller *Jaws* among the year's blockbusters.

★   ★   ★

The family is one of the most sacred and revered institutions in American society, but family dramas, like other serious pictures, have appeared in cycles. *Cavalcade,* the Oscar winner of 1932–33, was Fox's most prestigious production to date. Based on Noel Coward's play, adapted to the screen by Reginald Berkeley, it chronicles an upper-class British family. Spanning thirty years, the story begins on New Year's Eve 1899 and continues through the Boer War, the sinking of the *Titanic,* World War I, and the Depression.

Diana Wynyard gave a wonderful (nominated) performance as the strong mother who loses both of her sons in tragic circumstances. Receiving the largest number of Oscars at the time (three), *Cavalcade* won Best Picture in a tight competition with nine other pictures including *A Farewell to Arms, 42nd Street, I Am a Fugitive from a Chain Gang, Lady for a Day, Little Women, The Private Life of King Henry VIII, She Done Him Wrong* (the only Mae West picture ever to be nominated), *Smilin' Through,* and *State Fair.*

Like *Cavalcade,* John Ford's 1941 Oscar-winning family drama, *How Green Was My Valley,* was a hit at the box office even before earning Oscar nominations. Unlike the upper-class *Cavalcade,* however, it celebrates what Bosley Crowther described as "the majesty of plain people," and "the beauty which shines in the souls of simple honest folk." The film reaffirmed Ford's populist ideology, propagated the year before in another Oscar-nominated family saga, *The Grapes of Wrath.* However, *How Green Was My Valley* was not associated with the angry leftist politics of John Steinbeck's book. The story of a Welsh mining family narrated by its youngest son, it is one of Ford's most genuinely touching, if also sentimental, pictures. Andrew Sarris has described *How Green Was My Valley* as an elegiac poem with a portrait of a mining community's disintegration that is of epic, heroic dimensions.

How Green Was My Valley won five Oscars, honoring Ford's Direction, Arthur Miller's Cinematography, and Art Direction. Donald Crisp won the Supporting Oscar for his role as a stern father who's killed in the mine. Sara Allgood was nominated for playing a gentle mother, but did not win. It is significant that *How Green Was My Valley* was selected while the United States was at war. Its warm, sympathetic depiction of family unity struck deep chords in the country's collective consciousness, which may explain why its two major competitors, Orson Welles's *Citizen Kane* and William Wyler's *The Little Foxes,* each with nine nominations, lost. *Citizen Kane* and particularly *Little Foxes* were dark and somber visions of the American family. Once again, ideological considerations prevailed, though in Ford's defense, *How Green Was My Valley* is as visually distinguished as it is thematically acceptable.

If Ford's *How Green Was My Valley* is among of the most stunning celebrations of ordinary life, *Marty,* the next winning film about "ordinary little people," is possibly the most pedestrian, both intellectually and artistically. *Marty* tells the love story of a lonely bachelor-butcher (Ernest Borgnine) from the Bronx, and Clara (Betsy Blair) a shy teacher he meets in a dance hall.

Shot in the Bronx, its ethnic-American locale was captured with painstaking attention to detail, but the script patronizes its "little" protagonists, an attitude demonstrated in a scene in which Marty tells Clara, "You're not really as much of a dog as you think you are."

The competition in 1955 was one of the weakest in the Oscars' history. Three of the nominees were screen adaptations of Broadway stage hits — *Mister Roberts, Picnic,* and *The Rose Tattoo; Marty* was based on Paddy Chayefsky's television play. The fifth nominee was the tedious romantic melodrama, *Love Is a Many Splendored Thing.* In this case, movie politics might provide a clue as to why *Marty* was favored. *Marty* was the first American picture to win the Palm d'Or at the Cannes Film Festival, a fact that couldn't be ignored by the Academy or the critics — the film also won the New York Film Critics Award. Nominated for eight awards, *Marty* won four: Picture, Director (Delbert Mann), Screenplay (Chayefsky), and Actor (Borgnine). But the Oscar was not much help at the box office; *Marty* is still one of the least commercially successful Oscar-winning movies.

Two decades later, in 1976, an unemployed actor named Sylvester Stallone took some of *Marty*'s ideas, mixed them with conventions of the sports-prizefighting genre (*The Champ, Golden Boy, Champion,* and *Somebody Up There Likes Me*), and came up with a winning formulaic saga which he titled *Rocky.* This movie proved the impossible by becoming the first sports film to win Best Picture; *Chariots of Fire* was the second.

Each of the other 1976 contenders was more interesting than *Rocky.* Flawed but well-shot, *Bound for Glory* was the biopicture about the folk singer and labor organizer Woody Guthrie. Alan Pakula's *All the President's Men,* produced by Robert Redford, was an effective political thriller about the Watergate scandal, based on the best-seller by *Washington Post* reporters Carl Bernstein (Dustin Hoffman) and Bob Woodward (Robert Redford). Sidney Lumet made an outrageous satire, *Network,* about the power of television that, oddly, some critics perceived as a drama. Martin Scorsese followed up his breakthrough film *Mean Streets* with *Taxi Driver,* a disturbing anatomy of alienation, embodied by Robert De Niro in a forceful performance.

Of the five, *Rocky*'s message was the most upbeat. The rise to stardom of an obscure "nobody" paralleled both Stallone's life and the 1976 election of President Jimmy Carter, who also came out of nowhere. When the film premiered, it was cheered by Academy leaders and Oscar winners like Frank Capra. *Rocky* was also the most befitting of the nation's mood in the midst of its Bicentennial celebration.

The impact of *Rocky*'s success was profound. The film made Stallone a star — the most dominant male image of the 1980s, surpassing the powerful persona of Clint Eastwood in his Dirty Harry films, and led to four sequels. *Rocky* was not a family drama, but the romance between Rocky and Adrian (Talia Shire), a plain shy salesclerk whom he later marries, which parallels that of Marty and Clara in *Marty. Rocky* also paved the way for the production of other conventional, old-fashioned movies about ordinary folks. Having been saturated for a decade with action-adventure "disaster" movies, the American public seemed to crave simpler and more humanistic fare — something for the heart.

Moviegoers must have noticed that the family had almost disappeared from American films for most of the 1970s. Moreover, the last major pictures to have dealt with marriage or the family offered mostly negative portraits, such as Mike Nichols's back-to-back nominated films *Who's Afraid of Virginia Woolf?* and *The Graduate.*

The reentrance of family dramas into mainstream Hollywood was gradual, with such romantic melodramas as Herbert Ross' *The Turning Point* and Paul Mazursky's comedy, *An Unmarried Woman.* But it was Robert Benton's *Kramer vs. Kramer,* the 1979 Oscar-winner, which gave legitimacy and definition to a new cycle of family pictures. During this cycle, which lasted about four years, two family films won Best Picture, *Ordinary People* and *Terms of Endearment,* and five others were nominated: *Breaking Away, Coal Miner's Daughter, On Golden Pond, Tender Mercies,* and *Places in the Heart.*

Like other pivotal pictures that launch cycles, no one associated with *Kramer vs. Kramer* initially expected such extraordinary success. The film's carefully designed ad campaign, using different posters for different target audiences, proved this. Nonetheless, based on Avery Corman's novel, it was a timely movie that described the confusion of women who wished to establish firm identities independently of their roles as wives or mothers. Evocatively shot on location in Manhattan, *Kramer* vaunted a great cast, headed by Dustin Hoffman and Meryl Streep as the splitting couple, Justin Henry as their son, and Jane Alexander as their sympathetic neighbor. All four were nominated for their work, with Hoffman and Streep winning. The 1979 writing awards were divided between *Kramer vs. Kramer,* which won Adapted Screenplay, and *Breaking Away,* Peter Yates's comedy set in working-class Bloomington, for which Steve Tesitch won Original Screenplay.

In 1980, a year after *Kramer vs. Kramer*'s release, Robert Redford made a stunning directorial debut in *Ordinary People,* adapted to the screen by Alvin Sargent from Judith Guest's highly regarded novel. Emotional but decidedly unsentimental, *Ordinary People* concerned the disintegration of an upper-middle class suburban family. Following the accidental death of one son and a suicide attempt of another, this family is unable to communicate its feelings or deal with its strains.

Redford's direction was restrained, and the film was supported by an excellent cast, including Donald Sutherland as the sympathetic father, Mary Tyler Moore as the undemonstrative mother, Timothy Hutton (who won the Supporting Actor) as the surviving troubled brother, and Judd Hirsch as the sympathetic Jewish psychiatrist. Amazingly, *Ordinary People* was a low-budget film — it cost only $6 million — but its domestic grosses, greatly assisted by the Oscar, surpassed $20 million. By contrast, *Kramer vs. Kramer* would have become a box-office bonanza even without winning any Oscars.

At first sight, Dustin Hoffman's first Best Actor, for *Kramer vs. Kramer,* and his second, for *Rain Man,* have nothing in common but high-caliber acting.

However, thematically, both films celebrate the sanctity of the America family. The success of the 1988 Oscar-winning *Rain Man* could be attributed, among other things, to its ideological message, in this case, the rediscovery of sibling love between an autistic savant (Hoffman) and his hustler brother (Tom Cruise). Initially, the younger brother, a fast-talking car salesman, kidnaps the elder from an asylum, intending to rob him of their father's inheritance. But gradually, he gets to know a brother whose existence he had been completely ignorant of, and both realize not only their love, but also their need for each other. Blending motifs of the comedy-drama and road picture genres, *Rain Man* propagated mainstream family values: The predominance of blood ties against all odds and the importance of protecting the nuclear family. The public embraced the film, even before it was nominated for eight awards, winning four: Picture, Actor (Hoffman), Director (Barry Levinson), and Original Screenplay (Ronald Bass and Barry Morrow).

With nine nominations, *Driving Miss Daisy* had the distinction of being 1989's most nominated film. It then went on to win Best Picture and three other Oscars: Best Actress to Jessica Tandy, Adapted Screenplay to Alfred Uhry, and Makeup. *Driving Miss Daisy* competed against Oliver Stone's *Born on the Fourth of July,* Peter Weir's *Dead Poets Society,* Phil Alden Robinson's *Field of Dreams,* and Jim Sheridan's *My Left Foot.*

A virtuous, PG-13 movie, boasting values of decency and humanity, *Driving Miss Daisy* stood out by not featuring any sex or violence. As producer Richard Zanuck later said: "Anything that tugs at your heart and emotions has a good chance for Best Picture." *Driving Miss Daisy* had the cachet of being based on a Pulitzer Prize-winning play by Alfred Uhry. Its low budget (only $7.5 million) and noble but no-name cast must have commanded the Academy's attention. Genteel, theatrical, and sporadically entertaining, it tells the story of a simple black man (Oscar-nominated Morgan Freeman) who's hired as a chauffeur for a cantankerous old Southern matriarch (Jessica Tandy) and how he winds up being her loyal companion. Directed by Bruce Beresford in a smooth, understated style, the film was elevated by the lead performances, as well as a likable Oscar-nominated turn from Dan Aykroyd in an unusual "straight" role as Daisy's son.

The family featured prominently in a number of films over the past decade. Barbra Streisand's *The Prince of Tides* (1991), *Forrest Gump* (1994), *Secret & Lies* and *Shine* (both in 1996), *As Good As It Gets* (1997), *Life Is Beautiful* (1998), and *In the Bedroom* (2001) all had strong family plots or subplots, though, with a few exceptions, they were at once more and less than family movies per se.

The 1999 Oscar-winner *American Beauty* could be described as a dark comedy about the American family and the American way of life. Offering a startlingly incisive view of suburban angst, it was superbly directed by Sam Mendes, with dynamic performances from its entire ensemble, particularly Kevin Spacey in a brilliant Oscar-winning turn. The low-budget ($15 million) movie was a triumph for DreamWorks, which was disappointed the year before, when Spielberg's prestigious *Saving Private Ryan* was reduced to also-ran status as it lost the Best Picture to Miramax's more aggressively marketed comedy, *Shakespeare in Love. Entertainment Weekly's* Mark Harris depicted *American Beauty* as "a film that has more laughs than any other in the Best Picture category and is indisputably the grimmest as well." Among other qualities, the film defines its title subject by a plastic garbage bag tossed in the wind, mesmerizingly capturing the loveliness of a fleeting moment.

It was the fourth time in the past five years that the Best Picture was based on an original script — good news for the speculation script market. First-time scripter Alan Ball, who earlier won a Golden Globe and the Writers Guild prize, mines familiar suburban turf for profound pathos, vibrant characters, and one-liners. Released a year after *Happiness,* Todd Solondz's audacious expose of a dysfunctional family, and two years after Ang Lee's *The Ice Storm, American Beauty* seemed facile in its satirical elements. Even so, Ball took the concerns of a specific social class and turned them into a redemptive sermon on humanity, exploring the "comforts" of living in an economic boom and the continuing struggle to discover the true meaning of life.

American Beauty was compared to *The Graduate,* made thirty-two years earlier, by *San Jose Mercury News* critic Julie Hinds. It is as if Kevin Spacey were playing Benjamin Braddock (the Dustin Hoffman character), now stuck in an unhappy marriage, ready to quit his job at a plastics manufacturer. For Hinds, the movie was a time capsule and a work of art; it depicted what it is like to be alive at a specific time in America and the tendency to ignore the beauty of what's around you and instead dream of things you can't have.

Though British, Mendes shows an instinctive understanding for uniquely American character, tone, and dialogue. The entire cast is impressive, from Thora Birch as Spacey's sullen daughter, to Wes Bentley as the mysterious neighbor with hidden depths of wisdom, to Mena Suvari as Spacey's love interest, a girl who is not as precocious as she acts. In a year with a multitude of lengthy films, such as *Magnolia* and *The Green Mile, American Beauty* was just two hours long (122 minutes to be exact). Dealing with the here and now, *American Beauty* also had the distinction of being contemporary. In the last twenty years, only five contemporary movies have won Best Picture, the other four being *Ordinary People, Terms of Endearment, Rain Man,* and *The Silence of the Lambs.*

Sweeping 2001's most important Oscars, including Best Picture, Director, and Screenplay, *A Beautiful Mind* represents a borderline case, both in its time frame (the story begins in 1947 and ends five decades later), and in its genre: A biopic with strong emphasis on the redemptive power of love and the value of a durable marriage that survives against all odds.

The best moments are its domestic ones, which chronicle Nash's struggle to find his own "normalcy"; and with the help and renunciation of his loyal wife, combat a disease thought to be incurable and degenerative. Through sheer will power, motivated by the intoxicating demands of mathematical theory,

Nash continued his work, and in 1994 received the Nobel Prize that had earlier eluded him. By that time, Nash's insightful game theory has become one of the twentieth century's most influential ideas. His celebrity status and triumphant battle have turned him into a legendary man who continues to pursue his work today.

Supporting Actress winner, Jennifer Connelly, as Nash's loyal wife, offers the toughest presence and most exciting element in a movie that otherwise suffers from an overdose of sentimentality. As Alicia, Connelly conveys a passionate woman who never loses the glimpse of the charismatic man with whom she had fallen in love. Pure love fuels her sacrificial dedication to Nash, serving as his companion in what must have been a much more turbulent journey than the film and its title convey.

9

THE OSCAR-WINNERS—THE MASCULINE GENRES: HISTORICAL EPICS, WAR FILMS, AND WESTERNS

Historical epics have featured most prominently in the Oscar competition. No fewer than seventeen (23 percent) of the seventy-four Oscar winners have been epics:

> *Mutiny on the Bounty* (1935)
>
> *Gone With the Wind* (1939)
>
> *Hamlet* (1948)
>
> *Ben-Hur* (1959)
>
> *Lawrence of Arabia* (1962)
>
> *Man for All Seasons* (1966)
>
> *Gandhi* (1982)
>
> *Out of Africa* (1985)
>
> *The Last Emperor* (1987)
>
> *Dances With Wolves* (1990)
>
> *Schindler's List* (1993)
>
> *Forrest Gump* (1994)
>
> *Braveheart* (1995)
>
> *The English Patient* (1996)
>
> *Titanic* (1997)
>
> *Shakespeare in Love* (1998)
>
> *Gladiator* (2000)

Whereas not many epics are produced, those that do get made receive special attention from the Academy and stand a good chance to be nominated and win.

As a genre, the historical epic has to do as much with scope and intent as with locale and production values. Widely diverse in subject, historical epics are big-budgeted, large-scaled, sumptuously mounted productions with strong technical credits. The epic treatment has been given to Westerns (*Cimarron, Dances With Wolves*), war movies (*Saving Private Ryan, The Thin Red Line*), period romances (*Gone With the Wind, Out of Africa*), political dramas (*Gandhi*), disaster movies (*Titanic*), fantasy-adventures (*The Lord of the Rings: The Fellowship of the Ring*) and even comedies (*Tom Jones, Shakespeare in Love*).

Directed by Frank Lloyd, *Mutiny on the Bounty* relates the dramatic story of the famous 1787 mutiny aboard the British ship *HMS Bounty*. It features three great performances: Charles Laughton, as the ruthless and sadistic Captain Bligh; Clark Gable, as the dashingly romantic Christian Fletcher; and Franchot Tone, as the decent officer Byam. *Mutiny on the Bounty* is still the only film to have garnered Best Actor nominations for all three of its stars, though none won. The film was Gable's favorite work because, as he once said, "it was something you could get your teeth into, for it was history, the struggle of real he-men, with a refreshing absence of the usual load of love-interest." Acclaimed by critics, the movie enjoyed popularity with audiences too, but it won only one Oscar: Best Picture. The Director and Actor awards went that year to John Ford and Victor McLaglen for *The Informer.*

Mutiny on the Bounty has withstood the test of time, and it is vastly superior to its two remakes. MGM's 1962 version, which was also nominated for Best Picture, stars Trevor Howard in the Laughton role and Marlon Brando in the Gable role. The second remake, *The Bounty,* produced by Dino De Laurentiis in 1984 and starring Anthony Hopkins as Captain Bligh and Mel Gibson as Christian Fletcher, may be more accurate than its predecessors, but it's also dry, lacking the excitement and epic scale of the 1935 version.

Cecil B. DeMille, Hollywood's greatest showman, was represented in the Oscar contest with two expensive and expansive epics: *Cleopatra* (1934), starring Claudette Colbert, and *The Ten Commandments* (1956), with an all-star cast headed by Charlton Heston. *Cleopatra,* which won the Best Cinematography, is far more entertaining than the remake, directed by Joseph L. Mankiewicz and starring Elizabeth Taylor, which was a Best Picture contender in 1963.

Nominated for multiple awards, *The Ten Commandments* won only for Special Effects, best remembered for the parting of the Red Sea sequence. DeMille's next-to-last movie turned out to be one of the all-time top-grossers, often shown on television during the holidays. A new generation of viewers inevitably perceive the film as a prime example of Hollywood Kitsch.

Historical epics were also the specialty of David Lean. Two of his epics won the Best Picture: *The Bridge on the River Kwai* (1957) and *Lawrence of Arabia* (1962). A master filmmaker, Lean made large-scale epic-adventures that were also populated by intriguing characters. *Lawrence of Arabia* represents grand filmmaking, both visually and narratively, at its very best. The complex persona of T. E. Lawrence, the British officer who organized Arab tribes in an effort to drive the Turks out of their lands, remains an enigma in the film, but the portrayal by Peter O'Toole, then a newcomer, is stunning. Produced by Sam Spiegel, *Lawrence of Arabia* won seven Oscars: Director, Cinematography, Art Direction, Editing, Sound Recording, and Original Music Score.

Lean was represented in the Oscar contest with two other historical epics. *Doctor Zhivago* (1964), based on Boris Pasternak's novel, won five Oscars, including Adapted Screenplay to Robert Bolt, Cinematography to the veteran lenser Freddie Young, and Original Music Score to Maurice Jarre.

A Passage to India (1984), adapted to the screen from E. M. Forster's book, also received multiple nominations, but won only two: Supporting Actress to Peggy Ashcroft and Original Score to Jarre. All three of Jarre's Oscars were, in fact, for scoring Lean pictures. *A Passage to India* became the last picture of maestro David Lean, who died in 1991, the same year that Peggy Ashcroft passed away.

The 1959 winner, *Ben-Hur,* boasted a number of records, including being the most expensive film of its time, with a budget of $15 million, one-fifth of which was allocated for a massive ad campaign. Producer Sam Zimbalist constructed three thousand sets in Rome, for which he employed more than fifty thousand people. *Ben-Hur* was the first remake to ever win Best Picture, and it won the largest number of awards to date: Eleven out of its twelve nominations. The only category in which *Ben-Hur* lost was Adapted Screenplay, credited to Karl Tunberg, though at least four other writers worked on the text (Maxwell Anderson, S. N. Behrman, Christopher Frye, and Gore Vidal), which might have been the reason it lost. The winner was Neil Paterson for *Room at the Top.*

Inspired by Lew Wallace's popular novel about the rise of Christianity, *Ben-Hur* features spectacular visual effects, and a stunning chariot race choreographed by Yakima Canutt. Its acting, by contrast, is not spectacular, and Charlton Heston, who was cast after Universal refused to loan out Rock Hudson, is just decent. In the title role, Heston plays a converted Christian in conflict with Massalla (Stephen Boyd), the Roman commander and his former childhood friend. The shortcomings didn't matter; the film was endowed with a visual sweep and enough pageantry to entertain audiences for a running time of 217 minutes. Overcoming MGM's fears, *Ben-Hur* was such an instant hit that its grosses were reported week after week in the trades in an effort to label the movie as "a must-see" event, which it became. Good reviews and positive word of mouth resulted in worldwide grosses of over $80 million. The only historical spectacle in the 1959 contest, *Ben-Hur* was up against smaller, more intimate movies, such as Otto Preminger's *Anatomy of a Murder,* George Stevens's *The Diary of Anne Frank,* Fred Zinnemann's *The Nun's Story,* and Jack Clayton's *Room at the Top.*

Like other genres, historical epics have been more prominent in some decades than others. The strongest representation of epics was in the 1930s, followed by the 1950s and 1960s. The 1930s were dominated by MGM's prestige literary adaptations, such as *Viva Villa!* (1934), starring Wallace Beery as the Mexican rebel; George Cukor's *David Copperfield* (1935), based on Charles Dickens's novel; Irving Thalberg's production of Shakespeare's *Romeo and Juliet* (1936), also directed by Cukor, with the too-mature Norma Shearer and Leslie Howard as the adolescents in love; *A Tale of Two Cities* (also 1936), again from Dickens with Ronald Colman; and the film version of Pearl Buck's *The Good Earth* (1937), starring Paul Muni and Luise Rainer as the Chinese farmers.

Adapted from classic novels, these movies were marked by high literary values, though, like most films at the time, they were made on the studio lot. Their budgets were immense by the standards of the time. *The Good Earth* cost $3 million (the equivalent to over sixty million at present), partly due to its impressive and expensive locust attack sequence. Thalberg's death and changes in directors (George Hill began and Sidney Franklin finished) kept the film in production for three years. Winning two Oscars, *The Good Earth* brought a second Best Actress to Luise Rainer and Cinematography to Karl Freund, who was later nominated for two films in the same year (1941): *Blossoms in the Dust* and *The Chocolate Soldier.*

Not many historical epics were made in the 1940s, which is why David Lean's masterpiece *Great Expectations* and Laurence Olivier's Shakespearean adaptations, *Henry V* in 1946 and *Hamlet* in 1948, stood out on the American movie scene and were profusely honored by the Academy. *Henry V,* the more experimental and stylized of the two Olivier films, was shot in Technicolor. The movie begins at the Globe Theater, where the actors prepare for the performance, but then switches to a more realistic setting, including one spectacularly photographed battle scene. Nominated for four awards, *Henry V* won none, though Olivier received a Special Oscar for his "outstanding achievement as an actor, producer and director in bringing *Henry V* to the screen."

Hamlet, the 1948 Oscar winner, was filmed in a different style, emphasizing the camera as an active participant in the narrative. The film was shot in black and white; "it was like an engraving rather than a painting," Olivier later observed. The castle, with its massive, gloomy corridors, framed the human characters in a detached way — the Oscars for Art Direction and Costume Design were well deserved. Despite criticism of the adaptation, which omitted a number of characters and whole scenes, *Hamlet* is an exciting film with fine acting by Olivier and the very young Jean Simmons (nominated for her role as Ophelia).

With the advent of television in the 1950s, Hollywood believed that its survival depended on large-scale epic films flaunting the kind of production values that couldn't be seen on the small screen. Almost every year saw the nomination of epic movies, mostly dominated by MGM. The 1950s' epics were historical tales like *Quo Vadis?* (1951), the most expensive film of its time, starring Robert Taylor and Deborah Kerr. *Ivanhoe* (1952), a medieval romance based on Sir Walter Scott's novel, also starred Robert Taylor, this time with two leading ladies, Elizabeth Taylor and Joan Fontaine. Each of these pictures was nominated in multiple categories but won few, if any, awards. *Quo Vadis?,* for example, received eight nominations but no awards.

The trends of the 1950s continued into the 1960s. Along with David Lean's epics, the decade began with John Wayne's historical Western, *The Alamo* (1960), about the 1836 battle for Texan independence. In 1962, Lewis Milestone's version of *Mutiny on the Bounty* was nominated for seven awards but didn't win any. In 1963 *Cleopatra,* the picture that ultimately destroyed Twentieth Century-Fox, won only four technical awards out of nine nominations.

The following year, the British film *Becket,* based on Jean Anouilh's stage play about the conflict between church, represented by the Archbishop of Canterbury (Richard Burton), and state, King Henry VII (played by Peter O'Toole), was nominated in twelve categories. *Becket* won just one for Edward Anhalt's Adapted Screenplay.

One of 1966's most talked-about but severely flawed film was Fred Zinnemann's *A Man for All Seasons,* based on Robert Bolt's stage hit, concerning the battle of will between Sir Thomas More (Paul Scofield), the Roman Catholic Chancellor, and Henry VIII (Robert Shaw), who broke with the Vatican and established the Church of England with himself as its head. Simplifying his own play, Bolt's script accentuated the differences between the characters, making More an utterly noble saint, thus lacking the play's dramatic wit. Zinnemann's direction was barely serviceable, but it was elevated by Scofield's dignified acting and Shaw's eccentric turn. *A Man for All Seasons* must have been favored by the Academy for its compassionate humanistic message, particularly in a year in which its major competitor, Mike Nichols's *Who's Afraid of Virginia Woolf?* represented a new type of filmmaking that was grittier and more immediate, not to mention its foul language. Zinnemann's epic won six awards: Picture, Director, Actor, Adapted Screenplay, Color Cinematographer, and Costume Design.

The critical and commercial success of these historical films encouraged producers to make more epics. Franco Zeffirelli's handsome production of *Romeo and Juliet* (1968), cast two unknowns in the lead roles and stressed visual excitement at the expense of the Shakespearean text. In the same year, James Goldman's play, *The Lion in Winter,* was transferred to the screen without its original players, Robert Preston and Rosemary Harris. A gossipy, modern version of Henry II's court intrigues, it was marked by such anachronistic dialogue as the Queen saying, "Hush, dear, mother's fighting," or "Well, what family doesn't have its ups and downs?" which recalled *The Little Foxes* and *Who's Afraid of Virginia Woolf?* But Douglas Slocombe's cinematography, and O'Toole and Hepburn's acting made the viewing experience tolerable.

British royalty — this time the courtship between Henry VIII (Richard Burton) and Anne Boleyn (Genevieve Bujold) — featured again in the 1969 film, *Anne of the Thousand Days,* which received only the Costume Design (Margaret Furse) out of ten nominations.

Of the two historical epics nominated in the 1970s, one, *Nicholas and Alexandra* (1971) was extremely weak. James Goldman's script was based on Robert K. Massie's novel, which reconstructed the last years of tsarist history. Despite their tragic fate, the characters weren't interesting or moving enough. Even the Art Direction and Costumes (which won Oscars) weren't too imaginative, and in spite of aggressive publicity campaigns and multiple nominations, the movie died quickly at the box office. By contrast, Stanley Kubrick's *Barry Lyndon* (1975), based on William Makepeace Thackeray's eighteenth-century novel, represented a bold experiment in literary adaptation.

Boasting a breathtaking visual, albeit lacking in dramatic momentum, the film won four awards, including one for John Alcott's distinguished photography.

Roman Polanski's *Tess* (1980), inspired by Thomas Hardy's novel, and imbued with a contemporary viewpoint, excelled more in its production values — for which it won three Oscars — than in dramatic effect.

Reds (1981), Warren Beatty's endeavor as producer, co-writer (with Trevor Griffith), director, and star, was an ambitious attempt to make an historical epic, romantic adventure, and political drama all in one film. Beatty found an intelligent and original idea: To use informants, all contemporaries of John Reed, the adventurous journalist who was in Russia during the 1917 Revolution and wrote the influential book *Ten Days that Shook the World,* as interviewees. *Reds* also provided good parts for Diane Keaton as Louise Bryant, Reed's lover and then wife, Jack Nicholson as Eugene O'Neill, and best of all, Maureen Stapleton as the revolutionary Emma Goldman, who won the Supporting Oscar.

Spanning two decades (1913 to 1931), *Out of Africa,* starring Meryl Streep as Danish writer Isak Dinesen, was a tedious rendition of what must have been a passionate romance. Unclear about its heroine's psyche or soul, the film fails to provide either clues about the meaning of Africa for Dinesen, or how the exotic locale made her the kind of writer she later became. Nor does *Out of Africa* work as a love story since there is no chemistry between Streep and Robert Redford, as the white hunter. Episodic rather than dramatic, and with cinematography which is beautiful in the manner of *National Geographic, Out of Africa* does have redeeming qualities. A mature movie about adult characters for adult audiences, it stood out from the dominating teenage films at the time. Along with *The Color Purple,* the film was nominated for the largest (eleven) number of awards, winning seven, including Best Picture, Sydney Pollack's Direction, Kurt Luedtke's Adapted Script, and David Watkin's Cinematography.

Bernardo Bertolucci's epic *The Last Emperor* swept most (nine) of the 1987 awards. Though boasting stunning cinematography (the film was shot in China's Forbidden City), it suffers from an episodic narrative with no coherent story and no epic hero at its center. This may have accounted for the fact that none of the performers was nominated. Its protagonist, Pu Yi (who became emperor of China at the age of three), was a passive man who lacked any power over his life. But in terms of visual images, art direction, costumes, and editing, *The Last Emperor* offers an exciting treat to the eye. Bertolucci's win at his second nomination (the first was for *Last Tango in Paris*), made him the first and only Italian filmmaker to receive a competitive Oscar. His nine Oscars also made history, tying *Gigi,* the 1958 musical, which had also won nine Oscars — out of nine nominations!

Schindler's List, Steven Spielberg's three-hour Holocaust epic, was his most mature film to date. Made on a relatively small budget ($23 million), and shot in black and white, the narrative tackles an unusually tough subject matter. By holding himself back, Spielberg took a great leap forward, making a powerful yet restrained movie. The Academy finally "forgave" Spielberg for being the world's most commercial filmmaker and honored him with the Best Director accolade.

Spielberg and screenwriter Stephen Zaillian captured Thomas Keneally's 1982 book's matter-of-fact approach, making a film that's a huge canvas of locales, episodes, and characters. Schindler (Liam Neeson), a failed industrialist, takes over a major company that previously belonged to the Jews, and proposes to staff it with Jews — unpaid, of course. Schindler hires a Jewish accountant, Itzhak Stern (Ben Kingsley), and together they supervise a plant that becomes a major supplier of pots and pans for the German military. In the background is Krakow's disintegrating Jewish community, whose members are forced to identify themselves as Jews. The plot switches from the liquidation of the ghetto — and annihilation of a whole culture — to the confined life within the Plaszow Forced Labor Camp.

Schindler is depicted as a persuasive man who knew how to manipulate the Nazi elite, but one who was also willing to pay hard cash for every Jewish life saved. The portrait that Zaillian paints is far from heroic; there's no attempt to whitewash Schindler's motivation to be wealthy and live a good life. Ultimately, though, Schindler emerges as a complex character, torn by contradictory impulses. The most intriguing relationship in the film is between Schindler and Amon Goeth (Ralph Fiennes), the camp's vicious commander. Every frame of *Schindler's List* reflects Spielberg's anger, his urge to chronicle a catastrophe that defies rational understanding. The arbitrariness of life and death — who survived and who was exterminated — is effectively shown to be a function of fate or sheer luck.

Janusz Kaminski's kinetic camera records the traumatic events with the fury of a documentary. The film features top-notch, Oscar-nominated performances, with Neeson as Schindler; Kingsley in an understated performance as the accountant who reluctantly becomes Schindler's confidant; and most impressive of all, Fiennes, whose portrait of the Nazi commander goes way beyond the stereotypically nasty German officers seen in American movies. The ending, which was shot in Israel with the survivors from Schindler's List, is touching but too soft. *Schindler's List* chronicles a genocide of unparalleled proportions — what Hannah Arendt called the banality of evil. But the movie contains a hopeful note and proof of humanity — after all, eleven hundred Jews were saved by a Catholic German.

The next year, Spielberg presented the Best Director to his protégé, Robert Zemeckis, for *Forrest Gump.* Zemeckis showed shrewdness and technical skill in turning morally dubious material into a uniquely poetic American comedy, whose phenomenal commercial success suggests that it touched a deep chord in the American public. The hero is a mentally challenged man who is blessed with innate decency and courage. Though Forrest is simple, his heart is always in the right place. The film implies, as critic David Denby noted, that we the audience could be as good as Forrest if only we had the courage to be simple. Nonetheless, the film's approach was so smart that viewers ignored its sanctimonious tone and its packaging of innocence as a higher state of being.

As a character, Forrest belongs to the same type of idiot-savant that informed the 1966 French film *King of Hearts; Being There* (1979), with an Oscar-nominated role by Peter Sellers; and *Rain Man* (1988), which brought a second Oscar to Dustin Hoffman. Luckily, Forrest is embodied by Tom Hanks, the only star who could play the role without condescension. By 1994, a year after winning the Best Actor for *Philadelphia,* Hanks had become America's favorite son. Hanks plays a character who is limited in consciousness, but not in feeling, hence facilitating the audience's identification with him. As the glue that holds the episodic film together, Hanks never allows Forrest's eccentricities to become a comic caricature.

Forrest's charmed life leads him everywhere, from the White House, where Presidents Kennedy, Johnson, and Nixon greet him amiably, to an Alabama boarding house, where he's seen shaking hands with the yet unknown Elvis Presley. A loose string of vignettes, presented at a brilliant pace by Zemeckis, the film establishes Forrest as an accidental emblem of his times: A timid boy whose slowness is balanced by a talent for running and a genuinely sweet nature. We follow Forrest from his childhood in the 1950s through the 1980s; along the way, he becomes a celebrity several times over, though no one remembers him from one instance to the next.

Framed as an autobiography, the film centers on Forrest's love for his childhood sweetheart, Jenny (Robin Wright) — she is the only constant thing in his life. His solid qualities never change, whereas Jenny is presented as a victim of shifting ideologies. She is involved in the era's trendy politics and fashions (a hippie who demonstrates against Vietnam, a disco-coke junkie); Forrest, through his dim naiveté, is immune to them. As Denby suggests, the movie implies that Jenny reacts to the zeitgeist and gets nothing; Forrest stays out of it and gets everything. *Forrest Gump* served as a lyric poem to America as a country that ambles along happily while everything around it falls apart. Former President Reagan must have admired the movie: Forrest Gump ends up as a rich businessman proving that Reaganomics works.

In 1995, Paramount topped the list of Oscar nominations with ten bids for *Braveheart.* The studio's heart was indeed brave, entrusting movie star Mel Gibson with $35 million for his second feature as a director. Gibson went from making an intimate little film, *Man Without a Face,* to an epic — the choreography of the battle scenes with masses of people and horses was impressive. There was plenty of action and romance in this high-schoolish pageantry — a thirteenth century tale of the Scottish hero William Wallace (Gibson), who returns to his homeland after England's cruel king assumes power.

Braveheart became the fifth Best Picture in the last twenty years not to receive a screenplay Oscar, and deservedly so. Gibson became the sixth actor to win a directing Oscar, all in the past eighteen years, following Woody Allen in 1977, Robert Redford in 1980, Warren Beatty in 1981, Kevin Costner in 1990, and Clint Eastwood in 1992. Gibson also had the distinction of being the fourth Oscar-winning helmer not to have won the Directors Guild Award.

The DGA gave its prize to Ron Howard (who was not Oscar-nominated) for *Apollo 13,* his chronicle of the ill-fated mission to the moon.

One of the most artistically dubious Oscar winners, ultimately, *Braveheart* achieved notoriety as the most violent film to have won Best Picture to date, and one of the least commercial. With a $75 million price tag and underwhelming domestic grosses, *Braveheart* was released by Paramount several times (initially in September, then again after the nominations), but the public simply refused to see it.

The 1996 Oscar-winning epic, *The English Patient,* was an intelligent adaptation by Anthony Minghella of Michael Ondaatje's novel about a mysterious man (Ralph Fiennes) who is badly wounded in a World War II plane crash in the African desert. A Canadian nurse (Oscar-winning Juliette Binoche) tends to him in an abandoned monastery in Italy and slowly his story emerges. Fiennes and Kristin Scott Thomas are perfectly matched in this passionate romance about two people thrown together by chance during a tumultuous period. The story unfolds layer by layer. John Seale's striking photography draws in the viewer in its contrast between sensual images of an adulterous affair and jarring images of wartime brutality.

Upon winning Best Director, writer-director Minghella recalled: "Many people told me it was a novel that couldn't be adapted. Every day I felt I was hanging by my fingernails. I was helped by a great team, a great crew, and many of those people have been acknowledged by the Academy." The Oscar was "vindication, due to the troubles of getting the film made," to producer Saul Zaentz, who acknowledged Sydney Pollack's help. After reading the script, Pollack "went out on a limb for us, and, finally, Harvey Weinstein listened to him." Sweeping most (nine) of the Oscars that year, *The English Patient* also won Sound, Score, Costume, Editing, and other awards, easily beating out its American (*Fargo*), British (*Secrets & Lies*) and Australian (*Shine*) competitors.

Ridley Scott's *Gladiator,* which swept the largest (twelve) number of nominations in 2000, was a large-scale production that notwithstanding its blood and gore was basically a sand-and-sandals throwback to such historical adventures as *Ben-Hur* and *Quo Vadis?* With its central rebel-hero and old-fashioned mythic battle of good versus evil, safely placed in the past, it resembled the Mel Gibson vehicle, *Braveheart,* as well as numerous costume dramas of yesteryear.

A long (154 minutes), big-budgeted (over $200 million) picture, replete with royal intrigues, simplistic heroism, and grisly combats, *Gladiator* was set in 180 A.D. The aging Roman emperor, Marcus Aurelius (Richard Harris), is eliminated by his treacherous son, Commodus (Joaquin Phoenix), who resents the favored status of general Maximus (Russell Crowe). Sent away by Commodus, Maximus escapes death, becomes a prisoner, and is later sold by an entrepreneur (Oliver Reed, in his last role) who forces him to become a gladiator. After finding out that his wife and son were murdered by Commodus, Maximus conceals his identity. His idealized memory of his lost family serves as the vengeance motive for a life-long, single-minded pursuit. The story then moves to Rome and concludes, like most routine actioners, with a combat between the two men.

The CGI effects-driven Roman spectacle has its moments, such as the gladiators entrance into the Colosseum, which is a visual coup, and the dynamic and brutal gladiatorial contests. Its cliché evocation of the Roman empire, as scripted by David Franzoni, John Logan and William Nicholson, uses elements from previous epics, though there are fewer speeches and none of the Judeo-Christian conflicts that defined the genre in the 1950s. Reveling in the glory and horror of the games, they are presented as gaudy, lowbrow entertainment.

With the exception of *Variety, Gladiator* was generally dismissed as a popcorn movie blown to epic proportions. Some reviewers deemed it the least scintillating Oscar winner since *Gandhi,* while others dismissed it as one of the weakest films ever to win the top prize. For Roger Ebert, the choice represented "a case of temporary insanity on the part of the Academy." In a well-publicized rebuttal in the *New York Times,* Pauline Kael wrote: "I was shocked at how bad *Gladiator* was technically. It has the worst editing." Baffled by the praise showered on Crowe, as the silent hero-warrior, Kael observed: "It's absurd casting that actor as a gladiator. You look at him flexing his muscles and you want to laugh. He's like one of the Three Stooges."

War Films

War films have featured poorly in the Oscar contest, amounting to about 4 percent of the 432 nominated movies. However, the ratio of the winning war films to those nominated is three to one, showing the Academy's bias in favor of *epic* war films. All six Oscar-winning war films boasted a grand epic scale: *Wings* (1927–28), *All Quiet on the Western Front* (1929–30), *The Bridge on the River Kwai* (1957), *Patton* (1970), *The Deer Hunter* (1978), and *Platoon* (1986).

With the exception of William Wellman, who was not nominated for *Wings,* all the other directors were honored: Lewis Milestone for *All Quiet on the Western Front,* David Lean for *The Bridge on the River Kwai,* Franklin J. Schaffner for *Patton,* Michael Cimino for *The Deer Hunter,* and Oliver Stone for *Platoon.* Spielberg won a second Best Director for *Saving Private Ryan,* but the movie lost the Best Picture to *Shakespeare in Love.*

The only silent picture to have won the Oscar, *Wings* was in production for over a year due to its demanding aerial sequences, which are still exciting to watch. The film was the most expensive ($2 million) at the time and represented the first collaborative effort between Hollywood and the Air Force. It enjoyed the latter's assistance on the condition that the movie project a positive image of the military. This was the beginning of a more intimate connection between the film industry and the Armed Forces, one that would further develop during World War II.

If *Wings* celebrates heroism, action, and male camaraderie, the next winning film, *All Quiet on the Western Front,* has an antiwar message. Based on Erich Maria Remarque's novel, adapted to the screen by playwright Maxwell Anderson (and others), it describes the initial excitement, then disillusionment of a group of German soldiers in World War I, none of whom survives. The text uncompromisingly depicts a bleak picture of fighting in trenches, stressing the inanity of war for both sides, the Allies and the German. *All Quiet on the Western Front* proved popular at the box office — it was Universal's biggest success to date. But the film was poorly received in Germany prior to the Nazi regime and was officially banned after Hitler's rise to power. Reissued in the United States in 1939, in a truncated version, the film enjoyed a second successful run.

As one might expect, the largest number of war films (six) were nominated in the 1940s during World War II, but, interestingly, none won Best Picture. Furthermore, few of the nominees were action pictures about men in combat. Most were melodramas about the home front, such as the 1942 Oscar winner, *Mrs. Miniver,* about a "typical" British family during the Blitz, or *The Human Comedy* (1943), based on William Saroyan's book, about ordinary lives in a small California town, with Mickey Rooney as a Western Union messenger who delivers death telegrams.

In 1944, David Selznick produced an "American" version of *Mrs. Miniver,* which he entitled *Since You Went Away,* about a "typical" American family during the war. Claudette Colbert played the kind of indomitable mother that Greer Garson had embodied in *Mrs. Miniver.*

Most of Hollywood's good pictures about the war and its effects on its soldiers, and loved ones at home, were made after the war was over, such as MGM's *Battleground* and Fox's *Twelve O'Clock High,* both Best Picture nominees in 1949.

One exceptionally good film was Paramount's *Wake Island* (1942), a moving fictionalized report of the defense of the Pacific Island base and the heroic gallantry of three Marines, played by Robert Preston, Brian Donlevy, and William Bendix (who won a supporting nomination). Despite the fact that they were shot in California, the battle scenes seemed quite realistic. The film received rave notices, though the reviews themselves were tainted by the broader politics. The *Newsweek* critic wrote, "Although the U.S. has been at war for nine months, *Wake Island* is Hollywood's first intelligent, honest, and completely successful attempt to dramatize the deeds of an American force on a fighting front." Bosley Crowther, who saw *Wake Island* on a Marine base, noted that the film "deserves a sincere salute," and hoped that it would "bring a surge of pride to every patriot's breast."

The British were represented with two war pictures in the 1940s. The first, *The Invaders,* made in 1941 and released in America a year later, deals with six survivors from a Nazi submarine attempting to cross the Canadian border to the United States. Its cast was wonderful: Laurence Olivier, Leslie Howard, Raymond Massey, and best of all Eric Portman as a heartless, relentless Nazi. The other, *In Which We Serve,* was the creative effort of Noel Coward who, inspired by the sinking of HMS Kelly off Crete, re-created the biography of a ship from its construction to its last battle, interspersed with flashbacks of its crew's domestic lives.

The first Oscar-winning war films usually received few awards. *Wings* won two Oscars, Best Picture and Engineering Effects, a category which was discontinued the following year. *All Quiet on the Western Front* also won only two awards: Picture and Director. The tendency of one film to sweep awards began with *Gone With the Wind* in 1939, and became a trend in the 1950s. Lean's popular war epic, *The Bridge on the River Kwai,* was showered with seven Oscars.

Like other Lean movies, *The Bridge on the River Kwai* is rich in characterization and ambiguous in point of view — evident here in the depiction of the conflict between Colonel Nicholson (Alec Guinness), a rigid British officer committed to the military code of integrity at all costs, the Japanese commander of the prisoners' camp (Sessue Hayakawa), and the American man of action (William Holden). The bridge's construction has different meanings for these men and, at the end when the Colonel dies by falling on the detonator that destroys the bridge, the story's irony becomes explicit. Impressive as a psychological character study, *The Bridge on the River Kwai* is also strong in suspenseful action and visuals. As the critic Ivan Butler suggested, it is one of those rare movies that satisfy audiences emotionally, cerebrally, and aesthetically.

In the 1960s, three big war movies were nominated, beginning with *The Guns of Navarone* in 1961, an actioner about a tough sabotage team of Americans, British, and Greeks sent to destroy giant Nazi guns on a fictionalized island in 1943. *The Longest Day,* in 1962, about the preparations and landings of the Allies in Normandy on D day, June 6, 1944, was a more ambitious flag-waver. Were it not for the competition from *Lawrence of Arabia,* it would have probably won Best Picture. Of its five nominations, *The Longest Day* won two awards: Black-and-White Cinematography and Special Effects. However, Fox's 1966 attempt to make another blockbuster war movie, *The Sand Pebbles,* failed. An unabashed publicity campaign garnered the film eight nominations, but it lost in every category. Writer Richard Anderson and director Robert Wise were not exactly sure what kind of message they wanted to send in this 1926 story about an American gunboat patrol (led by Steve McQueen) trying to rescue American citizens and missionaries, with the involvement of Chinese warlords.

Patton, the 1970 Oscar-winning film, was also ambiguous in message, attempting to please both right-wing and left-wing audiences by letting each read the film in its own way. But unlike *The Sand Pebbles,* the film works on a number of levels. Made on a $12 million budget, with an original script by Francis Ford Coppola and E. H. North, the film presents a multifaceted view of General Patton as a noble hero, demented psychopath, genius strategist, megalomaniac, and even poet. In a brilliant performance, George C. Scott dominated every frame to the exclusion of the other actors, whose roles were underwritten. The response of the country, then in the midst of the Vietnam War controversy, to this basically one-character, one-star movie was overwhelming: The picture grossed over $28 million. *Patton* won seven major awards out of its ten nominations. In additions to Best Picture, the film won Oscars for Director (Franklin J. Schaffner), Actor (Scott), Original Screenplay, Art Direction, Editing, and Sound.

In 1978, two major films about the Vietnam War competed for Best Picture: *The Deer Hunter* and *Coming Home*. Both films were set in 1968, though they differed in their narrative, politics, and style. Michael Cimino's *The Deer Hunter* is more ambitious in its chronicle of five Pennsylvania steelworkers and their harrowing experiences in Vietnam. The film starts with the depiction of ordinary life in a small Pennsylvania steel town, then sharply switches to Vietnam. It says something about male camaraderie, physical and moral survival, violence in political and personal contexts, and even family life. There was no doubt, however, that the picture was stronger in its lyrical-expressive imagery than in its story or ideas. Sweeping all major critics awards, *The Deer Hunter* also won five Oscars.

Francis Ford Coppola's *Apocalypse Now* (1979) was inspired by Joseph Conrad's *Heart of Darkness*. Though intellectually vague and dramatically uneven, the film conveys effectively the Vietnam War as a disorganized, futile exercise. Paradoxically but cinematically exciting, each scene becomes at once more horrible and more spectacular in its audiovisual effects. The Academy responded like most moviegoers to the psychedelic spectacle of sights and sounds and honored the film with two Oscars: For the stunning cinematography of Vittorio Storaro and for the complex sound orchestrated by Walter Mursch, Mark Berger, Richard Beggs, and Nat Boxer.

Roland Jaffe's *The Killing Fields* (1984), about the civil war in Cambodia, was produced by David Puttnam, who three years earlier had won the Best Picture for *Chariots of Fire*. Nominated in seven categories, the film won three awards: Cinematography to Chris Menges, Supporting Actor to Haing S. Ngor, and Editing to Jim Clark.

In the 1980s, the war genre was alive and well, judging by the crop of belated films about Vietnam, some of which were produced under the guise of action-adventures but were imbued with a strong political subtext, reminiscent of the anti-Communist cold war movies of the 1950s. Prominent in this cycle were the Sylvester Stallone *Rambo* films, which, in their comic strip revisionism of the Vietnam War, proved to be a bonanza at the box office, but were expectedly ignored by the Academy.

The 1986 Oscar-winning *Platoon,* honored with four Oscars out of its eight nominations, was different in texture and ideology. Based on director Stone's tour of duty in Vietnam, it is a chronicle of "the everyday realities of what it was like to be a nineteen-year-old boy in the bush for the first time." Narrowly focused on the routine activities of a single infantry unit, *Platoon* gets its dramatic shape from the battle between the "Evil" sergeant Barnes (Tom Berenger) and the "Good" sergeant Elias (Willem Dafoe) over the soul of an innocent grunt named Chris (Charlie Sheen). It took Stone ten years to get his script produced due to the fact that the country seemed unwilling to deal with the issues of Vietnam. Released in December 1986, just as President Reagan's popularity began to decline, *Platoon* challenged the nation's collective consciousness and the ambivalent feelings toward Vietnam and its veterans.

Repeating the 1978 pattern two decades later, two of the 1998 Best Picture contenders were combat movies: *Saving Private Ryan* and *The Thin Red Line,* both about World War II. Revisiting a genre that was all but dead, Steven Spielberg made an epic that looked and sounded like no other war film. The shocking realization about *Saving Private Ryan* is how experimental it is. Spielberg challenged the basic foundations of film grammar — the construction of images, the notion of montage, the manipulation of sound and silence. As shot by Janusz Kaminski's piercing camera, the first twenty-three minutes represent the most revelatory battle ever recorded on-screen, a breathtakingly graphic portrayal of the violence and chaos at Omaha Beach on D day. The movie's violence set a new standard for Hollywood, which in the past tended to sanitize or mythologize the war.

Just as *Schindler's List* shed insight on the Holocaust, *Saving Private Ryan* confronts the sacrifices that Americans (and non-Americans) had to make during World War II. It was the fourth time that Spielberg explored this era — *1941, Empire of the Sun,* and *Schindler's List* previously — but each time, he depicts war on a grander physical scale while exploring more deeply its impact on individual lives. *Saving Private Ryan* takes familiar genre conventions and looks at them afresh. Unlike most war movies, it does not suggest that American soldiers were fighting for patriotic causes, but shows that in combat there's only one ideology: Survival. Refusing to glorify war, *Saving Private Ryan* doesn't shy away from depicting the fear, death, or the hesitancy of taking a human life, even if it belongs to the enemy. Going beyond the realm of war, *Saving Private Ryan* explores the burden of memory, the inevitable weight of the past on the present.

Tom Hanks, who once again played a sympathetic hero audiences (and Academy voters) could identify with, was nominated for Best Actor for the fourth time. Spielberg picked up his sixth nomination and second directorial Oscar. Janusz Kaminski got a second Oscar (and a third nomination; the second was for *Amistad*). John Williams was nominated for his score — the composer has received thirty-six nominations and five Oscars, three for Spielberg movies. Editor Michael Kahn (*Raiders of the Lost Ark* and *Schindler's List*) also won an Oscar.

The Thin Red Line brought Terrence Malick (of *Days of Heaven*'s fame) back to filmmaking after a twenty-year hiatus. Naturally, there were high expectations since word leaked out that Malick was shooting the James Jones's novel. Unfortunately, Malick's concern that his battle scenes would not match the intensity of *Saving Private Ryan,* and that American viewers would not support two war movies in the same season, proved valid. The film's story line was too amorphous and its pacing too elliptical for the Academy's more conservative voters. The Academy proved again that it doesn't know how to handle an ensemble film — none of the cast members, Sean Penn, Nick Nolte, Elias Koteas, Ben Chaplin, or Jim Caviezel received a nomination. *The Thin Red Line* received seven nominations, including Best Picture, Director, and Adapted Screenplay. Oscar-winning cinematographer John Toll (*Braveheart*) was up for his third nomination, but lost to Kaminski. *The Thin Red Line* also lost out commercially being released after *Saving Private Ryan*, which became a box-office bonanza ever since its July opening.

Action-Adventures

Action-adventures appeal to the mass public but are not much respected by the Academy. With their ceaseless entwining of special-effects, violence, stock characters, and simplistic one-liners, action movies are certainly not Oscar stuff. Indeed, only four adventures have won the Best Picture.

The first Oscar-winning adventure was Cecil B. DeMille's *The Greatest Show on Earth* (1952), which also earned, for no apparent reason, the writing award. Produced by Paramount, it was the only DeMille film to win Best Picture. Its inspiration derived from the Ringling Bros., Barnum and Bailey Circus, and depicted a romantic triangle between a tough manager (Charlton Heston), his beautiful aerialist (Betty Hutton), and a trapeze artist (Cornell Wilde). The movie's most spectacular sequence was a train crash with hundreds of animals running amok. A mass entertainment, *The Greatest Show on Earth* ranks as one of the least distinguished Oscar-winners. It is also the film that began the tradition of honoring big-budget, special-effects blockbusters with a large number of nominations.

Cecil B. DeMille got his first and only directorial nomination for this picture, but the winner was John Ford for *The Quiet Man*. The Academy must have anticipated DeMille's failure to win a competitive award, for it honored him with a Special Oscar in recognition of *The Greatest Show on Earth* and other blockbusters. This tribute was well-timed: DeMille made just one more film, *The Ten Commandments*, before his death in 1959 at the age of seventy-eight.

Mike Todd's *Around the World in 80 Days* (1956), the second winning adventure, was directed by Michael Anderson and based on Jules Verne's classic about a Victorian gentleman (David Niven) and his valet (Cantinflas) who go around the world in an air balloon on a wager. It was not the first film that used Todd-AO, which produced sharper images than Cinemascope, but it was an exciting travelogue that took audiences to exotic locales. With a budget of $7 million, well above the average at the time, the film boasts over fifty cameo appearances by famous stars such as Charles Boyer, Marlene Dietrich, Ronald Colman, Buster Keaton, Cesar Romero, and Frank Sinatra. Spotting the stars proved to be great fun for the audience, which set another trend: Casting large ensembles of stars in small roles in episodic films, such as *The Longest Day, How the West Was Won,* and the disaster movies of the 1970s (see below). *Around the World*'s five Oscars honored Picture, Adapted Screenplay, Color Cinematography, Editing, and Scoring. Victor Young, the noted Hollywood composer, won his first Oscar posthumously, after nineteen nominations. The picture ranked second, after *The Ten Commandments,* among the year's top-grossing films, and was the most commercially popular Oscar film until *Ben-Hur* in 1959.

While it was in production, no one expected William Friedkin's *The French Connection* to become such a major critical and commercial hit or to win the 1971 Oscar. But it did, capturing awards for its director, actor (Gene Hackman), screenplay (Ernest Tidyman), and editing (Jerry Greenberg). The Oscar legitimized *The French Connection*'s status as the decade's best "cop and caper" film. The movie contributed, as historian James Monaco has observed, to the resurgence of film noir in the 1970s, and to the rise of a viscerally exciting visual style. Preceding the release of *Dirty Harry* by a few months, *The French Connection* made the cop film the most popular genre of the entire decade.

Every element in *The French Connection* is effective in its own right, but even better as a part of the movie as a whole. It has a serviceable screenplay based on two real-life policemen, Eddie Egan and Sonny Grosso (who served as the film's technical advisers and also appeared in minor roles), obsessed with tracking down a large shipment of heroin hidden in a car transported from Marseilles to New York City. Along with being an exhilarating thriller containing one of the best and possibly most imitated car-chase scenes in American film, the narrative revolves around an interesting character. Popeye Doyle (Hackman) is a tough, vulgar, bigoted cop, obsessed with breaking up an international narcotic ring. That the filmmakers considered other actors for the role (Jackie Gleason and Steve McQueen, among others) is hard to believe, for Doyle provided Hackman with the best role of his career. *The French Connection* also boasts breathtaking cinematography, the sounds of the streets of New York, and well-paced editing, all of which contributed to a well-made and entertaining movie. Praised by most critics, *The French Connection* went on to rank third among the year's top grossers.

The nominated action or adventure films appeared in two major cycles: In the 1930s and in the 1970s. No adventure films were nominated in the 1940s and 1960s, and few in the 1950s. Adventure films are always strong in production values and special effects, but there are differences between the two cycles. In the first, adventures had melodramatic stories and well-constructed, if contrived, plots. MGM's *Trader Horn* (1931) was a jungle melodrama distinguished by its on-location shooting in Africa, which was a novelty at the time, and cast, with Harry Carey as a white hunter pitted against hostile tribes. Another MGM production, the popular *San Francisco* (1936), featured the most spectacular earthquake ever recorded, occupying close to ten minutes of screen time. A well-made film, *San Francisco* tells an emotionally engaging love story about a tough saloon owner (Clark Gable) and a singer (Jeanette MacDonald), although it's the third character, a no-nonsense priest (Spencer Tracy), who steals the show.

Two swashbuckling Warner adventures, both starring Errol Flynn, were additionally nominated in the 1930s. *Captain Blood* (1935) didn't win any awards, but *The Adventures of Robin Hood* (1938), the first Technicolor version of the legend, won three: Interior Decoration, Editing, and Original Score.

Paramount's *The Lives of a Bengal Lancer* (1935), for which Henry Hathaway received his only directing nomination, starred Gary Cooper, Franchot Tone, and Richard Cromwell as courageous British officers in India involved in some treacherous border intrigues. One of the year's most nominated (seven) pictures, *The Lives* was honored with only one Oscar, for Best Assistant Director.

The World War II years weren't particularly conducive to the production of adventure films due to the priority of war-themed movies. And they continued to be missing in the 1950s, a decade better known for its historical and biblical epics. MGM's *King Solomon's Mines* (1950) stands out as the decade's most entertaining adventure. Similar to *Trader Horn,* the film boasted exquisite color cinematography of Africa's jungles by Robert Surtees, and impressive editing by Ralph E. Winters and Conrad A. Nervig, all of whom won Oscars.

After a decade of no adventures nominated for the Best Picture, the 1970s brought a new cycle of actioners, labeled in the industry as "disaster movies." As such, they depicted natural and man-made catastrophes set on earth (*Earthquake,* 1974), in the air (*Airport,* 1970 and its sequels), on the sea (*Jaws,* 1975 and its sequels) and under the sea (*The Poseidon Adventure,* 1972). This genre exploited its narrative possibilities in a few years, saturating the market so fast that it resulted in a hilarious send-up (*Airplane,* 1980), of the Airport movies.

The disaster films were commercially packaged products that flaunted multigenerational, all-star casts. Most proved to be popular with the public, at once cashing in on and promoting collective fears of such ordinary activities as flying (*Airport*), swimming on Long Island's beaches (*Jaws*), and working in highrise building (*The Towering Inferno*). The pattern of these blockbusters was to receive a large number of nominations, in recognition of their technical aspects and commercial appeal, but few awards. Disaster movies provided employment to many actors, some of whom came out of forced retirement, but they were not generous to them — each actor had at best one or two scenes, and they had to compete with the machinery and special effects. This explains the large number of technical and the paucity of acting nominations. In the acting ranks, the Academy usually singled out elderly performers for sentimental reasons.

Helen Hayes won a second (Supporting) Oscar in *Airport* for portraying a compulsive stowaway who, upon being caught, says, "I don't think it would be very good public relations to prosecute a little lady for visiting her daughter." Reviewing the film in the *New York Times,* Vincent Canby wrote that Helen Hayes plays "with such outrageous abandon, you believe she must have honestly thought it would be her last performance," which it was not, but maybe the Academy thought so. The Academy also nominated Maureen Stapleton as the slow-witted, distraught wife of a mad bomber, played by Van Heflin. *The Poseidon Adventure* garnered Shelley Winters her fourth nomination for playing a Jewish grandmother-passenger in a sinking ship. Sentimentality, on-screen and off, also explains the first and only acting nomination of Fred Astaire, in *The Towering Inferno,* as a widower who loses his friend (Jennifer Jones) in the disaster.

Perplexed by its Best Picture nomination, Academy voter Burt Lancaster, who starred in *Airport,* didn't hesitate to describe the film as "the biggest piece of junk ever made." And *Time* magazine used the nomination of such mind-boggling mediocrity to deride the Academy in general, claiming that "in Hollywood, quality and high budgets are rarely synonymous."

By comparison the multiply nominated *Star Wars* received only one acting nomination for Alec Guinness as a whiskery wizard.

In fact, *Star Wars* began a new cycle of science-fiction films which, unlike its 1950s counterparts, was much more sophisticated in its technical and production values. The impact of *Star Wars,* its sequels, and imitators on American pop culture has been immense, influencing fashion, interior design, television programming, the toy industry, and even the way children are brought up. The Academy acknowledged the film's status and popularity with six competitive and one Special Award, though with respect to the other action-adventures, *Star Wars* might have been the exception.

The Academy has shown its respect for these blockbusters by showering nominations, but when it came to the "real thing," the Best Picture Oscar, a more cautionary vote was exercised:

> In 1970, *Patton* was selected over *Airport*
>
> In 1974, *The Godfather, Part II,* over *The Towering Inferno*
>
> In 1975, *One Flew Over the Cuckoo's Nest* over *Jaws*
>
> In 1977, *Annie Hall* over *Star Wars*
>
> In 1981, *Chariots of Fire* over *Raiders of the Lost Ark*
>
> In 1983, *Terms of Endearment* over *The Right Stuff*
>
> In 1993, *Schindler's List* over *The Fugitive*

The position of the disaster movie changed in 1997 with the release of James Cameron's $200 million *Titanic,* which successfully blended the conventions of the thriller, action-adventure, disaster movie and, above all, historical romance. With fourteen citations, the film tied *All About Eve* for the largest number of nominations. Cursed with an earnest, straightforward script, which received bad publicity, *Titanic* was sold as a kind of *Romeo and Juliet* love story.

Titanic faced only one serious competitor, Curtis Hanson's noir thriller, *L.A. Confidential,* which swept all the critics awards. But in terms of scale and size, no film could compete with this tentpole picture. The other 1997 nominees were small-scale, well-acted vehicles: *As Good As It Gets, The Full Monty,* and *Good Will Hunting.*

Talking to his peers at the DGA awards dinner, Cameron said: "*Titanic* was a labor of love, or, some might say, a crime of passion," referring to its inflated budget. Trying to explain the film's bonanza success, he noted: "This movie touched a common chord. It has been connecting on a heart level in every country, and we can hardly take responsibility for it. We were just a conduit." The most popular Oscar-winner ever, *Titanic* occupied the top spot at the box office for fifteen weeks, breaking the previous record held by *Tootsie* and *Beverly Hills Cop,* ultimately grossing $600.9 million in the U.S. alone.

Westerns

> I don't think a lot about honors, but I think it's demeaning to the Westerns
> that I have received honors for other films and none for my Westerns.
>
> — John Ford

For decades, the Western, arguably the most uniquely American film genre, was regarded as the "bread and butter" of the industry. Year after year, numerous "B-Grade" Westerns, which functioned as the bottom of the double-feature bill, were made. In the 1950s, the best decade for "A-Grade" Westerns in the genre's history, the production of Westerns amounted to one-third of Hollywood's entire output. Yet, only three of the seventy-four Oscar-winning films have been Westerns: *Cimarron* (1932–33), *Dances With Wolves* (1990), and *Unforgiven* (1992).

Based on Edna Ferber's best-selling novel about the opening of the Oklahoma frontier, *Cimarron* covers three decades in the Cravat family, beginning with the gold rush in the 1890s. Directed by Wesley Ruggles, the sprawling saga provided good roles for Richard Dix, as a dashing, adventurously romantic hero, and Irene Dunne, as his indomitable wife Sabra, who starts out as fragile and dependent but becomes the editor of a newspaper and then a congresswoman. *Cimarron,* which also won (writing) Adaptation and Interior Decoration, was a blockbuster with the public.

Actor-director Kevin Costner proved his critics wrong when *Dances With Wolves,* his epic ode to a West long gone, won seven Oscars, including Best Picture and Best Director. *Dances With Wolves* became the first Western since *Cimarron* to win the top prize. Costner directed himself as an idealistic officer whose solitary life at a frontier outpost is interrupted and then forever changes when he encounters the Lakota Sioux tribe.

When Costner was looking for finance, there was not much interest in a marathon-length Western featuring unknown actors speaking in a subtitled Lakota Sioux dialect. Hollywood skeptics, convinced that Costner had a flop the size of *Heaven's Gate* on his hands, had tagged his three-hour directorial debut, "Kevin's Gate." But by Oscar night, *Dances With Wolves* had accumulated more than $130 million in ticket sales. Michael Blake, who just a few years earlier was washing dishes and sleeping on friends' sofas, won an Oscar for his script, based on a novel which Costner had encouraged him to write.

The success of *Dances With Wolves,* which was Costner's first directing project, washed forgiveness over the much-scrutinized film. Despite his status as first-time helmer, the past shows that actors who turn to directing stand a chance at grabbing the Oscar. Costner, in fact, became Hollywood's new Golden Boy. One studio head rationalized the effects that *Dances With Wolves* had in breaking every conceivable Hollywood rule: "When pictures like that explode — and they're rare — they do something to us: All of our notions have to be reconceived. Forget the success of the flick or the problems Costner had or his achievement. We're all thinking differently now. About Westerns. About subtitles. About the length a picture can be. About movies with quills."

Costner's main competition was Martin Scorsese and his crime gangster film, *GoodFellas,* which swept all the critics awards: Los Angeles, New York, and the National Society of Critics. The same year also saw the release of the third, eagerly awaited film of Coppola's 1970s crime saga, *The Godfather, Part III.* The other nominees were *Awakenings,* a psychological drama with Robin Williams and Robert De Niro, which received multiple nominations but denied a nomination for its female director, Penny Marshall, and the romantic blockbuster, *Ghost.*

The great divide in 1990 was based as much on geography as on film sensibility. A New Yorker at heart, Scorsese was a graduate of NYU, setting most of his films in New York. *GoodFellas,* like most of Scorsese's films, feels like New York: Sharp, tough, and sometimes bloody. Costner hails from California, and *Dances With Wolves* was a romantic epic about the West. Consensus held that *GoodFellas* was brilliantly crafted, but that the blood and gore turned off the Academy voters who are old and live in Los Angeles. An Academy voter reflected the opinion of many when he said: "If the whole Oscar show was done at Radio City, I think *GoodFellas* would win."

Unforgiven, Clint Eastwood's chef d'oeuvre, swept the major awards from the Los Angeles Film Critics before winning Best Picture. A classic Westerns that is at once realistic and mythical, it boasted Eastwood's best work as an actor and director in a genre often regarded disreputable in Hollywood. Watching the film was particularly rewarding for those familiar with Eastwood's screen persona — *Unforgiven* deconstructs the myths of manhood and violence in the Old West. Eastwood set out consciously to humanize his superhero image in films that are not explicitly Westerns but have used elements of the genre, such as the Dirty Harry films, which are basically urban Westerns.

As the nameless gunslinger in Sergio Leone's Spaghetti Western of the 1960s, Eastwood established himself as a tight-lipped, steely-eyed icon. Now in the director's saddle, he turned that image on its ear with *Unforgiven.* Eastwood portrays William Munny, an aging pig farmer haunted by his blood-soaked desperado past, who emerges from retirement for one final bounty hunt to avenge the villains who cut a prostitute's face with a Bowie knife. A widower raising two children, Munny is doing it for the money he desperately needs for his farm. Based on David Webb Peoples's Oscar-nominated screenplay, *Unforgiven* is a debunking meditation on the irredeemable savagery of the West. A critical and box-office smash (one of the few Westerns to have grossed over $100 million domestically), the film earned four Oscars, including Best Picture and Director.

Of all genres, the Western has been the most peripheral in the Oscar contest. In addition to the three winning films, only seven Westerns have been nominated: *In Old Arizona* (1928–29), *Stagecoach* (1939), *The Ox-Bow Incident* (1943), *High Noon* (1952), *Shane* (1953), *How the West Was Won* (1963), and

Butch Cassidy and the Sundance Kid (1969). With the exception of John Ford (*Stagecoach*), the other nominated Westerns were directed by filmmakers who didn't specialize in the genre, which may have had something to do with their gaining nominations. "Prestige" filmmakers, such as Fred Zinnemann (*High Noon*) and George Stevens (*Shane*) were rewarded for making one impressive Western in their careers. (Stevens would later direct *Giant.*)

The lack of respect for the genre is also reflected by the paucity of directorial Oscars for Westerns. John Ford, undoubtedly the master of Westerns, was nominated five times, but only once for a Western (*Stagecoach*). Ford failed to win a nomination for what's considered to be his masterpiece, *The Searchers* (1956). Significantly, Ford's four Oscars were for other genres: *The Informer, The Grapes of Wrath, How Green Was My Valley,* and *The Quiet Man.*

Other directors excelling in Westerns have similarly skirted Academy recognition. Howard Hawks failed to get nominations for his two excellent Westerns, *Red River* (1948) and *Rio Bravo* (1959), but was nominated for the patriotic flag-waver, *Sergeant York,* though he did not win.

A typically masculine genre, the Western has offered better roles for men, which was acknowledged by the Academy: Eight men (four lead and four supporting), but no women, have won acting Oscars in a Western. The first was Warner Baxter, who played the legendary Mexican bandit the Cisco Kid in *In Old Arizona.* Gary Cooper gave one of his finest performances as Marshal Will Kane in *High Noon.* Lee Marvin played a dual part in *Cat Ballou:* Kid Shellen, a whiskey-soaked gunfighter, and Shellen's antagonist, Tim Straun, a villain with a silver nose. *True Grit* provided John Wayne with one of the richest roles of his career, as the fat, aging, eye-patched marshal Rooster Cogburn, who helps a teenager to avenge her father's death.

Four Supporting Oscars were given for roles in Western films, beginning with Thomas Mitchell as the drunken Doc Boone in *Stagecoach.* Walter Brennan won his third Supporting Oscar for playing Judge Roy Bean in William Wyler's *The Westerner.* Burl Ives won for his patriarch landowner in *The Big Country,* another Wyler Western, and Gene Hackman won a second Oscar as the sadistic sheriff in *Unforgiven.*

Few players have been nominated for a Western, not for lack of distinguished performances, but due to the genre's low prestige. Actors identified with some of the best Westerns failed to get recognition, including Henry Fonda, James Stewart, William Holden, Kirk Douglas, and Burt Lancaster. Moreover, those few who received recognition were nominated because of their status as players, not necessarily for a specific Western. Geraldine Page was nominated for a supporting role in a John Wayne Western, *Hondo,* because it was her first in Hollywood as Broadway's brightest star after appearing in Tennessee Williams's *Summer and Smoke.* Jennifer Jones and Lillian Gish were nominated for King Vidor's *Duel in the Sun* (an erotic but silly Western) because it was a blockbuster. Julie Christie won her second nomination for playing the frizzy-haired, opium-smoking whore in Robert Altman's *McCabe and Mrs. Miller* because she was then in vogue.

Ironically, only when the Western became a more reflexive genre, did it win some respect. Lee Marvin won Best Actor for a Western spoof, *Cat Ballou,* which caricatured the traditional Western hero and was sold to the public as a "put-on" Western. John Wayne won acclaim only when he poked fun at his own screen image. Madeline Kahn received a supporting nomination for Mel Brooks's spoof, *Blazing Saddles,* which pokes fun at every convention of the genre. As Lily von Shtupp, Kahn paid tribute to the numerous cabaret singers played by Marlene Dietrich in *Destry Rides Again* and other films.

10

THE OSCAR-WINNERS—
COMEDIES AND MUSICALS

Can Oscar Laugh? The Oscar-Winning Comedies

They don't recognize comedies. They don't have a comedy category. I have two Oscars and a plaque and a gold medal from the Academy, but I never won for acting. — Bob Hope, Comedian and Oscar Host

Screen comedy as a genre has been underrepresented in the Oscar contest — particularly in relation to the number of comedies made. Year after year, the Academy has displayed biases against comedy films and comedic performances. Only ten out of the seventy-four Oscar-winners (13.5 percent) have been comedies, which figure includes such serio-comedies and borderline cases as *The Apartment, Driving Miss Daisy,* and *American Beauty.*

It took seven years for a comedy to win the first Best Picture: Frank Capra's *It Happened One Night* (1934). And it won by surprise, as it was directed by a relative unknown and produced by a lesser studio, Columbia Pictures. For forty-one years, *It Happened One Night* held a record as the only film to have captured all five major awards: Picture, Director, Actor (Clark Gable), Actress (Claudette Colbert) and Writing (Robert Riskin). In 1975, *One Flew Over the Cuckoo's Nest* became the second film to boast such an achievement.

Structured as a "road" comedy, *It Happened One Night* concerns the evolving romance between a runaway heiress (Colbert) and a tough reporter (Gable) who, having been fired by his editor, plans a comeback by getting the exclusive story of the heiress's rebellious flight to marry a man her family doesn't approve of. The picture was rooted in the context of the Depression, embodying the values of upward mobility, individual success, and romantic love. *It Happened One Night* was influential in other ways. It is credited with exerting impact on the fashion industry: When Gable took off his shirt and exposed his sexy bare chest, the sale of undershirts declined substantially. The comedy also boosted domestic tourism, with a tremendous increase in the number of women traveling by bus hoping to meet their "white knights" on the road.

The second Oscar-winning comedy was also directed by Capra for Columbia, *You Can't Take It With You* (1938). Based on George S. Kaufman and Moss Hart's Pulitzer Prize-winning stage hit, it was adapted to the screen by Robert

Riskin. This zany comedy centers on a madcap family that believes in free enterprise, with each member dedicated to his/her own crazy habits. Nominated for seven Oscars, the film won two: Picture and Director. The comedy boasts a large, excellent cast, of which only Spring Byington was nominated for a supporting role for playing Penny, the eccentric mother who begins writing endless plays when a typewriter is left at her house by mistake. None of the rest of the cast — including Jimmy Stewart and Jean Arthur as the romantic couple, Lionel Barrymore as the charming grandfather, and Edward Arnold as the stuffy millionaire — was singled out for their acting.

The 1940s saw only one Oscar-winning comedy, *Going My Way* (1944), directed by Leo McCarey, and starring Bing Crosby as a progressive priest who turns a group of delinquents into a choir. Barry Fitzgerald plays an old, irascible priest who's still attached to his ninety-year-old mother. Both Crosby and Fitzgerald won acting awards, the former in the lead and the latter in the supporting category. *Going My Way* was the only nominated comedy in 1944. The other nominees are those exemplars of film noir, *Double Indemnity* and *Gaslight;* and two patriotic films, *Since You Went Away* and the biopicture *Wilson.* Sweeping seven Oscars, *Going My Way* proved to be a sentimental favorite of the public too, ranking as that year's top-grossing movie.

Not a single comedy won the Best Picture in the 1950s, and only two were cited in the 1960s: Billy Wilder's comedy-drama, *The Apartment,* and Tony Richardson's historical adventure-comedy *Tom Jones.* Among other distinctions, *The Apartment* (1960) was the last black and white film to win the Best Picture until 1993, when *Schindler's List* joined its ranks.

Though not one of Wilder's best films, *The Apartment* still offers biting commentary on big business, the ethos of success, and adultery — a consistent theme in the director's oeuvre. Lacking a clear point of view, the movie vacillates between sympathy and pity for its protagonists. Nonetheless, the acting of Jack Lemmon as the young, ambitious, upwardly mobile executive, and Shirley MacLaine as the elevator operator in his office building, was superb; both were nominated, though neither won. *The Apartment* opened to mixed reviews, ranging from outright rejection, with critic Dwight MacDonald charging that it lacked "style or taste," to moderate praise. The reviewer Hollis Alpert regarded the film as a "dirty fairy tale, with a schnook for a hero and a sad little elevator operator for a fairy princess." But 1960 was not a particularly strong year, which may have accounted for its win. *The Apartment* is still one of the few winners whose Oscar wasn't much help at the box office. With grosses of $6.6 million, it was the least commercially successful Oscar-winner of the 1960s.

By contrast, *Tom Jones* was a commercial success prior to winning the 1963 Oscar and a smash-hit afterward — it is one of the most popular films of the entire decade. The first all-British film to win the Oscar since *Hamlet* in 1948, *Tom Jones* made its star, Albert Finney, a household name in America. Based on Henry Fielding's famous novel, which was adapted to the screen by playwright John Osborne (who won an Oscar), it features Finney as the adventurous, amorous illegitimate son of a servant in eighteenth-century England. All three supporting women were nominated: Dame Edith Evans as the intrepid aunt, Diane Cilento as the gatekeeper's wild daughter, and best of all, Joyce Redman as a lady of easy virtue who seduces the hero over a large meal in what became the film's best-remembered sequence. Production values were high, particularly the cinematography by Walter Lassally (which won), editing, and music score. Influenced by the French New Wave, director Tony Richardson used his camera in a jazzy, dynamic manner. *Tom Jones* was far superior to all the other nominees in 1963: *America, America; Cleopatra; How the West Was Won;* and *Lilies of the Field.*

It took a whole decade for another comedy to win the Oscar, though by choosing George Roy Hill's *The Sting* (1973), the Academy found itself under severe attack from its more serious critics. Cashing in on the previous success of his comedy-Western *Butch Cassidy and the Sundance Kid,* Hill reteamed its stars, Paul Newman and Robert Redford, in a Depression-era comedy set in Chicago about the conceits of two con men (Newman and Redford) against a big-time racketeer (Robert Shaw). Released to mostly good reviews, *The Sting* ranks high on *Variety*'s All-Time Champions list. The abundantly charming movie boasts Scott Joplin's exuberant piano rags, which were adapted by Marvin Hamlisch and became popular throughout the country. Still, many felt that blockbusters like *The Sting* had no business being nominated for Oscars in the first place, let alone win Best Picture.

Woody Allen's semiautobiographical comedy, *Annie Hall* (1977), co-written by Allen and Marshall Brickman, is a bitter-sweet introspective look at the unstable affair between Alvie Singer (Allen), an anxiety-ridden Jewish comic, and Annie Hall (Diane Keaton), an insecure Waspish singer. The contrast between Jewish and Gentile, middle-American lifestyles is both touching and poignant. At once funny and sad, freewheeling and self-reflexive, *Annie Hall,* which originally was entitled "Anhedonia," is punctuated by Allen addressing the audience directly in some witty monologues. Establishing Allen as a major director, *Annie Hall* ranks as one of his most commercial movies; the other is the 1986 Oscar-nominated *Hannah and Her Sisters.*

Blending comedy and melodrama, *Terms of Endearment* (1983) was basically a TV sitcom expanded to the format of feature-length bigscreen entertainment. James Brooks's triple win, as producer, writer, and director, represented an astonishing achievement, considering that the screenplay had been turned down by several studios before Paramount decided to finance it. In its sentimental tone and traditional view of women, *Terms of Endearment* resembles many old-fashioned, "well-made" movies. However, most audiences enjoyed the honest, loving relationship between a possessive mother (Shirley MacLaine) and her stubborn daughter (Debra Winger). Especially amusing are romantic and sexual interludes between MacLaine's middle-aged widow and her boozy ex-astronaut neighbor (Jack Nicholson, who won the Supporting Oscar). The film's candid view of middle-age sexuality, expressed in the way that Nicholson courted MacLaine, was both refreshing and encouraging. Released at a time when most mainstream Hollywood movies were either action-adventure or teenage fare may explain the acclaim accorded by the Academy, and the film's huge commercial appeal.

The most recent comedy to win Best Picture was the crowd-pleaser *Shakespeare in Love* (1998), directed by the British John Madden in a manner that shrewdly combines poetry, art, and entertainment. Screenwriter William Goldman has pointed out that no Hollywood movie has been such a valentine to the theater in its depiction of actors as romantic fools who can only be happy and alive when they're on stage. Marc Norman's idea provides the basis for a clever script, co-written with Tom Stoppard: The Bard experiences a writing block. The movie presents a portrait of the artist (played by Joseph Fiennes) as a young hack struggling with both creativity and affairs of the heart. For director Madden, "there was nothing remotely academic about the film, it's all about first love."

All the ingredients seemed to be right for the taste of the Academy voters. The film's title has cachet too. Who can resist Shakespeare? Shakespeare signals the beginning of modern drama and pop culture as well. The 435-year-old writer is "hot" in Hollywood, as evident in numerous Shakespearean productions, from an MTV-influenced version of *Romeo + Juliet* to modern-costume renditions of *Richard III* and *Love's Labour's Lost*. David Denby complained in *The New Yorker* that *Shakespeare in Love* has bad jokes, silly sword fights, and a weak ending, yet conceded that overall the picture is charming. A celebration of populist entertainment, *Shakespeare in Love* was made with exuberant theatricality and wit. As a literary-erotic fantasy about the composition of the world's most famous love story, the film serves up a romantic romp about the Bard and his radiant muse.

Gwyneth Paltrow, who won the Best Actress for her irresistible Viola, gave a career-making performance in a role that Julia Roberts had turned down in a previous incarnation. It was a great part, allowing Paltrow to be a boy and a girl, with moods swinging from passionate and sexy to heartbroken. Geoffrey Rush won a supporting nomination as a theater owner shaken down by Elizabethan money men, and Dame Judi Dench won the Supporting Oscar for her authoritative portrait of Queen Elizabeth, a small but significant part. The result was massive box-office appeal and an Oscar bonanza, leading the contest with thirteen nominations, and winning Best Picture. The intelligent characters and colorful sets and costumes certainly help, but the real star of the picture is the feverish wordplay and whimsical plot by Tom Stoppard and Marc Norman, who won the Best Original Screenplay Oscar. Norman is credited with the story, but it is Stoppard who mixes aspects of philosophy and literature, fact and fancy, with wit and derring-do.

The Oscar-Nominated Comedies

The largest number (sixteen) of comedies were nominated in the 1930s, arguably the genre's golden age. Every brand of comedy was made, and nominated, in this decade, including Mae West's 1933 sex farce *She Done Him Wrong,* which would not have been nominated a year later due to restrictions imposed by the Production Code.

In 1934, the most popular of the nominated comedies was MGM's comedy-mystery, *The Thin Man,* which made William Powell and Myrna Loy certifiable movie stars as well as role models for married couples across the nation.

Charles Laughton gave a wonderful performance in Leo McCarey's 1935 political comedy, *Ruggles of Red Gap,* which contrasts the values of British aristocracy with those of American democracy. McCarey was also represented in the contest with the sophisticated marital comedy, *The Awful Truth* (1937), starring Cary Grant and Irene Dunne. Additionally, a number of MGM's female stars distinguished themselves in Oscar-nominated comedies: Jean Harlow in *Libeled Lady,* Garbo in Ernst Lubitsch's *Ninotchka.*

Of the nominated comedies in the 1940s, George Cukor's *The Philadelphia Story* (1940), starring Katharine Hepburn in one of her greatest performances, assisted by Jimmy Stewart and Cary Grant, stood out in its subtle staging and flawless acting. In the same year, Charlie Chaplin's *The Great Dictator,* in which he plays a dual role, Adenoid Hynkel, the dictator of Tomania (standing in for Hitler) and a Jewish ghetto barber, won recognition as both slapstick comedy and political satire.

Columbia's *Here Comes Mr. Jordan,* which won the 1941 writing awards (Original Story and Screenplay), recounts a fantasy in which a prizefighter (Robert Montgomery) is sent to heaven by mistake and then back to earth in search of a new body. This popular film later served as the inspiration for Warren Beatty's 1978 *Heaven Can Wait,* which also received Best Picture nomination. (The original *Heaven Can Wait* (1943) was Lubitsch's account of family life in nineteenth-century Hungary, with gorgeous sets and costumes.)

In 1943, George Stevens's *The More the Merrier,* a war comedy about housing conditions in Washington, D.C., starred Jean Arthur as a civil servant renting her small apartment to an old gentleman (Charles Coburn) who in turn rents it to an attractive man (Joel McCrea). Coburn, who was often cast as a British subject, won the Supporting Oscar for playing one of his many lovable grandfathers, here cast as a daffy millionaire.

Of the few comedies nominated in the 1950s, the most commercial one was the service comedy *Mister Roberts* (1955), starring Henry Fonda in his best-known role. Fonda plays the first officer on the Reluctant, a cargo ship miles away from the battle zone, whose route is described by him as "from Tedium to Apathy, and back again, with an occasional side trip to Monotony." The War is close to an end, and Mister Roberts is anxious to get into combat before it is too late. Fonda was unaccountably ignored by the Academy members, though they did put Jack Lemmon on the map by giving him the Supporting Oscar for playing Ensign Pulver, a flighty fellow assigned to laundry detail.

Like Fonda, Rosalind Russell re-created her successful stage role in the 1958 film version of *Auntie Mame,* which, with over $9 million at the box office, outgrossed the box-office receipts of the Oscar winner from that year, *Gigi.*

The most original of the decade's nominated comedies was George Cukor's *Born Yesterday* (1950), based on Garson Kanin's stage play, in which Judy Holliday's "dumb blonde" Billie Dawn is victimized by a rough and rude junk dealer (Broderick Crawford) and educated by a sensitive Washington correspondent (William Holden). The first part of the picture is funny, and many wished Billie didn't have to be tamed and socialized because the romantically "educational" sessions with Holden drag the picture down.

The appeal of *Born Yesterday* was also due to its political message. The nominal plot concerns the attempt of a scrap metal dealer to bribe a bill through Congress and the successful fight of a woman against political corruption. Condemning the dealers who profited from the war economy was a timely issue after World War II. Arthur Miller dealt with a similar issue in *All My Sons,* first done as a Broadway play, then as a Hollywood movie.

The 1950s also saw their share of romantic comedies. William Wyler's stylish romance, *Roman Holiday* (1953), starring Audrey Hepburn as a European princess, and Gregory Peck as an American reporter, was elegant and featured location shooting, albeit in black and white. The following year, the Academy nominated Fox's romantic comedy, *Three Coins in the Fountain,* also set in Rome, which received the Cinematography Oscar for Milton Krasner's sumptuous color lensing. It also won Best Song, by Sammy Cahn and Jule Styne, which contributed to the film's popularity. Like *High Noon*'s ballad, *Three Coins*'s title song showed how effectively music can be used to promote and market a movie.

The comedies nominated in the 1960s were of greater variability than in previous decades. In 1964, Stanley Kubrick's black comedy, *Dr. Strangelove; or, How I Learned to Stop Worrying and Love the Bomb,* was ahead of its time in its antinuclear warning, depicting military generals as irresponsible puppets enamored of their limitless power. Peter Sellers excelled in playing three widely contrasting roles: The American President, a British RAF Captain, and best of all, a mad German scientist whose heavy accent was inspired by the physicist Edward Teller. The film was popular with audiences, though not as much as *Mary Poppins,* which was also a 1964 Best Picture nominee. It was a good year for the genre, for a third comedy was nominated: Michael Cacoyannis's *Zorba the Greek,* based on Nikos Kazantzakis's best-selling novel. Anthony Quinn was cast in what became the signature role of his career. The no-nonsense, garrulous force of his virility contrasted with Alan Bates's British reserve.

Toward the end of the decade, two comedies that reflected the new zeitgeist of youth culture and racial diversity were nominated. Mike Nichols's second feature, *The Graduate,* was nominated for seven awards and won one, Best Director. Among other distinctions, the film reaffirmed youth counterculture and the generation gap. The central character of the passive nonconformist, Benjamin Braddock, was played to perfection by Dustin Hoffman. The other 1967 nominated comedy was Stanley Kramer's *Guess Who's Coming to Dinner,* one of Hollywood's first mainstream films about interracial marriage. Both pictures aimed at younger audiences, though *Guess Who's Coming to Dinner* was stronger in intent than in artistic execution, which is the reason it became outdated as soon as it hit American screens.

Among the few comedies nominated in the early 1970s was George Lucas's nostalgic view of youth, *American Graffiti* (1973), which was set in California in 1962 and used as its metaphor "what we once had and lost." Made on a shoestring budget, *American Graffiti* became a sleeper hit, launching a whole cycle of rock 'n' roll high-school movies. But as the decade came to an end, more comedies were made and more were nominated. Paul Mazursky's *An Unmarried Woman* (1978), starring Jill Clayburgh, was a timely comedy which reflected the changing position of women in American society.

Of the cycle of comedies about the changing definitions of gender, Sydney Pollack's *Tootsie* (1982) was the most accomplished and also the most honored, with ten nominations. A witty, topical comedy, written by Larry Gelbart and Murray Schisgal, it provides commentary on love, sex, and friendship. The film stars Dustin Hoffman as Michael Dorsey, an unemployed actor who becomes daytime television's most popular "female" star Dorothy Michaels. All members of the cast played their parts to the hilt, and four received nominations: Hoffman, Teri Garr as his also unemployed and rejected girlfriend, Jessica Lange as the submissive and sexy actress, and Charles Durning as Lange's widowed father who falls in love with Dorothy.

Both funny and sad, the 1997 Best Picture nominee, *As Good As It Gets,* followed in the footsteps of James L. Brooks's *Terms of Endearment,* except it was more eccentric, nutty, and at times, genuinely moving. Jack Nicholson won his third (and second Best Actor) Oscar, and Helen Hunt won her first Best Actress as the central romantic couple: He, a rich neurotic, who frequents the same restaurant every day; she, a working-class single mom. Some critics carped that the movie was too long and indulgent. Writers Mark Andrus and Brooks constructed a good beginning and a good ending, but a weak middle. The segments devoted to a gay painter (Greg Kinnear), forced to go to his disapproving parents to ask for money, slowed the picture down, though it offered opportunity for the indoor tale to get outside with a trip in which each of the three characters had some terrific moments of self-discovery. But in 1997, the ominous *Titanic* gave each of its competitors a run for its money. And yet in another disgraceful oversight, Brooks was snubbed by the Directors Branch, which failed to nominate him.

No Respect for Comedy Players

It's almost a fluke that Jack Nicholson and Helen Hunt won Oscars for *As Good As It Gets.* It's unusual for two performers to win the lead Oscars in the same film, and even more unusual for both winning roles to be in a comedy.

The Academy has shown a consistent lack of respect for comedic performances. For some reason, they are considered to be "easier," more effortless than dramatic performances. Leading actresses have seldom won an Oscar for a comedic role. It took twenty years after Audrey Hepburn's Best Actress for

Roman Holiday for the next woman to win the Oscar for a comedy, Glenda Jackson in *A Touch of Class,* and Jackson won due to paucity of good female roles that year. Men winning for performances in comedies have not been much more visible. No Best Actor won for a comedy role between Jimmy Stewart in *The Philadelphia Story* in 1940 and Lee Marvin in *Cat Ballou,* twenty-five years later.

Supporting Oscars for comedies have been more prevalent. Peter Ustinov won a second supporting Oscar for playing a con man talked into a robbery by Melina Mercouri in Jules Dassin's *Topkapi* (1964). Ustinov's misadventures as a tour guide afraid of his own shadow provided the most hilarious scenes in the movie. George Burns excelled as a veteran vaudevillian reunited with his old partner (Walter Matthau) after decades of hostility in Neil Simon's *The Sunshine Boys* (1975). Of the supporting comediennes, Josephine Hull gave a riotous performance in *Harvey* (1950) as Jimmy Stewart's distraught, scatterbrained sister, who ends up in a mental institution she had intended for him. Eileen Heckart received a well-deserved Supporting Oscar as the overbearing and overprotective mother of her blind son in *Butterflies Are Free* (1972).

That comedy has been overlooked by the Academy is also reflected in the underrepresentation of comedy writers-directors. Take Charlie Chaplin, whose contribution to the genre is indisputable. Of Chaplin's major works, only *The Great Dictator* was nominated for Best Picture though it did not win a single award. *The Circus* (1928), *City Lights* (1931), and *Modern Times* (1936) also failed to receive top nominations. Chaplin was nominated twice as Best Actor, for *The Circus* and *The Great Dictator,* but lost on both occasions.

Preston Sturges, another extraordinary filmmaker who specialized in the comedy genre, won only one Oscar, Best Original Screenplay, for his first film as a director, *The Great McGinty* (1940). Despite their originality, urbane sophistication, and biting humor, none of Sturges's comedies was nominated for Best Picture, though at least three deserved serious consideration: *Sullivan's Travels* (1941), *The Palm Beach Story* (1942), and *Hail the Conquering Hero* (1944). The Writers Branch was more appreciative of Sturges, and in 1944 he became the first scribe to have two scripts, *Hail the Conquering Hero* and *The Miracle of Morgan's Creek,* nominated for Original Screenplay; the winner was Lamar Trotti for the biopicture *Wilson.*

None of the "classical clowns" has ever won a legitimate Oscar or even a nomination. True, most of them did their best work in the silent era, prior to the Oscars' birth, but even those who contributed to the genre in later years were overlooked by the Academy. Members of the "clowns triumvirate," which included, along with Charlie Chaplin, Harold Lloyd and Buster Keaton, were eventually awarded Honorary Oscars as corrective measures. In 1952, Lloyd was awarded a special Oscar as "a master comedian and good citizen." Unlike Lloyd, Buster Keaton made some excellent comedies in the sound era, when he was under contract at MGM — *The Cameraman* and *Spite Marriage* — but he never won Academy recognition. A 1959 Honorary Oscar cited Keaton, THE

KING OF COMEDY for his "unique talents which brought immortal comedies to the screen."

The popular comedy team of Stan Laurel and Oliver Hardy was also underestimated during their lifetime. Joining forces in 1926, Laurel and Hardy delighted audiences with their inventive acts for decades. In 1960, three years after Hardy's death from cancer, the Academy honored his surviving partner, who had refused to perform after his colleague's death, with an Honorary Oscar "for his creative pioneering in the field of cinema comedy."

The Academy's bias against comedy was also apparent in the case of excellent comedians, who had to deviate from this genre to gain the Academy's respect. The best example of this trend is Cary Grant, who distinguished himself in romantic as well as screwball comedies. It was comedy which catapulted him to stardom and it was comedy which kept him up there on the pantheon for decades. The public preferred to see Grant in comedies, the best of which were those opposite Katharine Hepburn (*Bringing up Baby, Holiday*), Rosalind Russell (*His Girl Friday*), and Irene Dunne (*The Awful Truth*), but none of them brought him a nomination.

Grant had to step outside of his specialty to earn his nominations. The first was for a sentimental melodrama, *Penny Serenade* (1941), as a childless married man whose adopted daughter dies tragically at the age of six. The second nod was for a "serious-dramatic" role in Clifford Odets's pedestrian *None But the Lonely Heart* (1944), as a Cockney drifter. Grant's nominations had more to do with the fact that most Hollywood male stars were mobilized to the war effort than distinguished acting.

No other actor of Grant's generation contributed more to screen comedy, but the Academy took his acting for granted, which always seemed to be natural and too facile. In actuality, Grant's seamlessly polished style was a product of hard work and meticulous preparation. It took years of practice to perfect his genius timing, the spontaneity and naturalness in delivering lines which became Grant's trademark. The Academy "corrected" this injustice by honoring Grant with a 1972 Honorary Oscar, whose citation was simple and to the point, "for Cary Grant for being Cary Grant."

Jack Lemmon's Oscars also demonstrate the Academy's prejudices against comedy. Lemmon began his screen career in comedies, often cast opposite Judy Holliday (*It Should Happen to You, Phfft*). He later became the quintessential Billy Wilder actor, appearing in seven of the director's films, including *Some Like It Hot* (his first lead nomination) and *The Apartment* (his second). In later years, Lemmon starred in the Neil Simon comedies *The Fortune Cookie* and *The Odd Couple,* establishing him as the top comic actor of his generation.

Ironically, Lemmon received his acting accolades for straight dramatic performances, first for playing an alcoholic in *Days of Wine and Roses* (1962), a career breakthrough for which he earned his third nomination. Lemmon won the Best Actor (and his second) Oscar for *Save the Tiger* (1973), a film about the moral disintegration of a garment manufacturer who resorts to arson out of financial desperation. For some reason, the self-pity and disenchantment with the American value system of Lemmon's character deemed his acting more "serious" and "substantial" in the Academy's mind.

Tom Hanks also won two Best Actor Oscars for dramas, *Philadelphia* (1993) and *Forrest Gump* (1994). In the former, he plays an AIDS-stricken lawyer named Andrew Beckett who fights for his legal rights when he is fired from his job. Historically, Hollywood's top stars have steered clear from portraying gay characters for fear that it would harm their careers. *Philadelphia* represented a bold departure for Hanks, then best known for his comedy skills in *Big, Sleepless in Seattle,* and *A League of Their Own.*

Hanks was nominated again for *Saving Private Ryan,* for a role in which he delivered, as *Variety* wrote, "the kind of mature, thinking man's blend of guts and heart that the Academy loves." Lauren Shuler-Donner, who produced the Hanks-Meg Ryan vehicle *You've Got Mail,* released in the same year as *Saving Private Ryan,* said she would cast her vote for *Mail* since "Tom deserves another Oscar." But she conceded that out of the two pictures, Hanks would be nominated for *Saving Private Ryan,* because "the Academy goes for drama over comedy most of the time."

Overlooking comedy performers is not exclusive to the Academy. Other film associations have also failed to honor comedy films and comedy performers. Neither Cary Grant nor Jack Lemmon ever won the New York Film Critics Circle, for example. Steve Martin, honored in 1984 by the New York Film Critics and the National Society of Film Critics for his witty slapstick comedy, *All of Me,* is the exception rather than the rule. Most performers know when they are cast in comedies that their films may be popular with the public but will not get the Academy's attention. When British actress Julie Walters was nominated for *Educating Rita,* in which she played a hairdresser eager to better herself, she told reporters: "I won't win. They don't give Oscars for comedy." The Golden Globes and the Tony Awards distinguish between comedy/musical and drama to ensure that these genres get their fair representation and due respect. However, the Academy has refused to create comedy categories, claiming that it will not only increase the number of awards but also diminish their relative prestige.

The Oscar Musicals

> There is a strange sort of reasoning in Hollywood that musicals are less worthy of Academy consideration than dramas. It's a form of snobbism, the same sort that perpetuates the idea that drama is more deserving of Awards than comedy. — Gene Kelly

Unlike comedies, musicals have been *overrepresented* in the Best Picture category. Eight (eleven percent) of the seventy-four winning films have been musicals. Like comedies, however, musical performers have been consistently (and ironically) overlooked, both in the nomination and the final balloting.

As a genre, musicals featured most prominently during the Depression — about half of all Oscar-nominated musicals were made in the 1930s. By contrast, the weakest representation of musicals in the Oscar contest was in the 1940s, with only two nominees, *Yankee Doodle Dandy* and *Anchors Aweigh.*

But Hollywood was not willing to take risks with new ideas and new formats, and subsequently most of the nominated musicals from the 1950s on were based on Broadway hits. Among the few Oscar-nominated musicals that originated on the big screen rather than Broadway are *Seven Brides for Seven Brothers, Mary Poppins,* and *All That Jazz.*

There is no logical link between the number or quality of musicals made and their presence in the Oscar contest. More musicals won Oscars in the 1960s than in any other decade, despite the fact that not many films were made. Ironically, just as the musical genre began to decline, it gained in relative stature. The Academy showed its dutiful respect for the effort involved in making musicals by honoring more of them.

The first Oscar-winning musical, *The Broadway Melody* (1928–29), was also MGM's first musical and the first talking film to be honored by the Academy. It was advertised as ALL TALKING, ALL SINGING, ALL DANCING. *The Broadway Melody* also featured the innovation of color. One sequence, "The Wedding of the Painted Doll," was presented in two colors, though it would take another decade for color to be absorbed by Hollywood. A backstage musical, it is the tale of two sisters (Bessie Love and Anita Page) who seek fame in the New York theater, and in the process fall in love with the same song-and-dance man. Bessie Love's nominated performance as the older, wiser sister who sacrifices herself for her younger sister's career was truly touching. By today's standards, the story and characters are cliché-ridden, but in 1929, the novelty of sound, color, and form proved winning. A big-budgeted film (close to half a million dollars), *The Broadway Melody* opened to rave reviews, soon becoming the season's second top-grosser with $3 million in ticket sales. It was a good year for musicals: Fox's musical, *Sunny Side Up,* with Janet Gaynor and Charles Farrell at the height of their popularity, was 1929's biggest movie.

The Broadway Melody was such a hit that MGM made three more *Broadway Melody* films, of which *The Broadway Melody of 1936,* released in 1935, is considered to be the best. It is also one of the few sequels to be nominated for Best Picture. The supporting cast — particularly Jack Benny as the columnist, and June Knight as a no-talent who wants to become an actress — was more impressive than the leads, played by Robert Taylor and Eleanor Powell. The movie won one Oscar: Dance Direction for David Gould, who excelled in staging the number "I've Got a Feeling You're Foolin'."

In the 1930s, most studios produced musicals, each developing its own distinct style. MGM was represented in the Oscars with *The Great Ziegfeld* (1936), which became the second Oscar-winning musical, and later with *The Wizard of Oz* (1939). Paramount participated with some sophisticated operettas that flaunted "the Lubitsch touch," such as *The Love Parade* (1929), *The Smiling Lieutenant* (1931), and *One Hour With You* (1934), all starring Maurice Chevalier.

RKO left its imprint on the decade's musical map with the fabulous dancing of Fred Astaire and Ginger Rogers. Two of the couple's musicals were nominated for Best Picture: *The Gay Divorcee* (1934) and *Top Hat* (1935).

Of Warner's major Depression musicals, only one was nominated, *42nd Street* (1933), with Warner Baxter, Ruby Keeler, and Dick Powell, though it did not win any award. Harry Cohn, head of Columbia Pictures, was not in favor of making musicals, yet having Grace Moore, the Metropolitan Opera diva, under contract convinced him to produce *One Night of Love* (1934), a variation on the Svengali theme. Moore, as the rising star, was also nominated, and the film won Sound Recording and Score.

Alexander's Ragtime Band (1938), Twentieth Century-Fox's big-scale musical, with a wonderful score by Irving Berlin and a cast headed by Tyrone Power, Alice Faye, and Don Ameche, also received a Best Picture nomination and an Oscar for Alfred Newman's musical direction.

In the 1940s and 1950s, MGM dominated the musical genre in the Oscar Awards. Of the six nominated musicals, four were produced by MGM, and two of these were directed by Vincente Minnelli. *An American in Paris,* George Gershwin's musical about the romance of a young American painter (Gene Kelly) and a poor French girl (Leslie Caron), was the big winner of 1951, with six Oscars for Story and Screenplay (Alan Jay Lerner), Scoring (Johnny Green and Saul Chaplin), and other technical awards.

The second Oscar-winning Minnelli musical was *Gigi* (1958), based on Collette's story, again set in Paris and starring Leslie Caron as a shy girl groomed to become a "lady" by her aunt. Applying a uniquely French charm to the American-musical tradition, *Gigi,* an original movie musical, won the largest number of awards (nine) to date, including Director (Minnelli), Screenplay (Alan Jay Lerner), and Color Cinematography (Joseph Ruttenberg).

Four of the ten Best Pictures in the 1960s were musicals: United Artists's *West Side Story* (1961), Warner's *My Fair Lady* (1964), Twentieth Century-Fox's *The Sound of Music* (1965), and Columbia's *Oliver!* (1968), a British movie. All four musicals were based on Broadway hits, but each one involved a major cast change. The most publicized coup was the casting of Audrey Hepburn as Eliza Doolittle, a role played on stage with great success by Julie Andrews.

Each of these winning musicals represents a kind of landmark in the genre's history. Transporting Shakespeare's *Romeo and Juliet* to the slums of New York and boasting exuberant music by Leonard Bernstein and witty lyrics by Stephen Sondheim, *West Side Story* is the only Oscar-winner to be co-directed — Robert Wise and Jerome Robbins shared the Best Director Award. And the musical is also one of the few winners in the Academy's history to receive awards in all but one of its eleven nominations. *West Side Story* ranks third, next to *Ben-Hur* and *Titanic,* as the most Oscar-honored film.

The stylishly elegant *My Fair Lady,* which was nominated for twelve awards and won eight, was selected in 1964, a year that ironically saw the decline of the classic musical and the rise of a new kind of musical, beginning with

Richard Lester's Beatles movie, *A Hard Day's Night.* George Cukor, who won the Best Direction Oscar at his fifth nomination, directed an opulent production in a grand manner, with fabulous costumes designed by Cecil Beaton. With the conspicuous omission of Audrey Hepburn in the lead role, its three British players, Rex Harrison, Stanley Holloway (as Alfred P. Doolittle), and Gladys Cooper (as Mrs. Higgins were all nominated), and Harrison deservedly won. *My Fair Lady* won over another musical, *Mary Poppins,* the first of few Disney productions — *Beauty and the Beast* and *The Sixth Sense* are the other two — ever to be nominated for the Best Picture. Despite its win, *My Fair Lady* was much less commercially successful than *Mary Poppins.*

By contrast, the immense commercial success of the 1965 winner, Robert Wise's *The Sound of Music,* became a desirable goal for every studio in Hollywood to emulate. Winning five of its ten nominations, it is, along with *Titanic* and *Gone With the Wind,* among the most commercial Oscar winners. Based on Howard Lindsay and Russel Crouse's long-running Broadway hit, with music by Richard Rodgers and Oscar Hammerstein II, it represents Hollywood filmmaking at its most calculated. Set in Austria in 1938, *The Sound of Music*'s narrative consists of stilted devices, each aiming to appeal to a different demographic segment of the public. Advertised as entertainment for the whole family and a genuine celebration of life, it is high corn — American Kitsch.

The motherless Von Trapp family of seven children, headed by Christopher Plummer, becomes a troupe of singers under the benevolence of Maria, the nun-turned-governess (Julie Andrews), thus eluding the Nazis and successfully escaping first to Switzerland and then to America. Rather shrewdly, *The Sound of Music* includes two generational romances: Plummer and his haughty baroness (played by Eleanor Parker), whom he later deserts for the simpler and maternal Andrews; and a youthful romance. Ideologically, the musical cherishes family strength and religious benevolence. The film was shot in the stunning landscapes of the Austrian Alps and Salzburg, but the anti-Nazi political setting is fake.

Ingeniously packaged and sold to the public, *The Sound of Music* was released in March, while Julie Andrews was the talk or the town due to her triumph in *Mary Poppins,* and her position as front-runner for the Best Actress in the upcoming ceremonies (in April). Andrews's Oscar made *The Sound of Music* even more popular at the box office.

The 1965 competition for Best Picture was rather weak. Stanley Kramer's flawed and pretentious *Ship of Fools,* and the screen adaptation of the Broadway comedy *A Thousand Clowns* stood no chance of winning. The other two contenders were made by British directors, David Lean's *Doctor Zhivago,* a romantic spectacle, and John Schlesinger's *Darling,* clearly the most innovative of the nominees, earlier singled out by the New York Film Critics. For most Academy members, however, the choice was between *The Sound of Music* and *Doctor Zhivago,* each of which received ten nominations. At the end of the evening, the awards were also equally divided, with each movie receiving five, though, except for Screenplay (Robert Bolt), *Doctor Zhivago* won mostly technical awards, such as Color Cinematography (Freddie Young), Color Art Direction-Set Decoration (John Box and Terry Marsh), and Color Costume Design (Phyllis Dalton).

Fox hoped to repeat the success of *The Sound of Music,* dubbed in Hollywood as "the sound of money," with two subsequent musicals that were poorly conceived and executed: *Doctor Dolittle* (1967), starring Rex Harrison, and *Hello, Dolly!* (1969), starring Barbra Streisand. When these movies received multiple nominations — *Dolittle* nine and *Dolly* seven — it became abundantly clear that aggressive and expensive ad campaigns (see chapter 14) are far more important than artistic merits in securing the Academy's attention.

In the 1970s, only three musicals were nominated for Best Picture: *Fiddler on the Roof* (1971), *Cabaret* (1972), and *All That Jazz* (1979). Michael Apted's *Coal Miner's Daughter* (1980), was a biopicture of country singer Loretta Lynn rather than a conventional musical. Similarly, *Amadeus,* the 1984 Oscar winner, was at once more and less than a genre musical — one of its achievements was the specific and original way in which Mozart's music was integrated into the narrative. It took twenty-two years after *All That Jazz* for the next live-action musical to be nominated for Best Picture: Baz Luhrmann's *Moulin Rouge.* The animated musical feature, *Beauty and the Beast,* competed for the top prize in 1991.

Except for sharing similar setting and some common characters, Luhrmann's film has little in common with John Huston's 1952 *Moulin Rouge.* Huston's fictional biopic of Toulouse-Lautrec put dramatic emphasis on the love affair of the dwarfish artist, for which Jose Ferrer received a second Best Actor nomination. Huston showed strong interest in evoking the ambience of nineteenth-century Montmartre, especially in the film's first cancan sequence, though nothing else stood up to the initial exhilarating moments in a picture that slowly slides into tedium. In contrast, the new *Moulin Rouge* shows such technical prowess and dazzling visual virtuosity that even those who disliked the movie found it hard to ignore. Indeed, Catherine Martin, Luhrmann's collaborator and wife, won two Oscars: For Art Direction and Costume Design (with Augus Strathie).

Moulin Rouge had its passionate advocates, as well as vocal detractors. The distributor, Fox, had mounted a pugnacious, excessive and costly campaign, despite the "love it or leave it" status the film had acquired since its Cannes world premiere in May 2001. Trying to bolster its chances among the Academy's older voters, Fox prominently displayed quotes from such industry top guns as Robert Wise, Stanley Donen and actresses Cyd Charisse and Debbie Reynolds, all praising Nicole Kidman, who was nominated, and Luhrmann who was not.

Up to the 1950s, the directors of the Oscar-winning musicals were not honored by the Academy. Vincente Minnelli was nominated for *An American in Paris* but did not win; the winner was George Stevens for *A Place in the Sun.* Minnelli won his first and only Best Director for *Gigi,* at his second nomination. By contrast, all the directors of the winning musicals in the 1960s received an

Oscar, some long overdue. George Cukor is one of two filmmaker to have won the Oscar (for *My Fair Lady*) at his fifth nomination; the other is William Wyler.

British director Carol Reed was singled out for his direction of *Oliver!* at his third nomination. The separation between Best Picture and Best Director has been rare, but in 1972, the Academy chose Bob Fosse as Best Director for *Cabaret,* and *The Godfather* as Best Picture. Francis Ford Coppola was nominated but did not win.

Musicals have not been generous to their performers as far as acting Oscars are concerned. Only a few players, mostly women, have won an Oscar for a musical role. Luise Rainer was the first to win Best Actress for a musical, as Ziegfeld's first wife, Anna Held, in *The Great Ziegfeld.* The next musical winner was Julie Andrews, almost three decades later, as the magical governess in *Mary Poppins.* Two winners have appeared in musical biographies: Barbra Streisand as Fanny Brice in *Funny Girl,* and Sissy Spacek as Loretta Lynn in *Coal Miner's Daughter.* One of the most brilliant performances in a musical was delivered by Liza Minnelli in *Cabaret,* as Sally Bowles, the ambitious, sexually ambiguous nightclub singer in pre-Nazi Germany.

Only two males have won the Best Actor in the musical genre: Yul Brynner in *The King and I,* and Rex Harrison in *My Fair Lady.*

Most acting Oscars and nominations in musicals were selected after 1960. Fred Astaire and Ginger Rogers were never nominated for any of their musicals. Rogers won the Academy's recognition only when she proved she could handle a dramatic role in *Kitty Foyle,* as the Irish girl from the wrong side of the tracks. She herself was anxious to demonstrate that she was much more than Fred Astaire's dancing partner, though it's precisely in this capacity she is best remembered today. The biases against musical performers have been similar to those against comedy performers.

Thrillers and Horror Flicks

Judging by the scarcity of nominations, suspense films, like action-adventures, are more appreciated by filmgoers than Academy voters. For some reason, well-made thrillers are perceived in the industry as a product of sheer craftsmanship rather than genuine film art.

In the Academy's history, only two thrillers, Alfred Hitchcock's *Rebecca* (1940) and Jonathan Demme's *The Silence of the Lambs* (1991), have won Best Picture. Based on Daphne du Maurier's popular novel, *Rebecca* was Hitchcock's first American movie, in which he cast Laurence Olivier and Joan Fontaine in the starring roles. The film is distinguished by exquisite cinematography (George Barnes won the Oscar), and great ensemble acting, headed by Judith Anderson, as the malevolent housekeeper, in one of her most memorable portrayals.

In 1940, *Rebecca* competed against another Hitchcock film, *Foreign Correspondent,* which deals with espionage in Europe. The film was interpreted by some as an endorsement of the American involvement in the war, because its producer, Walter Wanger, was known for his antifascist views. Both *Rebecca* and *Foreign Correspondent* were popular with the public; *Rebecca* earned in film rentals a then-phenomenal $1.5 million.

Jonathan Demme began his career directing exploitation films for Roger Corman but, aware of the genre's disreputable status, he gave *The Silence of the Lambs* the treatment of an A-Grade Art Film. Based on Thomas Harris's best-seller, the suspenseful and gruesome thriller centers on the battle of nerves between an FBI trainee named Clarice (Jodie Foster) and a psychiatrist turned cannibalistic psychopath, who becomes Clarice's sparring partner in her efforts to hunt down a serial killer. The acting of the two stars is superb. Anthony Hopkins almost made a likable hero out of the sadistic, unruly demon Hannibal Lecter. As Clarice, Foster embodies the gentleness of an initially naive country girl who becomes susceptible to Hannibal's advances.

For some viewers, the movie was too creepy and disconcerting in its hints of romantic attraction between Hannibal and Clarice. Indeed, conservative movie-goers were outraged by the picture. First Lady Barbara Bush stormed out of the theater, protesting, "I didn't come to a movie to see people's skin being taken off."

Gay activists threatened to disrupt the Oscar show as a protest against Hollywood's representations of homosexuals in *The Silence of the Lambs,* as well as in Oliver Stone's *JFK* (also Best Picture nominee that year) and the Sharon Stone psycho-thriller, *Basic Instinct,* which was released during the 1992 nomination period.

The first of 1991's five nominees to be distributed theatrically, *The Silence of the Lambs* opened at an unusual time, in February. By Oscar time, the picture had grossed $130.7 million, which made it the last successful release by the then-recently bankrupt Orion Pictures, the company responsible for *Dances With Wolves,* the Oscar-winner of the previous year. This bizarre financial situation was not lost on director Demme, who remarked, "I know everyone feels the incredible irony of what's happened to Orion."

The Silence of the Lambs swept all five major Oscars: Picture, Director, Actor, Actress, and Adapted Screenplay. Only two other films in the Academy's history have accomplished this: *It Happened One Night* in 1934 and *One Flew Over the Cuckoo's Nest* in 1975.

Demme is the only filmmaker to have ever won a directorial Oscar for a thriller. Hitchcock, the genre's acknowledged master, was nominated five times: *Rebecca* (1940), *Lifeboat* (1944), *Spellbound* (1945), *Rear Window* (1954), and *Psycho* (1960), one of his last undisputed successes. And four Hitchcock films were nominated for the Best Picture: The aforementioned *Rebecca, Foreign Correspondent, Suspicion,* and *Spellbound.* Failing to give Hitchcock a competitive Oscar, the Academy compensated him with a 1968 Honorary Oscar. No wonder the master was cynical about the Oscar; he told a reporter that he wasn't disappointed for not winning, "What do I want with another doorstop?"

Other filmmakers specializing in the thriller genre have met similar fates. Carol Reed established an international reputation with two extraordinary suspense films, both based on Graham Greene novels: *The Fallen Idol,* starring Ralph Richardson, and *The Third Man,* with Orson Welles. Both pictures boasted high production values; Robert Krasker won an Oscar for his Black-and-White Cinematography of Vienna in *The Third Man.* Reed received nominations for these films, but won the Oscar at his third nomination, for a less characteristic movie, the musical *Oliver!*

Thrillers have also featured marginally among the nominees, amounting to only three percent of all pictures, mostly in the 1940s. In addition to Hitchcock's films, they included John Huston's first (and one of his best) features, *The Maltese Falcon* in 1941, George Cukor's gothic tale *Gaslight,* and Billy Wilder's *Double Indemnity,* both in 1944.

No noir-suspense films were nominated in the 1950s or 1960s, and only two in the 1970s: Roman Polanski's *Chinatown* and Francis Ford Coppola's *The Conversation,* both in 1974. Most of the nominated thrillers employed the thematic and stylistic vocabulary of film noir. Some, like *The Maltese Falcon* and *Double Indemnity,* have become classics of their genre.

"Craftsmanship, cultural impact, and box-office success. Now that's a trifecta Oscar may find hard to resist," is how *Entertainment Weekly* described the 1999 sleeper *The Sixth Sense,* a spiritual horror-thriller with strong performances from Bruce Willis (who was not nominated) and Haley-Joel Osment, who was. Osment must have uttered the most memorable line in any movie that year: "I see dead people." The most successful horror film in the genre's history, and yet one of the gentlest, was directed by the Indian-born M. Night Shyamalan, who, at twenty-nine, became one of the youngest Best Director nominees. *The Sixth Sense* made $284 million after its summer release, a level of success that must have deemed it too commercial for serious Oscar consideration (six nominations, zero awards).

The Academy's lack of respect for thrillers is also reflected in the paucity of acting awards in this genre. Not surprisingly, most of these roles were assumed by women who played victims, threatened with murder by their husbands, such as Joan Fontaine in *Suspicion* or Ingrid Bergman in *Gaslight* (see chapter 12).

Composers who specialized in the thriller and horror genres have also been neglected. In 1976, *The Omen* became the first horror film to receive a Music Oscar, honoring Jerry Goldsmith's score. Interestingly, he competed that year with Bernard Hermann, who was nominated posthumously for two pictures: *Obsession* and *Taxi Driver,* which turned out to be his last score. Herrmann had been nominated for two other films, *Citizen Kane* and *Anna and the King of Siam,* but not for any of his great Hitchcockian scores.

11

THE OSCAR AND
THE FOREIGN-LANGUAGE PICTURE

The Best Picture Nominees

In the Academy's entire history only a few foreign-language movies have been nominated for the Best Picture. Jean Renoir's antiwar masterpiece, *Grand Illusion,* competed for the 1937 top award, but that was before the creation of a distinct category for foreign-language pictures.

Officially, the first winner in this category was *La Strada* in 1956, which helped establish Federico Fellini as one of the most important European directors. Anthony Quinn, as Zampano, an itinerant strong man, and Giulietta Masina, as the young woman he buys and abuses as his clown and servant, gave memorable performances in a film that was also nominated for Original Screenplay (by Fellini and Tullio Pinelli).

Prior to the creation of a separate category, the Academy recognized several foreign films with an Honorary Award, beginning with Vittorio De Sica's neorealistic movie, *Shoeshine,* in 1947. Academy leader and board member Jean Hersholt held that "an international award, if properly and carefully administered, would promote a closer relationship between American film craftsmen and those of other countries." The citation for *Shoeshine* read: "The high quality of this motion picture, brought to eloquent life in a country scarred by war, is proof to the world that the creative spirit can triumph over adversity."

The following pictures were singled out for Special Awards before the foreign-language category was created:

1948	*Monsieur Vincent*	France
1949	*The Bicycle Thief*	Italy
1950	*The Walls of Malapaga*	France-Italy
1951	*Rashomon*	Japan
1952	*Forbidden Games*	France
1953	No citation	
1954	*Gate of Hell*	Japan
1955	*The Seven Samurai*	Japan

Since the establishment of the Best Foreign-Language Picture, only five foreign movies have been nominated for Best Picture. Costa-Gavras's political thriller *Z,* a French-Algerian co-production starring Yves Montand and Jean-Louis Trintignant, enjoyed a special position in 1969. *Z* won the Best Foreign-Language Picture, and it was also nominated in the general competitive category of Best Picture. According to Academy rules, foreign-language pictures that have opened in the United States are eligible to compete in all the other categories. Indeed, *Z* also won an Oscar for its editor, Françoise Bonnot. To qualify for the Best Foreign-Language Picture, however, a film must be sent by its country of origin to the Academy, where a committee selects the five nominees. *Z* qualified on both grounds; it was officially submitted as an Algerian entry, and it opened in the United States in December.

Two Swedish films received consecutive Foreign-Language nominations. In 1972, *The Emigrants,* which deals with the emigration of Swedish peasants to America in the nineteenth century, starred Liv Ullmann (who received Best Actress nomination) and Max von Sydow. Jan Troell was nominated as a director and co-writer of the film's adapted screenplay. In 1973, Ingmar Bergman's *Cries and Whispers,* a haunting film about death and dying, featuring unforgettable performances by Liv Ullmann, Ingrid Thulin, and Harriet Andersson, was nominated for Best Picture and four other awards. Bergman's ace collaborator, Sven Nykvist, won the Cinematography Oscar.

Two Italian movies were nominated for Best Picture in the 1990s, both distributed by Miramax. The 1995 *Il Postino* (*The Postman*) tells the story of an Italian postman who bonds with a legendary poet, Pablo Neruda, and wins the affections of a local girl through his heartfelt poetry. The film was based on *The Postman of Pablo Neruda,* a novel by Chilean author Antonio Skarmeta. Trying to re-create Southern Italy in the 1950s, New Delhi-born English director Michael Radford shot *The Postman* on two islands off the coast of Sicily. Massimo Troisi, who played the postman, suffered from heart problems, and died only one day after shooting was completed. Troisi headed an international cast, which included the noted French actor Philippe Noiret.

In 1998, *Life Is Beautiful* became the second film after *Z* to be nominated for the Best Foreign-Language and the Best Picture in the same year. A comedy-drama about the Holocaust, the film carried with it both gravity and importance. It received seven nominations, including Best Actor and Best Director, a record for a foreign-language film. The narrative concerns an accident-prone Italian bookshop owner (Benigni), who is imprisoned with his family in a World War II concentration camp. He bravely attempts to protect his son (Giorgio Cantarini) by making a game out of their tragic predicament. Benigni, known in the United States for his performances in *Down by Law* and *Johnny Stecchino,* came under fire when word got out that he was making a comedy about the Holocaust. Though not Jewish, the Italian director and co-writer had personal roots in the saga — his father served time in a German labor camp. Benigni recalled how "each evening my father was telling me a story, some awful and revolting tragedy things, always in a very light way. Maybe he was scared to make a trauma on me."

Citing Benigni's success at the European Film Awards (Best Actor) and at Cannes (where the film won the Grand Jury Prize), industry experts felt that Benigni had a strong shot at a lead performance award. Harvey Weinstein remarked that Miramax has gotten nominations in the past for Max von Sydow in *Pelle the Conqueror* and Massimo Troisi for *Il Postino,* which for him was "a testament that the actor category has been foreign-actor friendly." But it was the film's popularity with audiences that was the real ace up its sleeve — "Benigni's work pushes all the right emotional buttons."

Indeed, even before its American release, *Life Is Beautiful* showed the same trademarks as *Il Postino.* Ultimately, *Life Is Beautiful* shattered box-office records for foreign films, eventually outdoing *Il Postino'*s commercial success by far.

In 2000, another foreign-language film landed a spot in the Best Picture race — *Crouching Tiger, Hidden Dragon.* The thrilling fight sequences in this superbly mounted historical-romantic saga elicited heartfelt applause from audiences since its premiere at the Cannes Film Festival. Ang Lee's triumphant Hong Kong-style martial-arts film stars Chow Yun-Fat and Michelle Yeoh as fellow warriors who share an unspoken love; porcelain-lovely Zhang Ziyi portrays a dazzling young prodigy who hasn't yet found her true path.

Shrewdly marketed and platformed by Sony Pictures Classics, the Mandarin-language film clearly pushed the envelope. *Crouching Tiger, Hidden Dragon,* won Golden Globes for Best Foreign Film and for director Ang Lee, and was deemed best movie of the year by the Los Angeles Film Critics Association. The film set a new box-office record for foreign-language films in the United Sates with its impressive gross of $130 million. In February, it garnered ten Oscar nominations — the second most-nominated film of the year after *Gladiator.* *Crouching Tiger, Hidden Dragon* won four Oscars, matching Bergman's *Fanny and Alexander,* the previous Oscar record-holder for foreign-language films.

Foreign Winners and Nominees

I think we're carrying this foreign aid too far
— Bob Hope, 1958 Oscar show host

The foreign (non-British) nominees have generally come from countries with major film industries, such as France, Italy, Germany, Sweden, and Japan. Smaller countries, such as Greece, Israel, Egypt, and Hungary, have been represented in the Oscar race only if their players appeared in American-made movies. The notable exception is Polish stage actress Ida Kaminska, who was a Best Actress nominee for the Czech film, *The Shop on Main Street,* which was voted the Best Foreign-Language Picture in 1965.

However, most foreign male winners have received the award for American movies. German Emil Jannings earned the Best Actor for two American films

(*The Last Command* and *The Way of All Flesh*). Born in Switzerland, Maximilian Schell worked in Germany and Austria prior to winning the Best Actor for *Judgment at Nuremberg*. The same is true for the foreign nominees such as French Charles Boyer (*Conquest*), Austrian Oskar Werner (*Ship of Fools*), and Israeli Topol (*Fiddler on the Roof*).

The only actors nominated for performances in foreign-language pictures have been Italians: Marcello Mastroianni in *Divorce — Italian Style, A Special Day,* and *Dark Eyes;* Giancarlo Giannini in *Seven Beauties;* Massimo Troisi in *Il Postino,* and Roberto Benigni in *Life Is Beautiful.* Benigni is the only actor to actually win an Oscar for a foreign-language film.

In the Best Actress category, too, most foreign-born women have won the Oscar for American movies. Austrian actress Luise Rainer won her two Oscars for two American films, *The Great Ziegfeld* and *The Good Earth.* Italian actress Anna Magnani won for the movie based on Tennessee Williams's *The Rose Tattoo.* In 1961, Sophia Loren became the first and only foreign actress to win for a foreign-language film, Vittorio De Sica's *Two Women,* until Benigni joined her ranks thirty-seven years later.

None of the foreign actors (male or female) in the supporting categories has ever won for a role in a foreign language movie. But several foreign actresses earned the Supporting Oscar for an American film: Greek-born actress Katina Paxinou for *For Whom the Bell Tolls,* Japanese Miyoshi Umeki for *Sayonara,* Russian-French Lila Kedrova for *Zorba the Greek* and French Juliette Binoche for *The English Patient.* In 2000, Binoche received a second, this time lead, nomination, for *Chocolat,* which was also in English.

To get Academy recognition, foreign players must appear in commercially successful movies. A good performance has no impact if it is contained in a small art film seen by few. Similarly, most foreign pictures nominated for writing or technical awards have been box-office hits or ranked high on Ten Best Lists by major film critics.

Never on Sunday (1960), produced, written, and directed by Jules Dassin, who also starred in it with his wife-actress Melina Mercouri, would not have been nominated in major categories (Director, Best Actress) had it not been a commercial hit. A kind of contemporary Pygmalion, the movie focuses on the tempestuous relationship between a serious American writer and a joyous Greek prostitute. *Never on Sunday* won one Oscar, Best Song (written by Manos Hadjidakis), thus becoming the first song in a foreign-language picture to win an Oscar since the Academy began to recognize achievements in this category in 1934. The movie and its melodic score are credited with stimulating American and Western tourism in Greece. *Never on Sunday* also put its star, Melina Mercouri, on the international map; she went on to appear in such commercial films as *Topkapi* and others.

Fellini's satirical view of Italian high society, *La Dolce Vita,* would not have been nominated for the 1960 Screenplay, Director, and other awards had it not created a sensation with its decadent view of Italian high society. After the film's release, Rome's notorious Via Veneto, where some of the action takes place, became a major tourist site. Praised by critics, *La Dolce Vita* became one of the most popular foreign films in America, grossing over $8 million. By the time *La Dolce Vita* was shown in the United States, it had already received recognition at the Cannes Festival and had achieved immense popularity all over Europe. The movie, however, won only one Oscar — Black-and-White Costume Design for Piero Gherardi; the Academy failed to recognize the great acting of Marcello Mastroianni as the hip journalist whose experiences form the center of the narrative.

In 1976, Marie-Christine Barrault won a Best Actress nomination for the French comedy *Cousin, Cousine,* written and directed by Jean-Charles Tacchella, whose script was also nominated. The nomination of Barrault (niece of the famed French actor, Jean-Louis Barrault) had less to do with her acting than with the immense popularity of the movie in New York and Los Angeles. Recounting in a nonjudgmental way an open adulterous affair between two cousins, the nominated screenplay, by Jean-Charles Tacchella and Danièle Thompson, deserved recognition for its wit and originality.

In the same year, Giancarlo Giannini won Academy recognition for his performance in Lina Wertmuller's controversial movie *Seven Beauties.* This film put Wertmuller, nominated as writer and director, at the front rank of international filmmakers. Giannini excelled as the contemptible Neapolitan macho, driven to self-degradation in his attempts to survive. But his performance would not have been singled out if the movie had not been a critics' favorite and box-office hit.

Distinguished performances by foreign players in arthouse films that were not commercial hits have been consistently overlooked by the Academy. This list is too long to recite here, but a recent example demonstrates the point. One of Europe's best and busiest actors, Gerard Depardieu, didn't receive Academy attention, despite excellent performances in numerous films including the frustrated husband in *Get Out Your Handkerchiefs,* and the title role in Andrzej Wajda's *Danton,* until 1990 when he finally received a Best Actor nomination for the French version of *Cyrano.* Interestingly, Depardieu played the same role for which Jose Ferrer had won Best Actor exactly forty years earlier.

It's always encouraging when a foreign movie gets recognition in major categories, as did Wolfgang Peterson's *Das Boot,* a German film that chronicled the physical and psychological hardships endured by the Nazi crew of a U-Boat. This fascinating, claustrophobic movie occupied the fifth place among 1982's most nominated pictures, receiving six citations including Direction and Screenplay. Acclaimed by critics, *Das Boot* also proved popular with the public. Grossing $4.5 million, it is the most popular German film ever shown in the United States.

Recent foreign-language Oscar winners have been global blockbusters: *Kolya* (Czech) in 1996, *Life Is Beautiful* (Italy) in 1998, *All About My Mother* (Spain) in 1999, and *Crouching Tiger, Hidden Dragon* (Taiwan) in 2000. History would suggest that *Amélie* (France), with a worldwide gross of $138 million by Oscar time, would follow the same path. But it was not to be; the surprise winner of both the 2001 Golden Globes and the Oscars was *No Man's Land*. Since war-ravaged Bosnia hardly has any cinemas left, *No Man's Land*'s grosses there, $215,000, should be considered an extraordinary if not an impossible achievement. The film's distributor, Obala, took two Dolby projectors on a tour and screened the film in the country's sports' halls and public arenas.

The other three foreign contenders in 2001 were: *Son of the Bride, Elling,* and *Lagaan.* In Norway, *Elling* was the all-time number one local picture, grossing $6 million across Scandinavian. *Son of the Bride* was Argentina's biggest local movie. After topping charts in Argentina, the film went on to gross $4 million in Spain, where Latin American movies have routinely failed. *Son of the Bride*'s Spanish box office surged 60 percent in the weekend after the Oscar nominations. Sony Picture Classics opened the film in the United States on March 22, during the Oscar weekend, but, unfortunately, the film didn't find its audience.

Lagaan, the Indian nominee, is a blend of Bollywood and Merchant-Ivory costume drama. Despite its 223-minute running-time, *Lagaan* ranked number three in India. The film has played strongly both in India and in Bollywood theaters in the United States and United Kingdom, but it has yet to crossover to non-Indian audiences.

These four nominees had some distance to go on their international travels, and therefore much to gain commercially from an Oscar victory. But for *Amélie,* it was more a matter of pride and prestige. *Amélie* achieved its success despite being snubbed by the Cannes Festival. By nomination time, Jean-Pierre Jeunet's movie had already traveled wider and more successfully than any other French picture. Boffo figures in Germany and Spain, $14 million and $7 million, respectively, compounded the French grosses. Jeunet's charmer wowed crowds in most major territories: $29 million in the United States (by Oscar time), $7 million in the United Kingdom, $8 million in Japan. It also opened in Thailand, Indonesia, and the Philippines, territories that UGC International usually doesn't release pictures.

In contrast, the Cannes Festival was instrumental in elevating the visibility of *No Man's Land.* At the closing ceremonies, the film received an eight-minute standing ovation and the screenplay prize. "Cannes created this film and this director," said producer Cedomir Kolar. Nonetheless, it's a tough movie — an ironic drama and black comedy about the Bosnian war — and its box office beyond home turf reflected that.

For Kolar, the picture, a co-production between France, Italy, Belgium, the United Kingdom, and Solvenia, is "really no man's land." In France, *No Man's Land* won the César Award for best first film. In Belgium, the prize for best Belgian film. And in Italy it has been adopted as the country's standard-bearer after Nanni Moretti's 2000 Cannes Festival winner, *The Son's Room,* failed to secure a nomination. The Oscar nomination helped to sell the audacious film in smaller territories, such as Portugal, Singapore, Malaysia, and Taiwan. The box-office figures have been all right around the world for this sort of tough fare, but the movie broke records in Slovenia and Serbia, as well as Bosnia. The only blip was Croatia, where it grossed just $16,000, even though the film's two lead actors are local residents.

Foreign Artists in Other Categories

The best chances for foreign artists to get nominations are in the two writing categories: Original and Adapted Screenplay. The Swiss film, Leopold Lintberg's *Marie-Louise,* about a group of French children during World War II, was the first European (and foreign-language) movie to win the Original Screenplay, though 1945 was an admittedly weak year for writing achievements. The other nominees were: *Dillinger, Music for Millions, Salty O'Rourke,* and *What Next, Corporal Hargrove?*

Some of the best Italian neorealistic movies were also nominated for writing awards: Roberto Rossellini's *Open City,* with a script by Sergio Amidei and Fellini, and Vittorio De Sica's *Umberto D,* scripted by Cesare Zavattini, a major force in postwar Italian cinema.

In 1959, two of the five nominated original scripts were for foreign films: François Truffaut's stunning debut, *The 400 Blows,* which was one of the films to launch the French New Wave, and Ingmar Bergman's arthouse hit, *Wild Strawberries,* which boasted a legendary performance from Victor Sjostrom, as the old professor. Neither film won. The winner was an American comedy, *Pillow Talk,* scripted by Russell Rouse and Clarence Greene, based on Stanley Shapiro and Maurice Richlin's story.

Over the past few decades, the writers of the French *Day for Night,* the Italian *Seven Beauties,* the French *Mon Oncle d'Amerique,* the West German *Das Boot,* the Swedish *Fanny and Alexander,* the Argentinean *The Official Story,* Louis Malle's *Au Revoir, Les Enfants* (France), and Agnieszka Holland's *Europa, Europa* (Poland) have received writing nominations, if not awards.

It takes longer for foreign filmmakers to get recognition in the United States, particularly if they don't make American movies. Many good "art" films are not widely shown if they don't boast internationally known stars, or are not made by a prestigious director such as Fellini, Truffaut, or Bergman. The distribution of foreign movies in the American Heartland depends to a large extent on favorable reviews by major critics in New York and Los Angeles.

This is one reason why foreign players and foreign directors, particularly men, tend to be older than their American counterparts by the time they earn Academy nominations. Marcello Mastroianni is a prime example. He was not only one of the world's most distinguished actors, but also one of the few to be extremely popular outside of his native Italy. Mastroianni made his screen debut in 1949 at the age of twenty-five after studying acting and acquiring stage experience with Luchino Visconti's theatrical troupe. In the 1950s, he achieved stature in Italy, but he attained international stardom in 1960, with his starring role in Fellini's *La Dolce Vita.* A few years later, he starred in another

Fellini masterpiece, *8 ½,* which was even more commercially successful than *La Dolce Vita.*

The Academy, however, failed to nominate Mastroianni for either of these performances, though both movies were nominated — and even won — other awards. Mastroianni earned his first Best Actor nomination in 1962, at age thirty-eight, for the Italian comedy, *Divorce — Italian Style,* in which he excelled as the bored Sicilian baron who plans to get rid of his nagging wife. Mastroianni would probably not have received the nomination were it not for the publicity and awards that *Divorce — Italian Style* received from the Cannes Festival and the Hollywood Foreign Press Association. In 1987, Mastroianni garnered a third Best Actor nomination for Nikita Mikhalkov's *Dark Eyes,* in which he was perfectly cast as an aging womanizer recalling his affair with a young Russian woman.

Foreign players who work in the United States tend to be older than their American colleagues, because they first must excel in their own countries before being brought to Hollywood. Hence, Anna Magnani and Maggie Smith, both respected and established in their native countries (Italy and Great Britain, respectively), were older than American actresses of their generation when they won the Oscar.

American and foreign players make their debuts at more or less the same age. Women both foreign and American, tend to be younger than men both when they are first nominated and first win the Oscar. The gap between American and foreign players is wider among men. American actors win the Oscar at the average age of thirty-seven, whereas the foreigners average forty-four.

Despite a strong international dimension, the Academy is charged periodically with "chauvinism," or with favoring American over foreign artists. The question of just how distinctly American the Oscar is, compared with other prestigious prizes, such as the New York Film Critics Awards, is therefore an intriguing one. Though Americans have dominated both forums, the Oscar is a more American award (about 70 percent of all winners) than the New York Film Critics Award (60 percent). British players have occupied the second place in both contests, but their presence is stronger in the New York Film Critics than in the Oscar race.

In both organizations, there is more diversity among the female winners. Among the foreign women cited by the New York Film Critics Circle and the Academy are Italians Anna Magnani and Sophia Loren, and French Isabelle Adjani (two-time nominee) and Catherine Deneuve.

In 1988, Norma Aleandro became the first South American actress to be nominated for an Oscar for *Gaby — A True Story,* an Argentinean movie. Aleandro was already known in America, having starred in *The Official Story,* which won the 1985 Best Foreign-Language Picture. Noted Brazilian actress Fernanda Montengero joined Aleandro when she received a Best Actress nomination in 1998 for *Central Station.*

Some of the Oscar's greatest "losers" are foreign-born actresses who have won multiple awards from the New York Film Critics Circle. The British actress Deborah Kerr, a six-time Oscar nominee, won three New York Film Critics Awards, for *Black Narcissus; Heaven Knows, Mr. Allison;* and *The Sundowners.*

Swedish Icon Greta Garbo, a three-time Oscar nominee, was cited twice by the New York Film Critics Circle, for *Anna Karenina* and *Camille.* Liv Ullmann, Ingmar Bergman's quintessential actress, earned two Oscar nominations, losing both. She won three New York Film Critics citations, for *Cries and Whispers, Scenes from a Marriage,* and *Face to Face.*

No such striking cases exist among the men. Two British winners of the New York Film Critics Circle were not even nominated for their performances by the Academy: Ralph Richardson, for *Breaking the Sound Barrier,* and John Gielgud for *Providence.* Both actors were nominated by the Academy for other performances, and Gielgud won the Supporting Oscar for *Arthur.*

At most film festivals, nationalistic considerations do play a role beyond the quality of the competing performances. In 1980, a furor arose in the Cannes Festival when Peter Sellers's brilliant performance in *Being There* was overlooked by the jury for reasons that apparently had nothing to do with artistic merit. Kirk Douglas, the jury's president, was furious when his colleagues chose Michel Piccoli and Anouk Aimée (both for Marco Bellocchio's *Leap Into the Void*) because they felt it was time for French performers to win.

The 1980 Cannes acting prize is not an isolated incident. In other years too, political considerations have played a crucial role in determining the final winners. Critics felt that the motive for awarding the 1975 Palm d'Or to the Algerian film, *Chronicle of the Burning Years,* was political: Historically Algeria, and Third World cinema in general, had been vastly underrepresented. Similarly, rumors circulated on the Croisette that Roman Polanski's *The Pianist* won the 2002 Cannes Palme d'Or as much for its subject matter — a personal film about the Holocaust — and the fact that it was a comeback film for the Polish director, as for its artistic merits. Polanski, a French resident, had not produced a truly interesting work since *Tess,* twenty-two years earlier.

The relatively high number of ties at the Cannes Film Festival also attests to political compromise. In 1979, the Cannes Jury conferred the Palm d'Or on both the German picture *The Tin Drum* and the American *Apocalypse Now.* In 1980, a tie was declared between the Japanese film *Kagemusha,* by Akira Kurosawa, and the American entry, *All That Jazz,* by Bob Fosse. By contrast, there has never been a tie in the Best Picture Oscar.

All film forums and film juries are biased in their choices — that's the nature of awards determined by majority vote. Yet an argument can be made that the disagreements within a particular voting group, and the disparity among the various groups, play an important role in calling attention to the multiple criteria — artistic, ideological, political, and religious — in evaluating such a complex yet popular art form as film.

The Oscars' Foreign Directors

The foreign film directors nominated for an Oscar have generally made their debuts at a younger age than their American peers, but have been older when they received their first nomination. This difference increases among the Oscar winners. American filmmakers win at the average age of forty, whereas the foreign directors on average at forty-five.

Most foreign filmmakers have done their best work by the time they earn their first Oscar nomination. British director Carol Reed's international reputation reached a peak with *The Fallen Idol* (1949), earning him his first nomination, and *The Third Man* (1950), his second. Nonetheless, Reed won the Oscar many years later, and as seen for a musical, *Oliver!* (1968). It was a long overdue Oscar, received by an aging director (sixty-nine) then in decline. Jean Renoir received his one and only nomination for *The Southerner* (1945), a film he made in the United States at the age of fifty-two, years after making his French masterpieces, *Grand Illusion* and *The Rules of the Game,* for which he did not receive directing recognition by the Academy.

Fellini, another master filmmaker, never won a directorial Oscar despite four nominations: *La Dolce Vita, 8 ½, Fellini Satyricon,* and *Amarcord.* Fellini was older (forty-two) than his American peers at his first nomination and, like other foreigners, was not nominated for his earlier masterworks, *La Strada* and *Nights of Cabiria,* though both films won the Best Foreign-Language Picture (in 1956 and 1957 respectively). Fellini later received an Honorary Oscar in 1993, which was basically a compensatory gesture.

That the Academy tends to overlook the work of first-rate foreign filmmakers is clear from the career of Ingmar Bergman. It's hard to believe, but Bergman received his first nomination as late as 1973, for *Cries and Whispers,* when he was fifty-six. None of his earlier masterworks, *The Seventh Seal, The Virgin Spring,* or *Persona* was recognized by the Academy for their masterful direction, though *The Virgin Spring* and *Through a Glass Darkly* won the Foreign-Language Picture Oscar in 1960 and 1961 respectively. Bergman, like Fellini, did not win a Best Director Oscar, though he earned a second nomination for *Face to Face,* and a third for *Fanny and Alexander,* which also won the Foreign-Language Picture Oscar. In all likelihood, Bergman, like the late Fellini, will win an Honorary Oscar for his career, but the opportunity to confer the award on a uniquely talented artist while at his peak has been missed.

The revered Indian director, Satyajit Ray, who made such classics as *Pather Panchali* and *The World of Apu,* was awarded the 1991 Honorary Oscar. Too ill to attend the ceremonies, he appeared on videotape from his hospital bed in Calcutta, clutching the Oscar statuette in his arms.

Yet every once in a while foreign filmmakers feature prominently in the Oscar competition. In 1987, all five of the nominated directors were born outside of the United States: Italian Bertolucci (who won) for *The Last Emperor,* Briton John Boorman for *Hope and Glory,* Swedish Lasse Hallstrom for *My Life as a*

Dog, Canadian Norman Jewison for *Moonstruck,* and the British Adrian Lyne for *Fatal Attraction.*

In 1995, the noted Polish filmmaker Krzysztof Kieslowski received two Oscar nominations, Best Director and Original Screenplay, for *Red,* a Swiss-made picture and the last of his acclaimed Three Colors trilogy that won most of the critics awards for foreign film. A furor erupted when *Red* was disqualified to compete in the Foreign Language Picture category due to rigid bureaucratic rules.

Another Polish filmmaker, Andrzej Wajda, made history in 1999, when he became the first East European director to be given an Honorary Oscar. That he received the award from formerly more politically oriented actress Jane Fonda made his moment in the limelight all the more memorable. "I think to create film in a foreign language, and yet to be known and recognized by everyone, is the best kind of success one can expect," Wajda said in his eloquent acceptance speech.

In 1997, James Cameron became the first Canadian to win the Best Director, for *Titanic.* Though working in Hollywood, the Ontario-born Cameron has remained a Canadian citizen. Another Canadian-educated filmmaker, Atom Egoyan (who was born in Egypt), was nominated in the same year for adapting and directing *The Sweet Hereafter.*

In 2001, too, the five nominated directors represented an international mix: Robert Altman (*Gosford Park*), David Lynch (*Mulholland Drive*) and Ron Howard (*A Beautiful Mind*) are American, Peter Jackson (*The Lord of the Rings*) is from New Zealand, and Ridley Scott (*Black Hawk Down*) is British.

There's yet another dimension to Oscar's growing international dimension. In 1995, four out of the five Best Picture nominees were shot outside of America, highlighting the globalization of film production and blurring the definition of what constitutes a Hollywood studio product. The smorgasbord of locations, directors, casts, and crews gave that year's picks an international flavor usually seen only in the foreign-language film category.

This trend continues into the present. In a subtle statement about the state of the film industry, each of the 1998 Best Picture nominees did all or most of its shooting overseas. Indeed, in 1999, *American Beauty* became the first Best Picture in twenty-three years — since *Rocky* in 1976 — to be lensed entirely in Hollywood.

The production of foreign-language films has also reflected the growing internationalism of the movie industry. The UK entry, *Solomon & Gaenor,* was directed by a British subject (Paul Morrison), set in Wales, with actors speaking in Yiddish, English, and Welsh. Nepal's first-ever nomination, *Caravan,* was a French/British/Swiss/Nepalese co-production, set in the highest reaches of the Himalayas, with a French crew and cast, and Tibetans speaking in their native language.

12

BOYS WILL BE BOYS
AND GIRLS WILL BE GIRLS:
THE OSCAR-WINNING ROLES

The Oscar race is not wide open, and not every screen role stands an equal chance of nomination. Still, it is impossible to predict what kinds of screen roles will receive the Academy's attention. Quite disappointingly, gender segregation prevails in the typical Oscar-winning role — though this trend is not as distinct today as it was during the era of the studio system. Still typical Oscar roles for men and women continue as a reality.

The Oscar-winning roles are usually contained in popular movies, thus serving as barometers of what the American cinema has been telling its audience about the appropriate and inappropriate behaviors for men and for women. Since mainstream Hollywood movies are designed to appeal to the largest potential viewership, most filmmakers try to make movies that will be widely acceptable. The male and female Oscar-winning roles therefore shed light on the cultural guidelines, proscriptions and prescriptions, that the American cinema has provided for its viewers.

Macho Men and Chic Flicks:
Oscar and Movie Genres

Favoring biopictures over fiction films, the Academy has rewarded actors who play biographical roles: About one-fifth of all Oscar-winning roles have been inspired by real-life personalities and actual events. Re-creations on the big screen of real-life figures brings a measure of prestige to their performers, particularly if their characters are noble or accomplished in the line of work. That said, a clear gender-related bias is in operation: The number of biographical Oscar roles is twice as large among the men, particularly in the lead categories.

Male biographical roles have been more diverse, both historically and occupationally. Men have portrayed military figures, such as Gary Cooper as Alvin York, the Tennessee farmer who became a World War I hero in *Sergeant York,* and George C. Scott as General Patton, World War II's controversial but brilliant strategist, in *Patton.* Historical figures have included Charles Laughton as the English monarch in *The Private Life of Henry VIII,* and Paul Scofield as

Sir Thomas More in *A Man for All Seasons.* Men have also played political personalities such as the British prime minister in *Disraeli* (George Arliss), and the venerable Indian leader in *Gandhi* (Ben Kingsley).

Women, by contrast, have mostly portrayed showbiz figures such as Luise Rainer, Florenz Ziegfeld's first wife in *The Great Ziegfeld;* Barbra Streisand as musical star Fanny Brice in *Funny Girl;* or Sissy Spacek as country singer Loretta Lynn in *Coal Miner's Daughter.*

Most recently, Gwyneth Paltrow won the Best Actress as the Bard's muse in *Shakespeare in Love.* Paltrow gave a lively, sexy performance, which impressed her director and the Academy voters. Said John Madden: "With Gwyneth, you had to believe that she could inspire Shakespeare to write that play. She has incredible physical presence and beauty and a slightly kind of spiritual, ineffable quality as a muse. The range of things she has to accomplish — the comic moments with passionate intensity — was extraordinary."

The underrepresentation of women in biopictures that celebrate real-life achievements suggests that perhaps there have not been enough prominent women in science, politics, and literature for the movies to draw upon. However, this is clearly not the case, and the reason for overlooking women is rather simple. Hollywood movies were simply reluctant to use real-life heroines for screen biographies. Functioning as an agency of social control, Hollywood has kept women "in their place," confining them to the domestic arena or to show business, the two most traditional on-screen female domains.

The Oscar roles are contained in specific film genres. The most frequent, for both male and female roles, is the "serious" drama, with 60 percent of all Oscar roles belonging to this venerable genre. Few Oscar-winning roles have been in romances, musicals, thrillers, and Westerns. But there has been unequal distribution of male and female winners in these genres, attesting again to the prevalence of "more masculine" and "more feminine" Oscar roles.

The second most frequent genre among the men is the action-adventure (including war films and Westerns), amounting to one-fifth of all male winning roles. In contrast, there are only a few female roles in this genre, and usually in the supporting category.

The most "feminine" genre, the female equivalent of the action-adventure, is the romantic melodrama, particularly in the Best Actress category; no man has ever won the Best Actor for such a film. In suspense films, there are only two male winners, Fredric March in *Dr. Jekyll and Mr. Hyde* and Anthony Hopkins in *The Silence of the Lambs.* This compared to twice as many females, typically cast as victims (often of their husbands), such as Joan Fontaine in *Suspicion* and Ingrid Bergman in *Gaslight.*

The Oscar and Gender

According to the Oscar results, the American screen heroine is young: Three-fifths of all female Oscar roles have been young, compared with only one-fifth of the males. Characters in supporting roles, both male and female, are typically older than those in the leading roles.

Within each category, there is one dominant age group: Young for women, middle-aged for men. American pop culture, as expressed in Oscar-winning films, has prescribed consistent distinctions; screen heroines are younger than screen heroes. Attached to these biological attributes are also aesthetic norms: Leading ladies are young and attractive, whereas leading men are middle-aged or older and not necessarily handsome. Dustin Hoffman, Robert Duvall, Gene Hackman, and Tom Hanks are talented and appealing actors, but, by Hollywood standards, not typically or conventionally handsome. Since actors tend to receive the Oscar at an older age than actresses, their winning roles are often those of older characters.

These normative guidelines have confined the range of screen roles allotted to women: Lead roles are almost exclusively cast with young and beautiful actresses. Up to the late 1970s, leading actresses over the age of forty were forced to retire from the big screen, or to switch to smaller and secondary character roles.

Early retirement was not a matter of choice, and actresses were forced to quit while at the peak of their careers. Deborah Kerr, a leading lady and six-time Oscar nominee, retired in 1969, at the young age of forty-eight — after appearing in Elia Kazan's *The Arrangement* — because she did not want to play dotty aunts or eccentric grandmothers.

The Oscar roles also reveal different patterns of marital status for men and for women. Two-fifths of the female Oscar roles have been married compared with one-fourth of the men. And close to one-fifth of the male Oscar roles have made no reference to their marital status — in sharp contrast, the marital position of female roles is almost always clear. If knowledge of gender roles were entirely based on the movies, it would be impossible to understand women without knowing whether they are single, married, divorced, or widowed. By contrast, marital status would seemingly be less crucial to men's personalities and less important to their welfare and happiness. American film suggests that attributes other than marital status are more relevant in understanding men's place in society.

The number of male supporting roles with no reference to their marital status is also greater than that of the female roles. These differences are relevant as films usually do not provide much information about supporting roles due to limited time on-screen. In the case of female supporting roles, however, even if the characters have only one or two scenes, chances are those scenes will make references to their marital status.

Furthermore, in the course of the plot, a woman's marital position changes more frequently than that of the man. These transformations (from single to married, from married to widowed) constitute the focus of many melodramatic narratives. They also follow a consistent and predictable pattern — regardless of a heroines' initial status (single, widowed, divorced), by the end of the film, she is either married, going to be married, or attached to one man. Most stories make a point, at times using the most incredulous devices, to "resolve" their heroines' marital position. This explains the higher percentage of married or attached women at the end of the films than at their start.

The occupations portrayed in Oscar-winning roles distinguishes between men and women even more sharply than their depiction in terms of age and marriage. The vast majority of screen males claim identifiable occupations and are gainfully employed. By contrast, over one-third of the female characters have no gainful work. And while it is inconceivable for screen males not to engage in gainful employment unless they are criminals or convicts, showing women restricted to their homes is a non-issue. Whether they're happy or not, or whether the home is a paradise or a prison (as in Douglas Sirk's melodramas) is apparently irrelevant. Whereas there's always a "good" reason for screen males not to work, there's nothing "wrong" with women who don't work, or women who lack any ambition beyond playing the traditional roles of wives and mothers. Moreover, the range of occupations is much wider for men: Males have been portrayed in three times as many professions as women, from the power elite (kings, judges, governors, generals) to blue-collar occupations, such as butchers or miners.

Prevalent Male Roles

The men have played authority figures that are in charge of maintaining law and order. The most frequent occupations among the winning male roles are soldiers, sheriffs, policemen, and politicians.

Sixteen men have won the Oscar for portraying a military figure of which half were leading roles: Emil Jannings as ex-General in *The Last Command,* Gary Cooper in *Sergeant York,* Fredric March in *The Best Years of Our Lives,* William Holden in *Stalag 17,* Alec Guinness in *The Bridge on the River Kwai,* George C. Scott in *Patton,* Jon Voight in *Coming Home,* and, most recently, Russell Crowe in *Gladiator.*

The eight Supporting winners are: Harold Russell in *The Best Years of Our Lives;* Dean Jagger in *Twelve O'Clock High;* Frank Sinatra in *From Here to Eternity;* Jack Lemmon in *Mister Roberts;* Red Buttons in *Sayonara;* Christopher Walken in *The Deer Hunter;* Louis Gossett Jr. in *An Officer and a Gentleman;* and Denzel Washington in *Glory.*

The number of soldiers among the Oscar nominees is even more substantial. Montgomery Clift specialized in such roles, for which he was rewarded by the Academy. In Fred Zinnemann's *The Search,* Clift's first nomination, he plays a sensitive American soldier stationed in postwar Germany where he rescues and reunites a young boy, separated from his family, with his mother. Clift received his third Best Actor nomination (the second was for *A Place in the Sun*) for *From Here to Eternity,* also directed by Fred Zinnemann, in which he played Private Prewitt, a stubborn soldier who, having once blinded a man in the ring, refuses to join the boxing team.

Law enforcers (sheriffs, detectives, cops) have also been dominant among the males: Gary Cooper in *High Noon,* Lee Marvin in *Cat Ballou,* Rod Steiger in *In the Heat of the Night,* John Wayne in *True Grit,* Gene Hackman in *The French Connection,* and Sean Connery as the veteran Irish cop who takes Elliot Ness under his wing in *The Untouchables.*

In 1992, the two male Oscars went to Al Pacino's acerbic, blind lieutenant colonel in *Scent of a Woman,* and Gene Hackman's sadistic sheriff in *Unforgiven.* In the following year, Tommy Lee Jones won the Supporting Oscar for *The Fugitive,* in which he played the relentless Federal Marshal Sam Gerard.

In 2000, Benicio Del Toro won a well-deserved Supporting Oscar for *Traffic* as a mostly Spanish-speaking Tijuana cop. And last year, deviating from his established screen image, Denzel Washington won the Best Actor Oscar for playing a corrupt, decadent cop in *Training Day.* His co-star, Ethan Hawke, won supporting nomination for the naive rookie-trainee.

If all the male roles that deal with law and order are combined, their proportion will amount to over 40 percent of all Oscar roles. Along with military figures and sheriffs, this group would include kings (Yul Brynner in *The King and I*), politicians (Broderick Crawford in *All the King's Men,* Ed Begley in *Sweet Bird of Youth*), governors (Charles Durning in *The Best Little Whorehouse in Texas*), freedom fighters (Paul Lucas in *Watch on the Rhine*), and judges and lawyers (Lionel Barrymore in *A Free Soul,* Walter Brennan in *The Westerner,* Maximilian Schell in *Judgment at Nuremberg,* and Walter Matthau in *The Fortune Cookie*).

Priests, whose job is also relevant to maintaining the normative order, are also prevalent. In *Boys Town,* Spencer Tracy's Father Flanagan creates a school for tough and poor street children. And in *Going My Way,* Oscar-winners Bing Crosby and Barry Fitzgerald help rehabilitate a group of juvenile delinquents by turning them into a choir.

The Academy has honored seven men with the Best or Supporting Actor nomination for playing presidents, most of whom were based on actual politicians such as: Raymond Massey in *Abe Lincoln in Illinois,* Alexander Knox in *Wilson,* James Whitmore as Truman in *Give 'Em Hell, Harry,* and Anthony Hopkins in *Nixon.*

Lee Tracy was nominated for the Supporting Oscar as a pragmatic ex-president in *The Best Man.* Most recently, Jeff Bridges received a supporting nomination for *The Contender,* in which he played a president who's more interested in gourmet food than in discussing national issues.

Most roles have depicted men as committed to their careers, often at the expense of having any personal or domestic lives. Rod Steiger's Billie Gillespie in *In the Heat of the Night* is a thick-witted, bigoted sheriff, investigating a murder in his small Southern town. The film deals with Gillespie's relationship with Virgil Tibbs (Sidney Poitier), a black homicide detective from the North who's brought in to help Gillespie resolve the mystery. In the course of the movie, their relationship transforms from initial suspicion and contempt to mutual respect and understanding. *In the Heat of the Night* illuminates its male protagonists in terms of occupation and race, which are exclusively explored in the contexts of their jobs; nothing of their private lives enters into the narrative. Now try to imagine a female version of *In the Heat of the Night,* made in 1967. Wouldn't there be men and romantic affairs in the women's lives?

Similarly, *Patton* focuses on the career of the arrogant and authoritarian general who is in love with war, and is incapable of coping with peacetime. In fact, *Patton* deviates from the conventions of biopictures by *not* providing any information about its hero's personal life.

When there's conflict between job requirements and family duties, priority is always given to the job. Gary Cooper won a second Oscar for *High Noon* as Will Kane, a marshal facing a dilemma on his wedding day: Leave town, as his Quaker wife (Grace Kelly) urges him to do, or face the four outlaws by himself—nobody in this cowardly town is willing to help. Despite burdens of fear and isolation, the danger of losing his wife, and the fact that he has retired from the job, Kane decides to meet the challenge alone head on. A MAN'S GOT TO DO WHAT A MAN'S GOT TO DO, is the motto of screen heroes in all Hollywood genres, not just Westerns or war movies.

It is revelatory that two out of the four male Oscar roles primarily dealing with private life are of elderly or retired men. In *Harry and Tonto,* Art Carney's Oscar-winning role, Harry is an aging widower who, having been dispossessed from his New York apartment, goes on a transcontinental tour with his cat Tonto. Henry Fonda's Norman Thayer, the protagonist of *On Golden Pond,* is an eighty-year-old retired university professor spending what seems to be his last summer with his spunky wife (Katharine Hepburn) of fifty years.

Screen men have enjoyed greater freedom from the legitimate social order, with several men winning Oscars for playing criminals. Marlon Brando and Robert De Niro won Oscars for playing the same screen role: The former portraying Vito Corleone in *The Godfather,* and the latter playing the same character as a young man in *The Godfather, Part II.* De Niro studied Brando's performance meticulously, as he later explained: "I didn't want to do an imitation, but I wanted to make it believable that I could be him as a young man." For De Niro, the challenge was similar to "a mathematical problem—having the result first and then figuring out how to make the beginning fit."

By contrast, there are fewer Oscar roles of female deviants. Tatum O'Neal's Supporting Award in *Paper Moon,* as a tough-talking nine-year-old girl who becomes an accomplice to a con man, a Bible salesman (played by her real-life father Ryan O'Neal), is an exception, and so is Kathy Bates as a disturbed fan in *Misery.*

Even for men, there have been more nominations than actual Oscars for portraying criminals. In fact, some actors had to deviate from their screen image, if it were based on the crime genre before getting the award. To get the Oscar, actors who began their careers as heavies and villains had to switch to playing heroes. Wallace Beery played a wide array of villains in his silent Paramount pictures, but with the advent of sound, he shook off his image and began to be cast as the "lovable slob," or the "good-bad" guy. In his Oscar-winning role,

The Champ, Beery played an errant father, a drunk, gambling ex-champion who makes a comeback for the sake of his idolizing son (Jackie Cooper).

Ernest Borgnine's looks — wide face, beady eyes, gap between his teeth — made him a "natural" screen villain in Hollywood's eyes. Borgnine's appearance was exploited in his early years, when he was cast as a sadistic sergeant (*From Here to Eternity*) and other menacing villains (*Bad Day at Black Rock*). Nonetheless, Borgnine won the Oscar for a role that represented a change of pace — the lonely, sympathetic and kind butcher in *Marty.*

Great performances in crime-gangster movies are either ignored by the Academy or at best earn nominations, but they seldom win Oscars. None of the Warner's actors who specialized in crime movies ever won an Oscar for such a role. James Cagney's image is closely associated with the gangster film, but neither his performance in *The Public Enemy,* the film which made him a star, nor his role in the Freudian gangster movie *White Heat,* were nominated. Cagney received two nominations for such movies: *Angels With Dirty Faces,* which also won him the New York Film Critics Award, and *Love Me or Leave Me,* as the tough racketeer Martin Snyder married to singer Ruth Etting (Doris Day).

But to win the Oscar, Cagney had to step outside his realm and portray patriotic showman George M. Cohan in *Yankee Doodle Dandy.* However, Cagney's 1942 role did not change his screen persona. As Frank S. Nugent wrote in the *New York Times:* "Cagney has the faculty of being taken for granted. Although he is not in the least public enemy-ish off the screen, he has done so well in the role that producers entered a happy conspiracy to keep him there. His few breaks for freedom — *Boy Meets Girl* — have not been successful, whether through Cagney's fault or our inability to adjust ourselves to seeing him without an armpit holster."

Paul Muni, another noted Warner player, began his career in gangster films, delivering indelible performances in Howard Hawks's *Scarface* and others. But like Cagney, Muni won the Academy's respect when he played "important" historical figures, such as the French scientist in *The Story of Louis Pasteur,* his Oscar role, or the French writer-activist in *The Life of Emile Zola,* for which he received a nomination.

Even more revealing is the career of Humphrey Bogart, who for a whole decade played villains, usually shot down in the last reel; no other actor has died on-screen as often as Bogey. However, after *High Sierra* and *The Maltese Falcon,* Bogart's screen image underwent a radical transformation, and he was rewarded by the Academy for his new tough-but-romantic persona in *Casablanca,* his first nomination and most memorable film, and in *The African Queen,* for which he won the Oscar. Bogart was cast as Charlie Allnut, a tough, unshaven, gin-soaked riverboat captain who becomes a hero by helping a missionary (Katharine Hepburn) to torpedo a German battleship in Africa. As Andrew Sarris observed, the conservative Academy members are not likely to vote for anarchic, virile roles. The taming of Bogart by Hepburn in *The African Queen* — in one scene, she pours all his gin into the river — proves Sarris's point.

Until recently, mainstream roles rooted in dominant culture had better chances to receive Academy recognition than rebellious or anti-establishment roles. Take Dustin Hoffman's career, with its seven nominations and two Oscars. Hoffman received his first nomination for *The Graduate,* as the college graduate who violates sexual mores and has simultaneous affairs with both mother and daughter, then rejects the predatory older woman and the bourgeois lifestyle of his parents.

Hoffman's second nomination, in *Midnight Cowboy,* was for playing Ratso, a drifter-outcast living at the margins of society. For his portrait of Lenny Bruce, Hoffman received a third nomination, though embodying the foul-mouthed comedian almost guaranteed he would not get the Oscar. Hoffman continued to play other counter-cultural roles in films such as *Papillon, Devil's Island,* and *Straw Dogs,* for which he was not nominated. It was only when Hoffman was cast in a mainstream role in *Kramer vs. Kramer,* as a self-absorbed executive who's forced to learn how to become an affectionate and responsible father, that he won a long overdue Oscar.

For years, Hoffman was critical of the Oscar, which made him, among other reasons, one of Hollywood's enfants terribles. However, when polls predicted his likelihood to win for *Kramer vs. Kramer,* Hoffman mellowed his public utterances and also decided to attend the show. Gradually, Hoffman incorporated himself into — and was coopted by — mainstream Hollywood, along with other Hollywood "rebels," such as Jane Fonda and Barbra Streisand.

Anti-Hollywood and anti-establishment players are now all good citizens, abiding by the Academy and the industry rules. Their dissenting voices seem weaker and fewer, perhaps based on the realization that "rebelliousness" might have damaging effects on their careers and on their popularity. The 1980s and 1990s generation of stars, which includes Meryl Streep, Sissy Spacek, Sally Field, William Hurt, Tom Hanks, and Tom Cruise, have been "obedient" from the start, avoiding at all costs attacking Hollywood or the Academy. They either believe in the system or understand that to exercise power in Hollywood and win Oscars, they have to play by the rules of the game!

Female Stereotypes

Compared with the men, gainfully employed screen women are confined to stereotypical professions considered to be proper and appropriate for women. Two lines of work have rewarded women with Oscars: Service (teachers, nurses) and entertainment (actresses, singers, dancers). Indeed, the two most prominent professions among the female roles are actresses and prostitutes. One out of three gainfully employed women in the Oscar films is an actress or a prostitute, and at times both an actress and a prostitute.

In both professions, a woman is paid, as critic Molly Haskell has observed, for doing what already she did: "prostitution, in which she is remunerated for giving sexual pleasure, and acting, a variant on natural role-playing." What's common to both lines is "playing roles and adapting to others, aiming to please."

Neither acting nor prostitution enjoys high prestige in the occupational hierarchy, probably because it's possible to practice and excel in both without formal education or training.

Women playing actresses stand the best chance to win nominations and Oscars. The Actors Branch, which contains the largest number of members, is favorably biased toward portraits of showbiz personalities. Besides, playing a performer provides a meaty and juicy part that lends itself to the display of histrionics and wide gamut of intense emotions.

Two images of acting, both stereotypical, have informed Hollywood pictures. The first type is that of the fading star, an actress slipping from the top to skid row as a result of aging, declining looks, drinking problem, frustrated love, or unhappy marriage. The other image is the reverse, the young and ambitious ingenue who gets her big break at the very last moment, usually on opening night when the veteran actress is unable to perform.

Some movies, such as the 1950 Oscar-winning *All About Eve,* juxtapose the two stereotypes. Bette Davis, in the greatest performance of her career, plays Margo Channing, the aging star who cannot come to terms with her progressing age (forty), which by today's standards is young but in the 1950s was considered old. Anne Baxter plays the young, driven Eve Harrington, scheming to take over everything that Margo has — her roles, her friends, and even her lover.

Bette Davis specialized in portraying suffering actresses: Four out of her ten nominations were for such roles. In her first Oscar role, *Dangerous,* Davis plays Joyce Heath, a booze-swilling-once-famous stage actress bent on her own destruction until she meets an admiring young architect (Franchot Tone) who sponsors her comeback. When her husband (John Eldredge) refuses Joyce a divorce so that she can marry the architect, she attempts to kill both of them by driving her car into a tree. The couple survives, but Joyce's husband is crippled for life. Returning triumphantly to the stage, Joyce has learned the value of sacrifice.

In *The Star,* for which Davis received her ninth nomination, Davis's Margaret Elliot is a has-been, a former Oscar-winner who is now a pathetic, bitter and violent woman. As in *Dangerous,* an admirer (Sterling Hayden) saves Margaret by convincing her, as in *All About Eve,* to give up her career and live a more normal — that is, domestic life.

Davis's last nomination was for Robert Aldridge's cult horror flick, *What Ever Happened to Baby Jane?* She is cast as Jane Hudson, the genius child-star whose talent faded when she grew up, turning her into a demented alcoholic and sadist toward her crippled sister (Joan Crawford). Davis gave a flashy, grotesque performance, which opened a new phase in her career as a horror queen.

Gloria Swanson created an indelible shading in *Sunset Boulevard* as Norma Desmond, the aging silent movie queen terrified of the camera but still dreaming of a big comeback. Geraldine Page did her best work, on stage and on screen, as Alexandra De Lago in Tennessee Williams's *Sweet Bird of Youth,* as another aging, drug-addicted star, entertained by an opportunistic stud (Paul Newman), who finds out that her last film was not as disastrous as she had thought.

Screen actresses are often tragic, though the stereotype has been exploited in comedies, too. Maggie Smith won her second Supporting Oscar for Neil Simon's *California Suite,* playing a British actress named Diana Barrie, a hard-drinking, hard-talking woman who arrives in Hollywood for the Oscar ceremonies. Disenchanted after losing the Oscar, Diana charges at her bisexual companion (Michael Caine): "Acting doesn't win Oscars — what I need is a dying father." Italian actress Valentina Cortese was nominated for Truffaut's behind-the-scenes comedy *Day for Night,* in which she plays a fading movie star who hides a bottle on the set and cannot remember her lines.

The reverse stereotype of the young, stage-struck, wide-eyed ingenue was embodied by Katharine Hepburn in her first Oscar-winning role in *Morning Glory.* She plays Eve Lovelace (note the name *Eve*), a naive Vermont girl who creates a sensation when she steps in for the recalcitrant leading lady on opening night. Some lines from this picture have entered into movie lore. "How many keep their heads? You've come to the fore. Now you have the chance to be a morning glory, a flower that fades before the sun is very high." Or Hepburn's vow, "I'm not afraid of being like a morning glory. I'm not afraid. I'm not afraid." The best line is uttered pretentiously by Adolphe Menjou, as a tough producer, who tells Eve: "You don't belong to any man now, you belong to Broadway!"

The prostitute with a heart of gold is also an enduring screen image, and the second most prevalent Oscar role for women. Elizabeth Taylor won her first Oscar for *Butterfield 8* (based on John O'Hara's novel) as Gloria Wandrous, a New York call girl. Gloria describes herself as "the slut of all times," but basically she is a good-natured woman whose main aspiration in life is to gain respectability, marry a decent man, and live a suburban life. However, trapped in bad circumstances and unable to forget her past, there is no hope for Gloria. After a disastrous affair with a wealthy, married Yale graduate (Laurence Harvey), she finds her death in a fatal car crash.

Jane Fonda's first Oscar, for *Klute,* is generally acknowledged for being a great performance. For no apparent reason, the film was named after its detective (played by Donald Sutherland), but it should have been titled after its heroine, Bree Daniel, a tough New York call girl. Bree may be a victim of her circumstances, but she also enjoys the power she possesses over her clients. Like other films, *Klute* also makes an explicit association between the two traditional female professions, acting and prostitution. When Bree complains to her analyst that she has had no luck as an actress, the latter responds, "What's the difference? You're successful as a call girl, you're not successful as an actress." Other films have also made similar links. One of the three films for which Janet Gaynor was honored with the very first Best Actress was *Street Angel,* in which she plays a poor prostitute who takes refuge from the police with a circus, where she meets and falls in love with a painter (played by her frequent co-star Charles Farrell). Claire Trevor won the Supporting Oscar for *Key Largo,* in which she is cast as a gangster's alcoholic mistress and fading torch singer.

More Supporting than lead Oscars were bestowed on women playing prostitutes. In *East of Eden,* Jo Van Fleet plays James Dean's presumably dead mother, a woman who broke free of her family and is now a notorious madam. Dorothy Malone gave an intensely hysterical performance in Douglas Sirk's stylish melodrama, *Written on the Wind,* as a rich, frustrated nymphomaniac who seduces gas-station attendants in cheap motel rooms.

Woody Allen's films abound with prostitutes. In *Shadows and Fog,* Allen wasted the talents of two Oscar-winning actresses — Kathy Bates and Jodie Foster — by casting them as hookers; the film was ignored by the Academy and the public. In Allen's 1995 comedy, *Mighty Aphrodite,* Mira Sorvino became the eighth actress to win an Oscar for playing a hooker, albeit a bright and cheerful one. It took Allen decades to respond to the criticism that there are no speaking parts for black actors in his films, but then, in his self-referential, foul-mouthed comedy, *Deconstructing Harry,* the main female character is a black prostitute. So much for progress.

Some of the Oscars for screen prostitutes have rewarded actresses for deviating from their clean-cut, wholesome screen image. Anne Baxter began her career as the "girl-next-door" in patriotic war films (*The Pied Piper, Crash Dive, The Fighting Sullivans*), but she won the Supporting Oscar for a major departure from that image, in *The Razor's Edge,* as a woman who becomes a dipsomaniac prostitute after the death of her husband and child in a car crash.

Donna Reed built a name for herself as a sincere, wholesome girl, as in *It's a Wonderful Life* in which she plays Jimmy Stewart's loyal wife, but she won the Supporting Oscar for a role that was the exception, Alma, the good-hearted "hostess" in *From Here to Eternity.* Under pressures of censorship, that film was less explicit than the book in describing Alma's line of work; in the book, she's a prostitute.

In 1960, the two female awards were given to actresses who played prostitutes: Elizabeth Taylor in *Butterfield 8* and Shirley Jones in *Elmer Gantry.* Jones was recruited to Hollywood from the Broadway stage, having established herself as a singer. At first, she played shy, romantic girls in musicals (*Oklahoma!, Carousel, April Love*). However, only when Jones changed her image, playing Lulu Bains, the good-hearted prostitute in *Elmer Gantry,* did she earn the Academy's recognition. "I am sick of portraying ingenues with sunny dispositions, high necklines, and puffy sleeves, who are girlishly aggressive about happiness being just around the corner," Jones complained.

Cut to 1995, when three of the ten women nominated for acting awards played prostitutes, motivating emcee Whoopi Goldberg to quip: "Elizabeth Shue (*Leaving Las Vegas*) played a hooker. Sharon Stone (*Casino*) played a hooker. Mira Sorvino (*Mighty Aphrodite*) played a hooker. How many times did Charlie Sheen get to vote?" alluding to the scandalous reports that Sheen had spent thousands of dollars as a celeb customer of the high-profile Hollywood madam Heidi Fleiss (later celebrated in a documentary devoted to her life).

Other women's roles have conformed to familiar stereotypes of wives, mothers, and daughters. Family roles combined with sex and victimization have created some of the most enduring female screen stereotypes: The villainous adulteress, the self-sacrificing mother, the long-suffering wife, the oppressed spinster. These formulaic roles have persisted in mainstream American cinema for half a century with few alterations.

The Southern belle is a uniquely American literary and cinematic type. Mary Pickford won her first and only Best Actress for *Coquette,* a film version of the Helen Hayes Broadway vehicle, as a southern belle whose affair with a man beneath her class enrages her father, leading to disaster.

Bette Davis won a second Oscar for *Jezebel,* as the rich, spoiled, and willful Julie Marsden, whose entire behavior is motivated by her failure to win the love of Pres Dillard (Henry Fonda). Pres breaks their engagement when Julie disregards the norms, and wears a red gown to New Orleans's Olympus Ball — all the other girls wear a traditional white dress. Punished, Julie secludes herself, waiting for Pres to return, only to find out that he has married another girl. However, when Pres falls victim to a yellow-fever epidemic, Julie persuades his wife that she should accompany him to a quarantined island, promising to send Pres back to her if he survives.

Vivien Leigh gives a memorable performance as Scarlett O'Hara in *Gone With the Wind,* as a tempestuous, self-centered belle. Leigh's second Oscar was for playing Blanche DuBois in *A Streetcar Named Desire,* the sordid tale of the mental deterioration of a repressed Southern belle. Blanche DuBois, a challenge for every actress, is a perfect example of the kind of screen role that wins Oscars since it includes all the "necessary" ingredients of a substantial part, allowing for the display of wide range of emotions and technical skills.

A Streetcar Named Desire may be Tennessee Williams's best-known play, but most of his works contain memorable female roles for the stage and screen. The eccentricity of his characters, their richly nuanced inner selves, often dominated by repressed sexuality, has called for distinguished acting. Good or bad, films based on Williams's plays have earned nominations and awards, mostly for their women. In *Baby Doll,* Carroll Baker was nominated for playing "white trash," a retarded, thumb-sucking child-wife, seduced by her husband's revenge-seeking rival. In the same film, Mildred Dunnock was nominated for playing her pathetically demented aunt.

Though it lost in each of its six nominations, *Cat on a Hot Tin Roof* was one of 1958's most honored films, in which Elizabeth Taylor excelled as Maggie, the sexy wife punished by her alcoholic husband (Paul Newman, also nominated) who won't sleep with her. The scandalous *Suddenly Last Summer,* a chronicle of incest, cannibalism, and insanity, contrasts Katharine Hepburn, as a demented aristocratic mother in love with her homosexual poet-son, with Elizabeth Taylor as her niece, who almost goes mad after witnessing her cousin's rape and murder. Both Hepburn and Taylor received Best Actress nominations, though neither won. The winner was Simon Signoret for *Room at the Top.*

Vivien Leigh was not nominated for playing the widowed American actress who drifts into lassitude and decline in *The Roman Spring of Mrs. Stone,* but Lotte Lenya, as a vicious female pimp, was. In *Summer and Smoke,* Williams's drama about earthly and spiritual love, Geraldine Page was nominated as Alma, a sexually repressed spinster and the minister's daughter. Along with Page, *Sweet Bird of Youth* provided a Supporting nomination for Shirley Knight, who played the victimized daughter-girlfriend who had contracted syphilis from an irresponsible stud (Paul Newman). In *The Night of the Iguana*, Grayson Hall received the Supporting nomination as the leader of vacationing schoolteachers whose animosity toward the defrocked priest (Richard Burton) stemmed from repressed lesbianism and interest in the nymphomaniac teenager (Sue Lyon).

The spinster or the old maid is another enduring stereotype. Olivia de Havilland won her second Oscar for *The Heiress,* as the timid, ugly-duckling daughter of a domineering father (Ralph Richardson). She is deceived and bitterly disappointed when she finds out that her admirer (Montgomery Clift) is a scoundrel interested in her wealth. Other frustrated spinsters who received nominations include Agnes Moorehead's neurotic and spinsterish aunt in *The Magnificent Ambersons,* and Joanne Woodward in *Rachel, Rachel,* in which she plays a small-town spinster teacher who experiences her first sexual encounter at the age of thirty-five, only to be deserted by her lover.

Most of these screen spinsters have domineering mothers against whom they rebel, usually through the love of an older man. In one of Bette Davis's most popular films, *Now, Voyager,* she is cast as a humiliated mother-driven spinster who finds fulfilling love at a later age. In *Separate Tables,* too, Deborah Kerr starts as a timid, sexually repressed virgin, dominated by a cruel mother (Gladys Cooper), against whom she finally rebels.

It may not be a coincidence that Katharine Hepburn, the Academy's most celebrated actress, has played variations of each of the aforementioned female stereotypes. Hepburn's career can be conveniently divided into clear phases. In the earlier part, up to the 1940s, she played strongly independent but attractive women (*The Philadelphia Story, Woman of the Year*). When she began to age, Hepburn continued to play strong-willed women, but they were now unglamorous and spinsterish. If Tracy Lord in *The Philadelphia Story* summed up the first phase of Hepburn's screen career, *The African Queen* (her fifth nomination), in which she was cast as a missionary, offered a summation to the middle phase. Hepburn was cast in a similar role in *Summertime* (her sixth nomination), as a spinsterish teacher vacationing in Venice and falling in love with Rossano Brazzi. In *The Rainmaker* (her seventh nomination), Hepburn plays a tomboyish girl whose womanhood is brought to the surface by a con man (Burt Lancaster).

Suffering and Victimization

Suffering and victimization have been the chief attributes of the female Oscar roles. According to the Oscar annals, women have suffered a disproportionately large number of disasters, natural and man-made. While men are always in charge of their destiny, women exercise little or no control over their romantic and marital lives, all of which serve as causes for torment and anguish.

Sexual assault and rape are the most obvious forms of victimization. In *Johnny Belinda,* Jane Wyman plays a deaf-mute girl who becomes the victim of a brutal rape by a drunken fisherman, who later attempts to steal her baby. Blanche DuBois, the genteel belle of *A Streetcar Named Desire,* is tortured and raped by her brutish brother-in-law, which drives her into insanity.

A large number of Oscar roles depict women who are betrayed by their husbands. Adultery is one of the most consistent male privileges — and a continuous source of suffering for women. Janet Gaynor won Best Actress for *Sunrise,* in which she plays a loyal wife betrayed by her farmer-husband with a glamorous city woman who wishes her dead. Louise Rainer's second Best Actress Oscar was for *The Good Earth,* playing a selfless Chinese wife who is first neglected by her farmer husband, then further humiliated when he marries a younger women.

Serafina Della Rose, Anna Magnani's Oscar role in *The Rose Tattoo,* is a tempestuous widow who idolizes her dead husband; she's the last to realize his unfaithfulness. A religious woman, she is obsessed with sexual memories to the point of becoming a reclusive, domineering mother.

Women's status in American film can be instructively understood by the concept of stigma. Up until the 1970s, any attempt by screen women to deviate from society's prescribed roles was consistently punished. Strong-willed heroines are not only deviants but are also oppressed if their conduct is threatening to the status quo of male dominance. Forms of punishment for deviating from the normative order range from the most extreme sanctions, such as death, to humiliation, ostracization, and relegation to domestic life.

Wearing a red gown, Bette Davis's Julie in *Jezebel* is punished for violating dress conventions. The film suggests that Julie destroyed her chances at real happiness, through marriage, by defying social norms. Sexual promiscuity by women is also regarded as a severe violation of mores. Most screen prostitutes (Elizabeth Taylor's in *Butterfield 8*) pay with their lives for engaging in such a disreputable occupation.

Death by accident is also a common fate of adulteresses. Gloria Grahame, who specialized in playing floozies and loose girls (*Crossfire, The Big Heat*), received the Supporting Oscar for *The Bad and the Beautiful,* playing a social-climbing wife who urges her screenwriter-husband (Dick Powell) to move to Hollywood and live a glamorous lifestyle. The ruthless producer (Kirk Douglas) considers her to be disruptive to her husband's creativity and arranges for her to have an affair with a Latin lover. Needless to say, she dies in a tragic airplane crash.

Simone Signoret's Alice Abigal in *Room at the Top* finds her demise in a fatal car accident. An aging, unhappily married actress, she is desperate for affection, but she falls for the wrong man — an ambitious working-class man (Laurence Harvey) who mistreats her. At the end, Alice is sacrificed by him for a younger woman, the daughter of the town's tycoon, and she dies on his very wedding day.

Death resolves the problem of having to deal with women as equal partners, particularly if these women are actively involved in politics and the economy. Playing the title role in *Julia,* Vanessa Redgrave is a young intelligent woman who rebels against her aristocratic family by becoming a fighter in the antifascist movement. Julia, too, is killed in the course of the narrative, thus becoming a symbol of political heroism rather than a real, living woman, with whom men have to contend.

On-screen death functions as a safety valve, permitting audiences to admire courageous and independent women like Julia as martyrs, while relieving men of the burden of dealing with them as equals on a realistic level. If *Julia's* protagonist had been a man, he would probably have survived. Male screen fighters usually succeed in accomplishing their missions, as was shown by Paul Lukas's Oscar role in another adaptation of a Hellman work, *Watch on the Rhine.* Lukas, in fact, plays a similar role to Redgrave's in *Julia,* as an antifascist fighter.

Ambitious career women are consistently punished for stepping out of their place, for entering into men's domain, and competing for desirable jobs and rewards. In Joan Crawford's Oscar role as the suffering mother in *Mildred Pierce,* she plays a determined woman who builds up a chain of restaurants in order to provide her ungrateful daughter with all the luxuries she was deprived of as a girl. Throughout the movie, Mildred is penalized. Her younger daughter dies of pneumonia while she is spending her first weekend off from work with her lover. Mildred then throws herself into a second, loveless marriage with a playboy whom she ends up supporting. Her eldest daughter Vida (Oscar-nominated Ann Blyth) despises her mother's low-class origins and job as a waitress, and flirts with her stepfather, whom she later kills out of jealousy. At the end, having lost everything — her business, lover, and daughter — Mildred goes back to her first husband and to a second life as a housewife.

Mildred Pierce is by no means an exception. The portrayal of career women was quite consistent up to the late 1970s. That career women are typically single suggests that it is impossible for women to combine successful careers with satisfying personal lives — a task managed by men with relative ease. Even women choosing the perennial female occupation of acting are single. In *All About Eve,* Margo Channing is unmarried while she's successful; Eve is also solitary when her career begins to rise.

In American movies, career women are ridiculed and condemned as grotesque "unfeeling monsters." This dehumanization is illustrated by Louise Fletcher's Oscar role in *One Flew Over the Cuckoo's Nest,* as Big Nurse Ratched, a tyrannical nurse in charge of a mental ward. A severe, humorless woman, Nurse Ratched represents an oppressive establishment whose major goal is to tame patients — all of whom are men — using various methods of controls, including electroshock treatment and lobotomy. Endowed with a bureaucratic personality, Nurse Ratched is rigid, adhering strictly and blindly to the rules. She is sympathetic to her patients only when it promotes her interests and her authority; she drives one of her young patients (Oscar-nominated Brad Dourif), a mother-fixated kid, into suicide by consciously playing on his guilt complex. Ratched's character is not written or played on the same realistic level as her male patients. She is an abstract symbol of sexual inhibition and repressive authority.

Faye Dunaway's Oscar-winning role as Diana Christensen, a ruthless, power-hungry television executive in *Network,* is also more of an abstract type than a fully fleshed human character. Dunaway might have been rewarded just for being a good sport and poking fun at her own screen image as an ambitious career woman. Diana's chief goal in *Network* is to upgrade the station's ratings, unashamedly boasting, "All I want out of life is a 30 share and 20 rating," for which she is willing to use illegitimate and disreputable means such as co-producing a program with terrorists.

Obsessed with work, which permeates every aspect of her life, Diana talks about it nonstop, even during a sexual encounter. Diana is further ridiculed when she sets the tone and speed of this encounter with an older, sensitive married executive (William Holden). She sits on top of him and reaches orgasm prematurely, thus imitating what is considered to be a typically masculine sexual pattern. Needless to say, Diana is efficient and rational, but she's also incapable of any human feelings. Both *Network* and *One Flew Over the Cuckoo's Nest* suggest that their protagonists lack any meaningful personal lives outside of their work.

The most prevalent Oscar female parts have combined showbiz with suffering. The prototype for this role is still the movie *A Star Is Born* (in its various reincarnations), the story of a young actress who ascends to stardom while her husband's career goes on the skids. Janet Gaynor and Judy Garland were both nominated for the same role in the 1937 and 1954 versions, respectively. Based on simplistic formulas, showbiz pictures encourage the notion that achieving fame has a high price and that stardom doesn't last long.

Consider the following Oscar-nominated roles:

> Greta Garbo, as an opera singer conflicted between the love of a wealthy "patron" and a young clergyman, in *Romance*
>
> Eleanor Parker, as the crippled singer Marjorie Lawrence in *Interrupted Melody*
>
> Susan Hayward, as the alcoholic singer Lillian Roth in *I'll Cry Tomorrow*
>
> Katharine Hepburn, as Mary Tyrone in *Long Day's Journey Into Night,* a morphine-addicted woman who's unhappily married to a pompous and fading actor (Ralph Richardson)
>
> Vanessa Redgrave as Isadora Duncan, a dancer who dies prematurely in an accident, in *Isadora*
>
> Diana Ross, as the heroin-addicted, racially oppressed singer Billie Holliday in *Lady Sings the Blues*
>
> Bette Midler, as the drug-addicted rock star (loosely based on Janis Joplin's life) in *The Rose*

Jessica Lange, as the doomed, anti-establishment actress Frances Framer in *Frances,* who, tormented by an overbearing mother, turns to the bottle and is put in an asylum

Jessica Lange as country singer Patsy Kline who finds her untimely death in a plane crash in *Sweet Dreams*

Mary McDonnell, as the selfish, paralyzed soap-opera star in *Passion Fish*

Debra Winger, as Joy Gresham, an American divorcee who falls for Oxford literary critic, C. S. Lewis (Anthony Hopkins), only to die of cancer, in *Shadowlands* (1993)

Angela Bassett, as the abused singer Tina Turner in the biopicture, *What's Love Got to Do With It*

Meryl Streep, as a pill-popping actress caught in a problematic relationship with her mother-celeb, in *Postcards from the Edge*

Judi Dench, as Alzheimer-afflicted writer-philosopher Iris Murdoch, in *Iris*

Nicole Kidman, as the Camille-like courtesan-actress dying of tuberculosis, in *Moulin Rouge*

Suffering Mothers and Wives

During the heyday of the studio system, many actresses "specialized" in roles that called for a good deal of suffering. Though a versatile and subtle actress, who excelled in every film genre (including comedy), Margaret Sullavan was most typically used by Hollywood in tearful, soggy melodramas, such as her only Oscar-nominated role as Robert Taylor's tubercular wife in *Three Comrades,* for which she had earlier won the New York Film Critics Circle Award. Sullavan is best known for *The Shopworn Angel,* which she made in the same year, and, of course, for *Back Street* (the second version), in which she played a woman in love with a married man (Charles Boyer), who can't divorce because it will ruin his career.

At present, the lovely British actress Emily Watson has practically elevated physical suffering and emotional instability to a high art, for which she was rewarded with two Best Actress nominations. The first was for her astonishing performance as Bess McNeill in Lars Von Trier's 1996 emotional-spiritual drama, *Breaking the Waves,* which brought her international critical kudos. Two years later, Watson was nominated in *Hilary and Jackie* for playing Jacqueline du Pre, the world-renowned cellist who led an outwardly glamorous life but whose desperation placed a strain on her family, particularly on her sister (played by Oscar-nominated Rachel Griffiths). Adding to her emotional problems, du Pre developed multiple sclerosis, which first took its toll on her musical career, and eventually took her life. To prepare for her role, Watson withstood three months of practice in a rehearsal room, and took three cello lessons per week. She also met with an MS doctor and his patients as well as a movement teacher to approximate du Pre's precise gestures.

In 1994, most Best Actress nominees played victims calling for a good deal of suffering, both physical and mental. Jodie Foster received her third Best Actress nomination for *Nell*, as a young woman (the child of a hermit) without any communication skills, living in an isolated Appalachian cabin shut off from the outside world.

In *Tom & Viv*, directed by Brian Gilbert from a script by Michael Hastings and Adrian Hodges, and based on Hastings's play, Miranda Richardson is Vivienne Haigh-Wood, the passionate if unstable wife of the repressed and ambitious poet T. S. Eliot (Willem Dafoe). Viv's eccentricity (stemming from a hormonal problem, now easily treated) leads Eliot to commit her to a mental institution. Ultimately, it's the tragic story of a woman whose affliction was improperly diagnosed. The Best Actress that year went to Jessica Lange, who played yet another unstable woman in *Blue Sky*, the promiscuous wife of a military officer.

Oscar, Hollywood, and Male Dominance

Like all art, American films do not operate in a social or political vacuum. Rather, they're interrelated with the dominant ideology and politics of American society at large. Hollywood is an industry whose products have a strong technological foundation but they also embody and transmit cultural values. These two facets of film, as ideological constructs and commercial products, are intertwined in Hollywood's popular movies. As expected, American pictures have expressed the ideological dominance of one powerful group: White upper-middle class men. This group has defined and controlled the normative order and imposed it on less powerful groups, such as women and ethnic minorities. The notion of cultural hegemony or dominance is, therefore, crucial to the understanding of how specific but popular images have influenced American collective consciousness.

Screen heroes and heroines have differed in age, marital status, and occupation. Male roles have been contained in serious dramatic pictures dealing with important issues such as racism and injustice. Assigned to roles which control the social order, men have perpetuated the status quo symbolically, onscreen, and pragmatically, offscreen. Female roles, by contrast, have been based on fictional figures mostly contained in romances and melodramas known as "women's films." According to Oscar-winning roles, women's contributions to society are mostly in the marital and familial arena, as wives and mothers, or in service professions, as entertainers and prostitutes.

If the male Oscar roles can be described as types, the female roles can be defined as stereotypes. Types are shared, recognizable, easily grasped norms of how people are expected to behave, whereas stereotypes are based on more stringent and confining guidelines. Since stereotypes involve strong value judgments, both approval and disapproval, of particular behavior, they can be harmful as they confine people to narrowly defined conduct. Stereotypes imply that those who don't conform to the specified ways of appearing, feeling, and behaving are inadequate as males or females.

The function of female stereotypes, from the point of view of the dominant ideology, is to keep women in their place, to reward them for accepting traditional roles — for not challenging the status quo. Female screen roles provide the kinds of rationalization needed to reconcile women to marriage and family life. These images, which are all-embracing, go beyond the socio-economic area, offering a state of mind and a way of life. Their persistence for half a century suggests that most moviegoers have accepted (at least passively) the ideological messages prevailing in Hollywood movies.

However, the stereotypical portrayal of women also shows that Hollywood has been out of touch with reality, ignoring the progress women have made. Media images are not necessarily up-to-date: A "culture lag" prevails between society's material conditions and its cultural representations. A gap prevails in Hollywood pictures between women's occupational roles and their ideological treatment in texts and images. The most negative portrayal, trivializing women's domestic roles and condemning career women, occurred in the late 1960s and early 1970s — just when women were beginning to make their mark offscreen. Hollywood's ideological backlash in those years was manifest in three significant ways.

First, there was a paucity of screen roles, particularly leading ones, for women. For a while it seemed as if women had disappeared completely from the American screen. The worst year in the history of the Best Actress Oscar was 1975, when members of the Actors Branch had difficulties coming up with five lead actresses. No wonder Louise Fletcher won — there was not much competition. Under normal circumstances, Fletcher's role in *Cuckoo's Nest* would have qualified as a supporting category. The other nominees were Isabelle Adjani in *The Story of Adele H.;* Ann-Margret in the musical *Tommy;* Glenda Jackson in *Hedda,* the film version of Ibsen's play *Hedda Gabler;* and Carol Kane in the immigrant melodrama *Hester Street.* Ellen Burstyn, the previous year's winner, asked her colleagues in the Acting Branch not to nominate actresses in the lead category as protest against Hollywood's marginalization of women.

Men dominated Hollywood quantitatively and qualitatively. The era's typical big-budget movies were action-adventures, focusing on male heroism, male friendship, and male courage. Major movies of that era usually featured two males in the lead roles, with few if any women in their narratives. The list of these movies is too long to reproduce here, but it is sufficient to name some Best Picture nominees:

In the Heat of the Night, starring Rod Steiger and Sidney Poitier

Midnight Cowboy, with Jon Voight and Dustin Hoffman

Butch Cassidy and the Sundance Kid, with Paul Newman and Robert Redford

MASH, which boasted a male cast headed by Donald Sutherland and Elliott Gould

Patton, with George C. Scott and Karl Malden

The French Connection, with Gene Hackman and Roy Scheider

Deliverance, with Jon Voight and Burt Reynolds

The Godfather, Parts I and II, with an all-male starring cast, Marlon Brando, Robert De Niro, Robert Duvall, and Al Pacino

The Sting, with Paul Newman and Robert Redford

The Towering Inferno, with Paul Newman and Steve McQueen

Dog Day Afternoon, with Al Pacino, John Cazale, and Chris Sarandon

Jaws, with Richard Dreyfuss, Roy Scheider, and Robert Shaw

All the President's Men, with Robert Redford and Dustin Hoffman

Finally, most box-office stars in the late 1960s and 1970s were men — the only woman among the ten box-office champions was Barbra Streisand. The industry's biggest names were all male stars with tough "macho" images, such as Steve McQueen (*The Thomas Crown Affair* and *Bullitt*), Clint Eastwood (the *Dirty Harry* movies), Lee Marvin (*The Professionals* and *The Dirty Dozen*), and Charles Bronson (the *Death Wish* film series and its variants).

Changes in Oscar Roles

Some significant changes in women's Oscar roles began to take place in the 1970s. *Alice Doesn't Live Here Anymore* signaled a major change, because it was a film with a strong central role for a woman that challenged male cultural dominance, on- and offscreen. Ellen Burstyn, who won Best Actress for this film, was instrumental in bringing the project to the screen. Burstyn discovered Robert Gotchell's screenplay, persuaded a major studio, Warner, to distribute it, chose a rising director, Martin Scorsese, and even had a say in choosing its cast and crew. Thematically, however, *Alice Doesn't Live Here Anymore* was compromised and far from the feminist film it intended to be. Its eponymous heroine is a recent young widow struggling to launch a new career as a singer and a new life for herself and her son. But at the end, Alice becomes dependent again, settling into what seems to be a second, complacent relationship, albeit with a more sensitive man (Kris Kristofferson) than her husband. Even so, *Alice Doesn't Live Here Anymore* showed that there was interest in women's stories and that these films are commercially viable.

The turning point in female Oscar roles occurred in 1977, when for the first time, four of the five Best Picture nominees were about forceful women. The Oscar winner, Woody Allen's *Annie Hall* starring Diane Keaton, competed against Neil Simon's romantic comedy *The Goodbye Girl* (directed by Herbert Ross), with Marsha Mason, and Fred Zinnemann's *Julia,* a picture about the friendship between two strong women. The other nominee, Herbert Ross's *The Turning Point,* was about the costs and rewards of life choices, contrasting a dancer turned wife-mother (Shirley MacLaine) and her friend and competitor, now an aging and lonely ballerina (Anne Bancroft).

In the new movies, a new screen woman began to emerge: Professional and career-oriented but without the dehumanization and condemnation of Fletcher's Nurse Ratched in *Cuckoo's Nest* or Dunaway's TV executive in *Network.* The range of occupational roles allotted to women widened considerably, going beyond traditional "female" professions of actresses, secretaries, or prostitutes. Glenda Jackson won a second Best Actress for playing a fashion designer in *A Touch of Class.* Liv Ullmann was nominated for playing a psychiatrist in Ingmar Bergman's *Face to Face.* Ingrid Bergman was nominated for a concert pianist in another Ingmar Bergman film, *Autumn Sonata.* Geraldine Page was an interior decorator in *Interiors,* Jane Fonda an investigative reporter in *The China Syndrome.* Frances McDormand played a resourceful cop in *Fargo.* And Julia Roberts was a lawyer's clerk who uncovers corruption in *Erin Brockovich.*

The new screen woman was concerned not only with her career, but with asserting herself as a worthy human being whose status neither derives from nor depends upon her marital and familial role. Meryl Streep won the Supporting Actress as Joanna Kramer in *Kramer vs. Kramer,* playing a woman who walks out on her self-absorbed husband, leaving him the responsibility of raising their young son alone. Joanna is depicted as a confused woman, deeply dissatisfied with her mother-wife chores. *Kramer vs. Kramer* was the first major Hollywood movie to deal with a married woman who deserts her family in order to "find herself" and regain self-worth. In sharp departure from previous conventions, Joanna gives up her son willingly. After winning a cruel custody battle, she tells her ex-husband: "I came here to take my son home, and I realized he already is home."

This movie also changed the traditional image of the husband-father, played by Dustin Hoffman, who won Best Actor. Ted Kramer starts out as an egotistic advertising executive, so engrossed in his career that he neglects his family, forbids his wife to work, and is completely oblivious to her feelings. But he is capable of changing and, by the film's ending, Ted is transformed into a loving, caring father who learns basic lessons about responsible parenthood.

Screen women also began to show strong interest in the public and political domains. In the past, heroines were confined to their domestic lives, exhibiting little interest in what was happening in the "outside" world. But in the late 1970s, several new movies dealt with women gaining political consciousness.

At the center of Martin Ritt's *Norma Rae,* which won Sally Field her first Oscar, is the politicization of a Southern working-class woman in a small dormant town after meeting a Jewish labor-organizer (Ron Liebman) from New York. The movie describes Norma's feisty struggle to unionize a mill, which involves the organization of a strike. What is innovative from a gender point of view is that her relationship with the Jewish intellectual is not romantic or sexual, but based on mutual respect. At the end, they part with a friendly handshake rather than the clichéd kiss. Such camaraderie between unlikely partners (a simple, uneducated woman and a smart urban Jew) would have been impossible in years past, but in this film's context, they are mutually engrossing with each party learning and benefiting from the friendship.

The new screen woman also gained ground in sexual mores and conduct. In the past, it was the exclusive privilege of men to engage in illicit affairs. But recently women in the movies have become more sexually liberated — without being penalized. *Coming Home,* Jane Fonda's second Oscar, concerns Sally Hyde, a bored middle class wife married to a chauvinistic Marine captain (Bruce Dern, who was also nominated). Sally begins to become politically aware while volunteering in a veterans' hospital, where she falls in love with a sensitive war paraplegic (Jon Voight). For a change, and it is a big change, *Coming Home* does not condemn her adultery, which is described in a nonjudgmental way.

There were also changes in the perennial screen role of the mother. The new liberated mother is no longer suffering and self-sacrificing, like Mildred Pierce or Stella Dallas were for the future of their children. She is no longer weak or submissive, but determined, in control of her life and in charge of her emotions. Sally Field won a second Oscar for playing Edna Spaulding in *Places in the Heart,* a Texan housewife whose husband-sheriff is killed in an accident. After fifteen years of marriage, Edna suddenly finds herself with no talent and no skill for anything except cooking and taking care of her children. But with will power, steadfastness, and hard work, Edna faces a series of hardships: A bank foreclosure, a greedy cotton dealer, and even a tornado.

A very similar type of mother was portrayed by Jessica Lange (in *Country,* inspired by the farmers' plight in Iowa) and Sissy Spacek (in *The River*), both of whom were Oscar-nominated. These movies, labeled by journalists along with *Places* as "Hollywood's farm trilogy," also challenged the traditional screen images of men, depicting them as less committed, weaker, and often more emotional than their female counterparts.

A clear indication of changing gender roles — in film as well as in the larger society — was evident in 1988, a particularly strong year in the Best Actress competition. The winner, Jodie Foster in *The Accused,* plays Sarah Tobias, a fast-food waitress (a traditional female profession), who is gang-raped in a roadside bar (also a stereotype). However, in the course of the film, she transforms from a hard-drinking good-time girl to a woman fighting (with the assistance of a female attorney) for the decency and self-esteem she was never accorded.

Like Foster, Meryl Streep in *A Cry in the Dark* was cast as a defiant working-class woman held responsible for the death of her baby girl. Based on the 1980 story of Lindy Chamberlain, the complex role shows her to be proudly stubborn, a victim of the sensationalistic and merciless Australian media (she was acquitted in 1987). In *Dangerous Liaisons,* Glenn Close's Marquise de Merteuil is another proud woman who refuses to live by the sexual mores of her world. "I was born to dominate your sex and avenge my own," she tells the Vicomte de Valmont (John Malkovich) with whom she engages in sexual games of power.

In her assured portrayal of the late anthropologist Dian Fossey, Sigourney Weaver dominated every frame of *Gorillas in the Mist,* a film about Fossey's heroic struggle to save Africa's gorillas from poachers. Even Melanie Griffith's Tess McGill, in Mike Nichols's modern fairy tale, *Working Girl,* pointed to a new direction. Tess begins as a Staten Island secretary, victimized by a female executive (Sigourney Weaver, in another role reversal), who decides to take full charge of her life, and in the process also gets her boss's rich lover (Harrison Ford).

Changes in the women's Oscar roles became more evident in the last decade. Kathy Bates won the 1990 Best Actress for playing an obsessed fan in Rob Reiner's horror film, *Misery,* a genre that has not done much for women. In her acceptance speech, Bates thanked her co-star, James Caan (who played the fiction writer she torments), apologizing for the chilling scenes in which she uses a sledgehammer to break his ankles. Since *Misery,* Bates has been the butt of jokes about sledgehammers. Bates had an edge over the other nominees, both because of her stage credentials and her Plain Jane publicity that indicated a serious dedication to her craft. Coming out of nowhere, to use Hollywood parlor, Bates embodied the tale of the ugly duckling turning into a swan. Asked whether her victory might encourage directors to cast lesser-known actors in major roles, Bates noted, "I'm not sure. I just happened to be in the right place at the right time."

Bates felt no animosity toward producers who passed her over for film roles she had earlier popularized onstage, such as *Frankie and Johnny,* in which the female lead was later (mis)cast with Michelle Pfeiffer. But she was proud to say, "This one is for the actors." Bates later won Golden Globes and Screen Actors Guild awards for her work in film (*Fried Green Tomatoes,* 1991), and television (*The Late Shift,* 1996). In 1998, Bates received a second, supporting nomination in *Primary Colors* for playing a tough, openly lesbian character, seemingly based on President Clinton's aide Betsy Drake, who was in charge of controlling what she once famously termed "bimbo eruptions."

Another atypical Oscar performance — by an obscure, out of nowhere, actress — was Hilary Swank's Brandon Teena in *Boys Don't Cry* (1999). It was a truly revelatory performance, an indelible turn that won virtually every pre-Oscar trophy: The New York and the Los Angeles Critics, and Golden Globe Awards. It took years for director Kimberly Peirce to cast the role. Numerous actresses auditioned, but the director was determined to go with an unknown. For her test, Swank dressed as a boy, and when shooting began, she cut her hair, bound her breasts, and lost herself completely, which was crucial to the role.

Swank nudged Janet McTeer (*Tumbleweeds*) aside in the promising-newcomer sweepstakes with her portrayal of Brandon Teena, a doomed young woman who dresses and lives her life as a man. Beating out four actresses, Swank not only raised the profile of a tiny independent movie, but also transformed her career, which began inauspiciously with *The Karate Kid IV* and a part in TV's "Beverly Hills 90210." "I pray for the day when we celebrate our diversity," Swank said in her acceptance speech.

In the same year, it seemed fitting that Catherine Keener's star-making role — and first Oscar nomination — was for an indie film, *Being John Malkovich.* Keener is a truly independent spirit, having brought her wit to such high-quality, low-budget productions as *Living in Oblivion, Walking and Talking,* and *Your Friends & Neighbors.* Maxine, Keener's alluring Machiavellian character in *Being John Malkovich,* is, as *Entertainment Weekly* pointed out, one of the most aggressively sexual characters — male or female — ever seen on-screen.

Seldom has the American screen seen a woman so confident of her attractiveness that she doesn't feel the need to be polite and can crush a man with an offhand remark. "If you ever got me," she teases John Cusack's smitten Craig, "you wouldn't have a clue what to do with me." Though Cusack plays a puppeteer, it is Maxine who pulls the strings. As she entrances Craig, his wife (Cameron Diaz), and the eponymous actor, Keener seduces the audience with her off-kilter good looks and cut-to-the-quick delivery. Together with Diaz and Malkovich, Keener engages in one of the most mind-blowing three-way sex scenes ever conceived.

Add to Swank's Best Actress and Keener's Oscar-nominated turn in Angelina Jolie's Supporting Oscar for *Girl, Interrupted,* in which she played a rebellious youngster in an asylum — the female equivalent of Jack Nicholson's role in *One Flew Over the Cuckoo's Nest* — one begins to get a sense of how much female screen roles have changed over the past decade.

What better indication of the changes in the Oscar roles than the career of America's sweetheart, Julia Roberts, the most bankable female star in American film history, and the only one who belongs to the boys club in terms of her paychecks — north of $20 million per project. Julia Roberts's three nominations point to the slow but real progress made by women.

Roberts's first nomination was in the supporting league for *Steel Magnolias,* as Shelby, Sally Field's diabetic daughter about to get married. She was the only member to have secured a nomination out of a large, gifted, and mostly female cast that includes Oscar-winners Shirley MacLaine and Olympia Dukakis along with Dolly Parton, as the owner of the Louisiana beauty parlor where most of the story is set. A year later, Roberts surprised herself by winning a second, this time the Best Actress nomination, for playing a Los Angeles prostitute hired by a ruthless financial wheeeler-dealer (played by Richard Gere) in *Pretty Woman.*

In the 1990s, Roberts went through a cycle of small, mostly dissatisfying and uncommercial films — *Dying Young, Mary Reilly, Michael Collins* — in which she was often cast against type. The public stayed home, waiting for her comeback, which occurred in a series of romantic comedies such as *Notting Hill, Runaway Bride,* and *My Best Friend's Wedding.*

Actresses often gripe about the lack of good female roles, but few male roles have been as juicy as the feisty eponymous heroine in *Erin Brockovich.* As a single mom who takes a job and discovers an environmental cover-up, Roberts embodies one of the few roles about a real woman who juggles home and work. Proving her determination to be taken seriously as an actress, not just as a star,

Roberts played a larger-than-life figure, which became the jewel in the crown of her commercial vehicles.

Roberts's Oscar-winning performance vividly conveys the exhilarating experience of a woman who takes pride and pleasure in work. Dressed in a teasing array of miniskirts, platform heels, and bustiers, Roberts flaunts her long shapely legs and gorgeous hair. As critic Kenneth Turan notes, it was a part Roberts has long been looking for, allowing her, like the character, to use her allure for a good cause, to put her undeniable star qualities, her gift for humor, empathy, romance, and vulnerability at the service of a character with a real texture.

· 13 ·

THE IMPORTANCE
OF BEING ECCENTRIC

The best way to win awards in Hollywood is to plaster a young face with old-age makeup — artificial aging is interpreted as an infallible sign of "character" — for those who confuse the art of acting with the art of disguise. — Andrew Sarris

There are many roads to an Oscar nomination, but some are more effective than others. Here is a brief guide for actors eager to get an Oscar:

Play an eccentric, a genius or even a madman

Play a heroic role inspired by a real-life personality

Assume a heavy accent

Apply heavy makeup and age on-screen

Wear strange clothes

Play an alcoholic

Suffer on-screen (physically or mentally)

Die a tragic death on-screen

In short, avoid subtlety and delicacy

Do all of those things in the same role, and you've got yourself an Oscar nomination.

Various forms of eccentricity are a common attribute of both the male and female Oscar-winning performances. And they go way beyond the genre in which the performances are contained. Players have used a wide array of tricks to impress Academy voters. Such antics do not win awards in themselves, but they contribute to the overall impact of performances. Using tricks of the trade often result in making a decent work seem more visible and striking.

Heavy Accents

At present, the twelve-time Oscar nominee Meryl Streep is nicknamed "the queen of accents," for using a different accent in almost every film, from Polish in *Sophie's Choice,* to British in *Plenty,* to Danish in *Out of Africa,* to Australian in *Cry in the Dark.* Heavy accents have always been used to great effect as far as the Academy is concerned.

Spencer Tracy sported a thick accent for playing the Portuguese fisherman in *Captains Courageous.*

Mischa Auer used a droll accent for his eccentric role in the screwball comedy *My Man Godfrey.*

Loretta Young attempted a Swedish accent in *The Farmer's Daughter* (a role turned down by the real-life Swede Ingrid Bergman).

Ingrid Bergman used her native Swedish for the role of the neurotic missionary in *Murder on the Orient Express.* In the same film, Albert Finney was unrecognizable, donning a wig and speaking in a Belgian accent as detective Hercule Poirot.

Playing a Russian sailor, Alan Arkin employed a Russian accent in the comedy, *The Russians Are Coming, The Russians Are Coming,* for which he received his first lead nomination.

Michael Caine spoke directly to the audience with a heavy Cockney accent in *Alfie.*

Tom Hanks was slow and dim-witted, as required by his role, in *Forrest Gump.*

Russell Crowe's West Virginia accent contributed to the authenticity of his role in *The Insider.*

Fellow Australian Toni Collette put on a Philadelphian accent for playing the mother in *The Sixth Sense,* which probably increased her chances of receiving a supporting nomination.

Physical Transformation—Aging and Makeup

Deriving from a long theatrical tradition, the art of disguise encourages stage players to exploit mimicry and makeup as a form of sensationalism. In film too, heavy makeup and on-screen aging have been embraced by actors to impress the Academy.

Emil Jannings, the very first Best Actor winner, changed identities from a former Russian general to a Hollywood extra in *The Way of All Flesh.*

Fredric March's makeup transformation in *Dr. Jekyll and Mr. Hyde* was, of course, necessary, but it also contributed to the overall effectiveness of the film itself. The makeup man was the first to be acknowledged in March's acceptance speech.

Irene Dunne and Richard Dix aged considerably during the thirty-year-span of *Cimarron*'s story.

Greer Garson progressed from a boarding-house slave to wealthy matriarch in *Mrs. Parkington,* a story that covered half a century.

Peter O'Toole changed identities in *The Ruling Class* like he was changing hats. O'Toole played a man who, after the death of his eccentric father, becomes the Earl of Gurney. He has enough money and the persuasive powers to make people believe he's Jesus Christ, only to change identities again and become Jack the Ripper.

In *Big,* Tom Hanks played a boy, who, frustrated by the restrictions imposed on his age group, makes a special wish and wakes up in the body of a thirty-year-old man, with a twelve-year-old sensibility.

Tom Hanks played a person with AIDS in Hollywood's first major drama on the issue, *Philadelphia.*

In 1980, two of the Oscar frontrunners, Scorsese's *Ranging Bull* and David Lynch's *The Elephant Man,* dealt with grotesque human beings. British John Hurt received a lead nomination for playing John Merrick, a hideously deformed man who becomes a freak show for the upper class in turn-of-the-century England until he's rescued by a kind doctor, played by Anthony Hopkins.

Speaking of the talented and versatile Hopkins, in his best-known, Oscar-winning role, as serial killer Hannibal Lecter in *The Silence of the Lambs,* Hopkins spent most of his screen time in a mental institution. Most viewers remember Hopkins's grotesque gestures, particularly the way he rolled his tongue.

Deglamorization of Women

Attractive leading ladies have been rewarded for deglamorizing their looks, and for their willingness to appear drab or frumpy.

Bette Davis wore padding on her legs, donned glasses, and pulled her hair back tight in *Now Voyager.*

Olivia de Havilland played an ugly duckling in *The Heiress* and not a particularly attractive woman in *Hold Back the Dawn.*

Grace Kelly won the Best Actress for *The Country Girl,* as an embittered, humiliated wife, wearing the most unglamorous and unflattering wardrobe in her career; the same year, Kelly flaunted the most stylish costumes in *Rear Window* and *Dial M for Murder.*

Anne Bancroft in *The Miracle Worker* no doubt rendered a good performance as teacher Anne Sullivan, but she was also eccentric and in disguise: Hair pulled back, dark glasses, heavy accent, severe attitude toward work and employers. Bancroft also had a requisite show-stopping hysterical scene, in which she physically struggles with the blind and deaf Helen Keller (Oscar-winning Patty Duke).

At the young age of thirty-four, Elizabeth Taylor portrayed an older, fatter, gray-haired, harsh and deglamorized woman in *Who's Afraid of Virginia Woolf?*

For a decade, Lynn Redgrave couldn't shake her image in *Georgy Girl,* as a pathetic ugly duckling weighing 180 pounds! In 1998, as noted, Redgrave received a second, this time the Supporting nomination for *Gods and Monsters,* as director James Whale's senior and heavily accented housekeeper.

Cher was deglamorized as the lesbian roommate of Karen Silkwood (Meryl Streep) in *Silkwood.* And for her Oscar-winning performance, in *Moonstruck,* she began deglamorized as a widowed bookkeeper and ended up glamorized and in love.

Weight—Gaining and Losing

In *Hawaii,* Jocelyn LaGarde, who had never acted before and didn't even speak English (she learned the role phonetically with a coach) was cast for her role due to her weight—north of four hundred pounds.

Victor Buono was a mother-dominated fat boy in *What Ever Happened to Baby Jane?*

Newcomer Cathy Burns won a Supporting nomination for playing a tormented and bullied overweight girl in *Last Summer.*

The sexy and beautiful Ann-Margret gained at least twenty pounds to play Jack Nicholson's girlfriend in *Carnal Knowledge.*

Robert De Niro gained 56 pounds to play the gluttonous Jake La Motta in *Raging Bull,* forcing the production to shut down for four months to allow the actor to reach the 225 pounds required for the role. LaMotta himself supervised the training of De Niro for the prizefighting scenes.

James Coco received Academy recognition for his hysterical, overweight actor in *Only When I Laugh.*

Jack Nicholson also bloated for his aging astronaut in *Terms of Endearment* and for his Mafia don in *Prizzi's Honor.*

Russell Crowe gained considerable weight for *The Insider,* then lost it for *Gladiator.*

To impersonate the celeb-prizefighter in *Ali,* Will Smith gained weight and changed his posture.

For *Bridget Jones's Diary,* Rene Zellweger gained weight the old-fashioned way, eating lots of chocolate and pizzas.

Men in Drag—Transvestites and Transsexuals

Playing homosexuals, transvestites, or transsexuals has helped actors get recognition through the eccentric, campy behavior of their characters.

In *Some Like It Hot,* Jack Lemmon excelled in two roles: Jerry, the Chicago musician, who accidentally witnesses the St. Valentine's Day Massacre, which forces him to change into Daphne, a member of an all-girl orchestra, ending in the arms of billionaire Joe E. Brown aboard his yacht. The expression "nobody's perfect," has never been better used.

In 1982 alone, three actors were nominated for playing various kinds of cross-dressers. Dustin Hoffman won his second Best Actor as Michael Dorsey/Dorothy Michaels in *Tootsie.* Robert Preston, who played Julie Andrews's gay mentor in *Victor/Victoria,* received a his first and only supporting nomination—he had big showy scenes and flamenco-drag numbers. In *The World According to Garp,* John Lithgow was cast as Roberta, the former football player who had undergone a sex-change operation.

In Neil Jordan's romantic drama, *The Crying Game,* Jaye Davison played a character whose sex comes as a total surprise to both Stephen Rea (who received Best Actor nomination) and the audience.

Gender-Bender

Playing the opposite gender is a great challenge for actors. Screen characters who struggled with hiding their real gender, include two Oscar-winning Best Actresses: Gwyneth Paltrow as Viola De Lesseps/Thomas Kent in *Shakespeare in Love,* and Hilary Swank, as Teena Brandon/Brandon Teena in *Boys Don't Cry.*

Barbra Streisand deserved to be nominated, but was not, for playing Yentl/Anshel in the gender-bender *Yentl,* a movie that rewarded Amy Irving with a supporting nomination for playing the girl who falls for Streisand.

Winning the Supporting Actress Award for *The Year of Living Dangerously,* Linda Hunt is still the only performer to win the Oscar for actually playing a member of the opposite sex. Hunt was cast as Billy Kwan, an idealistic Indonesian vastly disillusioned by the Sukarno regime. When Hunt said in her Oscar acceptance speech, "the sky's the limit," she meant it literally.

Stigmatized Roles — Gay Characters

A number of straight actors have received the Oscar for playing homosexuals, among them William Hurt in *Kiss of the Spider Woman,* as a prisoner with a fertile imagination, and Tom Hanks in *Philadelphia,* as a person with AIDS. Peter Finch received his first Best Actor nomination for playing a homosexual Jewish doctor in *Sunday, Bloody Sunday.*

Changing Identities — Playing a Dual/Triple Role

Lee Marvin played a dual role in *Cat Ballou,* a drunken gunslinger and a killer with a silver nose.

In *Dr. Strangelove; or, How I Learned to Stop Worrying and Love the Bomb,* Peter Sellers played three roles, as powerless President Muffley, nuclear scientist Dr. Strangelove, and Captain Lionel Mandrake. Originally, Sellers was going to play a fourth role, Major King Kong (Slim Pickens's in the movie).

Other Tricks of the Trade

Yul Brynner shaved his head for *The King and I,* and continued to flaunt it as a trademark for the rest of his career.

John Wayne put on an eye patch in *True Grit* and won the Best Actor for a performance inferior to those in his other Westerns, *Red River* and *The Searchers* among others.

Marlon Brando puffed-out his cheeks for his audition and performance in *The Godfather.*

Alcoholism

The most common "deviant" trait of both male and female Oscar roles is alcoholism. Actors love to play dipsomaniac characters because they allow them to have "big," attention-grabbing scenes.

In *A Free Soul,* Lionel Barrymore won Best Actor as Norma Shearer's alcoholic lawyer-father.

Van Heflin played the alcoholic friend of Robert Taylor (vastly miscast as a gangster) in *Johnny Eager.*

Claire Trevor as Edward G. Robinson's alcoholic mistress in *Key Largo.*

In *Pillow Talk,* Thelma Ritter shone as Doris Day's perpetually hungover housekeeper.

In 1962, four of the Best Actress nominees played alcoholic and/or drug-addicted women: Bette Davis, *What Ever Happened to Baby Jane?,* Geraldine Page, *Sweet Bird of Youth,* Lee Remick, *Days of Wine and Roses,* and Katharine Hepburn, *Long Day's Journey Into Night.* The winner was the only sober woman, albeit an eccentric one, Anne Bancroft for *The Miracle Worker.*

In 1983, all five Best Actor nominees played drunks of one kind or another. The versatile Robert Duvall won the Best Actor for *Tender Mercies,* a drama about an alcoholic country singer who's rehabilitated through the love of a decent woman. Duvall had earlier received a Best Actor nomination for playing another alcoholic, the abusive father in *The Great Santini.*

Tom Conti played the drunken Scottish poet on a lecture tour in New England in *Reuben, Reuben,* written by Julius Epstein, the Hollywood vet best-known for his Oscar-winning script *Casablanca.*

Albert Finney and Tom Courtenay achieved the almost impossible task of receiving Best Actor nominations for the same film, *The Dresser,* in which Finney played an aging, alcoholic Shakespearean actor (based on the life of Donald Wolfit), and Courtenay played his abused, alcoholic dresser.

As Nick Nolte's abusive, alcoholic father in *Affliction,* James Coburn gave a chilling career-capping performance that garnered him his first nomination — and first Supporting Oscar at the age of seventy.

Ed Harris very much deserved his first lead (and third in all) nomination in *Pollock,* for embodying painter Jackson Pollock, the noted abstract expressionist whose short life (he died by crashing his car into a tree) was afflicted with alcoholism, insecurity, and a turbulent marriage.

The Oscar Pantheon of Screen Alcoholics

Men

Ray Milland, *The Lost Weekend*

James Mason, *A Star Is Born*

Jack Lemmon, *Days of Wine and Roses*

Dudley Moore, *Arthur*

Paul Newman, *The Verdict*

Albert Finney, *The Dresser* and *Under the Volcano*

Nicolas Cage, *Leaving Las Vegas*

Robert Duvall, *The Apostle*

Women

Susan Hayward, *Smash-up, the Story of a Woman, My Foolish Heart,* and *I'll Cry Tomorrow*

Deborah Kerr, *Edward, My Son*

Vivien Leigh, *A Streetcar Named Desire*

Piper Laurie, *The Hustler*

Elizabeth Taylor, *Who's Afraid of Virginia Woolf?*

Bette Midler, *The Rose*

Marsha Mason, *Only When I Laugh*

Simone Signoret, *Ship of Fools* (drugs)

Julie Christie, *McCabe and Mrs. Miller* (drugs)

Diana Ross, *Lady Sings the Blues* (liquor and drugs)

Jessica Lange, *Frances*

Jane Fonda, *The Morning After*

Eccentric Professions

Geena Davis was a dog trainer in *The Accidental Tourist,* her Supporting Oscar role.

Mercedes Ruehl won a Supporting Oscar for playing an aggressive hard-edged video store owner in *The Fisher King.*

In *Enchanted April,* Joan Plowright played an elderly, crotchety woman, living in the past and dropping names of all the famous authors she may (or may not) have met in her life.

Diseases—Physical and Mental

The Academy is a veritable dictionary of illnesses and diseases, both physical and mental.

Amnesia

Ronald Colman played an amnesiac who becomes enchanted with his own wife in his comeback role in *Random Harvest,* which earned him a Best Actor nomination.

Ingrid Bergman received her second Best Actress Oscar for playing an amnesiac in *Anastasia* (1956), as a woman pretending to be the youngest daughter of Tzar Nicholas II, rumored to have escaped the Bolshevik Revolution.

Blindness

Audrey Hepburn received her fifth Best Actress nomination for playing a victim in the stage-oriented thriller, *Wait Until Dark,* a blind woman who, unbeknownst to her, possesses a doll filled with drugs. Alone in her apartment, she has to confront two thugs (Alan Arkin and Richard Crenna) who invade her space. It was Hepburn's last nomination and last film before making a comeback nine years later in *Robin and Marian.*

Al Pacino was finally awarded Best Actor at his eighth nomination for *Scent of a Woman,* in which he played a brash and acerbic blind Lieutenant Colonel, saved from suicide by a younger protégé.

Mention has been made of Patty Duke's Supporting Oscar as the blind and deaf Helen Keller in *The Miracle Worker.*

Other thespians nominated by playing blind characters include:

Claude Rains as Bette Davis's blind husband in *Mr. Skeffington* (1944)

Arthur Kennedy as a blinded soldier in *Bright Light* (1951)

Elizabeth Hartman in *Patch of Blue* (1965)

John Malkovich as a blind man residing in Sally Field's Texas farm in *Places in the Heart* (1984)

Deaf-Mute

Receiving accolades in *Sweet and Lowdown,* British Samantha Morton was nominated for playing Sean Penn's randy and mute laundress-girlfriend.

In *The Heart Is a Lonely Hunter,* Oscar-nominated Alan Arkin played a deaf-mute man who changes the lives of the residents of a small-Southern town, including that of a sensitive adolescent girl, played by Oscar-nominated Sondra Locke in her very first screen role.

When John Mills played the mute village idiot in *Ryan's Daughter,* the critic Pauline Kael alerted her readers while deriding the Academy: "This is the kind of things that gets people Academy Awards because the acting is so conspicuous." Kael was right; Mills won the Supporting Actor.

Physical Deformity and Paraplegia

Harold Russell, a real-life hero who played himself in *The Best Years of Our Lives,* and Jon Voight, as a Vietnam vet in a wheelchair in *Coming Home,* won the Supporting and the Best Actor Oscars respectively.

Laurence Olivier donned a hunch for version of *Richard III.*

Jose Ferrer and Gerard Depardieu sported big noses in their respective versions of *Cyrano de Bergerac.* And Ferrer was nominated again as the French dwarf painter Toulouse-Lautrec in John Huston's version of *Moulin Rouge.*

Michael Dunn, a dwarf, was probably the best thing in *Ship of Fools,* serving as the narrative's moral consciousness and most balanced character.

Sheer Madness and Mentally Challenged Roles

The following winners have played characters that for one reason or another have descended into madness:

Emil Jannings in *The Last Command*

Vivien Leigh in *A Streetcar Named Desire*

Bette Davis in *What Ever Happened to Baby Jane?*

Leonardo DiCaprio first garnered attention as Johnny Depp's mentally retarded younger brother in *What's Eating Gilbert Grape.*

The questionable supporting nomination of Brad Pitt for Terry Gilliam's *Twelve Monkeys,* in which he played a rebel son escaping from an asylum. No doubt, Pitt was also rewarded for becoming a hot box-office star.

Mental Breakdowns

Gregory Peck, *Twelve O'Clock High*

James Stewart, *Harvey*

Humphrey Bogart, *The Caine Mutiny*

Bette Davis, *What Ever Happened to Baby Jane?*

Carrie Snodgress, *Diary of a Man Housewife*

Gena Rowlands, *A Woman Under the Influence*

Isabelle Adjani, *The Story of Adele H.* and *Camille Claudel*

Jack Nicholson and Brad Dourif, *One Flew Over the Cuckoo's Nest*

Ronee Blakley, *Nashville*

Peter Finch, *Network*

Peter Firth, *Equus*

Multiple Personalities and Schizophrenia

Fredric March, *Dr. Jekyll and Mr. Hyde*

Joanne Woodward, *The Three Faces of Eve*

Russell Crowe, *A Beautiful Mind*

Post-traumatic Stress Disorder

Bruce Dern, *Coming Home*

Christopher Walken, *The Deer Hunter*

Timothy Hutton, *Ordinary People*

Mental Retardation–Developmental Disabilities

An otherwise mediocre actor, Cliff Robertson received the Best Actor at his first (and only) nomination for *Charly* (1968), a poignant tale about a mentally retarded adult who undergoes brain surgery and blossoms into a genius only to learn that he is doomed to regress back to his initial state. Adapted by Stirling Silliphant from the novel *Flowers for Algernon,* which had been dramatized on TV with Robertson in 1961, *Charly* is a sentimental, outdated problem drama. Robertson fell in love with the role, bought the movie rights, and after years spent trying to place the film, a studio made it.

Penny Marshall's 1990 *Awakenings,* for which Robert De Niro received a Best Actor nomination, explores a similar theme as *Charly.* Indeed, Pauline Kael dismissed this adaptation of Oliver Sacks's tragicomedy of brain sickness as "a do-gooding synthesis" of three Best Picture winners: *Charly, One Flew Over the Cuckoo's Nest,* and *Rain Man.* For Kael, De Niro's patient doesn't exist except as fodder for pathos, and the whole movie epitomizes a "forced banalization" of the viewers' emotions into "showbiz shtick."

Other actors recognized by the Academy for playing mentally retarded roles include Peter Sellers in *Being There* and Tom Hanks in *Forrest Gump.* In 2001, Sean Penn received a lead nomination for *I Am Sam,* in which he played a mentally retarded father (with an I.Q. of a seven-year-old) who fights the court to maintain custody over his smarter daughter. Inevitable comparisons were made between Penn's performance and those of Hanks in *Forrest Gump* (I.Q. of seventy-five) and Dustin Hoffman in *Rain Man,* though the latter played an autistic, or idiot savant.

All of these movies represent Hollywood's idea of a prestige and noble "message" productions. They also demonstrate how deviant or merely hysterical acting is often mistakenly identified as "truthful realism."

Disclosed and Undisclosed Fatal Illnesses

Daniel Day Lewis had cerebral palsy in *My Left Foot.*

Dustin Hoffman died at the end of *Midnight Cowboy.*

Diane Keaton suffered valiantly in *Marvin's Room.*

Jessica Lange went through a painful lobotomy in *Frances.*

Excess for Excess's Sake – Eccentric Mannerisms

The Academy has always rewarded excessive performances that contain "big scenes" that call for hysteria and histrionics. Sadly, overacting of the worst kind has been noticed and rewarded by the Academy voters. How else would you explain the 1966 Supporting Oscar for the always-mannered Sandy Dennis in *Who's Afraid of Virginia Woolf?* in which she played Honey, the bird-brained wife of an ambitious and immoral academic (George Segal). Never at rest, Dennis's performance was a collection of tics, giggles, whizzes, and hiccups that made her role even less appealing than it must have been on the page.

In choosing scripts, actors, too, are aware that it is the easily identifiable — hysterical, flamboyant and hyperactive — qualities of their roles that will make their performances stand out among the Academy voters. Diane Ladd, first nominated for her worthy role as a waitress in *Alice Doesn't Live Here Anymore,* received a second nomination for an over-the-top role, as a wicked mother, smearing her face with lipstick and acting "big" in David Lynch's *Wild at Heart.* After being so out of control in this film, critics were amazed by Ladd's restrained performance as the sensitive and liberal wife-mother opposite Robert Duvall in *Rambling Rose,* for which she received a third supporting nomination.

Lillian Gish received her only nomination — a supporting one — for playing a wife driven to drink by her brutal cattle baron husband in the sweeping but silly Western, *Duel in the Sun.*

Richard Widmark was either blessed or cursed (depending on point of view) by his attention-getting film debut, the noir classic *Kiss of Death,* in which he played a giggling psychotic who gets a kick out of pushing old ladies down the stairs to their death.

Eileen Brennan as the nasty sergeant in *Private Benjamin,* torturing Goldie Hawn.

Joan Hackett played a narcissist actress terrified of growing old in *Only When I Laugh.*

Lesley Ann Warren gave an earthy performance as a low-voltage singer in *Victor/Victoria,* donning a platinum wig and speaking in a nasal, sexy voice ("I'm horny") to allure her boyfriend (James Garner). She added a wonderful interpretation to the archetypal dumb blonde, earlier played by Judy Holliday (*Born Yesterday*), Goldie Hawn (*Cactus Flower*) and others.

Glenn Close as Robin Williams's liberated mother, in *The World According to Garp,* running a camp of feminists and lesbians.

Meg Tilly was a possessed nun accused of murder in *Agnes of God.*

Edward Norton was nominated for *American History X,* as Derek Vinyard, a muscle-bound, shaved-head neo-Nazi psycho-killer who becomes a horrifyingly violent local hero to a gang of Los Angeles skinheads. In a much publicized bid, Norton added some twenty-five pounds for the role, and donned a large swastika tattooed on his chest. This was Norton's second (but first lead) nomination; his first was for playing a psychopathic choirboy-serial killer in *Primal Fear.*

Nudity

Elizabeth McGovern rendered a daffy portrait of a girl-in-a cage beauty, Evelyn Nesbit, in *Ragtime* (1981), in a role that included a memorable nude scene.

Annette Bening achieved notoriety and her first nomination for *The Grifters,* in which she was totally naked in a store scene.

Robin Williams played a homeless man, wild and crazy, running naked in Central Park in *The Fisher King* (1991).

In his Oscar-winning (*Shine*) and Oscar-nominated (*Quills*) roles, Australian Geoffrey Rush combined all the requisites for Oscar-caliber performances.

In the biopic *Shine,* Rush embodied pianist David Helfgott, an abused child prodigy tortured by his patriarchal, Holocaust-survivor father. As an adult, Helfgott grows up to be a neurotic (to say the least), an eccentric running around nude (or wearing just a raincoat) and shamelessly groping women. Speaking at breakneck speed and babbling half sentences, Helfgott was the kind of Oscar-caliber role actors like Rush dream of.

Following the career of an "all-purpose" stage actor, Rush then appeared as Queen Elizabeth's cunning adviser, Sir Francis Walsingham in *Elizabeth,* and as the theater manager Philip Henslowe in *Shakespeare in Love,* which earned him his first supporting, and second nomination. Two years later, Rush portrayed the impious eighteenth century French novelist Marquis de Sade, who died in an asylum in 1814, in *Quills.* Known for his prurient madness and maverick writings, de Sade spent thirty years in and out of prisons and asylums for acts of sexual offense, and for publishing his banned novels which melded philosophy and pornography. Among other things, Rush was asked to appear naked for long stretches of time.

The Oscar as a Reward for Mediocrity

> The curious thing about awards is that one receives them for work one does not expect to receive them for, and does not receive them for work one does.
> —Jule Styne, Composer

Styne received the Tony Award for *Hallelujah, Baby!* but not for *Gypsy.* Similarly, among Oscar annals, many performers have been nominated for mediocre work, not their best. And while there is agreement over the candidate's overall talent, there is disagreement over the particular film for which he or she receives Academy recognition.

Lew Ayres was not nominated for playing the pacifist soldier in *All Quiet on the Western Front,* but for his doctor in *Johnny Belinda,* because that picture was nominated in almost every category.

Cary Grant failed to earn recognition for any of his great comedies, *The Awful Truth, Bringing up Baby,* and *His Girl Friday,* or for his wonderful performance in Hitchcock's *North By Northwest.* Predictably, he was nominated for two pedestrian, sentimental movies — *Penny Serenade* and *None But the Lonely Heart.*

Lee Marvin undoubtedly gave a better performance in a more demanding role in *Ship of Fools,* as a vulgar Texan tycoon, than in *Cat Ballou.*

Steve McQueen's one and only nomination was for his inscrutable, alienated sailor in the big-budget *The Sand Pebbles,* not for his more interesting work in the intimate and sensitive *Baby, the Rain Must Fall,* Horton Foote's story of a violent parolee in a small Southern town.

Many British actors were nominated for mediocre American movies, not for their better work in British films. Sir Michael Redgrave was nominated just once, as Orin in *Mourning Becomes Electra,* but not for his teacher in *The*

Browning Version, or for Oscar Wilde's *The Importance of Being Earnest.* Sir Ralph Richardson received his first supporting nomination for *The Heiress,* but was not cited for his servant in *The Fallen Idol,* or his role in *Breaking the Sound Barrier.*

More than a few winners have received the Oscar for average work in popular films. Even the Oscar's supporters claim that while the winners might not be those who gave the best performance of the year, they are, nonetheless, Oscar-caliber artists, worthy of the award. The doubt is not over the awardee's deservability, but over the particular performance for which the award is given. Once again, the Academy claims that in the final account, the Oscars "even out the odds," that the Oscar eventually honors artists who have consistently made Oscar-caliber films. Some Academy voters are known to single out a nominee for the overall quality of their work rather than for a particular performance.

Bette Davis once said that her two Oscars, for *Dangerous* and *Jezebel,* didn't mean much to her, because they were for the "wrong films." She would have been more gratified to win for *The Letter* or *All About Eve.* James Stewart gave a finer performance in *Mr. Smith Goes to Washington* than in his Oscar role, *The Philadelphia Story.*

The twelve-time nominee and four-time winner Katharine Hepburn was nominated for distinguished roles, but won for merely good ones. Three of her nominated performances represent not only Hepburn's best but some of the best acting in American cinema: *Alice Adams, The Philadelphia Story,* and as Mary Tyrone in Sidney Lumet's brilliant version of Eugene O'Neill's *Long Day's Journey Into Night.* But Hepburn won for *Morning Glory, Guess Who's Coming to Dinner, The Lion in Winter,* and *On Golden Pond.*

Academy voters are naturally influenced by the selection of critics' groups, such as the New York Film Critics Circle. Several players received the critics' award for a role which brought them a nomination — but not the award. Almost invariably, they later went on to win the Oscar for a lesser performance. Jon Voight was singled out by the New York Film Critics Circle for his Joe Buck in *Midnight Cowboy,* for which he was also nominated. He lost, but received the Oscar for *Coming Home.* Jack Nicholson won the New York Film Critics Circle and an Oscar nomination for *Chinatown,* but the Academy Award was given to him a year later for *One Flew Over the Cuckoo's Nest.*

Some players actually won the Oscar for the weakest of their nominated performances. Jack Lemmon did not win for *Some Like It Hot, The Apartment,* or *Days of Wine and Roses,* but for *Save the Tiger.* Faye Dunaway lost twice, as Bonnie Parker in *Bonnie and Clyde* and as the mysterious femme fatale in *Chinatown,* but she won for *Network.* Dustin Hoffman's first Oscar, for *Kramer vs. Kramer,* was not on par with his other nominated roles.

No Reward for Subtlety

Once in a while there are pleasant surprises, and subtle, understated performances do get the Academy's attention. However, in the overall Oscar annals, these quiet performances have been in the minority. This may explain why a natural, untemperamental actor like Jeff Bridges has never received an Oscar, though he has been nominated four times.

In *Georgia,* it was Jennifer Jason Leigh who had the flashy role people associate with an Oscar-caliber performance. Leigh, who won the New York Film Critics Best Actress, was cast as an ungifted singer, jealous of her successful older sister, played by Mare Winningham. But Winningham received a supporting nomination. Subtle performances such as Winningham's, which accentuated the character's tense but repressed emotions, are often overlooked by the Academy since they appear easy. For many, Winningham personified the phrase "less is more," a quality that's rare in Oscar-winning performances.

In recent years, Kim Basinger in *L.A. Confidential* and Laura Linney in *You Can Count on Me* rendered clean, spare performances that were noteworthy for their lack of apparent technique. These so-called small performances stood in sharp contrast to the excessive technique used by Maggie Smith, for example, in most of her six Oscar-nominated performances, including *The Prime of Miss Jean Brodie, California Suite,* and *Gosford Park.* Or for that matter, note the difference between Smith and her *Gosford Park*'s co-star, Helen Mirren, also nominated in the same film for a supporting role as the head of the servants.

Most of the aforementioned eccentric roles have been good, if not distinguished. But they also raise an interesting question: Is the role, as written in the scenario, more important than the actual performance delivered on-screen? Sally Field said of her second Oscar-winning role that "The script of *Places in the Heart* was so well done that it brings more attention to the role. Edna is such a complex character that she gives the actor a lot to do." Vanessa Redgrave echoed the same feeling about her nominated role in *The Bostonians:* "All I've done is play the lady Henry James wrote." Is this modesty real or fake — noblesse oblige on the part of performers? Is the scripted role more critical for winning an Oscar than the specific interpretation by a particular performer?

1. *Wings,* the first film ever to win Best Picture (1927-28), also received a second Oscar for engineering effects. Its spectacular aerial sequences and running time (136 minutes) set a trend among Academy voters of favoring grand-scale epic films over small intimate ones.

2. Greta Garbo and John Barrymore in *Grand Hotel,* the 1931-32 Best Picture and the only Oscar winner to be nominated in one category. The two legendary players never won a legitimate competitive Oscar. Garbo won an Honorary Oscar. Barrymore was never even nominated.

3. Clark Gable and Claudette Colbert in Frank Capra's *It Happened One Night* (1934), the first comedy to win Best Picture and the first film to sweep all five major awards.

4. *Casablanca,* the 1943 Best Picture, features Humphrey Bogart (RIGHT) in his best-known role as Rick Blain, the most famous café owner in film history. Bogart should have won the Best Actor but did not. The winner was Paul Lukas for *Watch on the Rhine.*

5. Ray Milland in *The Lost Weekend* (1945), Billy Wilder's first Oscar-winning picture and Hollywood's first major film about alcoholism. Milland won the Best Actor for playing an alcoholic writer suffering a creative block. In the book, his character was a troubled homosexual.

6. Joan Crawford in her Oscar-winning role in *Mildred Pierce* (1945), her most famous film. The ambitious Crawford lucked out when both Bette Davis and Barbara Stanwyck turned down the role.

7. Gregory Peck at his best, a liberal-crusading journalist in Elia Kazan's 1947 Oscar-winning *Gentleman's Agreement.* It was Peck's third nominated performance.

8. A "meaningful look" between Bette Davis (LEFT) and Anne Baxter (RIGHT), playing the "aging" and "rising" actresses, respectively, watched by George Sanders (RIGHT) and Gary Merrill (CENTER) in *All About Eve,* the 1950 Best Picture, one of the two most-nominated (fourteen) films in the Academy's history—the other is *Titanic*—and the first to feature two Best Actress nominations.

9. Broderick Crawford and Judy Holliday, the 1950 Best Actress, as the "dumb blond" in *Born Yesterday,* George Cukor's comedy that was imbued with both erotic and political overtones.

10. Playing eccentric Southern belles became the "specialty" of British actress Vivien Leigh, here with Marlon Brando in her second Oscar–winning performance in *A Streetcar Named Desire* (1951), based on Tennessee Williams's prize-winning play. Leigh's first Best Actress was for *Gone With the Wind.*

11. The famous chariot race in William Wyler's blockbuster *Ben-Hur* (1959), the only remake to win the Best Picture Oscar and one of the few films to win eleven awards.

12. Rita Moreno, the first Latina to win the Oscar (Supporting Actress), in a production number from the musical *West Side Story* (1961), which won Best Picture and nine other awards. Moreno's award typecast her as a "Latin spitfire" for over a decade.

13. Peter O'Toole should have won the Best Actor for his lead performance in David Lean's magnificent historical epic *Lawrence of Arabia,* the 1962 Best Picture, re-released in 2002 for its fortieth anniversary. With seven nominations, all in the lead category, O'Toole is one of the greatest losers in the Oscars' history.

14. The two female Oscars in 1962 honored Anne Bancroft (as Annie Sullivan) and Patty Duke (as Helen Keller) in Arthur Penn's biopicture *The Miracle Worker*. Bancroft had earlier won a Tony for playing the same role on Broadway.

15. Paul Scofield (RIGHT) was honored with the Best Actor for his noble portrayal of Sir Thomas More in Fred Zinnemann's *A Man for All Seasons*, the 1966–Oscar winner. Robert Shaw was nominated as Supporting Actor for his interpretation of King Henry VIII.

16. *In the Heat of the Night* (1967), one of the least-distinguished Oscar winners, featured good performances by Rod Steiger (RIGHT), who won the Best Actor, and (LEFT) Sidney Poitier, who was not nominated. The movie launched a cycle of films celebrating male friendship.

17. Dustin Hoffman (RIGHT) and Jon Voight (LEFT) probably canceled each other out as Best Actor nominees in John Schlesinger's *Midnight Cowboy,* the 1969 Best Picture about an unlikely friendship set in a sleazy and impersonal New York City.

18. George C. Scott shocked the film world when he refused his nomination for *Patton* (1970), but his colleagues ignored his protests and honored him with the Best Actor. One thing was beyond doubt: the brilliance of Scott's performance as the controversial general.

19. Francis Ford Coppola's masterful crime sagas, *The Godfather* and *The Godfather, Part II,* won Best Picture of 1972 and 1974, respectively. Marlon Brando (Best Actor, 1972) and Robert De Niro (Supporting Actor, 1974) won the award for playing the same character, Don Vito Corleone, at different ages.

20. Faye Dunaway parodied her own screen image as a ruthlessly ambitious TV executive in Sidney Lumet's prophetic political farce, *Network* (1976), winning the Best Actress Oscar in her third nomination.

21. *Annie Hall,* the 1977 Oscar–winning comedy, established its confused heroine, Diane Keaton, as a household name and its director, Woody Allen, as one of
America's foremost auteurs.

22. Sally Field gave a stunning performance as the real-life working-class heroine who gains political consciousness in Martin Ritt's *Norma Rae* (1979), for which she was rewarded with her first Best Actress. Her second, largely undeserved Oscar, was for *Places in the Heart*.

23. Leonardo DiCaprio and Kate Winslet atop the sinking ship in *Titanic* (1997), a fictionalized account of the 1912 accident, which became the most successfully commercial Oscar–winning film due to director James Cameron's shrewd manipulation of narrative and technology, and his decision to focus on the romantic affair rather than the disaster.

24. In its critique of suburban life, the 1999 Oscar–winner *American Beauty* didn't break new thematic ground, but Sam Mendes's direction was smooth and the acting was flawless, particularly by Kevin Spacey, here with Annette Bening. Below is a shot of the two young girls, Thora Birch and Mena Suvari (on the bed), who gave meaning to the film's title.

· 14 ·

THE OSCAR AS
A POPULARITY CONTEST

Ideally, the selection of Oscar winners should be determined by two factors: The quality of achievement and the intensity of competition in a given year. If logic dictates, there should be a strong correlation between the intensity of competition and the quality of the Oscar achievements. In actuality, however, in years of fierce contest, the winning performance is not necessarily the strongest; at times, it is the weakest.

Intense Competition

In 1940, the competition in the two lead acting categories was particularly intense. The nominees for Best Actress were: Bette Davis in *The Letter,* Joan Fontaine in *Rebecca,* Katharine Hepburn in *The Philadelphia Story,* Ginger Rogers in *Kitty Foyle,* and Martha Scott in *Our Town.* That year, Hollywood consensus held that Hepburn gave the year's strongest performance, arguably the best of her career, for which she was cited by the New York Film Critics Circle. The Academy winner, however, was Ginger Rogers, earning an Oscar for her first and only nomination. In the same year, James Stewart's winning performance in *The Philadelphia Story* was also not the most distinguished, compared with Charlie Chaplin in *The Great Dictator,* or Henry Fonda in *The Grapes of Wrath.* The two other nominees were Laurence Olivier for *Rebecca* and Raymond Massey for the biopicture *Abe Lincoln in Illinois.*

The most impressive male performance in 1947 was delivered by William Powell in *Life With Father,* for which he won the New York Film Critics Award. Yet the Oscar winner was Ronald Colman in *A Double Life,* winning over stiff competition from Gregory Peck in *Gentleman's Agreement* and John Garfield in *Body and Soul;* the fifth nominee was Michael Redgrave in *Mourning Becomes Electra.* The female category that year was not particularly strong. The winner, Loretta Young in *The Farmer's Daughter,* was up against Joan Crawford in her second nomination, for *Possessed,* Susan Hayward in *Smash-up, the Story of a Woman,* Dorothy McGuire in *Gentleman's Agreement,* and four-time nominee Rosalind Russell in *Mourning Becomes Electra.*

Bette Davis was denied the 1950 Oscar for what is the most majestic performance of her career, as Margo Channing in *All About Eve,* but she competed against her co-star Anne Baxter in the same category. As noted, this must have split the votes. In fact, 1950 was a year of extraordinary performances, including Gloria Swanson's in *Sunset Boulevard*. The surprise winner was Judy Holliday in *Born Yesterday,* the only comedic role in a year of heavy dramatic roles; the fifth nominee was Eleanor Parker as the victimized wife in the prison drama *Caged.*

The historical epic *Ben-Hur* was the biggest winner in 1959, winning eleven of its twelve nominations, including Best Actor for Charlton Heston. An actor of limited range, Heston won his Oscar as a result of what's known as block voting, namely citing the same film in various categories — deservedly or undeservedly. The Best Actor competition that year was extraordinary: Laurence Harvey in *Room at the Top,* Jack Lemmon in *Some Like It Hot,* Paul Muni in *The Last Angry Man,* and James Stewart in *Anatomy of a Murder,* who won the New York Film Critics Award. Judged by the merits of his performance alone, Heston gave the least-impressive performance of the five nominated.

Similar trends prevail in the other acting categories. Take 1992, for example, when Marisa Tomei won the Supporting Actress for the comedy *My Cousin Vinny,* in which she played a feisty New York girl taken for granted by her lawyer boyfriend. Tomei was up against British and Australian "royalty": Judy Davis in Woody Allen's *Husbands and Wives* (cited by the Los Angeles Film Critics Association), Joan Plowright in *Enchanted April,* Vanessa Redgrave in *Howards End,* and Miranda Richardson in *Damage.*

When Tomei was nominated in 2002 for a second Supporting Oscar for *In the Bedroom,* her agents and friends hoped she would win — and finally live down one of Oscar's biggest myths. Since her win, Tomei has been dogged by talk that presenter Jack Palance had read the wrong name at the podium. Tomei has called the rumor incredibly hurtful and has refused to comment on it. The hubbub began when Palance called fellow nominee Judy Davis *Joan,* confusing her with the 1950s-sitcom star. But witnesses say that Tomei herself was utterly stunned when Palance named her over such grandes dames as Plowright and Redgrave. One voter recalled: "It seemed bizarre to everyone I knew that Marisa Tomei would win in such a year."

What if Palance had flubbed? "It's absolutely hogwash," insisted Frank Johnson, of Price, Waterhouse, Coopers Accountants, who remain alert during the show should a presenter make an error. Explained Johnson: "We have an agreement with the Academy that, if that happens, one of us would step on stage, introduce ourselves and say the presenter misspoke."

All five Supporting actors of 1993 were worthy nominees in an exceptionally strong category: Leonardo DiCaprio for *What's Eating Gilbert Grape,* Ralph Fiennes for *Schindler's List,* Tommy Lee Jones for *The Fugitive,* John Malkovich as the villain in *Line of Fire,* and Peter Postlethwaite as the wrongly convicted father for *In the Name of the Father.* How do you make an informed decision and choose *one* of those terrific turns? The feeling was that the talented Jones won because he was a known quantity and one who's paid his Hollywood dues — Jones was Sissy Spacek's husband in *Coal Miner's Daughter,* for which he wasn't nominated, though he was nominated in 1991 for *JFK.*

Errors of Omission

Year after year, the nominations have been criticized for slighting and bypassing worthy achievements. The Academy's apologetic response is consistent: There can be only five nominees and only one winner in each category. This inevitably means that not every worthy achievement will be nominated. Yet, errors of omission are particularly visible in years in which the nominees are mediocre, compared with the level of excellence of those overlooked.

The most glaring omission occurs when a movie is nominated for Best Picture, but its director fails to be recognized. The lack of correlation between the Best Picture and the Best Director is a function of the voting procedures: The Directors Branch nominates accomplishments in its league, but all Academy members nominate films for the Best Picture.

In 1995, although their films were cited in several categories, including Best Picture, directors Ron Howard (*Apollo 13*) and Ang Lee (*Sense and Sensibility*) came up empty-handed. Instead, the two slots in the directorial category were filled by Mike Figgis for *Leaving Las Vegas* and Tim Robbins for *Dead Man Walking.* Both films failed to receive Best Picture nomination though they were cited in other major categories, such as acting.

Two thousand one also saw the failure of two directors to receive recognition for Best Picture nominees. *In the Bedroom* secured five nominations (three for its actors), but left its novice helmer, Todd Field, in the cold. Similarly, and rather inexplicably, *Moulin Rouge* received multiple nominations, but not for Baz Luhrmann, its visionary director who's responsible for every frame of his postmodern musical. In lieu of Field and Luhrmann, the Directors Branch cited Ridley Scott (for the war film *Black Hawk Down*) and David Lynch (for *Mulholland Drive,* his noirish Hollywood fable-nightmare).

All the winners of major critics groups who have failed to receive the Academy's recognition probably deserved nomination. The most conspicuous omissions among performers, all cited by the New York Film Critics, include: Greta Garbo in *Anna Karenina,* Ida Lupino in *The Hard Way,* Tallulah Bankhead in *Lifeboat,* Ralph Richardson in *Breaking the Sound Barrier,* Liv Ullmann in *Cries and Whispers* and *Scenes from a Marriage,* John Gielgud in *Providence,* Glenda Jackson in *Stevie,* Norma Aleandro in *The Official Story,* and recently, James Broadbent, as the eccentric and repressed Gilbert (of the team Gilbert and Sullivan) in Mike Leigh's *Topsy-Turvy;* Broadbent won the Supporting Oscar in 2001 for *Iris.*

Some players have been consistently passed over by the Academy. Edward G. Robinson was never nominated, despite a number of estimable roles and considerable range in such films as *Little Caesar* and *Key Largo.* Robinson excelled in playing men on both sides of the law, like the good insurance-claims' manager in *Double Indemnity.* The Academy compensated Robinson with an

Honorary Oscar in March 1973, two months after he died. Robinson was informed about the award a week before he died and he asked his wife to read a personal note, in which he wrote: "It couldn't have come at a better time. Had it come earlier, it would have aroused deep feelings in me, still not so deep as now. I'm very grateful to my warm, creative, talented, and intimate colleagues who have been my life's association. How much richer can a man be?"

At least three of Jean Arthur's accomplishments should have been recognized by the Academy: *Mr. Deeds Goes to Town,* opposite Gary Cooper; *Mr. Smith Goes to Washington,* as Jimmy Stewart's secretary; and in George Stevens's classic Western *Shane,* in which she co-starred with Alan Ladd, Van Heflin, and Jack Palance. All three movies were nominated for Best Picture and most of Arthur's co-stars earned acting nominations: Cooper in *Deeds,* Stewart and others in *Smith,* and Brandon De Wilde and Jack Palance in *Shane.* Vastly underestimated, Jean Arthur was nominated only once, for George Stevens's war comedy *The More the Merrier.*

Some films have earned nominations for several of their players, but excluded the one or two who truly deserved to be nominated. Eleanor Parker and Lee Grant were nominated for *Detective Story,* but Kirk Douglas, in one of his best roles as the obsessively righteous detective, was not. Burt Lancaster and Shirley Jones earned awards for *Elmer Gantry,* but Jean Simmons, who played a devout evangelist, was conspicuously omitted. Spencer Tracy received a nomination for the courtroom drama, *Inherit the Wind,* but co-star Fredric March did not. Greer Garson was nominated for playing Eleanor Roosevelt in *Sunrise at Campobello,* but Ralph Bellamy, who re-created his Tony Award-winning role as President Roosevelt, failed to win a nod from the Academy.

The Sundowners was nominated in 1960 in many categories, including acting nominations for Deborah Kerr and Glynis Johns, but not Robert Mitchum. In his entire career, Mitchum earned only one supporting nomination, in the war film *The Story of G.I. Joe.*

Year after year, the critics compile lists of achievements bypassed by the Academy. Yet in some years, the omissions are more glaring than others.

Why was Leonardo DiCaprio snubbed by the Academy for his lead role in *Titanic,* a film that swept fourteen nominations? Perceiving it as a major injustice, DiCaprio's fans bombarded the Academy with hate mail and protest E-mails.

Why did it take so long for cinematographer Gordon Willis to receive recognition from his branch? After all, he lensed the first two *Godfather* movies and some of Woody Allen's best work (*Annie Hall*). Was it due to the fact that he was a quintessentially New York lenser? Willis finally received nominations for *Zelig* (1983) and *The Godfather, Part III* (1990).

What was wrong with Nicole Kidman's performance in the dark satire *To Die For* (1995), a film that garnered her a Golden Globe.

Laurence Olivier was recognized for his Shakespearean roles, including *Richard III* (1956), but when Ian McKellen did his own interpretation in the 1995 film he was unfairly denied a nomination.

Debbie Reynolds, one of MGM's most reliable stars, had a wonderful comeback role in the comedy, *Mother* (1996). Yet she too was overlooked by the Academy. Was Reynolds' performance in *The Unsinkable Molly Brown* (1964), for which she did receive her one and only Best Actress nomination, more deserving?

The Oscar as Popularity Contest

Artists' standing within the Hollywood industry and their popularity with audiences rather than the sheer quality of performance have often been yardsticks for being nominated. Bing Crosby was a dominant box-office draw in the 1940s, following his recordings and his Road movies with Bob Hope and Dorothy Lamour. His Best Actor, for *Going My Way,* and his second nomination, for *The Bells of St. Mary's,* were as much a reward for his long-enduring popularity as a tribute to his natural, effortless acting; it also helped that both movies were commercial hits.

Doris Day was the most popular female star in America for close to a decade. Her first and only nomination, for the comedy *Pillow Talk,* coincided with her appearance on the "Ten Most Popular Stars" poll in 1959. As she recorded in her memoir: "I was surprised at being nominated for an Academy Award for my performance in *Pillow Talk,* and even more surprised to find that by the end of that year, I had shot up to number one at the box office." But Day's performance in this film didn't match her work in Hitchcock's *The Man Who Knew Too Much,* or in the biopicture of singer Ruth Etting, *Love Me or Leave Me,* which is arguably the most accomplished of her career.

Robert Redford was catapulted to the pantheon of movie stars in 1969, after the success of *Butch Cassidy and the Sundance Kid,* which co-starred Paul Newman. Four years later, the two stars were reteamed in a bigger hit, *The Sting,* proving that a film could be a blockbuster without a love interest. Redford received his one and only nomination for *The Sting* (Newman did not), possibly due to its box-office appeal and to Redford's appearance in another blockbuster that year, *The Way We Were,* which kept him in the public eye. Redford would have preferred to be honored for his earlier work in Michael Ritchie's political satire *The Candidate,* or in Sydney Pollack's *Jeremiah Johnson.* But, by the time of the 1974 nominations, the Academy couldn't ignore that Redford ranked as America's most handsome and popular star.

Richard Dreyfuss's 1977 Oscar for *The Goodbye Girl* was probably also related to the fact that he had appeared in three of the all-time blockbusters of the 1970s, *American Graffiti, Jaws,* and *Close Encounters of the Third Kind.*

Some actors would not have been nominated had they not appeared in a commercial hit. Ali McGraw, a beautiful if below-average actress, began her career after a successful turn as a model, establishing herself as star material in *Goodbye, Columbus,* as the Jewish princess. McGraw's third movie, *Love Story,* based on Eric Segal's best-selling novel, opened to mixed reviews but was such a huge hit that it was nominated in every major category, including

Picture, Actress, Actor (Ryan O'Neal), and Director (Arthur Hiller). Similarly, John G. Avildsen's *Rocky* would not have been nominated for ten awards and won three, including Best Picture, had it not been the year's top money-maker. Popular films have the ability to make those associated with them appear more gifted than they are. Indeed, had Talia Shire's performance as *Rocky*'s shy girlfriend been in another film, she would not have received a nomination.

If the choice of winners is influenced by the candidate's popularity rather than talent, it's due to the fact that the final voting is done by the Academy's entire membership. Consequently, many artists stress the nomination because it is based more on peer evaluation, a process which is allegedly more matter-of-fact, less biased. Since the final selections are made by a large and varied body, many "irrelevant" factors — ad campaigns, studio politics, the nominees' personality, popularity within the industry — come into play. And while there is more of a consensus over the merits and deservedness of the five nominees, it is much harder to choose the one nomination that's the best. Almost inevitably, emotional and political factors impinge on the Academy's final selections.

The claim that the final choices are based on the "validity" or "morality" of the nominees *personalities offscreen* rather than their on-screen work is a double-edged charge. On the one hand, brilliant actors have been denied the Oscar (and nomination) because of real or alleged political factors. But mediocre artists have won the award for sentimental reasons, such as an impressive come-back, career longevity, old age, etc. In all of these cases, the Oscar signifies social acceptance and personal embracement, granted to previously wayward members of the film colony.

Joan Crawford had been in Hollywood for twenty years, an MGM star for a decade, and one of the highest-paid women in the United States. An extremely ambitious actress, Crawford lacked only one thing — peer recognition as epito-mized by the Oscar. In the 1940s, Crawford's career was in a rut, and she was proclaimed a wash-out. In fact, Louis B. Mayer "released" her from a long-term contract after eighteen years of loyal service. For two years, Crawford didn't make a picture until Warner came to the rescue with *Mildred Pierce,* for which she was not the first choice. In this movie, Crawford demonstrated as much will power as acting talent (which was limited). In a role that in many ways paralleled her life offscreen — a story of rise and fall, and rise — Crawford was as good as she could ever be; the Academy rewarded her with an Oscar. The 1945-Oscar award rejuvenated Crawford's career, which she enjoyed for another two decades, way beyond her MGM rivals. Greta Garbo and Norma Shearer both retired in 1942, and Greer Garson experienced a major decline in the early 1950s.

Olivia de Havilland, like Bette Davis, fought Warner for better roles and better contracts, for which she was occasionally suspended. At the end of de Havilland's seven-year contract, Warner refused to release her, demanding that the contract be extended to include the duration of her suspensions. De Havil-land sued the studio, winning a landmark victory with a court's decision setting the outside limit of a player's contract at seven years, including suspensions. Absent from the screen for three years, de Havilland celebrated her comeback with an Oscar for *To Each His Own.* Similarly, Gary Cooper's second Oscar for *High Noon* was also a comeback victory, after a faltering career in the late 1940s.

The impact of offscreen factors on winning the Oscar was abundantly clear with Ingrid Bergman. Bergman's career was severely damaged after she left her husband, Dr. Peter Lindstrom, and her daughter Pia, and went to Italy to work with director Roberto Rossellini. Bergman's s adulterous affair with Rossellini, and their out of the wedlock child, shocked the film community. After all, Bergman had been advertised as one of Hollywood's most "normal" and "wholesome" stars, living an idyllic family life. Bergman's screen roles, particularly that of Sister Mary Benedict in *The Bells of St. Mary's,* and in some of her Hitchcock's movies (*Spellbound*), perpetuated that image.

Bergman's affair with Rossellini, while married to another man, made her the subject of a vicious campaign. Fan magazines, the church, and even school organizations condemned her, and there was serious talk of boycotting her films in the United States. Senator Edwin C. Johnson denounced Bergman on the Senate floor as "a free-love cultist," a "common mistress, a powerful influence for evil," and "Hollywood's apostle of degradation," demanding that she be barred forever from the country on grounds of "moral turpitude."

For almost a decade, Bergman was "persona non grata" in the United States. Unfortunately, none of the pictures that she made with Rossellini in Italy was commercially successful. Neither artist benefited much from their professional collaboration; Bergman's star charisma was somehow foreign to Rossellini's neorealistic style that, among other things, relied on the use of nonprofessional actors. Soon the marriage itself was in troubled waters.

However, in 1955, producer Darryl Zanuck came to the rescue, offering Bergman the lead in *Anastasia,* as the amnesiac refugee who's passing as Tsar Nicholas and Alexandra's surviving daughter. This was done against the advice of Fox's executives who believed that the American public had not yet forgiven Bergman. But with Zanuck's insistence, and a new publicity campaign, which now sold Bergman as a courageous woman who sacrificed her career and family for true love, her image began to change. Bergman's comeback story reads like a Hollywood fairy tale. Ed Sullivan, the noted television host, flew to London, where *Anastasia* was shooting to interview her, though not before soliciting his viewers' opinion concerning her return to America. Many believed that it was Sullivan's popular show that turned the tide of public opinion in Bergman's favor. Bergman's reputation was restored with a second Oscar for *Anastasia,* though she did not accept it in person. Bergman returned to the United States in 1959, when the Academy asked her to be a presenter on the show.

In the 1950s, however, the very mention of Bergman's name evoked negative reactions. Shelley Winters recalls that during her affair with Italian actor Vittorio Gassman, her agents told her: "We have invested a great deal of money in you, and now you're destroying our investment." "You may not have noticed," they warned, "but Ingrid's career is finished in the United States and perhaps throughout the world. Are you ready to have that happen to you?" Winters was also asked to keep a low profile during the 1951 nominations, to secure her placement on the ballots. Winters's dispute with co-star Frank Sinatra on the set of *Meet Danny Wilson* infuriated Universal's Leo Spitz. "From all the rumors we hear," Spitz told her," you're going to be nominated as Best Actress for *A Place in the Sun.* If you keep your publicity as dignified as possible — given your explosive personality — there's a good chance the Academy will vote for your performance, and you will get the Oscar." Winters was surprised to hear that "most of the newspapers owe us favors and we can keep all this nonsense out of the press."

Most of Elizabeth Taylor's nominations and first Best Actress win were more dependent on events in her life offscreen than on-screen. Taylor's chances to win the award for her second nomination, *Cat on a Hot Tin Roof,* were good because MGM's publicity machine began an early campaign for her, and it was an estimable performance. Perhaps more to the point, the 1958 death of her husband Mike Todd in a plane crash guaranteed Taylor the sympathy of the industry and the press. However, a few months before the 1959 ceremonies, Taylor broke up Eddie Fisher's marriage to Debbie Reynolds, one of Holly-wood's most celebrated couples. Her ensuing rush to marry Fisher immediately changed public perception. The National Association of Theater Owners decided not to confer the "Star of the Year" Award on Taylor, instead giving it to Deborah Kerr. Taylor lost the Oscar. Even so, she was nominated in the following year for *Suddenly Last Summer,* but lost again, this time to Simone Signoret in *Room at the Top.*

Personal factors that had denied Taylor the 1958 Oscar operated in her favor in 1960, when she was up for *Butterfield 8.* This time around, it was Taylor's near-fatal illness that garnered sympathy — and the Oscar. The Academy, the press, and the public had "forgiven" Taylor for her sins; her bout with death restored her to favor.

Taylor herself believed that "the reason I got the Oscar was that I had come within a breath of dying of pneumonia." And although the Oscar "meant being considered an actress and not a movie star," she still felt that she won "for the wrong picture, since any of my three previous nominations was more deserving." In hindsight, Taylor's performance in *Butterfield 8* was not that bad — contrary to popular notion, it is not the worst performance ever honored by the Academy! Still, Taylor was delighted when she won her second Oscar for *Who's Afraid of Virginia Woolf?* As one critic noted, "this time, it was for what happened on the screen rather than off." In this picture, Taylor demonstrated once and for all to those who still doubted that she could really act.

The latest example of damaging effects of negative publicity is Russell Crowe. In February 2002, in the midst of an expensive "Academy" campaign, Crowe, then the undisputed front-runner Best Actor for *A Beautiful Mind,* added to his prevalent notorious bad-boy image by aggressively confronting Malcolm Gerrie, producer of the British Academy Film Awards show, over the way his acceptance speech was edited for British TV. Crowe was angry that his recital of a poem by Patrick Kavanagh was cut from the BBC broadcast. According to witnesses, Crowe pushed Gerrie up against the wall of a storage room in London's Grosvenor House Hotel where the aftershow party was held, and yelled obscenities at him. While his security men stood guard, Crowe reportedly said: "I don't give a fuck who you are. Who on earth had the fucking audacity to take out the best actor's poem? You fucking piece of shit, I'll make sure you never work in Hollywood."

Crowe's studios, DreamWorks and Universal, apologized to Gerrie. One witness said, "It was just awful. Crowe was incredibly intimidating." Gerrie, who heads indie company Initial (which produces the show) was "a complete gentleman." The problem arose because the show, which started at 6:00 P.M., ran thirty minutes long, and the editors had to choose between Crowe's speech and Warren Beatty's acceptance of his BAFTA Arts Fellowship. That decision was made by BBC executives, not Gerrie. Crowe, who had earlier won acting kudos from the Hollywood Foreign Press, later apologized, but the damage was done.

The Oscar as Compensation

Artists who do not win the Oscar are not forgotten — the Academy tends to compensate the losers, usually in the near future, with belated honors. The consolatory awards serve as corrective mechanisms to the imperfections of the Oscar as a reward system.

Bette Davis's Oscar for *Dangerous* (1935) is considered to be the first consolation or "hold-over" award, given to her for missing out on the previous year's nominations. The attempt to introduce new selection procedures in 1934, the write-ins, failed to get Davis a much deserved award for *Of Human Bondage.* After the nomination for *Dangerous,* Davis herself cited Katharine Hepburn's performance in *Alice Adams* as the best performance of the year.

Robert Donat's first nomination was for *The Citadel,* but he lost to Spencer Tracy in *Boys Town.* In the following year, Donat's loss was "corrected," and he won the Oscar for a nobler, but no better, performance in *Goodbye, Mr. Chips.* But by correcting this error, the Academy created a new error and a new "victim," Jimmy Stewart, who gave the best performance of 1939 in *Mr. Smith Goes to Washington.* This was corrected in 1940, when Stewart got the award for *The Philadelphia Story.* The fact that Stewart was already enlisted in the military, thus becoming Hollywood's first major star to join the war effort, was probably relevant to his win; Stewart accepted the Oscar in uniform.

In 1964, the film musical *My Fair Lady* was nominated in every major category except Best Actress, despite an elegant performance by Audrey Hepburn as Eliza Doolittle. Hepburn's casting was controversial; there was resentment in Hollywood over Jack Warner's refusal to cast Julie Andrews in a role she had played to great acclaim on stage. Under other circumstances, Hepburn would have been nominated, but the Acting Branch expressed its indignation by denying Hepburn a nomination and conferring the award on Julie Andrews for *Mary Poppins,* released the same year. Insiders felt that Andrews got the award for the wrong film — had she played Eliza, she would have won an Oscar. *Mary Poppins* served as an excuse to compensate Andrews for the injustice done to her by Jack Warner, though it didn't hurt Andrews that the film was a commercial hit.

Another corrective measure used by the Academy is to compensate artists who have been nominated multiple times. In theory, the number of nominations should not be a factor; in practice, however, chances to win increase with the number of nominations. About one-tenth of all winners have received the Oscar after at least three nominations.

Ellen Burstyn (*Alice Doesn't Live Here Anymore*) and Faye Dunaway (*Network*) won the Best Actress Award at their third nomination. Susan Hayward won the Oscar for a very good performance in *I Want to Live!* at her fifth nomination, but her previous losses were a factor, too.

Gregory Peck was honored with Best Actor for *To Kill a Mockingbird,* but the vote also acknowledged his status as a perennial nominee with four citations. Robert De Niro officially won the Best Actor for *Raging Bull,* but how could the Academy forget his memorable performances in *Taxi Driver* and *The Deer Hunter?*

The Academy has devised other mechanisms to counter the inevitable imperfections of its evaluation. The Honorary Awards, set apart from the competitive merit awards, are given "for exceptionally distinguished service in the making of motion pictures or for outstanding service to the Academy." The regulations stipulate that Honorary Oscars "are not limited to the awards year," and "shall not be voted posthumously."

As noted, Chaplin never won a competitive award, but he was honored with three Special Awards. The first of which in 1927–28, for his "versatility and genius," in writing, producing, directing, and acting in *The Circus.* Chaplin was nominated for this film in competitive categories, but did not win. Whenever the Academy sensed that a major contribution stands no chance of winning a competitive award, it voted an Honorary Oscar. Laurence Olivier received the 1946 Special Award for his first Shakespearean film, *Henry V.* ONE OF THE GREATEST FOREIGN FILMS, the citation stated, NO PLAY OF CLASSIC THEATRE WAS EVER TRANSLATED TO CELLULOID WITH SUCH FAITHFUL FLAWLESS ART. Olivier received Best Actor and Picture nominations for this film, but did not win.

Similarly, when rumors circulated that Fred Astaire was going to retire, the Academy immediately honored him with a Special Award in 1949, for "his unique artistry and contributions to the techniques of musical pictures." Astaire had never been nominated for his musical films, but received a supporting nomination for *The Towering Inferno.*

Over a short period of time, Greta Garbo, one of the screen's greatest actresses, was nominated four times (twice in the same year), but for one reason or another she never won. In 1954, Garbo received an Honorary Award for "unforgettable screen performances." Living up to her reputation, the reclusive actress didn't bother to show up, and the statuette was mailed to her home address.

In 1958, the Board voted on Honorary Award for French actor Maurice Chevalier "for his contribution to the world of entertainment for more than half a century." The Board denied rumors that there was a connection between the award and the fact that Chevalier failed to be nominated for *Gigi,* which swept most of the year's Oscars. But it was probably a compensation for this oversight as well as for having lost the Best Actor in 1929–30, when he was up for two films (*The Big Pond* and *The Love Parade*).

Lillian Gish, another screen legend, received an Honorary Award in 1970 for her cumulative work. Gish was nominated only once, for a supporting role in *Duel in the Sun.*

A look at the Honorary and the Jean Hersholt Humanitarian Awards shows that there is always some meaningful link with the legitimate and competitive Oscars. Edward G. Robinson, who was never nominated, received an Honorary Award in 1973 for a half-century career. Unfortunately, the ceremonies took place just months after he died of cancer. A four-time nominee, Rosalind Russell was honored with the Jean Hersholt Humanitarian Award in 1972 for her charity work. Barbara Stanwyck, a four-time nominee, received an Honorary Award in 1981. It was presented to her by William Holden, who made his film debut with her in *Golden Boy.* These have all been sentimental, but touching, moments in the history of the award.

Aware of their compensatory functions, most recipients of Honorary Oscars are quite sensitive about it. Mickey Rooney, a four-time nominee, was given the 1983 Honorary Award, in recognition of his sixty-year career, which began at age two. Standing at the podium, Rooney recited all the awards he had received lest the Academy think it was doing him a favor. "I'd been the world's biggest box-office star at nineteen and, at forty, unable to get work," Rooney said rather bitterly, reminding his colleagues of the inherent instabilities in his glamorous profession.

The recipient of the 1985 Honorary Award, Paul Newman was absent from the ceremonies; he was filming in Chicago. One of the Academy's great losers, Newman had received six Best Actor nominations. The special award was bestowed "in recognition of his many memorable and compelling screen performances and for his personal integrity and dedication to his craft." In his taped remarks, Newman made sure to state that unlike previous recipients, he was neither ill nor close to retirement. "I'm especially grateful that this didn't come wrapped as a gift certificate to Forest Lawn, my best work is down the pike in front of me." And it was. In the following year, injustice was corrected with a legitimate Oscar for *The Color of Money,* an inferior sequel to *The Hustler* (1961), which boasts Newman's finest work. Though Newman gave a decent performance as Fast Eddie Felson, now an aging pool player who becomes a mentor to a new protégé (played by Tom Cruise), doubts prevailed — was it a sentimental, compensatory vote for his previous defeats? The Academy could not do enough for Newman; after winning an honorary Oscar in 1985, and a competitive Oscar in 1986, he was given the Jean Hersholt Humanitarian Award in 1993, for years of donating money to various charities. In 1994, he was nominated again for Best Actor in Robert Benton's *Nobody's Fool.*

Deborah Kerr, a six-time Best Actress nominee, received an Honorary Award in 1993 IN APPRECIATION FOR A CAREER'S WORTH OF ELEGANT AND BEAUTIFULLY CRAFTED PERFORMANCES. Stanley Donen received the 1998 Honorary Oscar, "in appreciation of a body of work marked by grace, elegance, wit and visual innovation." Donen had produced and directed twenty-seven films, including *On the Town, Singin' in the Rain,* and *Charade,* yet had never been nominated for an Oscar.

Aside from Honorary Oscars, the Academy established the Irving G. Thalberg Memorial Award in 1937, to honor "the most consistent high level of production achievement by an individual producer." Producer-director Stanley Kramer received this award in 1961, coinciding with the release of *Judgment at Nuremberg,* for which he received a Best Director nomination but lost to Robert Wise and Jerome Robbins (*West Side Story*). Kramer had also been nominated for *The Defiant Ones,* but did not win. Alfred Hitchcock, a five-time directorial nominee, received the Thalberg Award in 1967, and Mervyn LeRoy, nominated for *Random Harvest,* received the award in 1975.

In 1974 Howard Hawks, nominated for *Sergeant York,* and French director Jean Renoir, also nominated once for his American-made *The Southerner,* both won Honorary Awards for their cumulative work.

King Vidor, who had been nominated five times as a director — for *The Crowd, Hallelujah, The Champ, The Citadel,* and *War and Peace* — received an Honorary Award in 1978 to make up for all of those losses. Federico Fellini, a four-time Oscar nominee, received an Honorary Award for lifetime achievement as one of the screen's master storytellers in 1992, two years before he died.

The Career Oscars

When the Oscar honors veteran artists who have been nominated multiple times, it is impossible to tell whether the award is given for a specific accomplishment or for an entire career. This is yet another corrective device, known as the "career Oscar." In such cases, the particular performance for which an artist wins serves as a vehicle to reward a body of stellar work. The career Oscar is not well-respected, as recipients can never be sure if their win was based on sentimental or meritorious considerations. As one critic observed, the gesture has been dismissed as "more of a back-scratching symptom of the film capital's love of saying thanks for past services than a genuine tribute for current achievements."

The first player to receive a career Oscar was Mary Pickford, who officially won for *Coquette,* her first talking movie (and the first acting award for a sound film). In actuality, the honor paid tribute to Pickford for being the first international movie star. Critics believed that the Oscar was "doubtless as much for past performances and for her service to, and eminence in, the industry, as for *Coquette,*" particularly since her performance in the film was not very good.

Marie Dressler's Best Actress for *Min and Bill* (1930–31) can also be considered a career Oscar: She had been a famous stage and screen actress for decades. At sixty-two, Dressler was the oldest female winner until Jessica Tandy, eighty-one, won Best Actress in 1989. Pickford retired from the screen in 1933 after making only three more films. Dressler's career was cut short by her death in 1934.

Geraldine Page was nominated eight times, five for Best Actress and three for Supporting. Her winning turn in *The Trip to Bountiful* was for a decent performance, though certainly not her best. Some of her nominations, particularly for *Sweet Bird of Youth* and *Interiors,* were far more impressive. Like Katharine Hepburn, Page did not win for her best work.

Ronald Colman had been an exemplary British actor in Hollywood for three decades, with fifty pictures to his credit before winning Best Actor for *A Double Life.* With a marvelous voice and impeccable diction, Colman was one of the few players who became even more popular with the advent of sound; Colman was rewarded as much for his box-office popularity as for previous nominations (*Bulldog Drummond, Condemned,* and *Random Harvest*). His belated Oscar, at the age of fifty-six, was a tribute to his enduring career in the silent and sound eras. After the Oscar, however, Colman's screen record was poor, making only a few films before his death in 1958, at the age of sixty-seven.

The 1969 vote for John Wayne's critically acclaimed performance in *True Grit* was based on sentimentality as well as a career of achievements. Wayne had been making films for over forty years, and had been a top star for twenty. With this Oscar, Wayne's colleagues essentially admitted that they had underestimated his acting skills. Wayne had been nominated once before, for his heroic role in *Sands of Iwo Jima,* which he lost to Broderick Crawford. Winning the Oscar at the age of sixty-two had no pragmatic effect on Wayne's career, but it was of great symbolic and prestige value to him.

Of Wayne's generation, Henry Fonda was the only major star without an Oscar. Fonda's first and only nomination was for his portrayal of Tom Joad in *The Grapes of Wrath.* In the late 1970s, the Academy and the American Film Institute realized that Fonda's achievements had never received their due recognition — and that he was not very healthy. Consequently, Fonda was showered with life achievement awards — the American Film Institute honor in 1978, the Golden Globe in 1980, and an Honorary Oscar "for his life-long contributions to the art of filmmaking" in 1981. "It's been a very rewarding forty-six years for me and this has got to be the climax," Fonda said.

Ironically it was not the climax; neither Fonda nor the Academy could have anticipated that a year later he would be named Best Actor for *On Golden Pond.* The Academy honored Fonda with the more prestigious legitimate Oscar at almost the very last minute. Daughter Jane Fonda received the Oscar for him in a lengthy and emotional speech. The cameras later followed Jane as she drove to her father's house to present the statuette in person. Henry Fonda died few months later.

Age Over Youth

The sentimentality factor is often reflected in the Academy's preference for older over younger, less experienced actors. Accused of erring on the side of conservatism at the expense of daring, the Academy has sometimes used the award as a compensation for survival in a volatile industry rather than strictly as a merit award.

There's some validity to this claim in the male categories. Of the sixty-six Best Actor winners, only eight were the youngest in their respective years, like Marlon Brando (thirty) in 1954, or William Hurt (thirty-six) in 1985. But even Brando and Hurt were experienced performers, having previously done notable work in the theater.

Of all the Best Actors, only Ernest Borgnine and Maximilian Schell were both young *and* unestablished. In most years, the award was bestowed on older, sometimes the oldest, nominees. In the 1970s, for example, the Oscar was conferred on John Wayne at sixty-two, Art Carney at fifty-four, Peter Finch at sixty, and Henry Fonda at seventy-six. This preeminence of age over youth is consistent with the fact that Best Actors are older than Best Actresses at their film debuts, first nomination, and first win.

A totally different picture prevails among the Best Actresses, half of whom have been the youngest nominees in their respective years. For example, Janet Gaynor was twenty-two, Katharine Hepburn twenty-seven, Claudette Colbert twenty-nine, Bette Davis twenty-seven when they won. Only a few Best Actresses have been the oldest of the nominees, like Marie Dressler, Katharine Hepburn at her second win, Shirley MacLaine, and Jessica Tandy. A larger number of Best Actresses — Grace Kelly, Audrey Hepburn, Joanne Woodward, Gwyneth Paltrow, and Hilary Swank — had only brief film experience before winning.

The Supporting winners, unlike the lead, have been either young and inexperienced or old and established. For each young winner, there's a counterexample of an older player. For instance, at winning, George Chakiris (*West Side Story,* 1961) was twenty-nine, but Ed Begley (*Sweet Bird of Youth,* 1962), was sixty-one, and Melvyn Douglas was sixty-two (*Hud,* 1963). Timothy Hutton, the youngest supporting nominee (twenty), and Cuba Gooding Jr. (twenty-eight) are the exceptions. As with the Best Actors, the predominant pattern is to select old and established performers for the Supporting Oscar:

> In 1968, Jack Albertson (58) won over Gene Wilder
>
> In 1969, Gig Young (56) over Elliott Gould
>
> In 1970, John Mills (62) over Richard Castellano
>
> In 1973, John Houseman (70) over Randy Quaid
>
> In 1975, George Burns (80) over Brad Dourif
>
> In 1976, Jason Robards (57) over Ned Beatty
>
> In 1981, John Gielgud (77) over Howard S. Rollins

In 1985, Don Ameche (77) over Klaus Maria Brandauer

In 1987, Sean Connery (57) over Albert Brooks

In 1991, Jack Palance (72) over Michael Lerner

In 1992, Gene Hackman (62) over Jaye Davidson

In 1994, Martin Landau (66) over Samuel Jackson

In 1998, James Coburn (71) over Billy Bob Thornton

In 1999, Michael Caine (66) over Tom Cruise

Almost the same pattern describes the Supporting Actresses, who have been either very old or very young. However, there have been more inexperienced, younger winners among the supporting women than in any other category — Teresa Wright and Anne Baxter were twenty-three, Patty Duke sixteen. But for each young recipient, there is an older counterpart. Jane Darwell won at sixty, Ethel Barrymore at sixty-five, Josephine Hull at sixty-six, and Margaret Rutherford at seventy-two. This conservative trend of honoring age over youth continued into the 1980s:

In 1968, Ruth Gordon (72) over Lynn Carlin

In 1970, Helen Hayes (70) over Karen Black and Sally Kellerman

In 1972, Eileen Heckart (53) over Jeannie Berlin and Susan Tyrrell

In 1975, Lee Grant (46) over Ronee Blakley and Lily Tomlin

In 1976, Beatrice Straight (60) over Jodie Foster

In 1981, Maureen Stapleton (56) over Elizabeth McGovern

In 1984, Peggy Ashcroft (77) over Christine Lahti

In 1989, Brenda Fricker (55) over Lena Olin

Inexperienced winners like Goldie Hawn, who was twenty-four, and Mary Steenburgen, who was twenty-seven, are a rarity. In the 1990s, younger winners such as Marisa Tomei, Mira Sorvino, Juliette Binoche, and Angelina Jolie (who was twenty-four when she won for *Girl, Interrupted*) have prevailed, perhaps reflecting the Academy's changing demographics.

· 15 ·

FROM TOTAL EMBRACEMENT
TO OUTRIGHT REJECTION:
THE VARIOUS MEANINGS OF THE OSCAR AWARD

> There are two types of people: One type asserts that awards mean nothing to them. The second type breaks into tears upon receiving an award and thanks their mother, father, children, the producer, the director, and — if they can crowd it in — the American Baseball League.
> — Producer Dore Schary

The Oscar Award, as former Academy president Howard Koch once noted, has been "sought and spurned, revered and reviled, called an incentive for excellence and a commercial tool." The subjective feelings of film artists toward the Oscar have ranged from complete embracement and joyous celebration to cynical ambivalence and outright rejection — even contempt.

Total Embracement:
The Oscar as Peer Recognition

The Oscar never gets old hat! — Billy Wilder

Before I made *Two Women,* I had been a performer. Afterward, I was an actress. — Sophia Loren

Peer recognition is the primary reward in most creative professions. Most film artists regard the winning of an Oscar as a great accolade, a supreme praise from colleagues, the ultimate goal in one's career. William C. DeMille, the second Academy president, explained in 1929: "The most valuable award a worker can get is to have the acknowledged praise of his fellow workers. It means a great deal more to us than just the acclaim of the public." The Oscar Award was considered to be the first occasion in film history in which "individual creative work is recognized, and meritorious achievements are passed upon by experts."

When Lionel Barrymore handed the Best Actress Oscar to Helen Hayes (*The Sin of Madelon Claudet*), he stressed the values of objectivity and fairness in judging an achievement: "There is no power, however great, in any branch of motion pictures that can exert an atom of influence beyond the marking of that secret ballot, and no smash of commercial significance can dilute the fairness of the awards when so many and such varied opinions are responsible."

The very nomination for an Oscar is perceived to be an important achievement in its own right. In 1930, the Academy Board announced: "Regardless of which ones of the nominees are finally chosen by the Academy to win the statuette trophies, there will be undeniable distinction in winning the preliminary nominations at the hands of their fellow workers." In the first year, all the nominees received an Honorable Mention, a practice that was later dropped. But the Academy still emphasizes the prestige of being nominated, conferring on every nominee a Certificate of Nomination.

All the contenders are now invited to an Annual Nominees Luncheon at the Beverly Hilton Hotel. The purpose of the luncheon is twofold: To encourage esprit de corps among the nominees for the last time before the show, and, more importantly, to generate more hype and publicity for the Oscar telecast and its sponsor ABC TV. The Nominees Luncheon takes place on Monday, the day after the Screen Actors Guild announces its awards, and two weeks before the Oscar ceremonies.

In 2002, a record turnout of 70 percent of all the nominees showed up. Other than talking to the press, there is a photo shoot, with all the nominees in attendance posing for a collective picture — just like a photo of high-school graduation.

Over lunch, the nominees emphasize the pride and the joy of being surrounded by their fellow-competitors. However, along with the blissful pride, there's tremendous anxiety that's barely concealable. Whoopi Goldberg remembers that after her first nomination, for *The Color Purple,* "I gave myself the hives. I got them so bad, I had to go to the dermatologist. I was totally freaked out."

Cicely Tyson took great pride in her first nomination (*Sounder*): "I'm proud and I want every person in the world to see the film." It was a special honor for a black actress to be nominated, and in a year in which Diana Ross was also a nominee; it was a double honor. Paul Winfield, Tyson's co-star in *Sounder,* also delighted in his nomination because he was up against "heady competition" (Marlon Brando, Michael Caine, Laurence Olivier, and Peter O'Toole). Even though Winfield lost, he felt he had won, because "the nomination came so soon, it took me by surprise."

The first nomination serves as a formal acknowledgment of talent. Penelope Milford, one of the youngest nominees (*Coming Home*), recalls: "The minute the nominations were announced, the telephone started ringing. A lot of people now are telling me they always knew I had talent and how wonderful it is that I've been nominated. They're the same guys who wouldn't take a phone call from me last week. I'd like to blast them, but let's face it, that's not the way to play the game. You've got to keep cool." After the nomination, Milford realized she had become "a known and valued commodity."

The significance of the first nomination is vividly recalled by Ray Milland. Apparently it was the sound mixer of *The Lost Weekend* who was the first to bet that Milland would be nominated. Milland drove home that night "in a very bemused state, trying not to think about it, but it kept filtering back. Could this wonderful thing possibly happen to me? To be acclaimed by one's colleagues in all the cinema crafts, for having given the best performance of the entire year? No! No, stop it! Don't even think about it. Think of the disappointment if nothing happens." Even before the nominations were announced, Milland sensed a change of attitude: "I had been getting smiles from people I didn't know, a little more deference from the people in the mailroom, and an unaccountable query from the studio's operations wanting to know if I'd prefer a parking lot right outside my dressing room instead of the one I now had."

The day of the nominations was deemed "judgment day," on which "five actors would be in purgatory until the 'Night' four weeks later." Early in the morning, Milland saw his wife, son, cook, butler, and nurse all sitting in the dining room with their eyes glued to the window. He asked them what was going on, why they were up so early. Together they replied: "Same as you. Waiting for the paper." "Later on, with the long-suffering look of a man forced to live with mental defectives, I went in to my breakfast. I was just lifting the cup to my lips, when I heard the scramble of the front door, and I froze. There was a moment of silence and then one big yelp of exuberance as they all came barreling through the door yelling, 'You made it? You're nominated!'"

The nomination confers on artists a measure of assurance, providing a standard of gauging the quality of their work. As Milland recalled, before the opening of *The Lost Weekend,* "I didn't know whether what I'd done was good or bad, a subject of this kind (alcoholism) hadn't been done before. I had no standards, and it had depressed me terribly." For Milland, the most important effect of the nomination was legitimacy: "Although I had been termed a movie star in the usual magazine concept for five or six years, I was now being accepted as an actor with dramatic merit. It was a wonderful feeling."

Esteem by peers is still one of the Oscars' most vital functions, even for veteran players. James Cagney believed that "praise from your peers generates a special kind of warmth." "I've always maintained," Cagney said in his *Yankee Doodle Dandy* acceptance speech, "that in this business, you are only as good as the fellow thinks you are."

For the young and inexperienced Mercedes McCambridge (*All the King's Men*), peer recognition was also the most valued reward. The Oscar literally changed McCambridge's life: Her salary skyrocketed overnight, she got more publicity, more invitations to parties, and her social life became much more active. All of these changes were, as she recalled, "highly enjoyable fringe benefits," but, best of all, was "the knowledge that you earned it from your peers, that actors voted for your acting."

Awards in the theater world perform the same vital role, but to a lesser extent, due to the fact that live performances are limited to the appreciation of the audiences able to see them. "There is something very special about having your work acknowledged by your peers," Joel Grey said after winning a Tony for *Cabaret.* "It is a milestone to work for, and the first time something like this happens to you, it is deeply satisfying."

Other film forums perform the same function even without conferring formal prizes. For Martin Scorsese, whose third feature, *Mean Streets,* was selected for the 1973 New York Film Festival, "it was the most important time of my life. The festival was a launching pad for my work." This kind of acknowledgment is crucial for artists like the young Scorsese, who are at the beginning of their careers: "A Festival can make the difference between recognition and disappearance."

The Oscar legitimizes the talent of movie stars who have not previously enjoyed much respect from their colleagues — and critics. "Before I made *Two Women,*" Sophia Loren said succinctly, "I had been a performer. Afterward, I was an actress." Loren had been a box-office star in Italy and America, but her 1961 Oscar assumed a special meaning: "I know some actors have deprecated the value and purpose of the Academy Award, but I'm certainly not one of them. As far as I'm concerned, if you are a professional actor who has pride in his work, the judgment of your peers should be important to you." Loren treasures each and every award she has ever received, and her Oscar is in "a place of honor." The Oscar fulfilled the same function for Julia Roberts, the most popular female star of the past decade, after winning the Best Actress for *Erin Brockovich.*

It's never too late to get such a recognition. Burt Reynolds, a veteran box-office star for four decades, was candid when he said upon receiving his first Academy nomination (for *Boogie Nights,* in 1997, at the age of 61): "I'm so truly humbled by it." Realizing the limitations actors his age endure in Hollywood, Reynolds hoped that the nomination would bring more "steady work."

"I've always been thought of as a personality," said Lauren Bacall, who reached the height her popularity in her films with Humphrey Bogart, *To Have and Have Not, The Big Sleep, Key Largo.* But Bacall did not receive a nomination until 1996, for playing Barbra Streisand's acerbic mother in *The Mirror Has Two Faces.* Bacall told Barbara Walters on her "Oscar Special Show" that "Bogie would be very happy that at long last I am given credit for being an actress because I never really have gotten it."

The Oscar nomination reinforces the determination of players to pursue careers in a profession that's inherently unstable. Asked how *Gandhi* changed his life, Ben Kingsley said, in addition to the barrage of scripts and a constantly ringing telephone, "I profoundly believe that I'm an actor now. I'm not saying I believe I'm a good actor. I just believe there is nothing else in the world I should be doing." The Oscar made Kingsley see the tip of the iceberg, as he said: "I know it's there and it's real."

Mercedes Ruehl, who won the Supporting Oscar for playing a video-store owner who nurtures a burned-out radio talk-show host in *The Fisher King,* recollected that success had not come easily to her. However, after winning, "all of these sort of doleful memories transform themselves into amusing and charming anecdotes."

Expressing the determination and pride of being a good actor, Whoopi Goldberg said, upon winning her Supporting Oscar for *Ghost:* "I come from New York. When I was a little kid, I lived in the projects. You're the people I watched, the people I wanted to be. I'm proud to be an actor."

Contrary to popular notion, most artists would favor peer recognition over large salaries. When Peter Finch's publicist first met her client, she asked him what his ambition was. Finch replied unequivocally that the only thing he really wanted was that when he died they would write on his tombstone: "He was a good actor." Finch's wish came true, though he didn't live to see it happen; his Best Actor for *Network* was awarded posthumously.

Another cherished star, Ingrid Bergman, indicated long before she died that she wanted her tombstone to read, "She acted on the last day of her life." Which she did: Bergman's last big screen appearance was in *Autumn Sonata,* for which she received the New York Film Critics Award and her sixth Best Actress nomination. Her very last acting job was in the TV mini-series *Golda,* which was broadcast after her death. Bergman's self-chosen epitaph was: "Here lies a great actress."

The Oscar is not an achieved goal that just happens. It is on most actors' minds early on in their careers. Loretta Young, who began her career as a child actress, won an Oscar after nineteen years in the business. "At long last," she sang out when her name was announced. And Shelley Winters shouted, when she won her first Supporting Oscar, "I've waited fifteen years for this."

Susan Hayward was determined to get an Oscar ever since she made her screen debut. When she lost for *Smash-up, the Story of a Woman,* she tried to take it with a sense of humor. But the defeat made her even more committed: "I'll be nominated for an Oscar again. Maybe the next year. Maybe I'll have to wait until the fifties. But I intend to win some day. That's my goal." After winning (*I Want to Live!*), at her fifth nomination and years of hard work, producer Walter Wanger commented: "Thank heaven, now we can all relax. Suzie got what she's been chasing for twenty years." Hayward herself was convinced that she now had everything she had ever wanted in life. "I used to make pictures for Academy Awards," she said, but, "I'm not concerned about winning Oscars anymore. I'm not retiring, but now I'll act for the joy of it and for the money."

Although Hayward's story is by no means unique, it attests to a displacement of goals — the Oscar was originally designed as a local gesture by Hollywood's artists to honor film achievements. The Award was an afterthought on the Academy's agenda, barely mentioned in the 1927 statement of goals. No one could have anticipated that it would become such a "sacred" end in its own right. It's no secret that artists set out consciously to make an "Oscar-winning" film, or render an "Oscar-winning" performance. For better or worse, winning the Oscar has become a major motive for choosing film projects, based on the knowledge of which films are potentially "Oscar caliber," namely, films that are likely to get them nominations and awards.

Shirley MacLaine turned down the title role in *Mistinguette,* a biopicture about the legendary French performer, in order to accept the part of the eccentric, possessive mother in *Terms of Endearment.* It was a conscious and rational decision. Long before it was made, MacLaine told her friends that the role might bring her an Oscar. "That's one reason I waited," MacLaine told the press, "and didn't work anywhere else for two years." MacLaine admitted that she wanted to win an Oscar, and if she did, "I would think I deserved it." She could not have been more perceptive: *Terms of Endearment* provided the best part of her career — and the coveted Oscar that had eluded her four times before.

It's no secret that actors want to win the Oscar for "the right stuff," a role they consider consequential, or one for which they feel strong professional and emotional affinity. Bette Davis said that she won her two Oscars (*Dangerous* and *Jezebel*) for the "wrong" films; she would have preferred to win the Oscar for *All About Eve.*

By contrast, Gig Young, was "crazy" about his part as the marathon dance emcee in *They Shoot Horses, Don't They?* and considered himself "lucky enough to win for the right picture." Young summed up his career as, "thirty years and fifty-five pictures, of which there were not more than five that were any good, or any good for me."

The Oscar assumes a special meaning for players who worked indefatigably on their winning film. Charlton Heston said that he had never worked so hard on a picture as he did on *Ben-Hur.* The Oscar never loses its value, even for those who have won. When Billy Wilder received his second directorial Oscar (*The Apartment*), Charlton Heston remarked, "I guess, this is old hat to you." To which Wilder replied, "The Oscar never gets old hat!"

Receiving an Oscar can also put pressure on the winners to prove that they are worthy of it. When Sally Field won her second Oscar (*Places in the Heart*), she shouted: "I've wanted more than anything to have your respect. And I can't deny the fact that you like me now. You really like me!" Field later told the *New York Times* that her response was emotional due to her "unorthodox career," having started on TV in such light fare as *Gidget* and *The Flying Nun.* Noted Field: "The first ten years of my career were in television, and it wasn't the finest television. It's taking me a while to get over that feeling."

When Marisa Tomei received a second supporting nomination for *In the Bedroom,* she felt that, "It's equally as thrilling and even more rewarding," than the first one (for *My Cousin Vinny*). "I really didn't have a context for it before," Tomei explained. The same feeling was shared by her *In the Bedroom* co-star, Sissy Spacek: "When I first went to the Oscars, I felt like an impostor, and I didn't know anybody. I felt like a little church mouse."

For some, the Oscar serves as a metaphor for glamour as well. Shelley Winters recalls that upon being introduced to Mrs. Roosevelt and Mrs. Stevenson, who congratulated her and Vittorio Gassman for their films, Vittorio behaved "as if we both has just won Oscars." Winters believes that there are "very definite rules" for public appearances in Hollywood's parties and opening nights: "You must always look beautiful and gloriously happy, and you must be photographed with someone more important than yourself, like people who have won Oscars."

The statue itself gets royal treatment from most of the winners. Joan Fontaine recalls "cradling the statue like a doll in my arms." After the ceremonies Ray Milland drove to Hillcrest Drive with the golden Oscar in his hand. He walked to the edge of Sunset and looked down at the lights. They seemed very bright that night. After a few moments, Milland quietly said, "Mr. Navarro. Tonight they belong to me!"

Asked if she had a mantel on which to put the Oscar, Mercedes McCambridge said, "Got one? I'll build one." And when a photographer asked McCambridge to pose while washing the Oscar in a basin, she refused, because she couldn't make fun of it. Regarding the statuette as "a remarkably beautiful piece of furnishing," McCambridge kept it in front of a mirror so that "it looked like two," a gimmick that has also been used by Louise Fletcher and other winners. For years, McCambridge wore a miniature Oscar on a golden chain around her neck.

Shelley Winters promised to donate her first Oscar (for *The Diary of Anne Frank*) to the Anne Frank Museum in Amsterdam after Otto Frank, Anne's father and the family's only survivor, visited the set and predicted she would win an Oscar. But after winning, Winters kept it on a mantel for fifteen years, because she couldn't bear to part with it. "I thought the other one (for *A Patch of Blue*) would get lonely!" she quipped. Years later, Winters brought the Oscar in person to Amsterdam. Initially, the statuette was put on open public display, but it became such an attraction, with people touching and holding it, that after three days, it was put inside a glass case.

A two-time Oscar and two-time Emmy winner, Peter Ustinov kept "two emasculated gentlemen and two emasculated ladies," on his desk, with the four of them making "a fine mixed-double match." Upon winning his third Emmy, Ustinov felt that he had built "an entire empire."

Sophia Loren's Oscar was stolen by thieves who believed it was solid gold. For a $60 check, she got a replacement from the Academy. Strange, thought Loren, how hard it is to win the Oscar, and how easy to replace it!

Ambivalence and Cynicism — Before and After

The Academy Awards — why don't we have awards for short order cooks or bus drivers? — Jim Jarmusch, independent filmmaker

I'm not going to thank anyone; I'm just going to say I damn well deserve it, I owe nobody nothing.
— Humphrey Bogart, before winning for *The African Queen*

You can't eat awards. Nor, more to the point, drink them.
—John Wayne, before winning for *True Grit*

The Oscar means a lot to me, even if it took the industry forty years to get around to it. —John Wayne, after winning

Although most film artists embrace the Oscar completely, some show a more cynical attitude toward its merits and fairness. Ambivalence toward the Oscar often characterizes players who have been nominated multiple times but have never won. Others are critical—until they win, at which time their criticism mellows. Total rejection of the Oscar, however, still describes the reaction of a very small minority of artists.

The 1929 speech made by Al Jolson, star of the first talkie, is still one of the most cynical and bitter ever made. "They gave *The Jazz Singer* a statuette, but they didn't give me one. I could use one. They look heavy and I need another paperweight. For the life of me, I can't see what Jack Warner could do with one of them—it can't say yes." Jolson, whose career went into severe decline in the mid-1930s, would never win a competitive Oscar or an Honorary Award, though his life story would be filmed twice, in *The Jolson Story* and *Jolson Sings Again*—and bring accolades to Larry Parks who "inhabited" the actor (Jolson provided the dubbed songs in both pictures).

Humphrey Bogart's cynicism toward the Oscar mellowed the moment he won the award. Bogart was the kind of actor who detested Hollywood's phoniness, but was extremely conscientious about his craft. Unlike Cooper or Brando, Bogie was really proud of his profession. However, the idea of awards was "diametrically opposed to his concept of noncompetitive acting." Bogart held that "awards are meaningless for actors, unless they all play the same part." For him, the only true test of ability would be to have all the actors don black tights and recite Hamlet, and then gauge who gave the most effective rendition of the same part.

Bogart was first nominated for *Casablanca* (1943) then for *The African Queen* (1951). He lost the first time to Paul Lukas, and the 1951 pre-Oscar polls predicted that all four actors of *A Streetcar Named Desire* would win. Bogart's friends were certain he would beat Brando, and he was just as certain he would lose. When Bogart's friends asked him what he would say in his speech if he won, he replied, "I'm not going to thank anyone; I'm just going to say I damn well deserve it." Bogart believed that he "owed nobody nothing," that his achievement was totally a product of hard work and talent. This attitude, as one critic suggested in the *New York Times,* was "in part making a shrewd bid for publicity, and in part he was giving irascible voice to his honest hatred of the crass and phony side of motion pictures." Before winning, Bogart described the Oscar as "silly and all bunk," and once, in a moment of uncontrollable anger, he even called it "fake."

However, when Greer Garson announced his name, Bogart, stunned, rushed onto the stage, took the Oscar gently, as though it were a newborn baby, and said, "It's a long way from the Belgian Congo to the stage of the Pantages, but it's a lot nicer here." He then proceeded to thank his colleagues: "No one does it alone. As in tennis, you need a good opponent or partner to bring out the best in you. John (Huston) and Katie (Hepburn) helped me be where I am now." Lauren Bacall claims that in spite of her late husband's seeming cynicism, he was very emotional and very humble. Bogart had really wanted to win — "for all his bravado, when push came to shove, he did care and was stunned that it was such a popular victory." According to Bacall, "he had never felt that people in town liked him much and hadn't expected such universal joy when his name was called." Bogart, too, used the Oscar as a symbol of achievement. Richard Burton recalls that once, when he dared to challenge Bogart over acting, Bogart stormed out of the room and came back with his Oscar statuette, which he thumped down on the table. "You were saying, Dick?" Bogart growled. Burton was dead silent.

John Wayne was another cynic who deprecated the value of the Oscar before he won. Asked how he felt about the possibility of winning, he would say, "You can't eat awards. Nor, more to the point, drink them." "My pictures don't call for the great dramatic range that wins Oscars," the Duke used to say, which was based on the unfortunate reality that his specialty, Westerns, have always been overlooked by the Academy. In 1969, however, when his prospects to win for *True Grit* seemed good, Wayne became more cautious in his public utterances. And after winning, Wayne praised the award as "a great accolade" and "a beautiful thing to have: It symbolizes appreciation of yourself by your peers. The Oscar means a lot to me, even if it took the industry forty years to get around to it."

Before Jane Fonda won her first Oscar (*Klute*), she used to say: "I don't care about the Oscars. I make movies to support the causes I believe in, not for any honors." But people close to her hold that she was extremely disappointed to have lost the Best Actress for *They Shoot Horses, Don't They?,* which she considered her best work to date. Indeed, despite her radical politics, Fonda accepted the New York Film Critics Award for *They Shoot Horses* modestly and appreciatively: "It's the biggest accolade I've ever been given. One tries to be blase about things, but now that it's happened, it's very nice."

Outright Rejection

The Oscar is a meat parade, offensive, barbarous, and innately corrupt.
— George C. Scott

George C. Scott and Marlon Brando received a lot of publicity for refusing the Oscar, but they were not the first to have done so. Dudley Nichols, winner of Best Screenplay (*The Informer*) refused his Oscar in 1935. A militant member of the Screen Writers Guild, Nichols resigned from the Academy, along with other members, during the 1933 labor crisis. The relations between the Academy and the guilds reached a low point at the eighth annual banquet (in 1936), when the guilds asked their members to boycott the ceremonies. Bette Davis and

Victor McLaglen, the winners of the acting awards, attended, but Nichols and director John Ford, also a winner, boycotted the show. Nichols felt that, "to accept the Oscar would be to turn my back on nearly a thousand members of the Writers Guild."

Nichols's negation was a minor incident compared with the controversy over George C. Scott's contemptuous rebuff. In 1971, upon notification of his nomination for *Patton,* Scott sent the Academy a telegram requesting that his name be withdrawn from the nominees. "I mean no offense to the Academy," wrote Scott, "I simply do not wish to be involved." Scott had not denied his first nomination, for *Anatomy of Murder,* in 1959. Many believed that Scott gave the best performance of the year, but the winner, *Ben-Hur*'s Hugh Griffith, benefited from the sweep factor. Scott's friends said that it was important for him to win, but after witnessing his peers' fierce campaigns for votes, Scott determined never again to have anything to do with the Oscar "meat parade."

Scott was nominated again for a supporting award (*The Hustler*). This time, however, he asked the Academy to withdraw his name from the list, but his request was denied by the Academy's President Wendell Corey. "You were nominated by a vote of your fellow-actors," Corey stated, "and the Academy cannot remove your name from the list of the nominated performances. The Academy nominates and votes awards for achievements as they appear on the screen. Therefore, any one person responsible for achievement cannot decline the nomination after it is voted." But Scott was told he could refuse the award, if he won. He lost, again undeservedly; the winner was George Chakiris for *West Side Story,* which, like *Ben-Hur,* swept most of the Oscars that year.

Scott regarded the politics of the Oscars as "offensive, barbarous, and innately corrupt," prizes that encourage the public to think that awards were more important than the work itself. Thus, when he received his third nomination for *Patton,* he declined it again: "Life isn't a race, and because it is not a race, I don't consider myself in competition with my fellow actors for awards or recognition." "I don't give a damn about the Oscar," Scott later told the *New York Daily News,* "I'm making too much money anyway."

Screenwriter Daniel Taradash, then-Academy president, ignored Scott's protests and made it clear that it was not Scott but his performance that was nominated. Taradash felt that to consent to Scott's demand would be demeaning to his fellow artists. Many actors believe that this was one of the Academy's finest hours, demonstrating that the vote was not personal but dispassionate — the kind of vote that could not have happened during the studio system.

Scott's attack of the film colony, thumbing his nose at the awards, had no damaging effects on his career. He won Best Actor for *Patton,* and a year later, was nominated again for Best Actor in *The Hospital.* This gesture was interpreted as yet another positive sign that the Academy was freeing itself from personal favoritism. Scott later claimed that he did not really mean to create a furor by his conduct. When the scandal grew to unprecedented proportions, he decided that if he would ever be nominated in the future, he would accept it. It was too much trouble not to accept.

Probably the biggest scandal in the Academy's history was created by Marlon Brando's refusal of his Best Actor Oscar for *The Godfather.* Brando's spurning of the Oscar, however, differed from Scott's. Brando protested against the mistreatment of Native Americans, on-screen and off. Brando did not refuse his first Oscar for *On the Waterfront,* even though his critical views of Hollywood were already well established. In fact, when Bette Davis announced him winner of the 1954 Best Actor, the then thirty-year-old Brando took the gum out of his mouth, walked to the podium and thanked everyone for "making me so very, very happy." As the couple walked off stage, Davis, who had heard a lot about Hollywood's new genius, turned to him and said, "it's nice to meet you, finally."

Is it the same Brando? That friendly smile feels like generations ago. As in case of George C. Scott, Brando's refusal had no impact on his standing, for a year later he was nominated for *Last Tango in Paris.* And in 1989, Brando received his first supporting — and eighth nomination — for playing a small but showy role in *A Dry White Season,* as an anti-Apartheid lawyer.

Katharine Hepburn has also been ambivalent toward the Oscar, though she never rejected any of her four awards. Hepburn's form of protest (some might call it eccentricity) was not to attend any of the ceremonies until 1968, when she broke her long-standing silence and appeared in a pre-recorded segment for the fortieth anniversary show. Hepburn made her first live appearance at the 1974 ceremonies, when she presented a special Oscar to her friend, producer Lawrence Weingarten. "I'm a living proof," said Hepburn, "that someone can wait forty-one years to be unselfish."

Dustin Hoffman attended the ceremonies when he was first nominated for *The Graduate,* but claimed to have been uncomfortable about it. "I hope to God I don't win an Oscar," he said. "It would depress me if I did. I really don't deserve it." In 1975, in a CBS interview aired just a few hours before the show, Hoffman voiced his contempt, calling the Oscar "ugly and grotesque." Frank Sinatra, one of the show's emcees, scolded him publicly for these remarks. For his part, Hoffman made a point not to show up at the awards presentations for his next two nominations.

Hoffman created another uproar when he questioned the validity of awards at the 1980 Golden Globes. "I think that awards are very silly," he said upon accepting the Best Actor Globe for *Kramer vs. Kramer,* "They put very talented and good people against each other, and they hurt the hell out of the ones that lose. And I think they relieve us that win." Addressing his fellow-nominees, Hoffman asserted that "awards make more sense when they are given for a life achievement to a man like Mr. Fonda's (recipient of the Hollywood Foreign Press Association's Cecil B. DeMille Career Achievement Award) and "particularly to a man like Mr. Lemmon, who recently gave one of the great performances of his life," in *The China Syndrome.*

Hoffman's criticism was along the same lines as Scott's — deploring the demeaning effects of the Oscar race. Both denounced and lamented the fact, as Scott said, that actors felt obliged to enter into a competition with each other, a contest that has nothing to do with the art of acting. They also resented the idea that actors have increasingly become award conscious. Unlike Scott, Hoffman didn't refuse his award, but he repeated his criticism in his Oscar speech, expressing resentment over the Academy's excessive spotlight on competition among fellow artists. "I refuse to believe that I am better than Jack Lemmon, Al Pacino, and Peter Sellers," said Hoffman, "and I refuse to believe that Robert Duvall lost. We are part of an artistic family and I am proud to share this award."

There is no doubt that Hoffman meant what he said, and there is no doubt that he expressed the opinions of many other artists. Yet, it is doubtful that this kind of criticism will change the Oscars' operations or effects. After all, the excitement generated by the Oscars depends and even thrives upon individual competition in all its nasty and cruel manifestations.

Defeat in the Public Eye

I managed not to shed any tears until everything was over. Then I sat down and had a good cry and decided that losing was just part of the game. — Susan Hayward, at her fourth nomination

I made history, I'm the only nominee who's lost twice in one night. It was horrible, everybody was so embarrassed for me that nobody wanted to talk to me. They should have made an anteroom for the losers. — Sigourney Weaver, losing both Lead and Supporting in 1988

Since it is not easy to face failure, some film artists cling to the prestige of the nomination itself. "My own disappointment," Gene Tierney observed, "was lessened by the conviction, new to me, that I had developed a difficult character (in *Leave Her to Heaven*), not just a pretty face on the screen." "I had been challenged by the role," she explained, "and to have been nominated for an Oscar was excitement enough."

Joan Fontaine lost at her first nomination (*Rebecca*), but she was not disappointed, because, as she said, "to have won it with my first good role would have been precipitous. The voters might well have thought Hitchcock was my Svengali, that after so many undistinguished performances in the past, surely it was Hitchcock who had mesmerized me into the performance I was nominated for."

Four-time nominee, and one of the Academy's greatest losers, Rosalind Russell recalled of her first nomination for *My Sister Eileen:* "Glad as I was about it, the honor put me under heavy pressure. It means too much to the studios to have their people win; I still can't think of the tension surrounding these races without breaking into a sweat." Of her subsequent nominations, Russell observed, "Half a loaf can feed you" (*Sister Kenny* and *Mourning Becomes Electra* had both been critical successes, bringing me two more Oscar nominations), but when you get the whole loaf, you know the difference." Apparently, Russell's 1947 loss threw her into complete shock; some suggested cynically that RKO changed the title of her picture, *Mourning Becomes Electra* to "Mourning Becomes Rosalind Russell." And if three misses were not enough, Russell lost a fourth race in 1958 for *Auntie Mame.*

That players are expected to care about the award is clear from Gloria Swanson's testimony of her *Sunset Boulevard* experience. Swanson could not attend the ceremonies because she was performing in New York, but she listened to the broadcast. She recalled: "I honestly didn't care, but I could see in the faces of everyone at La Zambra, and everywhere else I went in the weeks after that, that people wanted me to care. In fact, they seemed to want more than that. They expected scenes from me, wild sarcastic tantrums. They wanted Norma Desmond, as if I had hooked up sympathetically, disastrously, with the role by playing it." It soon became a problem. "If I said I didn't care, people would pity me and say I had a bad case of sour grapes. If I told them I was an Aries, that it was not in my nature to be dejected, they would think I was mad, and the Gloria-Norma identification would be made forever in the eyes of the press. It was easier to say nothing."

It is especially hard to accept failure for those nominees who are expected to win. Shelley Winters was sure that she would win at her first nomination (*A Place in the Sun*). On Oscar night, as she described, "I was a wreck," and the show seemed "interminable." When Ronald Colman opened the envelope, Winters was sure that he announced her name. She was almost on the steps leading to the stage, when her beau Vittorio Gassman tackled her. Winters remembered that "as we lay on the floor of the aisle, I thought he'd gone insane." Gassman then whispered, "Shelley, it's Vivien Leigh." They crawled back to their seats as inconspicuously as possible.

But Winters could not believe it, and, for the rest of the evening, felt "as if Ronald Colman had betrayed me. He could at least have said my name and swallowed the card, if he were any kind of English gentleman." Later, they went to the Governor's Ball, but Winters doesn't remember anything about it. "I just knew that the gold statuette was not on my table." To this day, Winters believes that Vivien Leigh had "taken her Oscar."

Frank Capra, whose *Lady for a Night* was up for four nominations, was extremely excited — "I became impossible to live with. I kept telling myself I would win four awards." In preparation for the event, Capra wrote and threw away a dozen speeches. As he recalled, "I ordered my first tuxedo, rented a plush home in Beverly Hills to be seen, sway votes in bistros." On Oscar night, when presenter Will Rogers said, "Well, well, well, what do you know. I've watched this young man come up from the bottom, and I mean the bottom," Capra was sure Rogers was talking about him. "It couldn't happen to a nicer guy," Rogers continued. "Come up and get it Frank." Capra rose and headed toward the spotlight, only to realize that the winner was another Frank, Frank Lloyd, for *Cavalcade*. Capra was shattered, standing "petrified in the dark, in utter disbelief, as I began the longest, saddest, most shattering walk of my life. I wanted to crawl under the rug. All my friends at the table were crying." After this awkward experience, Capra vowed that "if they ever did vote me one, I would never, never, never show up to accept it." But, as could be expected, just a year later, Capra changed his mind when his dream materialized, and *It Happened One Night* set a record, getting all five major awards.

Judy Garland experienced several Oscar defeats in her Hollywood career. Of her first nomination (*A Star Is Born*), biographer Gerold Frank writes: "It was inevitable that Judy be nominated, with almost everyone agreeing she was sure to get it. Though she had received a juvenile award for *The Wizard of Oz,* this was the real thing, and if it were to come true, what a triumph after everything." Prior to her nomination, her husband-producer Sid Luft went to an analyst, to help him cope with Judy, "as the time drew nearer, not only to the birth of her third child but to the resolution of the mounting uncertainty as to whether she would win the Oscar."

Though determined to attend the ceremonies, Garland unexpectedly gave birth on March 29, 1955, the night before the Oscar show. Extensive preparations were made at the hospital, with television cameras in Garland's room. The idea was that if Garland won, she would talk to Bob Hope from her bed. However, after learning of her loss (to Grace Kelly in *The Country Girl*), Garland said: "I knew I wouldn't get it. They wouldn't give it to me, although I deserved it." Garland's consolation prize was her newborn son, whom she labeled "My Academy Award." Garland's disappointment was profound — she accepted what was much more of a disaster to her than everyone knew. Realizing her anguish, comedian and friend Groucho Marx sent Garland a consolatory telegram that read: DEAR JUDY. THIS IS THE BIGGEST ROBBERY SINCE BRINK'S.

Even players who eventually win the Oscars have a hard time accepting earlier defeats. Susan Hayward took her first failure with humor. However, when she was nominated for the fourth time (*I'll Cry Tomorrow*) and lost, she confided: "I managed not to shed any tears until everything was over. Then I sat down and had a good cry and decided that losing was just part of the game."

The losers' reaction also depends on how worthy their competitors are, and who they lose to. Rod Steiger, who most people believed would win Best Actor for *The Pawnbroker,* was bitterly offended to have lost to Lee Marvin in *Cat Ballou*. Sylvia Miles, nominated for Supporting Actress in *Midnight Cowboy,* reacted similarly: "People think I was mad when I didn't win, but they're wrong. It's not that I mind losing, but losing to Goldie Hawn (*Cactus Flower*). That was an insult."

Peter Sellers perceived his role in *Being There,* as Chance Gardiner, the simple-witted fool who becomes politically powerful in Washington, as an "all-out bid" for the Oscar. Driven by an "obsessive quest" to make the film for seven years, Sellers hoped that this part would "purge" him of the coarse and exploitative roles he had taken in other films, such as the *Pink Panther* series. Sellers would finally achieve the perfection that had eluded him in the past. The role of Chance called for a simple, understated performance, devoid of any of the tricks, accents, and multiple impersonations that had made Sellers rich and famous in the *Pink Panther* movies as the bumbling eccentric Inspector Clouseau. In public, Sellers treated his loss to Dustin Hoffman

(*Kramer vs. Kramer*), with "little show of emotion, but deep down inside, he was tremendously disappointed."

Elizabeth Taylor, who won her second Best Actress for *Who's Afraid of Virginia Woolf?* was upset that her then-husband Richard Burton, lost. She believed that he gave the best male performance of the year. Burton knew he had no chance of winning after Paul Scofield (*A Man for All Seasons*) was cited by the New York Film Critics. To his credit, Burton didn't try to conceal the fact that he was hurt, having lost out on many occasions. "I want the Oscar," he told close friends, "I've won all kinds of little Oscars but not the big one."

Burton talked his wife out of attending the ceremonies, despite promises the couple made to Jack Warner. The excuse given by Hollywood's royal couple was their need to be on the set of their new film, *The Comedians,* in France. Taylor rationalized their decision: "I've gone to those award dinners four times, won it once, for not dying. The only time I didn't go was when I was nominated for *Raintree County* and the dinner was just two weeks after Mike (Todd) was killed. They didn't expect me to go. But most of the time you're supposed to, if you possibly can, whether you've got a chance of winning or not. It's for the industry." Anne Bancroft accepted the award for Taylor, which prompted emcee Bob Hope to quip: "It must be nice to have enough talent just to send for one." Taylor's absence was seriously criticized as all pre-award polls predicted she would win. "Everybody was talking about it backstage," Walter Matthau, the Supporting winner that year (*The Fortune Cookie*) recalled. "When the winners aren't present, it denigrates the whole thing, it cheapens it, it lessens the value, the drama, the excitement." In the same year, the other Supporting winner, Sandy Dennis (*Who's Afraid of Virginia Woolf?*) also didn't attend the show because she was performing in New York and, besides, she hated flying. "It's much easier to go than raise a storm of criticism," Dennis later said.

Contestants in all categories are expected to attend the ceremonies regardless of their chances to win. Indeed, in the last decade most nominees have been present. Even so, more than any other awards, the Oscar show may be fun for the winners, but not for the losers. It's the kind of show where every expression and gesture is mercilessly recorded, instantly broadcast, and just as instantly dissected and talked about by millions of viewers all over the world.

· 16 ·

I WOULD LIKE TO THANK...
THE ACCEPTANCE SPEECHES

Winning the Oscar—the Greatest Thrill of Life

The only other time in my life I really felt superb was when I gave birth for the first time.
>—Helen Hayes, Best Actress, *The Sin of Madelon Claudet*

This is the best drink of water after the longest drought in my life. I actually have friends who have won this before, and I swear I have never held one before. —Steven Spielberg, Best Director, *Schindler's List*

It's impossible to maintain one's composure in this situation.
>—Frances McDormand, Best Actress, *Fargo*

I didn't faint, but I went rather giddy. It was incontestably the greatest thrill of my life.
>—Sophia Loren, learning in Rome of her Oscar for *Two Women*

I was either on the verge of getting completely hysterical, or just kind of passing out. It's very surreal to see everyone standing up. I was constantly fighting the impulse to just dissolve into inarticulate sentimentality.
>—Susan Sarandon, Best Actress, *Dead Man Walking*

Is the thrill of winning an Oscar comparable to the thrill of becoming a parent? You would think so by the large number of recipients who have singled the win as "the most exciting" and "the most significant" event of their lives!

When Marie Dressler won the Best Actress for *Min and Bill,* she was "scared stiff," by her own admission, but that didn't prevent her from saying: "I have always believed that our lives should be governed by simplicity. But tonight, I feel very important. I think Dolly Gann, (sister of Vice President Charles Curtis, who attended the ceremony) should give me her seat." Utterly respectful, Mrs. Gann got up and gave Dressler her seat.

Winning the Oscar is considered to be a career climax, the greatest achievement of a film artist's life. The immediate reaction to winning, which follows a long period of anxiety — the six weeks between the nominations and the awards ceremonies — is slightly more spontaneous, or at least slightly less fabricated, than is the norm in Hollywood. With all the expectation and preparation to win, there's always unpredictability, as the numerous upsets have shown year after year. Ever since the awards began to be telecast, the reactions to winning (and losing) are shown live to a billion viewers all over the world, which is exciting for the winners, but can be terribly embarrassing for the losers. That's the glory and the drawback of the electronic age.

Halle Berry's weepy, over-the-top performance at the 2002 ceremony surprised most viewers — none, it turns out, more than Berry herself. "I wasn't in my right head all night," she told *Entertainment Weekly,* "It was like I was out of my body — but the next morning, when I saw it on tape, I thought, 'Oh, my God! I'm out of control.' " In London, following her triumph in *Monster's Ball* and modeling a retro Ursula Andress-style bikini for the latest James Bond picture (the twentieth!) *Die Another Day,* Berry confessed: "I had a breakdown, that's what I did. I couldn't utter a word. I felt like a babbling idiot." But Berry has no regrets: "I spoke from the heart and forced a lot of people to think, which always feels good."

In the first years, neither the ceremonies nor the awards were much publicized. Charles Laughton could not attend the 1933 banquet, as the ceremony was then called, because he was working in London. The Academy's telegram, congratulating Laughton for winning the Best Actor for *The Private Life of Henry VIII,* was placed on a bulletin board. And Laughton made no big fuss over it, partly because he didn't comprehend its meaning, and partly because the award itself didn't have much effect.

Joseph Schildkraut (*The Life of Emile Zola*) didn't attend the banquet either. "My agents discouraged me from going to the affair," he later recalled, "because they thought the recipient would be Ralph Bellamy or Thomas Mitchell." Schildkraut was already in bed when the telephone rang and the excited voice of a man who did not even bother to introduce himself bellowed: "Where in the hell are you? Why aren't you here? The awards are about to be handed and you are not here." Thinking it was some practical joke, Schildkraut blurted out, "If you don't tell me, I won't come." Then, the anonymous man replied, "Yes, you son of a gun, you won it. Get down here!" Schildkraut dressed in style, ordered out the car, and went to the Biltmore Hotel. He arrived just in time to be seated at the Warner's table and accept the Supporting Oscar from Frank Capra for his portrayal of Captain Dreyfus.

Similarly, fearing rejection, Joan Crawford decided not to attend the 1946 ceremonies. "I know I'm going to lose," she told her publicist, Henry Rogers. Even if she won, Crawford dreaded the idea of having "to get up in front of all those people and make a speech," worrying that she would be "tongue-tied and make an ass of myself." Neither her publicist nor producer Jerry Wald could persuade Crawford to go. However, Rogers, who had started an Oscar campaign earlier, arranged for photographers from all the fan magazines to be at Crawford's home. When Charles Boyer announced that Crawford won, cheers erupted over the radio from the Graumann's Chinese Theatre, and Crawford exclaimed, "This is the greatest moment of my life." Director Michael Curtiz, who had accepted the award for Crawford, came to her house to present it personally. The next morning, newspapers all over the world printed front-page stories of how Hollywood's Cinderella won the prize without even going to the ball. Highly moved, Crawford responded with a personal signed letter to each sender of flowers and telegrams.

Joining Crawford's ranks, Ingrid Bergman also did not attend the show — albeit for different reasons — when she was up for *Anastasia.* Performing in Paris, she asked Cary Grant to stand by, just in case she got lucky. After her performance, Bergman went to her hotel, only to be awakened at seven o'clock in the morning by a Fox publicity man shouting into the phone, "You've won! You've won!" Later, Bergman listened to a repeat broadcast of the ceremony over the French radio. She was taking a bath when Cary Grant began his speech, "Dear Ingrid, wherever you are in the world" (and she was saying, 'I'm in the bathtub!'), "we, your friends, want to congratulate you, and I have your Oscar here for your marvelous performance, and may you be as happy as we are for you."

When Sophia Loren heard she had been nominated for *Two Women,* she ecstatically announced that she would attend the Hollywood ceremonies. "I felt that just being nominated was an honor in itself and a rare one at that for an Italian-speaking actress in an Italian film." But then, upon reflection, Loren changed her mind, as she recalled: "My competition was formidable (Audrey Hepburn, Piper Laurie, Geraldine Page, and Natalie Wood). Besides, the plain fact was that in its long history, the Oscar had never been given to an actor or actress in a foreign-language film." Loren decided that she could not bear "the ordeal of sitting in plain view of millions of viewers while my fate was being judged. If I lost, I might faint from disappointment; If I won, I would also very likely faint with joy. Instead of spreading my fainting all over the world, I decided it was better that I faint at home."

Loren had no real expectations of winning. But, as she recalled, "hope being the eternal rogue that it is, on the night of the awards, I was too nervous to sleep." Photographer Pier Luigi came to Loren's Rome apartment to keep the vigil with her. At three o'clock in the morning, "I tried to go to bed, but my eyes would not close and my heart would not stop pounding, so I went back to the living room to talk to Pier." There was no coverage then of the awards on Italian television or radio. By six o'clock, Loren knew the ceremony was over and was sure she had lost. However, at 6:45 she was awakened by Cary Grant's pleasant voice telling her the good news. Recalled Loren: "I didn't faint, but I went rather giddy. It was incontestably the greatest thrill of my life."

The anxiety during the Oscar ceremonies is immense. All the nominees report that the show seems endless — that is, until winners are announced in their respective categories. As Ray Milland recorded in his memoir: "And we sat, and we sat, through the interminable minor awards, applauding dutifully each recipient and the endless speeches of acceptance." Milland remembered that after Ingrid Bergman tore the envelope open and a great big grin appeared on her face, he knew he hadn't won, because "Ingrid was smiling and I'd never even met her." But then "dimly, I heard the words, 'Are you nervous, Mr. Milland? It's all yours!' " In the applause that followed, Milland just sat there: "I never thought to move until I felt Mal's elbow in my ribs, a blow which I still feel to this day when it's raining. Get up there sweetheart!" his wife said. "Get up there! It's you! It's you!" Milland doesn't remember much of what happened after that, except for "a jumble of handshakes, microphones, people with notebooks and pencils, and flashing camera bulbs."

Gig Young, the 1969 Supporting winner, also kept looking away from the program, because he didn't want to know exactly when his category would be called. He kept telling himself, "I mustn't jump up if they call somebody else's name. I mustn't jump up."

Joan Fontaine recorded her experience of Oscar night, when she utterly froze: "I stared across the table, where Olivia was sitting directly opposite me. 'Get up there, get up there,' Olivia whispered, commanding. Now what had I done! All the animus we'd felt toward each other as children, the hair-pullings, the savage wrestling matches, the time Olivia fractured my collarbone, all came rushing back in kaleidoscopic imagery. My paralysis was total." Fontaine also remembers that "cries of 'Speak, Speak!' echoed through the room as she tried to find her voice." She doesn't have "the faintest idea of what she said in her acceptance speech — "God knows I hadn't rehearsed anything."

It's not easy to predict the winner. When Broderick Crawford (*All the King's Men*) was asked about his view of the polls, which had predicted he would win, he snapped back: "Polls! The polls predicted Dewey would win too!" referring to the failure of the 1948-presidential candidate. "I have no blood," Crawford said after the ceremonies, "I feel like I've been under an anesthetic all day." Crawford's wife was already in the car, with the motor running, "taking no chances on a recount."

Year after year, film critics, industry members, and avid moviegoers try to predict who will win. In some years, all pre-presentation favorites come through as expected. In others, though, there are major upsets, even shocks. In 1956, Anthony Quinn's Supporting win (*Lust for Life*) upset the pre-Oscar favorite, Robert Stack (*Written on the Wind*). In 1963, Sidney Poitier (*Lilies of the Field*) won to almost everyone's surprise; Paul Newman (*Hud*) and Albert Finney (*Tom Jones,* which would win the Best Picture) were considered more likely candidates.

In 1965, Rod Steiger (*The Pawnbroker*) was the critical favorite, and Richard Burton (*The Spy Who Came in from the Cold*) a runner-up, but the winner was Lee Marvin (*Cat Ballou*). In 1968, Peter O'Toole (*The Lion in Winter*) was considered the sure winner, but the Oscar went to Cliff Robertson (*Charly).*

In 1974, most predicted Fred Astaire (*The Towering Inferno*), a sentimental favorite, but the Supporting winner was Robert De Niro (*The Godfather, Part II*). In the same year, the polls predicted that Jack Nicholson (*Chinatown*) would win, but Art Carney (*Harry and Tonto*) was the upset recipient.

Liv Ullmann (*Face to Face*) was expected to win in 1976, but the winner was Faye Dunaway (*Network*). "I didn't expect this to happen quite yet," said the overwhelmed Dunaway. In 1985, William Hurt (*Kiss of the Spider Woman*) was the surprise honoree; Jack Nicholson (*Prizzi's Honor*) was expected to win.

Actors themselves are often surprised by their nominations and wins. Simone Signoret had no notion when she agreed to appear in *Room at the Top* "that this train I was boarding would lead me to my saying thank you in April 1960 in front of millions of TV viewers, to three thousand people seated in red-velvet seats in a Hollywood cinema." The film's critical acclaim shocked Signoret: "We had made this movie hoping that a few friends would like it." The picture's success in America came as a total surprise to her.

The uncertainty prior to the ceremonies adds to the overall excitement. "When the presenter finally gets the envelope open and the winner is you," Mercedes McCambridge recalled, "the giddiness of delirium sets in, and the long walk to the stage is like anesthesia. The dosage diminished slowly, its effects taking weeks to wear off."

Charlton Heston made the following entry in his diary, on April 4, 1960: "I made it. Looking across the orchestra, just before Susan (Hayward) read it off, something popped in my head, 'I'm going to get it.' And I did. I kissed Lydia and walked to the stage dripping wet, except for a pepper-dry mouth: Classic stage fright. I'll never forget the moment, or the night, for that matter."

Rita Moreno (*West Side Story*) was sure that Judy Garland (*Judgment at Nuremberg*) would win the 1961 Supporting Oscar. Extremely emotional and practically in orbit when her name was announced, Moreno shouted, "I can't believe it! Good Heavens. I never thought I'd win," Moreno said after the awards, "yet, at the same time I was wishing I would win. It's a strange emotional feeling to go around with for days. I'm glad it's over."

Gregory Peck was trying "not to work up either undue excitement or nerves," when he earned his fifth nomination for *To Kill a Mockingbird* — he had lost before and fully expected to lose again.

Sidney Poitier didn't expect to be nominated for *The Defiant Ones,* nor to win for *Lilies of the Field.* "My anxiety mounted until it was unbearable," he said of the 1964 Oscar night. "I was sitting there being ripped up internally, absolutely beside myself with nervousness." Poitier understood that "this is an important moment and I have to be here and in fact I want to be here for what it means to us as a people," but he also decided, "never again, under no circumstances, am I going to come here again and put myself through this." Although winning seemed a "long shot dark horse, I was switching from no chance at all to writing my acceptance speech."

When John Mills was watching the rushes of his scene with the lobsters in *Ryan's Daughter,* director David Lean asked him, "Johnny, have you ever won an Oscar?" to which the veteran actor said, "No, I haven't. Why?" "Nothing," said Lean, "I just wondered." A year later, Mills received a cable from the Academy congratulating him for his Supporting nomination. After the nomination, Mills recalled, "I [did] my best, because I wanted the damn thing so desperately, to persuade myself that I really didn't care, and that I had very little chance." Mills knew that his part, as the village's idiot, was small and "without a single line of dialogue." One day, Mills's daughter, Juliet, called from Hollywood to tell him that he had been awarded the Golden Globe. After that, Mills was even more anxious because he realized "that the recipient of the Golden Globe Award becomes a top tip for the Oscar."

On Oscar day, "the phone rang continually, reporters, gossip writers. Several of them told me that the rumors circulating around town made me favorite. The more of the stuff I listened to, the more convinced I was that I really didn't stand a chance." On Oscar night, Mills tried "to look cool and totally relaxed," but to no avail. He desperately wanted the Oscar, well aware that "at my age (sixty-three), it was in all probability my last chance of winning one." After "what seemed like an eternity, the moment arrived." Maggie Smith, the award's presenter, opened the envelope and smiled broadly, "I knew before she made the announcement, I'd made it."

To Mills's younger British colleague, Judi Dench, the Oscar ceremonies were also "unbelievable." As she recalled: "The first time (for *Mrs. Brown*) I took my daughter and it was so larky. I'm always terribly starstruck. We were black-and-blue from nudging each other the whole time, trying to draw attention to people. The next time we went, we were all rather blase about it. Our car was late. We got there and the place was all locked up. Somebody said, 'Oh, God, they want a shot of her while Whoopi Goldberg arrives as Elizabeth II.' So we were smuggled in."

For Dame Judi Dench, it was not revenge to win after being passed over for *Mrs. Brown,* because she really didn't think she was going to win either year. Dench doesn't remember much, "except my husband Mikey saying to me, 'I think you've won, "Jude." ' I don't remember getting up there. I remember Robin Williams curtsying. I remember crying in a lift. And then I remember meeting the Italian man Benigni."

I Would Like to Thank....

If you had won this, your price would have gone down so fast. Have you any idea what supporting actors get paid?
— Michael Caine to fellow-nominee Tom Cruise

I'd like to dedicate this to all the women who have come before me who never had the chances I've had. — Jodie Foster

Most Oscar thank-you speeches, often the most remembered part of the awards show, tend to sound like a speed-read version of the telephone book. Even Italian maestro Federico Fellini (recipient of an Honorary Oscar) had to shout his unintelligible last words off camera, without benefit of a microphone, when he overstayed the welcomed norm of forty-five seconds per speech. This is one aspect of the show that has changed a lot over the years.

Acceptance speeches used to be modest prior to public broadcasts of the show. Janet Gaynor, the first winner, simply said, "I am deeply honored," but she couldn't continue as her voice cracked and tears filled her eyes, thus setting a standard for future speeches by female winners. Embarrassed, Gaynor later sent a letter to the Academy: "This is an honor that I deeply appreciate. I regard the opinion of the Academy as so expert and unbiased that to be recipient of the award makes me very happy indeed."

Following in the Gaynor tradition, Mary Pickford, cited as Best Actress for *Coquette,* also cried heartily. But then, she quickly calmed herself and apologized for forgetting to bring "my prepared speech." So much for being genuinely surprised. The Best Actor that year, Warner Baxter for *In Old Arizona,* also fumbled his lines and apologized for being "truly overwhelmed."

Speeches have varied in length, content, and originality. A few have been brief, such as Vivien Leigh's speech for *Gone With the Wind,* in which she thanked "Mr. Selznick, all my co-workers and most of all Miss Margaret Mitchell."

In recent years, such brevity is a rarity. In 1990, Joe Pesci won the Supporting Oscar for playing a menacingly volatile gangster in *GoodFellas,* in what was the most competitive acting category that year. Collecting the statuette, Pesci gave the shortest speech in the Academy's history, leaving behind only five words. "It's my privilege. Thank you."

In the 2001 show, the Academy promised a free television set to the winner who gave the shortest speech. The winner came in at eighteen seconds; the speech belonged to Michael Dudok de Wit, honored for the Animated Short Subject, who said: "I would like to thank my two producers, Claire Jennings from London and Willem Thijssen from Amsterdam, and both for their dedication and hard work. And I would like to thank especially my wife Arielle for her support. Thank you, Academy members. This is fantastic."

Some speeches, such as Greer Garson's in 1943, have been extremely long. Garson thanked everyone, including "the doctor who brought me into the world." "I walked into the wings," she later recalled, "and a man said, 'you spoke for five and a quarter minutes.'" Garson realized that she had broken "a sacred rule," since "leading ladies aren't supposed to get further than, thank you, thank you, and burst into tears." Garson's speech soon became a joke in Hollywood, endlessly imitated at parties; in the next decade, the actress refused to speak in public at all.

By and large, this kind of long speech is impossible at present, in the age of television, when every minute of advertising costs a fortune. Still, in more-recent years, Beatrice Straight's speech was almost as long as her part in *Network,* practically two scenes. Dame Judi Dench's Oscar-winning role in *Shakespeare in Love* was also very short. Glancing down at the statuette in her hand, Dench said quietly and modestly: "I feel for eight minutes on the screen, I should only get a bit of him."

But there is long and boring, and long and entertaining. Julia Roberts audaciously broke the forty-five-second norm by first standing on stage and laughing hysterically and exuberantly — "I'm so happy...I love it up here." She then told conductor Bill Conti, "sir, you're doing a great job, but you're so quick with your stick, so why don't you sit because I may never be up here again."

Roberts acknowledged her director's (Soderbergh) contribution: "Steven, you made me want to be the best actor that I suppose I never knew I could be, or aspire to, and I made every attempt...so I thank you for really making me feel so." Her speech was considered a highlight of the show, probably its most spontaneous and joyous moment, and the audience didn't mind its length — three minutes and fifty seconds.

Who Do They Thank?

The "Thank You" note is customary in every speech, but different people and different objects have been thanked — for different reasons. The most routine and frequent thank you speech is the one that acknowledges family members, paying tribute to mom, dad, wife and kids.

Wearing a military uniform, Jimmy Stewart (*The Philadelphia Story*) thanked the entire film industry: "I assure you this is a very important moment in my life. As I look around this room, a warm feeling comes over me, a feeling of satisfaction, pride, and most of all, gratefulness for the encouragement, instruction, and advantage of your experience that have been offered to me since I came to Hollywood, and with all my heart I thank you."

Joanne Woodward tearfully expressed her thanks to Nunnally Johnson, who wrote, produced, and directed *The Three Faces of Eve,* "for having more faith in me than I ever knew anyone could have." Charlton Heston (*Ben-Hur*) thanked "the first secretary in a Broadway casting office who let me in to get my first job." In the same year, Shelley Winters thanked her agent for getting her the part in *The Diary of Anne Frank.*

Maureen Stapleton (*Reds*) outdid them all, thanking everyone she had met in her life, a speech that was almost repeated verbatim by Kim Basinger in 1997, when she won for *L.A. Confidential.*

Some of the fun in watching the Oscar show derives from the choice of presenters and the banter between them and the winners, particularly in a small community such as Hollywood.

Audrey Hepburn's choice as presenter of the 1965 Best Actor Award was ironic. She had not been nominated for *My Fair Lady,* but Rex Harrison was, and his chances to win were excellent. "It was a strange evening," Harrison reported. "I knew that if I won the award I would be on the stage, with two Fair Ladies. Julie Andrews had been nominated (*Mary Poppins*); Audrey Hepburn had not, but she was in Hollywood to present the awards."

It all happened — "I won it and Julie won it and things were fairly hectic backstage, trying to keep the factions in the right place for the photographs and interviews. The public relations people had a difficult time, but they are well equipped for this." "I have to thank two fair ladies," Harrison said in his speech. Hugged by Audrey Hepburn, the television camera caught a close-up of Julie Andrews extremely upset.

In the following year, when Harrison presented the Best Actress Award, another interesting incident happened. The two major contestants were named

Julie and both were British, Julie Christie (*Darling*) and Julie Andrews (*The Sound of Music*). Harrison ripped open the envelope and said with lips pursed, "Julie." He then paused for another second and said, "Christie." Christie, who had been trying to sit calmly, ran to the stage crying, clutching the Oscar and Harrison at the same time.

Burt Lancaster's address evoked laughter and applause when he thanked those who worked with him in *Elmer Gantry,* those who voted for him, and "those who didn't." Similarly, Sean Connery (*The Untouchables*) began his speech by saying, "Ladies and gentlemen, friends, and a few enemies." Connery then noted: "I realized just the other day that my first one and only attendance was thirty years ago — patience is truly a virtue."

Rod Steiger was gracious when he thanked his co-star in *In the Heat of the Night,* Sidney Poitier, "whose friendship gave me the knowledge to enhance my performance — and we shall overcome."

Gene Hackman (*The French Connection*) thanked his director, William Friedkin, who "brought me through this when I wanted to quit."

Jack Nicholson thanked "Mary Pickford who, incidentally, was the first actor to get a percentage of her pictures." "Speaking of percentages," he continued, "last but not least, I thank my agent, who about ten years ago said I had no business being an actor."

Jason Robards took the award "in honor of my producer, Robert Redford, who showed such integrity and perseverance" in creating *All the President's Men.*

One of the more charming speeches was given by Mary Steenburgen, who thanked "my patron, Jack Nicholson, for casting me in my first film, *Goin' South.*" She then concluded by thanking her then husband, actor Malcolm McDowell, "for making life so nice." "I feel like tap dancing," she said, quoting from her role in *Melvin and Howard.*

Fredric March, who split the 1931–32 Best Actor with Wallace Beery, said: "It just happened that this year Mrs. March and I adopted a child and Mr. and Mrs. Beery adopted a child. And here we are, both getting awards for the best male performance of the year." Claudette Colbert was boarding the Santa Fe train to New York when she was announced winner. The Santa Fe officials held up the train and she was taken by taxi to the ceremonies at the Biltmore Hotel. "I'm happy enough to cry," she said, "but I can't take the time to do so. A taxi is waiting outside with the engine running."

Bing Crosby thought he had only slim chances to win and subsequently decided to stay at home. However, around six o'clock in the evening of the awards, when Paramount learned that he might win, the executives had to persuade him to go. It was not an easy task. "All I can say," Crosby commented, "is that it sure is a wonderful work when a tired crooner like me can walk away with this hunk of crockery."

Edmund Gwenn, who won for his portrayal of Santa Claus in *The Miracle on 34th Street,* said: "Now I know there is a Santa Claus."

Jane Wyman, winning Best Actress for playing a deaf-mute in *Johnny Belinda,* said: "I accept this very gratefully for keeping my mouth shut; I think I'll do it again." Similarly, John Mills, who also won for playing a mute (*Ryan's Daughter*), remarked: "I was speechless for a whole year in Ireland, and I'm utterly speechless [at] this moment."

Eva Marie Saint (*On the Waterfront*) was far into pregnancy and feared, "I may have the baby right here out of excitement." "I hope this is not a mistake," Yul Brynner (*The King and I*) said, "because I won't give it back for nothing." And the same concern was expressed by Alec Guinness, recipient of the 1980 Special Award for career achievement, "I'm grabbing this while the going is good."

An excited David Niven (*Separate Tables*) admitted, "I'm so loaded down with good-luck charms I could hardly make the steps." The following day, he published a big "Thank You" in the trade magazines:

> In the full glare and under the stress of "Oscar Night" (if one is lucky enough to be the winner), it is almost impossible not to be corny in the wording of one's thanks. May I now, in the cold light of the morning after, thank from the bottom of my heart, not only those who voted for me, but those who did not vote for me, those who could not vote for me, and those who would not have voted for me in a million years even if they could have voted for me. In other words, I want to thank all show business where, in the midst of the most wonderful and crazy people, I have spent the happiest years of my life.
>
> Love to All
>
> DAVID NIVEN

Lee Marvin broke with the tradition of speeches when he simply said, "Half of this (Oscar) belongs to a horse someplace out in the valley," which helped him win in *Cat Ballou.* Gene Hackman suggested in the same vein, "maybe the award should really go to my car," referring, of course, to the breathtaking chase scene in *The French Connection.* Oscar-winning editor Jerry Greenberg, also felt that he should thank "the New York subway."

Estelle Parsons caused a wave of laughter when she gasped, "Oh, boy, it's heavy!" as she took the statuette from Walter Matthau. Her Broadway show closed down for the night so that she could attend the event. Dame Judi Dench's Broadway show, *Amy's View,* for which she would win a Tony Award, also closed for the night, but the star was allowed to fly to Hollywood on the condition that the show would run for an extra week.

Barbra Streisand simply looked at the statuette and said, "Hello, gorgeous," repeating her famous line from *Funny Girl.* In the following year, Streisand saw tears in John Wayne's eyes when she presented him the Best Actor for *True Grit.* Yes, the macho symbol broke down crying — on stage. "I thought some day I might win an award for lasting so long! But I never thought I would get this particular award."

Film critics are seldom acknowledged on Oscar night—why spoil the fun? Best Director Clint Eastwood, an underappreciated footsoldier for most of his career, was king of Oscar night: "This is pretty good," he said in a typically deadpan comment. He then graciously thanked not only his cast and crew but also the critics who supported *Unforgiven,* including the French. *Entertainment Weekly* described the evening as "Coronation for the Common Man."

And how about thanking teachers? In accepting her Best Actress for *The Piano,* Holly Hunter thanked her first piano teacher and her parents for letting her have piano lessons. Hunter also thanked director Jane Campion for "giving me a character and experience that was so difficult to say goodbye to."

Outing his gay drama teachers, Tom Hanks made an emotional impression in 1994, when he won for *Philadelphia.* With a standing ovation and a kiss from fellow Oscar nominee Liam Neeson, an emotional Hanks thanked the filmmakers of *Philadelphia* and his co-star, calling Antonio Banderas "the only person I would trade my lover for," and Denzel Washington, "an actor who really puts his film image at risk."

Honoring the Dead—Remember the Victims

Steven Spielberg credited Holocaust survivor Poldek Plefferberg for persuading Keneally to write the book, and for "carrying Oskar Schindler to us." Spielberg also thanked MCA President Sidney Sheinberg for "giving me the book" and screenwriter Steven Zaillian for his "inordinate restraint." Spielberg spoke of the six million Jews who died in the Holocaust, "who can't be watching this among the one billion watching the telecast tonight." Spielberg implored educators viewing the show not to permit the Holocaust to "remain a footnote in history."

A totally different tribute to the tragic subject of *Titanic* was made by James Cameron, when he won three Oscars for his tentpole picture. If Spielberg was modest and genuine about the Holocaust, Cameron was arrogant and insincere when he asked the audience at the Shrine Auditorium to pay tribute to the victims of the 1912 tragedy. "I'd like to do a few seconds of silence in remembrance of the fifteen hundred men, women, and children who died when the great ship died. The message of *Titanic* is that if the great ship can sink, the unthinkable can happen, the future's unknowable. The only thing that we truly own is today. Life is precious, so during these few seconds, I'd like you to listen to your own heart."

THE OSCARS' HUGE IMPACT

The Oscar Game: The Rich Get Richer

The expression, "the rich get richer and the poor poorer," based on Karl Marx's theory of "the haves and have nots," describes quite accurately the distribution of rewards in the film industry. The Oscar Award perpetuates the inequality that prevails in Hollywood between the haves and have nots in every respect: Money, prestige, and power.

How pervasive are the Oscar's effects on the winning and nominated films? Is the impact felt in the short run or in the long run? Some observers have stressed the "overnight success," winners who become international stars. Others talk about the Oscars' negative impact, or the Oscar as a jinx, citing winners who become victims of their accolades.

The Oscars' Impact on Films

The goal of every studio in Hollywood is to win the Best Picture, since the top prize carries with it both cash and prestige. The first film to benefit directly from winning, though not from the Best Picture, was John Ford's *The Informer,* which opened to good reviews but was not popular at the box office. However, after winning four Oscars, the largest number of awards for any film in 1935, including Director and Actor, the film became a hit.

A more dramatic impact was felt in 1947, when *The Best Years of Our Lives* turned out to be the most commercial Oscar-winner of its time, earning in domestic rentals over $11 million. Its eight Oscars, including Best Picture and a Special Award to Harold Russell translated into at least two million dollars more at the box office.

Even when the Oscar doesn't turn the winning movies into blockbusters, it does have some effect. A success d'estime, *Hamlet* (1948) was initially intended for select audiences in the arthouse circuit. But its surprise Best Picture Oscar made it a bigger draw, particularly for audiences who would not have seen it otherwise.

The Oscar's commercial value, as measured by grosses, wasn't immense in the first two decades of its operation. In the 1930s, the average domestic rentals of an Oscar-winner was about $2 million, as was the case of *Cimarron,* the 1930–31 winner and the year's top money-maker. *Grand Hotel,* the 1931–32 winner, was also that year's top grosser, with $2.25 million. *Cavalcade,* in 1932–33, ranked second among the season's blockbusters with $3.5 million, which made it the decade's second most popular Oscar-winner, after *Gone With the Wind* in 1939.

In the 1940s, the average earnings of the Oscar winners was $4.6 million, twice as much as that of the 1930s. The three most commercial Oscar films of the 1950s were: *Around the World in 80 Days,* with $23 million in domestic rentals; *The Bridge on the River Kwai,* with $17 million; and *Ben-Hur,* with $36 million. Each of these movies was a blockbuster prior to the nominations, but each then became a bonanza after winning Best Picture.

The Academy continued to honor small-scale pictures on which the Oscar had modest commercial influence. Contrary to public opinion, *All About Eve* was not a huge hit — it ranked as the year's eighth-biggest grosser with $2.9 million in rentals. On the other hand, it's doubtful that an intimate drama like *Marty* would have grossed $2 million in 1955 without the Oscar. MGM's musical *Gigi* was commercially successful before winning Best Picture, but the award added about $2 million to its rentals, thus making it the fifth top-grosser of the year, with $7 million.

The award's pecuniary effect became more apparent in the 1960s. Billy Wilder' *The Apartment* was the only Oscar-winner in the entire decade to have made less than $10 million in rentals; the average rentals were $21 million. More blockbusters were nominated for Best Picture in the 1960s than ever before, which means that most winners were hits before being nominated. *The Sound of Music* (nicknamed "The Sound of Money") didn't need the 1965 Best Picture to become the decade's biggest blockbuster, but the 1966 Oscar for *A Man for All Seasons* doubled its domestic receipts to about $13 million, a phenomenal amount for a historical film, based on a stage play, that lacked strong production values.

In the 1970s, an Oscar's cash value ranged from $5 million to $30 million in the United States. The 1971 Oscar for *The French Connection* added at least $15 million to its grosses. *Annie Hall,* the 1977 winner, had finished its run by nomination time with $12 million, but the film was rereleased after winning Best Picture, which added another $5 million to its rentals. The two films that benefited the most from their Oscars in the 1970s were *One Flew Over the Cuckoo's Nest* and *The Deer Hunter.* Ca. half of the former's $59 million and half of the latter's $30 million (rentals) could be attributable to the Oscar.

Two blockbusters were nominated for the 1973 Best Picture: William Friedkin's horror thriller, *The Exorcist,* and George Roy Hill' adventure-comedy, *The Sting,* which won. Both films were released at Christmas, a prime time movie-going season. In its first fourteen weeks, *The Exorcist* had a clear lead, earning close to $53 million, while *The Sting* followed with $30 million. However, in the first eight weeks after its Oscar, *The Sting* doubled its pre-award pace making an additional $30 million, whereas *The Exorcist* increased by only $12 million. The difference between the box-office status of these movies can be credited to *The Sting*'s multiple Oscars, which made it one of the all-time box-office champions.

The value of the Best Picture goes beyond box-office appeal, bestowing prestige on its filmmakers, turning the winning films into more visible and accessible fare. With the Oscar, these movies acquire the "must-see" label. The Oscar provides *legitimacy of approval,* as director Martin Scorsese once observed: "When people see the label ACADEMY AWARD WINNER, they go to see that movie." This may have negative effects too, as Scorsese noted, "the Academy voters feel a sense of responsibility," which means that they tend to choose movies by their "proper" subject matter rather than artistic merit.

Overall, the extent of the impact depends on the kind of films nominated. From the start, *Reds* was perceived as highbrow fare because of its overtly political content. Warren Beatty, its director and star, hoped that the Oscar would elevate and broaden its visibility, but failing to win the Best Picture, the epic didn't even recoup its budget at the box office. *Reds*'s two Oscars (for Beatty and Maureen Stapleton) were of no help.

For *The Turning Point,* however, a fledgling film, just receiving a Best Picture nomination made all the difference. Herbert Ross's 1977 ballet melodrama made more money in its second run, after it was nominated in eleven categories, than in its initial release. The nominations were helpful in getting booking dates across the country as the film's specialized topic, the internal intrigues of a ballet company, was initially an obstacle in attracting a mass audience.

The nominations performed a similar function for *The Elephant Man,* which, initially, Paramount released mostly in "sophisticated neighborhoods," based on the studio's belief that the appeal of David Lynch's somber black-and-white period saga was confined to educated audiences. But after receiving Best Picture and other nominations, *The Elephant Man* went into wider release, and helped Lynch secure funding for his next picture, *Dune.*

For smaller, independently produced films, the Best Picture nomination is a major help at the box office. Louis Malle's *Atlantic City,* nominated for five awards and cited as best film by the National Society of Film Critics, gained from its reissue after the Oscar nominations. Opening on April 3, *Atlantic City* completed its run before the end of the year with $3.3 million in domestic rentals. After the nomination, the film was rereleased and made another $1.7 million, a small amount in absolute terms but about one-third of its total grosses.

The specific date of a film's release is also a crucial variable. A December release, *Shakespeare in Love,* the 1998 Oscar-winner, enjoyed a significant box-office boost over the first post-Oscar weekend, with a three-day gross of $4.4 million, up 48 percent from the previous weekend. Miramax then wisely widened the film's number of play-dates by 52 percent, from 1,266 to 1,931 screens, in an effort to capitalize on *Shakespeare*'s seven Oscars. By contrast, *Saving Private Ryan,* which opened in July 1998, went into the Oscar show with roughly $210 million in domestic ticket sales, so obviously its five Oscars, including Spielberg's Best Director, were of lesser commercial impact.

The 1999 Oscar winner *American Beauty,* which had opened in September, reaped the benefits of its five Oscars the day after the ceremonies. The film grossed $727,544 on Monday, a day after taking Best Picture, Director, and Actor trophies, which represented a 132 percent surge from its total of $313,542 on the same day a week before. Monday is historically the weakest day of the box-office week. The post-Oscar start lent credence to DreamWorks's projections that *American Beauty* would add about $15 million to its domestic tally. As it turned out, reality proved much rosier for DreamWorks: By June 1, the picture's domestic grosses reached over $130 million.

The Oscar's effects are particularly noticeable for specialized, arthouse films. The other 1999 Oscar favorites, Miramax's *The Cider House Rules,* which won Adapted Screenplay and Supporting Actor for Michael Caine, and Fox Searchlight's *Boys Don't Cry,* for which Hilary Swank won Best Actress, also saw a box-office boost. *The Cider House Rules* collected $309,000 on post-Oscar Monday, up 35 percent from the previous week, and *Boys Don't Cry*'s receipts roughly doubled to an impressive $136,000.

Up to the 1980s, winning the top award almost always led to the reissuing of the honored films. *It Happened One Night,* the 1934 winner, was successful in its initial run in February, but a week after the ceremonies, it was rereleased by Columbia on the strength of its multiple Oscars, and enjoyed a second successful run.

However, at present, it takes three to five months for new movies to come out on video and DVD, which minimizes the reissuing prospects of Oscar-winning films. *Prizzi's Honor,* a 1985 Best Picture nominee, was available on video shortly after the Oscar show, which means that even if it had won Best Picture, it would have been a moot point to rerelease it theatrically.

Winning an Oscar for the Best Foreign-Language Picture is also commercially beneficial, though with considerably less impact. The 1959 winning French film, *Black Orpehus,* benefited in several ways: At least a 50 percent increase in bookings, particularly in cities seldom showing foreign fare, and a double in its gross at the box office. Pedro Almodóvar's serio-comedy-melodrama, *All About My Mother,* also added $2 to $3 million to its box office after grabbing the 1999 Best Foreign-Language Oscar. For the Best Foreign-Language films, even a nomination makes their directors instantly and internationally marketable. Polish director Agnieszka Holland, whose *Angry Harvest* was nominated for the 1985 Oscar, found it much easier to get funding for her future work.

Similarly, nominated director Mike Figgis refused to view the omission of *Leaving Las Vegas* from the Best Picture nominees as a snub, claiming: "Everything is a bonus. The other awards [Nicholas Cage won the Best Actor] will provide the film with an exposure to audiences it would not have otherwise had."

The Oscars' influence does not stop at the American border. In 1995, in addition to *Leaving Las Vegas,* movies that benefited overseas included *Sense and Sensibility, Dead Man Walking,* and *Nixon.* The foreign distributors of these pictures held off theatrical release until Oscar time. Global recognition, by way of Oscar nominations and awards, increased the films' commercial prospects abroad.

The acting Oscars are less influential, though quite instrumental for films that deal with unusually tough topics, or films that lack immediate box-office allure. Meryl Streep's Best Actress for *Sophie's Choice,* a film about a doomed Polish Holocaust survivor, is estimated to have increased box-office receipts by at least $4 million, and Geraldine Page's Oscar did a lot of good for the intimate family melodrama, *The Trip to Bountiful.*

No one expected *Kiss of the Spider Woman* to be nominated for Best Picture, but it was. And William Hurt's Best Actor contributed about $2 million to its overall box office. The very fact that clips from the movie were shown during the Oscar show brought *Kiss of the Spider Woman* to the awareness of millions of viewers who made a point to see the movie or at least rent it on video. Similarly, there's no denying that Hilary Swank's Best Actress Award for *Boys Don't Cry* is responsible for doubling the picture's grosses.

A major bonus for producers winning Oscars is getting better deals when their films are sold to television. In 1984, CBS paid $4.5 million to show the 1981 winner, *Chariots of Fire,* and NBC paid more than $12 million for the Oscar-nominated *On Golden Pond.* Enormous amounts were paid despite the fact that both films had enjoyed healthy theatrical runs and both were previously shown on HBO or Cinemax.

Oscar nominations and awards also increase the revenues of the video companies that distribute the winning movies. Retailers ordered more rental copies of *American Beauty, The Cider House Rules, Boys Don't Cry,* and *You Can Count on Me,* an indie that was nominated for major Oscars in 2000, as a result of their Academy support. To video retailers, the Oscar nominations are prime marketing tools that can trigger rental surges. Retailers benefit the most when movies come out on video just before the nominations are revealed, allowing them to profit from the media blitz that continues for the weeks leading up to the ceremonies.

In 2000, of the five Best Picture nominees, four have grossed more than $100 million at the box office, in no small part due to the Oscar attention. The exception was *Chocolat,* which considering how weak it was artistically, did rather well due to its Oscar visibility.

According to *Variety,* in 2002, of the five nominated pictures, *In the Bedroom* and *Gosford Park* enjoyed the biggest percentage Oscar box-office bump: The former gained 59 percent and the latter 52. However, *A Beautiful Mind* was the picture that enjoyed the largest monetary benefit: A $31 million increase in grosses (27 percent). By April 29, five weeks after the Oscar ceremonies, *A Beautiful Mind* was still playing in 746 theaters, with its cumulative gross topping $168 million. The other nominees, *The Lord of the Rings* gained 2 percent in box-office post-nomination, and *Moulin Rouge* only 0.2 percent, since the movie was already available on video and DVD.

The Oscars' Career Impact

Next to Best Picture, the other awards to exert strong impact are the lead acting Oscars, Best Actor and Best Actress, which have both symbolic and pragmatic effects on the winners' careers.

Skyrocketing Salaries

> Was my life changed by winning? Oh, yes, yes indeed, if change means money. My salary skyrocketed overnight, literally overnight.
> — Mercedes McCambridge, Supporting Actress

One of the immediate and most beneficial rewards for the Oscar is money: Every winner gets better pay after winning. The Oscar has always had cash value, though in its first two decades the issue was not discussed or publicly revealed. Claudette Colbert's fee jumped from $35,000 to $150,000 per picture after winning the Oscar for *It Happened One Night.* In 1936, Colbert became the highest-paid actress in the United States, based on her $302,000 annual income.

Not every artist enjoyed the Oscar's benefits during the studio system. Joan Fontaine was under contract to producer David O. Selznick, who made huge profits from loaning her out to other studios. Fontaine's loan-out fee jumped from $25,000 to $100,000 after her first nomination (for *Rebecca*), but she was still paid her usual fee, $1,200 per week. After Fontaine won the Best Actress for *Suspicion,* her fee went up, but she received only $100,000 out of the $385,000 that Selznick made. As noted, Fontaine's market value, like that of other winners, went up, but she didn't reap the rewards due to her exploitative contract with Selznick. Furthermore, Fontaine didn't work for long periods of time while Selznick was holding out for higher fees based on her new status.

Marlon Brando was paid $40,000 for his first major film, *The Men,* and $75,000 for his second, *A Streetcar Named Desire.* Brando's Oscar-nominated role brought his salary up to $100,000 for his third picture, *Viva Zapata!* In 1960, six years after his first Oscar for *On the Waterfront,* Brando was earning $1 million per picture. And after his second Best Actor for *The Godfather,* Brando's paycheck rose again. For *The Missouri Breaks,* which turned out to be a flop, Brando was paid $1.5 million plus a percentage of the profits.

It's hard to believe that Dustin Hoffman was paid only $17,000 for his first film, *The Graduate,* which made him an instant star and earned him his first nomination. Two years later, Hoffman received $400,000 for *Midnight Cowboy,* which brought him another nomination. In the 1970s, Hoffman commanded over $1 million per picture, and for *Tootsie,* his first movie after winning the Best Actor for *Kramer vs. Kramer,* Hoffman was paid $5 million.

The Oscars' monetary impact can be dramatic. Within a decade after Julie Christie's debut (in *Billy Liar*), for which she was paid the meager sum of $3,000, her salary went up a hundred times. For her Oscar-winning role in *Darling,* Christie was paid $7,500, but for her next film, *Doctor Zhivago,* she received $120,000. In the late 1960s, Christie commanded $400,000 or a percentage of the film's grosses, whichever was higher.

The Oscars' cash value is enjoyed by both lead and supporting winners. "All they wanted to know," said Martin Balsam, the 1965 Supporting winner, "was how much more money I wanted for my next project." The scripts that Balsam received were the same, but everything was reduced to money, or, as he put it, "I became an exploitable item." Tatum O'Neal also saw a dramatic increase in her fee after winning the Supporting Oscar for *Paper Moon,* commanding $300,000 and 9 percent of the net profits of *The Bad News Bears,* thus becoming Hollywood's highest-paid child actress.

The nomination itself can have a sudden impact on actors' box-office worth. Faye Dunaway's third film, *Bonnie and Clyde,* for which she received her first nomination, changed her status, and her paycheck rose from $30,000 to $300,000.

The enormous success of — and nominations for — *Love Story,* for which Ryan O'Neal earned only $25,000, resulted in his fee jumping to $500,000 against 10 percent of the gross profits. Known mostly until then as a television actor (*Peyton Place*), O'Neal became a bankable star whose name alone was sufficient guarantee to obtain financing for a movie.

International Stardom

The salary increase didn't whet my appetite, but world fame — wow!

— Frank Capra

The Oscar catapults the winners into the global media spotlight, resulting in extensive coverage of their lives both on-screen and off. For some artists, this effect is far more important than the pecuniary benefits. As director Frank Capra observed: "Those who grabbed off the little statuettes didn't give a hang how they got them. They just knew an Oscar tripled their salaries and zoomed them to world fame."

The Oscar's media effect is sudden and quite shocking. Joan Fontaine didn't exaggerate when she described the Oscar winners as "minor members of royalty suddenly elevated to the throne." After Fontaine's win, "the press clamored for some sittings, still photos, and a scrap or tidbit to fill the endless gossip columns, fan magazines, Sunday supplements." And this was back in the 1940s, when American society was not as obsessed with celebrities as it became over the past two decades. Elevated recognition has "pragmatic" benefits too, such as "the best table in restaurants, preferential treatment whenever one traveled." For Fontaine, this "was a fishbowl experience until the next year's awards, when a new winner would occupy the throne."

Mercedes McCambridge also realized that she really had entered into "the big leagues," after winning. Going to New York on a publicity tour, she was amazed to find out that, "for the first time in my life a baggage porter recognized me!" This meant, as she noted, that "I had moved into a new dimension: From now on my gratuities to such people would have to be stepped up to keep pace with my exalted station!" In a disgracefully broken down taxi, the driver knew who McCambridge was, and his flattery cost her another five bucks.

Even veteran star John Wayne failed to realize the worldwide importance of the Oscar — until *True Grit.* "What opened my eyes to how much it means to people," the Duke said, "was the flood of wires, phone calls, and letters I've been getting from all over the world." Wayne regarded them as "a tribute to the industry and to the Academy." This reaction reinforced Wayne's belief: "Never underestimate the power of the movies." After claiming for years, "I really didn't need an Oscar, I'm a box-office champion with a record they're going to have to run to catch," the Duke conceded that he was shocked by the massive media attention accorded to him after winning the Oscar.

For Charlton Heston, too, the day after winning an Oscar for *Ben-Hur* was "a fabulous round of phone calls and wires pouring in. It gets kind of frantic, but I wouldn't miss a minute of it."

The Oscars' impact is much more intense for obscure and lesser-known players. Few movie-goers knew who Audrey Hepburn, Joanne Woodward, or Hilary Swank were before the Oscars. Audrey Hepburn made her screen debut with a walk-on part in a British film, *Laughter in Paradise,* then appeared in a few more movies, but after her Oscar for *Roman Holiday,* she immediately became an international star. Hepburn would have become a star without the Oscar, but the award made her status official and legitimatized her talent. Joanne Woodward was virtually unknown before making *The Three Faces of Eve,* a film that put her in the front rank of leading actresses.

Mostly playing villains, Lee Marvin had also been relatively unknown until *Cat Ballou,* which made him an instant star. Marvin began his career as a supporting actor, specializing in Westerns and crime pictures usually as the heavy, but the Oscar led to a new screen image as a leading man, and to box-office popularity, with such films as *The Dirty Dozen* and *The Professionals.*

Some respectable actors became box-office attractions only after winning the Oscar. Fredric March enjoyed a reputation as a stage actor, but the Oscar for *Dr. Jekyll and Mr. Hyde* made him a full-fledged movie star. Marie Dressler was unlikely star material, but after the Oscar for *Min and Bill,* she became the top female star in America for four years. Some of these players would have become stars without the Oscar, but the award expedited the process and made them internationally popular.

Sidney Poitier's first nomination (for *The Defiant Ones*) was a turning point in his career, winning him recognition as a dramatic actor. Poitier's popularity rose gradually after winning the 1963 Best Actor for *Lilies of the Field.* In 1968, he was named America's box-office champion after the tremendous success of *To Sir, With Love* and *Guess Who's Coming to Dinner,* which were released back to back.

The Oscar as a Career Revitalizer

In the late 1940s, Frank (The Voice) Sinatra enjoyed success in every medium: Stage, radio, and in musical films. But in 1952, he was dropped by his record company when his vocal cords abruptly hemorrhaged. Sinatra's career seemed finished. But he fought back, literally begging Columbia to cast him as Angelo Maggio in *From Here to Eternity*, for which he was only paid $8,000. The Supporting Oscar for this performance salvaged Sinatra's career, establishing him as a leading dramatic actor with a wider range, which led to a Best Actor nomination two years later for *The Man With the Golden Arm.*

The Oscars' surprising effects were also experienced by veteran performers, such as comedian George Burns. In his autobiography, aptly titled *The Third Time Around,* Burns writes in a chapter called "A 79-Year-Old Star Is Born": "I hope the title of this chapter doesn't make you think I'm egotistical, calling myself a star, but I can't help it. That's what it says on my stationery." Burns explained: "I was seventy-nine years old when they asked me to play the part of Al Lewis in *The Sunshine Boys.* And it began a whole new career for me." Burns didn't stop working until his death, playing a variety of roles, including God in the Oh, God! comedies.

Stronger bargaining power for better films also comes hand in hand with the Oscar. This power, which translates into a forceful say over the choice of projects, directors, and co-stars, is just as important as bigger paychecks and increased international visibility. In Hollywood, power is the most crucial reward, even if it doesn't last long.

Meryl Streep's Supporting Oscar in *Kramer vs. Kramer* and her growing prestige as an actress helped to finance *The French Lieutenant's Woman,* based on the John Fowles novel and directed by Karel Reisz. Other noted directors, such as Mike Nichols and Fred Zinnemann, had tried to bring the project to the screen but no studio would finance it. Streep's star power was a crucial factor in convincing United Artists to invest $10 million in the production.

Streep also had a say over the choice of her leading man, opting for an English actor, Jeremy Irons, who was then unknown in America. After winning a third nomination for this film, and a second Oscar for *Sophie's Choice,* Streep became one of the few women in Hollywood with the ability to command any screen role. Streep's power has also allowed her to demand — and get — changes in screenplays submitted to her. Robert Benton, who directed Streep for the second time in the unsuccessful thriller, *Still of the Night,* observed after the experience: "Giving Meryl a script is like giving it to a second author."

For the Oscar-winning directors, the major reward is power rather than money. James Brooks noted after winning the Best Director for *Terms of Endearment:* "The Oscar gives you the right to make whatever movie you want next." However, this freedom could be negative as well as positive. Richard Attenborough fell flat on his face with the musical version of the Broadway hit *A Chorus Line.* It was an unsuitable film for his talents and skills, and one that Attenborough was able to make only on the strength of winning the Best Director Oscar for *Gandhi.*

The Oscar and Its Cumulative Advantage

The Oscars' multiple effects point to a broader phenomenon known to sociologists as *cumulative advantage.* This process, which creates and maintains inequality within the film industry, means that those who have done good work and earned peer esteem get more prestige and more recognition for their new work, and they get it faster due to winning. In other words, in Hollywood, the rich and famous get richer and more famous. The Oscar winners, and to a lesser extent the nominees, get better roles, more money, and more publicity at a rate that makes them even more famous and more successful, while increasing the gap between them and other members of their professions.

The accumulation of advantage begins to operate once actors "have made it," which can happen with a single movie, even a first film. Every player can point out his or her "breakthrough" role, the "turning point" in their careers. However, an effective film debut does not guarantee a successful career. Some players are early bloomers who fizzle quickly; others are slow to achieve and late bloomers. Many prominent players didn't make strong impressions in the early phase of their careers and had to wait for years to find their breakthrough role.

Jane Wyman made two abortive attempts to break into Hollywood: The first at the age of eight, the second at twenty-two. After the first effort, Wyman turned to radio, using the name of June Darrell. But she refused to sit idle or despair, and in 1934, she tried Hollywood again — a small part in *My Man Godfrey* led to a contract with Warner. After a long apprenticeship at Warner, playing chorus girls and bit parts, Wyman was cast as Ray Milland's long-suffering girlfriend in *The Lost Weekend.* This role was a turning point, and three years later, Wyman was given the chance of a lifetime in *Johnny Belinda,* her Oscar-winning role that made her a busy actress for the next decade.

Anne Bancroft began her career in television when she was nineteen, under the name of Anne Marno. Two years later, she made her film debut in *Don't Bother to Knock,* followed by six years of B-pictures. In 1958, disillusioned with Hollywood, Bancroft went back to New York and scored a huge success on stage in *Two for the Seesaw* opposite Henry Fonda. She received a Tony for this part and a second Tony the following year for her performance as the devoted teacher, Annie Sullivan, in *The Miracle Worker.* She repeated the role on-screen and earned an Oscar for it.

Leaving her Detroit home when she was eighteen, Ellen Burstyn was determined to seek fame and fortune in New York. At first, she worked as a chorus dancer in nightclubs, then in 1957, she landed a part on Broadway in *Fair Game.* Burstyn's study at the Lee Strasberg Actors Studio improved her skills and made her more committed to acting. Burstyn's first important role was playing Cybil Shepard's bitter mother in *The Last Picture Show,* earning her the Supporting nomination and the New York Film Critics Award. By the time Burstyn had "made it," she was thirty-nine, claiming at least three different screen names to her credit.

As expected, the outcome of winning an Oscar are far more dramatic for the winners than the nominees. The winners' increased popularity and prestige lead to additional nominations: About half of all winners have earned another Oscar and/or another nomination. This trend is stronger among the lead players: 60 percent of the Best Actors and Best Actresses but only 30 percent of the Supporting players have won another Oscar and/or another nomination.

Among the Supporting Actors, only one, Walter Brennan, received two more Oscars (*Kentucky, The Westerner*) and a nomination (*Sergeant York*) after his first win. Five supporting actors have received a second Oscar: Anthony Quinn, Melvyn Douglas, Peter Ustinov, Jason Robards, and most recently, Michael Caine. Caine's first Supporting Oscar was for *Hannah and Her Sisters,* in which he played Mia Farrow's adulterous husband, and his second Supporting Oscar was for *The Cider House Rules,* for playing a humanist doctor who performs illegal abortions.

Only two Supporting Actresses have received a second award. Shelley Winters won a second Supporting Oscar for *A Patch of Blue,* and another nomination for *The Poseidon Adventure,* as a brave Jewish grandmother. The two Supporting Oscars nabbed by Dianne Wiest were for appearances in Woody Allen's *Hannah and Her Sisters* and *Bullets Over Broadway.* In both she played an actress.

Of the four acting categories, the Oscar has been the most influential for the Best Actresses: 80 percent of the Best Actresses but only 40 percent of the Best Actors have been nominated again. And more Best Actresses than Best Actors have received a second Oscar. These variations arise from the fact that the Best Actresses win the award at their first nomination, whereas Best Actors are nominated two or three times before winning. While there is no difference between men and women in terms of the number of nominations, there are differences in the timing of these nominations. The Best Actors earn multiple nominations before their first win, whereas Best Actresses receive them after.

Katharine Hepburn received three Oscars and eight nominations after her first win, and Bette Davis another Oscar and eight more nominations. Ingrid Bergman got two more Oscars and two nominations, and Jane Fonda a second Oscar and four nominations. The same players are repeatedly nominated and repeatedly win. Indeed, 1961 stood out, because it was the first time in which all four winning actors (Maximilian Schell, Sophia Loren, George Chakiris, and Rita Moreno) won the Oscars at their first nomination.

In other years, previous winners can amount to half of the nominees. In 1964, for instance, five of the twenty acting nominees were former winners and six were previous nominees. In 1982 too, five of the nominees were former winners and four had been nominated before. The 1985 Best Actress nominees, Anne Bancroft, Whoopi Goldberg, Jessica Lange, Geraldine Page, and Meryl Streep, have collectively been nominated twenty-four times.

Cumulative advantage is also evident in the distribution of honors outside the Academy. The Oscar winners tend to be the recipients of awards from film critics and film festivals. Most of the critics' awards are announced in late

December, about six weeks before the nominations, which are in mid-February, thus inevitably affecting the Oscar's nominations.

There's consensus between the Academy's and the New York Film Critics' choices: About one-third of all Oscar winners have also received the Gotham Awards. The correlation between the two lead awards is even stronger: About half of all lead players have won both prizes. Some Oscar winners have been recipients of multiple critics' awards. Ingrid Bergman, Laurence Olivier, and Burt Lancaster hold the record with each winning three prizes from the New York Film Critics Circle.

The Golden Globes are announced in late January, but their nominees are announced in mid-December, two months before the Academy nominations. About half of all Oscar winners have also received Golden Globes, with a higher percentage among the lead categories. The stronger link between the Oscar and the Golden Globes, compared with that of the New York Film Critics, is due to the fact that the Globes are awarded by a small group (about ninety voters) whose diversity in age, and taste may parallel more closely the Academy's.

Multiple awards are usually conferred for the same performances. About one-third of the New York Film Critics winners have been cited for the same role that won them the Oscar. As Ray Milland observed in 1945: "I found myself the recipient of more awards than I ever knew existed." For his portrait of an alcoholic writer in *The Lost Weekend*, Milland received the Oscar, the New York Film Critics Award, the Golden Globe, the *Look* magazine award, and a citation from the Alcoholics Anonymous Unwed Mothers of America. Mercedes McCambridge was also surprised that for "the same short performance, I had already won two Golden Globes, one for Supporting Actress and one for Newcomer, the *Look* Award, and other awards."

There are now so many awards that actors can collect six or seven prizes for the same role. For her portrayal of the petty criminal Barbara Graham in *I Want to Live!* Susan Hayward won the Oscar, the New York Film Critics, the Golden Globe, the Cannes festival, and the Donatello (the Italian Oscar) awards. George C. Scott was singled out for the title role in *Patton* by the Academy, the New York Film Critics, the Hollywood Foreign Press, the National Society of Film Critics, the National Board of Review, and the British Film Academy.

The Triple Crown: Oscar-Tony-Emmy

A large number (one-third) of Oscar winners and nominees are distinguished stage actors and recipients of the Tony Award, the top award in the Broadway theater. But once again, the largest number of Tony winners and nominees is concentrated among the Best Actresses. As in film, a smaller number of women dominate the theatrical world, with the most interesting roles circulating among an elite.

Over a dozen players have won the Oscar and Tony awards for the same role. The Tony precedes the Oscar since the screen rights are purchased after a Broadway play has proven to be a commercial success. This lucky group includes: Jose Ferrer (*Cyrano de Bergerac*), Shirley Booth (*Come Back, Little Sheba*), Yul Brynner (*The King and I*), Anne Bancroft (*The Miracle Worker*), Rex Harrison (*My Fair Lady*), Paul Scofield (*A Man for All Seasons*), Jack Albertson (*The Subject Was Roses*), and Joel Grey (*Cabaret*).

The "success syndrome" in both the theater and film worlds often occurs within a short period of time. Shirley Booth won her first Tony for a featured role in *Goodbye, My Fancy* in 1949, then a second Tony as Dramatic Actress in *Come Back, Little Sheba* in 1950, an Oscar for the same role in 1952, and a third Tony for *Time of the Cuckoo* in 1953. With few screen credits, she's better known as a stage than film actress.

Several players have won the Oscar and the Tony in the same year. Fredric March was the first to claim both prizes in 1947, winning a second Oscar for *The Best Years of Our Lives* and a second Tony for *Years Ago*. Audrey Hepburn's 1954 Tony for *Ondine* followed the Oscar for *Roman Holiday* by only a few weeks. Ellen Burstyn's career peaked in 1975, when she won the Best Actress for *Alice Doesn't Live Here Anymore* and the Tony for the stage comedy *Same Time Next Year,* which she later re-created on-screen (receiving a Best Actress nomination for it). But the record holder is still Bob Fosse, who in 1973 became the only person in showbiz to win the Tony for the musical *Pippin,* the Oscar for *Cabaret* (which he didn't direct on stage), and the Grammy for the album *Liza With a Z* all in the same year.

Veteran performer Rita Moreno has provided inspiration for many women as one of the few artists to have won all the prestigious showbiz awards: A Supporting Oscar for her role as Anita in the musical *West Side Story;* a Tony for her performance in Broadway's *The Ritz;* a Grammy for her contribution to *The Electric Company Album,* and two Emmys, one for a stint on *The Muppet Show,* the other for a dramatic performance on *The Rockford Files* in 1978. On May 12, 2002, Moreno added another feather to her already-crowded cap when the State University of New York at Buffalo bestowed on her Honorary Doctorate of Letters. In her acceptance speech at the school's graduation ceremony, Moreno specifically addressed minority students, urging them to stand tall and proudly persevere through the hurdles they should expect to encounter in their post-college endeavors. Moreno made sure to emphasize that she was not only addressing Latinos and African Americans, but the disabled and gay students, too. Her impassioned speech was met with a standing ovation and huge applause.

As noted, Dame Judi Dench is still in awe of her meteoric rise to stardom. At a time when the industry is overrun with hot, young up-and-comers, Hollywood "discovered" Dench while in her sixties. In 1997, Dench became a certified film star with her Oscar-nominated performance as Queen Victoria in *Mrs. Brown,* for which she had won the Golden Globe. The next year she played another queen, Elizabeth, in *Shakespeare in Love,* and won the Supporting Oscar. Dench followed with a Tony for *Amy's View,* her first Broadway play in forty years, though she has been a staple of the London stage.

Dench was on-screen for only minutes in *Shakespeare in Love,* yet she was unforgettable. She fondly recalled: "I just played her like I imagined she would be. She was a fierce woman. People didn't like messing with her. I was in all those clothes and I couldn't do much but stay very still and pray I didn't have to go to the loo in the middle." Two years later, Dench was nominated for a supporting turn in *Chocolat,* which was followed by a lead nomination for the biopicture *Iris,* in which she played the Alzheimer-afflicted British writer, Iris Murdock. In five years, Dame Judi has been nominated for four Oscars.

Successful players "commute" effectively between stage and screen, and between the big and the small screens. This is yet another indication of accumulative advantage in showbiz. There is no short supply of talented actors, but those who are both talented and popular are in high demand. Theatergoers want to see the "hot" actors, and actors often become "hot" after winning an Oscar or a nomination, such as Glenn Close or Linda Hunt.

Popular screen players, like Vanessa Redgrave, Meryl Streep, and Jessica Lange, have all played interesting roles on television, often winning the Emmy, the most prestigious prize in that medium. Two fifths of all Oscar winners have won or were nominated for an Emmy. And again, lead players (particularly women) have an advantage over supporting in winning the Emmy.

Awards in the performing arts are concentrated within a small elite of actors whose success in one medium often leads to success in another. It's no longer true that most players begin their careers in the theater, then moved on to film and television. There is not one dominant route anymore. The strong correlation among the various awards points to the existence of multimedia stars — celebrities who are successful in all the media. This small minority of genuine media stars, headed by winners of the "triple crown" — the Oscar, the Tony and the Emmy — includes Helen Hayes, Thomas Mitchell, Ingrid Bergman, Shirley Booth, Melvyn Douglas, Jack Albertson, Paul Scofield, Anne Bancroft, Liza Minnelli, and Judi Dench.

Barbra Streisand became "the queen of the entertainment industries," because, as one observer noted, "at the staggeringly unprecedented age of twenty-seven, she accomplished an unheard of, indeed, undreamed of feat." Streisand was the only person, male or female, to have won every major entertainment award. Early on, Streisand vowed to scoop all major awards, a feat she achieved in only five years. She was nominated for a Tony for playing Fanny Brice in *Funny Girl,* which also provided Streisand's screen debut and earned her the 1968 Best Actress. Streisand won a Special Tony in 1970, as "the Actress of the Decade," then an extensive, multimillion-dollar contract, followed by a string of recordings and successful TV specials which earned her Grammys and Emmys.

One of America's most beloved and iconic actors, Henry Fonda was a media star in the full sense of the term, though he considered himself primarily a stage actor. One of the first screen stars to make a successful transition to stage and television, Fonda alternated regularly among those media. In 1959, he appeared in the TV series "The Deputy," two theatrical films, *Warlock* and *The Man Who Understood Women,* and a Broadway play. Fonda's string of prestigious awards included a Tony for *Mister Roberts,* the Oscar for *On Golden Pond,* Emmy nominations, and several Career or Lifetime Achievement Awards.

No personality validates the operation of accumulative advantage in showbiz better than Meryl Streep, Hollywood's hottest and most accomplished actress of the past generation. Streep achieved stardom on stage, television, and film in an astonishingly brief time. Upon graduation from the Yale School of Drama, she appeared in repertory at the Public Theater. For her Broadway debut, in the Phoenix Theater's production of Tennessee Williams's *27 Wagons Full of Cotton* and Arthur Miller's *A Memory of Two Mondays,* she received Tony and Drama Desk nominations and the Outer Critics Circle and Theatre World awards. This auspicious beginning led to a bit part in the film *Julia* and to a major role in the television series "Holocaust," for which she received an Emmy. In 1978, Streep earned her first supporting nomination and the National Society of Film Critics Award for *The Deer Hunter.*

The turning point in Streep's career occurred in 1979, with the release of Woody Allen's *Manhattan* and Robert Benton's *Kramer vs. Kramer,* which brought Streep her first Oscar and established her as a household name. In 1981, Streep made a smooth transition from supporting to leading roles in *The French Lieutenant's Woman,* which earned her a first Best Actress nomination. In the following year, there was critical consensus that as the doomed Polish heroine in *Sophie's Choice,* Streep rendered the most wrenching performance of the year, for which she won the Oscar and seemingly every other film award. In 1983, Streep won her fifth nomination for playing the title role in *Silkwood,* and two years later, she was singled out by the Los Angeles Film Critics for *Out of Africa,* for which she also received her sixth Oscar nomination and the Cannes Film Festival Award.

Over the past decade, Streep has been labeled the Queen of the Oscars because of her spate of nominations: *Ironweed* in 1987, *A Cry in the Dark* in 1988, *Postcards from the Edge* in 1990, *The Bridges of Madison County* in 1995, *One True Thing* in 1998, *Music of the Heart* in 1999. There's no doubt, that in the next decade, Streep will surpass the critical recognition of Katharine Hepburn, with whom she ties the all-time record of twelve nominations (though Hepburn's nominations are all in the Best Actress league, whereas two of Streep's dozen nods are in the supporting category).

For Helen Hunt, too, the Oscar arrived on a day when her blossoming movie and TV careers came together. On March 23, 1998, Hunt announced she would return for another year of her hit NBC sitcom "Mad About You," and in the evening, she won the Best Actress for *As Good As It Gets.* Hunt's movie and TV career now complement each other.

In the past, television actors were virtually "disqualified" from Oscar consideration. "I think the industry is finally changing," Hunt said about her crossover appeal. For Hunt, "the blacklist that existed between television and movies is gone. People have realized that work is work." The experience of making *As Good As It Gets* was "thrilling and fun and brutal and hard, a one-of-a-kind experience." Asked to compare her Oscar with her Emmys, Hunt joked: "Thinner? Without wings."

· 18 ·

OSCARITIS –

THE OSCARS' NEGATIVE EFFECTS

The Oscar also bears negative effects for some of the winners and for the film industry at large. Some recipients become victims of their own success when they are rushed by their agents into a succession of films, designed to cash in on their newly gained popularity.

After her stunning performance in *I Want to Live!,* Susan Hayward made mostly B-grade movies, which were meant to exploit her status as an Oscar winner. The studios held up the release of *Thunder in the Sun* and *A Woman Possessed,* hoping that audiences would flock to see them, regardless of their merits. They were wrong, both pictures did poorly, and Hayward never had another critical success before her retirement in the 1960s.

Quick attempts at uniting or reteaming Oscar winners to cash in on their visibility have usually failed. The two 1961 Oscar winners, Maximilian Schell and Sophia Loren, were cast in *The Condemned of Altona,* based on a Jean-Paul Sartre play, but the film failed both artistically and commercially.

A rare, fortunate exception was *The Bells of St. Mary's,* which reteamed three of the 1944 Oscar nominees, Bing Crosby, Ingrid Bergman, and director Leo McCarey, who all elevated the visibility of the new picture. Since Crosby played a priest, similar to his Oscar role in *Going My Way,* audiences believed that *The Bells of St. Mary's* was a sequel (though it was actually a quasi-sequel). It is one of the few Oscar-nominated sequels whose success surpassed that of the original movie on which it was modeled; even the *Godfather* sequels did not match the commercial success of the first film.

It is easy, but unfair, to single out the Oscar as the cause of a winner's dwindling career. For every case of an Oscar "casualty" or "victim," there is a counterexample of an Oscar winner whose career has been rescued and revitalized by the Award. Faltering careers are seldom a direct result of the Oscar — some Oscar winners are not distinguished performers in the first place.

Take for example Jennifer Jones, who was never a formidable actress. However, when cast in the right role, and working with a strong director, she could give a credible performance, such as her Oscar-winning role in *The Song of Bernadette.* Jones's later nominations are totally due to the aggressive ambitions and campaigns of her omnipresent husband-producer, David O. Selznick.

It is possible to distinguish between Oscar-caliber performers who have given many strong performances, and Oscar-caliber performances which have won an Oscar. Louise Fletcher, for example, has excelled in only one film, *One Flew Over the Cuckoo's Nest,* for which she was singled out by the Academy. By contrast, Vanessa Redgrave, Jane Fonda, Sissy Spacek, Meryl Streep, Holly Hunter, Emma Thompson, and Julianne Moore are Oscar-caliber actresses, who consistently deliver high-quality work for which they were rewarded with repeated Academy recognition.

Many players reach the pinnacle of their careers with their Oscar-winning roles, and are unable to surpass, or even match, that level. Sophia Loren (*Two Women*), Julie Christie (*Darling*), and Elizabeth Taylor (*Who's Afraid of Virginia Woolf?*) earned Oscars for their finest performances. Sophia Loren seldom reached the heights of her Oscar-winning role and, with the exception of her films opposite Marcello Mastroianni (*Marriage Italian Style* and *A Special Day*), she made mostly mediocre pictures.

Julie Christie is also an Oscar-winner who has never reached the artistic heights expected of her after *Darling,* though she appeared in many commercial hits such as *Doctor Zhivago* and *Shampoo.* Critics still wonder whether *Darling,* and to a lesser extent *McCabe and Mrs. Miller,* for which Christie received a second nomination, and *Afterglow,* a comeback performance for which she received a third nomination, were the only vehicles to bring out Christie's distinctive talent and intelligence as an actress.

Given the ratio of acting talent to the number of films produced, it is not surprising that gifted actors end up making bad pictures. Broderick Crawford began and ended his career making B-level movies. His Oscar-winning role in *All the King's Men* and a great performance in *Born Yesterday* might have been the notable exceptions in a long, largely undistinguished, career.

The most extreme case of an Oscar victim in Hollywood mythology is Luise Rainer, whose career prompted gossip columnist Louella Parsons to coin the phrase, "the Oscar as a jinx." Rainer was brought to Hollywood by Irving Thalberg to join MGM's great roster of female stars, headed by Garbo, Norma Shearer, and Joan Crawford. Rainer's career took off immediately, and she became the first actress to win two successive Oscars, for *The Great Ziegfeld* and *The Good Earth.* "Those two Academy Awards were bad for me," Rainer later observed." Expectations of her were so unrealistically heightened that when her next film failed, "I was treated as if I had never done anything good in my life." Rainer made only a few films after her second Oscar, and her career terminated abruptly with her last MGM failure, *Dramatic School,* in 1938. "After the Academy Awards, you cannot make mistakes," she complained. "In my day, making films was like working in a factory. You were a piece of machinery with no rights."

Some say Louis B. Mayer lost interest in Rainer after her MGM sponsor, Irving Thalberg, died. Others put the blame for Rainer's premature retirement on the poor choice of roles and bad advice that she received from her husband, playwright Clifford Odets. But judging by the quality of her two Oscar performances, Rainer was not a major talent, and the fact that she won two years in a row had to do more with internal studio politics than with her acting skills.

The decline in the quality of work of Oscar winners may be the combined result of producers rushing actors into unworthy film projects, as well as indiscriminating choices by actors themselves. Just look at Kevin Costner's career after *Dances With Wolves* — one debacle after another.

The Curse of Typecasting

If you play down-and-out loser parts, they send you down-and-out loser parts. — Marsha Mason

I wanted to break out of the kinds of roles I used to do because I was boring myself. — Glenn Close

Typecasting actors in parts similar to their Oscar-winning roles is another negative effect of Academy accolades. Actors complain that they tend to receive scores of offers that are similar or identical to their winning role, and that it becomes impossible for them to break away from the mold.

Most actors are aware of their potential range and of audiences' expectations of them in terms of screen roles. "When I appear on the screen," Cary Grant once said, "I'm playing myself," though he believed that "it's harder to play yourself." Grant attributed his success to his conformity to audiences' expectations. His philosophy was: "Adopt the true image of yourself, acquire technique to project it, and the public will give you its allegiance." Indeed, it is easily possible to describe the screen persona of Cary Grant or John Wayne due to their coherent and consistent screen choices.

Most actors understand the different responsibilities and rewards that are involved in being actors versus being movie stars. The critic John Russell Taylor once described "the penalty" of being a star as follows: "An actor is paid to do, a star is paid to be."

Indeed, some actors resent the screen images imposed on them by the public; images they see as limiting. Mary Pickford was best loved for playing the naive, innocent girl, for which she was dubbed "America's Sweetheart." Occasionally, Pickford would try to deviate from her standardized roles, but through public pressure she would be forced to play them again. In her late twenties, Pickford was still embodying on-screen teenagers in the mold of *Pollyanna*.

Pickford was cast against type in her Oscar-winning role, *Coquette,* which called for cutting her curls, and acquiring a new personality as well as a new hairstyle. But neither the film nor her persona convinced her fans. Pickford resented her public image, as she recorded in her memoir: "Every now and then, as the years went by and I continued to play children's roles, it would worry me that I was becoming a personality instead of an actress. I would suddenly resent the fact that I had allowed myself to be hypnotized by the public into remaining a little girl. A wild impulse would seize me to reach for the nearest shears and remove that blonde chain around my neck."

Greer Garson also got tired of the image that MGM had created for her — the graciously noble, English-like lady, epitomized in *Mrs. Miniver*. A professional actress, Garson felt qualified to play a wider range of roles, hence her strong interest in getting the part of the bitter, adulterous wife in *From Here to Eternity*, a role played with great success by Deborah Kerr. Kerr wanted this part for the same reason; she too was typically cast as the coolly elegant and reserved lady. Director Fred Zinnemann's decision to cast against type became a turning point in Kerr's career. After this part, she was able to demand any role, and the ensuing Oscar nomination enhanced her self-confidence as an actress.

Typecasting characterizes the careers of both leading and supporting players. Specializing in plump, middle-aged matrons, Jane Darwell was cast in over sixty standardized roles modeled on her Oscar-winning role as Ma Joad in *The Grapes of Wrath*. "Those mealy mouthed women, how I hated them," she once complained. "I played so many of them, those genial small-town wives, that I was getting awfully tired of them."

Glenn Close, too, was able to shake her earth mother screen image with the aid of one commercial hit, *Fatal Attraction*, for which she received an Oscar nomination. She recalled: "I wanted to break out of the kinds of roles I used to do because I was boring myself." After that 1987 success, Close was cast in another juicy, villainous role in *Dangerous Liaisons*, for which she garnered her second Best Actress (and fifth) nomination.

Since acting involves role-playing and film is perceived as a "realistic" medium, viewers often fail to separate between actors' lives on-screen and offscreen. Ray Milland recalled that after the release of *The Lost Weekend*, he found himself being looked upon as an authority on alcoholism. Jack Lemmon, who also played a hard-drinking character in *Days of Wine and Roses*, shared the same experience, as he told the *New York Times*: "You don't know how many people think of me as a drunk and send me letters telling me of the glories of Alcoholics Anonymous."

The trap of having an established screen image was most acutely felt by Julie Andrews, who won an Oscar (*Mary Poppins*) and another nomination (*The Sound of Music*) for similar roles: The virtuous, wholesome heroine. This image stuck so deeply in audiences' collective memory that Andrews couldn't rid herself of it. In 1964, Andrews replaced Doris Day as America's top female star, playing good-natured, reliable, and maternal women who represented traditional values.

However, as the critic Linda Gross observed, Andrews remained popular only as long as the status quo was maintained in American society; after four years, Andrews's image became outdated and out of step. Unfortunately, as Gross noted, Andrews was unable "to shake this sugary image in a time when sugary [was] out of favor, its place taken by conflict and conscience." The zeitgeist was now represented by a new generation of female stars: Jane Fonda, Diane Keaton, Ellen Burstyn, and Meryl Streep.

Andrews's clean-cut image was so solid that she couldn't change it even when she played vastly different characters, such as her role in *S.O.B.*, in which she dared to expose her breasts. "I hope I am not as square as some people might think," Andrews observed, expressing resentment at her public image. "I hope I have many facets." Andrews was aware that her career suffered because her image crystallized early on in her career: "If you have a large success at something, you are inclined to get typed."

Andrews further believes that "the lack of good roles for women and the bracketing" made her a victim of typecasting. She wanted play more dramatic roles, comedies, and musicals, without being typed. Children's films still interested her, though she didn't want to do anything that would seem a copy of *Mary Poppins*. Hoping that at least critics would recognize her as a better actress than she was given credit for, Andrews went out of her way to break her mold. In the musical comedy *Victor/Victoria*, she played a woman disguised as a man who impersonates women.

The effects of typecasting are severely felt by actors who play powerful roles that become their trademark. Gloria Swanson recalls that after her stunning 1950 performance, "more and more scripts arrived at my door that were awful imitations of *Sunset Boulevard*, all featuring a deranged superstar crashing toward tragedy." A strong woman, Swanson vowed: "I didn't want to spend the rest of my life, until I couldn't remember lines any longer or read cue cards, playing Norma Desmond over and over again." She resented that "serious directors were foolish enough to think that this was the only role I could play and get box-office returns."

Hollywood believes in repeating successful formulas, which means, among other things, recasting stars in similar roles. Sylvia Miles "specialized" in playing tough but vulnerable floozies, earning a first nomination for *Midnight Cowboy*, and a second for *Farewell, My Lovely*. Miles claims to have a drawer full of similar parts in her apartment — "whores with hearts of gold, waitresses, tough broads."

For her effective portrait of a prostitute in *Cinderella Liberty*, Marsha Mason received her first nomination, which was followed by numerous offers to play hookers — upscale and downscale, cheerful and tragic. Mason complained, "if you play down-and-out loser parts, they send you down-and-out loser parts."

Although women are more confined by typecasting, men are victims too. Bruce Dern played numerous villains, first on the CBS and NBC "Alfred Hitchcock Presents," then in *The Cowboys*, in which he "dared" to kill John Wayne on-screen. Dern holds that his recognition as an actor came rather late because "I was sold wrong." "I would have been much further along if I had gotten a better agent earlier. Everyone in this business is sold, and I was sold as a cuckoo, a bad guy, a psychotic." The Academy legitimized this typecasting when it nominated Dern for *Coming Home*, as the demented chauvinist captain, who commits suicide out of despair.

The second kind of typecasting is most severely felt by supporting actors, who are doomed to play "second bananas" for the rest of their careers. In some respects, the Academy itself is responsible for such typecasting, making the distinction between leading and character players official in the Academy Players Directory, the industry's chief casting tool. Until the late 1970s, players who won or were nominated for supporting awards tended to remain in this category.

A strong screen image, created in a first film and certified by an Oscar nomination, is that of Sidney Greenstreet, who made an auspicious debut as Kasper Guttman, the ruthless villain in *The Maltese Falcon.* This image suited Greenstreet's size, being a bulky man of three hundred pounds. Greenstreet went on to play so many master villains that he became Hollywood's classic screen heavy. Offended by Warner's relegating him to such a narrow range, Greenstreet became doubly sensitive to the critics' view that he was only capable of playing baddies. Warner never trusted his ability to carry a movie on his own and thus never cast him in a lead role.

After making his stage debut in London at seventeen, Peter Ustinov suffered from similar typecasting in Hollywood, where he mostly played older, often eccentric characters. Forever associated with screen roles of men much older than he, Ustinov never became a leading man. "It was a mistake," Ustinov later conceded. "For years I played nothing but old and freakish men."

A leading man in the theater but mostly a character actor in film Lee J. Cobb met the same fate. Cobb played secondary roles, often tough racketeers and stern politicians, earning nominations for *On the Waterfront* and *The Brothers Karamazov.*

Gig Young's lifelong dream was to be a leading man, but his Oscar (*They Shoot Horses, Don't They?*) and his two other nominations were all in the supporting league. Similarly, Angela Lansbury, Celeste Holm, Donna Reed, Shirley Jones, and Teresa Wright began and ended their screen careers as supporting actresses, especially after winning awards in this category, which legitimized their status.

In recent years, one of Oscar's greatest casualties has been Mira Sorvino. "When I won the Oscar," Sorvino told the *Los Angeles Times,* "my life became a total whirlwind and I got rocketed into doing one film after another very quickly. No one really tells you how to do it, what the rules are, and how to be the consummate professional." As a result, Sorvino made a quick string of undistinguished films (to say the least), such as *Romy and Michele's High School Reunion,* the sci-fi horror flick *Mimic,* and *The Replacement Killers,* a second-rate martial-arts film.

Reflecting on her hits and misses, Sorvino said, "I think in the past maybe some of my choices were more like 'OK, well this seems fun, let's do it.' But I was just starting out, and I was more innocent about the whole thing." The range of roles she was offered was extremely narrow, as she recalled, "I had done *Mighty Aphrodite,* the TV movie *Norma Jean & Marilyn,* and then *Romy and Michele,* that's three dumb blonds in a row. After that, I did get a lot of offers for dumb blonds, but I wouldn't do them." Sorvino credited Robert Redford, her director in *Quiz Show,* for giving her the best advice she ever received. "Beware the sex roles, Mira," Redford said, "they come to a dead end at 35."

Though typecasting is still a norm in Hollywood, it is not as rigid as it used to be, particularly for men. In the last three decades, several actors, including George C. Scott, Roy Scheider, Al Pacino, Robert Duvall, and Robert De Niro, began their careers and won Academy recognition as supporting players, but later made smooth transitions to leading roles.

Gene Hackman began his career as a character actor, distinguishing himself in secondary parts in films such as *Bonnie and Clyde* (his first nomination). Hackman's part in *I Never Sang for My Father* brought a second supporting nomination — "I guess the Academy is trying to tell me something," he said. Even so, Hackman was proud to state: "I never approach a film as if I'm playing a supporting character. If I do, then I'm just a supporting character. I approach it as if it's the most important thing in my life."

In 1971, Hackman won the Best Actor for *The French Connection;* since then he has played both leading and supporting roles by choice. For his role as a sadistic sheriff in *Unforgiven,* Hackman won a second, Supporting Oscar. Hackman belongs to the new breed of star character actors who get lead roles without conforming to Hollywood's traditional image of leading men as attractive and romantic.

In recent years, lead actors had to be neither attractive nor romantic to be cast in starring roles. Just look as Walter Matthau's career. In the 1950s, typically cast in villainous roles, Matthau seemed destined to stay in the supporting league. But he rose to sudden stardom in Neil Simon's *The Odd Couple,* in a role seemingly written for him. Matthau went on to star in a succession of comedies, earning the Supporting Oscar for *The Fortune Cookie,* and two Best Actor nominations for *Kotch* and *The Sunshine Boys.* Interestingly, the same slouching posture, awkward walk, and uncommon face, which had kept Matthau from becoming a leading man in the 1950s and 1960s, were used — and perceived by the public — to different effect in the 1970s. For the first time in his career, Matthau was asked to play romantic roles, beginning with *House Calls* opposite Glenda Jackson.

Oscaritis—Competition and Anxiety

The Oscar competition is terrifying. It's like blood sport. I hate public competition. It reminds me of *They Shoot Horses, Don't They?*
— Michael Ondaatje, author, *The English Patient*

Artists are very competitive. People tend to minimize it, but it's not true. You always want to win.
— Robert Duvall, Best Actor nominee, *The Apostle*

Did the Oscar belong to me, or did I belong to it? Which one of us would always be in debt to the other? — Mercedes McCambridge

The fierce competition doesn't stop once film artists reach the top of their professions. Membership in Hollywood's power elite is usually short — there are no guarantees of long-term security. As sociologist Philip Slater has observed: "The competitive life is a lonely one, and its satisfactions are very short-lived, for each race leads only to a new one."

One might ask: How do actors feel when they win the Oscar against all odds, in years in which the competition is particularly strong?

In 1956, the industry felt that Yul Brynner got the award that "belonged" to Kirk Douglas (*Lust for Life*). Bogart's *African Queen* out-polled Montgomery Clift's dazzling performance in *A Place in the Sun,* and also eliminated Brando's chances for his luminous turn in *A Streetcar Named Desire.* In 1992, Marisa Tomei won against top-notch actresses (three of whom were British and one Australian, Judy Davis).

In some years, there are too many acclaimed performances to wedge into the allotted five slots. Such was the case in the 1995 Best Actress competition, or the 1997 Best Actor race, which explains the long list of omissions compiled by critics year after year. In a piece in the *Los Angeles Times,* titled "Year of the International Women," I enlisted 20 great female performances in 2001, a year that was otherwise weak for mainstream Hollywood fare.

Yet the tough competition, the desirability of the Oscar, and its immense effects on the winners explains the growing obsession with winning the award. Those who have won the Oscar feel tremendous pressure to prove that they are worthy of it. Perpetual anxiety might indeed be one of the Oscar's most devastating consequences, for the winners and nominees alike.

Producers, directors, and actors go out of their way to grab the coveted award. Publishing tycoon William Randolph Hearst was so consumed with getting an Oscar for his mistress, actress Marion Davies, that his activities in the film industry were single-mindedly driven by this goal. First, Hearst joined forces with MGM, then with Warner. Hearst succeeded in getting Davies some good roles, but failed to get her the award; she was never even nominated.

David O. Selznick also worked hard to get a second Best Actress for his wife, Jennifer Jones, who had won the Oscar before they met. Though ultimately failing, Selznick used his power to get Jones nominations for unworthy performances, such as the one in the ridiculously campy Western, *Duel in the Sun.* Selznick's obsession continued for another decade, and he's responsible for Jones' another undeserving nomination in *Love Is a Many Splendored Thing.*

The Oscar also occasionally has damaging effects on the winners' interactions with their peers, family and friends. "A picture taken after the Oscar banquet of Brian (Aherne) sitting alone in an empty room," Joan Fontaine observes, "feet up on a chair, my fur coat over his arm, waiting patiently for the photographers to finish with the winners, graphically illustrates the plight of marriage when the wife is more successful than the husband." After winning, Fontaine herself felt that "there was many a doubter, many a detractor, many an ill-wisher. It's an uneasy head that wears the crown."

Mercedes McCambridge also believed that "there is a price tag and mischief in the lovely statue with my name on it." "I mustn't think that taking bows was all that would be expected of me," she recalled in her memoir. "Oscar was calling the tune now, and it gave me a funny feeling: Did the Oscar belong to me, or did I belong to it? Which one of us would always be in debt to the other?"

Hollywood is a small community, after all, where everybody knows everybody. In 1975, upon receiving her fourth supporting nomination for *Shampoo,* Lee Grant observed: "My big concern is would Brenda Vaccaro and Lily Tomlin (who were also nominated in her category) and I be talking to each other once it's all over." Being close friends could make the competition unbearable and even destructive.

The pressure to live up to the critics' expectations can make the award a burden for the winners. "The way to survive an Oscar," Humphrey Bogart said after winning the Best Actor for *The African Queen,* "is to never try to win another one." Bogart's rationale for his strange proposition was based on observing "what happens to some Oscar winners. They spent the rest of their lives turning down scripts while searching for the great role to win another one. Hell, I hope I'm never even nominated again. It's meat-and-potatoes roles for me from now on."

Well, it was not meat-and-potatoes for Bogart. After his win, Bogart received a third Best Actor nomination for *The Caine Mutiny,* and he continued to work until his untimely death from cancer, in 1957. "The nomination for *Tommy* made me realize that the nomination for *Carnal Knowledge* was not a fluke," said Ann-Margret with a sigh of relief, in 1971.

Two generations later, Meryl Streep reiterated Bogart's and Ann-Margret's fears even more succinctly: "I'm freaked out. It's like a mantel visited on me that has no relation to what I do or who I am." Some of Streep's friends didn't speak to her after she was hailed as "America's Best Actress" on the cover of *Time* magazine. It was a traumatic experience, as she noted: "Hype like that is very destructive. It takes a piece out of every other actress." Baffled by her meteoric rise, Streep has no explanation as to exactly how it happened. "It's very difficult. You get a big buildup and it's almost like nothing can live up to it."

The anxiety involved in winning the Oscar, and then living up to it, reflects the inherent problems that are unique to show business. Acting is one of the most precarious of professions. The rise to stardom can be meteoric, but the decline can be just as sudden and dramatic. One of Hollywood's saddest realities is expressed in the dictum, "You are only as good as your last picture." Two or three successive failures at the box office are enough to destroy careers of multiple achievements. Under these circumstances, no wonder film artists are inherently insecure — feeling the burden to prove with each and every film their commercial, not just artistic, worth. Unlike other professions, in which at some point security is granted, film artists must constantly struggle to maintain their status, over which they have much less control than other professionals.

"Looking back on Hollywood," Joan Fontaine observes, "I realize that one outstanding quality it possesses is not lavishness, the perpetual sunshine, the golden opportunities, but fear. Fear stalks the sound stage, the publicity departments, the executive offices. Since careers often begin by chance, by the hunch of a producer or casting director, a casual meeting with an agent or publicist, they can evaporate just as quixotically."

Hollywood has always been characterized by its here-and-now orientation. Ultimately, what counts is the bottom line, the commercial standing of films and the popularity of their directors and actors. The Oscar-winners of previous years are quickly forgotten, not just by the public, but by the Academy and the industry. Former winners are resentful that they are seldom invited to the Oscar ceremonies as guests of honor. Winners quickly become members of a "forgotten legion," unless they win another Oscar and remain active in the industry.

Frank Capra, a three-time Oscar-winner and one of the most beloved and iconic of American directors, observed after spending decades in Hollywood: "Show business is brutal to has-beens. Those pushed off the top are rolled into the valley of oblivion; often they are mired in degradation. I saw it all around me: D. W. Griffith, a forgotten man; Mack Sennett, walking unnoticed in the city he had once ruled as a King of Comedy; old stars pleading for jobs as extras."

Most artists are aware that success in show business, which the Oscar reflects, symbolizes, and perpetuates, is almost inevitably fleeting. Yet the Oscar exerts such pervasive influence on the winners' careers that artists continue to regard it as the ultimate achievement of their lives. And so long as they do, the Oscars' success mythologies — as well as anxieties — will continue to thrive.

19

CAN THE OSCAR BE BOUGHT?

The Oscar Awards, like movies themselves, do not exist in a social or political vacuum. As the premier award in the international film world, the Oscar is not immune to political pressures operating within and without the movie industry.

Studio Politics

> You'd have to be a ninny to vote against the studio that has your contract and produces your pictures. — Joan Crawford

From the first year, Academy voters were asked to exercise "rare discrimination and honest judgment" in their choices. Members were advised "to evince equal discrimination so that the final awards may be fairly representative of the industry's opinion of its best achievements." After the second ceremonies, the Academy Board was proud to report that "so far, there has been no evidence of studio politics," and that producers have "freely nominated pictures from studios other than their own." However, as David O. Selznick once noted, the Academy was always "influenced unduly by transient tastes, by commercial success, by studio log-rolling and by personal popularity in the community of Hollywood."

Both the nominations and final voting have been prejudiced by the studios' ad campaigns, even though there was always ambivalence toward outright politicking for a particular studio's movies and artists. Back in the studio system, ads were considered to be a violation of fair, dispassionate selection procedures. However, those in favor of ad campaigns claim that politicking is not unique or confined to the Oscar, that even the more esoteric and prestigious Nobel Prize is subject to extensive campaigning by scientists, both formal and informal. Still, the difference is that campaigns for the Nobel Prize are conducted by peers, whereas campaigns for Oscars are guided by the studios and the artists themselves.

Studios, directors, and actors gauge their careers in terms of the number of Oscar nominations and awards they receive. Independent producer David O. Selznick was proud to proclaim that his films had collectively received thirty-six nominations and that two, *Gone With the Wind* and *Rebecca,* won the Best Picture. It's understandable, therefore, that filmmakers campaign for their movies. The major studios have the resources and facilities to execute out sophisticated and effective campaigns on behalf of their movies and actors. During the heyday of the studio system, publicity departments could make stars out of contract players, sell their movies to the public, and persuade members to vote for their pictures. Not to be forgotten, the Academy began its existence as a guild-busting company union, led by the strongest studio, MGM. Louis B. Mayer, who ruled MGM for two decades, was one of the Academy's charter founders, and was instrumental in drafting its goals and recruiting its members.

During Mayer's reign, MGM received more than its fair share of nominations and awards. In the first decade, MGM earned a total of 153 nominations and 33 awards, more than any other studio. Paramount ranked a distant second, with 102 nominations and 18 awards, followed by Warner, with 71 nominations and 15 awards. Fox and Columbia fared poorly, the former with 54 nominations and 13 awards, the latter with 43 nominations and 10 awards.

In the Oscars' first twelve years (from 1927–28 to 1939), of the 102 Best Picture nominees, 28 were produced by MGM, 17 by Paramount, 10 by Twentieth Century-Fox, 15 by Warner, 8 by Columbia, 7 by RKO, and 4 each by United Artists and Universal. Only three of the nominees were produced outside Hollywood, the British-made *The Private Life of Henry VIII* and *Pygmalion,* and the French *Grand Illusion.* Independent producers justifiably complained that their movies stood little chance of being nominated. Samuel Goldwyn had only four films (*Arrowsmith, Dodsworth, Dead End,* and *Wuthering Heights*), and Selznick two (*A Star Is Born* and *Gone With the Wind*).

MGM's defenders claim that in the 1930s the studio produced more films than any other studio, and that MGM also made better films. What they mean is that MGM made films that were more suitable for winning Oscars. Of the first twelve Best Pictures, MGM made four: *The Broadway Melody, Grand Hotel, Mutiny on the Bounty,* and *The Great Ziegfeld; Gone With the Wind* was released by MGM, but was a Selznick production. In the early 1930s, MGM had at least two films nominated for Best Picture every year, and later in the decade even more. In 1936, no fewer than five MGM films competed for the Best Picture: *The Great Ziegfeld,* which won, *Libeled Lady, Romeo and Juliet, San Francisco,* and *A Tale of Two Cities.* MGM also dominated the 1930s acting Oscars: Ten out of the twenty Best Actors and Best Actresses were given to MGM players, including Norma Shearer, Marie Dressler, Helen Hayes, and Luise Rainer (in 1936 and 1937) among the women, and Lionel Barrymore, Wallace Beery, Spencer Tracy (in 1937 and 1938), and Robert Donat among the men.

Smaller studios had more limited opportunities of getting their productions nominated. Rising director Frank Capra assured his Columbia boss, Harry Cohn, that he would get nominations for his 1930 Barbara Stanwyck comedy, *Ladies of Leisure.* He was vastly disappointed when the film was ignored by the Academy. Quickly realizing the "disadvantage of working at Columbia," Capra learned that "the major studios had the votes. I had my freedom, but all the honors went to those who worked for the Establishment." The first Columbia movie to be nominated was Capra's 1933 comedy, *Lady for a Day,* and the first

Columbia film to win the Best Picture Oscar was Capra's *It Happened One Night,* a year later.

For two decades, the Academy was controlled by the big studios; nominations were dominated by a few powerful cliques within the studios. "The trick," as Capra observed, "was to get nominated by the clique of major studio directors who had achieved membership — and those Brahmins were not about to doff their caps to the 'untouchables' of Poverty Row," as the small studios were then labeled. "Making good pictures was not enough," Capra quickly realized. "I would have to gain status with big name directors to get them to nominate me."

Under the leadership of Adolph Zukor, Paramount was also strongly represented in the Best Picture category during the Depression. In the first year, four of the five nominated films were produced by Paramount, including the winner, *Wings.* A large number of these movies were produced and/or directed by Paramount's prestige filmmaker, Ernst Lubitsch.

Columbia's participation in the Oscar race in the 1930s was defined by its star director, Frank Capra. Six out of Columbia's eight nominated films were directed by Capra, who won three directorial Oscars (in 1934, 1936, and 1938) over a period of four years.

By contrast, the few RKO nominees were based on the strength of their performers. Three of Katharine Hepburn's vehicles were nominated — *Little Women, Alice Adams,* and *Stage Door,* and two were Fred Astaire-Ginger Rogers musicals — *The Gay Divorcee* and *Top Hat.* Similarly, two of Universal's four nominated films featured its biggest bankable star, Deanna Durbin, who helped save the studio from bankruptcy during the Depression.

In the 1940s, MGM's domination of the Best Picture category declined. The studio produced only ten of the seventy nominated films, most of which were Greer Garson vehicles. RKO and Paramount followed, each with seven nominated films. RKO gained prestige from the Orson Welles's films, two of which were nominated, *Citizen Kane* and *The Magnificent Ambersons.* Paramount also benefited from the work of writer-director, Billy Wilder. Three of Wilder's movies received nomination: *Hold Back the Dawn,* which he co-wrote with Charles Brackett but didn't direct; *Double Indemnity,* which he wrote and directed, and *The Lost Weekend,* which won Best Picture.

Up until the late 1940s, most of the nominations and awards were restricted to the big studios. In 1948, 72 out of the 102 nominees were featured in movies released by the major studios: MGM, Warner, Twentieth Century-Fox, Paramount, and RKO. The rest were in movies distributed by smaller companies, such as Universal, Columbia, and Republic. Universal's nominations were for the British-made *Hamlet,* which it distributed in America.

The studio that gained unexpected power in the 1940s was Twentieth Century-Fox, producing thirteen of the seventy nominated films, two of which won the Best Picture: *How Green Was My Valley* and *Gentleman's Agreement.* By comparison, the best decade for Columbia was the 1950s, in which three of its movies won the Best Picture: *From Here to Eternity, On the Waterfront,* and *The Bridge on the River Kwai.*

United Artists was fairly represented in the first two decades, though it distributed only one Oscar winner, *Rebecca.* However, from 1960 to 1990, no fewer than nine of the winners were distributed by UA, including *The Apartment, West Side Story,* and *Tom Jones.* UA also holds the record for being one of two studios to win three Best Pictures in a row: *One Flew Over the Cuckoo's Nest* in 1975, *Rocky,* and *Annie Hall.* The other is DreamWorks: *American Beauty* (1999), *Gladiator,* and *A Beautiful Mind.* DreamWorks also won the first animated Oscar for *Shrek* (2001).

In the studio era, artists were expected to be loyal to their home companies, upon which their livelihood depended. As Joan Crawford once noted: "You'd have to be a ninny to vote against the studio that has your contract and produces your pictures." This meant that essentially the employees nominated films and performers of their own studios. To assure nominations for their colleagues, their names were listed as first choice, followed by unlikely candidates from other studios, thus guaranteeing that there would be no serious competition.

Today, studios no longer wield the same power. But there are similar issues. As Peter Bart wrote in *Variety:* "If you were an Academy member, do you vote for what you really believe represents the best work in each category, even if it's an Australian or Italian movie, and, as such, a blunt indictment of Hollywood — and your employer?"

A more significant change in the Oscar operations is the increased visibility of some new players. Over the last fifteen years, smaller, independent companies — indies, as they are known in the industry — have become an important force in the American cinema with a strong presence in the Oscar contest.

Indies Grabbing Oscars

When independent producer Samuel Goldwyn's *The Best Years of Our Lives* swept most of the 1946 Oscars, it created shock waves, and the beginning of the decline of the studios' dominance. In the 1950s, three Best Picture winners — *Marty, Around the World in 80 Days,* and *The Bridge on the River Kwai* — were made outside of mainstream Hollywood.

The flowering of the independents became most visible in 1985, when *Kiss of the Spider Woman,* a small-budget film financed by Island Alive, was surprisingly nominated for the Best Picture. William Hurt won Best Actor for his performance in that film, and in the same year Geraldine Page won Best Actress for *The Trip to Bountiful,* also produced by a small, non-Hollywood company.

Then, in 1986, all five Oscar nominees were made outside of the Hollywood establishment: Oliver Stone's *Platoon,* which won, James Ivory's *A Room With a View,* Roland Joffe's *The Mission,* Woody Allen's *Hannah and Her Sisters,* and Randa Haines's *Children of a Lesser God.* The blockbuster success of the Vietnam war film *Platoon,* which grossed over $100 million even before winning the Best Picture, and the solid box-office receipts of *A Room With a*

View proved that there is money to be made out of specialized, quality films. These movies also showed that Hollywood was opening up its gates to offbeat, unusual work. The message was loud and clear: The indies are marching into the mainstream.

The box-office success of Steven Soderbergh's *sex, lies and videotape* in 1989 was yet another piece of evidence that there was vibrant life outside of the system. *sex, lies and videotape* was not an avant-garde film, but it was also not the result of consensus movie-making. Soderbergh's first film showcased a talented, self-assured director who came (in Hollywood terms) out of nowhere to win the Palme d'Or at the Cannes Film Festival. With production costs of $1 million against grosses of $25 million, *sex, lies and videotape* boasted a better profit ratio than the hugely successful *Batman* (which cost over $50 million and earned $245 million). This intimate film, which was nominated for Original Screenplay, may well have been the most profitable movie of the entire decade.

In 1992, *Howards End, The Crying Game,* and *The Player* were not only box-office smashes, they also garnered more Oscar nominations than the big studio releases. This led mainstream Hollywood to seek more extensive inroads into the independent community. Hollywood began to understand that indies are the soul of the medium in a way that the potboilers of Macaulay Culkin (of the *Home Alone* movies), Arnold Schwarzenegger (the *Terminator* pictures), Sylvester Stallone (*Cliffhanger, Demolition Man*) can never be.

Tim Robbins's *Dead Man Walking* featured prominently in the 1995 Oscar contest, with a Best Director nomination, and the Best Actress Oscar to Susan Sarandon. In 1996, four of the five Best Picture nominees were indies, financed and made outside mainstream Hollywood: *The English Patient, Fargo, Secrets & Lies,* and *Shine.*

The Oscar nominations and awards for the indies would seem to express the disgust of the Hollywood establishment for its own bloated and empty product. Indeed, while Hollywood was spending time, energy, and big bucks churning out and marketing big-budget, over-produced, special-effects and star-studded formulas (*Independence Day, Volcano, Speed 2, Batman and Robin*), something significant was happening out on the fringe. The American indie cinema was enjoying exhilarating years with young, bold filmmakers, critical support, receptive audiences, and the promise of an even better future.

The emergence of a viable alternative cinema, a second, Off Hollywood industry, with its own institutional structure and talent, is one of the most exciting developments in American culture of the last two decades. The Oscars have reflected this evolution particularly in the best Original Screenplay category: Neil Jordan's *The Crying Game* in 1992, Quentin Tarantino's *Pulp Fiction* in 1994, Christopher McQuarrie for *The Usual Suspects* (directed by Bryan Singer) in 1995, Billy Bob Thornton's *Sling Blade* in 1996. Paul Thomas Anderson, the new genius on the block, has received two writing nominations, for *Boogie Nights* in 1997 and *Magnolia* in 1999, both of which were made by mini-major company New Line. In 2000, Stephen Gaghan won the Adapted Screenplay Oscar for *Traffic,* made by the indie company U.S.A.

One studio that began truly independent and is now considered to be a mini-major dominated the Oscar contest in the 1990s: Miramax, owned by Disney since 1993. As run by its co-presidents, Harvey and Bob Weinstein, Miramax has been the most influential "studio" in Hollywood for a whole decade. Every year since 1992, Miramax has been represented in the Best Picture category with such innovative, envelope-pushing movies as *The Crying Game*. Since then, *The Piano* was nominated in 1993, *Pulp Fiction* in 1994, *Il Postino* (*The Postman*) in 1995, *The English Patient* in 1996, *Good Will Hunting* in 1997, *Life Is Beautiful* and *Shakespeare in Love* in 1998, and *The Cider House Rules* in 1999.

In 1998, Miramax outdid itself with two Best Picture nominees, *Shakespeare in Love* and *Life Is Beautiful*, which together garnered twenty nominations, winning ten: Seven for *Shakespeare in Love*, including Best Picture and Best Actress to Gwyneth Paltrow, and three for *Life Is Beautiful*, including Best Actor to Roberto Benigni. Miramax won the Best Screenplay in six of the past nine years: *The Crying Game, The Piano, Pulp Fiction, Sling Blade, Good Will Hunting, Shakespeare in Love,* and *The Cider House Rules*.

The weakest Miramax contender in the Best picture category was *Chocolat* in 2000 (one of the least deserving in Oscar's annals), though in 2001, Miramax was represented in the Best Picture race with one of the year's strongest film, *In the Bedroom*, a highlight of the independents and American cinema in general. *In the Bedroom* marked Miramax's tenth consecutive year with a Best Picture nominee, a record unmatched by any other studio.

Ad Campaigns

Ad campaigns are used by both studios and filmmakers to call the Academy's attention to "worthy" achievements. These campaigns have become extremely elaborate over the years, reaching their zenith in the 1990s. But it would be a mistake to believe that promoting and advertising is a recent phenomenon. There have always been efforts to persuade members to vote for a particular film, though they were not as explicit or expensive as they are today.

The studio for which artists worked and their position within its power structure has played a role in the Oscar race. There was a clear link between Mary Pickford's Best Actress for *Coquette* and the fact that her husband, Douglas Fairbanks Sr. was then the Academy president. Besides, Pickford may have conducted the first obvious campaign, when she invited the members of the Central Board of Judges to tea at her mansion, Pickfair.

It is doubtful that Norma Shearer would have received five nominations and one Oscar had she not been married to Wunderkind Irving G. Thalberg, MGM's head of production. There were always rumors that MGM employees were sent memos or received informal phone calls "encouraging" them to vote for Shearer.

Despite respect for her talent, even the great Greta Garbo might have been a victim of MGM's inner politics. On her first nomination, for *Anna Christie* (advertised as GARBO TALKS!), she lost out to Norma Shearer, who won for *The*

Divorcee, also an MGM movie. At her second nomination, for *Camille,* Garbo lost out to another lesser actress, Luise Rainer, in *The Good Earth.* Rainer was then supported by Louis B. Mayer, though three years later he would drop her and, as seen, her career would terminate. Then in 1939, when Garbo received her third nomination for *Ninotchka,* she lost when *Gone With the Wind* swept the major awards, including Best Actress, which went to Vivien Leigh. Unlike Garbo's previous competitors, Leigh at least did give a fine performance.

Studio politics also deprived Bette Davis of a nomination, and possibly an award, for her performance in *Of Human Bondage.* Davis was then under contract to Warner, which loaned her out to RKO for the film. Conceivably, neither Warner's nor RKO's members voted for Davis, whose name could be added to the nominees' list as a write-in. RKO knew that if she won, the rewards would be reaped by Warner, and Davis was not very popular at Warner. Davis later accused Jack Warner of asking his employees not to vote for her.

Clark Gable believed that he was outvoted for what he considered to be the best work of his career, Rhett Butler in *Gone With the Wind,* because of strained relations with producer David O. Selznick, and because MGM's publicity machine was not behind him. The winner was Robert Donat for *Goodbye, Mr. Chips,* which was also produced by MGM.

Columbia Pictures made no secret in 1953 that it was backing Burt Lancaster, not Montgomery Clift, in *From Here to Eternity.* Both were nominated for the Best Actor, though neither won; the winner was William Holden in *Stalag 17.* Clift was not supported because he was a Hollywood outsider, "suffering" from his reputation as a New York stage actor. Performers who came from New York and continued to appear in both films and plays, like Geraldine Page and Julie Harris, were regarded as "suspect" in the movie colony. In the same year, Van Heflin and Jean Arthur failed to get nominations for *Shane,* because neither was under contract to Paramount. Instead, the studio campaigned for William Holden, who had been at Paramount for years, and for Audrey Hepburn (*Roman Holiday*). Both Holden and Hepburn won.

The odds were against Judy Garland in 1954, despite an impressive performance in *A Star Is Born.* For one thing, Warner, which produced the movie, was then in conflict with the Academy, and for another, Garland was not supported by the studio. By contrast Grace Kelly, who won that year for *The Country Girl,* was supported by MGM, her studio, and by Paramount, which produced the film. Besides, Kelly was much in the news, having made four back-to-back pictures: *Dial M for Murder, Rear Window* (both from Alfred Hitchcock) and *Green Fire* were the other three.

In 1958, when Shirley MacLaine was first nominated for *Some Came Running,* MGM supported its veteran performer, Elizabeth Taylor, in the prestige blockbuster, *Cat on a Hot Tin Roof;* the winner was Susan Hayward in *I Want to Live!* In 1960, MacLaine gave the best performance of her career to date in *The Apartment,* but, once again, MGM launched a massive campaign in the trades supporting the ailing Taylor in *Butterfield 8.* As discussed, the

Academy's sympathy went for Taylor, whose bout with death was ultimately more responsible for her win than her acting in that particular picture.

How Effective Are Oscar Campaigns?

In 1945, Joan Crawford and her press agent, Henry Rogers, conducted one of the biggest campaigns in Hollywood history. According to biographer Bob Thomas, during the filming of *Mildred Pierce,* producer Jerry Wald sensed that something extraordinary was happening, upon which he called Rogers and suggested:

WALD: Why don't you start a campaign for Joan to win the Oscar?

ROGERS: But Jerry, the picture is just starting.

WALD: So?

ROGERS: So how would I go about it?

WALD: It's simple. Call up Hedda Hopper and tell her, "Joan Crawford is giving such a strong performance in *Mildred Pierce* that her fellow-workers are already predicting she'll win the Oscar for it."

ROGERS: Jerry, you're full of shit.

WALD: Possibly. But it might work. What have you got to lose?

In his daily reports to the famous gossip columnist, Rogers delivered some "confidential" reports. A few days later, Hopper wrote: "Insiders say that Joan Crawford is delivering such a terrific performance in *Mildred Pierce* that she's a cinch for the Academy Awards." Other columnists followed Hopper, all predicting an Oscar for Crawford.

One night, Wald called Rogers, triumphantly announcing, "I think we've got it made." Wald had just heard from producer Hal Wallis that "it looks like Joan Crawford has a good chance to win the Oscar." "I don't know where I heard it," Wallis said. "I may have read it somewhere." That's exactly what Rogers and Warner wanted — to create a favorable climate for Crawford. It helped, of course, that *Mildred Pierce* opened to good reviews and good business and that it was nominated for Best Picture.

How crucial was the campaign for Crawford's win? Wouldn't she have won the Best Actress without it? In 1945, Crawford competed against three stars, Ingrid Bergman in *The Bells of St. Mary's,* Greer Garson in *The Valley of Decision,* and Jennifer Jones in *Love Letters.* All three had recently won Oscars: Garson in 1942, Jones in 1943, and Bergman in 1944. The fifth nominee, novice Gene Tierney for *Leave Her to Heaven,* was unlikely to win.

A veteran of twenty years in Hollywood, Crawford enjoyed the sympathy of the press, which resented the way she was mistreated — and fired — by Louis B. Mayer. Furthermore, Mayer himself said in public that he would vote for Crawford, and not for his favorite star, Greer Garson, because "Crawford deserved it." Under these circumstances, Crawford might have won the Oscar even without the massive campaign.

Campaigning by individual performers made a point in 1943, when Teresa Wright called attention through "discreet" ads for her performances in *Mrs. Miniver* and *The Pride of the Yankees.* Wright received a supporting nomination for the former, and a lead for the latter, winning for *Mrs. Miniver.* Wright would probably have won even without all the publicity since *Mrs. Miniver* swept the awards.

A more mammoth and expensive campaign by an actress was mounted by Rosalind Russell, who spent thousands of dollars to get a Best Actress nomination for *Mourning Becomes Electra.* Additionally, RKO spent a huge (undisclosed) amount on her behalf and the movie's. Russell received a nomination, but lost the award, which some attributed to supersaturating the voters.

In 1961, Shirley Jones was advised to invest the $5,000 that she had intended to put toward building a new wing on her home into publicizing her work in *Elmer Gantry.* She won the Supporting Oscar, and it turned out to be the best bet she has made.

Even if campaigns for players do not result in winning, they pay off in other important ways. Peter Falk campaigned for his performance in *Murder, Inc.,* which cost him $5,000. It was his third picture, but the first made in Hollywood. Falk considered the investment worthwhile, because, as he said, "I'm a newcomer out here, thought of as a New York actor with some reputation, but they couldn't place me." *Murder, Inc.* was a small crime film, "the kind that usually gets passed by in the midst of all the big pictures." Falk's motive was "to stir up talk," so that "the talk itself will help the career." "Whether I get the nomination or not, I consider it the best investment I've ever made, and I don't have much money." It was a worthwhile investment: Falk earned his first supporting nomination, which established his reputation in Hollywood, and was cast in more important roles, including one in Frank Capra's *Pocketful of Miracles,* which earned him a second supporting nomination.

Personal campaigns can be shameless as well. Most Oscar veterans applaud the Academy's ongoing efforts to ensure fairness in voting through an increasingly stringent body of regulations governing the conduct of campaigns. Among the biggest changes: Parties are not what that used to be. Dale Olson, a four-decade publicist and now DreamWorks consultant recalled: "I was known for my parties. People like to come to my parties because I do my own cooking." Olson's Hollywood Hills home was the site of many schmooze festivals involving Academy voters back in the days when such soirees were allowed.

Olson recalled particularly his 1987 bash for actress Sally Kirkland, who starred that year in the small, widely unseen indie, *Anna,* in which she played an actress. Academy voters and press members were invited, and Olson whipped up a batch of chicken cordon bleu. The press then wrote glowingly about Kirkland's performance and she received a Best Actress nomination (the winner was Cher for *Moonstruck*). Olson makes sure to point out that it was not the chicken that won Kirkland the nomination, though a tiny film like *Anna* was not exactly getting loads of ink before his party.

The late Richard Harris, who received a second Best Actor nomination for *The Field,* a film no one saw, also conducted an ignoble campaign. The feeling in Hollywood was Harris should win, not for his performance in the picture, but for his performance in getting nominated. As one journalist put it, "Harris worked the town better than Ronald Reagan worked a room — there wasn't a voter's cheek he didn't kiss."

Those embarrassed by the current aggressive and disgraceful campaigning look back with nostalgia at Oscar's more dignified players of yesteryear. Two of Hollywood's most respected and most nominated players, Spencer Tracy and Katharine Hepburn, never campaigned for themselves, and never pressured their studios to do so for them.

Excessive politicking and advertising can have a boomerang effect, as John Wayne's patriotic campaign for *The Alamo* showed. One ad compared the Alamo's fighters with contemporary politicians, stating: "There were no ghost-writers at the Alamo, only men." The publicity cashed in on the fact that 1960 was an election year. *The Alamo* was released in July, four months before the presidential election. "Remember the Alamo," said Wayne on-screen as Davy Crockett, and offscreen as a political figure. Another full-page ad asked: WHAT WILL OSCAR SAY THIS YEAR TO THE WORLD? with a picture of the Alamo's battered fortress.

According to *Newsweek,* publicist Russell Bidwell received the highest amount of money ever paid to a publicist to promote a movie, $125,000, all costs and salaries of his New York and Hollywood offices for a year, plus a huge operating budget. With a high emotional and financial drive, Bidwell helped *The Alamo* get seven nominations, including Best Picture, but no acting or directing nominations for Wayne.

Much more criticized than Wayne was Chill Wills, who played Beekeeper, Crockett's humorous whiskey-drinking sidekick. Wills was charged with using deplorable means to seek a supporting nomination. At fifty-eight, after half a century in film, Wills realized this was his only chance to win the award. Thus, he didn't hesitate to print ads like: "We of *The Alamo* cast are praying harder than the real Texans prayed for their lives at the Alamo for Chill Wills to win the Oscar." "Cousin Chill's acting was great," he wrote, signing, "Your Alamo cousin." Another ad read: "Win, lose, or draw. You're still my cousins and I love you all."

Comedian Groucho Marx, appalled by Wills's methods, wrote back: "Dear Mr. Wills. I am delighted to be your cousin. But I'm voting for Sal Mineo (nominated for *Exodus*)." Wayne himself didn't approve of Wills's campaign tactics and reproached him in print, which prompted Groucho Marx's comment, "For John Wayne to impugn Chill Wills's taste is tantamount to Jayne Mansfield criticizing Sabrina for too much exposure." At the end of the day, neither Wills nor Mineo won; the supporting winner that year was Peter Ustinov for *Spartacus.*

The Alamo's ad campaigns led to heated controversies over the professional and moral ethics involved in promoting movies. Examining whether advertising for Oscar nominations paid off, critic Dick Williams saw "nothing reprehensible in artists or productions blowing their own horns, because it is done in almost every other phase of American life." Nonetheless, Williams objected to the fact that "Oscar voters are being appealed to on a patriotic basis," and resented the implication that "one's proud sense of Americanism may be suspected if one does not vote for *The Alamo*." At Wayne's request, Bidwell responded to the charge: "Along with the *Los Angeles Times,* you suggest very emphatically that we have conducted a campaign that to vote against *The Alamo* is un-American. This is a gratuitous and erroneous conclusion on your part."

Campaigns on behalf *The Alamo* might have helped in getting nominations, but not awards. The picture lost in every category but sound. *The Alamo* wasn't a bad film, but it was up against stiff competition from Billy Wilder's *The Apartment,* which won; Richard Brooks's *Elmer Gantry;* the British literary adaptation *Sons and Lovers;* and Fred Zinnemann's *The Sundowners.*

A year later, George C. Scott declined his nomination for *The Hustler,* deploring the demeaning effects of the Oscar race, particularly the explicit campaigning by press agents for their award-conscious players. However, Burt Lancaster, who won the previous year for *Elmer Gantry,* felt that "ads in the trade papers serve a purposeful function as part of the public relations of our business," akin to saying, "See my pictures before you vote." In response to Scott's accusations, Lancaster said, "No one's putting a gun to his head to buy any ads. Scott's attitude really doesn't make any sense. He's under no pressure to take out any ads."

The controversies over *The Alamo* and Scott's protests motivated the Academy's Board of Governors to take a public stance that called the attention of all potential nominees "for the importance of maintaining a standard of dignity in any and all media of advertising." Ever sensitive to public opinion outside of the film industry, the Board stated that "regrettably, in past years a few resorted to outright, excessive and vulgar solicitation of votes," which became "a serious embarrassment to the Academy and our industry." It therefore suggested "to eliminate those advertising practices which are irrelevant to the honest evaluation of artistic and technical accomplishments and violate the principles under which the Academy was established."

Ultimately, though, the Academy left the entire issue "up to the good conscience of the nominees, confident that they are well aware of the difference between that which enhances and that which lessens the status of the Academy." "The Academy can command respect," the statement concluded, "only as long as its members and the nominees take onto themselves the responsibility of dignified conduct." This request, as Murray Schumach noted in the *New York Times,* was "like asking Pavlov's dogs to ignore their conditioned reflexes."

Needless to say, the warnings didn't change the situation at all. On the contrary, in the 1960s, advertising campaigns for less than worthy films reached their peak, resulting in a severe decline in the Academy's public credibility. Fox outdid the other studios with its successful campaign for *The Sound of Music.*

In the next four years, Fox was determined to win nominations and awards at all costs for such clinkers as *The Sand Pebbles, Doctor Dolittle,* and *Hello, Dolly!* Through special screenings, fancy banquets with resplendent menus, and letters to each Academy member, Fox managed to get multiple nomination for these movies, which was enough to repudiate the Oscar's prestige in the public eye. Fox's campaigns showed that the most dismal films could get nominations, if they are sold and marketed with the right campaigns. Many began to suspect that Oscars' function had changed from honoring the best films to rescuing faltering films at the box office. Labeled as "Oscars' rescue mission," the whole issue soon became a public joke.

To be sure, the Oscars have always had effects on the commercial status of the winning films, and the ceremonies' ability to promote movies has always been acknowledged. Nonetheless, it is one thing to honor decent films such as *Chariots of Fire,* which was critically acclaimed but initially unsuccessful commercially, and quite another, to nominate mediocre films like *Cleopatra,* as a compensation for its immense budget. To honor a downright artistic failure like *Doctor Dolittle,* in order to help recoup its mammoth costs, was downright embarrassing.

At the same time, ad campaigns have helped small, specialized independent films that would otherwise have been buried. In 1968, *Rachel, Rachel,* directed by Paul Newman and starring Joanne Woodward, received four nominations including Best Picture, due to the efforts of Warren Cowan, a leading press agent. Conventional strategies were used to get free exposure for the artists in newspapers and talk shows and of course ads in the trades. But Cowan also set up private screenings for cliques of opinion-makers and public relations specialists who could get the word-of-mouth going.

A grand premiere for *Rachel, Rachel* was arranged in New York, with Newman and Woodward making appearances on all the television shows. The two stars spent Labor Day posing for the cover of *Life* magazine, which was not in their nature, but this movie was special to them. The campaign would not have been effective if *Rachel, Rachel* were not a good movie; the New York Film Critics cited Woodward as Best Actress and Newman as Best Director. Ultimately, the campaign proved more effective in the nomination process, for *Rachel, Rachel* did not win any awards.

Over the years, budgets for ad campaigns have grown steadily. In 1982, the major studios spent about $4 million between mid-December and mid-March on screenings, advertising, and promotion, a modest amount by today's standards. Ads generally appear in the two trades, *Hollywood Reporter* and *Daily Variety,* where a color page costs thousands of dollars. The trade ads have become a sticking point for both studios and the Academy. "It's a concern — anything that suggests that Oscar can be bought is damaging," said Rick Robertson, the Academy's administrator.

An extensive campaign doesn't ensure major nominations. Eighteen pages were bought for Bob Fosse's *Star 80* in *Daily Variety,* but the film did not get a single nomination. And Twentieth Century-Fox bought many ads for *Heart Like a Wheel* and its star, Bonnie Bedelia, but got only one nomination, for costume design. In 1983, *Silkwood* benefited from fifty pages in *Variety, Yentl* thirty-one, and *Terms of Endearment* twenty-eight. *Terms of Endearment,* which won, did not need as much publicity as *Yentl* or *Silkwood,* because it opened to rave reviews and immediately became a box-office hit. It was also a much easier film to sell than either *Yentl* or *Silkwood.*

Advertising ensures that a movie will not be accidentally overlooked, which was crucial to *Yentl,* since it divided critics and opened to lukewarm reviews — it received five nominations. It's hard to tell whether *Silkwood*'s five nominations were attributable to the ad campaign. Meryl Streep would have been nominated for Best Actress and Mike Nichols for Best Director without the campaign — anything with Streep gets extra attention. But Cher, nominated for supporting award, certainly benefited from the campaign.

It may be a coincidence, but in 1987, Streep and Cher found themselves competing in the same category, Best Actress, when the former was nominated for *Ironweed* and the latter for *Moonstruck.*

Admittedly, in *Ironweed* Streep and Nicholson, both Oscar-caliber performers, were nominated for typically "Oscar" roles: Alcoholic drifters in Depression-era Albany, and Streep even got to sing. But the mixed reviews of Hector Babenco's downbeat and flawed adaptation of the prize-winning novel by William Kennedy called for extra campaigning on behalf of the performers, especially since the film was a commercial failure. Hence, Streep agreed to pose for the cover of *Life* magazine, which ran a story entitled, "On Top — and Tough Enough to Stay There." And the distributor, TriStar, took many ads in the trade papers and organized special screenings for small groups of influential members.

As for Cher, she proved that timing is everything, and that campaigns can create a momentum for a film or a performance, start the buzz within the film colony. A veteran performer, Cher knew all too well the rules of the publicity game. During the run of *Moonstruck,* which got good notices and was popular with the public, Cher graced the cover of every possible magazine, from the more serious — *Newsweek* — to the more specialized — *Health and Fitness.* At the time, she was a also spokesperson for the Jack LaLanne Health Clubs.

It did not hurt that as a singer, Cher's new album hit the charts, or that she was dating a handsome beau, Robert Camilletti, who was almost half her age. One couldn't escape Cher's presence: She finally agreed to appear on the "The David Letterman Show" for a reunion with former partner Sonny Bono. In a moment of honesty, she confided in *New York* magazine: "Sometimes I feel like an old hooker. Just because they've stayed alive and stayed around, people start to respect them." That Cher won the Best Actress that year goes without saying.

New rules govern the industry, which changed a lot in the 1990s. The current, free-lance system, with no contract players or studio stars, and the evolving structure of the Academy membership, have resulted in the unanticipated nominations of films and artists that in the studio era would not have been recognized. At present, pictures that enjoy neither critical acclaim nor initial commercial popularity still have a chance to get nominated.

This applies to the stale comedy-drama, *Chocolat* — courtesy of Miramax's aggressive campaigning — as well as to smaller and more serious films. Martin Ritt's 1983 drama, *Cross Creek,* was panned by most reviewers and died quickly at the box office. Universal, which distributed the film, refused to keep the film on-screen, and thus it couldn't be seen during the crucial time of the nominations. Unfazed, producer Robert Radnitz booked *Cross Creek* at a Malibu theater and made up handbills for the members. With only six pages in *Daily Variety, Cross Creek* garnered four nominations, two for actors Rip Torn and Alfre Woodard in the supporting league.

The key to Academy nominations is getting a picture seen by as many voters as possible before the nomination season — that's the only justification for the ad campaigns. All the studios schedule free screenings for those films they believe hold strong Oscar potential. There are also free screenings arranged by the various guilds.

The studios try to boost the profile of their prestigious pictures. The common practice now is to send out video cassettes, making it convenient for Academy members who otherwise might not opt to attend special Oscar screenings. Despite rapid and vast changes in movie technology (the use of VCR, the ascent of DVD), the Academy's official line is that there is no substitute for viewing a movie in the theater on the big screen, though everyone realizes how indispensable videos and DVDs are in assuring films are seen by the Academy.

Screenwriter William Goldman has observed that if videocassettes had existed before, movies that had been overlooked would have been honored. Peckinpah's *Ride the High Country,* Scorsese's *Mean Streets,* and Lawrence Kasdan's *Body Heat* would have likely garnered Best Director and acting nominations, if not Best Picture. In recent years, Edward Norton in *American History X,* Nick Nolte in *Affliction,* and Ian McKellen in *Gods and Monsters,* to mention just a few distinguished performances in small, indie films, would probably not have been nominated for Best Actor without the benefit of videocassettes. How else would Julie Christie have been nominated for a tiny picture like *Afterglow,* which opened in December and barely grossed $2 million? Academy members are not youths brimming with vitality — they don't venture out of their houses to see so-called small pictures.

It is never too early to launch an Oscar campaign. The Samuel Goldwyn Company mailed out six thousand postcards in September 1993, touting its art house hit, *Much Ado About Nothing,* which starred Kenneth Branagh and Emma Thompson. Below the laudatory blurbs was the phrase: "For your consideration — all categories." They also sent the soundtrack CD to call attention to Patrick Doyle's score as well as paperback books that included the script. *Much Ado* had opened in May to glowing reviews, grossing more than $22 million, but there are seven months between May and January, and members tend to forget good movies. It is conventional wisdom in Hollywood that movies that open early in the year get overlooked at Oscar time. (See the conclusion).

Similarly, Sony Pictures Classics mailed out paperback copies of Virginia Woolf's novel *Orlando* to promote their film of the same name, which starred Tilda Swinton. Books, screenplays, and even trailers are now customarily sent for major movies by every studio.

Miramax, which boasts one of the industry's largest and most savvy publicity departments, enlists outside consultants to handle various aspects of its Oscar campaigns, screenings, and gossip-column items. Miramax learned how to conduct an effective campaign when they brought a tough, decidedly non-Oscar film such as *The Crying Game* into Oscar prominence.

In 1993, Miramax engineered an amazingly overblown ad campaign for *The Piano* in the trades, and mailed out elegant booklets printed on expensive parchment. One of the unusual aspects of *The Piano*'s campaign was its emphasis on the achievements of the women involved in the production. The picture garnered nominations for women in seven categories, including Director and Screenplay to Jane Campion, who won the latter. Harvey Weinstein claimed that the costs of the campaign were $250,000 for ads; his competitors tripled his figure. One sarcastic commentator said that it cost almost as much to promote the movie as to make it. Even so, by today's standards, these figures are minuscule.

While the race to win Oscars goes on for months, the five-week window between the nominations and the ballot deadline is crunch time for those who manage Oscar campaigns. The goal is to campaign aggressively without appearing desperate. According to Amy Wallace of the *Los Angeles Times,* for the 2000 race the studios ran ads for their nominees in New York and Los Angeles, where most of the Academy voters live. A recap of Annette Bening's vacuuming scene from *American Beauty* ran during NBC's "Friends," and nominated actor Michael Caine and *The Cider House Rules*'s director, Lasse Hallstrom, took time during an "NYPD Blue" episode to promote their film as an American classic.

The campaigns evoked more public appearances from those who are usually low-key performers. Kevin Spacey attended a number of high-profile evenings for *American Beauty,* and co-star Bening, days away from delivering her fourth baby, made an appearance with Jay Leno. Several other nominees appeared on award shows like the Golden Globes, banking on recognition from the television audience for a boost.

Nothing happens in a vacuum, according to Dawn Taubin, Warner's marketing executive. Warner aired a new TV ad in New York and Los Angeles that didn't even mention *The Green Mile*'s star (Tom Hanks) by name, instead opting to promote the Oscar-nominated screenwriter Frank Darabont. There is no magic formula, but shrewd Academy campaigns go for what Taubin called the cumulative effect of campaign: Trade publications, publicity appearances, the inclusion of movies and stars in articles about these events.

Although the studios do not reveal the costs of these campaigns, a four-week analysis by Amy Wallace, using the trade papers, shows how aggressive these campaigns are. The Best Picture front-runners were DreamWorks's *American Beauty* and Miramax's *The Cider House Rules,* and those projections were consistent with the ads tally from *Variety* since the nominations were announced.

Of the four studios with Best Picture contenders, Disney spent the least on advertising, about $141,000 on *The Sixth Sense,* and $198,000 on *The Insider.* Warner spent about $313,000 to promote *The Green Mile,* while Miramax paid about $350,000 for *Cider House.* DreamWorks spent the most by far on post-nominations ads — more than $774,000 on *Variety*'s most premium advertising (six full-page front cover ads at $29,100 a piece) for *American Beauty.* By contrast, Warner bought three full-page covers, and Disney two. Some of DreamWorks' spending was necessitated by congratulatory ads that are considered de rigueur after wins. *American Beauty* had already taken the Directors, Writers and Screen Actors Guild Prizes.

There is no ceiling on how much money the studios will spend to promote their nominees. In 2000, when a postal service mishap caused the Academy to postpone the ballot deadline by two days (March 23, rather than the 21st), the studios rallied to book ad space for the extra two days. More extensive advertising was placed for films that were still in wide release, such as *American Beauty* and *Cider House.* For those films, Oscar wins could mean at least a 15 percent increase at the box office. Even before the Oscar show, heavy advertising motivates moviegoers to see the nominees.

But a lesser campaign does not necessarily mean that the film will lose in its nominated categories. *The Silence of the Lambs* was released in February 1991, and was available on video before it was nominated for important Oscars. Orion didn't spend a lot on pre-Oscar buzz, but *The Silence of the Lambs* still won Best Picture, Actor, Actress, Director, and Adapted Screenplay.

Although ad bombardments may appear nonsensical, they are predicated on solid business decisions — relationships that need to be nurtured. As Amy Wallace pointed out, the relative lack of ads for *The Sixth Sense* didn't mean that Disney was more tasteful than the other studios. But Disney already had a first-look deal with *Sixth Sense*'s Oscar-nominated director, M. Night Shyamalan, and was committed to back his next film, *Unbreakable.*

Miramax gave *Music of the Heart*'s Best Actress nominee, Meryl Streep, a restrained bravado, based on the belief that "You don't have to prove anything to her with a bells-and-whistles campaign." But Streep may be the exception — many stars and directors pay close attention to how much money the studios spend to promote their films; both egos and reputations are at stake.

American Beauty's Best Picture represented, as Dana Harris wrote in *Variety,* a coming-of-age for DreamWorks, an upstart studio that began operation in 1994. The film's five Oscars, including Best Director and Actor, were a sweet victory after the disappointment the company had faced a year earlier, when *Saving Private Ryan* earned Best Director for Spielberg but lost the Best Picture to Miramax's *Shakespeare in Love.* DreamWorks's shrewd marketing, orchestrated by the gifted Terry Press, helped achieve the landslide victory. Some saw the 2000 battle between Miramax and DreamWorks as a rematch of the 1999 skirmish. In March, DreamWorks bought 38 percent more *Variety* pages for *American Beauty* than Miramax did for *The Cider House Rules.* Even so, the feeling was that Miramax got what they wanted out of the nominations for *Cider House,* doubling the movie's grosses to over $50 million.

Press's marketing campaign for *American Beauty* launched in September after the buzz began at the Toronto Film Festival, where the movie world-premiered. Despite word that the movie was too dark, that it engaged too many controversial issues — drugs, murder, adultery — for the Academy's older voters, the campaign stressed that the film was fresh and ultimately positive and humane. This was followed by a Christmas card from *American Beauty*'s Burnham family, inviting guests to an open house. At a Los Angeles restaurant, screenwriter Alan Ball, director Sam Mendes, and actors Kevin Spacey and Annette Bening mingled with guests as soundtrack artist Elliot Smith performed. The strategy worked — *American Beauty* emerged triumphant at Oscar time.

In the following year, there was mud-slinging in the Presidential elections, the SAG election (conducted twice due to dubious tactics), and even in the Olympic judging, wrote Tim Gray in *Variety.* So why should the Oscars be exempt? Universal's chair Stacey Snider first sounded the alarm, saying unidentified rivals were responsible for negative stories about *A Beautiful Mind* that were cropping up in newspapers, magazines, and Web sites. Everyone in Hollywood is convinced they know the culprit, but nobody has offered any proof. Rival studios privately insisted that, "It wasn't us!" Journalists were loath to admit they might have been manipulated. For some, it was a bigger whodunit than *Gosford's Park,* Robert Altman's nominated mystery.

The sniping worsened in the 2001 race. Attacking the moral fiber of seventy-three-year-old schizo-mathematician John Nash was pretty low, forcing him to appear on various shows, talking about his past and his anti-Semitic remarks. But it was not new. And it was not unique to the Oscars. When a film wins the Best Picture, rivals always nod cynically that the conquering studio "bought" the award. But when *Harry Potter* opened to $90.3 million in November 2001, nobody accused Warner of "buying" that record haul. Warner simply spent a lot of money promoting its product and succeeded — but did anyone care? That's what happens with the Oscar race: Studios promote those films they believe can win the top prize.

In the year of *Titanic,* studios weren't gunning for one another because they knew that they didn't have a chance to win. But in 2001, as noted, pulses were running high since there was potential for a surprise winner in virtually every race. And while *A Beautiful Mind* had an advantage over its rivals, it was certainly not a sure win. Just ask any of the publicists of DreamWorks, Miramax, Universal, and others about orchestrating campaigns and counter-campaigns, with a lot of blood, sweat, and tears.

20

STRANGE BEDFELLOWS?
THE OSCAR AND POLITICS

Historical and political factors have always influenced the types of films and artists nominated for the Oscars. Working in a popular art form, filmmakers are subjected to both stimulating and disruptive conditions of the socio-political contexts in which they operate.

Politics and Film Artists' Careers

World War II disrupted the careers of many actors and directors who were mobilized into the war. Some, in fact, lost the popularity they had previously enjoyed. Clark Gable, "The King," joined the Air Force in 1942, rising in rank from lieutenant to major, and receiving the Distinguished Flying Cross and Air Medal for his bombing missions over Germany. Gable's first film after being absent from the screen for four years, *Adventure,* was trumpeted by MGM as GABLE'S BACK AND GARSON'S GOT HIM. But this, and other Gable postwar films, failed, and his commercial standing began to decline. It didn't help that Gable was not aging well.

The career momentum of Mickey Rooney, who had been America's biggest box-office draw with the Andy Hardy series, reached its peak during the early years of the war. It's doubtful that he would have been nominated for *The Human Comedy,* had it not been for the shortage of nonactive men. But later, like other actors, Rooney's career was interrupted by military service, after which his popularity plummeted.

At the same time, other careers benefited from the war. Humphrey Bogart became a major star in the 1940s, after his appearances in *The Maltese Falcon* and *Casablanca,* the film that established him as a screen super-hero.

In other cases, the war delayed recognition that would have been received earlier. William Holden became a star with his very first film, playing the boxer-violinist in *Golden Boy* (1939). Then, mobilized to the Army, Holden did not make a single movie for three years. But after World War II, Holden's screen image ripened and his popularity rose, reaching a climax in 1950 with two films, *Born Yesterday* and *Sunset Boulevard,* both nominated for Best Picture. Three years later, Holden won the Best Actor for *Stalag 17,* after which his career blossomed for another decade.

The exposure of film artists, on-screen and off, has often made them the first "targets" to be affected by changes in the political climate. Film's strategic position as a powerful medium has always been recognized by the ruling elite, as was evident by its use and misuse by Hitler and Mussolini. Arguably the worst years for American film artists in terms of freedom of expression and organization were during Senator Joseph McCarthy's political witch-hunt in the 1950s. As a result, the careers of many first-rate Hollywood artists were destroyed. Gale Sondergaard, the first Supporting winner (*Anthony Adverse*), became one of the earliest political casualties because of her marriage to director Herbert Biberman, who was suspected of Communist leanings and later became one of the so-called Hollywood Ten. Blacklisted at the peak of her career, Sondergaard couldn't work for decades. Her appeal to the Screen Actors Guild for protection was rejected on the grounds that "all participants in the International Communist Party conspiracy against our nation should be exposed for what they are — enemies of our country and our form of government." Sondergaard emerged out of forced retirement in 1965 in a one-woman show off Broadway, and later attempted several comebacks, none of which succeeded. In 1978, as a gesture of reconciliation, the Academy asked her to be a presenter at Oscar's fiftieth anniversary.

Another Supporting winner, Anne Revere for *National Velvet,* was also at the peak of her craft when she was blacklisted for taking the Fifth Amendment before the House Un-American Activities Committee (HUAC), on April 17, 1951. By that time, Revere had made over thirty films. Her part as Montgomery Clift's mother in *A Place in the Sun* was severely cut, leaving only a few of her scenes. Rumor has it that actor Larry Parks named Revere (along with others) as a member of the Communist Party. (Parks's career reached its zenith with a Best Actor nomination for the title role in *The Jolson Story.* But his career plummeted when he was forced to admit to past membership in the Communist Party. Officially, Parks was never blacklisted, but Columbia didn't renew his contract, and other studios didn't hire him.) Revere was out of work for close to a decade. But, like many others, she found rescue in the Broadway theater, winning a Tony Award for Lillian Hellman's *Toys in the Attic.* The audacious director Otto Preminger, who helped restore the careers of many blacklisted artists, facilitated Revere's comeback in his movie *Tell Me That You Love Me, Junie Moon,* but at sixty-seven, she was too old to resume an active screen career.

Kim Hunter made a spectacular debut in *A Streetcar Named Desire,* for which she won Supporting Oscar. However, shortly thereafter, her career was ruined when her name appeared in "Red Channels," a Red-scare pamphlet. Hunter, too, was unable to get any work in Hollywood or New York and was finally rescued by the producers of the television series "Omnibus."

An auspicious Hollywood beginning marked Lee Grant's career, with a supporting nomination for her very first film, *Detective Story,* in which she played a shoplifter. Grant was married at the time to writer Arnold Manoff and was a close friend of actor J. Edward Bromberg, both of whom were suspected Communists. Grant did not get any work for ten years because she refused to cite her husband before the Committee. "The Committee wanted me to turn Arnold in," she later recalled. "I simply wouldn't do it. No work was ever important enough to make me turn in my husband!" Fortunately, Grant was still able to work in the theater — "Movies and TV were closed to us, but not the theater. But doing a play a year wouldn't support me, so I went to Herbert Berghof and he set me up in a class." Grant taught drama for many years, during which time her attorney worked hard to prove her innocence. Years later, Grant's name was taken off the list with a mild apology from Washington. Despite this experience, Grant never became bitter, as she told a reporter: "I was lucky, I was only 32 when it was over, I still felt I have time to make up for." Besides, she perceived it as a "a fascinating war, which fulfilled part of my life. I never would have believed it if I hadn't been part of it." Grant returned to films in an impressive role in *The Balcony,* and has not stopped working since, both as an actress and as director. In the 1970s, Grant won two more nominations, and a supporting Oscar for *Shampoo.* In her acceptance speech, Grant said: "I would like to thank the artistic community for sustaining me in my wins and losses, and sitting on the curb, whatever it was." Her remarks were greeted with considerable applause.

Few actors have arrived in Hollywood with the established reputation of John Garfield, a member of the famed Group Theater. For his very first film, *Four Daughters,* Garfield received a supporting nomination, and a few years later, a lead nomination for *Body and Soul.* However, in 1952, Garfield's career ended abruptly when he died of a heart attack the night before he was supposed to appear before the Committee. Garfield wasn't accused of anything in particular, but he was suspected of left-wing politics because of his membership in The Group Theater.

McCarthyism damaged the reputation of foreign artists as well. Maurice Chevalier, who was popular in the United States in the 1930s, was refused reentry into the country in 1951 for having signed a Communist-inspired decision, The Stockholm Appeal, which called for the banning of all nuclear weapons.

French actress Simone Signoret also encountered difficulties in getting offers from Hollywood, despite numerous promises made. As she recalled in her memoir: "Each time there had been a vague offer of my participation in an American production made in France, negotiations had rapidly broken off." In the late 1950s, despite assurance from American directors that times had changed, Signoret held onto her belief that "McCarthy was not dead, even if the citizens of this country thought they had buried him." Several films fell through for what she describes as "Washingtonian reasons."

When Signoret was offered the lead in *Room at the Top,* her feeling was "if I was going to lose as Alice, I wanted to know immediately." Signoret feared that if Americans were involved, "there was no point in beginning to negotiate." But it was a British production, and Signoret not only got the part, but also won the Best Actress for it.

Producers and directors also suffered from the fear induced by McCarthyism. The Hollywood Ten, a group of directors and screenwriters subpoenaed to appear before the HUAC in 1947, and cited for contempt of Congress because they refused to disclose their political affiliations, included: Producer-director Herbert Biberman, director Edward Dmytryk, producer-writer Adrian Scott, and screenwriters Alvah Bessie, Lester Cole, Ring Lardner Jr., John Howard Lawson, Albert Maltz, Samuel Ornitz, and Dalton Trumbo. Tried at a Federal Court in Washington, in April 1948, they were given the maximum sentence of a year in jail and a fine of $1,000. While blacklisted, some went abroad, others were forced to retire, and still others wrote scripts while using fronts.

Most of the Hollywood Ten were prominent artists with Oscar Awards and nominations to their credit. Edward Dmytryk was nominated for Best Director for *Crossfire,* which was also nominated for Best Picture. After his release from jail, he went into self-imposed exile in Europe. However, in 1951, Dmytryk cooperated with the Committee and became a "a star witness" in its second round of hearings. His testimony incriminated several colleagues, but he was able to work. In 1954, Dmytryk's version of Herman Wouk's *The Caine Mutiny* received a Best Picture and other nominations.

The Oscar-nominated director Robert Rossen was also blacklisted. In 1947, he was subpoenaed to appear before the Committee, but the hearings were suspended. Rossen continued to work and his film, *All the King's Men,* won the 1949 Best Picture, though he failed to win the directing award, probably because of his politics. There is usually a strong correlation between the two categories, but the 1949 Best Director was Joseph L. Mankiewicz for *A Letter to Three Wives.* In the second round of hearings, Rossen was identified as a Communist, and his refusal to testify resulted in blacklisting. Two years later, like Dmytryk, Rossen requested a second hearing in which he admitted membership in the Communist Party and was subsequently able to work, though he decided never again to return to Hollywood. In 1961, Rossen scored the greatest success of his career with *The Hustler,* which was nominated for nine awards, including the Best Picture, Director, Actor, and Actress, winning two technical awards.

Broken Arrow became a cause célèbre for another, equally important reason. Its screenplay, credited to Michael Blankfort, was nominated for an Oscar, except that Blankfort served as a front for blacklisted writer Albert Maltz. In 1947, Maltz became one of the Hollywood Ten, convicted of contempt for Congress for refusing to testify about membership in the Communist Party. Maltz served ten months in prison. Though he continued to do uncredited work on movies, after *Naked City* in 1948, his name would not appear on-screen. His status changed in 1970, when Clint Eastwood hired him for his Western, *Two Mules for Sister Sara.* In 1991, the Writers Guild of America corrected this injustice and Maltz received official credit for *Broken Arrow.*

Jules Dassin was identified as a Communist by his former colleague, Edward Dmytryk, which forced him into exile in Europe. He became one of the few American directors who was able to work abroad, making *Night and the City* in England, and *Rififi* in France. Even so, a major American company agreed to distribute *Rififi* in the U.S. on one of two conditions: That Dassin sign a declaration renouncing his past and stating he was duped into subversive associations, or that his name be removed from the film as writer-director. When Dassin refused, *Rififi* was dropped and released by a smaller distributor; earlier negotiations with United Artists failed because of hostile public opinion. Dassin's next picture, *He Who Must Die,* also could not get a major American distributor, and when the film was finally shown, only a few Hollywood figures came to see it, among them, Richard Brooks, Gene Kelly, and Walter Wanger. It took over a decade for Dassin's reputation to be restored with the release of *Never on Sunday* in 1960, his greatest commercial success, which won him his first and only directorial nomination.

Among the blacklisted writers was Carl Foreman, whose script for *High Noon* was nominated. Under pressure, Foreman left for England, working underground there for years, using the pseudonym Derek Frey for his script of Joseph Losey's *The Sleeping Tiger.* Foreman was given no credit for *The Bridge on the River Kwai,* which won all the major awards, including Adapted Screenplay to Pierre Boulle, the author of the book, who had nothing to do with the script. Ironically, Boulle had written the book in French and spoke very poor English. In 1984, the Academy corrected this injustice and awarded the Oscar posthumously to those who deserved it, Foreman and Michael Wilson.

The Academy itself became a victim of McCarthy's political hysteria, when, on February 6, 1957, it decided to enact the following rule: "Any person who, before any duly constituted federal legislative committee or body, shall have admitted that he is a member of the Communist Party (and has not since publicly renounced the Party) or who shall have refused to answer whether or not he is or was a member of the Communist Party or shall have refused to respond to a subpoena to appear before such a committee or body, shall be ineligible for any Academy Award so long as he persists in such a refusal."

More than any other talent group, writers suffered from this rule. Michael Wilson won the writing Oscar with Harry Brown for *A Place in the Sun,* but, refusing to answer charges of Communist affiliation, he found himself out of work.

In 1956, William Wyler's *Friendly Persuasion,* nominated for five awards, was released without giving credit to Michael Wilson's script, which he had written a decade before; the only credit mentioned on-screen was "from the book by Jessamyn West." Industry observers interpreted the writing nomination as an act of defiance by the Writers Branch, which always was more sympathetic toward its blacklisted members than the Academy, but Wilson never forgave director William Wyler and remained bitter to the end of his life.

An interesting incident occurred in the 1957 ceremonies, when the Best Story went to Robert Rich for *The Brave One,* but no writer claimed the award. The Writers Guild acknowledged that "it knew nothing about the man, who's as much of a mystery to us as he is to everybody else." Producer Frank King told the *New York Times* that he had no idea of his writer's whereabouts, but added that he was a brilliant young writer whom he had met in Germany, where he served while in the U.S. Army. To the Academy's embarrassment, it turned out that Rich was the pseudonym for blacklisted writer Dalton Trumbo, one of the Hollywood Ten. Trumbo received his long overdue Oscar in 1975, when producers Frank and Maurice King sent the Academy an affidavit verifying his identity.

One of the most acclaimed films of 1958, *The Defiant Ones,* earned nominations in most categories, including story and screenplay to Nathan E. Douglas and Harold Jacob Smith. But Douglas was the pseudonym of Ned Young, a blacklisted writer. The Academy, embarrassed for having to declare a member of the team ineligible, revoked its rules in January 1958. The Board of Directors denied that the motive for revoking the old rules was linked to *The Defiant Ones.* But it issued a statement calling the previous rule "unworkable and impractical to administer and enforce." According to the new regulations, the Academy would simply "honor achievements as presented." Dalton Trumbo hailed that decision as the official end of the blacklist, though he continued to wonder how the industry could officially rescind a blacklist that it had never acknowledged existed in the first place.

The fiery politics and feverish hysteria of the McCarthy era returned with a vengeance in 1998, when the Academy's Board of Governors decided unanimously to award its Honorary Oscar that year to the politically controversial, still unforgiven for naming names, Elia Kazan. With two directing Oscars to his credit (for *A Streetcar Named Desire* and *On the Waterfront*), Kazan's artistic record was beyond fault and everyone agreed with the Board's announcement that "Kazan is one of the most extraordinary directors of this century. Both on stage and on film, he made pronounced and lasting changes in the nature of our dramatic forms." However, beyond dispute were his dubious ethics and moral attitudes. It just happened that the Los Angeles Film Critics Association that year defeated a proposal to honor Kazan with a career Achievement award, instead honoring Abraham Polonsky, a victim of the McCarthy era, which garnered him a 1947 Original Screenplay nomination (the film was also nominated for editing and lead performance by John Garfield), followed by *Force of Evil,* a cult film noir.

Many people in and outside the industry still despised Kazan for his misconduct during the McCarthy era, though he himself had been a member of the Communist Party and influential member of the leftist troupe, The Group Theatre. Yet it also known that in 1952, he volunteered to give names of his former friends and colleagues to the HUAC. Within weeks, a major controversy erupted, first with the *Village Voice* caricature of Kazan on its cover, grasping a golden rodent with a caption stating, HOLLYWOOD #1 RAT; then editorials appeared in practically every newspaper and magazine in the country. Kazan's Honorary Oscar revived the political battles of the 1950s, showing again how divided the film industry was about this painful issue that destroyed numerous careers. At Oscar show time, there was a demonstration outside the Dorothy Chandler Pavilion, with protesters holding signs that stated BEST SUPPORTING SNITCH, BLACKLISTED DIRECTOR COULDA BEEN CONTENDER (paraphrasing

Brando's famous line from *On the Waterfront*) and KAZAN — THE LINDA TRIPP OF THE 1950S, referring to the Clinton-Monica Lewinsky sex scandal.

When presenters Martin Scorsese and Robert De Niro (who appeared in Kazan's last film, *The Last Tycoon*) invited Kazan to the stage, about half of the audience stood up and applauded, but others, including Steven Spielberg and Jim Carrey, clapped quietly while sitting down, and still others — Ed Harris, Amy Madigan, Nick Nolte — sat with their arms folded and angry faces.

Using the Oscar Show for Propaganda

There is singular lack of honor in this country today. — Marlon Brando

They confronted the wild charges of Joe McCarthy with a force and courage of a bowl of mashed potatoes. — Lillian Hellman

I salute you and I thank you, and I pledge to you that I'll continue to fight against anti-Semitism and fascism." — Vanessa Redgrave

I'm sick and tired of people exploiting the occasion of the Academy Awards for the propagation of their own political propaganda.
— Paddy Chayefsky

Most film artists believe that politics should be kept entirely out of the Oscars. In practice, however, this separation is impossible to achieve because film is an inherently political medium. Besides, the temptations to use the Oscar podium are too strong to resist for politically oriented filmmakers. There seems to be a dilemma between artists' need for freedom to express themselves candidly and the Academy's desire to neutralize the Oscar ceremonies and treat it as a strictly showbiz event, with no overt political dimensions.

Speeches with explicit political overtones tend to be the most outrageous aspects of the ceremonies because they are the least predictable; it is the only part of the show that cannot be rehearsed in advance. The show's live audiences and television viewers have come to expect such explosive incidents. That John Wayne and Jane Fonda, two of the most overtly political actors, did not use the Oscar platform for political speeches was held in high regard by some, but disappointed those who expected them to take advantage of the opportunity.

The explicit use of the Oscar show for advocating social causes was mostly a phenomenon of the 1970s. Jane Fonda was praised for her performance in *They Shoot Horses, Don't They?* for which she earlier won the New York Film Critics Award. However, many believed that Fonda's chances to win were spoiled by her radical politics: She supported the Black Panther Party, and conducted fund-raisers for various causes. There were other good performances in 1969, such as Liza Minnelli's in *The Sterile Cuckoo,* but majority opinion held that Fonda deserved the Oscar; the winner, however, was Maggie Smith for *The Prime of Miss Jean Brodie.*

Two years later, when Fonda received her second nomination for *Klute,* the industry speculated that she would either renounce her nomination or use the occasion to promote her politics. Earlier, she had sent a Vietnam vet to accept the Golden Globe from the Hollywood Foreign Press Association. For a while, Fonda considered declining the prize if she won, but on second thought, she decided to attend the ceremonies. Fonda explained: "A woman who is much wiser than I am said to me: 'You're a very subjective individual, an elite individual. The Oscar is what the working class relates to when it thinks of people in the movies. It's important for those of us who speak out for social change to get that kind of acclaim.' "

On Oscar night when Fonda's name was announced, there was a mixture of cheers and boos. But contrary to expectations, Fonda gave a restrained speech: "Thank you. And thanks to those of you who applauded. There's a lot I could say tonight. But this isn't the time or the place. So I'll just say thank you."

Shortly after, Fonda was informally blacklisted and didn't work for several years in America. Earlier, as part of her anti-Vietnam battle, she had formed with actor Donald Sutherland, "the Anti-War Troupe," which toured military camps in defiance of the Pentagon. In July 1972, Fonda went to North Vietnam, a move that put her career — and her life — on the line. When she got back, she was labeled by her opponents "a Commie slut" and "Hanoi Jane." Undaunted, Fonda co-produced F.T.A. (Free the Army and also Fuck the Army), a filmed version of the tour. She also campaigned with other actors for the presidential election of Senator George McGovern. In 1973, she married Tom Hayden, the antiwar militant activist. Joining forces with cinematographer Haskell Wexler, the three co-directed *Introduction to the Enemy,* which documented Fonda's visit to Vietnam.

For a decade, Fonda's record as a screen actress was rather poor. She appeared in Jean-Luc Godard's *Tout va bien* (*Everything's All Right*), a film about the 1968 student revolutions and strikes. She showed her commitment to socially relevant films by playing Nora, Ibsen's feminist heroine, in Joseph Losey's 1973 *A Doll's House.* But a cameo role in the 1975 American-Soviet co-production, *The Blue Bird,* was downright embarrassing.

For her American comeback, Fonda chose a comedy, *Fun With Dick and Jane,* co-starring George Segal. However, the turning point of her career was *Julia,* in which she was cast as playwright Lillian Hellman, a part that she said "means more to me than any movie I've ever made." When Fonda was asked to co-host the 1977 Oscar show, it was interpreted as a sign of Hollywood's forgiveness. In 1978, Fonda's second Best Actress for *Coming Home* proved that she emerged triumphantly from her aborted career. Her comeback was compared to that of Ingrid Bergman, whose second Oscar for *Anastasia* also represented a kind of reconciliation. Both Fonda and Bergman were restored to "respectability" while still young — in contrast to many blacklisted artists who had lost the most creative years of their lives.

In the 1980s, Fonda's politics mellowed and she has become accepted as a mainstream actress. Her new causes were the ERA (now defunct), opposition to nuclear weapons, rent control, and issues that were more accessible to the public. Fonda supported her then-husband's grassroots organization, CED (Campaign for Economic Democracy), whose goal was to curb the power of large corporations. Maturity and a second motherhood changed Fonda, though she was still committed to films with strong political convictions.

Looking back on her past, Fonda concedes to have been "a bit shrill." But she also reached the conclusion that "rallies and speeches aren't necessarily as effective as making one hell of a good movie." In the 1980s, Fonda became a media star due to the popularity of her books and videos, "The Jane Fonda Workout." Watching her co-host the 1986 Oscar show, in which she introduced Kermit the Frog, was an ironic commentary on the fate of a once-radical actress. Fonda received a Best Actress nomination for *The Morning After,* in 1986. But after two failures, *Old Gringo* and *Stanley and Iris,* she retired from the screen, and in 1991, married media mogul Ted Turner, a marriage that lasted a decade.

Charlie Chaplin, another political victim, was also "pardoned" by the industry and restored to legitimacy with an Honorary Oscar in 1972. Chaplin failed to win a single award for *The Great Dictator,* despite a brilliant performance. Politics had something to do with it: Chaplin was suspected of a leftist bent during World War II. He had declared that he was in favor of launching a second front in Europe to help the Russians. For some reason, the subjects of *Modern Times,* a satire on individual impotence in the technological age, and *The Great Dictator,* a satire of Hitler, made him suspect. At the end of this film, which shot before the United States joined the war, Chaplin stepped out of character and made an impassioned speech for freedom. There was also malicious gossip over Chaplin's reluctance to apply for American citizenship, which made him even *more* suspect. Public opinion turned against Chaplin after *The Great Dictator,* which was his last commercial American hit. Chaplin's subsequent films, *Monsieur Verdoux* and *Limelight,* were both box-office failures.

Chaplin refused to go on record and state that he was not interested in the politics of the Soviet Union, a country which he had never even visited. Threatened with a subpoena to testify before the HUAC, Chaplin decided to send a telegram: I AM NOT A COMMUNIST, NEITHER HAVE I EVER JOINED ANY POLITICAL PARTY OR ORGANIZATION IN MY LIFE. In 1952, when the Attorney General instructed the Immigration Authorities to deny Chaplin a reentry visa, he vowed never again to return to the United States. Chaplin's friends found it ironic that he was suspected of leftist politics because in his personal lifestyle he represented what they described as "the height of wealthy conservatism."

Twenty years after he left, Chaplin returned to the United States on a reconciliation tour. He was first honored by the Film Society of Lincoln Center, where he received a standing ovation from his fans. It was just the beginning of what Chaplin described as "my renaissance." The Academy's Honorary Oscar was given FOR THE INCALCULABLE EFFECT CHAPLIN HAS HAD ON MAKING MOTION PICTURES, THE ART FORM OF THIS CENTURY. Both of these gestures proved that the New Hollywood had finally overtaken the old guard.

A year later, in 1973, a major controversy erupted when Marlon Brando was named Best Actor for *The Godfather.* Brando's contempt for Hollywood had been a known fact for a long time. Upon making his first film, *The Men,*

Brando shocked the press when he stated that his only motive for being in Hollywood was his lack of courage to reject the tremendous amounts of money he was offered to make films. But somehow people got used to Brando's eccentricities, viewing them as part of his genius and personality. Besides, Brando was such a brilliant actor that he could get away with outrageous statements. Brando's derisive attitudes toward Hollywood didn't damage his career at all; they made him even more alluring and mysterious to the press, an image that he forcefully encouraged.

Prior to *The Godfather*, Brando was nominated five times for Best Actor, the last for *Sayonara*, which he made because he identified with the film's plea for racial understanding. In the 1960s, looking for interesting vehicles, Brando appeared in *Candy*, in which he played a guru; *Reflections in a Golden Eye*, playing a latently gay serviceman; and *The Countess from Hong Kong* (directed by Chaplin), as an American diplomat. Most of these films failed artistically and commercially.

Just when filmmakers declared Brando a has-been, he delivered a brilliant comeback performance, as Don Corleone in *The Godfather*, for which he was forced to take a screen test for the first time in his career. Paramount was at first reluctant to cast Brando in the lead role, holding that he had lost his box-office power, but his test was so convincing that he could hardly even be recognized!

Brando's performance got rave reviews and numerous awards. However, he turned down his sixth Oscar nomination with a short telegram: "There is singular lack of honor in this country today." The Oscar, according to columnist Bob Thomas, was an emotional gesture, "a sense of reaffirmation of an admittedly great, but wayward actor who had become alienated by and with Hollywood." It was a strange signal, to say the least, a welcome home extended to an actor who in no way wished to be welcomed home.

At the Oscar ceremonies, applause followed when Brando was announced the Best Actor. Thereupon, as noted earlier, a young Native American woman named Sacheen Littlefeather walked to the podium and read a statement from him. Brando voiced his protest against the treatment of Indians, on- and off-screen, through an Apache member of the Native American Affirmative Image Committee. He wrote: "I, as a member of this profession, do not feel that I can as a citizen of the United States accept an award here tonight. I think awards in this country at this time are inappropriate to be received or given until the condition of the American Indian is drastically altered." And he closed his speech with "if we are not our brother's keeper, at least let us not be his executioner."

Brando was criticized by those who felt he should have at least refused the award in person, not use an innocent girl. Brando later explained that he was on his way to Wounded Knee to support the Oglala Sioux's protest against discrimination. At the same time, Brando's rejection of the Oscar did not surprise those who knew him — and it didn't meet with unanimous criticism. During the same show, Oscar-winning writer Jeremy Larner, who wrote Robert Redford's political drama, *The Candidate*, could not resist the temptation of ridiculing President Richard Nixon, then in the midst of the Watergate scandal.

Said Larner, "I would like to thank the political figures of our time, who have given me terrific inspiration."

The next explosive incident occurred at the 1975 show, when Burt Schneider and Peter Davis were cited for their anti-Vietnam documentary, *Hearts and Minds*. In his acceptance speech, Schneider read a wire from a Vietcong leader: "Please transmit to all our friends in America our recognition of all they have done on behalf of peace for the application of the Paris Accords on Vietnam." This blatant propaganda outraged many viewers, who called NBC in anger. Consequently, Frank Sinatra, one of the show's emcees, was asked by the Academy to make the following statement: "We are not responsible for any political references made on this program tonight, and we are sorry that they are made." This was the first time that the Academy had taken an explicit stand as an organization against propaganda voiced on its platform.

After several years of controversy, the 1976 Oscar show was smooth and quiet. The magazine *Films in Review* described the ceremony as "negatively notable, no protests, no winners refusing awards, no political speeches, no surprises."

However, the following year saw another casualty of the McCarthy era, playwright Lillian Hellman, restored to legitimacy. Hellman's career suffered in the 1950s, after a successful decade in Hollywood as a screenwriter, during which she adapted to the big screen some of her Broadway plays, including *The Little Foxes*. Hellman was declared an uncooperative witness when she refused to testify before the Committee, sending her now-famous, often quoted letter. (Hellman has remained a controversial figure from both sides.)

The invitation to participate in the show, as presenter of the writing awards, was yet another attempt by the New Hollywood to offer reconciliation to the victims of the McCarthy era. Following an emotional standing ovation, which caught her by surprise, Hellman said: "My second reason for being here is perhaps only important to me. I was once upon a time a respectable member of this community. Respectable didn't necessarily mean more than I took a daily bath when I was sober, didn't spit except when I meant to, and mispronounced a few words of fancy French. Then suddenly, even before Senator Joseph McCarthy reached for that rusty, poisoned ax, I and many others were no longer acceptable to the owners of this industry. They confronted the wild charges of Joe McCarthy with a force and courage of a bowl of mashed potatoes." She then concluded: "I have a mischievous pleasure in being restored to respectability, understanding full well that the younger generation who asked me here tonight meant more by that invitation than my name or my history."

Warren Beatty, one of the show's co-hosts, remarked: "When I saw who was on this show tonight, Lillian Hellman, Norman Mailer, Jane Fonda, Donald Sutherland, I thought maybe the nicest thing to do was to say a few nice things about Reagan and Goldwater." Beatty, of course, could not know then that in two years Ronald Reagan would be elected President and would hold the office with great popularity for two terms.

A scandalous incident took place during the 1978 ceremonies, when Vanessa Redgrave won the Supporting Oscar for *Julia*. Before the show began, members of the Jewish Defense League (JDL) picketed outside the Dorothy Chandler Pavilion, protesting Redgrave's involvement in *The Palestinians*, an anti-Zionist documentary. Redgrave had taken an anti-Israeli stand when she became an outspoken proponent of the Palestine Liberation Organization (PLO). Neither the JDL signs, stating "Redgrave and Arafat: A Perfect Love Affair," and "Hell No to Vanessa Redgrave and the PLO," nor the PLO signs, "Vanessa: A Woman of Conscience and Courage," were seen by the TV viewers. The police and special security managed to keep the two groups apart and away from the media.

Redgrave's views sharply divided the industry. Jewish producers, heavily represented in Hollywood, supported artists' rights to express freely their opinions offscreen. JDL's demand from Fox, which produced *Julia*, never to hire Redgrave again and to repudiate her support of the PLO, were dismissed by the studio and the Screen Actors Guild. The studio's reaction was: "While Fox as a company and the individuals who work there do not agree with Redgrave's political philosophy, we totally reject and we will not be blackmailed into supporting any policy of refusing to employ any person because of their political beliefs." Redgrave's performance in *Julia* was brilliant, and it followed three previously nominated roles, in *Morgan, Isadora,* and *Mary, Queen of Scots.* Moreover, the 1977 competition in the supporting category was weak: Leslie Brown in *The Turning Point,* Quinn Cummings in *The Goodbye Girl,* Melinda Dillon in *Close Encounters of the Third Kind,* and Tuesday Weld in *Looking for Mr. Goodbar.*

The Academy's officials expected Redgrave to make a political speech if she won, and they did not mind when she spoke about the meaning of *Julia* for her: "I think Jane Fonda and I have done the best work of our lives, and I think this was in part due to our director, Fred Zinnemann. I also think it is in part because we believed in what we were expressing: Two out of millions who gave their lives and were prepared to sacrifice everything in the fight against fascist racist Nazi Germany." But then Redgrave proceeded with an impassioned propagandistic speech: "You should be very proud that in the last few weeks you stood firm and you refused to be intimidated by the threats of a small bunch of Zionist hoodlums whose behavior is an insult to the stature of Jews all over the world and to their great and heroic record against fascism and oppression. I salute that record and I salute all of you for having stood firm and dealt the final blow against that period when Nixon and McCarthy launched a worldwide witch hunt against those who tried to express in their lives and their work the truths that they believed in." And with a resolute attitude, she concluded: "I salute you and I thank you, and I pledge to you that I'll continue to fight against anti-Semitism and fascism."

Paddy Chayefsky, who presented the writing awards, chastised Redgrave: "I'm sick and tired of people exploiting the occasion of the Academy Awards for the propagation of their own political propaganda. Redgrave's win is not a pivotal moment in history, and doesn't require a proclamation." Charlton

Heston, who had voted for Redgrave, reflected many people's opinion when he said, "I thought it as much an error to interject what amounted to political commentary into her acceptance remarks as it was an error for people to oppose her nomination on political grounds." Redgrave's win was interpreted as yet another sign of the New Hollywood's "maturity" — it is unlikely that she would have won the Oscar in the 1950s.

Redgrave's politics were at the center of another controversy a few months later when she was cast as an Auschwitz concentration camp survivor in *Playing for Time,* Arthur Miller's television drama based on Fania Fenelon's memoir. This time, her casting drew sharp protests from the Jewish community and the entertainment industry alike. Rabbi Marvin Hier said it was like "selecting Edgar Hoover to portray Martin Luther King," and Sammy Davis Jr. felt "It would be like me playing the head of the Ku Klux Klan." Dore Schary, MGM's former chief and honorary chairman of the Anti-Defamation League, charged CBS with "a profound lack of sensitivity and understanding," calling the casting "a trick and a stunt."

In their defensive response, the producers said other actresses, such as Barbra Streisand and Jane Fonda, were considered for the part, and that Redgrave was the best actress available. Besides, some actresses refused to shave their heads, as was required by the role. The producers reiterated their philosophy that performers should not be penalized for their personal views, and that it was a matter of principle to remove politics from artistic decisions. Once again, Redgrave's performance was nothing short of splendid, earning her a well-deserved Emmy Award.

In 1982, following a storm of protests from subscribers and musicians, the Boston Symphony Orchestra canceled its performances of Stravinsky's *Oedipus Rex,* which were to feature Vanessa Redgrave. Other than that, Redgrave's politics have not marred her getting work. She continued to be cast in desirable roles, including *The Bostonians,* as Olive Chancellor, a wealthy suffragette, for which she received a fifth Oscar nomination and the National Society of Film Critics Award, and in David Hare's *Wetherby,* as the emotionally stifled teacher, for which she won another National Society of Film Award. Andrew Sarris noted, "I would have given the Oscar to Vanessa Redgrave for *Wetherby,* but I don't know if I would have waited around for her acceptance speech."

The uproar surrounding *Julia* was barely forgotten, when another dispute erupted in the 1979 ceremonies, caused by the nomination of two Vietnam War films for Best Picture: Michael Cimino's *The Deer Hunter* and Hal Ashby's *Coming Home,* each garnering a large number of nominations. Unlike World War II, which saw the immediate production of war films, it took almost a decade for Hollywood to make movies about Vietnam. The only exception was John Wayne's *The Green Berets,* in 1968, an unabashedly patriotic picture endorsing the American involvement in Vietnam. Both studios, Universal in the case of *The Deer Hunter,* and United Artists in *Coming Home,* had fears that the public would not support them, though they were proud of their artistic quality: *The Deer Hunter* opened to rave reviews, and *Coming Home* to mixed-to-positive reviews.

The Academy voters split the major awards between the two movies. *The Deer Hunter* won five: Best Picture, Director (Cimino), Supporting Actor (Christopher Walken), sound, and editing; and *Coming Home* received the two lead acting awards (Jane Fonda and Jon Voight), and Original Screenplay (Waldo Salt and Robert C. Jones, using Nancy Dowd's story). Ironically, John Wayne was chosen as the Best Picture presenter, though one could only speculate how he felt about handing it in to *The Deer Hunter;* this time, the Duke kept his mouth shut!

During the ceremonies, there were demonstrations outside the auditorium, mostly against the racist overtones of *The Deer Hunter,* and some in favor of the humanism of *Coming Home.* Director Cimino was accused of violating both historical truth and artistic responsibility, though he claimed that his aim was to make a dramatic picture about surviving the war. "My film has nothing to do with whether the war should or should not have been," he said. "This film addresses itself to the question of ordinary people of this country, who journeyed from their homes to the darkness and back. How do you survive that?" *The Deer Hunter* is a movie, Cimino explained, "It is not a newsreel."

But Cimino's rationale didn't pacify his critics. On the night of the awards, the police arrested members of "Vietnam Veterans Against the War," who protested against the film's misinterpretation of reality. Another dissenting group, "Hell No, We Won't Go Away Committee," denounced the film as "a racist attack on the Vietnamese people," citing the vicious violence, particularly the Russian Roulette sequences, used by the Vietnamese in the prison camp.

"We didn't want the film to be honored blindly," said Linda Garrett, who formed the Committee. "Even my progressive friends seemed blinded by the power of the film, its emotional impact. They felt it was a great film despite its racism, despite its misinterpretation of history." Other critics charged that the Americans were portrayed as innocent victims, which eliminated any discussion of the war's issues. A shocked Cimino continued to insist that his intention was to make an antiwar statement.

Furthermore, the winners' speeches and off-camera remarks were seen as violations of collegial professional ethics. Jane Fonda charged that *The Deer Hunter* was a racist film that represented the Pentagon's view of Vietnam. Referring to the demonstrators as "my friends," she said that *Coming Home* was a "better picture," even though she had not seen *The Deer Hunter.* And after winning the Best Actor for playing a sensitive paraplegic war veteran, Jon Voight said, "I accept this for every guy in a wheelchair."

Global politics have also entered the Oscar ceremonies through the nomination of foreign film and foreign artists. As was noted, the Polish government didn't approve of Roman Polanski's stunning debut, *Knife in the Water,* which was nominated for the 1963 Best Foreign-Language Picture, a denouncement that motivated the artist to leave his home country for Hollywood.

In 1981, the Hungarian producer of the Best Animated Short, *The Fly,* was unable to obtain a visa to attend the show. Instead, an official of the Hungarian Embassy in the United States was authorized to represent him, showing again how intricate the connection between politics and film is.

Documentaries and foreign films are more explicitly political than mainstream American features. The nominated foreign films are political in another way, given the particular regulations that govern this category. Films are sent for consideration by the equivalent academies of foreign countries. A particular form of censorship often comes into play, when a given country objects to sending a good film that is critical of its government, as was the case of *Man of Iron.* And conversely, foreign films are at times chosen because they project positive images of their respective countries.

Indeed, the Best Foreign-Language Picture category is particularly vulnerable to political pressures. Four of the five nominees of the 1985 Best Foreign-Language Picture were political works with strong ideological messages. The winner, the Argentinean *The Official Story,* is a disturbing emotional drama about an upper-middle class history teacher (played by Norma Aleandro), who suspects that her adopted daughter is a child of one of the "desaparecidos," the Argentineans abducted during the junta's counterinsurgency. In his speech, the film's producer Luis Perenzo said: "On another March 24, ten years ago, we suffered the last military coup in my country. We will never forget this nightmare, but we are certain now to begin with our new dreams."

The Official Story competed against the Yugoslavian entry, *When Father Was Away on Business,* a family tale set in Sarajevo in the 1950s, when the country was torn between Marshal Tito's policies and the Stalinist Soviet Union. The other nominees were the Hungarian film, *Colonel Redl,* about Alfred Redl, the powerful intelligence officer of the Austro-Hungarian Empire who, according to the movie, when threatened by the Russians with public revelation of his homosexuality, agreed to become their agent, then committed suicide. *Angry Harvest* was a psychological World War II drama about the relationship between a Jewish woman escaping the Nazis and a devout Polish farmer. The French comedy *Three Men and a Cradle* was the fifth contender, a film dealing with changing definitions of gender, particularly male roles.

Year after year, explicitly political remarks appear in the presenters' or winners' speeches. In March 1992, demonstrators outside the Oscar show waved signs that read "Stop Hollywood's Homophobia," and "Make Queer Films." Protesters complained about the negative portrayal of gays in *The Silence of the Lambs* and *JFK* (both Best Picture nominees), and *Basic Instinct,* which had just opened theatrically, a movie in which a bisexual killer uses an ice pick to slay her male lovers. Inside the auditorium, the ceremony was disrupted briefly during a commercial, when a tuxedoed man shouted statistics about Hollywood's neglect of the AIDS epidemic. Security guards pulled him from the auditorium, and TV viewers never saw or heard the incident.

There are also surprising and touching moments that reflect a different kinds of politics. One occurred in the 1996 show. Director Kary Antholis, the winner of the Documentary Short Subject, *One Survivor Remembers,* brought on stage the subject of his film, an old woman by the name of Gerda Weissmann Klein. Ms. Klein didn't leave the podium after her director's speech, and she decided to ignore the not-too-subtle music. Instead, she spoke in a determined voice:

> I have been in a place for six incredible years where winning meant a crust of bread and to live another day. Since the day of my liberation, I have asked myself the question, Why am I here? I am no better. I see those years, and those who never lived to see the magic of a boring night at home. On their behalf, I wish to thank you for honoring their memory. And you cannot do it in any better way than when you go to your homes tonight, to realize that all of you who know the joys of freedom are winners.

The show's director couldn't anticipate such a moment, but he was ready with his cameras to bring Klein's touching face in a big close-up to millions of viewers all over the world.

The same year, the winner of the Best Documentary Feature Oscar was also about the Holocaust, John Blair's *Anne Frank Remembered.* After thanking Steven Spielberg "without whose eleventh-hour intervention, I would never have been able to make this film," Blair introduced the real hero of Anne Frank's tale, Miep Gies, the Dutch woman who found the diary in the Franks's apartment — a diary which provided the basis of a book, play, and a movie, as well as this documentary. That Anne Frank loved movies and intended to visit Hollywood one day made the moment all the more special.

Over the past decades, various issues have been propagated on the Oscar podium. Oliver Stone, whose adapted screenplay for *Midnight Express* won an Oscar, said, "I hope this would lead to some consideration for all the men and women who are still in prison." Presenter Richard Gere made a plea, asking viewers to gather their vibes and drive the Chinese out of Tibet. And politically oriented actor-companions Tim Robbins and Susan Sarandon interrupted the scheduled programming to urge the United States to allow HIV-positive Haitians into the country.

Some critics think that turning the annual Oscar ceremonies into a political platform diminishes the prestige of the award and spoils the fun of the show itself. However, it would be a mistake to think that there will be no more political incidents or controversies in the future. Whether the Academy likes it or not, the Oscar ceremonies are bound to have explosive political occurrences due to film's inherent nature as a political medium and to the event's extraordinary exposure. After all, what other public occasion provides a captive and attentive audience of so many viewers?

21

NOBLE AND HEROIC—
OSCAR'S MIDDLEBROW SENSIBILITY

The Message's the Thing

There's talk that the motion picture we honor tonight may win a Nobel Prize. —Louis B. Mayer

Historical and political factors have always influenced the types of films and performances winning the Oscars. In other words, the social context, zeitgeist, and message are far more influential than the artistic quality in determining the winners.

From the first year, ideological considerations were taken into account. Carl Laemmle, head of Universal, spent over $1 million to film Erich Maria Remarque's antiwar novel, *All Quiet on the Western Front*. It concerns a group of German schoolboys who enlist in the army at the outbreak of World War I and become disillusioned as they face the reality of combat. The American Legion and other organizations were concerned about the sympathetic portrayal of Germans, but the movie became both a critical and commercial success.

It was a prestige production: Lewis Milestone directed and Broadway's noted playwrights, Maxwell Anderson and George Abbott, wrote the screenplay. *All Quiet on the Western Front* was nominated for four awards and won the Best Picture. When Louis B. Mayer handed the Best Picture Oscar to *All Quiet,* he solemnly said: "There's talk that the motion picture we honor tonight may win a Nobel Prize."

Indeed, the League of Nations could make no better or nobler ambassador for peace than *All Quiet,* or Warners' pictures of the era, for that matter. Prime among them was *Disraeli,* for which George Arliss, billed as "the first gentleman of the talking screen," and promoted by the studio as an important history lesson. The same could be said for the 1937 Oscar winner, *The Story of Emile Zola,* which, as noted also evidenced morality, respectability, and good taste, all the requirements — and qualities — that Will Hays, head of the industry's self-censorship board, lectured about at the 1929 show.

Citizen Kane

No other film in American history might better illuminate the intimate, complex, and intriguing interplay between studio politics and societal politics than *Citizen Kane*. Contrary to popular belief, the merits of *Citizen Kane* were recognized at the time, though not as fully as they should have been. It was gossip columnist Louella Parsons who began spreading the rumor, after seeing an advance preview, that *Citizen Kane* was "a repulsive biography" of her employer, William Randolph Hearst (played by Orson Welles). Hearst accepted her view at face value, without even seeing the movie, but because there was nothing libelous about it, all he could do was to demand that RKO shelve the movie and threaten to withdraw the support of his press empire from Hollywood. There was some talk to can *Citizen Kane,* and its release was postponed a number of times until it finally opened in May 1941. RKO had problems persuading theaters to book the movie, and Hearst's newspapers boycotting ads didn't help.

Citizen Kane received mostly good reviews, though it failed commercially across the nation. At Oscar nomination time, in January 1942, shortly after the United States declared war on Germany, *Citizen Kane* was hardly overlooked by the industry. The film was nominated for nine Oscars, including Best Picture, and Orson Welles received three nominations, as co-screenwriter (with Joseph L. Mankiewicz), director, and actor. The cinematography, editing, music, sound, and art direction also received nominations.

But the competition for Best Picture in 1941 was extremely intense: *Citizen Kane* was up against no fewer than nine other pictures: *Blossoms in the Dust* (four nominations), *Here Comes Mr. Jordan* (seven), *Hold Back the Dawn* (six), *How Green Was My Valley* (ten), *The Little Foxes* (nine), *The Maltese Falcon* (three), *One Foot in Heaven* (one), *Sergeant York* (eleven), and *Suspicion* (three). With so many good films in the race, it was inevitable that the Oscars would be spread among several films and that some excellent films would leave the ceremony empty-handed.

To the Academy's credit, the winning film, John Ford's *How Green Was My Valley* (sweeping five awards), might not have been a landmark in American film history, but it was an exquisitely executed movie with a strong visual component. It also dramatized more acceptable values and a more traditional morality than *Citizen Kane*. Ford's movie was chosen for various reasons: Its popular ideology cherishing the sacredness of the family (after all, the country was at war), as well as its aesthetic merits and fine acting.

Citizen Kane, by contrast, was dumped because of its downbeat, pessimistic message, Hearst's power in Hollywood, and Welles's status as an outsider. There is no doubt that *Citizen Kane*'s cinematic merits were not sufficiently recognized at the time. But this had as much to do with its revolutionary innovations, which were well ahead of their time, as with the dispute with Hearst. Furthermore, Welles was young, twenty-six, and a newcomer in Hollywood: *Citizen Kane* was his very first movie.

Ironically, the film's most controversial element, its screenplay, was the only category honored by the Academy. At the same time, William Wyler's *The Little Foxes* was another distinguished movie that lost out in each of its nine nominations. And John Huston's directorial debut, *The Maltese Falcon,* another classic of its kind, also failed to receive any award.

World War II Wins Oscars

World War II had a major impact on the film industry, influencing both subject matter and style of the films produced. About one-third of Hollywood's output (five hundred out of seventeen hundred films) between 1942 and 1945 dealt directly or indirectly with the war. Ultimately, most of these movies were more important historically than artistically, fulfilling, as Ken Jones and Arthur McLure have observed, a twofold goal: "to give unity of purpose for the war itself, and to give strength of purpose to the people on the home front." Heavily propagandistic, these movies served as morale boosters, dealing with issues that were of interest to most Americans at the time. Viewers often perceived and enjoyed these films as flag-wavers, refusing to apply to them any critical or artistic yardsticks.

All of the Oscar categories were influenced by the war, but especially the major ones: Best Picture, Best Director, the acting, and the writing awards. The male acting Oscars, as could be expected, were more determined by the war experience — the war film is a typically "masculine" genre. Four of the Best Actors in the 1940s were chosen for a role in a war-themed movie: Gary Cooper in *Sergeant York,* James Cagney in *Yankee Doodle Dandy,* Paul Lukas in *Watch on the Rhine,* Fredric March in *The Best Years of Our Lives.*

By contrast, only one Best Actress, Greer Garson in *Mrs. Miniver,* won for a film about the war. In fact, some of the female winners during the war were honored for stereotypical roles, such as victimized wives played by Joan Fontaine in *Suspicion* and Ingrid Bergman in *Gaslight.* Seen historically, these roles were traditional, unusual perhaps since for the first time in American history women directly participated in the economy during the war years.

The only Oscar-winning role that reflected the conflict between career and domesticity, which many American women must have faced at the end of the war was Joan Crawford's in *Mildred Pierce.* Though as noted, at the end of the movie the protagonist is punished for having stepped into a male world and is sent back to the kitchen, relegated to the traditionally female role of housewife-mother.

During the war, many films were lavishly praised by the critics and embraced by the public more for their patriotic rather than artistic values. Three films about the war won Best Picture: *Mrs. Miniver* in 1942, *Casablanca* in 1943, and *The Best Years of Our Lives* in 1946.

Mrs. Miniver, the least distinguished of the three, at once reflected and reinforced the mood of the home front through its description of a typical British family during the Blitz. Reviewers pointed out that it was actually the war, not the film, that earned the Academy votes. Released in July 1942, *Mrs. Miniver* became a blockbuster, and its six Oscars made it the most talked about movie of the year.

The war on pseudo-war films suited the times. Howard Hawks's *Sergeant York* reflected America's dominant ideology in July 1941, just months prior to the country's entry into the war. Its hero, Alvin York, starts as a conscientious objector and ends up totally committed to the cause of the World War I, a transformation that articulated the feelings of millions of Americans who initially were reluctant to join the fighting in Europe.

Celebrating George M. Cohan's life, *Yankee Doodle Dandy* was released in May 1942, just as American soldiers departed to fight in Europe. "What could be more timely," wrote the critic Patrick McGilligan, "than to have recalled for us the career of America's lustiest flag-waver."

Casablanca, the 1943 Oscar winner, was even more relevant in its message. The movie was released after the city of Casablanca had been chosen as the site of the Allied Forces Conference. The movie boasted a glorious cast headed by Humphrey Bogart, Ingrid Bergman, Claude Rains, and Paul Henreid. It is the movie that made Bogart an international star, crystallizing his immortal screen image as Rick Blain, the most famous café owner in film history. *Casablanca* was not a major box-office hit in its initial release, but over the years it has attained a status of a classic. In a recent American Film Institute (AFI) poll, *Casablanca* was chosen as one of the three most popular American films of all time.

William Wyler's *The Best Years of Our Lives* would have won Oscars in any year. However, released in 1946, it, too, cashed in on its timely issues: The adjustment problems of war veterans to civilian life. As shown, the inspiration for this movie came from an article in *Time* magazine.

The nominations and awards given to films about the war reflected profound changes in American society. In 1941, only one of the six major Oscars went to a war film: Gary Cooper in *Sergeant York.* In 1942 and 1943, five out of the six awards; the exceptions were Supporting Actor Van Heflin in the crime melodrama *Johnny Eager* (1942), and Ingrid Bergman in *Gaslight* (1943). In 1944, two of the Best Picture nominees were socially relevant: David O. Selznick's *Since You Went Away* (a pale, American imitation of *Mrs. Miniver*) and Fox's political drama *Wilson,* a dull, pompous biopicture.

Most of the writing awards in the 1940s also honored war movies: Emeric Pressburger won Original Story for *The Invaders;* the four screenwriters of *Mrs. Miniver;* William Saroyan for his original story *The Human Comedy;* the three screenwriters of *Casablanca;* Lamar Trotti for his original screenplay *Wilson;* and Charles G. Booth for the original script of Henry Hathaway's *The House on 92nd Street,* which depicts the destruction of a spy ring in America by the FBI.

After *The Best Years of Our Lives,* however, the war was quickly forgotten by Hollywood and by the Academy. In 1946, the Best Picture nominees included Olivier's *Henry V* and the spiritual melodrama, *The Razor's Edge,* based on

Somerset Maugham's book. Spiritualism, or rather pseudo-spiritualism, was also in vogue in 1947, with such nominated comedies as *The Bishop's Wife* and *Miracle on 34th Street.* These contrasted David Lean's literary adaptation, *Great Expectations.* A combination of prestige literary adaptations and middle-brow fare reappeared in 1948 with Olivier's *Hamlet,* Jean Negulesco's *Johnny Belinda,* and the British ballet melodrama, *The Red Shoes.*

The Oscars' Fear of McCarthy

The second era in which politics impinged directly on the Oscars was in the early 1950s, during Senator Joseph McCarthy's second round of Hollywood investigations — the first was in 1947. Most of the winning films in those years could be described as light, escapist fare. In sharp contrast to the 1940s, in which the Oscar honored socially relevant films, just a few years later Hollywood was so fearful of McCarthy that it went to the other extreme, honoring films that had little to do with the surrounding political reality. The 1950 Best Picture nominees included tales about Hollywood (*Sunset Boulevard*), the New York theater (*All About Eve*), a witty comedy with social messages (*Born Yesterday*), a family comedy about marriage and suburbia (*Father of the Bride*), and an adventure set in the African jungles (*King Solomon's Mines*).

The Oscar winners of 1951 and 1952 were also nonpolitical, escapist entertainment, showing again the Academy's fear of voting for films that were critical of the American Way of Life. MGM's musical, *An American in Paris,* inspired by George Gershwin's celebrated score, won the 1951 Best Picture, competing against such serious films as George Stevens's *A Place in the Sun,* based on Theodore Dreiser's novel, *An American Tragedy,* and Elia Kazan's powerful version of Tennessee Williams's *A Streetcar Named Desire.* The win must have surprised MGM itself, for the next day it took out ads in the trades that showed Leo the Lion smirking coyly at the Oscar statuette, with the caption reading: HONESTLY, I WAS JUST STANDING IN THE SUN WAITING FOR A STREETCAR.

The 1952 Best Picture, Cecil B. DeMille's circus adventure-melodrama, *The Greatest Show on Earth,* unaccountably won the Best Picture over Fred Zinnemann's psychological Western, *High Noon,* and John Ford's picturesque romance, *The Quiet Man. High Noon,* which was earlier cited by the New York Film Critics, earned the largest number of nominations, seven. The movie probably lost the important prizes for political rather than artistic reasons. More than a few critics perceive *High Noon* as an allegory of American foreign policy during the Korean War. Marshal Kane (Cooper) is eager to achieve peace after cleaning up the town five years earlier (World War II), but reluctantly, he's forced to face a new aggression (the Korean War). According to this ideological reading, the Quaker wife (played by Grace Kelly) stands in for the American pacifists and isolationists, though she too change her mind and ends up supporting her husband's cause. At the end, she violates her principles and kills to save her husband. In this and other messages, *High Noon* propagated the widely acceptable idea that war in certain circumstances may be both moral and inevitable.

The critic Philip French regards *High Noon* as a liberal statement, the archetypal Kennedy Western, standing in sharp contrast to *Rio Bravo,* which he considers the archetypal Barry Goldwater, right-wing Western. Considered in this light, *High Noon* is seen as an existential parable about a conscientious man, Marshal Kane, who stands alone to defend his moral principles in the McCarthy era. The townsfolk, who refuse to help the marshal, desert him one by one, and are viewed as prototypes of the American masses, people who are afraid to stand up and fight for their rights.

These particular readings may or may not be valid, but most commentators would at the very least agree that *High Noon* deals with civic responsibility, passive versus active involvement in public life, and heroic behavior in political crises — all issues with explicitly political overtones in the 1950s. The filmmakers responsible for *High Noon,* producer Stanley Kramer, director Fred Zinnemann, and screenwriter Carl Foreman, were all known for their liberal politics. This was Foreman's last Hollywood film, after which he was forced into exile to England.

Cooper, known for his Republican leanings, claimed to be unaware of the political message imbued in his role. But some of Cooper's colleagues, like John Wayne, objected strongly to the film's message, claiming that the rugged men of the West, who fought nature and the Indians would unite — not cower — in the face of four villains. In a 1971 *Playboy* interview, Wayne described *High Noon* as "the most un-American thing I've ever seen in my whole life," referring to "ol' Coop putting the marshal's badge under his foot and stepping on it." Proud of his patriotic politics, the Duke declared, "I'll never regret having helped run Foreman out of this country."

The Oscar during Vietnam

Arguably the worst movies in the Academy's history were nominated for the Best Picture in the late 1960s and early 1970s, mostly escapist entertainment, perhaps in counter-reaction to the daily TV reportage of Vietnam carnage, the "Living Room War" as Michael Arlen has noted, and the first visual war in American history.

The downbeat mood of Sydney Pollack's *They Shoot Horses, Don't They?* must have worked against its inclusion in the 1969 Best Picture contest, despite the fact that it was critically acclaimed and nominated for nine awards, including Jane Fonda for the lead, and Susannah York and Gig Young for the supporting categories. Its omission among the five top contenders was conspicuous. Based on Horace McCoy's Depression-era novel, the narrative depicts a harrowing six-day marathon dance contest, stressing the fantasies, illusions, and madness of young people in Los Angeles of the early 1930s. The shabby locale and despair of the characters, most notably of Gloria (Jane Fonda), a suicidal would-be actress, and another starlet (Susannah York), whose fantasy is to be the next Jean

Harlow, must have depressed the Academy. In 1969, voters favored lighthearted fare such as *Hello, Dolly!* and *Butch Cassidy and the Sundance Kid* for Best Picture nominees over Pollack's disturbing parable.

Gandhi versus *Tootsie*

That Academy members, like ordinary moviegoers, tend to judge a film by the importance of its subject and relevance of its issues was also clear in 1982, when Richard Attenborough's *Gandhi* swept most of the Oscars. Cinematically, it is a rather conventional, solemn biography of the noble political figure, lacking epic scope and visual imagination. *Gandhi* could have been a better movie had it been directed by a more subtle and inventive filmmaker like David Lean. However, Mohandas Gandhi was so inspirational and his anti-violent preaching so timely in the context of the 1980s that Academy voters favored the movie over Steven Spielberg's *E.T.* and Sidney Lumet's *The Verdict.*

Once again, Sydney Pollack lost the Oscar for the wrong reasons. His comedy, *Tootsie,* was accomplished on every level, but it lacked the noble intent and "important" theme that *Gandhi* delivered. The *New York Times* critic Vincent Canby described *Gandhi* as having "the air of an important news event, something that is required reading." Faulting it for its earnestness, Canby wrote: "All films about saintly men tend to look alike, even though the men themselves may be radically different." But Canby understood the Academy's motivation: "To honor a film like *Gandhi,* a perfectly reverent if unexceptional film about an exceptional man, they are paying their dues to the race (human), certifying their instincts (good), and also the belief that movies about worthy subjects can make money.

Variety's chief editor, Peter Bart, recalled: "Frankly, I was aghast, when *Gandhi* beat out *E.T.* and *Tootsie.* I felt my colleagues in the Academy were so eager to vote with their heads they abandoned their hearts." It is worth noting that the Academy's taste didn't differ much from the critics'. *Gandhi* opened to almost unanimously favorable reviews. The only dissenting voices among the major critics were Andrew Sarris and Pauline Kael. And it won the New York Film Critics, the National Board of Review, and the Golden Globe awards. However, there was no consensus among critics that year: The Los Angeles Film Critics cited *E.T.* as Best Picture, and the National Society cited *Tootsie.*

The Oscars: Politically Correct Entertainment?

The Oscar contests in 2000 and 2001 were again as much about politics as about art. It's always been that way. How else would you explain that, year after year, the films nominated for Best Picture — and especially those that win — are not necessarily the most artistically distinguished, but those whose ideological messages are timely and widely accepted. More than other films, the Oscar nominees may serve as America's storehouse of recorded values.

So, judging by the five nominated films, what was the country's mood at the dawn of the new millennium? With the notable exception of *Traffic,* Steven Soderbergh's richly complex chronicle of the drug war, the other four nominees represent safe and noble entertainment, a throwback to old-fashioned fare. They were movies that integrate with varying degrees of success new and sophisticated technology into rather conventional and crowd-pleasing narratives, a trend epitomized in 1997 by the Oscar-winning blockbuster *Titanic.*

Who will disagree today with the anti-big business message of *Erin Brockovich,* a well-made biopicture centering on a working-class woman, a classic American underdog, who, with feisty determination and commitment to the cause, triumphs against all odds. That's safe and noble entertainment. In its crowd-pleasing qualities and bravura star performance by Julia Roberts, *Erin Brockovich* offers a similar message — and emotional pleasure — of *Norma Rae,* Martin Ritt's 1979 biopicture that earned Sally Field her first Best Actress.

Lasse Hallstrom's fluffy, insubstantial *Chocolat* is the kind of compassionately humanistic film that's not only old-fashioned in its values and looks, but also set in the past — in this case a remote French village in the early 1950s. Structured as a romantic fable, basically a fairy tale, it cherishes similar values to those flaunted a year earlier in Miramax's Oscar-nominated *The Cider House Rules,* also directed by Hallstrom and also set in the past. *Chocolat* is an enjoyable, well-acted film whose liberal anti-censorship, anti-repression morals are both timeless and universal, but there's nothing challenging about it.

The Academy's most audacious act in the 2000 race was nominating Ang Lee's *Crouching Tiger, Hidden Dragon,* a foreign-language film, for the Best Picture and nine other categories — an all-time record in the Oscar's annals. Yet once you overcome the shock of novelty — after all, as we have seen, only a few foreign films have garnered Best Picture nomination — it's easy to understand the members' motivation. A hybrid action-romance-costume drama, *Crouching Tiger* shrewdly positions at its center two bright and beautiful women who are just as expertly skilled in martial arts as their male counterparts. Moreover, once the resistance to a subtitled film (and Mandarin at that) is surmounted, it's easy to understand why the movie broke box-office records, conquering the American heartland where foreign fare is seldom shown.

One can't deny the good, honorable politics behind voting for a film like *Crouching Tiger,* particularly in a year which featured no black-themed movies and few performers of color. Showering this film with multiple nominations addressed PC cultural diversity, and a global one at that, and showed respect and hospitality to a talented ensemble from Asia, which has become a major market for American movies. It also provided compensation for snubbing *Crouching Tiger*'s gifted helmer, Ang Lee, who had never been nominated, despite the fact that his 1995 literary comedy, *Sense and Sensibility,* was singled out in seven categories, winning Adapted Screenplay for Emma Thompson, its star.

Of the five nominees, *Traffic* stands out both for its stylistic innovation, and its attempt to deal with the contentious issue of drug wars across the American and Mexican borders. Yet a closer look at Soderbergh's ambitious movie, which tells not one but three stories, shows that it, too, is a compromising and old-fashioned narrative, albeit in a different way from *Erin Brockovich,* Soderbergh's other nominated contender.

Traffic may well have been the most exciting and complex American movie of the year, but it's marred by a soft and balanced last reel that somehow negates the story's predominantly tough and bleak tone. In treating a polemic issue in a personalized, individualistic manner, by centering on the intergenerational strain between a new drug kingpin, played by Michael Douglas, and his drug-addicted teenage daughter, *Traffic* follows the tradition of most social-problem films (*All the President's Men, The China Syndrome, Wall Street*) that reduces and deflates ills of the social system to more easily comprehendible individual problems.

Film after film suggests that any problem, political or economic, can be treated and often resolved in individual terms by an ordinary personality. Never mind that "ordinary" in Hollywood terms means casting an attractive star like Jane Fonda and Robert Redford in the past, and more recently Julia Roberts in *Erin Brockovich,* and Michael Douglas and Catherine Zeta-Jones in *Traffic.* As *Traffic*'s multilayered story unfolds, the initially established mysteries, double meanings, and ambiguities gradually give way to an orderly narrative that goes out of its way not to upset its viewers too much. That's good entertainment, and good box office. Is there a better combination?

The same priorities dominated the 2001 Oscar race, when the Academy favored the inspirational, noble and upbeat — Ron Howard's *A Beautiful Mind* — over the ambitious and artistically audacious — Peter Jackson's *The Lord of the Rings: The Fellowship of the Ring.* Besides, Ron Howard was a favorite son, a child star and homegrown director.

With its more conservative membership, which is about a generation older than Hollywood's movers and shakers, and two generations older than most American moviegoers, the Academy has always favored noble and inspirational fare that propagates political correctness — even before the concept existed. This bias, toward earnest movies that deal with "important" issues over audacious movies that are more artistically innovative or politically charged, is easily documented. The Academy's preference is always for safe, mainstream, noncontroversial films imbued with widely acceptable values:

In 1937, *The Life of Emile Zola* over *The Awful Truth* and *Lost Horizon*

In 1941, *How Green Was My Valley* over *Citizen Kane*

In 1942, *Mrs. Miniver* over *The Magnificent Ambersons*

In 1944, *Going My Way* over *Double Indemnity*

In 1951, *An American in Paris* over *A Place in the Sun*

In 1952, *The Greatest Show on Earth* over *High Noon*

In 1956, *Around the World in 80 Days* over *Giant*

In 1964, *My Fair Lady* over *Dr. Strangelove*

In 1966, *A Man for All Seasons* over *Alfie* and *Who's Afraid of Virginia Woolf?*

In 1967, *In the Heat of the Night* over *Bonnie and Clyde*

In 1971, *The French Connection* over *A Clockwork Orange*

In 1976, *Rocky* over *Network* and *All the President's Men*

In 1980, *Ordinary People* over *Raging Bull*

In 1981, *Chariots of Fire* over *Reds*

In 1982, *Gandhi* over *Tootsie and E.T.*

In 1983, *Terms of Endearment* over *The Right Stuff*

In 1989, *Driving Miss Daisy* over *My Left Foot*

In 1990, *Dances With Wolves* over *GoodFellas*

In 1994, *Forrest Gump* over *Pulp Fiction*

In 1997, *Titanic* over *L.A. Confidential*

In 1998, *Shakespeare in Love* over *Saving Private Ryan*

In 1999, *American Beauty* over *The Insider*

In 2000, *Gladiator* over *Traffic*

In 2001, *A Beautiful Mind* over *The Lord of the Rings*

One might ask what are the most crucial attributes of winning the Oscar, a question that can be answered by examining the filmmakers who have dominated the competition. John Ford, William Wyler, Fred Zinnemann, and David Lean have occupied special positions in the Academy annals in two ways: Many of their films were nominated for Best Picture, and many performers in their films have received Oscar nominations and awards.

Mention has been made that John Ford's directorial Oscars were not for his specialty, the Western, but for what the Academy deemed as "more important" social problem pictures, such as *The Informer, The Grapes of Wrath,* or *How Green was My Valley* (the fourth was for *The Quiet Man*).

Of the aforementioned quartet, Wyler is the most diverse, at least in genre, having directed serious dramas, Westerns, romantic comedies, and even musicals. Three of Wyler's films won the Best Picture: *Mrs. Miniver, The Best Years of Our Lives,* and *Ben-Hur.* Wyler often brought out the best from his performers, with thirteen Oscar-winning roles in his films: Walter Brennan (*Come and Get It,* co-directed with Howard Hawks, and *The Westerner*), Bette Davis and Faye Bainter (*Jezebel*), Greer Garson and Teresa Wright (*Mrs. Miniver*), Fredric March and Harold Russell (*The Best Years of Our Lives*), Olivia de Havilland (*The Heiress*), Audrey Hepburn (*Roman Holiday*), Burl Ives (*The Big Country*), Charlton Heston and Hugh Griffith (*Ben-Hur*), and Barbra Streisand (*Funny Girl*).

William Wyler is the Academy's most respected and most honored director: Over half of his thirty-five sound movies brought their players nominations.

Wyler's films may contain the largest number of Oscar-winning or nominated performances due at least in part to his use, with cinematographer Gregg Toland, of long takes and deep-focus. In these shots actors appear in the same frame for the duration of entire scenes, thus enabling them to achieve real dramatic continuity and coherence. These strategies required discipline and concentration on the part of screen players, most of whom were used to acting in bits and pieces, the predominant norm of shooting in Hollywood. A meticulous craftsman, he was nicknamed "90–take Wyler" due to the numerous takes he demanded. Accused of being a tyrant, Wyler often clashed with his actors, yet most of them have done their best work in his movies.

However, the Wyler films that won Best Picture and Best Director do not necessarily represent his most distinguished or characteristic work, among which are *Dodsworth, The Letter,* and *The Little Foxes.* Wyler was at his best adapting literary works to the screen. *Mrs. Miniver* won for political rather than artistic reasons, and the historical epic *Ben-Hur* did not bear Wyler's signature as a filmmaker.

Wyler's reputation suffered in the 1960s and 1970s, along with Zinnemann's, when auteurist critics could not discern consistent or idiosyncratic elements in his work compared with more obvious auteurs such as Fritz Lang, John Ford, and Howard Hawks. Yet as Vincent Canby observed, Wyler was best at "submerging his own personality to obtain the most effective realization of the work of others," and it is this "extraordinary consistency of purpose and achievement" that is his distinctive trademark.

If consistent artistic quality is Wyler's signature, Zinnemann's trademark was a middlebrow humanism, which defined mainstream Hollywood in the 1950s and 1960s. Zinnemann directed two Oscar-winners, *From Here to Eternity* and *A Man for All Seasons,* and four Oscar-nominated pictures, *High Noon, The Nun's Story, The Sundowners,* and *Julia.* Considering the duration of his career, over half a century, his film oeuvre was rather small: Twenty-two features. Nonetheless, the number of Oscar-winning performances in Zinnemann's films is disproportionately large. Eighteen players were nominated in his movies, some more than once, such as Montgomery Clift in *The Search,* as a sensitive American soldier befriending an orphan in Europe right after the war, and in *From Here to Eternity,* as yet another sensitive soldier.

Six of Zinnemann's actors won Oscars: Gary Cooper (*High Noon*), Frank Sinatra and Donna Reed (*From Here to Eternity*), Paul Scofield (*A Man for All Seasons*), and Vanessa Redgrave and Jason Robards (*Julia*). Some performers have done very fine work in his films — Marlon Brando in his debut, *The Men,* Audrey Hepburn in *The Nun's Story,* and Julie Harris and Ethel Waters in *The Member of the Wedding.*

Zinnemann was considered to be a "dream director," due to his respect for actors. His movies were "perfect Oscar material," with their sensitive subject matter, humanistic orientation, and conflicted characters. Zinnemann's films also displayed thematic consistency. Asked to describe the narratives that attracted him, he said: "I just like to do films that are positive in the sense that they deal with the dignity of human beings and have something to say about oppression. Moral courage has interested me the most. I look for the universal theme that will allow the audience to identify with the characters." What fascinated him about *Julia,* his last-nominated film, was "the friendship of the two women and the issue of conscience. I always find questions of conscience very photogenic. That kind of interior drama is to me very exciting."

Zinnemann's early films were produced by Stanley Kramer, who was highly committed to films propagating liberal causes such as racial equality (*Home of the Brave, The Defiant Ones*), political justice (*Judgment at Nuremberg*), and interracial marriage (*Guess Who's Coming to Dinner*). Kramer was one of the first Hollywood filmmakers to make mainstream movies about pressing social issues. Several of his films were nominated for Best Picture, despite unimaginative approaches and flat, static direction.

Ship of Fools was nominated for eight Oscars in 1965, including Best Picture, because it was considered to be "important," dealing with a group of passengers (*Grand Hotel* or *Stagecoach* on water) aboard a ship bound for Germany in 1933. The movie was pretentious, technically crude and shapeless, yet a number of powerful performances and a symbolic message must have overshadowed its formal weakness; the Academy again proved the primacy of subject matter over style and form. Like Zinnemann, Kramer was a "sociological" director, though he lacked the veteran director's command of technical skills.

Zinnemann's humanist approach to filmmaking is almost nonexistent in Hollywood today. When British producer David Puttnam (*Chariots of Fire, The Killing Fields*) was appointed chair of Columbia in 1986, he hoped to reinstate Zinnemann's kind of vision. As he said, "If I had to characterize the films I like in terms of another filmmaker, they're not unlike Fred Zinnemann's films. They're about people finding within themselves resources they didn't know were there, and coming from the best of them." Puttnam didn't stay in power long enough to implement his ambitions, and it is doubtful that he would have succeeded even if he had.

One of the few filmmakers to combine intriguing issues, complex characters, and grand epic style was David Lean, whose work is a perfect example of the kinds of films that win Oscars. Six of Lean's movies have been nominated, from *In Which We Serve,* co-directed by Noel Coward, to *Great Expectations, Doctor Zhivago,* and *A Passage to India.* Unlike other directors, Lean was also effective at making more intimate films (*Brief Encounter*), literary adaptations (*Oliver Twist*), and documentary-style narratives (*Breaking the Sound Barrier*), but he achieved international recognition when he switched to epic-style movies, beginning with *The Bridge on the River Kwai.*

CONCLUSION:
THE OSCARS, HOLLYWOOD,
AND AMERICAN CULTURE

With the exception of the two months immediately after the show, the Oscar Awards dominate the Hollywood film industry all year round. In June 2002, barely two months after the ceremonies, the Academy issued a call for Scientific-Technical Achievements for the 2003 Oscars. This public announcement officially began the seventy-fourth Oscar race. Entry forms for these awards were mailed to eight hundred companies and individuals in the film-related scientific community around the world, as well as to all past winners. Scientific and Technical Awards are considered for advances which have proven significant to the film industry through successful application. Entry forms, which must be submitted to the Academy no later than August 1, 2002, are brought to the attention of the Scientific and Technical Awards Committee and are evaluated by sub-committees of engineers and scientists before being voted upon by the Academy's Board of Governors.

The Oscars have changed the entire operation of the film industry through their pervasive influence on every element of the filmmaking process: The studios and production companies, the various film artists, moviegoers, and even film critics.

To begin with, the big studios release their most prestigious and "important" pictures in the late fall and early winter, particularly in the month of December. The thinking behind this practice is that these movies will be fresh in the Academy voters' minds when they receive the nomination ballots in January.

Indeed, other things being equal, films released in December stand a better chance to get nominated than those released in any other month of the year. Of the fifty films nominated for Best Picture in the 1980s, eighteen (40 percent) were released in December, and thirty-four between September and December. By contrast, only six of the fifty films opened in the first quarter of the year. *Missing, Witness,* and *Hannah and Her Sisters* were released in February, and *Coal Miner's Daughter, Tender Mercies,* and *A Room With a View* in March. These six movies were released in the winter because, initially, their producers didn't consider them to be "Oscar stuff" or "Oscar caliber." In other words, they didn't qualify as serious contenders for the kinds of movies the Academy likes.

In some years, all five Best Picture nominees were released in December. This was the case in 1988, when *The Accidental Tourist, Dangerous Liaisons, Mississippi Burning, Rain Man,* and *Working Girl* all opened during the crucial month of December. Many films would have stood stronger chances of getting major nominations had they been released at more strategically fortuitous times. For example, Martin Scorsese's *The King of Comedy* and David Jones's *Betrayal,* both released in January 1983, would have featured more prominently in the nominations had they been released in the fall. It is doubtful that *The King of Comedy* would have been more successful at the box office — it was a fiasco — or that it would have garnered the Best Picture nomination, but the three superb performance by Robert De Niro, Jerry Lewis, and Sandra Bernhardt would have received more serious attention for acting nominations. Similarly, the British film *Betrayal,* with a screenplay by Harold Pinter from his own play, also contained three superlative performances by Ben Kingsley, Jeremy Irons, and Patricia Hodge, each of whom deserved but failed to be nominated.

The film's release date has not always been a crucial variable. In the 1930s, only seven (8 percent) of the ninety-two nominated films, and in the 1940s, ten (14 percent) of the seventy films, premiered in December. The specific month began to play a strategic role in the 1950s, when ten (20 percent) of the nominated films opened in December. And it became even more important in the 1960s, when sixteen (32 percent) were released in December, many around Christmas Day. The Award Year's rule stipulates that films must play at least one week in the Los Angeles county prior to December 31.

Though a strategic release certainly contributes to a film's visibility, one should not jump to the conclusion that the release date counts more than artistic merits. With his thirteen nominations, Woody Allen, a highly respected figure for his many talents, has shown complete disregard for the timing of his films' showing. Most of Allen's pictures have been released in the winter or spring — the worst season as far as Oscars are concerned. As noted, *Hannah and Her Sisters* opened in February, and *Bullets Over Broadway,* Allen's last film to receive Best Picture nomination, was released in September, almost in defiance of Oscar norms. The Oscars' effect on release dates and distribution patterns is a prime example of unanticipated consequences.

Another displacement of goals in the Oscars' operation has been its gradual acceptance as an institutionalized yardstick of evaluating artistic quality. The Oscar has become an integral part of the film world, used by critics in gauging films' various merits (acting, writing, direction). For better or for worse, the Oscar has become a legitimized measure of cinematic excellence.

For instance, in 1958, the critic Anthony Carthew wrote about David Niven's performance in *Separate Tables:* "I knew I was seeing a piece of acting worth an Oscar." Niven did win the Best Actor for this film. In 1969, the *National Observer*'s Clifford A. Ridley was so smitten with Liza Minnelli in *The Sterile Cuckoo* that he predicted: "She does not play nineteen-year-old Pookie Adams, she *is* Pookie Adams, and you may mark your Oscar ballots right now." Minnelli received her first Best Actress nomination for this role. *Variety,* the popular trade magazine, known for using "inside Hollywood" jargon in its reviews, can also be to the point. Reviewing *Arthur,* the *Variety* critic noted that "John Gielgud gives a priceless performance, truly the kind that wins supporting Oscars." Gielgud won.

But film critics have used the Oscar label for praise as well as condemnation. The *New Yorker*'s Pauline Kael did not like Gena Rowlands's performance in *A Woman Under the Influence,* noting that Rowlands was doing too much, "enough for half a dozen tours de force, a whole row of Oscars." The Oscar is often used as a tool for derogation, as in David Denby's *New York* magazine review of *Places in the Heart,* a film he didn't like because it was "too pious." "Parched and academic," wrote Denby, "the movie is too square for art, though it's perfectly designed for Oscars." Denby was right, at least as far as Oscar nominations are concerned — *Places in the Heart* received seven nominations, including Best Picture and Best Director.

Both film critics and film audiences have incorporated the Oscar into their everyday lingo, making value judgments in terms of "Oscar caliber" movies and other achievements. In fact, shortly after the release of a major film, critics try to predict that film's chances of getting nominations and Oscars. In 1983, *The Big Chill* opened to rave reviews, with Richard Corliss writing in *Time* magazine, "the eight star actors deserve one big Oscar." And Andrew Sarris stated in his *Village Voice* review of *Twice in a Lifetime* that Amy Madigan "deserves an Oscar." Madigan was indeed nominated. That critics are able to predict quite accurately the Oscar nominees and winners demonstrates again that the parameters of what constitutes a so-called "Oscar film" or "Oscar-caliber" performance are rather established in our movie consciousness.

That the Oscar has also been institutionalized as a legitimate symbol of success is also reflected in the award's portrayal in Hollywood movies about Hollywood. *The Bad and the Beautiful,* Vincente Minnelli's glossy melodrama, was one of the more successful "Hollywood on Hollywood" films. Using flash-backs as a device, the film's narrative consists of a series of recollections by a director (Barry Sullivan), a glamorous star (Lana Turner), a screenwriter (Dick Powell), and a studio executive (Walter Pidgeon) about their encounters with a ruthless Oscar-winning producer (Kirk Douglas). Offering an inside view of Hollywood, *The Bad and the Beautiful* received special attention from the Academy with six nominations and five awards, including Best Screenplay to Charles Schnee and Supporting Actress to Gloria Grahame.

Curiously, most of the "self-examination" movies have provided a downright negative and unflattering view of Hollywood as an industry, and a disparaging attitude toward the Oscar itself. Joseph Levine's 1966 production *The Oscar,* based on Richard Sale's novel and directed by Russell Rouse, is a vulgar soap opera about the informal machinations of the award. The story centers on a selfish actor, Frankie Fan (Stephen Boyd), who, waiting impatiently to be de-clared an Oscar winner, recalls in a flashback the abuse he took from the drama coach (Eleanor Parker) who launched his career, his unhappy marriage to a glamorous star (Elke Sommer), the betrayal of an old friend (Milton Berle), and a ruthlessly aggressive Oscar campaign. Frankie's illusions are shattered when, much to his shock and chagrin, another actor wins the Oscar.

As a movie, *The Oscar* was the worst publicity Hollywood could have devised for itself. Panned by all critics, it was also a fiasco at the box office. "Obviously the community doesn't need enemies so long as it has itself," wrote the *New York Times*'s Bosley Crowther. Other critics noted that "discriminating moviegoers prefer to watch the real thing — the Oscarcast — on television and hypothecate to themselves as to the behind-the-scenes chaos involved."

On-screen, the Oscar has been depicted in both humorous and cynical ways. With a characteristically biting irony, Billy Wilder cast Henry Fonda in his 1979 film, *Fedora,* as an Academy President who's sent to a remote island to present an Honorary Oscar to an aging but legendary star (Marthe Keller), possibly standing in for Garbo or Gloria Swanson — actresses who never won a legit Oscar. By 1979, Fonda himself had not won an Oscar — he received his first and only Best Actor in 1981.

Blake Edwards also played a cruel joke on Hollywood when he cast his wife-performer Julie Andrews in *S.O.B.* as an actress who has won an Oscar for *Peter Pan* (i.e., *Mary Poppins*), and is now going out of her way to change her wholesome screen image by willingly exposing her breasts.

Sheer ambivalence has always dominated some filmmakers' attitude toward the Oscar. Pioneer D. W. Griffith is reported to have said at the mention of the Academy of Motion Picture Arts and Sciences, "What art? What science?" Hitchcock, who never won a competitive Oscar despite five directorial nominations, described the Oscar as "a coveted annual prize whose previous year's winners nobody can ever remember."

Director Hal Ashby, who began his career as an editor, created a flurry of controversy when he told the press, upon winning the Best Editing for *In the Heat of the Night,* that he was going to use his Oscar statuette as a doorstep.

Still, the fact remains that the Oscar has become, as producer Walter Mirisch said, "movies' most effective ambassador throughout the world. The nickname stuck." "I have never been in any country in the world," Mirisch explained, "where the word Oscar has not entered its common language." Indeed, what better proof of the Oscar's legitimization than its entrance into the most respectable dictionaries?

At present, the Oscar is more widely embraced as the ultimate symbol of professional achievement than ever before. Asked for his attitude toward the Oscar, William Hurt, the 1985 Best Actor, said, "If this was the way they chose to tell me that they liked my work, then I was going to accept it. There are enough people that I now know and trust and admire and respect, who are members of that institution, that I can't piss on it."

The acceptance of the Oscar as a cultural symbol is virtually universal. As the 1959 Best Actress Simone Signoret observed: "In the French industry, there's always a smart guy who says before the umpteenth take of the same shot: 'Come on, let's do it again and we'll get the Oscar.' "

The Oscars' Preeminence in American Culture

As noted in this book, the Oscar show is watched by one billion people in and outside America, many of whom are not moviegoers. These global dimensions extend the Oscars' visibility way beyond the borders of the film world, and way beyond the borders of the United States. The Oscar has become a preeminent symbol of success and achievement in mainstream American culture. Watching the show, viewers get a microcosm of American movies, American television, American culture, and American society at large. Explicitly and implicitly, this function contributes to a form of American cultural imperialism all over the world. The Oscar Awards and the Oscar show serve as effective propaganda not just for American movies but also for American capitalism and the American Way of Life.

Watching the annual ceremonies has become obligatory for most Americans. The Oscar functions as a secular ritual in American culture. Like other religious rituals, the Oscar ceremonies are prescheduled, occurring every year at the same time. Like other rituals, the Oscar ceremonies are highly organized, following a strict set of rules; there are hundreds of Academy rules and commandments. The Oscar ceremonies are collective, requiring the participation of a large public, live and via television. Most important of all, like other rituals, the Oscar reaffirms the central values of mainstream American culture.

The Oscar Awards embody such basic American values as democracy, equality, individualism, competition, upward mobility, hard work, occupational achievement, and monetary success. The Oscars also highlight all the inherent contradictions that accompany these values, the dilemmas between the significance of cultural myths and their corresponding reality. Each value exemplified by the Oscars can be stated as a dichotomy of opposite orientations: Democracy versus elitism, equality versus discrimination, universalism versus particularism, individualism versus collectivism, competition versus collaboration, hard work versus sheer luck, success versus failure.

More than any other Oscar category, it is the acting awards that express the cultural contradictions inherent in the dominant American value system. In no other profession is the conflict between the ideal of democracy and the reality of elitism more apparent. Acting is one of the most democratic professions, with a broader social class base than that of other occupations. The choice of acting as a career continues to provide a channel for upward mobility. Over half of the Oscar-nominated players have come from poor, uneducated families, and over one fourth are members of ethnic minorities. Acting is still one of the most accessible professions, easily entered but also easily left. Entry into acting requires less formal education and less training than those required by other professions. On-the-job training and actual experience are far more valued and important than formal schooling.

Most actors' biographies are replete with rags-to-riches and overnight success stories, myths that are still powerful in attracting new members into the acting profession. One of the most startling success stories is exemplified by

Oscar-nominated writer-actor Sylvester Stallone. The product of a broken home, Stallone grew up in New York's Hell's Kitchen, then in Silver Springs, Maryland, and then in Philadelphia. After growing up in foster homes, he was booted out of fourteen schools in eleven years. Stallone attended the drama department of the University of Miami for a while, where his instructors discouraged him from pursuing acting as a career. He then tried his hand at various jobs, the most glamorous of which was as an usher at the Baronet Theater in New York City.

Determined to become an actor, however, Stallone managed to get some bit roles in films such as *Bananas* and *The Prisoner of Second Avenue*. When his career seemed to have reached a dead end, Stallone decided to create his own opportunity and write a screenplay. The result was *Rocky:* the script was reportedly completed in three days, with a narrative that is similar to his own life story. It's a tale of a down-and-out prizefighter who rises to stardom against great odds. The rest is film history: *Rocky* won the 1976 Best Picture and established Stallone as the preeminent male star of his generation.

Though accessible and democratic, acting is also one of the most sharply stratified professions. The Oscar winners and nominees constitute a small elite composed of the most accomplished actors, who occupy the highest echelon in the film world in terms of money, prestige, and power. In acting, the gap in rewards between the elite and rank-and-file members is immense. The supply of film artists continues to surpass demand, which means that most actors are unemployed most of the time. By contrast, most Oscar-winners go from one film project to another, and from screen to stage and television, and vice versa. Cumulative advantage, as mentioned, is in operation in Hollywood and showbiz: The rich players become richer and the famous more famous, while the unsuccessful ones become progressively less successful.

The contradiction between hard work on the one hand and sheer luck on the other as two determinants for successful careers is also exemplified by the careers of the Oscar players. The Protestant ethic of hard work is still a legitimate avenue for achieving success. In acting, there is strong emphasis on motivation, ambition, self-discipline, and energy, all crucial requirements for professional success. Veteran actors like John Wayne rationalized their success by stressing the hard work involved in making movies, the physical rigor, the irregular time schedules, the long hours, and the grim and demanding working conditions. Walter Matthau was not joking when he once described acting as "the hardest job known to mankind."

But despite emphasis on hard work, most actors realize that they have little or no control over their career opportunities, that luck and fate play just as important a role in shaping their careers. Gary Cooper, a two-time Oscar-winner, regarded acting as "just a job," which made him successful because he was "the right man at the right time." Cooper also differed from his colleagues in considering screen acting as "pretty silly business for a man because it takes less training, less ability, and less brains to be successful at it than any other business I can think of." The men's attitudes toward acting range from Jack Lemmon's — "I have never lost a total passion to my work" — and William

Hurt's — "I am proud to be an actor" — all the way to Marlon Brando's — "acting has never been the dominant force in my life."

Whatever the case may be, most artists acknowledge the impact of luck and other contingencies on their screen careers. Some men have become actors by accident, without ever making a conscious or deliberate decision to pursue such a line. Jimmy Stewart, who majored in architecture at Princeton but never practiced, once summed up his career: "If I hadn't been at some particular place at some particular time and some man hadn't happened to say so-and-so, and I hadn't answered this-and-that, I'd still be hunting for a job in an architect's office."

Another Oscar star, Bing Crosby, viewed his popularity as a series of lucky coincidences, titling his autobiography *Call Me Lucky.* "I'm not really an actor, I was just lucky," Clark Gable used to say about his meteoric success, "If it hadn't been for people like Howard Strickling (MGM publicity director), I'd probably have ended up a truck driver."

Luck also plays a considerable part in getting the "right" screen roles, i.e., roles that are easily recognized and acknowledged with the Oscars. The Academy's history is fraught with Oscar-winning roles played by actors who were neither intended nor originally cast in them. What would have happened to Jack Nicholson if Rip Torn hadn't turned down the part of the dropout lawyer in *Easy Rider,* Nicholson's breakthrough film after ten long years in Hollywood? One also wonders if this part would have made Rip Torn a more visible star?

The conflict between individualism and collaboration is also demonstrated by the Oscar Award. Rugged, romantic individualism is most fully expressed in competitive achievement, which thousands of Hollywood films have portrayed on-screen. But romantic individualism also means rewarding artists for their contributions in their specific area of expertise. Since film is a collaborative art, it is often hard to single out the relative contribution of each element (writing, direction, acting, cinematography, editing) to the overall success or failure of the final work because the various elements are so interdependent. However, the Oscar Award follows the primacy of individualism in American culture and honors individual achievements.

It is almost impossible to define the elements of an effective screen performance, though one knows a good performance when one sees it. Along with talent, individual performances depend on the support from other players, on the way they are photographed and edited. Not surprisingly, screen players resent their lack of control over the final shape of their work — often opting to work in the theater where they feel more directly responsible.

Ironically, more than other elements, it's acting that's often blamed for the film's overall low quality, and, conversely, actors are often undeservedly praised when they appear in good or commercial films. When a film is powerful, every aspect of it seems to be good. Good films tend to overcome mediocre performances, but effective acting has a harder time overcoming a bad movie. This is one of the inherent problems in evaluating films — the ability to distinguish the input of each element to the overall quality. Good films tend to get nominations and awards in most categories, even in those which do not merit a nomination. By contrast, excellent individual contributions are often ignored if they are contained in average or bad pictures.

Moreover, the structure and impact of many films depend on ensemble acting, when a group of players complement each other. As noted, only Sam Shepard was nominated in *The Right Stuff,* Glenn Close in *The Big Chill,* Julianne Moore and Burt Reynolds in *Boogie Nights,* Tom Cruise in *Magnolia,* and Helen Mirren and Maggie Smith in *Gosford Park* — all films that rely heavily on large casts and ensemble acting. It is in such cases that other, less relevant factors, such as actors' former work, previous nominations, and popularity begin to play a role in determining their chances to win the Oscar.

Some critics have proposed to establish a supplementary category, for the best ensemble acting, a category that exists at the SAG awards, honoring the collective achievements of a team. However, this notion is unlikely to happen with the Oscars. It not only runs against the individualistic nature of the awards, but also against individual competition and achievement, values that are highly cherished in American culture. "The comparatively striking feature of American culture," the sociologist Philip Slater once observed, "is its tendency to identify standards of excellence with competitive occupational achievement." And competition bears negative effects as well, as Slater noted: "The competitive life is a lonely one and its satisfactions are very short-lived, for each race leads only to a new one."

The Oscar also functions as an arena for conflict between universalism and particularism. Had the Oscar operated on completely factual and rational principles, quality of work would have been the sole criterion for evaluating film artists. A universalistic ethos requires that artists producing high-quality work would be rewarded regardless of ascribed statuses such as age, gender, race, religion, or nationality. However, such a reward system is utopian and does not exist even in science. Indeed, one of the Oscar's effects is to call attention to the operation of multiple of yardsticks in evaluating film art. Hence, the more disagreement there is about the Oscars, the more critically aware the public becomes of the problems involved in judging film.

What is amazing about the Oscar is its public and immediate manifestation of these cultural values. Through the Oscar show, viewers get to participate in the making or breaking of careers, in the rise and fall of artists, in upholding overnight success stories, all of which happen on their TV sets right before their eyes.

Finally, the Oscar Award embodies the inherent tension in Hollywood between art and commerce, which explains the title of the following discussion.

The Oscar—Longer, Bigger, Uncut—Size Matters

The first massive film to win the Best Picture was *Grand Hotel,* in 1931–32, which led the *Los Angeles Times* to observe: "*Grand Hotel* filled the requirements of bigness," with the reviewer altogether avoiding the issue of quality.

Over the years, the Academy has denied the charge that the Oscar Award has become a commercial tool, and the Oscar ceremonies a monetary spectacle. Academy leaders still insist that the Oscar is first and foremost "a merit award," designed to honor excellence, not to promote or enhance visibility at the box office. However, observant members have conceded that in some years a disproportionate number of awards and nominations have been given to movies that are commercial successes though they hasten to point out that awards have also been given to commercial failures.

This is where the defense of modest art films and small independent films comes in. On the one hand, there is clear correlation between the caliber of the Oscar nominees and the ratings of the Oscar show. On the other, the Academy takes pride in nominating such small but impressive artistic endeavors as *Lenny, Bound for Glory, Taxi Driver, The Elephant Man, Raging Bull, Atlantic City, Missing, The Dresser, Tender Mercies, Kiss of the Spider Woman, Hope and Glory, The Remains of the Day,* and *The Insider,* most of which have underperformed at the box office, and some of which were downright commercial failures. The Academy would like the public to believe that, give or take a specific year, the Oscar-winning and Oscar-nominated films have represented worthy attainments regardless of perceived or real commercial grosses.

The Academy has always promoted its image as a standard-setter, an organization that "reminds the public of worthy achievements," and "calls the attention of millions of viewers to the significance of motion pictures as a fine art as well as popular entertainment." The members still wish to believe that the Academy functions as "a constant incentive for better work" and as a stimulus "for hundreds of millions of people to think and to talk about the best in motion pictures."

But once the Academy became aware of the Oscar's influence, the tendency to shower mediocre films with multiple nominations and awards in order to boost their commercial standing became more prevalent. This was particularly evident in the late 1960s and early 1970s, when such artistically unworthy films as *Anne of the Thousand Days, Hello, Dolly!, Airport, Love Story,* and *Nicholas and Alexandra,* were inexplicably nominated for the Best Picture and other major awards.

Genre and subject matter aside, one might ask, what are the most crucial attributes of winning the Oscar? The answer may be simpler than the question. Most Oscar-winning and Oscar-nominated films have flaunted glossy production values expressed in grand visual style and pseudo-epic vision, manifest in large production budgets and epic running times.

Ordinary People, Terms of Endearment, American Beauty, and *A Beautiful Mind* were among the few "modest" films to win the Best Picture. Most Oscar winners have been big-budgeted, large-scaled, and super-produced, from the very first Best Picture, *Wings,* through *Gone With the Wind, Ben-Hur, Lawrence of Arabia, Tom Jones,* and *The Godfather* movies. The 1980s were defined by such colossal Oscar winners as *Gandhi, Amadeus, Out of Africa,* and *The Last Emperor.* In the 1990s, too, most Oscar winners were epics safely set in the past: *Dances With Wolves, Schindler's List, Forrest Gump, Braveheart, Titanic, Gladiator.* If the 1940s are conspicuously underrepresented in this list, it's due to the impact of the austere war economy on Hollywood's film production and the dominance of war pictures.

Size Over Quality

1928–29	*The Broadway Melody* over *The Patriot*
1930–31	*Cimarron* over *The Front Page*
1931–32	*Grand Hotel* over *One Hour With You*
1932–33	*Cavalcade* over *Lady for a Day*
1935	*Mutiny on the Bounty* over *The Informer*
1936	*The Great Ziegfeld* over *Mr. Deeds Goes to Town*
1959	*Ben-Hur* over *Anatomy of a Murder*
1965	*The Sound of Music* over *Darling*
1973	*The Sting* over *American Graffiti*
1984	*Amadeus* over *The Killing Fields*
1985	*Out of Africa* over *Prizzi's Honor*
1995	*Braveheart* over *Babe* and *Sense and Sensibility*
1996	*The English Patient* over *Secrets & Lies*
1997	*Titanic* over *L.A. Confidential*
2000	*Gladiator* over *Traffic*

Lengthy running time continues to impress the Academy voters. The running time of over half of the Oscar winners has been in excess of the 100–120 minute norm. *Wings*'s running time is 136 minutes, *The Great Ziegfeld* 179, *Gone With the Wind* 220, *The Best Years of Our Lives* 182, *Around the World in 80 Days* 178, *Out of Africa* 150, *The Last Emperor* 166. This is especially true of the Oscar-winning pictures in the 1990s: *Dances With Wolves* 181 minutes, *Schindler's List* 195, *Forrest Gump* 142, *Braveheart* 177, *The English Patient* 162, *Titanic* 194, *Gladiator* 154.

Delbert Mann's *Marty* and Woody Allen's *Annie Hall* are still the notable exceptions: The former claims a running-time of 91 minutes, the latter of 93. Together, they are the shortest of all Oscar-winning features. The briefest film to have ever been nominated for the Best picture is the 1933 Mae West vehicle, *She Done Him Wrong*, with a running time of 66 minutes. Yet, what West said in an hour or so is priceless, outshining in wit, humor, and originality most of the Oscar comedies.

Regardless of changing times and tastes, we continue to watch — in breathless anticipation.

Table 1: Awards in Six Categories by Year, 1927/28–2001

Year	Picture	Director	Actor	Actress	Supporting Actor	Supporting Actress
1927/28	Wings	Frank Borzage (Seventh Heaven) Lewis Milestone (Two Arabian Nights)	Emil Jannings (The Way of All Flesh; The Last Command)	Janet Gaynor (Seventh Heaven; Street Angel; Sunrise)		Gale Sondergaard (Anthony Adverse)
1928/29	The Broadway Melody	Frank Lloyd (The Divine Lady)	Warner Baxter (In Old Arizona)	Mary Pickford (Coquette)		
1929/30	All Quiet on the Western Front	Lewis Milestone	George Arliss (Disraeli)	Norma Shearer (The Divorcee)		
1930/31	Cimarron	Norman Taurog (Skippy)	Lionel Barrymore (A Free Soul)	Marie Dressler (Min and Bill)		
1931/32	Grand Hotel	Frank Borzage (Bad Girl)	Fredric March (Dr. Jekyll and Mr. Hyde); Wallace Beery (The Champ)	Helen Hayes (The Sin of Madelon Claudet)		
1932/33	Cavalcade	Frank Lloyd	Charles Laughton (The Private Life of Henry VIII)	Katharine Hepburn (Morning Glory)		
1934	It Happened One Night	Frank Capra	Clark Gable	Claudette Colbert		
1935	Mutiny on the Bounty	John Ford (The Informer)	Victor McLaglen (The Informer)	Bette Davis (Dangerous)		
1936	The Great Ziegfeld	Frank Capra (Mr. Deeds Goes to Town)	Paul Muni (The Story of Louis Pasteur)	Luise Rainer	Walter Brennan (Come and Get It)	

Year	Picture	Director	Actor	Actress	Supporting Actor	Supporting Actress
1937	*The Life of Emile Zola*	Leo McCarey *(The Awful Truth)*	Spencer Tracy *(Captains Courageous)*	Luise Rainer *(The Good Earth)*	Joseph Schildkraut *(The Life of Emile Zola)*	Alice Brady *(In Old Chicago)*
1938	*You Can't Take It With You*	Frank Capra	Spencer Tracy *(Boys Town)*	Bette Davis *(Jezebel)*	Walter Brennan *(Kentucky)*	Fay Bainter *(Jezebel)*
1939	*Gone With the Wind*	Victor Fleming	Robert Donat *(Goodbye, Mr. Chips)*	Vivien Leigh	Thomas Mitchell *(Stagecoach)*	Hattie McDaniel
1940	*Rebecca*	John Ford *(The Grapes of Wrath)*	James Stewart *(The Philadelphia Story)*	Ginger Rogers *(Kitty Foyle)*	Walter Brennan *(The Westerner)*	Jane Darwell *(The Grapes of Wrath)*
1941	*How Green Was My Valley*	John Ford	Gary Cooper *(Sergeant York)*	Joan Fontaine *(Suspicion)*	Donald Crisp	Mary Astor *(The Great Lie)*
1942	*Mrs. Miniver*	William Wyler	James Cagney *(Yankee Doodle Dandy)*	Greer Garson	Van Heflin *(Johnny Eager)*	Teresa Wright
1943	*Casablanca*	Michael Curtiz	Paul Lukas *(Watch on the Rhine)*	Jennifer Jones *(The Song of Bernadette)*	Charles Coburn *(The More the Merrier)*	Katina Paxinou *(For Whom the Bell Tolls)*
1944	*Going My Way*	Leo McCarey	Bing Crosby	Ingrid Bergman *(Gaslight)*	Barry Fitzgerald	Ethel Barrymore *(None But the Lonely Heart)*
1945	*The Lost Weekend*	Billy Wilder	Ray Milland	Joan Crawford *(Mildred Pierce)*	James Dunn *(A Tree Grows in Brooklyn)*	Anne Revere *(National Velvet)*
1946	*The Best Years of Our Lives*	William Wyler	Fredric March	Olivia de Havilland *(To Each His Own)*	Harold Russell	Anne Baxter *(The Razor's Edge)*
1947	*Gentleman's Agreement*	Elia Kazan	Ronald Colman *(A Double Life)*	Loretta Young *(The Farmer's Daughter)*	Edmund Gwenn *(Miracle on 34th Street)*	Celeste Holm

Table 1 (continued)

Year	Picture	Director	Actor	Actress	Supporting Actor	Supporting Actress
1948	Hamlet	John Huston (Treasure of Sierra Madre)	Laurence Olivier	Jane Wyman (Johnny Belinda)	Walter Huston (Treasure of Sierra Madre)	Claire Trevor (Key Largo)
1949	All the King's Men	Joseph L. Mankiewicz (A Letter to Three Wives)	Broderick Crawford	Olivia de Havilland (The Heiress)	Dean Jagger (Twelve O'Clock High)	Mercedes McCambridge
1950	All About Eve	Joseph L. Mankiewicz	Jose Ferrer (Cyrano de Bergerac)	Judy Holliday (Born Yesterday)	George Sanders	Josephine Hall (Harvey)
1951	An American in Paris	George Stevens (A Place in the Sun)	Humphrey Bogart (The African Queen)	Vivien Leigh (A Streetcar Named Desire)	Karl Malden (Streetcar)	Kim Hunter (Streetcar)
1952	The Greatest Show on Earth	John Ford (The Quiet Man)	Gary Cooper (High Noon)	Shirley Booth (Come Back, Little Sheba)	Anthony Quinn (Viva Zapata!)	Gloria Grahame (The Bad and the Beautiful)
1953	From Here to Eternity	Fred Zinnemann	William Holden (Stalag 17)	Audrey Hepburn (Roman Holiday)	Frank Sinatra	Donna Reed
1954	On the Waterfront	Elia Kazan	Marlon Brando	Grace Kelly (The Country Girl)	Edmond O'Brien (The Barefoot Contessa)	Eva Marie Saint
1955	Marty	Delbert Mann	Ernest Borgnine	Anna Magnani (The Rose Tattoo)	Jack Lemmon (Mister Roberts)	Jo Van Fleet (East of Eden)
1956	Around the World in 80 Days	George Stevens (Giant)	Yul Brynner (The King and I)	Ingrid Bergman (Anastasia)	Anthony Quinn (Lust for Life)	Dorothy Malone (Written on the Wind)

Year	Picture	Director	Actor	Actress	Supporting Actor	Supporting Actress
1957	*The Bridge on the River Kwai*	David Lean	Alec Guinness	Joanne Woodward *(The Three Faces of Eve)*	Red Buttons *(Sayonara)*	Miyoshi Umeki *(Sayonara)*
1958	*Gigi*	Vincente Minnelli	David Niven *(Separate Tables)*	Susan Hayward *(I Want to Live!)*	Burl Ives *(The Big Country)*	Wendy Hiller *(Separate Tables)*
1959	*Ben-Hur*	William Wyler	Charlton Heston	Simone Signoret *(Room at the Top)*	Hugh Griffith	Shelley Winters *(The Diary of Anne Frank)*
1960	*The Apartment*	Billy Wilder	Burt Lancaster *(Elmer Gantry)*	Elizabeth Taylor *(Butterfield 8)*	Peter Ustinov *(Spartacus)*	Shirley Jones *(Elmer Gantry)*
1961	*West Side Story*	Robert Wise; Jerome Robbins	Maximilian Schell *(Judgment at Nuremberg)*	Sophia Loren *(Two Women)*	George Chakiris	Rita Moreno
1962	*Lawrence of Arabia*	David Lean	Gregory Peck *(To Kill a Mockingbird)*	Anne Bancroft *(The Miracle Worker)*	Ed Begley *(Sweet Bird of Youth)*	Patty Duke *(The Miracle Worker)*
1963	*Tom Jones*	Tony Richardson	Sidney Poitier *(Lilies of the Field)*	Patricia Neal *(Hud)*	Melvyn Douglas *(Hud)*	Margaret Rutherford *(The V.I.P.s)*
1964	*My Fair Lady*	George Cukor	Rex Harrison	Julie Andrews *(Mary Poppins)*	Peter Ustinov *(Topkapi)*	Lila Kedrova *(Zorba the Greek)*
1965	*The Sound of Music*	Robert Wise	Lee Marvin *(Cat Ballou)*	Julie Christie *(Darling)*	Martin Balsam *(A Thousand Clowns)*	Shelley Winters *(A Patch of Blue)*
1966	*A Man for All Seasons*	Fred Zinnemann	Paul Scofield	Elizabeth Taylor *(Who's Afraid of Virginia Woolf?)*	Walter Matthau *(The Fortune Cookie)*	Sandy Dennis *(Who's Afraid of Virginia Woolf?)*
1967	*In the Heat of the Night*	Mike Nichols *(The Graduate)*	Rod Steiger	Katharine Hepburn *(Guess Who's Coming to Dinner?)*	George Kennedy *(Cool Hand Luke)*	Estelle Parsons *(Bonnie and Clyde)*

Table 1 (continued)

Year	Picture	Director	Actor	Actress	Supporting Actor	Supporting Actress
1968	Oliver!	Carol Reed	Cliff Robertson (Charly)	Katharine Hepburn (The Lion in Winter); Barbra Streisand (Funny Girl)	Jack Albertson (The Subject Was Roses)	Ruth Gordon (Rosemary's Baby)
1969	Midnight Cowboy	John Schlesinger	John Wayne (True Grit)	Maggie Smith (The Prime of Miss Jean Brodie)	Gig Young (They Shoot Horses, Don't They?)	Goldie Hawn (Cactus Flower)
1970	Patton	Franklin J. Schaffner	George C. Scott	Glenda Jackson (Women in Love)	John Mills (Ryan's Daughter)	Helen Hayes (Airport)
1971	The French Connection	William Friedkin	Gene Hackman	Jane Fonda (Klute)	Ben Johnson (The Last Picture Show)	Cloris Leachman (The Last Picture Show)
1972	The Godfather	Bob Fosse (Cabaret)	Marlon Brando	Liza Minnelli (Cabaret)	Joel Grey (Cabaret)	Eileen Heckart (Butterflies Are Free)
1973	The Sting	George Roy Hill	Jack Lemmon (Save the Tiger)	Glenda Jackson (A Touch of Class)	John Houseman (The Paper Chase)	Tatum O'Neal (Paper Moon)
1974	The Godfather, Part II	Francis F. Coppola	Art Carney (Harry and Tonto)	Ellen Burstyn (Alice Doesn't Live Here Anymore)	Robert De Niro	Ingrid Bergman (Murder on the Orient Express)
1975	One Flew Over the Cuckoo's Nest	Milos Forman	Jack Nicholson	Louise Fletcher	George Burns (The Sunshine Boys)	Lee Grant (Shampoo)
1976	Rocky	John G. Avildsen	Peter Finch (Network)	Faye Dunaway (Network)	Jason Robards (All the President's Men)	Beatrice Straight (Network)
1977	Annie Hall	Woody Allen	Richard Dreyfuss (The Goodbye Girl)	Diane Keaton	Jason Robards (Julia)	Vanessa Redgrave (Julia)

Year	Picture	Director	Best Actor	Best Actress	Best Supporting Actor	Best Supporting Actress
1978	*The Deer Hunter*	Michael Cimino	Jon Voight *(Coming Home)*	Jane Fonda *(Coming Home)*	Christopher Walken	Maggie Smith *(California Suite)*
1979	*Kramer vs. Kramer*	Robert Benton	Dustin Hoffman	Sally Field *(Norma Rae)*	Melvyn Douglas *(Being There)*	Meryl Streep
1980	*Ordinary People*	Robert Redford	Robert De Niro *(Raging Bull)*	Sissy Spacek *(A Coal Miner's Daughter)*	Timothy Hutton	Mary Steenburgen *(Melvin and Howard)*
1981	*Chariots of Fire*	Warren Beatty *(Reds)*	Henry Fonda *(On Golden Pond)*	Katharine Hepburn *(On Golden Pond)*	John Gielgud *(Arthur)*	Maureen Stapleton *(Reds)*
1982	*Gandhi*	Richard Attenborough	Ben Kingsley	Meryl Streep *(Sophie's Choice)*	Louis Gossett Jr. *(An Officer and a Gentleman)*	Jessica Lange *(Tootsie)*
1983	*Terms of Endearment*	James L. Brooks	Robert Duvall *(Tender Mercies)*	Shirley MacLaine	Jack Nicholson	Linda Hunt *(The Year of Living Dangerously)*
1984	*Amadeus*	Milos Forman	F. Murray Abraham	Sally Field *(Places in the Heart)*	Hang S. Ngor *(The Killing Fields)*	Peggy Ashcroft *(A Passage to India)*
1985	*Out of Africa*	Sydney Pollack	William Hurt *(Kiss of the Spider Woman)*	Geraldine Page *(The Trip to Bountiful)*	Don Ameche *(Cocoon)*	Anjelica Huston *(Prizzi's Honor)*
1986	*Platoon*	Oliver Stone	Paul Newman *(The Color of Money)*	Marlee Matlin *(Children of a Lesser God)*	Michael Caine *(Hannah and Her Sisters)*	Dianne Wiest *(Hannah and Her Sisters)*
1987	*The Last Emperor*	Bernardo Bertolucci	Michael Douglas *(Wall Street)*	Cher *(Moonstruck)*	Sean Connery *(The Untouchables)*	Olympia Dukakis *(Moonstruck)*
1988	*Rain Man*	Barry Levinson	Dustin Hoffman	Jodie Foster *(The Accused)*	Kevin Kline *(A Fish Called Wanda)*	Geena Davis *(The Accidental Tourist)*

Table 1 (continued)

Year	Picture	Director	Actor	Actress	Supporting Actor	Supporting Actress
1989	Driving Miss Daisy	Oliver Stone (Born on the Fourth of July)	Daniel Day-Lewis (My Left Foot)	Jessica Tandy	Denzel Washington (Glory)	Brenda Fricker (My Left Foot)
1990	Dances With Wolves	Kevin Costner	Jeremy Irons (Reversal of Fortune)	Kathy Bates (Misery)	Joe Pesci (GoodFellas)	Whoopi Goldberg (Ghost)
1991	The Silence of the Lambs	Jonathan Demme	Anthony Hopkins	Jodie Foster	Jack Palance (City Slickers)	Mercedes Ruehl (The Fisher King)
1992	Unforgiven	Clint Eastwood	Al Pacino (Scent of a Woman)	Emma Thompson (Howards End)	Gene Hackman	Marisa Tomei (My Cousin Vinny)
1993	Schindler's List	Steven Spielberg	Tom Hanks (Philadelphia)	Holly Hunter (The Piano)	Tommy Lee Jones (The Fugitive)	Anna Paquin (The Piano)
1994	Forrest Gump	Robert Zemeckis	Tom Hanks	Jessica Lange (Blue Sky)	Martin Landau (Ed Wood)	Dianne Wiest (Bullets over Broadway)
1995	Braveheart	Mel Gibson	Nicolas Cage (Leaving Las Vegas)	Susan Sarandon (Dead Man Walking)	Kevin Spacey (The Usual Suspects)	Mira Sorvino (Mighty Aphrodite)
1996	The English Patient	Anthony Minghella	Geoffrey Rush (Shine)	Frances McDormand (Fargo)	Cuba Gooding Jr. (Jerry Maguire)	Juliette Binoche
1997	Titanic	James Cameron	Jack Nicholson (As Good As It Gets)	Helen Hunt (As Good As It Gets)	Robin Williams (Good Will Hunting)	Kim Basinger (L.A. Confidential)
1998	Shakespeare in Love	Steven Spielberg (Saving Private Ryan)	Roberto Benigni (Life Is Beautiful)	Gwyneth Paltrow	James Coburn (Affliction)	Judi Dench
1999	American Beauty	Sam Mendes	Kevin Spacey	Hilary Swank (Boys Don't Cry)	Michael Caine (Cider House Rules)	Angelina Jolie (Girl, Interrupted)
2000	Gladiator	Steven Soderbergh (Traffic)	Russell Crowe	Julia Roberts (Erin Brockovich)	Benicio Del Toro (Traffic)	Marcia Gay Harden (Pollock)
2001	A Beautiful Mind	Ron Howard	Denzel Washington (Training Day)	Halle Berry (Monster's Ball)	Jim Broadbent (Iris)	Jennifer Connelly

Table 2:
Best Picture Winners and Nominees by Genre,
1927–2001 (in percentage)

Genre	Nominees	Winners	All
Drama	48.6	39.2	47.0
Comedy	18.2	13.5	17.4
Historical Epic	9.8	16.2	10.9
Musical	7.8	10.8	8.3
Action-Adventure	6.1	5.4	6.0
War	4.5	8.1	5.1
Suspense	3.1	2.7	3.0
Western	1.9	4.1	2.3
Total	100.0	100.0	100.0
	(358)	(74)	(432)

Table 3:
The Oscar-Winners by Nominations, Awards, and Appeal

Year	Film	Noms	Awards	Domestic Rentals*
1927–28	Wings	2	2	n/a
1928–28	The Broadway Melody	3	1	3.00
1929–30	All Quiet on the Western Front	4	2	1.50
1930–31	Cimarron	6	3	2.00
1931–32	Grand Hotel	1	1	2.20
1932–33	Cavalcade	4	3	3.50
1934	It Happened One Night	5	5	n/a
1935	Mutiny on the Bounty	7	1	n/a
1936	The Great Ziegfeld	7	3	n/a
1937	The Life of Emile Zola	10	3	n/a
1938	You Can't Take It With You	7	2	n/a
1939	Gone With the Wind	11	8	76.70
1940	Rebecca	10	2	1.50
1941	How Green Was My Valley	10	5	2.80
1942	Mrs. Miniver	12	6	5.50
1943	Casablanca	8	3	3.70

*In millions of dollars

Table 3 (continued):
The Oscar-Winners by Nominations, Awards, and Appeal

Year	Film	Noms	Awards	Domestic Rentals
1944	Going My Way	9	7	6.50
1945	The Lost Weekend	6	4	4.30
1948	Hamlet	7	4	3.25
1946	The Best Years of Our Lives	9	7	11.30
1947	Gentleman's Agreement	8	3	3.90
1949	All the King's Men	7	4	2.40
1950	All About Eve	14	6	2.90
1951	An American in Paris	8	6	4.50
1952	The Greatest Show on Earth	5	2	14.00
1953	From Here To Eternity	13	8	12.20
1954	On the Waterfront	11	8	4.50
1955	Marty	8	4	2.00
1956	Around the World in 80 Days	8	5	23.12
1957	The Bridge on the River Kwai	8	7	17.19
1958	Gigi	9	9	7.30
1959	Ben-Hur	12	11	36.65
1960	The Apartment	10	5	6.65
1961	West Side Story	11	10	19.45
1962	Lawrence of Arabia	10	7	16.70
1963	Tom Jones	10	4	16.95
1964	My Fair Lady	12	8	12.00
1965	The Sound of Music	10	5	79.75
1966	A Man For All Seasons	8	6	12.75
1967	In the Heat of the Night	7	5	10.91
1968	Oliver!	11	6	16.80
1969	Midnight Cowboy	7	3	20.32
1970	Patton	10	7	28.10
1971	The French Connection	8	5	26.31
1972	The Godfather	10	3	86.27
1973	The Sting	10	7	78.20
1974	The Godfather, Part II	11	6	30.67
1975	One Flew Over the Cuckoo's Nest	9	5	59.24
1976	Rocky	10	3	55.92
1977	Annie Hall	5	4	18.09
1978	The Deer Hunter	9	5	27.53
1979	Kramer vs. Kramer	9	5	60.00
1980	Ordinary People	6	4	23.12
1981	Chariots of Fire	7	4	30.60

Table 3 (continued):
The Oscar-Winners by Nominations, Awards, and Appeal

Year	Film	Noms	Awards	Domestic Rentals*
1982	Gandhi	11	8	24.75
1983	Terms of Endearment	11	5	50.25
1984	Amadeus	11	8	22.82
1985	Out of Africa	11	7	43.10
1986	Platoon	8	4	69.74
1987	The Last Emperor	9	9	18.82
1988	Rain Man	8	4	43.60
1989	Driving Miss Daisy	9	4	50.50
1990	Dances With Wolves	12	7	91.53
1991	The Silence of the Lambs	7	5	59.88
1992	Unforgiven	9	4	44.40
1993	Schindler's List	12	7	44.16
1994	Forrest Gump	13	6	156.00
1995	Braveheart	10	5	31.81
1996	The English Patient	12	9	32.76
1997	Titanic	14	11	300.00[†]
1998	Shakespeare in Love	13	7	42.00[†]
1999	American Beauty	8	5	66.62
2000	Gladiator	12	7	90.00[†]
2001	A Beautiful Mind	8	4	80.00[†]

[†]Estimates

Table 4:
The Most Nominated Films, 1927–2001

10 nominations: 30 movies

Year	Film	Nom.	Awards
1937	The Life of Emile Zola	10	3
1939	Mr. Smith Goes to Washington	10	1
1940	Rebecca	10	2
1941	How Green Was My Valley	10	5
1943	The Song of Bernadette	10	4
1953	Roman Holiday	10	3
1956	Giant	10	1

Table 4 (continued):
The Most Nominated Films, 1927–2001

10 nominations: 30 movies

Year	Film	Nom.	Awards
1957	*Sayonara*	10	4
1960	*The Apartment*	10	5
1962	*Lawrence of Arabia*	10	7
1963	*Tom Jones*	10	4
1965	*Doctor Zhivago*	10	5
	The Sound of Music	10	5
1967	*Bonnie and Clyde*	10	2
	Guess Who's Coming to Dinner?	10	2
1969	*Anne of the Thousand Days*	10	1
1970	*Airport*	10	1
	Patton	10	7
1972	*Cabaret*	10	8
	The Godfather	10	3
1973	*The Exorcist*	10	2
	The Sting	10	7
1976	*Network*	10	4
	Rocky	10	3
1978	*Heaven Can Wait*	10	1
1981	*On Golden Pond*	10	3
1982	*Tootsie*	10	1
1991	*Bugsy*	10	2
1995	*Braveheart*	10	5
2000	*Crouching Tiger, Hidden Dragon*	10	4

11 nominations: 18 movies

Year	Film	Nom.	Awards
1939	*Gone With the Wind*	11	8
1941	*Sergeant York*	11	2
1942	*The Pride of the Yankees*	11	1
1950	*Sunset Boulevard*	11	3
1961	*West Side Story*	11	10
1968	*Oliver!*	11	5
1974	*Chinatown*	11	1
	The Godfather, Part II	11	6

Table 4 (continued):
The Most Nominated Films, 1927/28–2001

11 nominations: 18 movies

Year	Film	Nom.	Awards
1977	*Julia*	11	3
	Star Wars	11	7
	The Turning Point	11	0
1982	*Gandhi*	11	8
1983	*Terms of Endearment*	11	5
1984	*Amadeus*	11	8
	A Passage to India	11	2
1985	*The Color Purple*	11	0
	Out of Africa	11	7
1998	*Saving Private Ryan*	11	5

12 nominations: 11 movies

Year	Film	Nom.	Awards
1942	*Mrs. Miniver*	12	6
1948	*Johnny Belinda*	12	1
1951	*A Streetcar Named Desire*	12	4
1954	*On the Waterfront*	12	8
1959	*Ben-Hur*	12	11
1964	*My Fair Lady*	12	8
1981	*Reds*	12	3
1990	*Dances With Wolves*	12	7
1993	*Schindler's List*	12	7
1996	*The English Patient*	12	9
2000	*Gladiator*	12	5

13 nominations: 5 movies

Year	Film	Nom.	Awards
1953	*From Here to Eternity*	13	8
1961	*Judgment at Nuremberg*	13	2
1964	*Mary Poppins*	13	5
1994	*Forrest Gump*	13	6
1998	*Shakespeare in Love*	13	7
2001	*The Lord of the Rings*	13	4

14 nominations: 2 movies

Year	Film	Nom.	Awards
1950	*All About Eve*	14	6
1997	*Titanic*	14	11

Table 5:
The Ten Highest-Grossing Oscar Winners

Film	Year	Box-Office Gross* (in Million-Dollars)
Titanic	1997	600.8
Forrest Gump	1994	329.7
Gone With the Wind	1939	198.6
Gladiator	2000	187.7
Dances With Wolves	1990	184.2
Rain Man	1988	172.8
A Beautiful Mind	2001	170.8
The Sting	1973	156.0
Platoon	1986	138.5
The Godfather	1972	135.0

*The figures are not adjusted for inflation.

Table 6:
Best Picture Winners by Year and Date of Release

Picture	Year	Release Date
Wings	1927–28	Aug 13
The Broadway Melody	1928–29	Feb 9
All Quiet on the Western Front	1929–30	Apr 30
Cimarron	1930–31	Jan 27
Grand Hotel	1931–32	Apr 13
Cavalcade	1932–33	Jan 6
It Happened One Night	1934	Feb 23
Mutiny on the Bounty	1935	Nov 9
The Great Ziegfeld	1936	Apr 9
The Life of Emile Zola	1937	Aug 12
You Can't Take It With You	1938	Sep 2
Gone With the Wind	1939	Dec 20
Rebecca	1940	Mar 29
How Green Was My Valley	1941	Oct 29
Mrs. Miniver	1942	Jun 5
Casablanca	1943	Nov 27
Going My Way	1944	May 3
The Lost Weekend	1945	Dec 3
The Best Years of Our Lives	1946	Nov 22
Gentleman's Agreement	1947	Nov 12

Table 6 (continued):
Best Picture Winners by Year and Date of Release

Picture	Year	Release Date
Hamlet	1948	Sep 30
All the King's Men	1949	Nov 9
All About Eve	1950	Oct 14
An American in Paris	1951	Oct 5
The Greatest Show on Earth	1952	Jan 11
From Here to Eternity	1953	Aug 6
On the Waterfront	1954	Jul 29
Marty	1955	Apr 12
Around the World in 80 Days	1956	Oct 18
The Bridge on the River Kwai	1957	Dec 19
Gigi	1958	May 16
Ben-Hur	1959	Nov 19
The Apartment	1960	Jun 6
West Side Story	1961	Oct 19
Lawrence of Arabia	1962	Dec 11
Tom Jones	1963	Oct 8
My Fair Lady	1964	Oct 22
The Sound of Music	1965	Mar 3
A Man for All Seasons	1966	Dec 13
In the Heat of the Night	1967	Aug 3
Oliver!	1968	Dec 11
Midnight Cowboy	1969	May 26
Patton	1970	Feb 5
The French Connection	1971	Oct 8
The Godfather	1972	Mar 16
The Sting	1973	Oct 26
The Godfather, Part II	1974	Dec 13
One Flew Over the Cuckoo's Nest	1975	Nov 20
Rocky	1976	Nov 22
Annie Hall	1977	Apr 21
The Deer Hunter	1978	Dec 17
Kramer Vs. Kramer	1979	Dec 19
Ordinary People	1980	Sep 19
Chariots of Fire	1981	Sep 26
Gandhi	1982	Dec 8
Terms of Endearment	1983	Nov
Amadeus	1984	Sep 19
Out of Africa	1985	Dec 18
Platoon	1986	Dec

Table 6 (continued):
Best Picture Winners by Year and Date of Release

Picture	Year	Release Date
The Last Emperor	1987	Nov
Rain Man	1988	Dec
Driving Miss Daisy	1989	Dec
Dances With Wolves	1990	Nov 9
The Silence of the Lambs	1991	Feb 13
Unforgiven	1992	Aug 7
Schindler's List	1993	Dec 15
Forrest Gump	1994	Jul 6
Braveheart	1995	May 24
The English Patient	1996	Nov 15
Titanic	1997	Dec 19
Shakespeare in Love	1998	Dec 11
American Beauty	1999	Sep 15
Gladiator	2000	May
A Beautiful Mind	2001	Dec

Best Picture by Month of Release

January–April		
The Broadway Melody	1928–29	Feb 9
All Quiet on the Western Front	1929–30	Apr 30
Cimarron	1930–31	Jan 27
Grand Hotel	1931–32	Apr 13
Cavalcade	1932–33	Jan 6
It Happened One Night	1934	Feb 23
The Great Ziegfeld	1936	Apr 9
Rebecca	1940	Mar 29
The Greatest Show on Earth	1952	Jan 11
Marty	1955	Apr 12
The Sound of Music	1965	Mar 3
Patton	1970	Feb 5
The Godfather	1972	Mar 16
Annie Hall	1977	Apr 21
The Silence of the Lambs	1991	Feb 13

May–August		
The Life of Emile Zola	1937	Aug 12
Mrs. Miniver	1942	Jun 5

Best Picture by Month of Release

May–August

Going My Way	1944	May 3
From Here to Eternity	1953	Aug 6
On the Waterfront	1954	Jul 29
Gigi	1958	May 16
The Apartment	1960	Jun 6
In the Heat of the Night	1967	Aug 3
Midnight Cowboy	1969	May 26
Forrest Gump	1994	Jul 6
Braveheart	1995	May 24
Gladiator	2000	May

September–November

Mutiny on the Bounty	1935	Nov 9
You Can't Take It With You	1938	Sep 2
How Green Was My Valley	1941	Oct 29
Casablanca	1943	Nov 27
The Best Years of Our Lives	1946	Nov 22
Gentleman's Agreement	1947	Nov 12
Hamlet	1948	Sep 30
All the King's Men	1949	Nov 9
All About Eve	1950	Oct 14
An American in Paris	1951	Oct 5
Around the World in 80 Days	1956	Oct 18
Ben-Hur	1959	Nov 19
West Side Story	1961	Oct 19
Tom Jones	1963	Oct 8
My Fair Lady	1964	Oct 22
The French Connection	1971	Oct 8
The Sting	1973	Oct 26
One Flew Over the Cuckoo's Nest	1975	Nov 20
Rocky	1976	Nov 22
Ordinary People	1980	Sep 19
Chariots of Fire	1981	Sep 26
Terms of Endearment	1983	Nov
Amadeus	1984	Sep 19
The Last Emperor	1987	Nov
Dances With Wolves	1990	Nov 9
Unforgiven	1992	Aug 7
The English Patient	1996	Nov 15
American Beauty	1999	Sep 15

Best Picture by Month of Release

December

Gone With the Wind	1939	Dec 20
The Lost Weekend	1945	Dec 3
The Bridge on the River Kwai	1957	Dec 19
Lawrence of Arabia	1962	Dec 11
A Man for All Seasons	1966	Dec 13
Oliver!	1968	Dec 11
The Godfather, Part II	1974	Dec 13
The Deer Hunter	1978	Dec 17
Kramer Vs. Kramer	1979	Dec 19
Gandhi	1982	Dec 8
Out of Africa	1985	Dec 18
Platoon	1986	Dec
Rain Man	1988	Dec
Driving Miss Daisy	1989	Dec
Schindler's List	1993	Dec 15
Titanic	1997	Dec 19
Shakespeare in Love	1998	Dec 11
A Beautiful Mind	2001	Dec

Table 7:
Best Picture Winners by Year and Running Time

Picture	Year	Running Time (Min.)
Wings	1927–28	139
The Broadway Melody	1928–29	100
All Quiet on the Western Front	1929–30	133
Cimarron	1930–31	124
Grand Hotel	1931–32	113
Cavalcade	1932–33	110
It Happened One Night	1934	105
Mutiny on the Bounty	1935	132
The Great Ziegfeld	1936	176
The Life of Emile Zola	1937	116
You Can't Take It With You	1938	127
Gone With the Wind	1939	222
Rebecca	1940	130
How Green Was My Valley	1941	118
Mrs. Miniver	1942	134

Table 7 (continued):
Best Picture Winners by Year and Running Time

Picture	Year	Running Time
Casablanca	1943	102
Going My Way	1944	126
The Lost Weekend	1945	101
The Best Years of Our Lives	1946	172
Gentleman's Agreement	1947	118
Hamlet	1948	153
All the King's Men	1949	109
All About Eve	1950	138
An American in Paris	1951	115
The Greatest Show on Earth	1952	153
From Here to Eternity	1953	118
On the Waterfront	1954	108
Marty	1955	91
Around the World in 80 Days	1956	167
The Bridge on the River Kwai	1957	160
Gigi	1958	116
Ben-Hur	1959	212
The Apartment	1960	125
West Side Story	1961	151
Lawrence of Arabia	1962	216
Tom Jones	1963	129
My Fair Lady	1964	170
The Sound of Music	1965	174
A Man for All Seasons	1966	120
In the Heat of the Night	1967	109
Oliver!	1968	153
Midnight Cowboy	1969	113
Patton	1970	169
The French Connection	1971	104
The Godfather	1972	175
The Sting	1973	129
The Godfather, Part II	1974	200
One Flew Over the Cuckoo's Nest	1975	133
Rocky	1976	119
Annie Hall	1977	94
The Deer Hunter	1978	183
Kramer Vs. Kramer	1979	104
Ordinary People	1980	123
Chariots of Fire	1981	123

Table 7 (continued):
Best Picture Winners by Year and Running Time

Picture	Year	Running Time
Gandhi	1982	188
Terms of Endearment	1983	132
Amadeus	1984	158
Out of Africa	1985	161
Platoon	1986	120
The Last Emperor	1987	160
Rain Man	1988	133
Driving Miss Daisy	1989	99
Dances With Wolves	1990	181
The Silence of the Lambs	1991	118
Unforgiven	1992	127
Schindler's List	1993	195
Forrest Gump	1994	142
Braveheart	1995	177
The English Patient	1996	162
Titanic	1997	194
Shakespeare in Love	1998	122
American Beauty	1999	121
Gladiator	2000	154
A Beautiful Mind	2001	134

The Longest Best Picture Winners
(151 or more minutes)

Picture	Year	Running Time
Gone With the Wind	1939	222
Lawrence of Arabia	1962	216
Ben-Hur	1959	212
The Godfather, Part II	1974	200
Schindler's List	1993	195
Titanic	1997	194
Gandhi	1982	188
The Deer Hunter	1978	183
Dances With Wolves	1990	181
Braveheart	1995	177
The Great Ziegfeld	1936	176
The Godfather	1972	175
The Sound of Music	1965	174
The Best Years of Our Lives	1946	172
My Fair Lady	1964	170

Table 7 (continued):
Best Picture Winners by Year and Running Time
The Longest Best Picture Winners (continued)

Picture	Year	Running Time
Patton	1970	169
Around the World in 80 Days	1956	167
The English Patient	1996	162
Out of Africa	1985	161
The Bridge on the River Kwai	1957	160
The Last Emperor	1987	160
Amadeus	1984	158
Gladiator	2000	154
Hamlet	1948	153
The Greatest Show on Earth	1952	153
Oliver!	1968	153
West Side Story	1961	151

Best Picture Winners
(121–149 minutes)

Wings	1927–28	139
All About Eve	1950	138
Mrs. Miniver	1942	134
A Beautiful Mind	2001	134
All Quiet on the Western Front	1929–30	133
One Flew Over the Cuckoo's Nest	1975	133
Rain Man	1988	133
Mutiny on the Bounty	1935	132
Terms of Endearment	1983	132
Rebecca	1940	130
Tom Jones	1963	129
The Sting	1973	129
You Can't Take It With You	1938	127
Unforgiven	1992	127
Going My Way	1944	126
The Apartment	1960	125
Cimarron	1930–31	124
Ordinary People	1980	123
Chariots of Fire	1981	123
Shakespeare in Love	1998	122
American Beauty	1999	121

Table 7 (continued):
Best Picture Winners by Year and Running Time
The Longest Best Picture Winners (continued)

Picture	*Year*	*Running Time*
Best Picture Winners		
(less than 120 minutes)		
A Man for All Seasons	1966	120
Platoon	1986	120
Rocky	1976	119
How Green Was My Valley	1941	118
Gentleman's Agreement	1947	118
From Here to Eternity	1953	118
The Silence of the Lambs	1991	118
The Life of Emile Zola	1937	116
Gigi	1958	116
An American in Paris	1951	115
Grand Hotel	1931–32	113
Midnight Cowboy	1969	113
Cavalcade	1932–33	110
All the King's Men	1949	109
In the Heat of the Night	1967	109
On the Waterfront	1954	108
It Happened One Night	1934	105
The French Connection	1971	104
Kramer Vs. Kramer	1979	104
Casablanca	1943	102
The Lost Weekend	1945	101
The Broadway Melody	1928–29	100
Driving Miss Daisy	1989	99
Annie Hall	1977	94
Marty	1955	91

Table 8:
Best Foreign-Language Winners by Year and Country

Year	Film	Country
1947	*Shoe Shine*	Italy
1948	*Monsieur Vincent*	France
1949	*The Bicycle Thief*	Italy
1950	*The Walls of Malapaga*	France/Italy
1951	*Rashomon*	Japan
1952	*Forbidden Game*	France
1953	Not Given	
1954	*Gate of Hell*	Japan
1955	*Samurai*	Japan
1956	*La Strada*	Italy
1957	*The Nights of Cabiria*	Italy
1958	*My Uncle (Mon Oncle)*	France
1959	*Black Orpheus*	France
1960	*The Virgin Spring*	Sweden
1961	*Through a Glass Darkly*	Sweden
1962	*Sundays and Cybele*	France
1963	*8 1/2*	Italy
1964	*Yesterday, Today and Tomorrow*	Italy
1965	*The Shop on Main Street*	Czech Republic
1966	*A Man and a Woman*	France
1967	*Closely Watched Trains*	Czech Republic
1968	*War and Peace*	USSR
1969	*Z*	France/Algeria
1970	*Investigation of a Citizen Above Suspicion*	Italy
1971	*The Garden of the Finzi-Continis*	Italy
1972	*The Discreet Charm of the Bourgeoisie*	France
1973	*Day for Night*	France
1974	*Amarcord*	Italy
1975	*Dersus Uzala*	Japan/Russia
1976	*Black and White in Color*	Ivory Coast/France
1977	*Madame Rosa*	France
1978	*Get Out Your Handkerchiefs*	France
1979	*The Tin Drum*	West Germany
1980	*Moscow Doesn't Believe in Tears*	USSR
1981	*Mephisto*	Hungary
1982	*To Begin Again*	Spain
1983	*Fanny and Alexander*	Sweden

Table 8 (continued):
Best Foreign-Language Winners by Year and Country

Year	Film	Country
1984	*Dangerous Moves*	Switzerland
1985	*The Official Story*	Argentina
1986	*The Assault*	Netherlands
1987	*Babette's Feast*	Denmark
1988	*Pelle the Conqueror*	Denmark
1989	*Cinema Paradiso*	Italy
1990	*Journey of Hope*	Switzerland
1991	*Mediterraneo*	Italy
1992	*Indochine*	France
1993	*Belle Epoque*	Spain
1994	*Burnt by the Sun*	Russia
1995	*Antonia's Line*	The Netherlands
1996	*Kolya*	Czech Republic
1997	*Character*	The Netherlands
1998	*Life is Beautiful*	Italy
1999	*All About My Mother*	Spain
2000	*Crouching Tiger, Hidden Dragon*	Taiwan
2001	*No Man's Land*	Bosnia